Ingrid Betancourt was born in 1961 [...] Pulecio, served in Colombia's Congress, and her father, Gabriel Betancourt, was a government minister and the Colombian ambassador to UNESCO in Paris. Ingrid was educated in France and England and has dual Colombian and French nationality. She lived in France and returned to Colombia in 1989 to become involved in national politics. Elected to the Chamber of Representatives in 1994 on an anti-corruption ticket, she then formed her own party, Oxígeno Verde (Green Oxygen), and became a senator in 1998. She was a Colombian presidential candidate when she was kidnapped by the FARC, who held her captive from 2002 to 2008.

Ingrid Betancourt has received numerous awards and honours, including France's *Légion d'honneur*.

'For all its horror and injustice, the experience of the political prisoner held in inhuman conditions has often been transformed into compelling literature; just think of Aleksandr Solzhenitsyn and *The Gulag Archipelago* . . . Ingrid Betancourt joins that distinguished company . . . Gripping not just for its heart-wrenching portrayal of captivity, but also because of the sharp and useful psychological insights it offers' Larry Rohter, *New York Times*

'Ingrid Betancourt's resilience is astonishing. She not only endured, but constantly plotted doomed escapes, Steve McQueen style – she broke out seven times, and spent days on the run three times. Her *Légion d'honneur*, granted by France in 2008, is entirely deserved' Brian Schofield, *Sunday Times*

'The story of her ordeal is no less powerful because you know about the happy ending; the suspense comes from Betancourt's internal battle to keep her essential self intact through all the degradations of her imprisonment . . . This brave woman's story truly inspires' Kate Saunders, *The Times*

'Harrowing . . . The most interesting part of Betancourt's book is her relationship with her fellow captives, and the transformation of her own character' Janine di Giovanni, *Observer*

'This thoughtful and moving account of her ordeal is a memorable tribute to the resilience of the human spirit' *Waterstone's Books Quarterly*

'Gripping . . . As much a story of relentless introspection as is it a tale of survival . . . The significance of Betancourt's memoir must not be obscured' Caroline Elkins, *New York Times Book Review*

Also by Ingrid Betancourt

SI SABÍA

UNTIL DEATH DO US PART: MY STRUGGLE
TO RECLAIM COLOMBIA

LETTERS TO MY MOTHER

Even Silence Has an End

INGRID BETANCOURT

virago

VIRAGO

First published in Great Britain in 2010 by Virago Press
This paperback edition published in 2011 by Virago Press
Reprinted 2011 (twice)

Copyright © Ingrid Betancourt 2010

Translated from the French by Alison Anderson, with the
collaboration of Sarah Llewellyn

The moral right of the author has been asserted.

"Noches de Bocagrande" © Maestro Faustino Arias, performed by Trío
Martino. Translation by the author.

"Stairway to Heaven" © Jimmy Page and Robert Plant, performed by
Led Zeppelin

A CIP catalogue record for this book
is available from the British Library.

ISBN 978-1-84408-613-9

Typeset in Sabon by M Rules
Printed and bound in Great Britain by
Clays Ltd, St Ives plc

Papers used by Virago are from well-managed forests
and other responsible sources.

MIX
Paper from
responsible sources
FSC www.fsc.org   FSC® C104740

Virago Press
An imprint of
Little, Brown Book Group
100 Victoria Embankment
London EC4Y 0DY

An Hachette UK Company
www.hachette.co.uk

www.virago.co.uk

To my brothers who are still held hostage.

To my companions in captivity.

To those who fought for our freedom.

To Melanie and Lorenzo.

To my mother.

1

ESCAPING THE CAGE

December 2002. I had made my decision to escape. It wasn't the first time. This was my fourth attempt, but after my last one the conditions of our captivity had become even more terrible. They had put us in a cage made of wooden boards, with a tin roof. Summer was coming, and for over a month now we had not had any storms at night. And a storm was absolutely necessary. I spotted a half-rotten board in a corner of our cage. By pushing hard with my foot, I split it enough to make an opening. I did this one afternoon after lunch, when the guard was dozing on his feet, balanced on his rifle. But it made a dreadful noise. The guard, edgy, walked all around the cage slowly, like a pacing animal. I followed him, peering through the slits between the boards, holding my breath. He stopped twice, put his eye up to a hole, and for a split second our eyes met. He jumped back, terrified. Then, to regain his composure, he planted himself at the entrance to the cage; this was his revenge. He would not take his eyes off me.

I avoided his gaze and thought carefully. Could someone squeeze through that opening? In principle, if you could get your skull through, your body would follow. In my childhood games, I squeezed through the bars of the fence at Parc Monceau, headfirst. It was always your head that blocked everything. But I was no longer so sure. It worked for the body of a child, but for an adult were the proportions the same? I was all the more worried because although we, Clara and I, were terribly thin, I had noticed over the last few weeks a sort of swelling of our bodies, probably liquid retention from enforced immobility. In my companion it was very visible. It was harder for me to judge my own condition, because we didn't have a mirror.

I had talked to her about this, and it had irritated her no end. We'd made two previous escape attempts, and the subject sowed tension between us. We didn't talk much. She was touchy, and I was prey to my own obsession. All I could think of was freedom, finding a way to escape from the hands of the FARC.

So I spent the entire day plotting, preparing in detail the equipment for our expedition, giving importance to stupid things. For example, I could not conceive of leaving without my jacket. I had forgotten that the jacket was not waterproof, and once it got wet, it would weigh a ton. I also thought we ought to take the mosquito net along.

I'll have to figure out what to do about the boots. At night we always leave them in the same place, at the entrance to the cage. I'll have to start bringing them inside, so they get used to not seeing them when we're asleep . . . And we'll have to get hold of a machete. To protect ourselves from wild beasts and to clear our way through the vegetation. It will be almost impossible. They're on their guard. They haven't forgotten that we already managed to steal one when they were setting up the old camp . . . Take scissors — they lend them to us from time to time. I have to think about food, too. We have to stock up without their realizing. And it all has to be wrapped up in plastic, because we'll have to swim. It can't be too heavy, or we'll have difficulty making headway. We have to be as light as possible. And I must take my treasures: I can't possibly leave behind the photos of my children and the keys to my apartment. I spent the day turning such questions over and over in my mind. Twenty times or more, I thought about our route once we were out of the cage. I tried to calculate all sorts of things: where the river must be, how many days it would take us until we could get help. I imagined the horror of an anaconda attacking us in the water, or an enormous cayman like the one whose red and shining eyes I had seen in the guard's flashlight when we were coming down the river. I saw myself wrestling with a jaguar; the guards had regaled us with a ferocious description. I thought of everything that might possibly frighten me, to prepare myself psychologically and be ready to respond. I had to know how to control my emotions. I'd decided that this time nothing would stop me.

I could think of nothing else. I no longer slept, because I understood that my brain worked better in the quiet of the evening. I observed, and I took note of everything: what time the guards changed watch, where each one stood, who stayed awake, who fell asleep, who would report to his replacement on the number of times we'd got up to pee . . .

I also tried to continue communicating with my companion, to prepare her for the effort the escape would require, the precautions to take, the noises we must avoid making. She listened to me in silence, exasperated, and would only answer to refuse or disagree. We had to prepare decoys to leave where we slept, to give the impression of a body curled up on the bed. I was not allowed outside the cage, except to go to the *chontos** when nature called. This was an opportunity to rummage through the garbage dump in the hope of discovering some precious item.

I came back one evening with some bits of cardboard and an old sack that had been soaked in decomposing food: ideal to build our decoys. My behaviour annoyed the guard. Because he didn't know whether he ought to forbid me from taking things, he shouted at me to get a move on, reinforcing his invective with a wave of his gun. As for Clara, my booty disgusted her, because she couldn't understand what possible use it might be.

I realized the gulf between us. Stuck together, reduced to a regime of Siamese twins who have nothing in common, we lived in opposite worlds: She was trying to adapt, I could only think of escape.

After a particularly hot day, the wind rose. The jungle went silent for a few moments. Not a single peep from a bird or rustling of a wing. We all turned toward the wind, to breathe in the weather – a storm was approaching rapidly.

Activity in the camp became feverish. Everyone hurried to his task. Some checked the ropes on their tents, others set off at a run to pick up laundry drying in a patch of sunlight, others with greater foresight went

---

* The FARC word for the makeshift toilets they dug in the ground for us.

to the *chontos*, in case the storm lasted longer than they could hold out. I watched all this agitation, my stomach twisted in anxiety, and I prayed to God to give me the strength to go through with it. *Tonight I shall be free.* I repeated this sentence over and over, to ward off the fear that was contracting my muscles and draining my blood, while I struggled to make the gestures I had planned a thousand times during my sleepless nights: I waited until nighttime to build my decoy, folded the big black plastic sheet and slipped it inside my boot, unfolded the little grey plastic bag that would serve as a waterproof poncho, and checked to see if my companion was ready. I waited for the storm to break.

From my previous attempts, I had learned that the best moment to slip away was at dusk, the hour when wolves look like dogs. In the jungle this meant precisely 6.15 P.M. During the few minutes while our eyes adjusted to the darkness and before night fell completely, we were all blind.

I prayed for the storm to break at that time. If we fled the camp just before night took possession of the forests, the guards would change watch without noticing and the alarm would be sounded only the next morning at dawn. That gave us enough time to get away and hide during the day. The teams sent out to look for us would go much faster than we could, because they were much fitter and they had the daylight in their favour. But if we covered our tracks, the farther we got, the greater the area they would have to search. To cover the search area, they would need more men than they had available in the camp. I thought it would be possible to move at night, knowing that they wouldn't look for us in the dark, and if they did, we would see the beams of their flashlights and hide before they could locate us. After three days, if we walked all night, we would be about twelve miles from the camp, and it would be impossible for them to find us. Then we could start walking during the day, near the river – but not too close, because that would probably be where they would con-tinue their search – to reach a place where, at last, we could find help. It was feasible, yes, and I believed we could do it. But we had to leave early, to gain enough time the first night to maximize the distance from the camp.

That night, though, the opportune moment had come and gone and the storm had still not broken. The wind was blowing incessantly, but the thunder rumbled far away, and a certain tranquillity had returned to the camp. The guard had wrapped himself up in a big black plastic sheet, which made him look like some ancient warrior braving the elements with his cape whipping in the gusts. And everyone waited for the storm with the serenity of the old sailor who thinks he has already secured his cargo.

The minutes passed with infinite slowness. From a radio somewhere in the distance, we could hear strains of happy music. The wind continued to blow, but there was no more thunder. From time to time, a bolt of lightning pierced the cathedral of vegetation, and my retina caught the negative print of the camp. It was cool, almost cold. I could feel the electricity charging the air, making my skin crawl. And then gradually my eyes swelled from trying to see in the dark, and my eyelids grew heavy. *It's not going to rain tonight.* My head throbbed. Clara had curled up in her corner, overcome by drowsiness. And I, too, was drawn by the wait into a deep sleep.

A drizzle spraying through the boards awoke me. The hair on my arms started bristling. The sound of the first drops of rain on the tin roof finally wrenched me from my torpor. I touched Clara's arm; it was time to go. With each passing moment, the drops were getting heavier, thicker, closer together. But the night was still too light. The moon was doing its job well. I peered outside through the planks: It was as if it were broad daylight.

We would have to run straight out of the cage in the hope that no one in the neighbouring tents would think to look over at our prison just then. I stopped to think. I had no watch; I was counting on my companion's. She usually got annoyed when I asked her the time. I was reluctant to ask even now, then went ahead. "It's nine o'clock," she answered, aware that this was not the moment to create unnecessary tension. The camp was already asleep, which was one good thing. But for us the night was getting shorter and shorter.

The guard was struggling to protect himself from the torrents of water, and the thud of the rain on the tin roof drowned the sound of my feet kicking the rotten boards. By the third kick, the board shattered to bits. But the opening that appeared was not as wide as I had hoped.

I shoved my little backpack through and left it outside. My hands were drenched when I brought them back in. I knew we would have to spend entire days soaked to the bone, and just the thought of it was repugnant. I was furious with myself for thinking that some notion of comfort might interfere with my struggle for freedom. It seemed ridiculous to waste so much time trying to convince myself that I would not get sick, that my skin would not shrivel up at the end of three days of bad weather. I told myself that I'd had life too easy, conditioned by an upbringing where fear of change was disguised as caution. I had observed the young people who held me prisoner, and I could not help but admire them. They didn't get hot, they didn't get cold, nothing stung them, they displayed remarkable skill in any activity requiring strength and flexibility, and they moved around the jungle at three times my own pace. The fear I had to overcome was made up of all sorts of prejudices. My first attempt to escape had failed because I was afraid I would die of thirst, because I could not bring myself to drink the brown water in the puddles on the ground. So for months now I had practised drinking the muddy river water, to prove to myself that I could survive the parasites that must already have colonized my stomach.

Moreover, I suspected the commander of the front who had captured me, "El Mocho" Cesar, of having ordered the guerrillas to "boil the prisoners' water" in front of me so that I would remain mentally dependent upon this antiseptic measure and be afraid to escape into the jungle.

To instil terror they ordered us to the riverbank to watch the killing of an immense snake they'd caught just as it was about to attack a swimming *guerrillera*. The creature was truly a monster, I measured it by counting my steps, it was 25 feet long and 20 inches round – the same diameter as my waist. Three men were needed to pull it out of the water. They called it a *guío*, I thought it was an anaconda. They had wanted me to see it with my own eyes. For months I could not get it out of my nightmares.

I saw these young people who were so at ease in the jungle and I felt clumsy, handicapped, worn out. I was beginning to get the impression that it was the idea I had of myself that was in crisis. In a world where I inspired neither respect nor admiration, without the tenderness and love of my family, I felt I was ageing without reprieve and, worse still, that I'd been made to despise what I had become – so dependent, so stupid, and utterly useless at resolving even the most trivial everyday problems.

For a few more minutes, through the narrow opening and beyond, I observed the wall of rain that awaited us. Clara was crouching next to me. I turned back to the door of the cage. The guard had disappeared into the storm. Everything was frozen, except the water mercilessly streaming down. Our gazes met. We reached out and clung to each other so tightly it was painful.

We had to go. I pulled away, smoothed my clothes, and lay down next to the hole. I put my head through the boards with encouraging ease, and then my shoulders. I twisted to get my body through, felt stuck, then wriggled nervously to get one of my arms out. Once my arm was clear, I pushed. With the strength of my free hand, digging my nails into the ground, I managed to get my entire upper body out. I edged forward, painfully contorting my hips, so that the rest of my body would slide sideways through the opening. I could tell that the end of my struggle was near, and I began to wiggle my feet, with a dread that I might not be able to free myself. At last I was out and I jumped to my feet. I took two steps to the side so that my companion could get out more easily.

But there was no movement near the hole. What was she doing? Why wasn't she already outside? I got down on all fours to have a look inside. Nothing; except for the forbidding womblike darkness of the cage. I ventured to whisper her name. No answer. I slipped one hand inside and groped about. Nothing. Nausea was choking me. I stayed crouching by the hole, scanning every millimetre of my field of vision, sure that at any moment the guards would spring at me. I tried to calculate how much time had gone by since I'd come out. Five minutes? Ten? I could not tell. I was thinking at full speed, undecided, listening for the slightest noise, watching for the faintest light. In despair I bent down by the opening, calling to Clara so loudly this time that she must hear me on the far side of the cage, but somehow I already knew that there would be no reply.

I stood up. I was facing the dense jungle and the torrential rain, which had come to answer all my prayers of the previous days. I was outside, there was no going back. I would be alone. I had to be quick, leave right away, not try to understand. I checked to see if the rubber band holding my hair was still in place. I didn't want the guerrillas to find even the tiniest clue of the path I would take. I counted slowly: one . . . two . . . At the count of three, I dashed straight ahead, into the forest.

I ran and ran, driven by an uncontrollable panic, avoiding trees instinctively, unable to see or hear or think, forging straight ahead until I was exhausted.

At last I stopped and looked behind me. I could still see the clearing in the forest, like a phosphorescent light through the trees. When my brain began to work again, I realized that I was automatically retracing my steps, incapable of resigning myself to leaving without her. Carefully I went back, reviewing all our conversations one by one, reexamining all the instructions we had agreed on. There was one in particular that I remembered, and I seized upon it: If we got lost on the way out, we would meet up at the *chontos*. We had mentioned it once, fleetingly, without really believing it.

Fortunately, my sense of direction seemed to be working in the jungle. In the grid of a big city, I could easily get lost, but in the jungle I could find my way. I emerged exactly level with the *chontos*. Of course there was no one. The place was deserted. I looked around, disgusted by the swarms of insects above the holes of excrement, and my dirty hands, and my fingernails black with mud, and this incessant rain. I did not know what to do. I was ready to sink into despair.

I heard voices and quickly went back to hide in the thick of the jungle. I tried to see what was going on over by the camp, and I circled it to get nearer the cage, taking cover at the very spot where I'd come out. The storm had given way to a biting and persistent drizzle, and now you could hear other sounds. The commander's loud voice reached my ears. It was impossible to understand what he was saying, but his tone was threatening. A flashlight lit up the inside of the cage, and its beam shone harshly through the hole in the board and then swept over the clearing from left to right, only inches from my hiding place. I stepped backward, sweating abundantly in my clothes; I had a terrible urge to throw up, and my heart was racing. That's when I heard Clara's voice. The suffocating heat now instantly gave way to a mortal chill. My entire body began to tremble. I could not understand what might have happened. Why had she been caught? Other lights appeared, other orders were given, a group of men carrying flashlights scattered; some of them were inspecting the area around the cage, the corners, the roof. They took their time over the hole, then shone their beams toward the edge of the jungle. I could see them talking among themselves.

The rain stopped completely, and darkness fell like a lead curtain. I thought I could see my companion's silhouette inside the cage, thirty yards or so from my hiding place. She had just lit a candle, a very rare privilege; as prisoners we were not allowed to have light. She was talking with someone, but it wasn't the commander. Their voices were calm, as if restrained.

As I looked at this inaccessible world, I found myself almost regretting the fact that I was alone and drenched and shivering. It would have been so easy, so comfortable, so tempting to admit defeat and return to that warm, dry place. I contemplated the patch of lights and told myself that I couldn't afford any self-pity, and I said over and over, *You have to go, you have to go, you have to go!*

Painfully I tore myself away from the light and plunged into the thick, matted darkness. It had begun to rain again. I had my hands out in front of me to avoid obstacles. I hadn't managed to get hold of a machete, but I did have a flashlight. The risk of using it was as great as the fear of doing so. I went slowly into this threatening space and told myself I would switch it on only when I couldn't take the darkness any longer. My hands collided with wet, rough, sticky surfaces, and at any moment expected to feel the burn of some lethal poison.

The storm was raging again. I could hear the thundering of the rain pounding on the canopy of vegetation that for a few more minutes would protect me. I expected the fragile roof of leaves to yield at any moment and open under the weight of water. The prospect of the flood that would soon submerge me was overwhelming. I no longer knew whether it was raindrops or my own tears that were flowing down my cheeks, and I hated to have to drag along this relic of a snivelling child.

I had already made considerable headway. A bolt of lightning tore through the forest, landing a few yards from me. In a burst of light, the space around me was revealed in all its horror. I was surrounded by gigantic trees and was only two steps from falling into a ravine. I stopped short, totally blinded. I squatted to catch my breath among the roots of the tree just there before me. I was on the verge of finally taking out my flashlight when I noticed intermittent flashes of light in the distance, headed my way. I could hear their voices now. They must be very near, because I heard one of them shout that he had already seen me. I camouflaged myself among the roots of the old tree while praying to the Lord to make me invisible.

I followed their progress from the swinging of their beams of light. One of them aimed his beam at me and dazzled me. I closed my eyes, unmoving, waiting for their shouts of victory before they seized me. But the light left me, strayed, came back for an instant, then went away for good, leaving me in silence and darkness.

I got up, scarcely daring to believe it, still trembling, leaning against the hundred-year-old tree to recover my wits. I stayed like that for minutes on end. Another bolt of lightning lit up the forest. From memory I cleared a path where I thought I'd seen a passage between two trees, while I waited for the next flash of lightning to free me from my blindness. The guards were gone.

My relationship with the night world began to evolve. It was easier to move ahead, my hands reacted faster, and my body was learning to anticipate the lay of the land. The sensation of horror was beginning to fade. My surroundings were no longer totally hostile. I began to think of these trees, these palms, these ferns, this intrusive undergrowth, as a possible refuge. The fact of being soaked, bleeding from my hands and fingers, covered with mud and not knowing where to go – all of this lost its importance. I could survive. I had to walk, keep moving, get away. At dawn they would resume the chase. But with each step I kept repeating, *I am free*, and my voice kept me company.

Imperceptibly the jungle became more familiar, changing from the flat, dark world of the blind to a land in monochromatic relief. Shapes became more distinct, and finally the universe took possession of its colours: It was dawn. I had to locate a good hiding place.

I hurried my step, imagining their reaction, trying to guess their thoughts. I wanted to find some dip in the terrain where I could roll myself in my black plastic sheet and cover myself with leaves. The forest changed from grey-blue to green in the space of a few minutes. It must already be five o'clock in the morning, and I knew they'd be upon me at any moment. And yet the forest seemed so isolated. Not a sound, not a movement; time seemed to stand still. Deceptively reassured by the tranquillity of daylight, I found it difficult to maintain a heightened state of alert. I continued on my way, cautiously all the same. Suddenly, without warning, the space ahead of me filled with light. Intrigued, I looked around. Behind me the forest remained just as opaque. I then realized what it meant. A few feet away, the trees were thinning to make room for sky and water. The river was there. I could see how it flowed in fits and starts, angrily sweeping along entire trees that seemed to be calling for help. The roiling water frightened me. And yet there lay my salvation.

I stood motionless. The absence of imminent danger repressed my survival instincts, and I listened to the voice of caution that told me not to jump in. Cowardice was taking shape. Those tree trunks swirling on the water, disappearing under the surface only to bounce back up farther down, their branches reaching to the sky – that was me. I saw myself drowning in that liquid mud. My cowardice invented pretexts to postpone my diving in. With my companion I probably would not have hesitated; I would have recognized those trunks carried along by the current as perfect lifebuoys. But I was afraid. My fear consisted of a series of pathetic little fears. Fear of being soaked again, now that I had managed to get warm by walking. Fear of losing my backpack and the meagre supplies it contained. Fear of being carried away by the stream. Fear of being alone. Fear of dying carelessly.

These thoughts shamefully exposed to me who I was. I understood that I was still such an ordinary, second-rate human being. I had not suffered enough to find the rage in my guts I needed to struggle to the death for my freedom. I was a dog who, no matter how beaten up, would still wait for a bone. I looked around anxiously for a hole to hide in. The guards would come to the river, too, and search here more thoroughly than elsewhere. Of course I could go back into the thick of the jungle. But they were already on my heels, and I risked running into them.

Near the river there were mangroves and old rotting trunks, relics of long-ago storms. One tree in particular, difficult to get to, had a sizeable recess on one entire side. The mangrove roots created a barrier all around it, and it seemed to provide the best hiding place. On all fours, then crawling and wriggling, I managed to make my way inside the hollow. I carefully unfolded the big plastic sheet that had been tucked within my boot since my escape. My socks were full of water, as was the plastic. I shook it out without thinking and frightened myself with the noise it made. I stopped everything and held my breath, alert to the slightest movement. The forest was already waking, the buzzing of insects getting louder. Reassured, I went back to my task of making the cavity of the trunk a safe haven, wrapped in my plastic sheet.

That is when I saw her. Yiseth.

She had her back to me. She had arrived at a trot, without her rifle, but with a revolver in her fist. She was wearing a sleeveless vest in camouflage material, and its femininity made her seem harmless. She turned around very slowly, and her eyes found mine instantly. She closed them for a second as if to thank the heavens and then walked toward me warily.

Her smile was sad as she extended her hand to help me crawl out of my hiding place. I no longer had the choice. I did as I was told. She was the one who carefully folded up my plastic sheet and flattened it lengthwise so that I could put it back in my boot. She nodded, and then, satisfied, she addressed me as if I were a child. Her words were strange. She did not use the self-conscious speech of the guards, who were always worried that a comrade might tell on them. At one point she looked at the river and, as if she were talking to herself out loud, her words filled with regret as she confessed that she, too, more than once, had thought of running away. I talked to her then about my children, my need to be with them, how urgent it was for me to go home. She told me about the little baby that she had left with her mother, although he was only a few months old. She was biting her lip, and her black eyes welled with tears. "Leave with me," I said. She took my hands, and her expression turned cold again. "They would find us and kill us." I begged her, squeezing her hands even harder, obliging her to look at me. She refused outright, took up her weapon, and stared at me. "If they see me talking to you, they will kill me. They're not far. Walk ahead of me and listen carefully to what I have to say to you." I obeyed, picking up my things, putting my backpack over my shoulder. She stuck right behind me and whispered, her lips against my ear. "The commander has ordered the men to abuse you. When they get here, they will scream at you, insult you, shove you around. Above all don't react. Don't say anything. They want to punish you. They're going to take you away . . . Only the men will stay with you. We women have to go back to the camp. Do you get it?"

Her words echoed in my brain, empty shells, as if I had lost my Spanish. I was making a great effort to concentrate, trying to go beyond the sounds, but fear had paralysed my brain. I was walking without knowing that I was walking, I was looking at the world from the inside, like a fish in an aquarium. The young woman's voice came to me distorted, alternately very loud, then inaudible. My head felt very heavy, as though it were being squeezed in a vice. My tongue was covered with a dry paste, stuck to my palate, and my breathing had become deep and heavy. As I was walking, the world was rising and falling to the rhythm of my steps. The resonant beating of my heart filled my inner space, causing my skull to vibrate. I did not see them arrive. One of them circled me, his face red like a little pig's, his blond hair bristling. He held his rifle above his head, arms outstretched, and he was jumping and gesticulating, indulging in a ridiculous, violent war dance.

A blow to the ribs made me realize that there was a second man, a short, dark man with powerful shoulders and bowed legs. He had just thrust the barrel of his rifle into the flesh above my hips, and he pretended he was restraining himself from doing it again. He was shouting and spitting, insulting me with crude, absurd words.

I could not see the third man. He pushed me from behind. His laugh was nasty, and his presence seemed to excite the other two. He grabbed my bag and emptied it on the ground, poking through things he knew were precious to me with the toe of his boot. He laughed and crushed them in the mud with his heel, then forced me to pick them up and put them back in my bag. I was on my knees when I saw the flash of a metal object in his hands. That is when I heard the clank of the chain, and I leaped up to face him. The young girl had stayed there beside me, holding me firmly by the arm and pushing me forward to walk. The guy who was laughing motioned to her to leave. She shrugged her shoulders, accepted defeat, avoided my gaze, and left me there.

I was tense and absent, my heart pounding between my temples. We went forward a few yards. The storm had caused the water to rise, which had transformed the place. It was now a pond littered with trees that stubbornly refused to go elsewhere. Farther away, beyond the stagnant water, you could sense the violence of the current from the persistent quivering of the shrubs.

The men were circling me, barking. The clank of the chain became insistent. The guy was playing with it as if to bring it to life, as if it were a snake. I would not let myself make any eye contact. I tried to rise above all this agitation, but my peripheral vision apprehended gestures and movements that made my blood run cold.

I was taller than they were, I held my head straight and high, and my entire body was tense with anger. I knew there was nothing I could do against them, but they were not sure of that. They were the ones who were afraid, more afraid than I was – I could feel it. However, they had hatred on their side, and group pressure. All it would take was one gesture to destroy the equilibrium in which I still had the upper hand.

I heard the man with the chain speak to me. He said my name, over and over, with a familiarity that was meant to be insulting. I had decided that they would not hurt me. Whatever happened, they would not touch the essence of who I was. I had to cling to this fundamental truth. If I could remain inaccessible, I might avoid the worst.

My father's voice spoke to me from very far away, and a single word came to mind, in capital letters. But I discovered with horror that the word had been completely stripped of its meaning. It referred to no concrete notion, only to the image of my father standing there, his lips set, his gaze uncompromising. I repeated it again and again, like a prayer, like a magical incantation that might, perhaps, break the evil spell. *DIGNITY*. It no longer meant a thing, but to say it repeatedly sufficed to make me adopt my father's attitude, like a child who copies the expression on an adult's face, smiling or weeping not because he feels joy or pain but because by miming the expressions he sees, he triggers in himself the emotions they are meant to represent.

And through this game of mirrors, without my thoughts having anything to do with it, I understood that I had gone beyond fear, and I murmured, "There are things that are more important than life."

My rage had left me, giving way to an extreme coldness. The alchemy taking place inside me, imperceptible from the outside, substituted the rigidity of my muscles with a bodily strength that would prepare me to ward off the blows of adversity. This was not resignation, far from it, nor was it a headlong flight. I observed myself from within, measuring my strength and resistance not according to my ability to fight back but rather to submit to those blows, like a ship that is battered by the tides yet will not sink.

He came very close to me and tried to loop the chain quickly around my neck. Instinctively I dodged him and took a step to the side, out of reach. The other two did not dare come forward, but they shouted abuse to encourage him to try again. His pride wounded, he held himself back, gauging the precise moment to attack again. We glanced at each other, and he must have read in my eyes my determination to avoid violence. He must have taken it for insolence. He leaped forward and struck me with the chain, landing a blow to my skull. I collapsed on my knees, the world spinning around me. After the initial blackness, I held my head between my hands and stars appeared in flashes before my eyes, until gradually my eyesight returned to normal. I felt intense pain, compounded by a great sadness that washed over me in successive waves as I registered what had just happened. How could he have done this? It wasn't so much indignation that I felt, but something far worse: a loss of innocence. I opened my eyes again upon the world, and again my gaze met his. His eyes were bloodshot, his lips distorted by a snarl. He could not bear for me to look at him – he was stripped naked before me. I had caught him looking at me with the horror that his own gestures inspired in him.

He regained his composure and, as if to eradicate all trace of guilt, redoubled his efforts to fasten the chain around my neck. I stubbornly fought off his gestures, each time avoiding physical contact as much as possible. He took hold of himself and, gathering momentum, came at me yet again with the chain, making hoarse grunts to multiply the strength of his blow. I fell down in the darkness, senseless, losing all notion of time. I knew that my body was the object of their violence. I could hear their voices around me echoing loudly.

I could feel I was being assaulted, driven to convulsions, as if borne away by a high-speed train. I don't think I lost consciousness, but although I suppose I had my eyes open wide, the blows I'd received no longer allowed me to see. My body and my heart were frozen during the short span of an eternity.

When I finally managed to sit up, I had the chain around my neck and the man was pulling on it, jerkily, to oblige me to follow him. He was foaming at the mouth as he shouted at me. The way back to the camp seemed very long, under the weight of my humiliation and their sarcasm. One in front of me, two others behind, they were loudly exulting in their victory. I did not feel like crying. It wasn't pride. It was just the scorn required to ensure that the cruelty of these men and the pleasure they derived from it had not reached my soul.

During the suspended time of that endless march, I felt myself becoming stronger with each step, because I had become more aware of my extreme vulnerability. Subjected to every humiliation, obliged to walk on a leash like an animal, paraded through the entire camp to the victory cries of the rest of the troops, arousing the basest instincts of abuse and domination – I had just witnessed, and been victim of, the worst.

But I was surviving, with a newly acquired lucidity. I knew that in a way I had gained more than I'd lost. They had not managed to transform me into a monster thirsting for revenge. I expected the physical pain to hit when I was at rest, and I prepared myself for the onset of my mental torment. But I already knew that I had the ability to free myself from hatred, and I viewed this as my most significant conquest.

I arrived back at the cage and decided to isolate myself, to hide my emotions. Clara was sitting facing the wall with her back to me, by a wooden board that served as a table. She turned around. I found her expression disconcerting; I sensed a surge of satisfaction, which hurt me. I brushed by her, aware of the gulf that separated us once again. I sought out my little corner, to find refuge under my mosquito net, on my mat, trying not to think too much, because I was not in a state to make clearheaded judgements. For the time being, I was relieved that they had not found it necessary to attach the other end of my chain to the cage with a padlock. I knew that later they would. My companion did not ask me any questions, and I was grateful for that. After a long silence, she said, simply, "I won't have a chain around my neck."

I lapsed into a deep sleep, curled up on myself like an animal. The nightmares had returned, but they were different. It was no longer Papa whom I encountered when I fell asleep, it was myself, drowning in deep and stagnant waters. I saw the trees looking at me, their branches yearning toward the shuddering surface. I felt the water trembling as if it were alive, and then I lost the trees and their branches from view. I was submerged in the briny liquid that was drawing me down, each time deeper and deeper, my body straining painfully toward that light, toward that inaccessible sky, despite my struggle to free my feet and rise up to the surface for air.

I awoke exhausted and bathed in sweat. I opened my eyes on my companion, who was looking at me attentively. When she saw I was awake, she went back to her business.

"Why didn't you follow me?"

"The girl put on a light just as I was about to go out. She must have heard a noise . . . And I hadn't prepared my decoy very well. She saw right away that I wasn't in my bed."

"Who was it?"

"Betty."

I didn't want to probe further. In a way I was angry at her for not trying to find out what had happened to me. But on the other hand, I was relieved I didn't have to talk about things that hurt too much. Sitting on the ground, with that chain around my neck, I went back over the entire course of the past twenty-four hours. Why had I failed? Why was I back in this cage again, whereas I had been free, totally free, all through that fantastic night?

I forced myself to think of the ordeal I had just lived through in the swamp. I made an extreme effort to make myself recognize the bestiality of those men. I wanted to give myself the right to name it, to be able to cauterize my wounds and clean myself.

My body rebelled: I was overcome by spasms. Quickly picking up the lengths of metal coiled at my feet, I jumped up, and in a panic I asked the guard for permission to go to the *chontos*. He didn't bother to reply since he saw I was already on my way there, taking great strides to cover the distance to the makeshift latrines. My body knew the distance by heart – and also knew that I would not make it. The inevitable occurred three feet too soon. I squatted at the foot of a young tree and vomited my guts out. I stayed there, my stomach empty, still racked by dry, painful contractions that brought nothing more to the surface. I wiped my mouth with the back of my hand and looked up at an absent sky. There was nothing but green. Foliage covered the space like a dome. Faced with the vastness of nature, I felt even smaller, and my eyes were moist with effort and sorrow.

"I have to wash."

The wait for the appointed bathing time seemed to take forever, far too long for someone who had nothing better to do than ruminate on her own repugnant state. In addition, my clothes were soaked from the night before, and I stank. I wanted to talk with the commander, but I knew he would refuse to receive me. And yet the idea of disturbing the guard with my request gave me the energy to emerge from my apathy and formulate my request. At the very least, he would be so annoyed at having to respond to me that he was bound to do something.

The guard looked at me warily and waited for me to speak. As a precaution he had straightened his rifle, and now he held it vertically across his stomach, one hand on the barrel, the other on the butt, at attention.

"I threw up."

He didn't answer.

"I need a shovel, to cover it up."

He still said nothing.

"Tell the commander I need to speak to him."

"Go back to your cage. You're not allowed out."

I did as I was told. I saw him thinking, rapidly, warily, making sure I was far enough away from the guard station. Then, with an authoritarian air and a boorish gesture, he shouted to the nearest guerrilla, who sauntered over. I saw them whispering as they looked at me, and then the second guerrilla went off. I followed him with my eyes, unmoving. He came back with an object hidden in his hand.

Once he was near the entrance to the cage, he hopped nimbly inside. He grabbed the free end of my chain, looped it around a beam, and locked it all with a huge padlock.

It was clear that this chain was more than just a burden and a constant source of discomfort; it was also a confession of their weakness: They were afraid I might escape. To me they were pathetic, with their guns, their chains, so many men just to take care of two defenceless women. Their violence was cowardly, their cruelty was spineless. They knew it was something they could get away with, because they practised it with impunity and without witnesses. The words of the young *guerrillera* came back to me. I had not forgotten. What she had wanted to warn me about was that it had really been an order. She had told me so.

How could someone give such an order? What went on in a man's head that he would require such a thing of his subordinates? I felt very dumb in this jungle. In this environment that was so hostile to me I had lost a large part of my faculties. Now it was vital for me to open a door that would help put me back in my place in the world or, better still, put the world back in its place in me.

I was a grown woman. I had a solid head on my shoulders. Would it be a relief to understand? No, probably not. There are orders that must be contravened, no matter what. Of course, peer pressure was considerable. Not only that of the three men among themselves, who had all received the order to bring me back and punish me and who had tried to outdo each other in their brutality, but also the pressure of the rest of the troops, who would hail them for acting ruthlessly. It wasn't the men but the image of themselves that had proved fatal for me.

Someone called my name, and I was startled. The guard was standing before me. I hadn't heard him coming. He unfastened the padlock, and I still did not understand what was happening. I saw him kneel down and run the chain in a figure eight around my feet, then lock me up again with the same huge padlock. Disappointed, I began to sit back down, which annoyed him. He condescended to inform me that the commander wanted to see me. I looked at him with my eyes open wide, asking him how he thought I could possibly walk with all this scrap iron between my legs. He grasped me by the arm to make me stand and shoved me out of the cage. The entire camp had taken a front-row seat to watch the spectacle.

I looked at my feet, careful to coordinate my steps and avoid meeting anyone's gaze. The guard waved to me to hurry up, showing off in front of his comrades. I didn't respond, and when I didn't even pretend to obey, he got truly upset, worried he might look like an idiot.

I arrived at the opposite end of the camp, where the commander, Andres, had his tent, and I tried to anticipate what sort of tone he might adopt for this private audience.

Andres was a man who was just reaching maturity, with the fine features of a Spaniard and copper-coloured skin. I had never found him truly dislikeable, even though from the day he took command of this mission he had made a point of being as inaccessible as he could. I sensed that he had a strong inferiority complex. He managed to emerge from his pathological mistrust when the conversation turned to everyday life. He was madly in love with a pretty young thing who hungered for power, and she had him wrapped around her little finger. She was obviously bored with him, but being the commander's woman gave her access to some of the luxuries of the jungle. She reigned over the others, and as if somehow it went with being queen, she was putting on weight before our very eyes. Perhaps he thought I might be of use to him in decoding the secrets of this female heart he coveted more than anything. On several occasions he would stop by to talk with me, beating around the bush, lacking the courage to come straight out with his thoughts. I helped him to relax, to talk about his life, to share his personal thoughts. In a way it made me feel useful.

Andres was above all a peasant. His greatest pride was that he had learned how to adapt to the demands of life as a guerrilla. Small but sturdy, he was better than anyone at doing what he required his men to do. He earned respect by fixing his subordinates' slapdash work himself. His leadership resided in the admiration he galvanized in his troops. But he had two weak spots: alcohol and women.

I found him sprawled on his camp bed, indulging in a tickling session with Jessica, his partner; her squeals of pleasure carried beyond the river. He knew I was there, but he hadn't the slightest intention of allowing me to think they might interrupt their game for my sake. I waited. Eventually Andres turned, gave me a disdainful look, and asked what I wanted.

"I'd like to talk to you, but I think it would be better if we were alone."

He sat down, ran his hands through his hair, and asked his girlfriend to leave, which she did, pouting and dragging her feet. After a few minutes, he asked the guard who had come with me to leave as well. Finally he looked at me.

The hostility and harshness he displayed signalled that he was not the least bit sensitive to the sight of this ravaged creature in chains who stood before him. We were sizing each other up. It was odd for me to be this pivotal in a scene where all the workings of human machinery were becoming so patently obvious. I knew there were far too many things at stake, things that, like the jagged cogs of a clock, depended upon one another to be set in motion. First of all, I was a woman. Faced with a man, he might have been indulgent; it would have revealed his nobility of heart and thereby increased his prestige. But in this case he knew he was surrounded, that dozens of pairs of eyes were watching him all the more eagerly since they could not hear him, so his body language had to be flawless. He must treat me fiercely, to avoid any risk of appearing weak. Still, what they had done was hateful. The written codes to which they were supposed to abide left no room for doubt. So they had to seek refuge in grey zones, justifying themselves with what they called the casualties of war: I was the enemy, I had tried to escape. The punishment they had inflicted upon me could not be considered an error that they might have to explain, or even a blunder they could try to hide. They pretended that what had happened was the price I must pay for the affront I had made them suffer. There would therefore be no sanctions against his men, let alone any consideration for me.

I was an educated woman and consequently terribly dangerous. I might be tempted to manipulate him, to bamboozle him and cause his undoing. As a result he was more than ever on his guard, stiff with all his prejudice and guilt.

I stood before him, filled with the serenity of detachment. *I* had nothing to prove. I was defeated, mortified beyond bounds, there was no place left in me for pride. I could live with my conscience, but I wanted to understand how he could live with his.

The silence that came between us was the fruit of my determination. He wanted to get it over with, while I wanted to observe him at leisure. He was looking me up and down, while I was examining him. The minutes went by one by one. "Well, what do you have to say to me?" He was defying me; he could not stand my presence, my obstinate silence. Then I heard myself continue out loud, very slowly, a conversation I had been carrying on in my head ever since I'd returned to my cage. He was transported imperceptibly into the secret place of my pain, and as I gradually revealed to him the depth of my wounds, as if he were a doctor to whom I could exhibit the full horror of my suppurating gash, I saw him turn pale, incapable of interrupting, both fascinated and disgusted. I no longer needed to talk to free myself from what I had experienced. That is why I was able to describe it to him with precision.

He let me finish. But as soon as I raised my eyes, which betrayed my secret desire to hear what he had to say, he regained his composure and delivered the blow he had meticulously prepared before I'd even got there: "That's what you say. But my men tell me otherwise . . ." He was lying on his side, leaning on his elbow, casually fiddling with a twig he had in his mouth. He raised his eyes and looked straight out at the other tents in a semicircle around his own, where his troops had settled in to watch our conversation. He paused, then continued, ". . . And I believe what my men tell me."

I began to weep, uncontrollably, unable to staunch the flood of tears — a reaction that was all the more unexpected given that I was unable to identify the feeling that had triggered it. I tried to contain the onslaught of tears with my sleeves, which smelled of vomit, and by brushing aside the strands of hair that stuck to my streaming cheeks as if deliberately increasing my confusion, but I hated my lack of restraint. My anger left me pitiful, and the knowledge that I was being observed only intensified my clumsiness. The idea of leaving, of heading back across the camp, enchained as I was, obliged me to concentrate on the simple mechanics of movement and helped me to lock up my emotions.

When Andres felt he was no longer under scrutiny, he relaxed, giving free rein to his malice. "I have a sensitive heart . . . I don't like to see a woman cry, still less a prisoner. Our regulations stipulate that we must show consideration for our prisoners." He grinned, aware that he was delighting his audience. With one finger he beckoned to the man who had brutalized me. "Take her chains off. We're going to prove to her that the FARC knows how to show consideration."

It was unbearable to endure the touch of that man's hands, brushing my skin as he put the key into the padlock hanging from my neck.

He was smart enough not to make too much of it. Then he knelt down, not looking at me, and removed the chains that hobbled my feet.

Relieved of the weight, I wondered what I should do. Should I leave without asking for anything more or thank the commander for this gesture of mercy? His indulgence was a move in a pernicious game. The aim was to go one better in snubbing me, by means of an ingenious stunt that left me indebted to my torturer. He had planned it all, enrolling his subordinates as his henchmen. He had gone from being the instigator of his villainy to pretending to be its judge.

I chose a way out that would once have cost me so dearly. I thanked him, in the proper manner. I needed to cloak myself in rituals, to regain whatever it was that made me a civilized human being, shaped by an upbringing that was part of a culture, a tradition, a history. More than ever, I felt the need to mark my distance from the barbarity. He looked at me with astonishment, uncertain whether I was making fun of him or whether I had capitulated.

I headed back to my cage, aware of all the mocking gazes of disgust that, in spite of everything, I had got off lightly. They all must have concluded that the old crying trick had finally got the better of their commander's obstinacy. I was a dangerous woman. Surreptitiously, the roles had been reversed – no longer a victim, I was now feared: I was a politician.

Politician. It was a word that contained all the class hatred with which they were brainwashed daily. Indoctrination was one of the commander's responsibilities. Each camp was built on the same model, and each featured a classroom where the commander communicated and explained his orders, where everyone was expected to denounce any non-revolutionary attitude displayed by their comrades. They risked, if they failed to do so, being considered an accomplice, being brought before a court-martial for sentencing and being shot.

They'd been told that I had run for president of Colombia. I belonged, therefore, to the group of political hostages whose crime, according to the FARC, was that they voted to fund the war against the FARC. As such, we politicians had an appalling reputation. We were all parasites, prolonging the war in order to profit from it. Most of these young people did not really understand the meaning of the word "political." They were taught that politics was an activity for those who managed to deceive and then amass wealth by stealing taxes.

For me the problem with their explanation was that to a large degree I shared it. Moreover, I'd gone into politics in the hope, if not of changing things, at least of being able to denounce injustice.

But, for them, anyone who wasn't on the side of the FARC was scum. It would be pointless for me to wear myself out explaining my struggle and my ideas to them. They weren't interested. When I told them that I had gone into politics in order to fight against everything I hated – corruption, social injustice, and war – their argument was irrefutable: "You all say the same thing."

I headed back to the cage, freed from my chains but burdened with this hostility mounting against me. It was then that I heard for the first time that FARC song, set to a childish little tune:

Esos oligarcas hijueputas que se roban la plata de los pobres,
*Esos burgueses malnacidos, los vamos a acabar, los vamos a acabar.**

In the beginning it was a humming sound, coming very quietly from one of the tents; then it began to move around with me wherever I went. I was so lost in my ramblings that I didn't even react. Only when the men's voices began to chant the verses, deliberately articulating very loudly, did I raise my head. Initially I did not grasp the meaning of the words, since their regional accent often distorted them, but they were raising such a fuss about this little ditty that it ended up making everyone laugh, and the change of mood brought me back to reality.

The man singing was the very same one who had removed my chains. He was singing with a sneer on his face, very noisily, as if to set the rhythm for his gestures, pretending the whole time to be putting his things away inside his backpack. The other one singing, who had come all the way from his tent on the far side, was a puny, bald, pathetic sort, in the habit of closing his eyes every two seconds as if to ward off a blow. One of the girls was sitting on the guy's mat ogling me and clearly thought it was great fun to accompany her stare with this tune that, visibly, they knew by heart. I

---

* "Those sons of bitches oligarchs who steal the poor man's silver, / Those ill-bred bourgeois, we'll destroy them all, we'll destroy them all."

hesitated, wearied by everything I'd been through; I told myself that in the end I did not need to feel targeted by the words of the song. Their attitude conveyed the meanness of a playground at recess. I knew that the best thing would be to turn a deaf ear, but I did the opposite and stopped. The guard who was glued to my heels nearly collided clumsily with me, which made him mad. He yelled at me to keep moving, enjoying the fact that he had an entire audience he'd won over effortlessly.

I turned to the girl who was singing to herself. I heard myself say, "Don't sing that song around me any more. You have guns, and the day you want to kill me, you can just go ahead."

She continued singing with her companions, but her heart wasn't in it. They could not make a nursery rhyme out of death. At least not in front of their victims.

The order to bathe arrived soon enough. The afternoon was nearly over, and they informed me that the time allowed would be very short. They knew that bathing was the best moment of the day for me. To have it curtailed was an indication of the regime that I should come to expect.

I said nothing. Escorted by two guards, I went to the river and jumped into the grey water. The current was still very strong, and the water level had not stopped rising. I clung to a protruding root by the riverbank and kept my head underwater: I opened my eyes wide, hoping to wash away everything I'd witnessed. The water was icy. It awoke every painful spot in my body, and it hurt to the very roots of my hair.

The meal arrived as I got back to the cage. Flour, water, and sugar. That evening I huddled in my corner, with dry, clean clothes, and I drank my *colada** not because it was good but because it was hot. "I will not have the strength to face any more days like this one," I said. I had to protect myself, even against myself, because it was clear that I did not have the strength to endure for much longer the treatment to which they were subjecting me. I closed my eyes before night fell, hardly breathing, while I waited for it all to subside: my suffering and anxiety, my solitude and despair. During the hours of that night without sleep, and

---

* A popular hot drink made of water, flour and sugar.

during the days that followed, my entire being undertook a curious path that led to the hibernation of my body and soul, waiting for freedom like the coming of spring.

The next day dawned, as on all the mornings of all the years of my entire life. But I was dead. I tried to fill the endless hours, occupying my mind with anything that could distract me from my own self. But the world no longer interested me.

I saw them coming from the other end of the camp. They had crossed it silently, one behind the other, or rather one pushed by the other. When they had drawn level with the guard station, Yiseth spoke in the guard's ear. He motioned with his chin for them to go through. She whispered something that seemed to bother him and pushed him forward.

"We would like to speak to you," she said to me, while I tried my best to not seem concerned.

She was wearing the same sleeveless camouflage shirt as the night before. And had the same hard, secretive air, which aged her.

I looked up at her, my eyes heavy with bitterness. Her companion was one of the three men who had brutalized me in the swamp. His presence alone gave me a shiver of repulsion. She realized and nudged her companion with her shoulder. "Go ahead, tell her."

"We are . . . I came to say that . . . I'm sorry. Please forgive me for what I said to you yesterday. *Yo no pienso que usted sea una vieja hijueputa. Quiero pedirle perdón. ¡Yo sé que usted es una persona buena!*"*

The scene was surreal. This man had come to apologize, like some kid scolded by a strict mother. Yes, they had called me every vile name. But that was nothing compared to the horror they'd put me through.

It was all absurd. Except for the fact that they had come. I was listening. I thought I was indifferent. It took me time to understand that these words, and the way in which they'd been said, had actually soothed me.

---

* "I don't think you're an old son of a bitch. I want to apologise. I know that you are a good person!"

2

FAREWELL

February 23, 2009. It is exactly seven years to the day that I was abducted. On every anniversary, as soon as I wake up, I wince when I realize what day it is, even though I've known for weeks that it is getting closer. I consciously count backward, wanting to mark this day so that I never forget it, so that I can dissect and ruminate over every hour, over every second of the chain of events that led to the prolonged horror of that interminable captivity.

I awoke this morning, as I have every morning, giving thanks to God. And also as I do every morning since I was freed, I take a few moments, just seconds, to realize where I've been sleeping. On a mattress, without a mosquito net, and under a white ceiling instead of a sky of green camouflage. I awake naturally. Happiness is no longer a dream.

But on this particular day, February 23, a split second after waking I feel remorseful for forgetting. My guilt and anxiety drive my memory to distraction, causing such a flood of recollections that I have to leap out of bed to escape my sheets, as if mere contact with them could cast some irreversible evil spell upon me and engulf me once again in the depths of the jungle.

Once out of danger, my heart still pounding yet anchored in reality, I realize that the relief that comes from recovering my freedom cannot in any way be compared to the intensity of the suffering I have known.

I'm reminded of a Bible passage that had struck me while I was in captivity, a hymn in the book of Psalms that described the harshness of crossing the desert. The conclusion had come as a surprise to me. It said that the compensation for the effort, courage, tenacity, and endurance displayed during that journey was not happiness. Nor glory. What God offered as a reward was only rest.

You need to grow old to appreciate peace. I had always lived in a whirlwind of activity. I felt alive. I was a cyclone. I had married young, my children, Melanie and Lorenzo, fulfilled all my dreams, and I undertook to transform my country with the strength and stubbornness of a bull. I believed in my lucky star, and I worked hard and could do thousands of things at once, because I was sure I would succeed.

January 2002. I was on a short trip to the United States, accumulating sleepless nights and back-to-back meetings while seeking support from the Colombian community for my party, Oxígeno Verde, and my presidential campaign. My mother was travelling with me and we were together when I received a call from my sister, Astrid. Papa was unwell, although it was nothing serious. My parents had separated many years earlier, but they had stayed close friends. When my sister explained that Papa was tired and had lost his appetite, we immediately thought of my uncles and aunts, who had all died suddenly after feeling a little unwell. Two days later Astrid called: Papa had suffered a heart attack. We had to return immediately.

The journey home to Bogotá was a nightmare. I adored my father. Time spent with him was always interesting. I could only imagine life without him as a desert of boredom.

I arrived at the hospital to find him hooked up to a frightening-looking machine. He awoke, recognized me, and his face lit up. "You're here!" he exclaimed before falling back into a deep, barbiturate-induced sleep, only to open his eyes ten minutes later and exclaim once again, "You're here!"

The doctors told us to prepare for the worst. The parish priest came to administer a blessing. In a moment of lucidity, Papa beckoned all of us to his bed. He had chosen his words of farewell and lavished blessings on each of us with the precision of the sage who can peer into people's hearts. Then my sister and I were left alone with him. I realized that it was time for him to go, and I was not prepared. I broke down in sobs, desperately clinging to his hand. The hand that had always been there for me, that had warded off danger, had consoled me, had held on to me when I crossed the street, had strengthened me at those difficult times in my life, and had led me into the world. This was the hand I took whenever I was near him, as if it belonged to me.

My sister turned to me. "Stop it!" she said sharply. "We are in a logic to fight for life. Papa is not going to die." Taking his other hand, she assured me that everything would turn out fine. She was holding him tight. In the midst of my sobs, I felt that something extraordinary was happening. A wave of electricity was running from my arm and flowing through my fingers into his arteries. The tingling left me in no doubt. I looked at my sister. "Do you feel it?" Without a trace of surprise, she replied, "Of course I feel it!" We probably spent the entire night in that position, shrouded in silence, feeling the circuit of energy that had formed among the three of us, fascinated by an experience that had no explanation except that of love.

My children also came from Santo Domingo, where they were living with their father Fabrice, to see Papa. Fabrice was still very close to him, even though he and I were no longer married. Papa considered him to be like his own son. When I was with Melanie and Papa alone, she also experienced the strange wave of electricity when holding his hand. My father opened his eyes when Lorenzo kissed him; Astrid's young children, Anastasia and Stanislas, were there too, wanting to be cuddled by him. Papa was so happy to have his family reunited by his bedside that he started getting better.

My mother and I stayed with Papa throughout his two-week recovery, living with him at the hospital. I knew that I would not have the strength to carry on if he were no longer by my side.

I'd been in the middle of a very important campaign time for our party. Oxígeno, the Green Party, was still young – created four years earlier, it brought together a collection of passionate independent citizens who were fighting against years of political and military corruption crippling Colombia. We were putting forward an alternative ecological and pacifist platform. We were "green," we were about social reform, we were clean, in a country where politics too often went, as far as we were concerned, hand in hand with the drug kingpins and the paramilitaries.

Papa's illness had suddenly halted all my political activities. When I disappeared from the public spotlight, my poll numbers plummeted. Some of my colleagues deserted my campaign in panic to swell the ranks of rival candidates. After I left the hospital, I found myself with a much smaller team to prepare for the final sprint. The presidential elections were to be held in May. We had only three months left.

During the first meeting with the entire team, we set out the agenda for the remaining months. The discussion was heated. The majority wanted to go ahead with a long-planned visit to San Vicente del Caguán. My campaign managers were eager for us to help out the mayor of San Vicente, who was the country's only elected mayor to bear the colours of Oxígeno Verde. Our staff wanted me to make an extra effort to compensate for the weeks I'd been at Papa's bedside and to put all my energy into the campaign. I felt I owed it to them, so I reluctantly agreed to go to San Vicente. We announced the trip at a press conference during which we explained our peace plan for Colombia.

In the 1940s, Colombia was plunged into a civil war between the conservative party and the liberal party, a conflict so merciless that those years were called *la violencia* – "the violence." It was a power struggle that spread from the capital of Bogotá and brought bloodshed to the countryside. Peasants identified as liberals were massacred by conservative partisans and vice versa. The FARC* was born spontaneously as the peasants' effort to protect themselves against that violence and to safeguard their land from being confiscated by the liberal or conservative landlords. The two parties reached an agreement to share power in government and end the civil war, but the FARC was not a part of it. During the Cold War of the 1950s and beyond, the movement shifted from being a rural, defensive organization to being a communist, Stalinist guerrilla group seeking to

---

* The official initials are FARC-EP, which in Spanish stands for Colombian Revolutionary Armed Forces–People's Army.

take power. They built a military hierarchy in their ranks and opened fronts in different parts of the country, attacking the military and the police and carrying out indiscriminate kidnappings. During the 1980s the Colombian government offered a peace agreement to the FARC, and a truce was signed and political reforms were voted in Congress to support the agreement. But with the rise of drug trafficking, the FARC found a way to finance its war and the peace agreement collapsed. The FARC brought terror to the countryside, killing peasants and rural workers who would not accept their rule. A rivalry between the drug traffickers and the FARC, vying for control of the drugs trade, gave rise to a new surge of violence. The paramilitaries emerged as an alliance between the political far right – in particular the landlords – and the drug traffickers, striving to confront the FARC and expel them from their regions. President Andres Pastrana, a member of the Conservative Party, had won the elections on a platform offering a new peace process with the FARC.

Oxígeno Verde's aim was to establish dialogue simultaneously with everyone involved in the conflict, while maintaining strong military pressure to ensure that the illegal factions had an incentive to sit at the negotiating table. To better convey our message at the press conference, I had sat in the middle of a long table between life-size cardboard cutouts of Manuel Marulanda, the supreme leader of the FARC (which was now the oldest communist guerrilla group in South America); Carlos Castaño, his fiercest adversary, the head of the paramilitaries; and the generals of the Colombian army that fought both.

A few weeks earlier, on February 14, a televised meeting had taken place at San Vicente del Caguán between all the presidential candidates and members of the FARC secretariat. That meeting had been organized by the outgoing government, and we'd been allowed to use the presidential plane for the round trip. The government was seeking support for its peace process with the FARC. It had been the object of increasingly harsh criticism for handing over to FARC the control of a demilitarized zone of sixteen thousand square miles – an area more or less the size of Switzerland – in exchange for a guarantee that they would turn up at the negotiating table. San Vicente del Caguán was located at the heart of this zone.

We had gathered around a table, members of the FARC on one side and the candidates and government officials on the other. The meeting turned into an indictment of the guerrilla movement, which was accused of stalling the negotiations.

When it was my turn to take the floor, I asked the FARC representatives to prove they were serious about peace. The country had just witnessed with horror the death of Andres Felipe Pérez, a twelve-year-old boy in the final stages of terminal cancer, who had begged the FARC to allow him to talk to his father through a radio link-up before he died. His father, a soldier in the Colombian army, had been held hostage by the FARC for several years. The FARC had refused. I expressed the bitterness we all felt over this and our utter dismay at the lack of humanity from a group that claimed to be defending human rights. I concluded my speech with a declaration that peace in Colombia had to begin with the release of all the hostages – more than a thousand – being held by the FARC.

The following week, the FARC hijacked a plane in the south and captured the region's most important senator, Jorge Eduardo Géchem. The president abruptly ended the peace process. In a televised address, he announced that within forty-eight hours the Colombian army would regain control of the demilitarized zone and evict the FARC.

In the ensuing hours, the government informed us that the FARC had left the San Vicente region and that everything had returned to normal. As proof, the press announced that President Pastrana would travel to San Vicente the following day, precisely when we had planned to go.

The telephones at our headquarters were ringing off the hook. If the president was going to San Vicente, then surely we would be going, too! My campaign team made contact with the president's office to ask if we could fly with the president's retinue, but the request was refused. After many long hours of discussion, it appeared that we could fly to Florencia – a city 230 miles south of Bogotá – and complete the rest of the journey by car. San Vicente's airport was under military control and closed to civilian flights. The security services confirmed we would have a solid escort: Two armoured cars would meet us when we disembarked from the aircraft, and motorcycles would be at the head and rear of the convoy.

I spoke on the telephone with the mayor of San Vicente. He, too, was very insistent that I come. Military helicopters had been flying over the village all night long, and the population was afraid. People feared reprisals, as much from the paramilitaries as from the guerrillas, since the village of San Vicente had supported the peace process.

The mayor was counting on the media exposure I would get as a presidential candidate to highlight the risks being run by his people. My presence would help shield them from violence. In a final effort to convince me, he said that the bishop of San Vicente had taken the road that morning and reached his destination without a problem. The trip was not dangerous.

So I agreed to go to San Vicente, provided that security measures on the ground be confirmed before our departure, scheduled for five o'clock the following morning.

That night when I left our HQ I was exhausted. But my evening was only just beginning. I had a meeting with friends of the Colombian left who were seriously committed to a peace settlement. In the face of the renewed hostilities, our goal was to draft a joint strategy. I left the meeting to attend a dinner at the home of a campaign worker who had gathered together the hard-core members of the group. We all felt the need to be together, to discuss the recent turn of events.

Midway through the evening, I received a call from one of the newcomers to my campaign, Clara. She was on the team and had replaced the administrator who had recently left our campaign to support one of our competitors. She wanted to join us on the trip to San Vicente. I told her that she didn't need to, there was plenty to be done during the days ahead, and I repeated to her a number of times that she could better spend the weekend preparing for what was coming up. She insisted. As a new member of the campaign, she wanted to become more involved and get to know our San Vicente team. So we agreed that I would pick her up in the car at dawn.

I left the meeting at ten. I was desperate to be in Papa's arms again. He would not have eaten because he was waiting for me, and I wanted to put him to bed before going home. Ever since he left the hospital, I'd made it a rule to end my working day by dropping in to give him a kiss. It was always a relief to share all the latest minor crises with him. He looked at the world from above. Where I saw threatening waves, he saw tranquil water.

I always arrived with chilled cheeks and frozen hands. He would lift his oxygen mask and pretend to be disagreeably surprised. "Ha! You're like a toad," he would say, as if he were angry with me for bringing in the cold with my hugs. It was all a game, and then he would laugh and shower me with kisses.

Yet when I arrived that particular evening, the face behind the oxygen mask was serious. He asked me to sit down on the arm of the chair, and I complied, intrigued. Then he said, "Your mother is very worried about your trip tomorrow."

"Mom worries about everything," I replied, feeling unconcerned. Then, after thinking about it a little longer, I added, "What about you? Are you worried?"

"No, not really."

"You know, if you don't want me to go, I will cancel."

He said nothing.

"Papa, it doesn't matter if I don't go. Besides, I don't really want to go. I would much rather stay with you."

At that point, the overriding priority in my life was my father. The day he had been discharged from hospital, his physician took my sister and me aside and led us into a small room full of computers to show us a beating heart on one of the monitors. He pointed to an erratic-looking line on the screen. "That's the vein that is keeping your father alive. It is going to stop working. When? Only God knows. It could be tomorrow, the day after, in two months, or in two years. You need to be prepared."

"Papa, tell me that you want me to stay and I'll stay."

"No, my darling, do what you have to do. You gave your word. The people of San Vicente are expecting you. You have to go."

I was holding his hand, as always. We looked into each other's eyes in silence. Papa always based his decisions on principles. I had frequently rebelled against this; as a child I found it strict and stupid. Then, as it came time for me to make my own decisions, I understood that when I was in doubt, his course was always the best one. I had devised my own motto from his example, and it had stood me in good stead. That evening I, too, saw that the trip to San Vicente was a matter of principle.

Suddenly, in a kind of irrational outburst, I heard myself say to him, "Papa, wait for me! If anything should happen to me, you wait for me! You are not going to die!"

Still shaken, his eyes widened in surprise, he replied, "Of course I will wait. I am not going to die." I immediately regretted letting myself go like that.

Then his face relaxed, and he took a deep breath and added, "Yes, I will wait for you, my darling. God willing."

And he turned toward the picture of Christ that had pride of place in his room. His expression was so intense that I, too, turned toward it. I had never really looked at that picture before, even though it had been there for as long as I could remember. In fact, viewed with my adult eyes, it looked very kitsch. Yet it was Christ resurrected, full of brightness, his arms open and his heart vibrant. Papa made me stand in front of him, beneath the saintly picture.

"My good Jesus," he said, "take care of this child for me."

Mi buen Jesús, cuídame a esta niña.

He patted my hand to indicate that it was me he was talking about, as if his request might have been misconstrued.

I was startled, just as he had been a few minutes earlier. His words seemed strange. Why did he say "this child" and not "my child"? But why even give it a second thought? It was of no importance whatsoever. Papa often came out with old-fashioned expressions. He was born before the streetcar, in the era of horse-drawn carriages and candles. I remained motionless, scrutinizing the expression on his face.

"*Cuídame esta a niña.*" He repeated it, and it permeated my entire being, as if water had been poured over my head.

I knelt before him, hugging his legs, my cheek pressed against them.

"Don't worry," I said. "Everything will be fine."

It was more for my own reassurance that I uttered these words. I helped him back into bed, taking care to place the bottle of oxygen next to him.

He switched on the television, which was airing the last news bulletin of the day. I curled up against him, my ear against his chest listening to the beating of his heart, and dozed off in his arms, unafraid.

Toward midnight I got up, put out the lights, and kissed him good night, making sure he was well covered up. He held out his hand to give me a blessing and was asleep before I even reached the door. That evening, as on all previous evenings, I turned to look at him one more time before I left.

I didn't know that it would be the last time I would ever see him.

3

THE ABDUCTION

February 23, 2002. The security escort arrived as planned, a little before four in the morning. It was dark, and I was wearing my campaign uniform: a T-shirt printed with our campaign slogan — FOR A NEW COLOMBIA — jeans, and hiking boots. I put on my fleece jacket and just before leaving, on an impulse, removed my watch.

No one in the house except Pom, my dog, was awake. I kissed her between the ears and left with a small bag containing only what I would need for one night away.

Once I arrived at the airport, I checked that all the security arrangements were in place. The captain in charge of coordinating the security team pulled a fax from his pocket and showed it to me. "Everything is in order. The authorities have provided you with armoured vehicles." He smiled at me, satisfied that he had done his job.

The rest of the group was already there. The plane took off at dawn. We were stopping first at Neiva, a town 150 miles from Bogotá, before crossing over the Andes to land in Florencia, the capital of the Caquetá department in the Llanos Orientales, a stretch of lush, flat grassland between the Amazon rainforest and the Andes. After that we would go by car to San Vicente.

The stopover was expected to be half an hour but ended up lasting just over two hours. I barely noticed, as my mobile phone did not stop ringing;

a vicious article in the local press was reporting the split that had occurred within our campaign team. The journalist quoted only the biting comments of those who had deserted our ranks to endorse my competitors. My team was outraged and wanted to get out our side of the story as quickly as possible. I spent most of the time on the telephone going back and forth between my HQ and the editor of the newspaper in question to have our version of the facts published.

We got back on the plane in sweltering heat, and by the time we reached Florencia, we were already behind schedule. However, we could still make the sixty-mile drive to San Vicente in less than two hours.

Florencia Airport had been taken over by the military. A dozen Black Hawk helicopters were lined up on the tarmac, blades rotating, waiting for the order to lift off. As soon as I disembarked from the aircraft, I was met by a colonel in charge of local operations, who led me into an air-conditioned office while my security team contacted those responsible for our journey on the ground and prepared the final details of the next leg.

The colonel was respectful, and with great courtesy and deference he offered to fly us by helicopter to San Vicente.

"They leave every half hour. You can be on the next one."

"That's very kind, but there are fifteen of us."

"Let me see what I can do."

He left the room, returning ten minutes later looking frustrated, and announced, "We can only take five people on board."

The captain in charge of my security escort was the first to react. "Some of the security team can remain behind."

I asked if the chopper could accommodate seven. The colonel nodded. "That's no problem." He asked us to wait in his office for the next helicopter.

We expected a half-hour wait. My security team was conferring among themselves, probably deciding who would go with me. One of the escorts began to clean his pistol and put back the bullets that had been removed for the plane journey. While he was handling the gun, he accidentally pulled the trigger, and a shot rang out, thankfully with no consequences.

The bullet landed right next to me, and I nearly jumped out of my skin, suddenly aware of how edgy I was.

I hated these small incidents, not because of the incidents themselves but because of the conflicting thoughts that entered my head immediately afterward. *Bad omen,* resonated a monotone voice within me. The other voice retorted, *What a stupid thing to say. On the contrary, it's good luck!* My team was on the alert, watching for my reaction, and the poor guy who'd fired the shot was now scarlet with embarrassment, apologizing profusely.

"Please, don't worry. But let's be careful. We're all tired," I said, bringing the incident to a close.

My thoughts turned to Papa, but I remembered that phone coverage was sketchy in this region. The wait continued. Some of my group wandered off to the restrooms or to get drinks. I had already seen at least three helicopters depart, and it still wasn't our turn. I didn't want to appear impatient, especially since the offer seemed very generous. Finally I went to see what was happening.

The colonel was outside talking to my security officers. When he saw me, he cut short his conversation.

"I'm very sorry, madam, but I have just received instructions not to take you by helicopter. It's an order from the top, and there's nothing I can do about it."

"Well, in that case, we must revert to Plan A. Gentlemen, can we leave right away?"

The silence of my escort team was palpable. Then the colonel stepped forward with the suggestion that I should appeal to his general, who was on the tarmac. "If anyone can give you authorization, it's him."

I spotted a large, surly guy issuing orders from the landing strip. Before I had a chance to ask, the colonel nodded; he was indeed the general.

The general's aggressive tone was disconcerting. "There's nothing I can do for you. Please leave the runway!" For a moment I thought he had not recognized me, and I tried to explain why I was there. But he knew very well who I was and what I wanted. He was irritated; he kept talking to his subordinates, handing out orders, ignoring me, letting me talk to myself. He surely was prejudiced against me, probably because of the debates in

Congress during which I had exposed incidents of corruption among high-ranking officials. Without realizing it, I had raised the tone of my voice. Cameras appeared out of nowhere, and suddenly we were surrounded by a group of journalists.

The general put an arm around my shoulders and steered me toward the terminal to get me off the runway and away from the cameras. He explained that he was acting on an order, that the president would be arriving shortly, that he had a hundred journalists with him, and that they needed the helicopters to transport them to San Vicente. He added, "If you want to wait here, he'll walk past. You will be able to speak to him. It's the best I can do." I stood there, my arms dangling, wondering if I really ought to go along with this whole charade. A pack of journalists rushed over to film the landing of the presidential plane. Leaving was no longer an option. It would be interpreted as discourteous.

The situation was all the more embarrassing because the previous day we had asked to travel with the group of journalists going to San Vicente, and the president himself had refused. For the last twenty-four hours, the television news had been repeating incessantly that the region had been liberated and that the FARC had completely withdrawn. The president's trip to San Vicente was planned to prove it. The government had to show the world that the peace process had not been a huge mistake, that it had not led to the loss of control to the guerrillas of a sizeable portion of national territory. From what I could see, the zone was under military control; helicopters belonging to the armed forces had not stopped taking off for San Vicente since our arrival. If Pastrana were to refuse again, we simply needed to go by road as originally planned and not waste any more time.

The president's plane landed, a red carpet was unfurled on the tarmac, and the staircase was placed at the aircraft door. But the door remained closed. Faces appeared at the windows, then quickly withdrew. I stood there, stuck between the row of soldiers on guard and the horde of journalists behind me. I had only one desire: to slip away.

Relations between President Pastrana and Oxígeno Verde hadn't been easy. I had supported him during his campaign on the condition that he implement major reforms against political corruption, in particular by amending the electoral system. But he'd broken his word, and I had crossed over to the opposition. He turned against my team and managed to fracture it by luring away two of my senators.

Nevertheless, I always supported him in his peace process. We had met up again earlier that month at a cocktail party at the French embassy, and he thanked me for my unfailing support of the peace negotiations.

Finally the aircraft door opened. It was not the president who stepped out first, but his secretary. I suddenly remembered an incident that had slipped my mind until this moment. During the televised meeting with the FARC commanders nine days earlier, I had supported the theory that both parties needed to show consistency between their words and actions to establish trust between the government and the FARC. There was no doubt that my criticisms of the FARC had been sharp, but no more so than those aimed at the government. In particular, I had explained that a government complacent about corruption lacked credibility in the peace process. And I mentioned a scandal in which the president's secretary had been accused of manipulating to his own benefit a contract for the supply of uniforms to the security forces, and said he should resign. But the two men were close friends. To make his secretary disembark first was a clear message to me from the president: He was furious with me for what I'd said. He made his secretary go first so that I would know that he had his full support.

What happened next confirmed my suspicions. The president brushed past me, not even stopping to shake my hand. Taking the snub without a word, I spun around, biting my lip. More fool me. I shouldn't have waited.

I walked over to my group, who were waiting for me, perplexed.

"We need to get going. We're already really late!"

My captain was as red as a lobster. He was sweating miserably in his uniform. I was about to cheer him up with a kind word, when he said, "Madam, forgive me, I have just received a peremptory command from Bogotá. My assignment has been cancelled. I can't go with you to San Vicente."

I stared at him, incredulous.

"Wait. I don't understand. What order? From whom? What are you talking about?"

He stepped forward stiffly and handed me the paper he was nervously crumpling in his hands. It was indeed signed by his superior. He explained that he had just spent twenty minutes on the telephone with Bogotá, that he had tried his best, but that the order came "from the top." I asked him what he meant by that, and letting out a long, almost laboured sigh, he said, "From the president's office, madam."

I was flabbergasted as I began to grasp the implications. If I went to San Vicente it would once again be without protection. It had happened before, when the government had refused to increase my one-man escort while we were crossing the Magdalena Medio, the banned territory of the paramilitaries. I looked around. The runway was now almost deserted, the last journalists of the presidential committee were boarding a half-empty helicopter, and three other helicopters, blades rotating, remained on the ground with no passengers to transport.

The general came up to me and in a loud, patronizing voice said, "I told you!"

"Okay, so what do you suggest?" I asked him, irritated. After all, if I hadn't been offered transport in one of those choppers, I would have left for San Vicente long before and would already be there by now!

"Do as you originally planned! Go by road!" he retorted, and I watched him and all his military stripes disappear inside the terminal.

It wasn't that simple. We still needed armoured vehicles. I walked over to my security personnel to find out what the local team had arranged for our transport. They all faltered, not knowing what to say. One of them had been sent to find out what was happening and came back looking contrite. "The guys of the local team have gone, too. They were ordered to abort the mission."

Everything had been orchestrated to prevent my going to San Vicente. The president probably feared that my appearance in San Vicente might reflect badly on him. I sat down for a moment to think things over. The heat, the commotion, my emotions – my mind was a blur. I wanted to do what was best.

What would become of our democracy if we, the presidential candidates, were forced to change our campaign strategy because of the government's withdrawl of our security teams? If we agreed not to go to San Vicente, it would mean accepting suicidal censorship. We would lose the freedom to express ourselves on war and on peace, lose our ability to act in the name of the marginalized populations who did not have a voice. Whoever held power could quite simply appoint his successor.

One of the security men had managed to establish a good relationship with officials from the airport's security division. There was an official vehicle at the airport that might be made available to us for the trip to San Vicente. He went off to obtain more details and came back with the authorization.

It was a small, four-by-four pickup truck. There was room for only five people; it was a far cry from the armoured car we'd been counting on. I turned to the group. Some laughed, others shrugged. My logistics manager, Adair, stepped forward, offering to drive. Without hesitating, Clara said she would come too. Our press officer declined. He wanted to leave room for our cameraman and one of the French journalists covering the campaign. Two French journalists were deep in discussion. Finally the young female reporter decided not to come. She did not feel safe and preferred for her older colleague to go with us, since he would be able to take some good photos.

A member of my security team took me by the arm and asked if he could speak to me in private for a few minutes. He was the longest-serving member on the team and had been protecting me for more than three years.

"I want to come with you." He looked nervous and uncomfortable. "I don't like what they're doing to you."

"Have you spoken to your superior?"

"Yes."

"If you come with me, won't you risk losing your job?"

"It's bound to cause problems."

"No, listen. This is not the time for more difficulties."

Then, seeking his advice, I asked, "What do you think about the road? Do you think it could be dangerous?"

He smiled sadly. And, with a resigned look on his face, replied, "No more than anywhere else."

Then, as if to tell me what he was really thinking, he added, "There are soldiers everywhere. It's almost certainly less dangerous than when we crossed the Magdalena! Call me as soon as you get to San Vicente. I will do whatever is necessary to ensure that the return goes more smoothly."

My team had plastered the vehicle with improvised signs spelling out my name and the word "Peace." We were about to leave when the man from the security division who had secured the pickup for us rushed back over, visibly agitated. He was brandishing a set of papers and panting as he said, "You can't leave until you have signed a discharge form! It's a government vehicle, you understand, and if you have an accident, you'll have to cover the costs!"

I closed my eyes. I felt as if I were in a slapstick Mexican movie. Clearly they wanted to do their utmost to delay our departure. I smiled, mustering some patience. "Where do I sign?"

Clara took the form. "I'll take care of it," she said kindly. "Hopefully, my years in law will serve some purpose!"

I laughed and let her handle things. It was already noon. The heat was becoming suffocating, and we couldn't wait any longer.

We hit the road, the air-conditioning on full blast. Just the prospect of spending two hours in this small metal oven breathing artificial air was excruciating.

"There's a military checkpoint at the exit to Florencia. It's purely routine, to check our ID papers," I said.

I had made this journey many times. The military cordon was always a rather tense moment. We reached it very quickly. Cars were lined up one behind the other, waiting patiently. Everyone would be searched. We pulled over, parked the truck, and got out.

At that moment my phone rang. I rummaged in my bag to retrieve it. It was Mom. I was astonished that her call had got through to me. Usually there was no network once you left Florencia. I brought her up to date with all the details of our journey. "My escort received an order not to accompany me. It seems it came from the president himself. I still have to go, though. I gave my word. I wish I were with Papa. Tell him I send my love."

Mom had been a senator and knew well how demanding an electoral campaign could be. "Don't worry, darling, I'll tell him. And I'll be with you every second. Every step of the way, I'll be with you. Be careful."

While I was talking to Mom, the soldiers had taken our vehicle and were meticulously examining the carpets, the glove compartment, and our bags. When I hung up, I refrained from calling Papa. Instead I walked over to the officer who was standing a short distance from all the activity and who seemed to be in charge of operations, to inquire about the traffic situation.

"Everything is normal. Up to now we haven't had any problems."

"What is your opinion?"

"I have no opinion to give you, madam."

"Very well. Thank you anyway."

We took to the road behind a bus and alongside a small motorcycle being ridden at top speed by a young woman, her arms bare, her hair flowing in the wind, her eyes glued to the asphalt. She was in full throttle but having a hard time keeping up with us; she looked like she wanted to race us. The scene was rather comical, and we laughed. But the noise of her engine was unbearable. We picked up a little more speed to get ahead of her and arrive more quickly at the fuel station at Montañitas, an unavoidable stop-off point. Every time I'd been along this road, I would stop here to fill up with gas, get a drink of cold water, and chat with the owner.

As usual, she was at her post. I greeted her, happy to see a friendly face.

"I'm so relieved they've gone!" she confessed. "Those guerrillas moved into the region as if it belonged to them. They gave me a lot of problems. Now the army has cleared the zone. They have done a good job."

"What about the control posts the guerrillas set up along the road? Are they still there?"

"No, no. The road is completely clear. I am the first to know, because any car that is forced to return stops here to give the alert."

I got back into the car, feeling satisfied, and shared with my companions what the owner had to say, before confiding bitterly, "I'm convinced they don't want us to go to San Vicente. Too bad. We'll get there late, but we'll get there all the same."

We headed off, and fifteen minutes later we noticed some people up ahead, sitting in the middle of the road. When we got closer, we saw that a bridge was being repaired. On the previous trip, we'd had exactly the same problem on the way back from San Vicente. That was during the rainy season; the river had burst its banks, and the force of the water had weakened the bridge's structure. Then, as now, we'd had to bypass the bridge and drive through the river. Today the water was no more than a trickle, and it would mean just a small detour from our route. Two people stood up to show us which way to go. We veered left and drove down the embankment.

In front of us, a Red Cross vehicle was heading down toward the water on the same course we were about to take. Once it reached the top of the opposite bank to rejoin the road, it disappeared from view. We followed suit.

As soon as we crested the embankment, I saw them. They were dressed in military garb, rifles slung across their shoulders, and they had gathered around the Red Cross vehicle. Instinctively I looked down at their shoes. They were black boots, the sort often worn by peasants in the swamps. I'd been taught how to identify boots. If they were leather, it was the army; if they were rubber, it was the FARC. These were rubber.

One of the guerrillas, carrying a rifle, noticed our arrival and jogged over.

"Turn around!" he ordered. "The road is closed."

Our impromptu driver looked at me, not knowing what to do. I hesitated for a moment, two seconds too many that would prove fatal. I'd been stopped at FARC checkpoints before. You talked to the group commander, he radioed for authorization, and you were allowed to pass. But that was during the era of the "demilitarized zone," when peace negotiations were taking place in San Vicente. Everything had changed in the last twenty-four hours.

"Turn around, quickly!" I ordered Adair. It was not an easy manoeuvre. We were stuck between the Red Cross vehicle and the embankment. He began to make the turn; the pressure on him was intense.

"Quick, quick!" I shouted. I had already spotted the gun barrels trained in our direction. The guerrillas' leader issued a command and yelled to us from a distance. One of his men came running over, looking menacing. We had completed three-quarters of the manoeuvre when he caught up with us and put his hand on the door, motioning at Adair to lower the window.

"Stop right there! The commander wants to talk to you. Don't make any fast moves."

I had not reacted fast enough. We should have turned around and retraced our path without hesitating. I was angry with myself. I looked behind me. My companions were white with fear.

"Don't worry," I told them, to force myself to believe. "Everything will be all right."

The commander put his head through the driver's window and looked intently at each of us, one at a time. He stopped when he got to me and asked, "Are you Ingrid Betancourt?"

"Yes, I am."

It was hard to deny it with my name emblazoned all over the car.

"Good. Follow me. Park the car on the side of the road. You'll have to pass between the two buses."

He kept hold of the door, forcing us to drive slowly. It was then that I noticed a strong smell of gasoline. A man with a yellow drum in his hand was splashing the contents over the two buses. I heard the sound of an engine and turned around. The young girl on the motorcycle had, like us, stumbled into the trap. One of the guerrillas made her get down from her bike and took it from her, signalling for her to leave. She stood there, arms dangling, not knowing what to do. Her motorcycle was also doused with gasoline. She understood and hurried away toward the bridge.

A heavyset man with copper-coloured skin and a large black moustache, sweating profusely, was pacing up and down across the road, nervously fanning himself with a red handkerchief and wringing his hands until his knuckles were white. His features were distorted in anguish. He had to be the driver of the bus.

After passing between the two buses, we momentarily lost sight of the

Red Cross vehicle's passengers, who were still held on the shoulder of the road, a gun trained on them. They did not take their eyes off us.

The commander stopped our truck after a few yards. On the order of the commander, the man who had doused the girl's motorcycle with gasoline left it at the base of the bus and ran toward us. Just as he was crossing the verge about ten yards away, an explosion made us all jump with fright. I saw the man hurled into the air and fall to the ground in a crumpled heap. He lay in a huge pool of blood, his shocked gaze locked on mine as he stared at me, bewildered, not understanding what had just happened to him.

The commander was shouting, yelling abuse and cursing at the top of his voice. At that moment the wounded man began screaming in horror as he reached behind him and picked up his boot — containing the bloody flesh and exposed bone of a piece of leg that no longer belonged to him.

"I'm going to die, I'm going to die!" he howled. He was covered in blood that had spurted in every direction. Strips of dripping flesh had been blasted all over, splattering the body of our vehicle and the windscreen. Bits were stuck to people's clothes, their hair, their faces. The smell of burned flesh, combined with the smell of blood and gasoline, was nauseating.

I heard myself say, "We can drive him to the hospital. We can help you!"

I was talking to the group leader in the same way I might have addressed a road-accident victim.

"You will go where I tell you to go," he said.

Then, turning back, he ordered the wounded man to shut up, which he did at once, whimpering softly like a dog caught between pain and fear. The commander appeared satisfied. He then ordered his men to put the injured guerrilla onto the back of the pickup.

"Go ahead," he ordered our driver. "Keep it steady, but make it quick!"

Without hesitating, Adair pulled away as the last members of the group were jumping onto the bed of the truck. One pushed my friends onto the rear bench with the enormous barrel of his rifle and sat inside the vehicle, placing the rifle upright between his legs. He apologized for the inconvenience and smiled as he looked straight ahead. They were all wedged against one another, elbow to elbow, trying to avoid contact with the latest arrival.

To the journalist accompanying us, I said in French, "Don't worry. I'm the one they want. Nothing is going to happen to you."

He nodded, not at all reassured. Beads of sweat were forming on his brow. As I looked through the rear window, I watched a terrifying scene unfolding on the bed of the truck. The wounded man was crying as he held the stump of his leg in both hands. His comrades had tried to make some semblance of a tourniquet with one of their shirts, but the blood kept flowing, seeping up through the already soaked fabric. The car was jerking every two seconds, making it virtually impossible to apply a new tourniquet. The commander tapped the side of the vehicle and shouted something incomprehensible, and the vehicle slowed down. The wounded man's head was lolling back; he had purple shadows under his eyes and was already half unconscious.

We drove along a small, bumpy, dusty road for twenty minutes in the diabolical heat before the leader gave the order to halt, just ahead of a bend that curved around a promontory.

A group of young people in uniform appeared from all sides. There were women, their hair braided into buns, smiling broadly, strangers to the drama, all teenagers. Several helped carry the wounded man from the truck toward a semi-secluded area where we could just make out the roof of a house.

"It's our hospital," the youth sitting with us in the cab declared proudly. "He'll pull through. We're used to this."

We had been there less than a minute when the leader ordered us to leave. Other armed men jumped onto the bed in the back, standing up in spite of the jolts and speed of the vehicle.

After ten minutes the vehicle stopped again. One of the recent arrivals jumped out and opened the doors. "All of you, out! Quickly!" He pointed his gun at us and grabbed me by the arm. "Give me your phone. Show me what you've got in there!" He searched my bag and pushed me forward, pressing the barrel of his gun into my back.

From the beginning I had held on to the hope that they were taking us to a place where they would care for the wounded man and that we would then be permitted to turn around and leave.

Now I had to face what was happening to me. I had just been taken hostage.

4

"EL MOCHO" CESAR

I had shaken the hands of the FARC leader, Marulanda, and his men, Mono Jojoy, Raúl Reyes, and Joaquín Gómez – the last time being just two weeks earlier – and this led me to believe that we had established a dialogue, protecting me from their terrorist actions. We had discussed politics for hours, we had shared a meal. How could these affable individuals be the same men who had ordered our abduction?

And yet their subordinates were threatening to kill me as they forced me to follow them. I tried to retrieve my travel bag from the vehicle, but the person shoving me with his gun yelled at me not to touch it. He ordered hysterically that I be separated from the others, and I saw my companions in misfortune line up pitifully on the other side of the road, each held at close range by an armed man.

I prayed with all my strength that nothing would happen to them, already accepting the fate I believed to be mine. My mind was operating in a thick fog, and I registered sounds and movements only after they happened. I had a sense of déjà vu. Or maybe I had just imagined it. I remembered a photo in the newspaper that had filled me with horror. In it, a car was parked beside this very road, or perhaps a road just like it, the way ours had been. Corpses were lying face down, scattered around the vehicle with its doors still open. The woman who had been shot along with her escorts was the mother of a member of Congress. When looking at the photo, I had imagined everything – her terror at the immediacy of death, her resignation to the inevitable, and then the end of life, the gunshot, the nothingness. Now I understood why it had obsessed me. It was a mirror of what awaited me, a reflection of my future. I thought of all the people I loved, and I thought it was so stupid to die like this. I was in a bubble, curled up within myself. So I did not hear the engine, and when he pulled up beside me in his huge, latest-model Toyota pickup truck and lowered the automatic window to speak to me, I was unable to look at his face or understand his words.

"*Doctora*** Ingrid . . . *Doctora* Ingrid . . . Ingrid!"

I snapped out of my torpor.

"Get in!" he ordered. I landed in the front seat, next to this man who was smiling at me, taking my hand as he would a child's.

"Don't worry. You're safe with me."

"Yes, Commander," I answered without thinking.

It was Cesar, "El Mocho" Cesar, leader of the FARC's fifteenth front. There was no mistaking it. He was definitely the commander. He seemed delighted that I had guessed as much.

He looked around. "Who are these people?"

"That's my assistant."

"And are those your body guards?"

"Not at all. They're working with me on the campaign. One of them is in charge of logistics. He arranges our trips. The other is a cameraman we hired. The oldest one is a foreign journalist, a photographer from France."

"Nothing is going to happen to you. But them . . . I need to verify their identity."

I blanched, only too aware of what he meant.

"Please, believe me, none of them are security agents . . ."

He gave me a cold look, lasting no more than a second; then, imperceptibly, his attitude softened. "Do you have everything you need?"

"No, they wouldn't let me take my bag."

---

* In Colombia, this is a polite way to address someone and replaces madam and sir.

He put his head out of the window and gave some orders. I understood what they meant more from the gestures that accompanied them than from the words themselves. I was trembling from head to toe. I saw that Clara had been separated from the group and ordered to get into the rear of the truck. A man ran to fetch my bag and quickly slid it between my legs before jumping onto the bed of the truck, just as Commander Cesar was putting it into reverse. I turned around. Clara was now sitting on one of the two benches that had been installed on the bed, wedged between a dozen armed men and women whom I had not noticed earlier. Our eyes met. She gave me a faint smile.

I turned back in time to see the rest of my friends being pushed roughly inside the vehicle that until now had been ours, with a guerrilla behind the wheel.

"Does the A/C bother you?" Cesar asked, his tone courteous.

"No, thank you, it's fine like that." He was a small, dark man, his skin burned by the sun. He had to be in his fifties, with a prominent belly betraying what must once have been an athletic body. I noticed that he was missing a finger.

He followed my inspection of his person with amusement and said, "They call me 'El Mocho'* for obvious reasons!" He displayed his stump, adding, "A small gift from the military."

I said nothing.

"Do I scare you?"

"No, why would you scare me? You are actually very polite."

He smiled broadly, delighted by my response.

"The commanders asked me to say hello to you. You'll see, the FARC is going to treat you very well."

I looked away.

"Do you like music? What sort do you like? *Vallenatos*,† boleros, salsa? Open the glove box. There's everything you want in there. Go on! Pick something!"

---

* *Mocho* means "chopped off" in Spanish.
† Lively music from Valledupar on the Caribbean coast.

The conversation was completely surreal. But I acknowledged the effort he was making to put me at ease, so I played along. Dusty CDs had been tossed in haphazardly. I didn't know any of the artists and had difficulty reading what remained of their names on the labels of the obviously pirated discs. I rejected them one by one and noticed Cesar's impatience at my lack of enthusiasm.

"Take that blue one. Yes, that one. I'm going to let you listen to the music we make. This is a pure FARC product. The songwriter and the singer are guerrillas!" He wagged his index finger to emphasize the fact. "We recorded them in our own studios. Listen to this!"

It was grating, ear-shattering music. The car's sound system was ultra-modern, with fluorescent lights shooting in all directions like the dashboard of a spaceship. *Worthy of a drug trafficker!* I couldn't help thinking. A second later I felt bad when I saw the man's childlike pride. He fiddled with the dials with the dexterity of an airline pilot, while somehow controlling the wheel, along that hellish road.

We passed through a village. I was dumbfounded. How could he drive around so nonchalantly with me, his hostage, in front of everyone?

Once again Cesar read my thoughts.

"I'm the king here! This village belongs to me. It's La Unión-Penilla. Everyone loves me here." As if to prove the point, he rolled down the window and waved to passersby. Along the village's main road, a shopping street by all appearances, people returned the gesture, as they might greet the mayor.

"Being the king of a village is not good for a revolutionary!" I remarked.

He looked at me in surprise. Then he burst out laughing. "I have been wanting to meet you. I saw you on TV. You're prettier on TV."

It was my turn to laugh. "Thank you, that's very kind. You make me feel a lot better."

"You're starting a new life with us. You must be prepared. I'll do my best to make things easier, but it's going to be hard for you."

He was no longer laughing. He was calculating, planning, making decisions. Inside that head, vital things were being formulated for me, things I could neither anticipate nor assess.

"I have a favour to ask you," I said. "My father is ill. I don't want him to learn of my abduction on the news. I want to call him."

He looked at me long and hard. Then, as if carefully weighing his words, he replied, "I cannot allow you to call him. They could locate us, and that would place you in danger. But I will allow you to write to him. I'll fax it. He'll get your letter by the end of the day."

More than three hours had passed since we'd driven through Unión-Penilla. I desperately needed to relieve myself. Cesar assured me that we would be arriving in a few minutes, but minutes turned into an hour, and we were still surrounded only by empty fields.

Suddenly, after we'd come around a bend, I saw six small wooden huts lined up in threes on either side of the road. They all looked the same, like shoe boxes – no windows, rusted tin roofs, all covered in a veneer of dust that turned what must once have been brightly painted walls into a uniform shade of grey.

Cesar braked sharply in front of one of them. The door was wide open, and you could see through to the end of the back garden. It was a small house, modest but clean, dark and no doubt cool.

He pushed me inside, but I refused to take another step until I knew that Clara was right behind me. She got out of the vehicle and took my hand to make sure we would not be separated.

"Don't worry. You'll stay together." Cesar indicated the toilets at the end of the garden. "Go ahead. A girl will show you the way."

The garden was full of flowers of every colour. I thought then that if our place of imprisonment were to be this little house, I could resign myself to my misfortune.

A small shed with a wooden door appeared to be the toilet. I didn't see the young girl until a few seconds later. She could not have been more than about fifteen, and I was struck by her beauty. Dressed in camouflage, gun held firmly across her chest, she stood astride, swaying her hips coquettishly. Her pretty face, her flaxen hair coiled on her head, like a little bird's nest, and the femininity of her earrings contrasted with the severity of her uniform. Almost shyly she greeted me with a beautiful smile.

Inside the shed the smell was revolting. There was no toilet paper. The drone of large green flies hovering over the putrid hole made the experience all the more vile. Once outside, I nearly fainted.

Cesar was waiting in the house with a cold drink for us and two sheets of paper that he laid on a small table in the living room. He explained that we could use the paper to write a message to our families.

I spent a long time thinking about the words I would choose in writing to Papa. I told him that I had just been taken hostage but that I was being treated well and that I was not alone because Clara was with me. I described the conditions under which we had been captured, how distressed I was to see one of the guerrillas lose his leg by stepping on an antipersonnel mine they had planted, and finally I said I hated the war.

I wanted him to sense through my words that I was not afraid. And I wanted to prolong our last conversation, to ask him to wait for me.

Cesar returned, telling us that we could take as long as we needed but that we were not to give any indication of our location or of the time, nor should we mention any names, because if we did, he would not be able to send our letters.

Of course he was going to read my letter. He could even censor it! He had left again, but I still felt his breath on my neck as if he were peering over my shoulder. Never mind. I wrote what I had planned to write, taking care not to let my tears fall onto the paper. All I could see was darkness. My lucky star had just vanished.

Cesar left but soon returned; a small, barrel-shaped man with a large, bushy moustache and greasy hair was with him. When he saw us, he looked panic-stricken, as if he had set eyes on the devil. He interlaced his fingers nervously and was clearly waiting for instructions from his leader.

"This is Doctora Ingrid," said Cesar.

The newcomer extended an enormous hand covered in soot, which he quickly tried to wipe on his jeans and holey T-shirt.

Cesar continued in a measured voice, articulating every word, as if to make sure he would be properly understood and not have to repeat himself.

"Go and buy some clothes: trousers, jeans, something chic, and short-sleeved shirts, pretty ones, for women, do you understand?"

The man nodded quickly, his eyes rooted to the floor in extreme concentration.

"Get some underwear, too. Make sure it's feminine. The best quality."

The man's head moved up and down, as if on a spring, and he held his breath.

"And rubber boots. Get the good ones. The Venus. Not the Colombian-made ones. And also get me a good mattress, double thickness, and a mosquito net. But make sure they're decent. I don't want the useless stuff you dug up last time! Send everything straight to Sonia's. I'm counting on you. I want quality, do you understand?"

The little man took his leave, backing out of the room before pivoting on the step and disappearing.

"If you're ready, we'll get going right away."

It was the end of the day. The heat became tolerable as we bumped along a wretched, dusty track pitted with craters full of stagnant mud. Large, centuries-old trees blocked the horizon, and the sky winding above the road was blood red. Now Clara and I were in the front cab. The sound system had finally been switched off, and our silence was invaded by the cheeping of millions of invisible birds that burst into the sky in small black clouds as we passed by, only to turn back almost immediately and resume their positions in the cover of the foliage. I tried to lean my head out the window to watch the silhouettes of these magical, free birds above the treetops. If I had been with Papa, he would have wanted to gaze at them just as I was doing. This marvellous spectacle was painful – the happiness of these birds was hurting me, and so was their freedom.

"You'll have to get used to eating everything," Cesar remarked. "The only meat here is monkey!"

"I'm a vegetarian." It wasn't true, but I felt the need to come up with a witty remark. "You have to get me salad, fruit and vegetables. With all this greenery, I don't suppose that'll be a problem."

Cesar remained silent. He seemed, however, to be enjoying my conversation. I pushed it a bit further.

"And if you really want to make me happy, get me some cheese!"

Ten minutes later he stopped the truck in the middle of nowhere. The guerrillas who were in the rear of the vehicle got out to stretch their legs and piss matter-of-factly in front of everyone. Cesar also got out and issued instructions, then headed off with two of the guerrillas toward a small house I hadn't noticed initially, hidden between the trees. He came back smiling, a plastic bag in each hand; the other two men were just behind him, carrying a case of beer.

He handed me one of the plastic bags.

"Here, this is for you. I'll get you some whenever I can, but it's not easy here."

I couldn't help smiling. Inside the bag was a large piece of fresh cheese and a dozen small limes. I noticed the men's sidelong glances and placed the bag in the shade under the seat.

The track had now narrowed, and the trees seemed to have taken over. We could no longer see the sky through the canopy of vegetation.

Suddenly, after crossing a furrow, the vehicle swung sharply to the left and crashed through the bush. I put my forearm over my eyes to protect myself from the impact, but instead of hitting something the truck just barged its way onto a path and ended up in the middle of an open area of beaten earth. All the vegetation had been cut away. We stopped. It was starting to get dark.

The squealing of brakes had announced our arrival, and a large German shepherd came trotting over, barking diligently, doing its duty.

Cesar got out of the vehicle. I did the same on my side.

"Be careful," he warned. "This dog is fierce."

The dog lurched toward me, barking with all its might. I allowed it to come close and smell me, and then I stroked it lightly between the ears. Cesar was watching me out of the corner of his eye.

"I love dogs," I ventured. I didn't want Cesar to think he could intimidate me.

The clearing was surrounded by huts; a little farther away were some tents, and a large open shelter lined with low wooden trestle tables every few feet. One of the huts had an earth wall all the way around it; another was open, with rows of benches laid out like church pews facing a small television set that hung from the branch of a large tree protruding through the side. It was the first time I had set foot in a FARC camp.

"Let me introduce you to Sonia."

A large woman with dyed-blonde hair sticking up military style held out her hand to me. I hadn't seen her arrive and somewhat belatedly held out mine. Her handshake was bone-crushing, and I yelled in pain. She let go, and I shook my hand vigorously to bring back the circulation. Cesar was amused.

Sonia was bent double, laughing uncontrollably. Then, catching her breath, she said, "I'm sorry. I didn't mean to hurt you."

"So now you know. You have to treat her gently," said Cesar, and he left.

Before I even had a chance to say good-bye to Cesar, Sonia put her arm around my shoulders, like an old schoolmate, to take me on a tour of the camp. Clara followed.

Sonia was the commander of this camp. She lived with her partner, a younger man of lower rank; she ostentatiously gave orders to him to leave no doubt who was in charge. She took us into her hut, the only one, in fact, that had a wall and therefore a degree of privacy. Standing in the centre of the room between a mattress on the floor and a plastic chair was a small refrigerator: she opened it proudly. It contained only two soft drinks and three bottles of water.

"It's for medicine," she explained, as if to apologize for having such a luxury.

I looked at her, not understanding.

"Yes, this camp is a FARC hospital. All the region's wounded come here – those waiting for surgery in town and those who are recovering."

She then took us over to the large shelter. At the end of one of the tables, a couple of girls were rummaging through the contents of some large black plastic bags. Next to them was a rolled-up mattress tied with string and a thick roll of mesh.

"Isabel and Ana. Take turns guarding them. Make up the bed and get them settled."

The low tables were beds. At the opposite end of the shelter, some guerrillas were starting to set up mosquito nets or lying down to sleep on black plastic sheets they had laid over the top of the wooden planks. At each corner of the shelter, a man stood watch. It would have been difficult to leave without being seen.

The girls finished making up one bed. I looked around and saw nothing with which to make up a second. I asked about this, and one of them replied that the order was for us to sleep in the same bed. A huge moon lit up the camp. I asked Clara if she wanted to walk with me a little. We were soon outside, breathing in the light air of a beautiful tropical night. I still felt free and refused to think of myself as a hostage. The girls who were following us gave each of us a flashlight.

"Only use it if absolutely necessary. Never point it toward the sky. Switch it off as soon as you hear the sound of a plane or helicopters, or when we tell you to. You have to go back now. If you need anything, call us. One of us will stay at the foot of your bed."

The girl who had spoken moved a short distance away and stood in front of us, setting down her rifle and leaning her elbows on the butt. I assumed she was our personal guard and that the four others were sentries standing at their usual posts.

I sat on the edge of the mattress, lacking the energy to look inside the bags containing our new clothes. I had eaten nothing all day. I saw Cesar's plastic bag – it was empty. The limes were floating in the water from the cheese. Clara was already asleep, stretched out under the mosquito net, fully clothed and covered by a beige sheet with brown flowers. I lay down myself, trying to take up as little space as possible. I examined the mosquito net with my flashlight. I did not want to find any bugs on the inside. Then I switched it off. Where were the others? Adair? The French photographer? I was suddenly overwhelmed with sorrow. I wept silently.

5

SONIA'S CAMP

I lay awake all night. I watched the guards more carefully than they watched me. Every two hours new men arrived to take over. I was too far away to hear what they were saying, but it was brief. A slap on the back and one group left, leaving the others standing in their place in the dark. The girls taking turns at our bedside ended up sitting on the empty bed opposite, and gradually they succumbed to their drowsiness. How could we get out of there? How could we get to the road? How could I get home? Would there be more guards farther away? At the exit to the camp? I had to watch more closely, ask questions, observe. I pictured myself leaving with my friend toward freedom. Would she agree to follow me? I would go straight to Papa. I would surprise him in his room. He would be sitting in his green leather armchair. He would be wearing his oxygen mask. He would open his arms wide, and I would snuggle into them and cry from happiness at being with him. Then we would call everyone. What joy! Perhaps Clara and I would have to get a bus along the road. Or walk until we came to a town. That would be safer. The guerrillas had spies everywhere. We would have to find a military base or a police station. When he had stopped to get the cheese and beers, Cesar had pointed toward the right. He'd laughed and explained that there was a military base nearby. He said the *chulos* were stupid. I didn't know that guerrillas called the soldiers "vultures." It hit me, as if it were an insult directed at me. But I didn't say anything. *From now on I will always be on the side of the military*, I thought.

How would the country react when they learned of my abduction? What would the other candidates do? Would they show solidarity? I thought of Piedad Córdoba, a colleague from the Senate. She had arranged for me to meet Manuel Marulanda, the leader of the FARC. We had travelled together by taxi from Florencia to San Vicente. It was the first time I'd been there. We took a terrible road, a real roller coaster. On several occasions we got stuck in the mud, and at times we were forced to get out and walk to lighten the vehicle's load. We had all pushed, pulled, and lifted before arriving covered in dust at the meeting place, which was at a camp on the edge of the virgin forest. I saw how the old Marulanda had absolute control over all his men. At one point he complained about the mud beneath his chair. They literally picked him up in his chair like an emperor, while other commanders laid planks of wood on the ground, crafting an improvised floor for him. Six months after our visit to the FARC, Piedad Córdoba was abducted by the paramilitaries. Castaño, their leader, accused her of being an ally of the guerrillas. I had gone to speak with an old farmer who was said to have the ear of Castaño. I asked him to intervene in favour of Piedad's release. Many had pleaded in her favour. A few days later, she was released. I hoped my own case would be similar to hers. Perhaps it would just be a matter of a few weeks before my freedom was secured. All these questions that blended fantasy and reality preoccupied me the entire night.

Day was breaking, the first day of my life in captivity. The mosquito net we had been given was white, with tightly woven mesh. I gazed through it, following the strange world awakening around me, under the illusion that I could look out but no one could look in, as if I were protected in a cocoon. Contours of objects started to emerge from the darkness of the night. A chilly breeze caused me to shiver. It was four-thirty in the morning when one of the guerrillas switched on the radio loud enough for me to hear it. The talk was about us, and I strained to get closer to the radio without daring to leave my refuge. The voice confirmed that I'd been taken hostage by the guerrillas. I heard Mom's appeals, and my heart contracted in pain, so much so that I was unable to listen properly. Then they were talking about Clara. I woke her so that she could follow the bulletin with me. The guerrilla kept changing stations, and every time he did, he landed on a station broadcasting news about us. Someone else, farther away, tuned in his radio to the same station, as did a third. The sound reached us in stereo, which made listening easier.

Just before five o'clock, someone went by our bed making a very loud and unpleasant noise with his mouth, which galvanized the camp into action. It was called *la churuquiada*, another typically FARC term referring to an imitation of the call of the monkey. It sounded the wake-up of the jungle.

The convalescent guerrillas who were sleeping with us in the shelter all rose immediately. They removed the mosquito nets, quickly folded them, and rolled them into tight oblongs which they secured with the same string used to hang them from the four corners of their beds. I watched them work, fascinated, as I listened to the news bulletins. Clara and I got up, and I asked to use the toilet.

Our guard was Isabel. She was short, about thirty, with long, frizzy hair pulled back in a bun. She had on pretty gold earrings and childish barrettes to keep her unruly bangs away from her face. Slightly overweight, she wore heavy cotton camouflage trousers that looked a bit too tight for comfort. She responded to my request with the nicest of smiles, was clearly excited to be looking after us.

Taking me by the hand, she then tucked my forearm under her elbow in an unexpected gesture of affection and complicity. "You'll like it here with us, you'll see. You won't want to leave!"

I followed her to the toilets, expecting to find a latrine similar to the one I had used in the old house along the road and getting ready to hold my breath to stave off the stench.

After no more than twenty yards, we were pushing our way through the thick vegetation. I still couldn't spot an outhouse in the vicinity. We emerged into a fairly large clearing. The earth looked like it had been churned up more or less all over. I was suddenly aware of the sound of an engine running. I asked Isabel what it could be.

She didn't know what I was talking about; then, listening more closely, she said, "No, no. There's no engine running."

"But there is! Wait, I'm not crazy – there's a very loud noise. Listen!"

Isabel once again listened intently, then burst out laughing, squeezing her nose like a little girl so as not to make a noise.

"Ah, no! That's the sound of the flies!"

I looked down in fright. Swirling around my feet were thousands of flies of all species – fat ones, long ones, yellow ones, green ones, all in a mass, so excited that they were bumping into each other and falling to the ground, feet in the air, wings flapping in vain against the earth. I was in the process of discovering a world of extraordinarily active insects. Wasps attacking flies before the latter could get up. Ants attacking wasps and flies and transporting their still-quivering spoils back to their nests. Shiny-green-backed beetles flying about loudly before crashing into our knees. I let out a nervous yelp when I realized that an army of minuscule ants was storming up my trousers and had already got as far as my waist. I tried to shake them off by stamping up and down vigorously on the spot to stop them from climbing any farther.

"So where are the toilets?"

"They're right here!" Isabel said with a laugh. "These are the *chontos*. See? There are still some holes you can use. You squat over them, do your business, then cover it up with the earth next to it, like this, with your foot."

I looked more closely. A number of holes had been dug in the ground. The sight inside each was nauseating. Insects were crawling all over the matter that had not been covered properly. I was already feeling sick, and instinctively I doubled over in disgust, gripped by spasms as the putrid odour filled my nostrils. Without warning I threw up over both of us, splattering even our shirts.

Isabel was no longer laughing. She wiped herself with the sleeve of her jacket and covered my vomit with the nearest pile of earth.

"Right then, I'll wait for you over there."

I was hysterical at the idea of remaining alone in this hell. Through the vegetation I could perceive shadows moving.

"But everyone can see me!"

Isabel handed me a roll of toilet paper. "Don't worry. I won't let anyone near."

I returned unsteadily to the camp, already missing the latrine of the little house along the road. I would have to wash my vomit off and put on the clothes they had given us. There were four pairs of trousers, all jeans of different sizes and styles, T-shirts with childish motifs, and underwear, some very plain and made of cotton, some covered with brightly coloured lace. Distribution was simple: We each took the size closest to ours. There were also two large bath towels and two pairs of rubber boots, the same ones that had enabled me to identify the guerrillas. Instinctively I put them to one side, with no intention of ever using them.

A very young girl whom I had not seen before came over to us. She appeared uneasy. Isabel introduced us. "This is María, your *recepcionista*." My eyes widened. I could not fathom how, in the middle of nowhere, there could be a "receptionist."

"She is in charge of your meals," explained Isabel. "What would you like?"

It had to be six-thirty in the morning at most. I was therefore thinking of breakfast, the simpler the better.

"Fried eggs?" I ventured.

Panic-stricken, María headed off toward the back of the camp and disappeared behind an embankment.

Then Isabel left, before I had a chance to ask her about taking a shower. Clara sat down, boredom written over her face. I looked around. There were no sick people in bed. Every one of them was busy with manual work: some chopping wood with machetes, some sewing straps onto their backpacks, and some using a very bizarre technique to weave belts. Their hands were so quick that it was impossible to follow their movements.

"Let's go for a walk around the camp!" I suggested to my companion.

"Yes, let's!" she replied enthusiastically.

We arranged our things as best we could on a corner of the bed and were getting ready to leave the shelter when a woman's voice behind me stopped us.

"What are you doing?"

It was Ana. She was holding her FAL rifle in both hands and looking at us sternly.

"We're going to walk around the camp," I replied, surprised.

"You need to ask permission."

"From whom?"

"From me."

"Really? Well, then, will you give us permission to take a walk around the camp?"

"No."

Just then María returned with a boiling-hot pot giving off a strong aroma of coffee. In the other hand she was carrying two small bread rolls and two stainless-steel cups. Sonia was right behind her, smiling broadly.

"So, Ingrid, how are you?"

She slapped me on the back, throwing me off balance, and continued, beaming. "All the talk on the radio is about you! The Secretariado" – which was the highest governing body in the FARC hierarchy – "announced that they are going to be issuing a press release this evening. It's going out around the world!"

The guerrillas were very proud of the media coup that my capture had generated for them. But I was far from thinking about the news capturing international attention. I was hoping above all that the announcement would prompt the government to speed up its efforts to obtain our release. I imagined that now more than ever the government would want to obscure the details of the events leading up to my abduction, as they could prove embarrassing.

"Can we watch the news this evening? I noticed you have a television . . ."

Sonia grew serious and reflective, a look I had seen before in "El Mocho" Cesar. All faces turned toward Sonia, everyone holding their breath in total silence, as if their lives depended on her response. She took her time, then gave her verdict, carefully weighing each word. "The television is banned because of the air force," she said. "But I will make an exception this evening."

A wave of happiness swept through the camp. Lively conversations started up again, and the sound of distant laughter filtered through the air.

"Commander Cesar has informed us he will be visiting. Come and see me in my *caleta* whenever you want," Sonia announced before turning to leave.

I stood there trying to digest these new codes, this confusing vocabulary. The *caleta* must be her hut, just as the *chontos* were the toilets and the *recepcionista* was a girl who served meals. I supposed that in a revolutionary organization certain words must be taboo. Enlisting in the FARC to end up working as a maid had to be unthinkable. Naturally, it was better to be called a *recepcionista*.

Ana returned with instructions to take us to bathe. She was visibly annoyed.

"Go on, hurry up. Fetch your clean clothes and bath towels. I don't have all day!"

We quickly gathered up our things and threw them into a plastic bag, thrilled at the idea of being able to freshen up. We took the same path as to the *chontos* but turned right well beforehand. There, under a tin roof, was a cement tub that they were filling with water from a hose. Ana gave us a bar of laundry soap and went off into the bushes. The pump was silenced, and the water stopped running. "So much for my shower!" I mused. Ana returned, still in a bad mood. Isabel had followed us. She stood there, feet planted wide, gun over her shoulder, watching Ana in silence.

I looked about me; the place was surrounded by thick vegetation. I tried to spot somewhere to put my things.

"Go and cut them a rail," instructed Isabel curtly.

Ana pulled out her machete and selected a thick branch from the nearest tree. She severed it in a single blow and caught it with astonishing dexterity as it fell. Then she cleaned it and peeled off the bark, transforming it into a broom handle so perfect it could have come straight from a factory. I couldn't believe my eyes. Next she installed it, placing one end on the edge of the tub and the other on the fork of a conveniently located bush. She tested the soundness of her handiwork and returned her machete to its sheath. I carefully hung my fresh clothes over the rail, still impressed by her performance. Then, looking around for Clara, I saw that she was removing all her clothes. Yes, of course. That was what you were supposed to do. The girls watched her impassively.

"And what if someone shows up unannounced?" I asked hesitatingly.

"Everyone is made the same," retorted Ana. "What does it matter if someone sees?"

"No one will come, don't worry," said Isabel, as if she had not heard her comrade's remark. Then she added softly, "Use the *timbo*."

I had no idea what a *timbo* might be. I looked around and saw nothing. Except that yes, in the water there was an oil can cut in half so that the handle and base formed a scoop. The *timbo* became indispensable. Clara and I took turns using it.

Ana was getting impatient, shuffling around in the bushes, grumbling. She had decided to restart the water pump.

"There, are you happy? Now, hurry up."

The final shower lasted only a few seconds. Two minutes later we were dressed and ready to receive Commander Cesar.

Cesar's truck was parked in the clearing. He was talking to Sonia. We walked up to him, escorted by two female guerrillas. Sonia dispatched them immediately.

Smiling, Cesar held his hand out to me. "How are you?"

"Not good. I don't know what happened to my friends. You told me that—"

Cesar cut me off. "I told you nothing."

"You told me that you were going to check their identity—"

"You told me they were foreign journalists."

"No, I told you that the older one was a photographer with a foreign magazine; the young one is a cameraman employed by my campaign and the other, the one who was driving, is my logistics manager."

"If you're telling me the truth, I'll spare them. I confiscated all their video equipment and viewed the footage last night. The military is not too fond of you! Nice discussion you had on the tarmac with the general. That cost him his job! And they are already hot on your heels. There's fighting near Unión-Penilla. You will have to get out of here fairly quickly. Did they bring you your things?"

I nodded mechanically. Everything he said was worrying. I wanted assurance that my companions were safe and would be freed shortly. The fighting at Unión-Penilla was a source of hope. But if there were confrontations, we risked being killed. How did he know that the general had been dismissed? That general was the one in the best position to mount a successful rescue operation. He was the man who knew the area, he was in the field, and he was the last one to have seen me.

Cesar took his leave. There was nothing to do but wait, without knowing what we were waiting for. The minutes stretched into an oppressive eternity, and to fill them required a determination I didn't have. I could do nothing but ruminate. We noticed a game of chess on the corner of what was meant to be a table. That such a thing could exist in the middle of this self-contained world was both unexpected and surprising. We were the pawns. Our existence was being defined according to a logic that our abductors were concealing from us. I pushed the game away. How long was this going to last? Three months? Six months? I observed the people around me. The blithe attitude to life, the gentle rhythm of routine – it all sickened me. How could they sleep, eat, and smile while keeping us away from our loved ones?

Isabel had finished her guard duty and had come to have lunch. She looked with manifest longing at the red and black-lace underwear still in its packaging. I offered it to her. She turned it over in her hands with childlike delight, then put it back where it was, as if pushing away too great a temptation. Finally she stood up, driven by a sudden fervour, and said in a loud voice for her comrades to hear, "I am going to make a request." As I later learned, "requests" were a fundamental part of FARC life. Everything was controlled and monitored. No one could take the slightest initiative or give or receive a gift without asking permission. You could be refused the right to stand up or sit down, to eat or to drink, to sleep or to go to the *chontos*. Isabel came running back, her cheeks flushed. She had obtained permission to accept my gift. I watched her walk away, trying to imagine what life must be like for a woman in the camp. The commander was a woman, but I counted just five girls among about thirty men. What could they hope for here that would be better than elsewhere? Their femininity did not cease to amaze me, even though they were never without their guns and had masculine reflexes that did not appear to be feigned. Just as with this new vocabulary, these peculiar songs, this peculiar habitat, I looked with surprise at these young women who all seemed to be cast in the same mould and to have sacrificed their individuality.

Being a prisoner was bad enough. But being a female prisoner in the hands of the FARC was another matter entirely. It was difficult to put it into words. Intuitively I felt that the FARC was exploiting these women with their consent. The organization worked subtly, words were chosen deliberately, appearances were carefully cultivated, and there was more to everything than met the eye . . . I had just lost my freedom, but I was not willing to surrender my identity.

When night fell, Sonia came to fetch us to watch the news on TV. The camp was convened in the hut that boasted the small screen. She assigned us our places, then left to switch on the generator. A solitary light bulb swayed from the ceiling like a hanged man. It came on, and the group went into raptures. I had trouble understanding their excitement. I sat there waiting in the middle of a band of armed men, their rifles propped up between their legs. Sonia switched on the television and left again; the picture was fuzzy and the sound full of static. No one moved, all eyes glued to the screen. Sonia finally came back, turned a couple of knobs, and a blurred picture appeared. But the sound was clear. The news had started. I saw Adair, my logistics manager, on the screen. He and the other members of our group had just been released. They were speaking emotionally about their final moments with us. I leaped up with joy. My commotion irritated some of the guerrillas and they called gruffly for silence. I slumped back down on the bench, my eyes moist.

That night I didn't feel like sleeping. It was a bright, huge moon again and the temperature outside was pleasant. I wanted to walk to clear my mind. Isabel was on guard. She had no problem agreeing to my request. I set off across the clearing to the *chontos*, passing in front of Sonia's hut and alongside the shelter. Some of the convalescents had switched on their radios, and echoes of tropical music drifted toward me. I imagined the world without me, this Sunday that had brought sorrow and anxiety to those I loved. My children, Melanie, Lorenzo, and Sebastian, my stepson by Fabrice, had already heard the news. I expected them to be strong. We had often talked about the possibility that I might be abducted. I had always been more afraid of being taken hostage than of being assassinated. I had told them that they must never give in to blackmail and that it was better to die than to submit. Now I was not so sure. I no longer knew what to think. What was most intolerable to me was the pain they had to be feeling. I wanted to live. I did not want them to become orphans, and I was determined to give them back their carefree spirit. I imagined them talking to each other, bound by mutual torment, trying to reconstruct the events leading up to my abduction, trying to understand. I was in pain.

I understood only too well the significance of the press release issued by the Secretariado. It confirmed that I had been taken hostage and that I was part of the group of "interchangeables."* My captors threatened to kill me one year to the day after my capture if there was no agreement to release the guerrillas detained in Colombian prisons. To spend one year in captivity and then be assassinated – that was my possible fate. Would they carry out their threat? It was hard to believe, but I did not want to be around to find out. We had to escape.

The thought of preparing our escape calmed me. I created a mental map of our environment and tried to reconstruct from memory the road we had taken to get here. I was certain that we had travelled in what was almost a straight line, southward. It would mean a lot of walking, but it was feasible.

I finally got into bed, fully clothed, but I still couldn't close my eyes. It must have been around nine in the evening when I heard them in the distance. Helicopters, several of them, were rapidly approaching. Suddenly the camp went into a frenzy. The sick jumped from their beds, pulled on their backpacks, and started running. Orders were shouted in the darkness as the commotion reached its peak. "Turn out the lights, goddamn it!"

---

* "Interchangeable" is the FARC term used to describe political prisoners who can be exchanged for FARC prisoners held in Colombian prisons.

yelled Sonia, her voice like a man's. Ana and Isabel rushed toward us, grabbing the mosquito net and pushing us out of bed. "Bring what you can, we're leaving immediately! It's the air force!"

My mind went blank. I heard hysterical voices around me and went into a trance: put on shoes, roll up clothes, put them in the bag, take bag, check that nothing is left behind, walk. My heart was beating slowly, as it did when I went diving. The echo of the outside world reached me in the same way, as if filtered by an enormous wall of water. Ana continued to yell and push me. The guerrillas were already advancing in single file. I turned around. Ana had rolled up the mattress and was carrying it under her arm. Wedged under the other arm was the mosquito net, twisted into a roll. She was also carrying her huge backpack, so heavy that it forced her to lean forward. "Talk about a dog's life!" I muttered, more irritated than anything else. I was not afraid. Their hastiness was none of my concern.

About a hundred yards from camp, we were ordered to stop. The moon was sufficiently bright through the trees so that I could distinguish the people around me. The guerrillas were sitting on the ground, leaning against their backpacks. Some had taken out their black plastic sheets and were covering themselves with them.

"How long are we going to stay here?" I whispered to Isabel. We could still hear the sound of the helicopters, but it seemed that they were no longer close.

"I don't know. We have to wait for instructions from Sonia. We could be in for days of walking."

"Days of walking?"

Isabel didn't respond.

"Our boots are still at the camp," I said, hoping to have a reason to retrace our steps.

"No, I have them." She showed them to me. They were folded in a bag she was using as a cushion. "You should put them on. You won't be able to walk in the mountains otherwise."

"The mountains? We're going to the mountains?"

That threw me. I had thought we'd be going south, toward the inmost depths of the Llanos, the tropical plains to the east of the Andes. Beyond that was the Amazon. Mountains meant turning back on ourselves toward Bogotá. The Andes formed a natural barrier that was almost impossible to cross on foot. Simón Bolívar had done it with his army but it was considered an exploit!

My question struck her as suspicious, as if I were trying to trap her into divulging secret information. Isabel looked at me warily.

"Yes, the mountains, *al monte*,* the *selva*†!"

For them, *monte* meant the forest and any land covered by vegetation untouched by man. Curiously, that was indeed the ancient meaning of the word *monte*. They had assimilated it into the word *montaña* and used both without making a distinction. Their dialect tended to be confusing. I started learning it as if it were a foreign language, and I tried to memorize the false friends between my Spanish and theirs. Once I understood that we were headed toward the Llanos, my mind started to race.

The helicopters were returning, the sounds rapidly getting louder. They were hedgehopping above the trees. I could see three overhead, lined up in formation, and guessed there must be more. They passed right over us, and the sight of them moved me to joy: they were looking for us! The guerrillas were visibly anxious. Their faces were turned toward the sky, their jaws clenched in defiance, hatred, and fear. I knew that Ana was watching me. I avoided letting my feelings show. Now the helicopters were moving away. They would not be returning. Those around me had been aware of my moment of hope. They were animals trained to sniff out other people's happiness. I had done the same. I had got a whiff of their fear, and I had delighted in it. Now I could smell their satisfaction at my disappointment. I belonged to them. Their sense of victory excited them. They nudged each other, whispering and looking me straight in the eye. I lowered my gaze. I was powerless. The line loosened up; they all went back to preparing their little space for the night. I walked over to Clara. We held hands in silence, sitting next to each other on our travel bags, stiff and formal. We were used to the city. The night was closing in and large clouds were

---

* "The forest" in the peasants' vernacular.
† Jungle.

gathering above us, filling the sky. The moon became blurred. There was a flurry of activity. The guerrillas were kneeling before their backpacks, undoing the thousands of straps, buckles and knots that secured them.

"What's going on?" I asked.

"It's going to rain," replied Isabel as she, too, worked on her backpack.

"And what about us? What are we supposed to do?"

Her response was to hand me a black plastic sheet. "Cover yourselves with this!"

The first drops of rain began to fall. We heard them tapping on the leaves on the forest canopy, not yet penetrating the vegetation. Someone threw us another plastic sheet, which landed at our feet. It came just in time. The storm unfurled like a biblical deluge.

At four-thirty in the morning, we filed back into the camp. Radios were switched on, and familiar voices announced the news. The smell of black coffee marked the start of another day. I collapsed onto the planks before I even had a chance to unpack.

María brought over a large plate of rice and lentils, plus two spoons.

"Do you have any forks?" I asked.

"You'll have to put in a request with the commander," she said.

"You mean Sonia?"

"No, Commander Cesar!"

He had arrived at the camp earlier in the afternoon in his large red pickup, which was far too luxurious for a rebel. I smiled when I thought of the story he'd told me. He had got a FARC militiaman to buy it for him in Bogotá and drive it to the demilitarized zone, where he'd handed it over. The militiaman then declared it stolen and received the insurance payment. That was the FARC way. More than insurgents, they acted like gangsters. A large construction truck full of young guerrillas followed the pickup.

Cesar greeted me, looking pleased.

"There was fighting last night," he informed me. "We killed half a dozen soldiers. They were coming to get you. They have come to realize they will never succeed! You have to leave at once. This place has already been spotted. It's for your own safety. Get your things together."

This time Cesar did not accompany us. The driver was the same fat man who had bought the mattress and other items. The fifteen guerrillas who had arrived with Cesar continued on with us, standing in the back of the truck, holding their rifles. Clara and I climbed into the cab with the driver.

After the previous night's storm, the track had become a slimy mud chute. It was impossible to travel at more than twelve miles per hour. We continued southward, deeper and deeper into the Llanos. The landscape became thickly forested, with just a few open fields lying fallow and some terrain razed by controlled fires. The experts called it the "agricultural frontier." The Amazon rainforest could not be far away.

The sky was ablaze as the sun set with great ceremony. We had gone many hours without stopping, and the farther we travelled, the more my heart constricted. It meant even more miles separating me from my home. I tried to stay calm by calculating that we could put aside enough provisions for our escape to last for one week's walk. We would have to get away at night when the guards relaxed their vigilance. We would walk until dawn and hide during the day. We wouldn't ask civilians for help. They might be working for the FARC. The driver's attitude was revealing: Like many in the region, he was bound to the guerrillas in an almost feudal relationship that was based on dependency, submission, allegiance, interest, and fear.

I was deep in thought when the vehicle stopped. We were at the top of a butte, the full splendour of the sunset spread before us. On the left were hacienda-style gates. The property was enclosed not by a wall but by green oilcloth, which circled the perimeter and completely concealed from the road what lay inside.

The guerrillas jumped out of the truck and, in groups of two, dispersed to each corner of the property. A tall man with a thin moustache opened both entrance gates wide. He was very young, probably in his early twenties. The truck entered silently. The sky was turning green, and night fell swiftly.

The tall man walked over and held out his hand.

"I'm honoured to meet you. I'm your new commander. If you need anything, you come to me. My name is Cesar. And this is Betty. She will look after you. She is your *recepcionista*." Betty was not her real name. The guerrillas all had aliases chosen by the commander who recruited them. Often it was a foreign name, or a biblical one, or a name from a national television show. *Ugly Betty** had been a favourite soap opera in Colombia for years. And here was another commander called Cesar. *Hardly surprising — all the commanders here are Cesar*, I mused.

Our Betty was not ugly, but she was so small she resembled a dwarf. She switched on her flashlight and asked us to follow her. The truck, empty, went away, and the gates closed. Betty led us toward an old shed with a rotten roof, half of which had fallen to the ground. Under the half that remained were two beds, similar to those we had used at the hospital, except that the boards were also rotten and crumbling.

Betty set down her backpack in a corner and with her rifle over her shoulder began the task of recuperating the few planks still solid enough to make one bed. She held the flashlight between her teeth to keep both hands free and work more quickly. The beam of light followed her movement. She was about to put her hand on one of the planks when she jumped back, losing the flashlight, which rolled onto the floor. I saw it at the same time: an enormous furry red tarantula, puffed up on its fat legs, ready to pounce. I grabbed the flashlight to look for the beast, which had since bounced under the bed and was scuttling toward the rotten roof and a pile of straw. With her machete Betty chopped the creature in two.

"I can't sleep here. I hate those beasts. What's more, they live in pairs, so the other one can't be far away!" My voice was shrill, betraying my anxiety. It was astonishing. I sounded just like my mother. *She* was the one who dreaded "those beasts," not me. I found them fascinating because it seemed as if their massive size took them from the world of insects and bugs to that of vertebrates.

"We'll give the place a thorough clean. I'll have a good look under the bed and all around. And then I'll sleep here with you, don't worry." Betty was trying her best not to laugh.

---

* The American show *Ugly Betty* was based on the Colombian series *Yo soy Betty, la fea*.

As soon as the mattress and mosquito net were in place, Clara lay down on the bed. Betty came back with an old broom she'd found lying around, and I borrowed it to help her. I put our belongings on a plank of wood that Betty had fashioned into a shelf, then got into bed, although it was dawn before I was able to sleep. My insomnia gave me the opportunity to locate the positions of the guards, and I soon formulated an escape plan for the following evening. I even spotted a knife in Betty's backpack that could come in handy.

But our hopes for escape were short-lived. El Mocho turned up around noon, and we took to the road again, still travelling southward. I was once again gripped by anxiety; I figured that it would now take us more than a week to retrace our steps. The situation was becoming critical. The farther we travelled, the fewer our chances of success. We had to act as quickly as possible and equip ourselves to survive in a region that was becoming more hostile by the mile. We were no longer crossing flat country but starting on the climbs and descents of an increasingly rolling landscape. The peasants were now a population of lumberjacks, whose presence you could detect from the damage they left behind. Helpless spectators to an ecological disaster no one cared about, we crossed the ravaged space as if we were the sole survivors of a nuclear war.

El Mocho stopped the vehicle on a hill. Down below, half-naked children played on the floor of a small house built in the middle of a cemetery of trees. Smoke rose wearily from the chimney. El Mocho dispatched a group of guerrillas to fetch some cheese, fish, and fruit. Fish? I examined my surroundings. I couldn't see any rivers. At our feet stretched a vast expanse of vegetation: trees as far as the eye could see. I did a complete turn, 360 degrees – the horizon was a single, continuous green line.

El Mocho stood next to me, following my gaze. I was moved without knowing why. I felt that he was, too. He put his hands on his forehead to protect his eyes from the glare, looking far into the distance, and after a long silence he said, "This is the Amazon." He said it with great sadness, almost resignation. His words echoed in my mind. There was something about his voice and his tone that this time really set me on the edge of panic. I looked out before me, incapable of speaking, my heart pounding, searching the horizon for a response. Yes, I was very frightened. I sensed danger. I couldn't see it. But it was there, before me, and I didn't know how to avoid it.

Once again, as if reading my mind, El Mocho said, "That is where you are going."

6

THE DEATH OF MY FATHER

March 23, 2009. I am alone. I am here. No one is watching me. In these hours of silence that I cherish, I talk to myself and reflect. That past, entrenched in time, motionless and infinite, has vanished into thin air. None of it remains. Why, therefore, am I hurting so much? Why did I bring back with me this nameless pain? I followed the path I set for myself, and I have forgiven. I do not want to be chained to hatred or resentment. I want to have the right to live in peace.

I have become my own master. I get up at night and walk barefoot. There is no one to blind me with a flashlight. My noise does not bother anyone, my behaviour intrigues no one. I do not have to ask for permission, and I do not have to explain myself. I am a survivor. The jungle remains in my mind, even if there is nothing around me to bear witness to it. Except for the thirst with which I drink life.

I stay a long time under the shower. The water is scalding, barely tolerable. Steam is everywhere. I can take water in my mouth and let it run slowly, warmly, down my face and neck. No one is disgusted by it; there are no sidelong glances. There is no longer anyone judging me. I am no longer accessible. I turn the tap. I want the water to run cold now. My body doesn't flinch. It has been trained by too many long years of freezing water.

Seven years ago today, Papa died. I am free, and I weep. From sorrow and happiness, from bitterness and gratitude too. I have become a complex being. I can no longer feel just one emotion at a time. I am torn between opposite emotions that inhabit me and shake me.

I am my own master now, but I am small and fragile, humbled through force of circumstance, and all too aware of my vulnerability and inconsequence. My solitude relaxes me. I can accept my inconsistencies without worrying about other people. Without having to hide and without the burden of someone who mocks, barks, bites.

Seven years ago on this very day, I saw the guerrillas gather together in a circle. They were looking at me from a distance and talked among themselves. We had settled in a new camp. The group had grown in number. Betty was joined by other women: Patricia, the nurse, and Alexandra, a very pretty girl with whom all the boys seemed to be in love.

Ten days before that, there had been a warning that the *chulos* were on the river. We were on the run. We walked for days. The road was wide enough for two-way traffic and linked the bank of one river to the mouth of another, miles away. In this labyrinth of rivers that make up the Amazon, the guerrillas had built a network of roads that they kept secret. They knew exactly how to use a GPS and computerized maps to find their way.

At one point we had to cross a new river. I couldn't see how we were going to do it. It was less than a month since I'd been captured. I had a few small things the guerrillas were carrying in a bag of provisions that I saw change hands throughout the journey. It had been set down on the riverbank, as if the bearer had had enough. I was about to take it when the girls pushed me roughly into the scrub. I lost my balance and found myself on the ground.

"*¡Cuidado, carajo! Es la marrana.*"*

"*¿La marrana?*"

I was expecting to be charged at any moment by a rabid pig, and I tried to get up as quickly as possible. But the girls held me down by the shoulders, increasing my panic.

---

* "Shit, look out! It's the Fat Pig!"

"*¡Arriba, mire arriba! ¡Allá está la marrana!*"*

I looked up to where one of the girls was pointing. Above our heads, through a large opening in the trees and high in the clear sky, was the miniature cross of a white aircraft.

"*¡Ésos son los chulos! Así es cómo nos miran para después 'borrbardiarnos.'*"†

She mispronounced the verb *bombardear*, "bombard", as *borrbardiar,* like a child who had not yet learned to talk properly. They also used "look" when they meant "see". I smiled. Would the plane be able to spot us from such a distance? It seemed unlikely. But I felt that it was not even worth worrying about. For me what mattered was the realization that the military was continuing its search and that this *marrana* was the enemy for them – and therefore hope for me.

We were moving deeper and deeper into the jungle, and each step was taking us farther from civilization. But the military was following our tracks. We had not been abandoned. After half an hour, the aircraft turned around and vanished from sight. Just as quickly the sky filled with large black clouds. Once again bad weather sided with the guerrillas. The plane's engine faded. The girls handed me a black plastic sheet.

Heavy droplets of rain made circles on the calm surface of the river. I heard the cry of a rooster, not far away, on the opposite bank.

My God, there must people around here! I was overjoyed. If someone saw me, the alert would be given and the military would come to rescue us.

Young Cesar arrived looking proud. He had found a dugout to cross. On the opposite bank was a large *finca.*‡ The forest had been cleared to create a huge pasture, and in the middle stood a pretty wooden house, brightly painted in green and orange. I was able to make out chickens, pigs, and a tired-looking dog, which started barking as soon as we emerged from the heavy foliage to get into the dugout.

Cesar ordered us to cross the river well covered up, so that the "civilians" wouldn't see us. The storm broke overhead, and I was soaked to the

---

* "Look up there! The Fat Pig is overhead!"
† "It's the vultures. That's how they look at us, and then they bomb us."
‡ A *finca* is a property.

skin, walking in the rain for hours until it was pitch black. The guerrillas erected a tent in the middle of the road between two trees, just above the ground. We slumped into it, dripping wet.

The following day we continued on foot to a spot where other guerrillas had obviously slept before. It was a pretty place. Clusters of coloured butterflies constantly twirled around us. We were again close to the road, and I told myself that escape was still possible.

But the next day, at dawn, we were told to pack everything up. During the night a large number of bags of provisions had been piled up beside the road, I had no idea where they came from. The guerrillas, already laden with their heavy backpacks, divvied up the extra provisions and, spines bent under the weight, carried them across the jungle on their backs.

After an hour of walking, we reached the trunk of a huge tree that had fallen across the road, so we branched off onto a side path covered with crawling plants. The path wound unpredictably through the trees. I had to concentrate so as not to lose sight of the markers left by those who had gone on ahead to clear our passage. It was very humid, and I was sweating profusely.

We crossed a small, half-rotten wooden bridge. Then a second, and a third. The deeper we went, the longer the bridges became. Some were more like roads built on stilts throughout the forest. I was distraught, because I could see how difficult it would be to grope our way along the path at night in the opposite direction.

By nightfall we'd arrived at a sort of clearing on a gentle slope. A tent had been put up at the top. In the middle of the wilderness, they had constructed a proper bed with a forked pole at each corner, some five inches from the ground to support the slats laid crosswise to hold the mattress. The mosquito net was fastened canopy-bed style to tall corner posts they called *las esquineras*.*

It was in this camp that I saw the guerrillas in hushed discussion in a circle near the *economato*, the name given to the shelter where they stored the provisions.

---

* Corners.

It was March 23, one month to the day since my capture. I knew that France had issued an ultimatum: I'd heard it on a guard's radio. If I was not released, the FARC would be put on the European Union's list of terrorist organizations. Since our arrival at the new camp ten days earlier, a routine had been established with the guard changes every two hours and the meal breaks. I had pinpointed the ideal moment to get away. Clara had agreed to follow me.

They were talking among themselves and giving me surly looks. I assumed they had heard the announcement, and I felt a certain relief at the thought of their being under pressure to release me. In any event, it didn't matter. In a few days I would be home, in Papa's arms. I had set myself this coming Sunday as a deadline for my escape. I was convinced I would succeed. It was the beginning of Holy Week. I wanted to flee on Easter Sunday.

I watched them talking; it was obvious they were worried. Young Cesar finally dismissed everyone, and Patricia, the nurse, came over to speak to us, acting as if she had been entrusted with a delicate task. She knelt in front of our *caleta*.

"What have you been hearing lately in the way of news?"

"Nothing special," I ventured after a silence, trying to understand the reason for her visit.

She was being particularly nice in order to gain our trust. She said she sympathized with our situation and made it seem as if she had come over to make us feel better. She explained we had to be just a little more patient, that we had already waited "a long time" and that now we could wait "a short time." She said we would soon be released. I sensed she was lying.

I could think only of one thing, and that was to mask any hint of our planned escape. But in fact that was not what was troubling them. Her eyes were not searching every corner of our *caleta*. She was calm and measured, examining rather *my* eyes, as if she were trying to read my thoughts.

She went away again. I felt triumphant; she had no inkling of our plan! I thought she was annoyed at her inability to get anything out of us. But

I was wrong. She was relieved. My father had just died. They were just making sure that I hadn't found out. From then on, they prevented me from listening to the radio. They were concerned that grief might push me over the edge.

7

FALLING INTO THE ABYSS

April 3, 2002. Three days after our second attempted escape, we were back at the camp, being shoved forward by the two guards who had captured us. Clara's feet were swollen, and she could barely walk. I was mortified, furious with myself: My reflexes were too slow. I had lacked foresight. I had been careless. I thought of Papa. I wouldn't be with him for his birthday. I wouldn't be there for Mother's Day. My daughter's seventeenth birthday was next. And if I still wasn't released, it would be my son's turn. I so wanted to be there for his fourteenth birthday.

The guards were pushing us. They were laughing at us. They had fired shots into the air when we got back to the camp, and the rest of the pack sang and cheered when they saw us. Young Cesar watched from afar, his eyes dark. He had not wanted to join in the celebrations our recapture had elicited. He motioned to the receptionists to take care of us. He was not the same man; I saw him in his *caleta* pacing around in circles like a wild animal in a cage.

The camp nurse came over to see us. She searched through our belongings and gleefully confiscated all the things we cared about: the little cooking knife, the effervescent vitamin C tablets, the fishing hooks and line that one of the boys had given us. And, of course, the flashlight.

She asked us a ton of questions. I remained as evasive as possible. I didn't want her to deduce the hour or the path we had taken to escape. But she was clever. She made so many comments, slipping in trick questions here and there, that I had to concentrate hard and bite my lip not to fall into her trap.

Clara was injured, and I asked the nurse to take care of her. She sensed that her interrogation could not continue and stood up abruptly.

"I'll send someone over to tend to you," she said to my companion.

I saw her walk directly toward the commander's tent. It looked as if she and Cesar were having a heated discussion. He was a tall guy, very slim, and probably younger than she was. He seemed exasperated by what she was saying to him. He did an about-face and left her talking to herself while he marched up the slope to our *caleta*.

He arrived, a grave expression on his face. After a long moment of silence, Cesar made a speech. "You did a really goddamn stupid thing. You could have died in that jungle and been eaten by who knows what. There are jaguars, bears, and caymans out there, just waiting for prey like us. You put your own lives in danger and those of my men. You are not to step outside your mosquito net without the guards' permission. When you go to the *chontos*, one of the girls will follow you. We will not take our eyes off you." Then, lowering his voice, in an almost intimate tone he said, "We all lose people we love. I'm suffering as well. I'm a long way from those I love. But I'm not going to throw my life away because of it. You have children waiting for you. You have to be sensible. It's staying alive that you need to be thinking about now."

He turned on his heel and left. I stood there in silence. His speech was absurd. He could not possibly compare suffering like ours with his own, when he had chosen his fate and we had no say in ours. Of course he must have spent many dark hours living with the anxiety of being blamed for our escape by his superiors, or even of being put before a war council and executed. I was expecting him to be violent and ruthless like the rest of his men. But instead he was the one restraining them. The mockery that had been heaped on us by the guerrillas on the way back to the camp had dissipated in his presence. It was as if he had been more afraid for us than for himself. That evening they held another assembly in a clearing in the middle of the camp. I could see them gathered in a circle. They spoke in hushed voices. Only the drone of their conversation reached me. But now and then someone would speak a little louder. I could tell that things were tense.

A girl was standing guard next to me, leaning against one of the posts holding up the mosquito net. It was the first time that guards had actually been positioned inside the tent; the conditions of our detention had obviously changed. The moon was so bright we could see as if it were daylight. The girl was following the assembly's progress fervently, more practised than I was at listening from a distance.

She became aware that I was watching her, and, looking embarrassed, she shifted her rifle to the other shoulder and said, "Cesar is furious. They told the leaders too soon. If they had just waited, no one would have known. Now he'll most likely be replaced as commander." She spoke in a low voice without looking at me, as if she were thinking aloud.

"Who told them?"

"Patricia, the nurse. She is second-in-command. She would like to take his place."

"Really?"

I was stunned. I could scarcely imagine there would be court intrigues in the middle of the jungle.

The following morning Patricia's "associate" – in FARC jargon meaning her romantic partner – turned up at our tent armed with some heavy, half-rusted chains. He stood there a good while, playing with the chains, taking pleasure in the clanking noise they made as he jangled them between his fingers. I was not going to stoop to asking him what the chains were for. And he was enjoying the mortification that the uncertainty of our situation was producing in us.

He approached us, eyes shining, lips snarling. He was determined to put the chain around our necks. I wouldn't let him.

He tried to impose it by force. I resisted, sensing that he was afraid of overstepping the mark. He looked behind him. He was alone. He shrugged in defeat and declared, "All right then, it'll be your ankles! Your loss. It will be more uncomfortable, and you won't be able to wear your boots."

I felt sick to my stomach. The thought of being chained up was nothing in comparison to the reality of it. I pursed my lips, knowing that I had no choice but to submit. From a practical standpoint, it didn't make a great deal of difference. We had to ask permission anyway to make the slightest move. But psychologically it was devastating. The other end of the chain was attached to a large tree, and it was taut if we decided to remain seated on our mattress, under the mosquito net. The tightness meant that the chain cut into our skin, and I wondered how we could sleep in such conditions. But most of all there was the dismay of losing hope. The chains ruled out escape. We would not even be able to dream up a new means of fleeing; the lead curtain had come down once again. Clinging to the irrational, I whispered to Clara, "Don't worry, we'll still manage to get away."

She turned toward me and screamed, "It's over! You're the one they want, not me. I'm not a politician. I'm nothing to them. I'm going to write a letter to the commanders. I know they'll let me go. I have no business here with you!"

She picked up her travel bag and rifled through it irritably. Then, at the peak of her anger, she yelled, "Guard! I need some writing paper!"

Clara was a single woman in her forties. We had worked together in the Ministry of Commerce. She had helped on my first campaign when I ran for Congress and decided after that to go back to the Ministry. I hadn't seen her for years. Two weeks before our abduction, she approached me, asking to join the campaign team. We were friends, but I really didn't know her that well before.

She was right. I could not hold it against her. We had reached the point where we had to face the facts: Our release could take months. Any new attempt to escape would be all the more difficult now that we had such little leeway. The guards were on the qui vive, closely watching whatever we did and severely restricting where we could go. They took the chains off only when we went to the *chontos* and at bathing time. But I suppose we had to consider ourselves lucky. One of the guards had wanted us to keep the chain around our ankles when we went to bathe, which would have meant dragging behind us the length that had been unchained from the tree. I was forced to appeal to Cesar, who showed clemency. But in every other respect, our situation had grown substantially worse. We had no access to radio. The guards on duty had been ordered to respond to all our requests as evasively as possible. That was the FARC way. They did not say no. They just put us off and lied to us, which was even more humiliating. It was the same for the flashlights. Whenever we needed them, they had always left them behind in their *caletas*. Yet they were always pointing them at us, shining the beam in our faces all night long. We had to remain silent. We could no longer use their machetes, even for the most basic of tasks. We had to ask someone to help us, but no one ever had the time. We would spend the entire day in boredom under our mosquito net, unable to move without disturbing each other. Yes, I understood her reaction. But naturally I was hurt by her attitude. She had turned her back on me.

She wrote her letter and passed it to me to read. It was a strange letter, because she had written it in legal jargon, as if it were addressed to a civil authority. Its formality seemed incongruous with the world in which we found ourselves. But so what? After all, these guerrillas had well and truly imposed their authority on us.

She insisted on handing the letter directly to the commander. But Young Cesar did not come. Instead he sent the nurse, who assured us it would be delivered into the hands of Marulanda. The response would take two weeks. Two weeks was an eternity. With a bit of luck, we would be released before then.

One evening, as Clara and I discussed the letter and the possibility of release, we explored the shifting sands of our hypotheses and fantasies. She was anticipating her return to Bogotá, certain that the leaders would reconsider their decision and give her back her freedom. She was worried about the plants in her apartment that must have dried out by now through lack of care. She was angry with herself for never having given a set of keys to her mother and was bitter about how alone she was in life.

Her regrets aroused my own. Overcome by a sudden fervour, I gripped her arm and said, with uncalled-for intensity, "When you are released, swear to me that you will go and see Papa immediately!"

She looked at me in surprise. My eyes were moist, and my voice was trembling. She nodded, sensing that I was racked by an emotion she had not seen in me before. I broke down, sobbing, clutching her arm, and spoke to her the words that I wanted to say to Papa. I wanted him to know that his blessing was my greatest solace. That I constantly went over in my mind the moment he had placed me in God's hands. I regretted not calling him that last afternoon in Florencia. I wanted to tell him how much it hurt me not to have had more time for him in my life. In the whirlwind of activity in which I found myself at the time of my capture, I had lost sight of my priorities. I had been focused on my work. I had wanted to create change in the world, but in the end all I'd created was more distance between myself and those who were dearest to me. I understood now why he would tell me that family was the most important thing we had in life, and I was more determined than ever, the moment I regained my freedom, to change the way I lived. "Tell him to wait for me," I implored Clara. "Tell him to hold on for me, because I need to know that he is alive in order to have the courage to go on living."

My companion listened to this tragic confession like an intruder in a drama that did not concern her. She was indifferent to it; she had her own tragedy to deal with. She did not want to carry mine on her shoulders as well.

"If I see him, I will tell him you are thinking of him," she said evasively.

I remember that night, lying on the edge of the mattress, my face pressed against the mosquito net, trying not to wake her with the persistent gulps produced by my irrepressible sobs. Since my childhood, Papa had always done his best to prepare me for the time when we would be separated permanently. "The only sure thing is death," he would say, like a wise man. Then, once he was certain that I understood he was not afraid of dying, he would say jokingly, "When I pass away, I will come and tickle your feet underneath the covers." I had grown up with the idea that even beyond death this unwavering complicity would enable us to communicate with each other. I resigned myself to the thought that whatever happened, God would allow me to be with Papa and hold his hand when it was time for him to cross to the other side. I almost considered this my right. When Papa had almost died a month earlier in the hospital, my sister Astrid's presence had been my greatest recourse. Her fortitude, her control, and her assurance had made me realize that the strong hand helping him cross the Acheron was not mine but that of my older sister. In contrast, my own might hold him back like a weight, making his departure more painful.

I had not envisaged the possibility that I would be absent from his bedside on the day of his death. That had never entered my mind. Until dawn this very morning. After coffee at breakfast time, the sun commenced its reign, piercing through the jungle in every direction. Nighttime vapours started to rise from the ground, and each of us tried to hang our laundry under its most powerful rays.

Two guerrillas arrived, their shoulders laden with recently stripped wooden poles, which they tossed at the base of our tent. Some of the ends were pronged, and it was with those that they began to work first. They drove them deep into the ground in each corner of an imaginary rectangle. They repeated the exercise with four more poles that they cut into much shorter lengths, and they dug those into the corners of another, more elongated rectangle. They had also brought vines, rolled into a spool, and they used them to bind sticks that they placed between the corner prongs. It was fascinating to watch them work. They did not speak but seemed to work in perfect unison, one cutting, the other pitching into the ground, one binding, the other measuring. An hour later, there in front of our *caleta* were a table and bench, made entirely from tree trunks and close enough that we could reach them in our chains.

The guard gave us permission to sit there. Sunshine fell directly onto the bench. I scooted into it at once, seeking to rid my clothes of the jungle dampness. From where I sat, I had an unobstructed view of the *economato*. Toward eleven in the morning, guerrillas arrived carrying large bags of provisions on their backs. To our surprise there was a delivery of cabbages wrapped in newspaper. Vegetables were an extremely rare commodity, as we had come to realize. But even more extraordinary was the presence of a newspaper at the camp.

I asked if we could have the newspaper and insisted that my request be given to the commander before the newspaper was thrown into the rubbish pit. Cesar agreed. Our *recepcionista* was assigned the task of reclaiming the newspaper, and after lunch she brought over a small stack of sheets, still damp but nevertheless legible.

We sorted them into two piles and sat down with our reading material, happy to have found something to pass the time and a suitable use for our table. The guards had been changed. It was now the turn of the nurse's boyfriend. He had positioned himself almost hidden by the large tree to which our chains were attached. He wouldn't take his eyes off me, and I felt uncomfortable being watched so closely. Never mind. I had to learn to shut it out.

The sheet in front of me was out of *El Tiempo* from a Sunday in March, more than a month earlier. It was the gossip section dealing with the world of entertainment, politics, and the country's social scene — required reading if you wanted to be up on the capital's gossip. I was about to turn over the sheet to look for more substantial news when my attention was caught by a photograph in the middle of the page. I looked again and examined it carefully. A seated priest was wearing an embroidered chasuble in purples and greens on top of his alb. He was looking at two photographers holding large cameras with ridiculously long telephoto lenses that were pointed toward an invisible target. What struck me was not the photo itself, but the priest's expression, the tension on his face, his obvious pain, yet also a certain anger that came across in the sheer stiffness of his body. Curiosity led me to read the caption. It described the priest watching with consternation a crowd of journalists jostling to photograph the coffin of Gabriel Betancourt.

I felt an invisible hand pushing my head underwater. The words danced before my eyes, and I had trouble understanding them. I read them again and again, and the concept took shape slowly in my numbed brain. When I finally made the link between the word "coffin" and my father's name, I froze with shock and could no longer control my breathing. There was no more air entering my lungs. I was in a void, my mouth wide open, like a fish out of water. I was suffocating without understanding why; I felt as if my heart had stopped and I was going to die. Throughout my agony, I thought, *It can't be him. It must be someone else. They made a mistake.* I grabbed the edge of the table, sweating from the chill, witnessing the dual horror of his death and mine, until I managed to tear my eyes from the newspaper and beseech the sky for air.

And then my gaze met his. The guard had been watching me from behind his tree, fascinated by my transfiguration, like a child in front of a fly whose wings he wants to pull off. He knew everything – he knew about Papa's death, and he was waiting for me to discover it. He had chosen the best seat in the house and was revelling in my suffering. I hated him instantly. My hatred forced me to regain my self-control, as if I had been lashed across the face.

I quickly turned away, red with fury. I didn't want him to see me. He had no right to look at me. I was going to die, I was going to implode, I was going to end my days in this shithole of a jungle. Good. I would be joining Papa. I wanted to go. I wanted to disappear.

That's when I heard his voice. He was there, just a few yards from me. I couldn't see him, but I could smell him. It was the smell of his white hair, the hair I'd kissed when I said good-bye. He was standing to my right, like the centuries-old tree that covered me with its shadow, just as tall and just as solid. I looked toward him and was blinded by a white light. I closed my eyes and felt the tears running slowly down my cheeks. It was his voice – no words, no speech. He had kept his promise.

I turned to my companion and, mustering all my strength, articulated the words: "Papa is dead."

8

TAMING THE HORNETS

A month earlier, March 2002. It was Easter Sunday. The camp was still under construction. Young Cesar had organized the building of a *rancha** next to the stream that circled the camp, the *economato* for storing provisions and, in the middle of the circle of tents, the *aula*, or classroom.

I liked to walk around the *rancha* to see how they prepared the food. At first they cooked over wood fires. Eventually a heavy gas stove arrived, transported on a man's back along with an enormous gas cylinder. But my real interest was focused on two kitchen knives always sitting on the table in the *rancha,* and I would gaze at them longingly. I told myself we would need them for the escape we were planning. While I sewed, wrapped, sorted, and selected items for our departure under my mosquito net, I observed life at the camp. There was one young man in particular who was having a difficult time. He was called "El Mico," the monkey, because his ears stuck out and he had a big mouth. He was greatly smitten with Alexandra, the prettiest of the *guerrilleras,* and had succeeded in seducing her. But at the end of each day, a tall, strong, handsome guy would turn up at the camp who also had his heart set on Alexandra. They called him the *masero.*† His role was to connect two worlds: the legal world, where he

---

* FARC word for cooking area.
† Because he dealt with "the masses," meaning the peasants, the people living in the region.

lived in a village just like the next person, and the illegal world, where he brought provisions and information to the FARC camps. Alexandra responded to his advances, while El Mico went around in circles, racked with jealousy. So badly was he affected that during his turn at guard duty he was incapable of taking his eyes off his girlfriend, and he completely forgot about watching over us. I prayed that on the day of our escape he would be the one on duty. I was convinced that we could leave right under his nose and he wouldn't notice a thing.

During these days of preparation, luck served us well. While the camp was in turmoil and the guerrillas were working like dogs, cutting wood and bringing it back for all sorts of construction, one of them left his machete near our tent. Clara spotted it, and I had managed to hide it in the *chontos*. The *chontos* they had made for us here were located between some bushes. Anticipating future needs, they had dug six square holes, each three feet deep. Once the first was full, it would be well covered and the next one would be started.

I hid the machete in the last hole and covered it with earth. I had attached a piece of string to the handle and let it poke discreetly through the top of earth, so that on the day of our escape we would only have to pull on the string to recover the machete and not have to put our hands in the dirt to look for it. I took the precaution of carefully explaining to my companion where the machete was buried so that she didn't use that particular hole, which would have made recovering it very unpleasant.

It was already Holy Week. I meditated every day, drawing courage from my prayers. Papa's birthday was at the end of April, and I worked out that by leaving one month beforehand, we had every chance of being able to surprise him.

I went through my list of tasks one by one and concluded with satisfaction that we were ready for the big departure. I thought this Sunday would be a good day to attempt our escape. I had noticed that on Sunday evenings Young Cesar gathered his troops together for some recreational activities. They played, sang, recited, and invented revolutionary slogans, which diverted the attention of the guards who wanted to join in but couldn't.

We had to wait for the right opportunity, and so every evening at nightfall we were ready, as if it were a practice session. I was tense beyond description, incapable of sleeping, thinking in my insomnia of all the obstacles we might have to face.

One afternoon, on my way back from the *chontos*, I noticed Clara hastily hiding something in her bag. Out of curiosity and playfulness, I tried to find out what she was trying to conceal. To my astonishment I discovered that she had already broken into our reserves of cheese and vitamin C tablets. I felt betrayed. That significantly reduced our chances, but more than that, it created a climate of distrust between us.

That was the one thing we had to avoid at all costs. We had to remain united and bound to one another; we had to be able to rely on each other. I attempted to explain my concerns to her as best I could. But she was staring straight through me. I took her hands in mine to try to bring her back.

That Sunday had been a slow day. The camp had lapsed into a dozy calm. We had everything ready, and there was nothing to do but wait. I had tried to sleep, telling myself that we were in for a terrible ordeal and that we had to conserve our strength. I made every effort to be easygoing and was careful about what I did and what I said in order to avoid arousing any suspicion. I was only too aware that I was not myself. I was gripped by immense feverishness at the thought of putting an end to our captivity, but I was also deeply anxious about being caught. If I didn't control myself, I would be swallowing my food whole, forgetting to rinse after bathing, and asking the time every two minutes. As it happened, I did the opposite: I chewed my food slowly, I took my time over the day's tasks and threw myself into performing them as best I could in order to mimic what I believed to be my usual behaviour. I spoke without seeking conversation. It was one month and one week since we had been captured. They were proud to be keeping us prisoner. I felt a thrill at the thought of leaving them.

The guerrillas pretended to be nice, and I pretended to be getting used to living among them. Anxiety hovered over all our words, each of us trying to gauge what lay behind the other's mask. The day went on,

slowing down as my impatience intensified. My anguish became suffocating. So much the better: This mounting, unbearable surge of adrenalin
was more effective to help us flee than the fear that our captivity would be
endless.

At exactly 6.00 P.M. on Sunday, March 31, 2002, there was a change of
guard. The person taking over was El Mico, the very one who was madly
in love with Alexandra, the pretty *guerrillera*. My heart leaped – it was a sign
from destiny. We had to go. Six-fifteen was the ideal moment to leave the
caleta, walk toward the *chontos*, and disappear into the forest. By 6.30 it
would be night. It was already 6.10. I left my rubber boots in plain view
outside the *caleta* and started putting on my own shoes, which I was going
to wear for our escape.

"We can't leave, it's too risky," said Clara.

I looked around me. The camp was getting ready for the night.
Everyone was busy. "El Mico" had left his post. He had moved away and
was waving madly at the object of his desire at the very moment the handsome *masero* made his entrance into the camp. The young girl had been
about to come up toward us but stopped dead when she saw her other
admirer arrive.

"I'll wait for you at the *chontos*. You have three minutes, no more," I
whispered to Clara in response, my feet already outside the mosquito net.

I cast a final glance at the guard and was immediately annoyed with
myself for doing so. If he'd looked at me at that moment, it would have
given the game away. But he was caught up in his own drama. He was
next to a tree, observing his rival's success. Nothing else in the world
interested him. I headed straight for the hole in which we had buried
the machete. The string I'd left poking out was still there.
Unfortunately, the hole had been used, and the smell was disgusting.
Take it easy, take it easy, I repeated silently to myself, pulling on the string and
retrieving not just the machete but all sorts of other unspeakable matter.

Just then Clara arrived, breathless, and knelt down next to me, trying
to hide herself from the guard's view. We were concealed by palm leaves.

"Did he see you?" I asked.

"No, I don't think so."

"Do you have everything?"

"Yes."

I showed her the machete, which I quickly cleaned with some leaves. Her face screwed up in disgust.

"I hadn't realized," she apologized with a nervous giggle.

I took the cane that I'd hidden in some nearby shrubs and rushed into the bush, continuing straight ahead. The sound of the cicadas was deafening in the forest, flooding the brain to the point of dizziness. It was exactly 6.15. The cicadas knew better than we did – they were as punctual as a Swiss watch. I smiled. No one would ever hear the din we were making as we walked through the leaves, the dry branches snapping horribly under our feet. Once night fell completely, the noise of the cicadas would give way to the croaking of the toads. Our steps would then be audible, but by that point we would be far enough away. Through the bushes I could make out the light coming from the camp. I could see human shapes entering and leaving the *caletas*. Under the cover of the vegetation we were already in darkness. They would no longer be able to see us.

Clara held on to my shoulder. An enormous tree trunk had fallen to the ground and was blocking our path. I climbed onto it in order to get by and turned to help her, and it was as if someone had just switched off the lights. All of a sudden, we were in the most intense darkness. From now on we would have to feel our way. I used the cane like a blind person to identify obstacles before us and cut a path for us between the trees.

At a certain point, the trees started to thin out and eventually clear. This made the walk easier and encouraged us to talk. I had the impression the path was gradually sloping downward. If that was the case, we were better off moving back into the forest. A path was synonymous with guards, and I had no idea how many security rings had been set up around the camp. We risked walking straight into the arms of our captors.

We'd been heading like this for almost an hour, in darkness and silence, when I suddenly sensed we were not alone. The feeling was immediate, and I stopped dead in my tracks. Someone was definitely moving around in the dark. I distinctly heard the rustle of leaves underneath his feet, and I almost thought I could hear his breath. Clara tried to whisper something in my ear, and I put my hand over her mouth to stop her. The silence was leaden. The cicadas had gone quiet, and the toads were late starting their chorus. I could hear my heart pounding in my chest and was convinced that whoever was out there would be able to hear it, too. We had to stay absolutely still – if he had a flashlight, we were doomed.

He approached slowly. His footsteps glided noiselessly, as if he were walking on a carpet of moss. He seemed able to see in the dark, because there was no hesitation in his step. At just two paces away from us, he stopped. I had the feeling he knew. I felt him looking at us.

A cold sweat ran down my spine, and a new surge of adrenalin chilled my veins. I was paralysed, unable to make the slightest movement or produce the slightest sound. And yet we had to move, distance ourselves one step at a time, find a tree, try to get away from him before he could switch on his flashlight and grab us. That was impossible. The only part of my body I could move was my eyes, rotating them in their sockets. I strained to pick out even a shadow, but it was so dark that I thought I truly had gone blind.

He came closer. I could feel the heat from his body. A dense steam clung around my legs, and his odour rose to my nostrils, feeding my panic. It was strong and rancid. But it was not what I was expecting. My brain was working at full speed, processing all the signals my senses were sending it. Out of instinct I looked down. What was near me was not a man.

The creature growled at my feet. It came up as high as my knees and was close to brushing up against me. It was a wild animal; I was certain of that now. Minutes that lasted forever went by in the deathly silence. And then it moved off, just as it had come, in a ripple of wind and a rustle of leaves.

"It was a jaguar," I whispered in Clara's ear.

"Are you sure?"

"No."

"Let's switch on the flashlight. We have to see what it was."

I hesitated. We could not be too far from the camp. They would be able to see the light and come after us. However, there was no noise, no voices, no lights.

"We'll switch it on for a second and then turn it off."

The animal disappeared in the undergrowth like a yellow spark. In front of us, a small trail wound its way downward. We took it instinctively in the hope that it would lead somewhere. A few feet below, it came out onto a small wooden bridge that crossed a dribble of water. On the other side, the terrain grew flatter and barer, the soil sandy and spotted with clusters of mangroves. I was no longer afraid. The light had given me back my faculties.

But I was worried, because taking a path was not a good idea and using the light made us dependent on it. We decided to follow the riverbank. We walked quickly to gain as much ground as we could. Lightning flashed across the night sky, and the wind picked up, sweeping through the trees and crushing the leaves. With no time to lose, we set to work. We had to build a shelter as quickly as possible. A piece of string between two mangroves, the large plastic sheet over the top, and we would have ourselves a roof. We sat underneath, huddled up so we would both fit. I laid the machete I'd just used at my feet, and I slumped forward onto my knees, overcome by desperately needed sleep.

I awoke shortly afterwards with the unpleasant sensation of having my backside in water. We were being drenched. A long, eerie creaking sound followed by an explosion made sure I was completely awake – a heavy tree had just crashed to the ground a few yards from our shelter. It could have crushed us. I reached out for the machete and put my hand into two inches of water. The storm was raging. The water level was actually rising and flooding us. How long had we been asleep? Long enough for the stream to increase its volume tenfold and burst its banks.

I was still crouched down, groping for the machete, when I felt the water around my feet gathering speed – we were in the middle of a current!

I switched on the flashlight. No point continuing the search for the machete. It had been swept away. We had to gather our things together and get out as quickly as possible. That was when I remembered what the guerrillas had said. In winter the land on either side of the stream flooded, hence the wooden paths built on stilts, which I'd taken for randomly erected bridges. Winter had hit us in a matter of minutes, and we could not have picked a worse place to spend the night.

Without the machete, and with our fingers swollen from the water and the cold, dismantling the shelter became an arduous task. I was still trying to undo the knots and retrieve the precious string when the water reached our knees. I looked up. The branches of the mangroves were woven into a tight mesh a few inches above our heads. Water was rising fast. If we didn't find the way out, we were going to drown in the limbs of the mangrove trees. I quickly glanced around; the trail was engulfed in water.

The pounding rain, water up to our waists, and the strength of the current were all conspiring against us. The flashlight stopped working. My companion was panicking and shouting, not knowing what to do in the dark, trying to go around me and putting me off balance in a current that was already extremely dangerous.

"Listen," I said, "we're going to get out of here. Everything will be all right. The first thing we need to do is put new batteries in the flashlight. We'll do it together, slowly. Take the batteries out of the bag one by one and pass them to me, and make sure you put them securely in my hand. I have to find the right end. There. Give me the other one. That's it, done."

The operation took many long minutes. I wedged myself between the branches of a small bush to stabilize myself against the current. I had just one fear: that the batteries would slip from my fingers and get lost in the water. My hands were trembling, and I had trouble keeping a good grip on them. By the time I finally managed to push the switch, the water was up to our necks.

At the first sweep of light, my companion forged straight ahead. "This way!" she shouted, going deeper into the water. It wasn't worth arguing. I remained perched on my bush, scanning the area, trying to find an indication of which direction we should take.

She returned defeated and looked at me in confusion.

"Over there," I told her.

It was more than intuition. It was like a calling. I let myself be guided, and I walked. *An angel!* I thought, without finding it absurd. Now, looking back, I like to think that angel was Papa. He had just died, and I didn't yet know.

I went deeper into the water but continued in the same direction, stubbornly. Farther on, the terrain rose steeply. Three more strides and we were out of the water, looking over a huge swamp. The small bridge had disappeared, as had the stream. It was now a flowing, raging river, flooding everything in its path.

We walked on, our backs hunched, soaked to the skin, shivering with every step and exhausted. The first glimmer of dawn was cutting through the thick vegetation. We had to take stock of our losses and wring out our clothes. Most of all we had to prepare our hideout for the day. They were surely on our tail already, and we had not made sufficient headway.

The sun came out. Through the thick foliage, we could see patches of pale blue, evidence that the clouds were breaking up. Slanted rays of light pierced the vegetation, heating the ground with such intensity that the soil released fragrances that seemed to turn the place into an enchanted forest. The jungle had lost the sinister aspect of the previous night. We spoke in whispers, planning meticulously the tasks we would each be allocated during the day. We'd decided not to walk at night, given that there was no moon to light our path because it was hidden behind the heavy clouds of the rainy season. But we were afraid of walking during the day, since we knew that the guerrillas would be searching for us and were probably pretty close. I looked around for somewhere to hide and spied a hole left by a gigantic root that had been literally ripped out of the soil by the weight of the falling tree. The exposed earth was red and sandy – filled with small creatures crawling around. Nothing too nasty – no scorpions or "Indian beards," the large, rainbow-coloured venomous caterpillars. I thought we could spend the day camouflaged in this hollow. We needed to cut some young palm leaves to hide ourselves. The kitchen knife I had "borrowed" was a good substitute for the machete.

We had finished fabricating a screen by crisscrossing branches and palm leaves when we heard Young Cesar's loud voice bellowing out orders, followed by the sound of several men running a few yards to our right. One of them was cursing as he bolted past us. He moved farther and farther away before disappearing altogether. Instinctively we huddled together tightly and held our breath. Then calmness returned; the wind blew through the treetops, water could be heard babbling all around us as it found its way toward the river, the birds started to sing. Man was conspicuous by his absence. Had we been dreaming? We hadn't seen them, but they'd been very close. It was a warning. We had to move. Our clothes had already dried on us. Our leather boots were full of water. Placed in the right spot under a powerful ray of sun, they produced a beautiful swirl of steam. The smell had attracted a swarm of bees that clung to them in clusters and took turns sucking them to relieve them of their salt. Covered in bees like that, they looked more like a hive than a pair of boots. After a while I noticed that the bees' activity was having a beneficial effect: They were like a team of cleaners, replacing the rancid odour with the sweet smell of honey. Encouraged by this discovery, I had the unfortunate idea of drying my underwear on a branch in full sun. When I went to check on it, I burst out laughing. The ants had cut out and carried off circles of fabric, and what was left had been invaded by termites using it as material to build their tunnels.

We decided to leave at dawn the next day. We would use the cut palm leaves as a mattress. One of the plastic sheets could go on top, and the other could be draped to serve as a roof. We were at the crest of a hill. If it started raining again, at least we would not be flooded. We broke off four branches and pushed one into each corner of our makeshift tent. We could thus enjoy the luxury of our mosquito net.

We had just completed our first twenty-four hours of freedom! Outside the mosquito net, shiny hard beetles tried in vain to get through the mesh. I closed my eyes after making sure there were no gaps in the net; it was well secured by our body weight.

When I woke up with a start, the sun was already high in the sky. We had slept too long. I hastily gathered our things, scattered the palm leaves so as not to leave any trace of our presence, and listened intently. Nothing. They had to be far away. They'd probably already struck camp. The realization that we were completely alone made me calm and anxious in equal measure. What if we went around in circles for weeks and got lost forever in this labyrinth of chlorophyll?

I didn't know which direction to take. I moved forward by instinct. Clara followed. She had insisted on bringing a host of small items – medicine, toilet paper, anti-inflammatory cream, Band-Aids, a change of clothes, and of course food. She had wanted to take my overnight bag, which was not only bursting at the seams but weighed a ton. I'd done everything I could to dissuade her. But I hadn't wanted to push the argument too far, because I realized that in this small bag she was storing all the antidotes to her own fear. After an hour of walking, she was doing her best not to appear handicapped by the load and I was doing my best to appear not to notice.

I tried to get my bearings from the sun, but large clouds had filled the sky with a layer of grey, turning the world beneath the trees into a flat space with no shadows and therefore no clues as to direction. We both kept our ears open for any sound that would alert us to the presence of another living soul, but this was an enchanted forest, suspended in time, absent from the memory of men. There was only us, and the sound of our footsteps on the carpet of dead leaves.

Without warning, the forest changed. The light was different, the jungle sounds were less intense, the trees seemed farther apart, and we felt more exposed. We slowed our pace and proceeded with more caution. A couple of steps later and we were on a road, wide enough to accommodate a vehicle, a proper road in the middle of the jungle. I turned around immediately, taking my companion by the arm to hide in the vegetation, where we crouched among the enormous roots of a tree. A road! It was the way out! But it was also the greatest danger.

We were fascinated by our find. Where could the road lead? Was it possible that by following it we would end up somewhere inhabited, in some corner of civilization? Was this the location of the guerrillas whom we'd heard the previous day? We talked this over in hushed tones, looking at the road like a forbidden fruit. Any road in the jungle was the work of the guerrillas.

It was their domain, their territory. We decided to walk alongside it, albeit at a reasonable distance, and keep ourselves under cover at all times. We wanted to make as much headway as possible during the day, as cautiously as possible.

For hours we followed our initial plan. The road climbed and fell steeply, wound its way around sharp bends and appeared to have no end. I hastened my step, to try to gain as much distance as possible during daylight hours. Little by little, my companion started to lag behind, biting her lip so as not to admit she was suffering from the weight of her load.

"Give it to me, I'll carry it."

"No, it's okay. It's not heavy."

The road became significantly narrower, and it was increasingly difficult to stay to the side of it. The landscape was insane. Ascents became climbs, and descents became toboggan rides. We stopped after three hours at a small wooden bridge over a creek. The water was crystal clear and babbled tunefully over a bed of small white and pink stones. I was dying of thirst, and I drank like a horse, kneeling on the riverbank. Then I filled my small water bottle. Clara did the same. We laughed like children at the simple pleasure of drinking clean water. What we'd been ruminating over in the solitude of our individual thoughts now became the subject of discussion: We had walked all morning without encountering a soul. The guerrillas knew we were unaware that this road existed. If we took it, we could cover ten times the distance. We agreed to walk in strict silence so we could jump for cover at the slightest sound, and I kept my eyes focused well into the distance in an effort to discern any movement whatsoever. We became wrapped up in the mechanics of walking, and my mind gradually grew more absorbed in concentrating on the physical effort than in observing the vigilance we had promised each other.

After turning a bend, we came to a fairly long bridge that crossed a dry riverbed. Our boots were encrusted with mud, and the latest rains made the wooden bridge look as if it had been washed down with soap and water. We decided to pass underneath to avoid leaving footprints. As I edged my way along the underside of the bridge, I noticed creeper tendrils hanging down in twists over the moss. I had already observed this bizarre form of vegetation on a few trees and thought it bore a strange resemblance to dreadlocks. I could have imagined any number of things, except that it was hornets' nests. I spotted them clustered on one of the bridge's beams and jumped back in fright. I warned Clara, who was a few steps behind me, pointing to a ball foaming with insects. Had it not been for an increasingly loud buzzing sound a second earlier, I would have slammed right into it. As it was, the noise alerted me to the fact that the wasps had taken flight and were about to punish us for having disturbed them.

I saw the squadron in triangle formation rushing toward me. I shot like an arrow to the other end of the bridge and ran as fast as I could along the path until I thought had distanced myself from the noise. I stopped, breathless, and turned around, only to be met with the most nightmarish vision: My companion was standing a few yards away from me, black with hornets. The insects, having noticed that I had stopped, abandoned their initial prey to come toward me like a fighter squadron. There was no way I could start running again and leave Clara at the mercy of the warring swarm. Before I could give it any further thought, I, too, became covered in raging insects; they latched onto me everywhere, curling up on themselves to drive their powerful stingers into me as deeply as they could. I remembered one of the guards talking about African wasps whose sting could kill livestock within seconds.

"They're African wasps!" I heard myself scream.

"Stop it! You'll excite them even more!" replied Clara.

Our voices echoed in the forest. If our captors had heard us, they would know where to come and find us! Gripped by panic, I continued to cry out from the pain of each sting. Then, all of a sudden, reason returned. I left the road and rushed toward the nearest bush. I noticed that by moving I was able to shake off some of the wasps. I felt emboldened again. The proximity of denser vegetation had confused some of them, and others simply abandoned me to rejoin the main swarm. But there were still a lot stuck to my trousers. Using two fingers, I grabbed them by their furiously beating wings and plucked them off one by one, mercilessly crushing them under my foot. I shuddered at the crunching sound but forced myself to continue methodically. Most of the time I ended up breaking them in two, leaving the still-quivering abdomen embedded in my skin. I thanked heaven it was I who had experienced this and not my mother or my sister; they would have died of fright. I made a major effort to control myself, in part because of fear but mainly because I was in the grip of a nervous aversion to touching the cold, damp bodies of these insects – I was trembling with revulsion. Finally I won the battle, surprised not to feel any pain, as if I had been anaesthetized. I saw that Clara had won her battle, too, except that her attack had been far worse than mine, and she'd managed to keep her cool better than I had.

"My father kept hives in the country. I got used to them," she said testily. The hornet attack had shaken us. I thought about the noise we'd made and could not dismiss the idea that our pursuers had dispatched a reconnaissance mission.

The hornet bridge was the first in a long series of wooden bridges erected every fifty yards, similar to those we had crossed to reach the camp from which we'd escaped. At times these bridges looked like viaducts because they went on interminably, meandering between the trees over hundreds of yards. They must have been built in previous years and abandoned. The planks were rotting and the sides crumbling, eaten away by hungry vegetation. We walked over them, six feet above ground, inspecting each plank and beam as we made our way forward, terrified we might fall through at any moment. We were aware of the risk of being spotted if guerrillas were in the area, but these bridges saved us from getting trapped in the tangle of roots and creepers that were lurking underneath.

We decided to take turns carrying the bag. Having eaten nothing and drunk little, we had succumbed to exhaustion.

Once the bridges became less frequent, we decided to hang the bag over the stick I'd been using as a cane, placing one end of the stick on the shoulder of the person in front and the other on the shoulder of the person behind. This technique made the walk easier, and we continued like this at a faster pace for a few more hours.

The forest began to lose its colour, and the air gradually became cooler. We had to find somewhere to spend the night. Straight ahead the path climbed, with a final wooden bridge awaiting us after a bend. Beyond the bridge, the forest seemed less dense; the light filtering through was different. We might be very close to the river and, who knows, to finding peasants, a boat, or any type of help.

But my companion was exhausted. I could see how her feet had doubled in size. The wasps had stung her all over. She wanted to stop before we crossed the bridge. I thought for a moment. I was aware that tiredness was a very poor counsellor, and I prayed that I would not make any mistakes. Or maybe it was because I sensed I *was* making a mistake that I called to the heavens for help. In less than an hour, it would be dark, and the guerrillas would be back at camp, reviewing another day they had returned empty-handed. The thought calmed me down. I agreed to stop, and I explained to Clara the precautions we needed to take. What I didn't see was that she had left the bag propped up against a tree in full view of the path, before going down to drink from a spring flowing just below us.

I heard their voices. They had come up from behind and were talking normally as they walked, not imagining for one moment that we were a few yards away. My blood froze. I saw them before they saw me. If Clara hid in time, they would pass by without noticing us. There were two of them, the pretty guerrilla who in spite of herself had served to distract the guard and thus facilitate our escape, and Edinson, a wily-looking youth who was always guffawing. They were talking loudly enough to be heard from a distance.

I took my eyes off them and turned toward Clara. She dashed up to get her bag, moving completely into the open – and came face-to-face with Edinson. The kid stared at her, his eyes popping out of his head. Then she turned to look at me, the blood draining from her face, fear and pain deforming her features. Edinson followed her movement to where I was standing. We looked at each other. I closed my eyes. It was all over. I heard Edinson's carnivorous giggle, which cut through the air like a razor, then the sound of a machine gun being fired into the air to celebrate their victory and announce it to the others. I hated them for their happiness.

9

THE STRAINS OF COMMUNAL LIFE

I was with Papa. He was wearing his square, horn-rimmed glasses that I had not seen on him since the happy days of my childhood. I was hanging on to his hand and crossing a busy road, swinging my arm back and forth to get his attention. I was a little girl. I was laughing from the delight of being with him. Once on the pavement, he stopped abruptly without looking at me and inhaled deeply. He pressed my hand, still held in his, against his heart. His voice became strained as he grimaced in pain, and my joy suddenly turned to anguish.

"Papa, are you all right?"

"It's my heart, my darling, it's my heart."

I looked everywhere for a car, and we bundled into the first taxi heading toward the hospital. But it was at home that we arrived, it was into his bed that I put him; he was still unwell, and I tried frantically to reach his doctor, my mother, my sister, but the phone remained silent. Papa collapsed against me. I caught him and shook him, but he was too heavy, his weight was smothering me, he was dying on me, and I didn't have the physical strength to put him back into bed or help him, save him. A muted scream remained lodged in my throat, and I found myself sitting under my mosquito net, panting, covered in sweat, wide-eyed, and blind. *Dear God! Thank goodness it was only a nightmare! But what am I talking about? Papa is dead, and I am a prisoner. The real nightmare is waking up here.* I cried for hours and hours, waiting for daybreak so that I could bury my pain in the everyday gestures I would perform mechanically, to give myself the impression of still being alive. My companion was head to tail next to me and was annoyed.

"Stop crying, you're keeping me awake."

I took refuge in my silence, my soul ravaged to the core at having to endure a fate that would not even allow me to cry in peace. I was angry at God for turning against me. *I hate you, I hate you! You don't exist, and if you do, you are a monster!* Every night for more than a year, I dreamed that Papa was dying in my arms. Every night I would wake up terrified, disoriented, in emptiness, trying to work out where I was, only to discover that my worst nightmares were nothing compared to my reality.

The months went by in devastating sameness, empty hours that needed to be filled, punctuated only by meals and bathing. Lassitude set in, creating a distance between Clara and me. I no longer spoke to her, or at least very little – just what was required to move forward or sometimes to give us heart. I refrained from revealing my feelings so as not to start a conversation I wanted to avoid. It began with the little things – a silence, embarrassment at having seen in the other something we did not want to discover. It was nothing; we were just settling in to daily life in spite of the horror.

In the beginning we shared everything without keeping count. Very soon we had to divide meticulously what was allotted to us. We gave each other dark looks, we were annoyed with the space we each took from the other, and we slid imperceptibly toward intolerance and rejection.

The feeling of "every man for himself" was gradually surfacing. It was definitely not something to verbalize. There was a boundary or, better still, a bulwark, between us and our abductors, composed of our secrets, our conversations that were inaccessible to them in spite of their constant surveillance. As long as we maintained our unity, I felt we would remain armoured. But daily life was wearing us down. One day I asked the guard for a piece of line to hang our laundry on. He didn't want to help. The line nevertheless turned up the following day, and I set about installing it between the trees, using the entire length as efficiently as possible. I went to fetch my laundry, and when I came back, I discovered that there was no room for my things. Clara had taken up all the space with hers.

Another day the area under the mosquito net became a problem. Next it was the issue of hygiene to control odours. Then noise management. It was impossible to agree on the most basic rules of behaviour. In this enforced intimacy, there was a major risk of becoming indifferent and cynical and ending up forcing the other person, shamelessly, to put up with you. One evening, after asking Clara to move over because I had no room in the bed, she exploded. "Your father would be ashamed of you if he could see you!" Her words stung my heart as if she'd slapped me. I was overwhelmed by the gratuitousness of the insult and devastated to realize that I would no longer be able to lean on her.

Every day brought a new dose of pain and acrimony. I saw us drifting apart. It took considerable strength not to seek relief from the guards' constant humiliation by humiliating in turn the person sharing the same fate. It was surely neither conscious, nor desired, but it was a form of release for our bitterness.

Yet, estranged as we now were, we were still chained to a tree twenty-four hours a day, sitting crammed together in a space six feet long by four feet wide.

I persuaded them to bring us fabric and thread, and I thanked heaven I had spent time listening to my elderly aunt Lucy, who, when I was a teenager, insisted on teaching me the art of embroidery. My cousins were too bored to stick around, but I stayed out of curiosity. Now I realized that life supplies us with everything we need for the journey. Everything I had acquired either actively or passively, everything I had learned either voluntarily or by osmosis, was coming back to me as the real riches of my life, even though I had lost everything.

I was surprised to find myself repeating my aunt's gestures and using her words and mannerisms to explain to Clara the rudiments of cross stitch, straight stitch, and blanket stitch. Before long, when they weren't on guard duty, the young women of the camp started coming over to watch us work. They, too, wanted to learn.

The hours, the days, and the months went by less painfully. The concentration required for embroidery lightened our endless silences. There was a kinship in our gestures, which made our fate more bearable. It lasted many months and many camps until the thread ran out.

A few weeks after our failed escape, with no explanation, they made us gather our belongings to leave in the opposite direction from what I had been calling "our way out." We ventured even deeper into the jungle, and for the first time there was no path, no sign of human life. We walked in single file, one guard up front, another at the rear. These sudden changes in location filled me with immense anxiety. The coincidence of this feeling, which we sensed was the same for both of us, made our war of silence – a war fed by the constant strain of defining our space and our independence from each other – vanish instantly.

We would look at each other and all was said. It was in these terrible moments, when our destiny seemed to be sinking even further into the abyss, that we acknowledged defeat, recognizing only then how much we needed each other.

While the guerrillas finished breaking down the camp and we witnessed the dismantling of this space, which we had ended up adopting as "ours," while the last of them were pulling up and throwing into the bushes the stakes that had supported our tent until there was nothing left but an indistinct, muddy area, and any proof of our existence in this place had just been eliminated, Clara and I would take each other silently by the hand in an instinctive effort to give strength to the other.

I applied myself to memorizing everything in the hope of retaining some spatial consistency in my brain that could potentially enable me to find my way back. But the more we walked, the more new obstacles had to be incorporated into my calculations. Feverish chills ran over my skin, and my hands were so damp that I had to wipe them continually on my trousers. Then came the nausea. I was well aware of the process that took place each time a departure was announced. In one and a half hours, at most, I would have to dash behind a bush, where I could throw up without being seen. I always made sure to have a small roll of tissue to wipe my mouth and clothes, a somewhat superfluous gesture given that I was already covered in mud.

The new camp that awaited us was very different from the previous one. The guerrillas thought it prudent to build our *caleta* away from their own dwellings. From where they placed us, it was impossible to see what they were doing or how they organized themselves. We were isolated, with a gloomy-looking guard posted a few feet from our mosquito net, obviously unhappy at being condemned to the boredom of being separated from his comrades and the embarrassment of being so close to us.

I preferred it this way. It would be easier, if circumstances permitted, to dupe the surveillance of just one man.

We had already got our bearings again and had resumed our embroidery when I saw Patricia, the nurse, walking toward us with a man I'd never seen before. He was young, in his thirties, with copper-coloured skin, a small, shiny black moustache, and short hair. He was wearing regulation khaki trousers, the usual rubber boots, and a shirt unbuttoned to the navel, revealing a hairy bulk that stopped just short of being fat. Around his neck hung a gold chain bearing a large, yellowed tooth.

He arrived all smiles, rolling his shoulders, and I couldn't help thinking that there was something bloodthirsty about him. Patricia made the introductions.

"This is Commander Andres!" she said with an adulation that took me by surprise.

The man obviously wanted to make a bold entrance and impress the troops who had gathered a few yards away to witness the scene.

"What are you doing?" he asked me, half authoritarian, half friendly.

"Hello," I replied, looking up from my work.

He looked me straight in the eye, as if trying to read my thoughts, and burst out laughing as he stroked his moustache. Then, still smiling, he continued, "What is that?"

"This? It's a tablecloth for my mother."

"Let me see!" he ordered.

I passed him my sewing, taking care not to raise my mosquito net too much. He pretended to inspect my work with the eye of a connoisseur and was about to return it to me with a "not bad" when a striking young woman who was standing behind me and whom I had not seen before snatched my work from his hands with a confidence that left no doubt as to the nature of their relationship. "Oh! It's so pretty! I want to do this! Please!" She rolled her hips with the full intention of enticing him. Andres looked delighted. "Maybe later," he replied, laughing.

Patricia chimed in. "He is the new commander!"

So this was the man with whom we had to get along from now on. I was already missing Young Cesar, who had obviously been dismissed because of our escape attempt.

"What's that you have around your neck?" I asked.

"This? It's a jaguar's tooth."

"A jaguar's?!"

"Yes, it was huge. I killed it myself."

His black eyes shone with pleasure. His expression changed, and he became almost charming.

"Those animals are on the verge of extinction. You shouldn't kill them."

"Oh, we're eco-conscious in the FARC! We don't kill, we execute!"

He turned on his heel and left, followed by his retinue of women.

My companion stared at me. "You're an idiot!"

"Yes I know, but I couldn't help it."

I plunged back into my work, thinking about Papa. I hadn't eaten for ten days; I needed to say good-bye to him, to mark his death in my flesh and etch in my memory these painful days spent in a time and place void of any distinguishing features. *I have to learn to hold my tongue*, I told myself, wincing as I pricked myself with a needle.

My deepest regrets assailed me when darkness fell. The memory of Papa was their primary trigger. I had stopped fighting it, telling myself that it was better to cry until my pain ran dry. But I also had the feeling that my suffering, instead of dissipating, was increasing and that as a result, instead of easing my burden, it was simply compacting it. I decided therefore to confront my distress in stages. I permitted myself to wallow in the sorrow of recalling the moments that had created my love for my father, but I would not permit myself any thoughts at all of my own children. That, for me, was quite simply unbearable. The times when I had opened up a small crack at the mention of them, I thought I would go mad. I could not think of Mom either. Now that Papa had died, I had begun to torture myself thinking that she, too, could go at any moment. And this thought, which always accompanied my memories of her like a perverse dread, filled me with terror: I had also imagined Papa might die, and it had become a reality, as if I had acquired the abominable power to transform my fears into reality.

I knew nothing of my family. Since March 23, the day we ended our first month in captivity, and also the day on which the order was issued denying us further access to radios, we had lost contact with the world of the living. Only once had Young Cesar shared some news with us. "Your father spoke on the radio. He asked you to hold on, to be strong, and he wants you to know that he will take care of himself and wait for you!" After learning of Papa's death, I wondered whether Cesar hadn't lied to me, whether he hadn't invented this story to keep me calm. But I didn't want to believe that. It was good for me to think that Papa had wanted to reassure me before dying.

However, with nightfall I would soon be joining him, and perhaps because I had the conviction that we both belonged to the world of the dead, I could let myself speak to Papa and cry in the darkness we shared, curling up in it, the way I used to in his arms.

Insomnia had a bewitching effect on me. Those hours of wakefulness gave me access to another dimension of myself. Another part of my brain took over. In the physical immobility imposed on me by sharing the small mattress on which we were living, my mind would wander and I would talk to myself as I would to Papa and to God, turning those long hours of darkness into my only moments of privacy.

At night another kind of nature emerged. Sounds resonated deeply, revealing the immensity of this unknown space. The cacophony of the fauna's croaking reached a painful volume. It exhausted our brains with its vibrations. This was also the hour of major surges in heat, as if the earth were discharging what it had stored up during the day, expelling it into the atmosphere and giving us the sensation of having succumbed to fever. But it passed quickly. An hour later the temperature dropped steeply and we

had to protect ourselves against a chill that left us yearning for the sweltering heat of dusk. As coolness set in, the night birds left their nests,
breaking up the air with the dry flutter of their wings, and crossed the sky,
screeching eerily like solitary souls. I followed them in my imagination,
joining them as they dodged the trees, flying at high speed beyond the
forest, higher than the clouds, toward the constellations where I dreamed
of happiness from the past.

The moon would move between the thick foliage. It was always late,
always capricious and unpredictable. I forced myself to rethink carefully
what I thought I knew about it but had never truly grasped – the moon's
dance around the earth, its phases and its power. Absent, the moon
intrigued me even more.

On the nights of a new moon, a spell was cast on the forest. In the
total darkness of its privation, the ground would be lit with thousands of
fluorescent stars, as if the sky had been scattered on the ground. At the
beginning I thought I was delirious. But later I had to admit that the
jungle was enchanted. I put my hand under the mosquito net and picked
up the phosphorescent nuggets that were strewn across the ground.
Sometimes I brought back a stone, at other times a twig or a leaf. But as
soon as I touched them, their supernatural light disappeared. And yet I
only had to put them back on the ground for them to regain their power
and light up again.

The inanimate world emerged from its torpor, and life held its breath.
On such evenings the sounds of the forest were magical. Thousands of jin-
gling bells would start to chime cheerfully, and this mineral noise seemed
to eclipse the call of the insects. As strange as it seemed to me, there was
a melody to this nocturnal chiming, and I could not help but think of
Christmas bells, in mid-July, and wept bitter tears at the thought of lost
time.

On one of those moonless nights, I could hear voices carried far into the
distance and whispered conversations of my guards as if they had been
speaking in my ear.

That was how I overheard one of the guards tell Yiseth that we had
almost succeeded in escaping. At the end of the road of rotten bridges

there was a *caserío*, a small village. Soldiers had recently moved in there and were starting infiltration operations for the army's intelligence services. My remorse was even greater; we should never have stopped by the side of the road.

I also heard them say that they would spy on us while we were bathing. I demanded the very next morning that Andres put up some cabins beside the river to block off the view; he replied that his men had "better things to do than look at an old hag." Nevertheless, he had a cubicle built the following day.

During another of those sleepless nights, I heard one of the guards say, "Poor woman. By the time she gets out, her hair will be down to her ankles!"

The comment startled me. I couldn't believe that such a thing was even conceivable. I had made a huge effort to be patient and accept that we would have to wait for negotiations to go through before we could be released, but the more time went by, the more complicated the elements leading to our release became.

10

PROOF OF LIFE

One morning, El Mocho Cesar, the front leader who had captured me, returned. Even though we couldn't see what was happening, the guerrillas' nervous comings and goings, along with their turnout in full uniform, signalled that a leader was on site.

I was sitting cross-legged under the mosquito net, barefoot, with the large chain attached to my ankle, starting some new work. I was aware of how distorted my sense of time had become. In "civilian life," to borrow from the FARC terminology, the days had gone by with staggering speed and the years had passed slowly, giving me a sense of accomplishment, of leading a full life.

In captivity my perception of time was the exact opposite. The days seemed endless, stretching cruelly and slowly between anguish and boredom. In contrast, the weeks, months, and, later on, years seemed to accumulate at breakneck speed. My awareness of time irreparably wasted stirred up an agonizing feeling of being buried alive.

When Cesar arrived, I was still trying to flee those demons by focusing my mind on threading a needle.

Cesar looked at my feet, swollen from the numberless bites inflicted on me by invisible bugs. His gaze embarrassed me, and I hid my feet under my buttocks, which set off shock waves of pain as the chain cut into my skin.

"Why did you escape into the jungle like that? You could have been attacked by a jaguar. It was madness! In fact, it was goddamn stupid. What would I have had to do? Send your corpse to your children? I don't understand. You know you don't stand a chance."

I looked at him in silence. I knew he didn't like seeing the state I was in; deep down I think he felt ashamed.

"You would have done the same thing. Except that you would have succeeded. It is my duty to regain my freedom, just as it is yours to prevent me from doing so."

His eyes shone with disturbing brightness. He stared at me, but it was not me that he was seeing. Was it memories he was watching unfold before his eyes? He suddenly aged a hundred years. He turned around, his back bent, as if overcome by enormous fatigue, and before leaving he said to me in a deep voice, as if talking to himself, "We're going to take the chains off. I won't allow them to be put on again. I'll send you some fruit and cheese."

He kept his word. At dusk a young guerrilla came to remove the chains. He made a constant effort to be pleasant, trying to start a conversation that I always managed to avoid. I hadn't recognized him at first, but he was the guerrilla sitting in the back of our vehicle's cab on the day of our capture. He opened the padlock carefully; my skin was bruised from the chain.

"You know, this gives me more relief than it gives you!" he said, smiling broadly.

"What's your name?" I asked, as if I had just awoken from a dream.

"My name is Ferney, *Doctora*!"

"Ferney, please call me Ingrid."

"Yes, *Doctora*."

I burst out laughing, and he ran off.

The fruit and cheese also turned up. Cesar sent us a large box full of at least thirty green and red apples and some big bunches of grapes. When I opened the box, I automatically offered some to Jessica, the commander's *socia*,* who had delivered it. She tightened her lips and replied, "The instructions were to take fruit to the prisoners. We can't accept anything from you!"

---

* A partner or girlfriend in FARC jargon.

Puffing out her chest, she turned on her heel and left. I realized that it could not be easy for her. I knew only too well by now that fruit and cheese were a rare luxury in a FARC camp, where our staple diet was rice and beans.

Cesar reappeared a week later.

"I have good news for you!" he announced.

My heart started to race. The hope of imminent release preyed on my mind constantly. As nonchalantly as possible, I said, "Good news? Now, there's a surprise! What is it?"

"The Secretariado has authorized you to send your loved ones proof that you are still alive."

I wanted to weep. Proof we were still alive – that was anything but good news. It confirmed the prolongation of our captivity. I thought that secret negotiations might have been initiated with France. I knew that the guerrilla movement had been damaged by the inclusion of its name on the European Union's list of terrorist organizations, and I imagined that the FARC would have sought negotiations to have its name removed in exchange for our release. These hopes had just been shattered into a thousand pieces.

The presidential elections were imminent: Within two months Colombia would have a new government, and Álvaro Uribe, the extreme right-wing candidate, had the best chance of winning. If the FARC was eager to produce proof we were alive a few days before the first round, it was a sign that nothing was being done about our release and that the guerrillas were getting ready to pressure whoever won. If it was Uribe . . . well, the FARC hated him as much as he hated them. And yet my spirits rebounded at the thought that it was easier for hardened enemies to negotiate. I thought of Nixon reestablishing diplomatic relations with Mao's China and de Gaulle leading a policy of reconciliation with Germany. I believed that Uribe could succeed where his predecessor had failed because as the FARC's fiercest opponent he would not be suspected of the weakness or secret bargaining that had undermined the outgoing president's previous initiatives.

I asked Cesar how much time I had to prepare my message. He wanted to tape me that same afternoon.

"Put on a bit of makeup," he said.

"I don't have any makeup."

"The girls will get you some."

I realized then why we'd been given the fruit and cheese.

They set up a table in an open space where we normally hung out our laundry and where the light was better. The session lasted twenty minutes. I resolved not to let my emotions get the better of me. I wanted to present my family a calm face, a determined voice, and gestures that would reassure them that I had lost neither my strength nor my hope. When I mentioned Papa's death, I pressed the pencil deep into my hand until it bled. I had to focus on something else to stem the flood of tears streaming down my face.

I'd wanted to speak on behalf of the other hostages who, like me, were waiting to return home. On the trees next to our *caleta*, the bark was gouged in a very strange way. Years earlier there had been a prison at this very spot where other hostages had also been chained to trees. I didn't know these hostages, but I'd heard that some had just completed their fifty-seventh month in captivity. I'd been shocked, unable to imagine what that represented, not knowing that my own torment would end up lasting considerably longer. By refusing to speak of our situation and condemning us to oblivion, it seemed to me, the Colombian authorities were throwing away the key to our freedom.

In the years to come, the government's strategy would be to let time pass, hoping that our lives would become less valuable, forcing the guerrillas to release us without obtaining anything in return. We were being given the heaviest sentence that could be inflicted on a human being, that of not knowing when our captivity would end.

The psychological weight of this revelation was crushing. The future could no longer be viewed as a time for things to be created, battles to be won, and goals to be achieved. The future was dead.

El Mocho was visibly satisfied with his day. Once they had finished taping the proof of life, he insisted on speaking with me, sitting astride the tree trunk.

"We're going to win this war. The *chulos* are powerless against us. They are too stupid. Two days ago we killed dozens of them. They rush after us like ducks in formation. We just hide and wait for them."

I said nothing.

"And what's more, they're really corrupt. They're bourgeois, only interested in money. We buy them, and then we kill them!"

I knew that there were indeed individuals within the Colombian army for whom the war was an unlimited source of dishonest earnings. In the Colombian parliament, I had denounced the inflated price of arms contracts that allowed for the generous distribution of bribes. But Cesar's comment hurt me deeply. In civilian life I'd felt that the war did not concern me. I was opposed to it out of principle. Now, having just spent months in the hands of the FARC, I saw that the situation of the country was a lot more complex. I could see what the FARC really were. I could no longer remain neutral. Cesar could criticize the armed forces, but they were the ones who confronted the FARC and limited its expansion. And they were the only ones who were fighting to rescue us.

"Everyone is interested in money," I said, "particularly the FARC. Look at how your commanders live. And yes, you kill, but you get killed, too! Who knows if you'll still be alive at the end of the year!"

He looked at me surprised, incapable of imagining his own death. "That would not be in your interest!"

"Yes, I know. That's why I hope you live a very long time."

He squeezed my hand in both of his and bade me good-bye, adding, "Promise me you will look after yourself."

"Yes, I promise."

Two months later El Mocho Cesar was killed in a military ambush.

11

THE LITTLE WOODEN HOUSE

One night, under a full moon, we received the order to march. We ended up at a road where a large, brand-new truck was waiting for us. How was it that in the middle of nowhere there was a road and this vehicle? Were we close to civilization? The driver was a nice guy, around forty, dressed in a T-shirt and jeans. I'd seen him a couple of times before. His name was Lorenzo, like my son. Andres and his companion, Jessica, sat in the back. The rest of the troop followed on foot. I had the impression we were travelling north, turning back on ourselves. I was excited by the thought of retracing our steps. What if a settlement was in the works? What if freedom was imminent? I became talkative, and Lorenzo, who was outgoing, gave free rein to his spontaneity.

"You created problems for us!" He glanced over at me as he drove, keen to gauge the effect of his words. "They've gone and put us on their list of terrorist organizations, but we're not terrorists!"

"If you're not terrorists, then don't act like terrorists! You kidnap, you kill, you gas-bomb people's homes, you sow terror. What do you want to be called?"

"That's all part of war."

"Maybe so, but your way of waging war is sheer terrorism. Fight the army, don't attack civilians if you don't want to be called terrorists."

"It is because of you! It's France that has included us in the list of terrorists."

"Well, if it's because of me, set me free!"

We reached an immense prairie beside a river. A pretty little wooden house looked out across the landscape. Its attractive wraparound veranda and brightly painted balustrades lent it a colonial air. There was no mistake: I recognized this house. We'd passed by it a few months earlier during a tropical storm that broke out just after we'd spotted the famous *marrana*, the army's reconnaissance aircraft.

For the first time in months, I could see the horizon again. My heart contracted at the feeling of magnitude. I filled my lungs with as much air as they could hold, as if in doing so I were taking possession of the vast space before me, which stretched as far as the eye could see. It was an interlude of joy, a joy I'd known only in the jungle, a sad, fragile, fleeting joy. A summer breeze swayed the lonely palm trees that had so far been spared by man to stand proudly along the riverbank, faithful witnesses to a war against the jungle that man was winning. They made us walk to the landing stage, which was nothing more than an enormous gnarled *sangre toro**. I would like to have stayed in that pretty house on the banks of this tranquil river. I closed my eyes and imagined my children's joy at discovering this place. I imagined my father's expression, ecstatic at the beauty of this tree whose enormous branches spread six feet above the ground like gigantic vines. Mom would already have started singing one of her romantic boleros. It didn't take much to be happy.

The roar of the outboard motor snapped me from my reverie.

Clara took my hand and squeezed it in anguish. "Don't worry. Everything will be okay."

As I got into the boat, I checked the direction of the current. If we went downstream, we would be heading even deeper into the Amazon. The driver of the boat lined up the craft with the current and moved off slowly. I was immediately overcome with nausea. The river narrowed. Now and again the branches of the trees on both banks would interlace above our

---

* Meaning "bull's blood," the name of a tree in Amazonia, with a wood particularly prized for its easy combustibility.

heads. No one spoke. I made an effort not to succumb to drowsiness; I wanted to observe and memorize what I saw. After hours I was startled to hear the sound of tropical music. Just around a bend, three wooden huts were lined up on the riverbank, as if waiting for us. In the centre of one of them, a light bulb swung gently from an electric wire, casting a myriad of sparkles across the surface of the water. The driver turned off the engine, and we let the current carry us in silence, to avoid attracting any attention. I kept my eyes firmly on the huts in the hope of seeing a human being – someone, anyone – who might spot us and raise the alarm. I stayed like that, straining my neck, until the huts disappeared from sight. And then nothing.

Three, four, six hours. Always the same trees, the same bends, the same unremitting roar of the engine, and the same despair.

"We're here!"

I looked around. The forest seemed to have been cleared at the point where we'd stopped. A small, dingy-looking wooden house stood in the middle of the empty space. Voices came out to greet us, and I easily recognized some of the group that had gone on ahead of us.

I was tired and on edge. I dared to hope that our captors would allow us to spend the rest of the night inside the little house. Andres quickly disembarked. He issued instructions for his bags to be brought into the hut and designated guards to take us "to the site."

We set off in single file, our path lit by a large flashlight at the head of the line. We crossed the garden of the house, then what had to be a vegetable patch. We passed a cowshed that I gazed at wistfully, and suddenly we entered an enormous cornfield, with stalks over six feet high bearing ears ripe for the picking. I heard Mom's voice from when I was a child, forbidding me to go near them: "They're full of snakes and trapdoor spiders." I clutched my bag against my chest with one hand and used the other to chase away the bugs that were jumping on me, their legs and wings getting tangled in my hair, millions of giant grasshoppers and owl butterflies fleeing in fright. The plants were so close together that I had to fight my way through with my elbows and knees. I tried my best to protect my face from the green corn leaves that were as sharp as a razor.

Suddenly, in the middle of the cornfield, we stopped. They had cleared a square area with the machete and had put four posts in the ground to support our mattress and the mosquito net, which was unfurled as a canopy. The insect population, attracted by the strange construction, had completely colonized it. Glistening red crickets, larger than a man's fist, seemed to be ruling the roost. The guard chased them away with the back of his machete, and they soared laboriously into the sky, emitting a high-pitched screech.

"You'll be sleeping here." The guard was ogling us, clearly revelling in our distress.

I slid under the mosquito net, trying to stop the breathless creatures from getting in, and I looked up at the open sky above my head, heavy with black clouds, before I sank into a fitful sleep.

They had started to build the camp in the *monte*,* beyond the cornfield and behind the coca plantation that surrounded the house. While crossing the plantation, we filled our jackets with limes picked from an enormous lime tree that towered majestically over the coca trees.

They had brought a chain saw with them, and from morning to night I heard them relentlessly felling trees. Ferney came to help us get set up and busied himself with building us a small shelf to put our things on. He spent the afternoon peeling the bark off some posts, proud to be doing such "meticulous work."

Ferney left as soon as he had finished his task, forgetting his machete, which lay concealed under the wood shavings. Clara and I both noticed it at the same time. My companion asked permission to go to the *chontos*. When she returned, she stopped to exchange a few words with the guard, giving me more than enough time to pick up the machete, wrap it in my towel, and hide it in my bag.

Possessing the machete made us euphoric. Now we could venture again into the jungle. But we could be searched at any moment. The following morning we were put to the test. Ferney came with four of his comrades, and they combed the area without saying a word to us. We were sitting

---

* The bushes.

cross-legged under our mosquito net. Clara was reading aloud a chapter from her copy of *Harry Potter and the Philosopher's Stone*, which she had thrown into her bag before leaving Bogotá. We had agreed to take turns reading pages aloud. In that hour, while they searched, we read out loud mechanically, without absorbing a word. We were both focused on following Ferney's team, doing our best not to appear concerned by their movements.

Finally one of them turned toward us and snarled, "Did you take Ferney's machete?"

A surge of adrenalin blocked my brain.

"Why?" I responded obtusely.

"Ferney left his machete here yesterday evening," he retorted, his tone threatening.

I stammered, not knowing what to respond, petrified that Clara might be interrogated as well.

It was all too obvious that I was frightened. I knew they were going to search us, and I panicked at the thought.

Then Ferney came to my rescue.

"I don't think I left it here. I remember taking it with me. I think I left it where we were cutting the wood, when I went to fetch some planks. I'll take a look later. Come on, let's go."

He had spoken without even looking at me and turned on his heel with his companions following, delighted to be relieved of their chore.

My companion and I were drained. I took the book from her trembling hands and tried to resume reading. But it was impossible to focus on the page. I let the book drop onto the mattress. We looked at each other as if we had just seen the devil, and we burst into nervous laughter, bending forward so the guard couldn't see us.

As ridiculous as it seemed, that evening I felt the stirrings of guilt for fooling the too-trusting Ferney.

The chains were not put back on. We could move freely around the *caleta*. However, we spent most of the day sitting in the five by five-feet space of our mosquito net, because we were used to it. The veil separating us from the outside world formed a psychological barrier, protecting us from the contact, curiosity, and sarcasm of the other side. For as long as we were under the mosquito net, they didn't dare speak to us. But the feeling of being able to leave "our *caleta*" and walk a hundred feet in front of it if we so chose was a freedom we appreciated all the more now that we understood how easily it could be taken away from us. We used it sparingly, for fear that they would detect how thrilled we were and might use it as an instrument of blackmail.

Little by little I was beginning to detach myself from both the small and the big things, for I did not want to be subjugated to my desires or my needs, because having lost the ability to satisfy them only made me more a prisoner in my jailors' hands.

They also brought us a radio. It was so unexpected that we weren't even pleased. El Mocho had sent it, in all likelihood because in our last conversation I'd said that I no longer knew what was going on in the world and, to my astonishment, didn't care. In fact, since I'd learned of Papa's death, the outside world seemed foreign and distant to me. Back then the radio was a nuisance.

It was a large Sony that the youngsters called "the brick" because it was black and shaped like one. It had a powerful speaker, so it was popular among the guerrillas, since they could listen to the latest pop music at full blast all day long. When Jessica brought it to us, it was immediately obvious that she did not approve of her commander's gesture. Worse still, she was outraged by our indifference.

"This is as good as it gets around here!" She took our reaction as a sign of contempt, believing that in civilian life we were used to much better. She could not understand that in our mental state all we were interested in was freedom.

She took revenge in her own way. The following day she came to look for the penknife El Mocho had given me before he left. When she came to get it on the pretext that Commander Cesar had asked for it, I knew very well she was going to keep it for herself. She was the commander's girlfriend. She could do whatever she wanted. I gave it to her reluctantly, arguing that it was a gift, but that only added to her pleasure.

Gradually the radio became a source of friction. At the beginning Clara and I would take turns following the news bulletins during the day. The radio was temperamental, and you had to move it around like a radar gun, turning it in all directions before finding the most effective angle and the best reception, which was always full of interference. What I found surprising was that in the *caleta* next door they had exactly the same "brick," but theirs, in contrast, had perfect reception. I discovered that they tampered with the sets by "poisoning" the circuits and inserting pieces of cable to increase the reception. I asked if they could "poison" my brick. They sent me to Ferney.

"Of course, I'll take care of it. We'll do it when you move into your new house."

I was stunned. "What new house?"

"The wooden house that Commander Cesar ordered to be built for you. You'll be very comfortable there. You'll have your own room, and you won't have to worry any more about people peeping at you!" he said.

That was the least of my concerns. A wooden house? They were going to keep us prisoner for months! I would not be home for Melanie's birthday, or for Lorenzo's birthday – he was turning fourteen. He wouldn't be a child any more. It broke my heart to miss that too. My God, what if this went on until Christmas?

Unable to rid myself of the anguish, I lost my appetite completely.

Once the planks were cut, the house was built in under a week. It had been constructed on stilts, with a roof made of woven palm leaves that had been assembled with astonishing beauty and skill. It was a simple rectangular structure, with wooden walls six feet high on three sides and the fourth side completely open and facing the camp. In the left-hand corner of the space, they had erected two interior walls to create a bedroom with a proper door. Inside, four planks resting on trestles constituted the bed, and pieces of wood in the corners provided shelving. Outside the bedroom were a table and a small bench for two people.

Andres was eager to show us our new lodgings. He was proud of his team's work. I could barely hide my distress. The door would be locked with a huge padlock at night, and it was hard to see how we would escape. I tried my luck.

"It needs a window. The room is very small and dark. We'll suffocate!"

He threw me a highly suspicious look, and I let it drop. But the following day a team was sent over with a chain saw to open one up. With a window we might have a chance.

Our life changed. Paradoxically, although this space was definitely an improvement compared to our previous living conditions and enabled us to dictate our own schedule and create our own routine, the tension between Clara and me became unbearable.

I fixed a daily schedule that allowed me to remain active while staying out of her way. Her reactions were unpredictable. If I swept, she would follow me around and snatch the broom from my hands. If I sat at the table, she would want my seat. If I paced to get some exercise, she would block my path. If I closed the door to rest, she would demand I leave. If I didn't, she would pounce on me like a cat with its claws out. I no longer knew what to do. Another morning, on discovering a hive in a corner of the kitchen, she began to scream. Snatching the broom and swinging it wildly, she sent everything on the shelves along the wall crashing to the ground. Then she ran off toward the jungle. The guards brought her back, shoving her with their rifles.

When Ferney came to fix our radio, he brought a brand new broom he had made especially for us.

"Keep it. It's better that you don't ask to borrow things. It annoys people."

He spent time explaining which broadcasts we could pick up and what times they came on. Before six-thirty in the morning, there was nothing. In the evening we were spoiled for choice with all the national stations. However, he forgot to tell us the most essential thing: We did not know there was a special programme for hostages, and it aired messages every weekend from our families.

Tension mounted one morning at dawn when I was disturbed by a terrible crackling sound. Clara was sitting against the wall with the radio between her legs, turning the knobs back and forth, oblivious to the noise she was making. The padlock to our door was not removed until six. I sat there waiting, my increasingly black mood filling the room. I reminded her as calmly as I could that there was no reception before six-thirty in the morning, hoping that she would turn off the set. Yet she dismissed me. She wanted nothing more than to make the set crackle. I stood up, sat back down, paced in circles between the bed and the door, showing how irritated I was. Just before they removed the padlock, she finally agreed to silence the "brick."

The following day the scene played out exactly the same way, except that this time I could not get her to switch it off. I watched her listen intently to the crackling noise and thought, *She's going mad.*

One morning after I had already gone outside to clean my teeth in a bucket of water that a guerrilla usually dropped off at the other end of the house, I heard a crash in the bedroom. Dreading what I might find, I ran back to see Clara, arms hanging at her sides, with the radio broken at her feet. She explained that it had slipped out of her hands. "Never mind. We'll see if someone can fix it," I said, doing my best not to hold this against her.

12

FERNEY

Every evening at six, while it was still daylight, the guard would come by to put the padlock on our door. He would walk around behind the house to lock the solitary window with another large padlock before moving to the front of the house to take up his post for the night. I followed his movements with intense interest, trying to find a flaw in the system that would enable us to break out.

We would have to execute our escape in two stages. Before six, Clara would jump down from the window and run into the bushes behind the house, taking the bag containing our supplies. The guard would come by at six on the dot to lock the door. He would see me and a decoy beside me in the bed. He would put on the padlock and go to lock the window at the back, giving me just enough time to jump out the window myself and climb up onto the roof to hide. After padlocking the window, he would assume his position at the front of the house, leaving me free to join Clara at the back. We would then veer to the right to get away from the camp and make a ninety-degree turn to the left, which would take us to the river. We would have to swim and let the current carry us as far as possible. We would hide during the day, as they would be on our tail, combing the entire area. But after two nights of searching, without knowing which way we had gone, they would not be able to trace us. We would run into a peasant dwelling and risk asking for help.

I was anxious about swimming in the dark waters of this jungle in the night, having seen the shining eyes of the caymans, camouflaged on the riverbanks, scoping out their prey. We would need a rope to tie ourselves together so we wouldn't get separated by the current and lose each other in the darkness. If one of us were attacked by a cayman, the other could come to the rescue – and, fortunately, we had the machete. We had to make a sheath for it so we could carry it on our belts without being hindered while we swam. We would take turns carrying the backpack. The contents would have to be wrapped meticulously in plastic bags and sealed tightly with rubber bands. Surviving in the water was a major challenge. We needed to make flotation devices so we could swim for hours.

I solved this problem by using a Styrofoam cooler in which the nurse had received some medicine. When I asked if I could keep it, Patricia laughed. She obviously found my request odd and handed me the box as if handing a child a broken button to play with. Proud of my acquisition, I returned to the room, and with the door tightly shut Clara and I used the machete to saw it into pieces, loudly talking and laughing to mask the squeaking noise of the blade on the Styrofoam. We took the unbroken side panels off the box and made them into devices large enough to rest our bodies on and small enough to fit in our knapsacks.

The rest of our preparations were easier to take care of. One evening, just before they shut us in for the night, I discovered an enormous scorpion, a female with all her offspring attached to her abdomen, more than five inches long, on the strut of the door. The guard killed it with a blow of his machete and put it in a jar with some formalin. It would yield an antidote, which, he said, would perform miracles. I emphasized the danger of having no light inside the room and stressed the fact that the creature could easily have landed on the back of my neck when I closed the door. Andres sent us the flashlight I was dreaming of for our escape.

However, although we were ready to leave, our plan kept getting delayed. First came a week of extremely low temperatures, especially at dawn. "It's the freeze from Brazil," the guard told me knowingly. I was thankful we had not yet left. Then we were held up by my catching a cold.

As they refused to give us medicine, the fever and cough had persisted. But the greatest obstacle to our escape was Clara's manic-depressive behaviour. One day she explained that she was not going to escape because she wanted to have children, and the effort of escaping could disrupt her capacity to conceive.

Another afternoon, seeking refuge in the bedroom, I overheard an astonishing conversation. Clara was telling the girl on guard about an episode in my life that I had revealed to her, describing it with exactly the same words I'd used. I recognized my expressions, my pauses, the intonation of my voice. It was all there. What was disturbing was that Clara had substituted herself for me in her narration. *It will only get worse*, I said to myself.

I felt we needed to talk. "You know, they could switch our camp at any moment," I said one evening before she fell asleep. "At least here we already know their routine. We know how they operate. And now that we're in this house, they're less watchful. This is a good time. Of course it will be hard, but it's still possible. There are dwellings two or three days' swim from here – it's not the other end of the world." For the first time in weeks, she was the person I used to know. Her comments were sensible and her questions constructive. I felt a genuine sense of relief at being able to share my thoughts with her. We set our departure date for the following week.

When that day came around, we washed our bath towels and had hung them on a line strategically placed to block the guard's view. I checked that from where he was standing, our guard would not be able to see our feet under the house between the stilts when we jumped out the back window. We followed our regular routine exactly. But we ate more than usual perhaps, which raised the eyebrow of our receptionist. It was a beautiful sunny afternoon. We waited until the last possible moment.

When the time came, Clara climbed up to the window as planned but got stuck, one part of her body outside and the other inside. I pushed her with all my might. She landed off balance but quickly recovered. I threw the bag out the window, and just as she was running toward the bushes, I heard a voice calling me. It was Ferney. He was coming from the direction of the *chontos*. Had he seen her?

"What are you doing?"

"I'm trying to see the first stars," I replied, as if I were Juliet gazing out from her balcony.

I gaped at the sky, hoping he'd leave. Darkness was falling rapidly. The guard was about to padlock the door. I had to cut the conversation short. Furtively I glanced over to where Clara was. There was no sign of her.

Ferney continued, "I know you are very upset about your father. I wanted to say something earlier, but I didn't find the right moment."

I felt like an actor in a bad play. If anyone had been watching us, they would have found the scene comical. There I was, leaning against my window, looking up at the stars, attempting to trick a guerrilla in order to escape, with him at my feet, or rather below my window, as if he were about to serenade me. I stayed there silently, imploring providence to come to my rescue.

Ferney took my silence and my anxiety for emotion.

"I'm sorry, I shouldn't make you think of sad things. But have faith — one day you will get out of here, and you will be a lot happier than before. You know, I never say so because we're communists, but I am praying for you."

He said good night and walked away. I turned around at once. The guard was already there, inspecting the room. I had no time to make a suitable decoy.

"Where is the other prisoner?"

"I don't know. At the *chontos*, probably."

Our attempt had failed miserably. I prayed that Clara would realize that and return as quickly as possible. But what would she do if they found her with the bag? And in the bag the machete, the ropes, the flashlight, our food. I broke out in a cold sweat.

I decided to go to the *chontos* myself without asking the guard's permission, hoping to distract his attention so that my companion could get back into the room.

The guard ran after me screaming and struck me with the butt of his rifle to force me to turn around. Clara was already back in the room when we got there. The guard swore at her and locked the door.

"Do you have the bag?"

"No, I had to hide it beside a tree."

"Where?"

"Near the *chontos*."

"Dear God! We have to think . . . How can we get it back before they discover it?"

I couldn't sleep the whole night. Dawn was breaking. I heard voices and shouts from near the *chontos*. People were running toward the house, they had discovered our bag. Once this conclusion turned into certainty, all the anguish that had been building up in me during the night vanished. I instantly found absolute peace and serenity. They would punish us. Of course. It didn't matter. They would be cruel, humiliating, maybe even violent. That no longer frightened me. I would never give up.

The door opened before six in the morning. It was Andres, surrounded by a large portion of the troop. In an imperious voice, he ordered, "Search them from top to bottom." The girls took over, combing through all our belongings. They had found our bag and emptied it out. I was numb. The search complete – they had taken everything from us – they dispersed. Only Andres remained.

"Go ahead," he said to someone behind me. I turned around.

Ferney was standing there with a large hammer and an enormous box of old, rusty nails. He strode into the room and in a frenzy began hammering nails into every board. After two hours he had not yet covered the entire room. From the start he had wrapped himself in absolute silence and carried out his task with unhealthy zeal, as if he wanted to pin me to the boards. Then he climbed up onto the roof and continued his job, sitting astride a beam, angrily nailing areas where it was clearly unnecessary, until his complete stock of nails ran out.

I knew exactly what he must be feeling. He had found his machete and felt duped. He was remembering the conversation we'd had at the window. In the beginning I was embarrassed, feeling terrible for having deceived him. But as the hours passed, I found him grotesque, with his hammer and nails, his obsession, and this room he had transformed into a bunker in fury.

He brushed past me, enraged.

"You are ridiculous!" I yelled, unable to stop myself.

He did an about-face, slammed both hands on the table as if he would like nothing better than to jump on me, and hissed, "Repeat what you just said."

"I said I find you ridiculous."

"You steal my machete, you make fun of me, you try to escape, and *I* am ridiculous."

"Yes, you are ridiculous! You have no reason to be angry with me."

"I'm angry with you because you betrayed me."

"*I* did not betray *you*. You abducted me, you are keeping me prisoner. I have every right to escape."

"Yes, but I offered you my friendship. I trusted you," he retorted.

"And the day your leader tells you to put a bullet in my head, will I still have your friendship?"

He did not reply. I did not see him again for some time. Then one evening he arrived for guard duty once again. Before putting on the padlock, he produced a fistful of candles from his jacket pocket and handed them to me.

He closed the door before I had time to thank him. These forbidden candles were his answer. I stood there with a lump in my throat.

13

LEARNING TO WEAVE

In my boredom I read the Bible and wove. I had been given a Bible, a very large one with maps and illustrations at the back. Could I have discovered the riches of the Bible in any other way? I don't think so. The world in which I'd lived had no place for meditation, or for silence. But given the absence of distractions, my brain kneaded the words back into shape, as if they were clay being moulded to create something new. And so I would reread passages, and I would discover why they had stayed with me. It was like finding chinks, secret passages, links to other thoughts, and different interpretations of the texts. The Bible became a fascinating world of codes, insinuations, and hidden meanings.

Perhaps that was also why it was easy for me to devote so much time to weaving. Thanks to manual activity, my mind entered a state of meditation, and I could reflect on what I had read while my hands were moving.

It all began one day when I was on my way back from talking to the commander.

Ferney was sitting on his mat, repairing the straps of his backpack. Beto, the boy who shared a tent with him, was standing in front of one of the supporting poles, focused intently on weaving a belt with nylon thread. I had often seen them do this. It was fascinating. They had acquired such dexterity and moved their hands so quickly that they looked like machines. At each knot a new shape appeared. They could make belts with their own name written across them. They would then dye them at the *rancha* by boiling them in large cauldrons of fluorescent water.

I stopped for a moment to admire his work. Beto's lettering was the most attractive of any I'd seen so far.

"He's the best of all of us!" said Ferney unreservedly. "The time it takes me to make one, Beto can make three."

"Really?"

I had trouble seeing why it was an advantage to go fast in a world where there was so much time to kill. That night during my nocturnal musings, I began to think that I would like to learn to weave belts, too. The idea excited me. But how would I go about it? Ask Andres for permission? Ask one of the guards? I had learned that in the jungle there is nothing to be gained by acting impulsively. The world where I was a prisoner was an arbitrary one. It was an empire of whims, ruled by those who had the ability to say no.

One day there was a terrible storm. The downpour lasted from morning to night. I was sitting on the floor watching the spectacle of nature unleashed. Sheets of rain formed a screen so dense you could only see the *caletas* nearest to you; the rest of the camp seemed to have disappeared. The guards remained at their posts without moving, like lost souls, covered from head to toe with black plastic covers. They looked like they were floating on a lake. Unable to absorb all the rain, the ground was under several inches of brown water as far as the eye could see. Whoever ventured outside returned covered in mud. The camp came to a standstill. Only Beto kept on weaving his belt, oblivious to the storm. I couldn't take my eyes off him.

The following day Beto and Ferney came over together, smiling. "We thought you might like to learn to weave," said Beto. "We asked for permission, and Andres agreed. Ferney will get you nylon thread, and I'll show you how to do it."

Beto spent several days with me. First he taught me how to prepare the warp. They had a small hook to secure the warp. Ferney made me a pretty one, and I felt set up like a pro. Beto came by in the evening to review what I had done during the day. "You have to stretch the thread more tightly over the hooks," he told me. And then, "The knots need to be tighter" and "You have to pull on it twice – otherwise it will run." I put all my energy into learning the proper technique, correcting my mistakes, and following his instructions to the letter. I had to wrap my fingers in pieces of fabric so that the nylon thread wouldn't cut into my flesh when I pulled it. With my work in front of me, I no longer felt the burden of time. The hours passed quickly. *Just like monks* I thought, who, when practising meditation, dedicated themselves to crafting precious objects. I felt that reading the Bible and the meditations that arose from my hours of weaving were doing me good. I was more peaceful, less defensive.

Beto came to tell me one day that I was ready to make a real belt. Ferney turned up with a full reel of thread, and we cut it into the appropriate lengths. The measurements were jungle measurements. Two "armfuls" of thread were needed to make one "quarter" of a belt. An "armful" was the distance between a hand and the opposite shoulder, and a "quarter" was the distance between the thumb and the small finger with the hand open wide.

I wanted to make a belt with Melanie's name woven into it with hearts at the beginning and end of it. I asked around, and no one knew how to do it. So I improvised and found a way, which started a new fashion in the camp, because all the girls wanted to have hearts on their own belts.

The opportunity to be active, creative, and inventive brought respite. There were only two weeks left until Melanie's birthday. I decided that the belt would be ready before then, even if I had to spend entire days on it. The exercise sent me into a trance. I felt as if I were communicating with my daughter – and therefore in touch with the best part of myself.

Beto came to see me again. He wanted to show me another belt with different colours he had made using a new technique. He promised to teach me how to do it. Then, for some reason, during the course of the conversation he said, "You must be ready to run when we tell you to. The *chulos* are close by. If they get here, they will kill you. They want to be able to say that the guerrillas did it, and that way they won't have to negotiate your release. If I'm here, I'll run. I'm not going to get killed for your sake. No one will."

On hearing his words, a strange sensation came over me. I felt sorry for him, as if, by admitting that he would think only of himself at the moment of great danger, he was condemning himself to receiving no help from others when he would most need it.

He left the camp the following day "on an assignment," which meant he was probably in charge of our provisions for the coming months. One evening as the guards were talking among themselves, convinced we were sound asleep, I learned that he had been killed in an ambush by the Colombian army – the same operation in which El Mocho had lost his life. It was a terrible shock. Not just because the echo of his final words and, with them, his fierce desire to live came back to me, but all the more so because I could not understand how his companions, his comrades, could speak of his death without a shadow of regret, as if they were talking about the latest belt he was finishing.

I could not rid my thoughts of that macabre wink from destiny, that fateful connection, understanding that in a way he did get killed "for me" after all, because of this particular chain of events that had brought us together in spite of ourselves: he as my keeper, I as his prisoner. As I was finishing the belt he'd helped me to start, lost in my meditation, I thanked him in the silence of my mind more for the time he'd spent talking to me than for passing on his art. For I was discovering that the most precious gift someone can give us is time, because what gives time its value is death.

14

MELANIE'S SEVENTEENTH BIRTHDAY

The days were all alike and seemed to last forever. I had trouble remembering what I'd done on the previous day. Everything seemed to be happening in a thick fog, and all I could remember were the camp transfers, because I found them so difficult. Nearly seven months had gone by since I was kidnapped, and I could feel the changes. My centre of interest shifted; the future no longer interested me, nor did the outside world. They were simply inaccessible to me. I was living the present moment as in an eternity of relentless pain, without the hope that it would ever end.

And yet before I knew it, it was my daughter's birthday, as if time had accelerated capriciously just to annoy me. For two weeks I'd been weaving a belt for her. I was proud of it. The guerrillas would file past the shack to come and inspect my work. "The old girl is learning!" they said, with a hint of surprise, as a compliment. Calling me the *cucha* in their particular slang had no pejorative connotation. They used the same word to speak to their commander, in a tone meant to be familiar and respectful at the same time. However, I was having trouble getting used to it. I felt as if I'd been shoved irrevocably into a closet of relics. But the fact remained, my daughter was turning seventeen — I was old enough to be their mother.

So I went on weaving, lost in the hundreds of thoughts that laced themselves together like the knots I patiently added to my handiwork. For the first time since I'd been captured, I was in haste to finish something.

The day before Melanie's birthday, at six o'clock in the evening, just before they locked us up, I completed the last knot of her belt. I was proud.

Melanie's birthday had to be a day of joy. I told myself it was the only way to honour her, my little girl, who had shed light on my life, even in the depths of this green hole. All night long I'd gone through her life in my mind – the day of her birth, her first steps, the terrible fright she got from a wind-up doll that walked better than she did. I saw her again as she was on the first day of school, with her pigtails and her white toddler boots, and I watched her gradually grow up, following her until the last time I'd held her in my arms. I cried. But my tears now were of a different kind altogether. I was thankful, thankful that I had been there, that I had known so many moments I could now draw on in my thirst for happiness. To be sure, it was a sad happiness, because I felt so acutely my children's physical absence, but it was the only happiness I could reach.

I got up long before they unlocked the door. I was sitting on the edge of the bed, singing "Happy Birthday" in my head, hoping the vibrations would reach my daughter, travelling mentally from the wooden house, above the trees, above the jungle, above the Caribbean, and all the way to her room on the island of Santo Domingo. I could picture her sleeping just as I'd left her. I imagined waking her up with a kiss on her cool cheek. I firmly believed that she could sense my presence.

The day before, I'd asked for permission to make a cake, and Andres had granted it. Jessica came to help me, and we prepared the batter with flour, powdered milk, sugar, and dark chocolate (extraordinary concessions) that we melted in a separate saucepan. Because we had no oven, we fried it. Jessica took care of the icing. She had used a packet of the powder for making strawberry-flavoured drinks, mixing it with powdered milk and a little bit of water. The thick paste that resulted transformed the black cake into a candy-pink disk, and on it she wrote: FROM FARC-EP.

Andres allowed us to borrow his cassette player, and Jessica came back into the house with it, the cake, and El Mico, under whose nose we had escaped. He was there as a dancing partner, because Jessica was determined to make the most of the occasion. As for me, I had also got ready. I had dressed up, wearing the jeans I'd had on when I was kidnapped –

jeans that Melanie had given me for Christmas – and the belt I'd made for her, because I had lost a lot of weight and my trousers were sliding down.

For a few hours, these young people changed as if by magic. They were no longer guards, or terrorists, or killers. They were young people, my daughter's age, having fun. They danced divinely, as if they'd never done anything else their entire life. They were perfectly synchronized with one another, dancing in that shack as if it were a ballroom, whirling around with elegant self-awareness. You couldn't help but watch. Jessica, with her long, curly, black hair, knew that she was beautiful. She moved her hips and shoulders, just enough to reveal the contours of her curves. El Mico was a rather ugly boy, but that night he was transformed. The world was his. I wanted so much to have my children there! It was the first time I thought this. I would have liked for them to know these young people, to discover their strange way of life, so different and yet so close to theirs, because all adolescents in the world are alike. These young people could have been my children. I had known them to be cruel, despotic, humiliating. I could only wonder as I watched them dance whether my children, under the same conditions, would not have acted the same way.

That day I understood that we are all fundamentally the same. I thought back to my tenure in Congress. For a long time, I had singled out people as a way to unmask corruption in my country. Now I wondered whether that had been right. It was not that I doubted the truth of my accusations, but rather I had grown aware of how complex we human beings are. Because of that, compassion appeared to me under a new light, as an essential value for dealing with my present. *It is the key to forgiveness*, I thought, wanting to set aside any inclinations of vengeance. The day of Melanie's birthday, I understood that I did not want to miss the opportunity to hold out my hand to my enemy, when the time came.

After that day my relationship with Jessica changed. She came and asked me if I could give her English lessons. Her request surprised me: I wondered what a little *guerrillera* could do with English lessons in the jungle.

Jessica showed up on the first day with a brand-new notebook, a pen, and a black pencil with an eraser. Being the girlfriend of the commander had certain advantages. But it was also true that right from the start she had all the characteristics of a good student – neat handwriting, spatial and mental organization, excellent concentration, very good memory. She was so happy to learn that this in turn pushed me to better prepare my lessons. I was surprised to find myself looking forward to her visits. As time went by, we mingled English lessons with more intimate conversations. She shivered as she shared with me descriptions of her father's death – he had also been part of the guerrilla movement – and of her own recruitment. She talked about her relationship with Andres. From time to time, she raised the tone and talked about communism, about how glad she was to have taken up arms to defend the people, how women were not discriminated against in the FARC, how sexism was strictly forbidden, too. She would lower her voice to talk to me about her dreams, her ambitions, and the problems in her relationship. I realized she was worried that the guards might be listening.

"I have to be careful, because they might misunderstand and ask for an explanation at the *aula*."

That was how I learned that problems were discussed out in the open. They were all under scrutiny and were obliged to inform the commander in the event of any suspicious behaviour on the part of a comrade. Informing was an intrinsic part of their regime. They were all subject to it, and they all practised it, indiscriminately.

Once she came with the words to a song in Spanish that she loved. She wanted me to translate it into English so that she could sing it herself. She wanted to sing like an American. She worked hard perfecting her accent.

"You are so gifted, you should ask Joaquín Gómez to have the FARC send you abroad to train. I know that a lot of the sons of members of the Secretariado are in the best universities in Europe and elsewhere. They might be interested in having someone like you who speaks good English . . ."

I saw her eyes light up for a moment. Then she quickly took hold of herself and raised her voice to be heard saying, "We are here to give our lives to the revolution, not to go to some bourgeois university."

She never came back to her English lessons. I was sorry. One morning when she was on guard, I went up to her to ask her why she had dropped the English classes when she was learning so well.

She glanced around her and said in a hushed voice, "I had an argument with Andres. He forbade me from continuing the English lessons. He burned my notebook."

15

RESENTMENT AND REMISSION

One morning almost at dawn, Ferney came to see us. "Pack up all your things. We're leaving. You have to be ready in twenty minutes."

I felt my guts turn to liquid. The camp had already been half disman-tled. All the tents had been folded up, and the first guerrillas were leaving with their backpacks, hiking in single file over by the river. They made us wait.

Right at noon Ferney came back, took our things, and ordered us to follow. Crossing the coca fields was like walking through a furnace, the sun was so strong. As we went by the lemon tree, I picked up a few lemons and filled my pockets. It was a luxury I could not pass up. Ferney looked at me impatiently, and then he decided to take some, too, while ordering me to go on walking. We went back into the *manigua* – the swamp-like terrain cov-ered with tropical bushes. The temperature changed immediately. We had moved from the stifling heat of the coca field into the damp coolness of the undergrowth. There was a smell of rot. I hated this world that was decom-posing perpetually, inhabited by horrendous swarming insects. It was truly a living tomb – all it would take was a slight inadvertent gesture on our part and we would be doomed. The water was only twenty yards or so away; we were near the banks of the river. So we could expect to be trans-ported by boat. But there were no boats waiting.

The guard flung himself on the ground, pulled off his boots, and made as if he were settling down for a while. I looked everywhere in the hope of finding a decent spot to sit. I turned in circles, undecided, like a dog trying to sit down on its tail. Ferney reacted with a laugh. "Wait a minute!" He pulled out his machete and vigorously cleared a space around a dead tree, then cut down some huge leaves from a wild banana tree and carefully spread them onto the ground.

"Have a seat, *Doctora!*" he said mockingly.

We were made to wait all day long, by an old tree trunk on the riverbank. Through the thick foliage, the sky was turning a darker shade of blue by the minute, and it filled my soul with regret. *Lord, why? Why me?*

The sound of an engine roused us from our drowsiness. We all got to our feet. In addition to the captain, who turned out to be Lorenzo, Andres and Jessica were already on the boat. I relaxed when I saw we were headed upstream. We came out on a river that was twice as wide as the previous one. In the pale gloom of twilight, I could see more and more little lights shining here and there, the lights of houses. I tried my best not to yield to the hypnotic effect of the engine's vibrations. The others were snoring around me, curled in twisted, uncomfortable positions to avoid the wind that blew straight into our faces.

We disembarked two days later by a small house. There were horses waiting for us, and we were led by the bridle across an immense farm with enclosures filled with well-fed cattle. Once again I prayed, *My God, please make this be the path to freedom!* But we left the farm behind and followed a little dirt road that was very well maintained, with freshly painted fences scattered here and there. We were back in civilization. A feeling of lightness came over me. This had to be a good omen. We came to a crossroads and were told to dismount; the guerrillas gave us back our belongings to carry, and we were ordered to start walking. I looked up and saw a column of guerrillas ahead of us, marching into the forest again, making their way up a very steep slope. I didn't know how I would manage to do the same. But with a rifle in my back, I succeeded, one foot in front of the other, like a mule. Andres had decided to set up his new camp at the top.

It seemed to be easier to get supplies at this new camp. There was a delivery of the shampoo and care products that I had been requesting for months. Yet when I saw the box full of supermarket bottles, I grew weary, knowing that my release was not on the agenda. They expected me still to be there at Christmas. We also received a delivery of underwear. There must be a store not too far away. The road we'd taken had to lead somewhere. And what if there was a police station nearby, or perhaps even a military detachment?

I decided to start up a daily routine that would allay their suspicions, and I made it a regular habit to keep an eye on all their movements. Clara and I were living in a *caleta* they had put together for us beneath a huge black plastic sheet. We were also entitled to a little table with two facing chairs and a bed just big enough for our one mattress and our mosquito net. I had asked Andres for permission to have a *pasera** built so that we would have somewhere to put our things. Jessica was just behind him, and she scoffed wryly, "They're set up like queens, and still they complain!" Her resentment surprised me. A slope that turned muddy overnight led to a dreamy brook that wound its way along the bottom of our hill. The water was absolutely transparent, flowing over a bed of aquarium pebbles that reflected the light in a multitude of coloured beams. Going there was the best moment of the day. We would descend to the brook at the beginning of the afternoon in order not to disturb the cooks in their work; this was where they came to fetch water and wash the pots in the morning.

Two girls were our escorts for the time it took to wash our laundry and bathe. I had the unfortunate idea of mentioning how extraordinary the spot was and how much I liked diving into the crystal water. Worse than that, I had lounged in the water for just an instant too long when my eyes met the spiteful gaze of one of the guards. From that moment on, the girls who guarded us stared at their watches and made us hurry from the second we got there.

But I was determined not to let them spoil my pleasure. I spent the shortest time possible on my laundry in order to enjoy my bath. On one particular day, it was Jessica's turn to escort us, along with Yiseth. As soon

---

*A shelf.

as we arrived, she went away annoyed, because I had jumped into the water playfully. I guessed she would go and complain, irritated, arguing that I took too long to bathe. But we had passed Ferney on the way down, and I was counting on him to clear things up. I was not at all prepared for what happened.

We were naked, rinsing out our hair, our eyes full of soap, when we heard male voices shouting insults as they came down the path to the river. I didn't have time to cover myself before two guards ordered us to get out of the water, their rifles pointed at us. I wrapped myself up in my towel, protesting, demanding that they go so we could get dressed. One of the guards was Ferney, and he looked at me viciously as he ordered me to leave the place immediately. "You're not on vacation here. You'll get dressed back in your *caleta*!"

October 2002. I shielded myself behind the Bible, turning to what was easiest, the Gospels. These texts, written as if there were a hidden camera following Jesus everywhere, stimulated my imagination. And thus a character came to life before my eyes, a man who had relations with people around him and whose behaviour intrigued me all the more in that I felt I would never have reacted like him.

Yet my reading triggered something in my mind. For instance, the story about the wedding at Cana. There was a dialogue between Jesus and his mother that struck me, because I could have experienced something similar with my own son. Mary, realizing that there is no more wine for the feast, says, "They have no wine." And Jesus, who understands perfectly that behind her simple remark there is a request for him to act, replies in a bad mood, almost annoyed at feeling manipulated. Mary, like all mothers, knows that despite his initial refusal her son will end up doing what she suggested. This is why she goes to speak to those who are serving, asking them to follow Jesus's instructions. Just as Mary suggested, Jesus transforms water into wine, beginning his public life with this first miracle. There was something undeniably pleasing and almost pagan about his first miracle – to make sure the feast could continue. The scene stayed with me for days. Why had Jesus refused at first? Was he afraid? Intimidated? How could he be mistaken about the fittingness of the moment, when he was supposed to know everything? The story fascinated me. Thoughts spun around in my brain. I searched, I reflected. And then suddenly it dawned on me: He had the choice! How silly – it was obvious. But this changed everything. This man was not some robot programmed to do good and suffer punishment in the name of humankind. Of course he had a destiny, but he'd made choices, he'd always had the choice! . . . As for me, what was my fate? In this state of total absence of freedom, did I have the possibility to make a choice? And if so, which one?

The book I held in my hands became my trusted companion. What was written there had so much power that it forced me to stop avoiding myself, to make my own choices as well. And through some sort of vital intuition, I understood I had a long way to go, that it would bring about a profound transformation within me, even though I could not determine its essence, or its scope. In that book there was a voice, and behind that voice there was an intelligence that sought to establish contact with me. It was not merely the company of written words that assuaged my boredom. It was a living voice, speaking. To me.

Aware of my ignorance, I read the Bible from the first line to the last, like a child, asking all the questions that might come to mind. For I noticed that often, when some detail in the narrative seemed incongruous to me, I would put it to one side in a mental basket that I had created to store things I did not understand, stamping it consciously with the word "errors" – and this led me to go on reading without asking any questions and receptive to the voice as the words progressed.

My initial interest lay in the Virgin Mary, quite simply because the woman I had discovered at the wedding at Cana was very different from the ingenuous and somewhat simple-minded adolescent I thought I'd known up to now. I went over the New Testament painstakingly, but there was very little about her. She never spoke, except in the Magnificat, which took on a new dimension, and I decided to learn it by heart.

I had found something to do with my days, and my anxiety receded. I opened my eyes in the morning impatient to start my reading and my weaving. Lorenzo's birthday was coming soon too, and I intended to make it as joyful as Melanie's. I had made it a life precept. It was also a spiritual exercise, that of forcing oneself to find happiness in the midst of the greatest distress.

I had set about making Lorenzo a special belt, weaving little boats that stood out on either side of his name. Because I was getting rather skilled at it, I managed to finish it well before the date. My innovative design had promoted me to the rank of a "pro." I exchanged high-flying technical conversations with the top weavers in the camp. Having a creative outlet made me feel I was capable of something new in a world that had rejected me, and it freed me from the burden of failure that my life had become.

I also continued to exercise. Or at least that's how I thought about it, because what I really needed was a pretext to do the physical exercise that would enable me, in the future, to escape.

The Bible reading had helped to smooth my relationship with Clara. One afternoon, during a torrential storm, when we were confined together under our mosquito net, I ventured to share with her the results of my nocturnal ruminations. I explained to her in detail how to get out of the *caleta*, how to avoid the guard, how to erase our tracks, how to find the road that would lead us to freedom. The rain made such a din on the plastic roof that we had trouble hearing each other. She asked me to speak more loudly, so I raised my voice to go on with my explanation. It was only when I'd finished outlining my detailed plan to her that I noticed a movement behind our *caleta*. Ferney was hidden inside, behind the shelf that Andres had finally agreed to build for us. He'd heard everything.

I collapsed. What would they do? Would they chain us up again? Would they search us again? I could have killed myself for being so careless. Why had I not taken all the necessary precautions before speaking?

I kept a close watch on the guards' attitude in order to try to detect any change. I fully expected to see Andres arrive with the chains in his hand. Then it was Lorenzo's birthday. I asked for permission to bake a cake, sure that they would refuse to let me anywhere near the *rancha*. However, they did grant me permission, and this time Andres asked us to make enough cake for everybody.

As I had sworn it would be, it was a day of remission. I was able to let go of all my thoughts of sadness, regret, and uncertainty, and I immersed myself in a task that would bring pleasure to everyone, as a way of giving back, in return for having received so much with the birth of my child.

That evening for the first time in months, sleep overcame me. Dreams of happiness, where I was holding three-year-old Lorenzo in my arms and running through a field scattered with yellow flowers, invaded these few hours of respite.

16

THE RAID

At two o'clock in the morning, I was violently awoken by one of the guards shaking me and shouting, the beam of his flashlight shining in my face. "Get up, bitch! Do you want to get killed?"

I opened my eyes, not understanding, panicking at the fear I could hear in his voice.

Military planes were flying very low over the camp. The guerrillas were grabbing their backpacks and running away, leaving everything behind them. The night was pitch black, you couldn't see a thing except the shadows of the aeroplanes you could sense above the trees. Instinctively I grabbed everything within reach: my handbag, a bath towel, the mosquito net.

This only made the guard bleat all the louder. "Leave everything! They're going to bomb us, don't you get it?"

He was trying to wrench my things out of my hands, and I was clutching onto them and grabbing more things on the way. Clara had already fled. I rolled everything in a ball and began to run in the same direction as the others, pursued by the guard's cries of rage.

I had managed to save my children's belts, my jacket, and some clothes. But I'd forgotten my Bible.

We crossed the entire camp and took a footpath I did not know existed until then. I stumbled every other step, grabbing onto whatever was within reach, and my skin was lacerated by the vegetation. The guard was annoyed, insulting me, all the more spiteful because he had no witnesses. We were the last, and we had to catch up with the rest of the group. The engines of the military planes droned above us, flying off, then coming back, with the result that we were often plunged into terrible darkness, because the guard would not switch on his flashlight until the planes were well away. I managed as I ran to put the few belongings I'd rescued into a satchel, but I was out of breath and my burden slowed me down.

The guard poked the end of his rifle into my ribs, trotting behind me all the while, but the more he mistreated me, the more I lost my balance, and I often found myself on my knees in fear of an immediate bombardment. He was beside himself with rage, accusing me of doing it deliberately, dragging me by the hair or my jacket to pull me to my feet. During the twenty-plus minutes that we ran over flat terrain, I more or less managed to make headway, like a hounded beast, not really knowing how. But then the terrain changed, with steep downward slopes and difficult climbs. I couldn't stand it any longer. The guard tried to take my bag, but I was afraid that his aim was not to help me but rather to get rid of it along the way, as he had threatened to do. I clung to my little bag of belongings as if it were my life. Then suddenly, without any transition, I began to walk slowly, indifferent to his shouts and threats. Run? Why? Flee? Why? No, I wasn't going to run. Never mind about the bombs, never mind about the planes, never mind about me, I was not going to obey, nor was I going to submit to the whims of an overexcited, panicky young man.

"Stupid bitch, I'm going to stick a bullet in your head to teach you how to walk!"

I turned around like a wild animal to face him. "If you say one more word, I won't take another step."

He was surprised, and regretted having lost face. He went to shove me with the butt of his rifle, but I reacted more quickly than he did. "I forbid you to touch me."

He restrained himself, suddenly made of stone. I then realized that it was not I who had intimidated him in this way. Andres was taking great strides toward us along the footpath.

"Quickly, quickly, hide in the *manigua*. Total silence, no lights, no movement."

I found myself sprawled in a ditch, crouched over my bag, certain I would see soldiers at any moment. My mouth was painfully dry, prey to a mortal thirst, and I wondered where Clara was. Andres stayed there for a while, crouched next to me, and then he went away again. But before he left, he said to me, "If you don't strictly obey orders, the guards have very precise instructions, and you run the risk of not being here tomorrow."

We stayed there until dawn, when Andres ordered us to walk toward the valley, cutting through the forest.

"Those *chulos* are so stupid that they flew over our heads all night long and didn't even locate the camp! They're not going to bomb. I'll send a team to pick up everything that stayed behind."

We did as he said. We were on a hill. Through the thick foliage, I could see spread below us an immense wooded savanna, crisscrossed with emerald green pastures, as if the English countryside had appeared by magic in the middle of the Colombian jungle. It must be wonderful to live down there! Such a world existed outside, and it was forbidden to me—it seemed unreal. And yet it was just beyond the trees, beyond their rifles.

Right then we were shaken by an enormous explosion. We were already quite far away, but it must have come from our camp.

As soon as we ran into other guerrilla troops, they talked of nothing else.

"Did you hear?"

"Yes, they bombed the camp."

"Are you sure?"

"I've no idea. But Andres sent a team back to reconnoitre. It's almost sure."

"They only bombed once."

"What do you mean? We heard several explosions. There was a series of attacks."

"At least all the planes are gone now. That's something."

"We have to watch it. They made a landing. They've got troops on the ground. We'll have helicopters over us all day long."

"Those sons of bitches, I can't wait to see them face-to-face. They're chickens, every one of them."

I watched in silence. The most cowardly ones were the most aggressive.

We stopped in a tiny clearing where a small stream ran alongside. Clara was already there, sitting against a tree with dense foliage and generous shade. I needed no coaxing – I was exhausted. From where I sat, I could see the roof of a little house and a column of blue-grey smoke rising from the chimney. In the distance I could hear the voices of children playing, like an echo of happy days lost in my past. Who were those people? Could they know that just behind their garden there were guerrillas, hiding captive women?

One of the girls, in her camouflage uniform, her boots shining as if for an important military parade, her hair perfectly styled in a large braid rolled into a chignon, came over to us, smiling from ear to ear, with two enormous plates in her hands. How did she manage to look so impeccable after running the whole night?

We were given the order to start marching once more. We set off in single file along a footpath that began to climb, again following the crest of the hill. I was surprised by the stamina of the girls who carried burdens as heavy as those the men carried and walked as quickly as they did. Little Betty was astonishing. She looked like a tortoise with the enormous pack twice as big as she was, which she carried hunched over as if she had a piano on her back. Her little legs scurried along not to be left behind, and she still found a way to smile.

The helicopters were after us. I could feel the throbbing of their engines on the nape of my neck. William, the guard who had been assigned to me for the march, ordered me to walk faster. Even if I'd wanted to, I couldn't.

A sharp blow to my spine took my breath away. I turned around, outraged. William was poised to hit me again with a rifle butt in my stomach.

"Shit, you want to get us killed? Can't you see they're almost on top of us?"

Indeed, above our heads, sixty yards from the ground, the undersides of the helicopters in formation seemed to be brushing the tops of the trees.

I could see the feet of the soldier manning the artillery, hanging in the void on either side of the gun. They were there. They must have seen us! If I had to die, I would rather die like this, in a confrontation where I might at least have the chance to get free. To die for nothing, swallowed up by that damned jungle, thrown in a hole and condemned to vanish without my family even being able to retrieve my remains – that was what filled me with horror. I wanted my children to know that at least I'd tried, fought, done everything I could to get back to them.

The guard must have read my thoughts. He loaded his rifle. But in his eyes I saw a primal, visceral, most basic fear. I couldn't stop myself from looking at him with scorn. He was not so proud now, this guy who liked to swagger around the camp all day.

"Run like a rabbit if you want to. I'm not going any faster!"

His girlfriend spat on the ground and said, "I'm not about to get myself killed for the sake of this old bitch!" She headed off at a trot and disappeared around the first bend.

After a few minutes, the helicopters disappeared. I could still hear two of them, but even then they peeled away before reaching us and left for good. I was furious. How could they have failed to see us? With an entire column of guerrillas right under their nose!

Unconsciously I had begun to walk more quickly, frustrated and disappointed, sensing that we'd come so close to a chance at being set free. When we arrived at the bottom of the hill, Andres had had a mixture of water and sugar made up, with a little bit of an orange-flavoured, powder-based beverage mixed in.

"Drink! It will help you avoid dehydration."

He didn't need to tell me again – I was soaked in sweat.

He then explained that we would cross the cornfield in front of us in groups of four. He pointed toward the sky. Far in the distance, I could see a tiny white aeroplane against the blue sky. "We have to wait until it's gone. It's the phantom aeroplane."

His orders were followed to perfection. I crossed the open field looking at the aeroplane directly overhead. I was sorry I didn't have a mirror to try to make signals. Once again my captors had managed to slip through the net of the army. On the far side, in the undergrowth, a toothless, sun-baked peasant was waiting for us.

"This is our guide," whispered someone ahead of me.

Without warning, a cold wind began to blow, filling the forest with a shiver. The sky turned grey in an instant, and the temperature immediately dropped by several degrees. As if they had received a peremptory order, the guerrillas all dropped their packs onto the ground, pulled out their huge black plastic sheets, and covered themselves.

Someone gave me one, and I wrapped myself up in it the way I had seen them do. A moment later a torrential storm broke over us. Despite all my efforts, I was very quickly soaked through to the bone. It would go on raining like this all day long and all the night that followed. We walked one behind the other until the next day, passing through the forest for hours in silence, hunched over to avoid the water that the wind blew into our faces. Then at twilight we took a path that went along a hillside, and it became a veritable quagmire as the whole column marched over it. With each step I had to reach for my boot that had become mired in eighteen inches of thick, stinking mud, losing my balance. I was exhausted. I was shivering, worn out from the effort. Then we left the cover of the under-growth, with its steep ups and downs, and came out on flat, warm land, cultivated and inhabited. We went past farms with dogs that barked and chimneys that smoked. They seemed to be looking at us with scorn as we went by. How desperately I wanted to go home. Just before twilight we reached a magnificent *finca*. The landlord's house was built in the finest drug-trafficker style. The stable alone would have fulfilled all my dreams of a place to sleep. It was late, I was thirsty and hungry, I was cold. My feet were ravaged by enormous blisters that had burst and stuck to my soaked socks. I'd been bitten from head to toe by tiny fleas that I couldn't see but I could feel, swarming all over my body. The mud had stuck to my fingers and beneath my nails, swelling them, infecting the skin, which cracked. I was bleeding, and yet I couldn't identify my multiple sores. I collapsed on the ground, determined to move no more.

Half an hour later, Andres gave the order to leave again. We were back on our feet, dragging our misery, marching like convicts in the darkest

night. It wasn't fear that made me walk, and it wasn't their threats that
made me put one foot in front of the other. None of that mattered to me.
It was fatigue that made me carry on. My brain had disconnected, and my
body was moving without me.

Before dawn we reached the top of a small hill that overlooked the
valley. A fine drizzle continued to persecute us. There was a sort of shelter
in beaten earth, with a thatched roof. Ferney hooked up a hammock
between two beams, stretched a black plastic sheet on the ground, and
handed me my bag.

"Get changed. We're going to sleep here."

I woke up at seven o'clock in the morning in the cocaine laboratory
that had served as our shelter. Everyone was already up, including Clara,
who was smiling: She was happy that I had dry clothes to give her. The
new day promised to be equally long and difficult, and we decided to
put our dirty, wet clothes from the day before back on and keep the dry
clothes for sleeping. I really wanted to take a bath, and I'd got up determined to find a place to have a wash. There was a spring ten yards away.
They allowed me to go there. They had given me a piece of potassium
soap, and I rubbed my body and scalp furiously with it to try to get rid of
the lice and ticks I'd picked up during the march. The girl escorting me
was urging me to finish, annoyed that I was washing my hair when the
order had been to have a quick wash. However, there was nothing pressing: once we got back up to the shelter, we found the guerrillas sitting idly,
waiting for new instructions.

The toothless, emaciated peasant from the day before reappeared. He
had a *mochila* slung over his shoulder, one of those bags that the local tribes
weave so nicely, and inside the *mochila* there were two hens tied up, their
legs in the air, wriggling with convulsive spasms. He was relieved of his
burden with cries of victory: Breakfast was turning into a feast. Once the
euphoria had subsided, I went up to the peasant and asked him, with a
boldness that was unusual for me, if he would let me have his *mochila*. It was
grimy, stinking, and full of holes. But for me it was a treasure. I could fill
it with the things I needed for the walk and keep my hands free, and once
it was washed and stitched, it would be useful for hanging supplies to

keep them out of reach of rodents. The man looked at me, astonished, failing to understand the value I placed upon his bag. He handed it to me without protesting, as if he had received not a request but an order. I thanked him with such an effusion of joy that he burst out laughing like a child. He tried to start up a conversation with me, and I was about to reply only too gladly when we heard Andres's voice curtly calling us to order. I went back to sit down in my corner and glanced over at Andres, astonished by the violence in his gaze as he stared at the gift I had just received. *It won't be mine for long*, I said to myself.

The day seemed endless. Immediately after a solid breakfast, at which, to my great pleasure, I was given one of the hen's feet to share, we went back down toward the valley to follow a road that wandered through the forest. Ferney and Jhon Janer, a young man who had recently joined the troops and whom I found more mischievous than disagreeable, had been assigned as our guards. Visibly, the rest of the troops had taken a different route. We came to a crossroads, by which time I was dragging myself, limping on the edges of my feet, and in the distance, like a mirage, I could make out my toothless peasant holding two old nags by the bridle. As soon as he saw us, he began to walk toward us, and I collapsed on the ground, incapable of taking another step. What a joy it was to see the old man again and to be able to exchange a few words with him. I knew he would have liked to do more.

We were each given one of the nags, and we set off again at a slow trot. The guards ran by our side, holding the horses firmly by the neck. We had to catch up with the troops, and they expected that it would take us most of the day. On horseback I thought, *I don't mind — they can take all day if they want, and all night and the next day, too*. I silently thanked the heavens for this godsend, only too aware, now, of what I'd gained.

The forest we were going through was different from the thick jungle where we'd been hiding all those months. The trees were immense and sad, and the rays of the sun reached us only after they had penetrated the thick layer of branches and leaves far above our heads. The undergrowth was bare, with neither ferns nor shrubs, just the trunks of those colossal trees like the pillars of an unfinished cathedral. The place was strange, as if a curse had been cast upon it. My mood seemed to correspond to the nature around me, and it opened up old wounds that had never completely healed. And now that my physical pain had been assuaged, with my bloody feet hanging loose and relieved from any excruciating contact, it was the pain in my heart that was aroused, for I was incapable of letting go of my past life, a life I so loved and that was no longer mine.

The rain fell with a brute force, as if someone were gleefully tipping buckets of water on us from the treetops. Once again the road had become a quagmire. The water covered the guerrillas' boots almost completely, and the suctioning mud held them prisoner with each step. We had caught up with the troops, and now we began to pass them one by one, as they were bent beneath the weight of their burdens, their faces hardened. I felt pity for them: Someday I would get out of this hell, whereas they had knowingly condemned themselves to rot in this jungle. I did not want to meet their gazes as I rode by. I knew only too well that they were cursing us.

The march continued all day long through the endless storm. We left behind the tree cover and crossed *fincas* rich with fruit trees. The rain and fatigue left us indifferent. The guerrillas didn't have the strength to stretch out their hands to pick up the mangoes and guavas rotting on the ground. I didn't dare, from the height of my horse, pick the fruit on my way, for fear of irritating them.

Turning a corner, we came upon some children playing, jumping in the puddles. They had bags full of mandarin oranges that they had left to one side. When they saw us arrive, because we were on horseback they took us for the guerrilla commanders, and they gave all of us some fruit from their reserve. I accepted with gratitude.

It was still raining at dusk, and I was shivering feverishly, wrapped up in a plastic sheet that no longer protected me from the rain but did help me stay warm. We had to give up our horses and continue on foot. I was biting my lips to keep from complaining, as with each step I felt a million needles stabbing my feet and penetrating my limbs. We walked for a long time, until we reached an ostentatious *finca*. An opulent house majestically overlooked countryside that undulated like velvet in the evening twilight. We were guided toward a landing stage, where we were allowed to sit down and wait for the arrival of a motorboat, an enormous iron launch with enough room for all the guerrillas, all the backpacks, and a dozen sturdy plastic bags filled with provisions.

Clara and I were made to sit in the centre. Andres and Jessica sat just behind us, next to William and Andrea, his attractive but disagreeable girlfriend, who'd been escorting us when we were chased by the helicopters. They were talking loudly, so that we would overhear.

"I guess we got rid of the *chulos* again!"

"If they think they're going to get hold of our cargo that easily, they're in for a surprise."

They were laughing maliciously. I didn't want to listen to them any more.

"They took everything that was left after the bombing and burned the rest. The old women's mattress, their Bible, all the shit they had collected."

"So much the better – there's less to carry now!"

"And to think they wanted to swim away from us, stupid old bags. Now they're with us for years!"

"They'll be grandmothers by the time they get out."

That made them laugh even harder. There was a silence, and then Andres turned to me and said disdainfully, "Ingrid, hand over the *mochila*. It's mine now."

17

THE CAGE

We travelled for days, heading down rivers that grew ever wider. Most often we moved at night, so no one would see us. Sometimes, but rarely, we risked travelling during the day, beneath a baking sun. And I always made sure to look into the distance, to search the horizon, to fill my soul with beauty, because I knew that once we went into the forest, I would no longer see the sky.

Walls of trees rose a hundred feet above the riverbanks in a compact formation that blocked all light. We glided through the jungle, aware that no human beings had ever ventured here before, on a mirror of water the colour of emerald that parted like velvet as we passed. The sounds of the jungle seemed to grow louder inside this tunnel of water. I could hear the cry of monkeys, but I couldn't see them. As a rule, Ferney would sit next to me and point out the *salados*. I stared at the riverbank, hoping to see some mythological beast emerge, to no avail. I confessed that I didn't know what *salados* meant. He laughed at my expense, but he eventually explained that *salados* was where the tapirs, the lapas* and the deer went to drink. This was the place hunters always looked for. No one, however, was able to name any of the thousands of birds that crossed our sky. I'd been surprised to see kingfishers, egrets, and swallows, and I was delighted

---

* A rodent.

that I could recognize them just as if they were flying out to me from the pages of a picture book. The parrots and parakeets with their brilliant, deceptive feathers were outraged by our passage. They flew away from their shelter, then returned as soon as we went by, giving us a chance to admire their magnificent wings. There were also those that flew off like arrows, skimming the water alongside us, as if they were racing our boat. They were little tiny birds with marvellous colours. Sometimes I thought I could see cardinals or nightingales, and I remembered my grandfather watching out for them for hours from his window, and now I understood him, the way I understood so many things I hadn't taken the time to grasp before.

One bird fascinated me more than all the others. It was turquoise, the underside of its wings was fluorescent green, and its beak was blood red. When I saw it I alerted everyone, not only in the hope that someone might be able to tell me its name but above all from a need to share the sight of this magical creature.

I knew these visions would remain etched forever within me. But not as good memories, for good memories are only those you can share, especially with your loved ones. If I had only known the name of that bird, I would have felt that I could bring it back with me. But there was nothing left. We finally reached the end of our journey. We had sailed down a wide river, which we then left behind to head up a secret tributary hidden behind thick vegetation and winding unpredictably around a small hill. We disembarked in dense jungle. We sat on our belongings and waited while the guerrillas went at it with their machetes to clear a space for our camp.

In a few hours, they built a wooden dwelling with a zinc roof, closed on all sides, with a narrow opening for a door. It was a cage! I was afraid to go in. I anticipated that this new walled-in space would exacerbate the tension between Clara and me.

After my fourth escape attempt when Yiseth had recaptured me near the river, a group of six guerrillas, including Ferney and Jhon Janer, erected an iron fence all around the cage. At night they locked us in with a padlock.

Behind the metal fence, the feeling of imprisonment plunged me into unbearable distress. I stood there for days praying in an attempt to find an explanation, some meaning behind my misfortune. *Why, why?*

Ferney was on duty once and came over. He handed me a tiny radio that he could just squeeze through the mesh of the fence. "Here, listen to the news, it will take your mind off things. Hide it. Believe me, this fence hurts me more than it does you."

After they had locked us in like rats, they spent several days digging a hole behind our cage, taking turns. At first I thought they were setting out to dig a trench. Then, when I saw that the hole was getting deeper and that they weren't digging it all the way around the cage, I concluded it must be a grave, so they could kill us and throw us in. I had not forgotten that the FARC had threatened to assassinate us after one year of captivity. I lived in terrible dread. I would have preferred for them to announce my execution. Uncertainty was eating away at me. It was only when the porcelain toilet made its appearance that I realized they were merely building a cesspool. They had just finished digging nine feet down, as they'd been ordered. They thought it was great fun to jump into the hole and climb out again without any help, just the strength of their arms, slithering up a wall so smooth and shiny it looked polished by a machine. Someone came up with the idea of letting me have a go, too, and I refused at once, adamantly.

My obstinacy only served to get them all the more excited. They pushed me in, and I found myself at the bottom of the hole, frightened yet determined. They had placed their bets. Everyone was shouting and laughing, eager for the show to commence.

Clara came up to the hole and gave a doubtful look. "She'll make it," she predicted.

I did not share her conviction. Ultimately, however, I proved her right, with much effort and just as much luck. The joy of the two guerrillas who had placed their bets on my success made me laugh. For a moment the barriers that kept us apart had fallen and another division, subtler, very human, had surfaced. There were those who disliked me because of what I represented. They saw in me everything that they were not. And then there were the others, like Ferney and Jhon Janer, the ones who were curious to know who I was and who were ready to build bridges rather than walls. And there was Clara, who had played the referee this time, and who had come out in my favour. In spite of the tension between us, she had wanted me to succeed, and I was grateful to her for that.

This interlude of peace among all of us helped us to prepare our first Christmas in captivity. We had to let bitterness flow between our fingers like water you can't hold back anymore.

To me the most unbearable thing of all was the distress I must be causing my family. This was their first Christmas without my father, and without me. In a way I felt more fortunate than they were, because I could imagine them together at Christmas, which is also my birthday. But they knew nothing about what had happened to me, and they didn't even know whether I was still alive. The idea of my son, Lorenzo – who was still a young boy – of my teenage daughter, Melanie, and of my stepson Sebastian, already an adult, all tormented by the horrors their imagination might construe regarding my fate was driving me mad.

To escape from my labyrinth, I busied myself with making a manger from the clay that had been dug up for the cesspool, moulding figurines dressed in the tropical bulrush that grew abundantly in the surrounding swamps. My work attracted the attention of the young girls. Yiseth wove a lovely garland of butterflies with the metallic paper from cigarette packs. Another came to cut out cardboard angels with me, and we hung them from the tin roof just above the manger. Finally, two days before Christmas, Yiseth came back with an ingenious system of Christmas lights. She had obtained a supply of little flashlight bulbs that she'd fastened to an electric wire. All it took was contact with a radio battery and we had Christmas lights in the middle of the jungle.

I was surprised to see that they had also decorated their *caletas* for the occasion. Some of them had even put up Christmas trees, the branches draped with surgical cotton and decorated with childish drawings.

On Christmas Eve, Clara and I hugged each other. She gave me some soap from her supply. I made a greeting card for her. We had somehow become a family – and as is the case with real families, we hadn't chosen each other. Sometimes, like that day, it was reassuring to be together. We prayed and sang our few *villancicos*, traditional Colombian carols, and we knelt on the ground by our makeshift manger, as if our songs could take us home again, even if just for a few moments.

Our thoughts bore us far away. Mine travelled to another space and another time, to the place where I had been a year earlier with my father, my mother, and my children, amid a happiness I thought was unshakeable – and that only now could I fully appreciate.

Lost in our meditation, we had not noticed that there was a crowd behind us: Ferney, Edinson, Yiseth, El Mico, Jhon Janer, and the others had come to sing with us. Their strong, steady voices filled the forest and seemed to resonate ever louder, beyond the barriers of thick vegetation, toward the sky, beyond the stars, toward the mystical North, where it is written that God dwells, and where I imagined he could hear the silent quest of our hearts only He could answer.

18

FRIENDS WHO COME AND GO

We had a new recruit. William and Andrea had captured a baby monkey. One evening when we had just set up camp for the night by the river, we saw a family of monkeys swinging from branch to branch in the tree-tops, stopping just long enough to throw sticks at us or piss to mark their territory. A mother with her baby hanging from her back clung care-fully to make sure her baby was holding on. William shot the mother. The baby fell at his feet, to become Andrea's mascot. The same bullet that had killed its mother had injured its hand. The little animal cried like a child and licked its fingers, not understanding what had happened. Now it was tied by a rope to a bush near Andrea's *caleta*. Rain had begun coming down, and the little monkey was shivering, all alone, looking wet and wretched. I had a small flask of sulfamide in my belongings that I'd man-aged to hang on to since the day of my abduction. I decided I would treat the baby monkey. The little animal was screaming with fear, pulling on the rope and nearly choking itself. Bit by bit I took its tiny hand, all black and soft like a human hand in miniature. I covered its wound with the powder and made a bandage around its wrist. It was a baby female. They had baptized it "Cristina."

Once we settled into the camp, I asked for permission to go to say hello to Cristina. When she saw me coming, she would call out with joy. I would keep something from my morning food ration to give to her.

She would grab it from my hands and run off to eat it with her back to me.

I heard Cristina shrieking violently one morning. The guard explained that they were bathing her because she smelled bad. Finally I saw her coming at a run, dragging her rope behind her and moaning with sorrow. She grabbed hold of my boot desperately, looking behind her to see if anyone was following. She then clambered up to cling to my neck and eventually fell asleep with her tail wrapped around my arm so she wouldn't fall.

They had given her hair a military haircut that they called *la mesa* (the table), which gave her a flat head, and they'd dunked her in the water to give her a good rinse. Cristina's bath became a regular torture. Andrea had decided that the little monkey had to get used to her daily grooming, like a human being. Cristina in response would shit everywhere, which made Andrea and William hysterical. Whenever she managed to escape, she came to me. I cuddled her, I talked to her, and I trained her as much as I could. When Andrea would come to get her, she would shriek and cling to my shirt. I had to force myself to hide my sorrow.

One day the guy who brought the supplies in the motorboat brought with him two little dogs that Jessica wanted to train. I never saw Cristina again. Andrea came one evening to explain that she and William had gone deep into the forest to release Cristina. It made me very sad; I'd grown so fond of Cristina. But I was relieved that she was free, and whenever I heard monkeys overhead, I would look up in the hope of seeing her again.

One night when I was again prey to insomnia, I overheard a conversation that made my blood run cold. The guards were joking together, saying that Cristina had been the best meal Jessica's dogs had ever had.

Cristina's story shook me profoundly. I was so angry at myself that I hadn't done more to help her. But above all I knew that I could not afford the luxury of any attachment while in the hands of the FARC, as they could use it to blackmail me and alienate me further. Perhaps that was why I tried to keep my distance from everyone, in particular Ferney, who was often kind.

After my abortive escape, he had come to see me. He felt terrible about what his comrades had done to me. "Here, too, there are good people and there are bad people. But you mustn't judge the FARC on the basis of what the bad people do."

Every time Ferney was on duty, he managed to start up a conversation, taking care to speak loudly so that the entire camp could follow. His invariable topic was politics. He justified his armed struggle on the basis that too many people in Colombia lived in poverty. I answered that the FARC wasn't doing anything to combat poverty – on the contrary, the organization had become an important cog in the system it was claiming to fight against, because it was a source of corruption, drug trafficking, and violence. "You are becoming a part of this," I argued.

He was born nearby. He came from a very poor family; his father was blind, and his mother, a peasant, did what she could with an acre of land. All his brothers had gone into subversive activities. But he liked what he was doing. He was learning things, had a career ahead of him, had friends among the guerrillas.

One afternoon he escorted me to work out in the gym Andres had built on the border of the camp. There was a jogging track, parallel bars, a horizontal bar, a hoop for practising somersaults, and a beam three yards from the ground for practising jumps. Everything had been built by hand, by removing the bark from young trees and fixing the bars to sturdy trunks with lianas. Ferney showed me how to jump from the beam to land properly on the ground, which I did – in spite of my fear – just to impress him. I couldn't keep up with him when he did push-ups or other endurance exercises. But I beat him in some of the acrobatics and exercises that required suppleness. Andres joined us and gave us a demonstration of his strength that confirmed he'd had years of training. I asked to use the gym on a regular basis, but he refused. He did, however, allow us to take part in the guerrillas' training, which started every morning at four-thirty. Some days later he had parallel bars put up near the cage for Clara and me to use.

Ferney had intervened in our favour. I thanked him.

"If you find the right words, the proper tone of voice and you ask at the right moment, you're sure of getting what you want," he replied.

After a quarrel I had with Clara, Ferney came over to the fence and said, "You're letting it get to you. You have to create a distance; otherwise you'll go insane, too. Ask them to separate you. At least you'll get some peace."

He was very young – he must have been seventeen. And yet his remarks made me reflect. He had a generous soul and an uncommon sense of honesty. He had gained my respect.

Among the things I lost in the raid was the rosary I had made out of a wire that I had found lying on the ground. I decided to craft a new one by removing the buttons from the military jacket I'd been given and using bits of nylon thread I had left over from my weaving.

It was a fine day in the month of December, the dry season in the jungle, the best in the year. A warm breeze caressed the palm trees, filtering down to us through the foliage, bringing a rare sensation of tranquillity.

I was sitting outside the cage, in the shade, working furiously in the hope of finishing my rosary that same day. Ferney was on duty, and I asked him to cut me some little pieces of wood to make a crucifix that I could hang from my rosary.

Clara was getting lessons in belt weaving from El Mico, who would stop by to check on her progress from time to time. As soon as her teacher left, seeing that Ferney was bringing the little cross to me, she stood up, frowning. She dropped her weaving and threw herself at Ferney, as if she wanted to tear his eyes out.

"So you don't like what I'm doing? Go on, say it!"

She was much taller than he was, and she was taking a provocative pose, thrusting her torso forward, which obliged Ferney to duck his head so as not to brush against her body. He gently took his rifle to put it out of her reach and withdrew, cautiously stepping backward, saying, "No, no, I like what you are doing a lot, but I'm on duty. I can't come and help you right now."

She pursued him for a dozen yards or so, provoking him, shoving him, lunging at him, while he continued to move backward to avoid physical contact. Andres was alerted by the other troops and came to order us back into our cage. I silently complied. Maturity had nothing to do with age. I admired Ferney's self-control. He trembled with rage but had not reacted.

When I shared my thoughts with him, he replied, "When you carry a weapon, you have a responsibility toward other people. You can't afford mistakes."

I, too, could choose how to react. But I was often wrong. Life in captivity had not removed the necessity to act in the right way. It was not about pleasing others or gaining support. I felt I had to change – rather than trying to adapt to the ignominy of the situation, I had to learn to be a better person.

Drinking my usual hot drink one morning, I saw a red and blue flash overhead in the foliage. I pointed to show the guard the extraordinary guacamaya that had just landed a few yards above us. It was a huge parrot, a vision of paradise with carnival colours, and it sat watching us, intrigued, from up on its perch, unaware of its extreme beauty.

What had I done! The guards sounded the alarm, and Andres hurried over with his hunting rifle. The bird was easy prey; it was no feat to kill this magnificent, naive creature. A second later its inert body lay on the ground, blue and orange feathers scattered everywhere.

I took it out on Andres. Why had he done something so pointless and stupid?

He answered, spitting his words out like a machine gun, "I can kill what I want! Especially pigs and people like you!"

There were reprisals. Andres felt that I had judged him, and his behaviour changed abruptly. We had to stay within six feet of the cage at the most and were not allowed to go to the *rancha* or walk around the camp anymore. The bird ended up in the garbage, and for weeks its beautiful blue feathers were scattered all over the camp, until the new rains brought the mud and buried them completely. I vowed to be cautious and keep quiet. I observed myself as I never had before, and I understood that spiritual fulfilment required a constancy and rigour that I needed to acquire. *I had to watch myself, to stop repeating the same mistakes,* I concluded, *keep my impetuous nature in check.*

The days had been warm. The streams had all dried up, and the river where we went to bathe had decreased by half. The young people played games of water polo in the river with the plastic balls they had saved from roll-on deodorants. They looked like miniature ping-pong balls and they vanished easily in the water. The battles to catch them degenerated into free-for-alls that were always fun. I had been invited to play with them. We spent a few afternoons like children. Until the weather changed, and Andres's mood with it.

The rains brought bad news. Ferney told me he was going to be transferred to another camp. Andres had taken an intense dislike to him, accusing him of being too kind and standing up for me. Disheartened, Ferney said to me, "Ingrid, you must always remember what I'm going to say to you: if they treat you badly, always respond with goodness. Never lower yourself, don't react to insults. You must know that silence will always be your best response. Promise me that you will be careful. Someday, I will see you on television when you will get back your freedom. I am waiting for that day. You do not have the right to die here."

His departure was wrenching, because despite everything that separated us, in Ferney I had found a sincere heart. I knew that in this abominable jungle I had to detach myself from everything, to avoid more suffering. But I was beginning to think that in life there might be some suffering that was worth enduring. Ferney's friendship had lightened my first months of captivity, especially the suffocating confinement with Clara. His departure would force me to be tougher, to find greater psychological strength. I was even more alone, now.

19

VOICES FROM THE OUTSIDE

The radio that Clara had broken now worked only half the time. And the only broadcasts we managed to get were a Sunday mass transmitted live from San José del Guaviare, the capital of one of the departments in the Amazon and a station that played some popular music the guerrillas adored and I was sick of.

One morning out of the blue, the guards called me urgently because the radio had announced that my daughter would be on the air. Standing outside the *caleta*, I listened to Melanie's voice. I was surprised by how clearly she reasoned, how well she expressed herself. She was barely seventeen at the time. My pride in her was stronger than sadness. Tears flowed down my cheeks at the moment I least expected. I went back inside the cage, warmed by a feeling of great peace.

Another time when I was already stretched out in my corner under my mosquito net, I heard Pope John Paul II pleading for our release. His voice was unmistakable, and to me it meant everything. I thanked the heavens above, not so much because I thought that the leaders of the FARC would be moved by the Pope's appeal but because I knew that his gesture would lighten my family's burden and help them bear our cross.

Of the few lifelines we received during this period, one gave me hope that I could recover my freedom – that was Dominique de Villepin. We had met when I was just starting my studies in the Paris Institute of

Political Studies and had not seen each other again for almost twenty years. In 1998, recently elected President Pastrana decided to go to France before his inauguration; he wanted to attend the soccer World Cup. I knew that Dominique had been appointed Secretary-General of the Élysée Palace, and I suggested to Pastrana that he call him. Dominique arranged an official welcome, and Pastrana called to thank me. Shortly thereafter Dominique and I renewed our friendship. He had not changed, he was as generous and considerate as I remembered him to be. From then on, whenever I went to Paris, I made sure to call him. "You have to write a book, you have to make sure your struggle to reclaim Colombia exists in the eyes of the world," he'd said. I followed his advice and wrote a first book.

One evening at dusk, I was getting ready to put my work away. The guard was already rattling the keys to the padlock to let us know it was time to lock us up. In the nearest *caleta*, a radio had been squawking all afternoon. I'd learned to shut out the outside world and live in my own silence, so I heard it without really listening. I suddenly froze. I searched with my eyes where it came from, a familiar sound from another time, another world: I recognized Dominique's voice. I turned around and ran between the *caletas* to place my ear against the radio, which was swinging from a post. The guard behind me screamed at me to go back into the cage. I waved to him to be quiet. Dominique was speaking perfect Spanish. Nothing he said seemed to have anything to do with me. The guard, intrigued by my reaction, put his ear up against the radio like me. The newscaster intoned, "On an official journey to Colombia, the French Minister of Foreign Affairs, Dominique de Villepin, wanted to express his country's commitment to ensure that the French-Colombian citizen be returned alive as soon as possible, along with all the hostages."

"Who is it?" asked the guard.

"My friend," I replied, moved, because Dominique's tone betrayed the pain our situation was causing him.

The story spread like wildfire through the camp. Andres came to hear the news. He wanted to know why I was attaching so much importance to this information.

"Dominique has come to Colombia to fight for us. Now I know France will never let us down!"

Andres was looking at me incredulously. He was completely resistant to notions of greatness or sacrifice. For him the only thing that mattered was the fact that I had a French passport, and France – a country he knew nothing about – wanted to negotiate our release. He saw vested interests where I saw principles.

After Dominique's speech everything changed. For better and for worse. My status as a prisoner went through an obvious transformation. Not only with regard to the guerrillas, who now understood that their booty had increased in value. But also with regard to the others. From that time on, the radio stations felt duty-bound to hammer home that I was a "French-Colombian" – sometimes as an almost indecent advantage, sometimes with a touch of irony, but most often with a concern to mobilize hearts and minds. I was indeed a dual national: Born in Colombia, raised in France, I had engaged in Colombian politics to fight against corruption. I felt as much at home in Colombia as I did in France. But it was above all on my future relations with other hostages that the support of France would have deep repercussions. "Why her and not us?"

I first sensed this during a discussion with Clara about our chances of getting out.

"Why should *you* complain? At least you've got France fighting for you!" she burst out.

The New Year started off with a surprise. One morning we saw the new commander from Front Fifteen arrive, the one who had replaced El Mocho Cesar after his death.

He was escorted by a tall brunette entrusted with a delicate mission.

"I've come to convey some very important news," she said tensely. "You will be allowed to send a message to your families!"

She had a movie camera strapped to her wrist and was ready to film us. I looked down on her, uptight and distant. This was neither a favour to us nor important news. I remembered how shamefully they'd edited my previous proof of life. They had cut the parts where I described the conditions of our detention, the chains we had to wear twenty-four hours a day, as well as the declaration of gratitude to the families of soldiers who had died fighting to rescue us.

"I have no message to send, thank you all the same." I turned on my heel and went back into the cage, followed by Clara, who grabbed me by the arm, infuriated by my response.

"Listen, if you want to do it, go ahead," I told her. "You don't need me to send a message to your family. You should do it. It would be very good if you do it."

She wouldn't let go of me. She absolutely had to know why I refused to send proof that I was alive.

"It's very simple. They are holding me prisoner, so be it — there's nothing I can do. What I do not accept is that in addition they manipulate my voice and my thoughts. I haven't forgotten the way they treated us last time. We recorded twenty minutes, and they sent ten, arbitrarily choosing whatever suited them. Raúl Reyes makes declarations in my place, stealing my voice. That's unacceptable. I refuse to play along with their tricks."

After a long pause, Clara went to speak to the brunette. "I don't have a message to send either," she told the woman.

A few days later, Andres showed up, visibly excited. "There's someone from your family who wants to talk to you through the radio."

I never dreamed that this could be possible. He had set up a table with the machine beneath a sophisticated installation of thick cables arranged in a pyramid. The radio technician, a young, blond guerrilla boy with blue eyes, whom they called "Chameleon," was repeating a series of codes and changing the frequency.

After an hour had gone by, he handed me the microphone. "Speak!" blurted Chameleon.

I didn't know what to say. "Yes, hello?"

"Ingrid?"

"Yes?"

"Good, Ingrid, we're going to connect you with someone important, who is going to speak to you. You won't hear their voice. We'll repeat their questions, and we'll transmit your answers."

"Go ahead."

"To verify your identity, the person wants you to provide the name of your childhood friend who lives in Haiti."

"I want to know who I'm talking to. Who's asking that question?"

"It's someone who's connected with France."

"Who?"

"I can't answer that."

"Right. Well then, I can't answer either."

I felt manipulated. Why couldn't they simply tell me whom I was talking to? And what if it was all just a trick to obtain information they would use against me at some later point? For a few minutes, I had believed I might hear their voices—Mom, Melanie, or Lorenzo.

20

A VISIT FROM JOAQUÍN GÓMEZ

A few weeks later, as I was beginning the fourth belt in my project of weaving a belt for each member of my family, I heard the sound of an engine, which usually meant our supplies were being delivered. The chaos that had suddenly erupted in the camp – everyone trying to tidy up, put on uniforms, comb hair – made me realize that along with the normal supplies some big fish must have just arrived.

It was Joaquín Gómez, the chief of the Southern Bloc and adjunct member of the Secretariado, and as such the most important authority in their organization that these guerrillas had ever seen. He was born in La Guajira and had the dark skin of the Wayo Indians of the north of Columbia.

He was taking great strides through the camp, his back bent in the manner of men who carry very heavy responsibilities, and he spread his arms as he walked toward me before hugging me for a long time, like an old friend.

I was strangely moved to see him. The last time we'd met was during the televised debate for presidential candidates, in the presence of government negotiators and members of the FARC, during Pastrana's peace process, in San Vicente del Caguán, two weeks before my abduction. Of all the members of the Secretariado, he was my favourite. He was relaxed, always smiling, affable, even funny, and he possessed none of the sectarian, sullen attitude that was typical of the hard-line FARC commanders.

He had two chairs brought over, and he sat with me behind the cage, in the shade of a huge ceiba.* He took a box of cashew nuts from his pocket on the sly, and without a fuss he placed it in my hands. What a treat! He laughed to see my delight and, as if to impress me still more, asked if I liked vodka. Even if I hadn't, I would have said yes – in the jungle you don't refuse anything. He gave instructions to one of the men to go and look in his equipment, and a yellow-labelled bottle of lemon and lime Absolut eventually ended up in my hands. This was a promising beginning for conversation. I used it sparingly, wary of the effects the alcohol might have on my weakened body.

"How are you?"

I shrugged my shoulders in spite of myself. I would have liked to be more courteous, but what was the point in replying to something so obvious?

"I want you to tell me everything," he continued, sensing that I was holding back.

"How long will you be staying here?"

"I'm leaving the day after tomorrow. I want to have time to arrange some things in the camp, but above all I want us to have a talk."

We got down to business immediately. He wanted to know why France was interested in me and why the UN wanted to get involved in negotiating our release.

"In any case we'll have nothing to do with the UN. They're gringo agents."

His remark surprised me. He didn't know anything about the UN.

"It really would be in your best interests to accept the UN's gestures. They're an indispensable partner in any peace process."

He burst out laughing and retorted, "They're spies! Exactly like the Americans we've just captured."

"Who are they? Have you seen them? How are they?"

I had heard the news on the radio. Three Americans flying over a FARC camp had been captured a few days earlier.

---

* A large tree, the Amazonian version of the African baobab, it can grow up to 230 feet high; also known as a kapok.

"They're doing great, they're big sturdy guys. A little stay with us will do them a world of good. To guard them, Comrade Jorge has assigned the smallest men we have. Just a lesson in humility to remind them that size is not proportional to courage!" He burst out laughing.

The sarcasm in his words hurt me. I knew that those men must be suffering. Joaquín must have sensed my restraint, because he added, "In any event it will be good for everybody if the Americans put pressure on Uribe to obtain the gringos' release, and you'll be out that much faster."

"You're wrong. You made a mistake with me. You're doing a huge favour to all those people who found me too much of a troublemaker in Colombian politics. The establishment won't budge even a little finger to get me out of here."

Joaquín looked at me for a long time, his gaze so melancholy that it ended up making me feel sorry for myself. I had begun to shiver despite the heat.

"Come on, then, let's go for a little peripatetic walk!" He took me by the shoulders and led me over to the jogging track, laughing with a mischievous air.

"Where did you get that? 'Peripatetic'!" I asked in disbelief.

"What? Do you think I'm illiterate? My poor child, I have read all the Russian classics! Just remember that I went to the Lumumba!"*

"Well, *tovarich*! We have Aristotle to thank, then, because I want to talk to you frankly. But that's impossible with all the guards around."

We calmly moved away, following the sandy path to the athletic track. We walked for hours, going round and round the same track until twilight. I told him everything we'd been enduring at the hands of these often cruel and insensitive men – the constant humiliation, the scorn, the stupid punishments, the harassment, the jealousy, the hatred, the sexism, all the everyday details that poisoned our lives, with the number of things Andres forbade us to do increasing by the day, the absence of all communication or information, the abuse, the violence, the meanness, the lying. I even told him stupid details, like the story about the chicken coop

---

* Communist university named after Patrice Lumumba, the Congolese independence leader.

Andres had built opposite our cage to taunt us and the fresh eggs they ate each day, and the smell that came from the *rancha* to tease our nostrils in the morning, yet there were never any for us.

I told him everything, or almost. For I found it impossible to evoke certain things.

"Ingrid, I'm going to do all I can to improve your conditions here. You have my word. But now you must tell me sincerely, why do you refuse to let us record your proof of life?"

Joaquín Gómez came back to get me at my cage the following morning. He had given the order to kill the hens, and at the *rancha* the cooks were busy preparing them "in the pot," which made my mouth water all morning. He wanted us to have lunch all together, with Fabián Ramírez, his second-in-command, whom I'd seen very little because he had dealt only with Clara. I had already met him when I spoke with Manuel Marulanda before my capture. He was a young man of average height, blond, with milky-white skin that visibly suffered from the continual exposure to the region's implacable sun. I concluded that he must not live under the forest canopy as we did, that he was probably always on the move on a small motorboat along the innumerable tributaries of the Amazon.

When Joaquín came to see me, he seemed preoccupied. "Has your companion spoken to you about the request she made to us?"

I had no idea what he was talking about. In fact, Clara and I were not communicating very much.

"No, I don't know anything. What's it about?"

"Listen, it's rather delicate. She's claiming her rights as a woman, talking about her biological clock, saying she's running out of time to become a mother – in short, I think we should talk about it before I submit her request to the Secretariado."

"Joaquín, I appreciate what you are trying to do. But I want to be very clear about this: I have no opinion in the matter. Clara is a grown woman. Her private life is no one's business but her own."

"All right, if you think you have nothing to say, I respect that. However,

I want her to repeat to both of us in person what she said to Fabián. So I'll ask you to come with me."

We sat down at a little table, and Fabián went to collect my companion, who was still in the cage. She sat down next to me, opposite Fabián and Joaquín, and she repeated word for word what I'd already been told. It was clear that Joaquín not only wanted me to be informed but also wanted me to be a witness.

Clara's request surprised me and left me puzzled. I decided I had a responsibility to talk to her. And I asked myself what my father's advice would have been if I could have consulted him. I spoke to her as sincerely as possible, wiping the slate clean of our everyday difficulties, to offer her some thoughts that might help her evaluate the consequences of her request. We had both been cornered, burdened with a terrible fate. We had each, independently, called upon whatever psychological resources we had at hand in order to survive. I drew from an enormous reserve of memories, feeling thankful for the incredible store of happiness I had accumulated over the years and for the strength I'd found in my children. I knew that because they were waiting for me I would never give up my struggle to return home alive.

Clara's situation was different. I could understand that she felt there was nothing holding her to her past. But I truly thought her plan was senseless. I made an effort to choose my words carefully, in the right tone. I did not want to hurt her feelings. I listed all the reasons I could think of to deter her from her request, telling her she could adopt a child once she was free. I evoked the difficulties for a baby born in such distressing conditions, and the uncertainty of not even knowing if the FARC would free the child with her when the time would come . . . I spoke to her in desperation, the way I would have wanted someone to speak to me or to my daughter. She listened carefully to my every word. "I'll think about it," she concluded.

Joaquín came back to see me at the end of the afternoon. He was worried about the proof of life. I could tell he was under pressure. His organization must have a plan that required other people to know I was alive.

"If you can guarantee that my entire message will be transmitted to my family, that you're not going to cut anything, then we can discuss it again."

"Right now I can't promise anything. What I can tell you at this point is that there are some rules. You won't be able to mention any places, you won't be able to give the names of those who are guarding you, you won't be able to make any references to your conditions of detention, because the army's intelligence could find out where you are."

"I'm a prisoner, but I can still say no."

I saw something devilish in his eyes. Of course they could film me without my consent. I immediately understood what had occurred to him, and I added, "You wouldn't do that. It would be in very poor taste . . . and it would end up backfiring sooner or later!"

He embraced me affectionately and said, "Don't worry. I'm watching over you. As long as I'm here, there are things that won't happen."

I smiled sadly. He was too distant and too high up in the hierarchy to really be able to protect me. He was as inaccessible to me as I was to him because of both the distance and the stubbornness of his subordinates. He knew this. He was already heading out again, the way he had come, his back bent. He was about to disappear from view when suddenly he returned. "In fact, I think what would be best is if I have them build a little house for each of you," he said. "What do you think?"

I sighed, because this meant that our release was not coming any time soon. He read my thoughts, and before I replied, he said gently, "Go on. As Ferney would say, at least you'll have some peace!"

Dear Lord, I was happy to have news of Ferney. My face lit up. "Please say hello to him for me."

"I will do, promise!"

"He's with you?"

"Yes."

As Joaquín had promised, he had two separate houses built, a reasonable distance apart, not facing each other. The model was identical to the previous wooden house but smaller. I had a room with a wooden door that I could close and that was never locked. I could go there in privacy and not feel like I was in prison. Clara and I shared a porcelain toilet, set up in a shed covered with palm leaves and closed with canvas from a rice sack. There was also a large plastic tank that they filled with water from the river, thanks to a motorized pump, which allowed us to wash privately, away from indiscreet gazes and whenever we felt like it.

At last I had some peace. Joaquín came to see the house once it was finished, and he said to the guards there before me, "This is Ingrid's home here. None of you has the right to set foot in this house without her permission. It's like an embassy — she's protected by extraterritoriality."

My life changed. I found it hard to grasp how the guards could be kind and then nasty, as if to order. And yet that is what I was witnessing. The transformation applied to every detail of our daily life, and even if I was well aware that their attitude toward me was far from spontaneous, I could rest and use this lull to my advantage. I endeavoured to regain my emotional stability. Gradually I began to sleep again, several hours a night, and above all to take longer naps that did me a world of good.

I was seized with the idea of asking for an encyclopaedic dictionary. I had no idea how much of a luxury this was. Very quickly I was hooked on it. I spent my mornings sitting at my worktable with my view of the river, and I would travel through time and space as I turned each page. In the beginning I did this more or less in a whimsical fashion. But gradually I established a methodology that allowed me to do research into a predefined topic, following the logic of a treasure hunt. I could not believe my good fortune. Time no longer dragged. When they brought me my plate of rice and beans, I ate everything, still lost in my scholarly deductions as I finalized the next stage of my exploration. Art, religion, medicine, philosophy, history, aircraft, war heroes, women in history, actors, statesmen, monuments, countries — I was interested in everything. And since all the information was by definition distilled, my curiosity was all the keener to go and look elsewhere for the missing details.

My solitude became a sort of liberation. Not only because I was no longer exposed to the whims and mood swings of my companion but also and most of all because I could be myself again, I could order my life according to the needs of my heart. After my intense reading in the morning, in the afternoon I subjected myself to a gruelling physical work-out. I closed the door to my bedroom, raised the real bed that Joaquín had got them to make for me against the wall, and I transformed the free space into a gym. I practised the acrobatics I had learned as a child but abandoned as an adult. One after another, as the memories of the move-ments returned to me, I overcame my fear of risk and learned once again to push back my limits ever further.

Then I would take my bath, watching the birds fly overhead, and I managed to admire them without envy. When I returned to my house, I sat down with my legs crossed in the lotus position and went into a med-itation that had nothing religious about it but invariably led to an awareness of the presence of God. He was there, everywhere, too big, too strong. I did not know what he could expect of me and even less what I was allowed to ask of him. I thought of begging him to get me out of my prison, but I immediately found that my prayer was too trivial, too petty, too focused on my little self, as if thinking of my own well-being or requesting his kindness were a bad thing. Perhaps, too, what he wanted to give me was something I did not want. I remember reading in the Bible, in one chapter in the Epistle of St. Paul to the Romans, that the Holy Ghost helped us in our communication with God, because he knew better than we did how to ask what was right for us. When I read this, at the time I thought I did not want the Holy Ghost to ask for anything other than my freedom. By formulating it in this way, I understood that I was missing the essential point, that there was probably something else, greater than free-dom, that he could seek to give me, something that for the time being I did not know how to appreciate. I had questions. Never any answers. They pursued me during my meditation. And in this circular thinking that went on day after day, I saw events as they unfolded, and I analysed them with precision. I would stop to examine certain moments. I reflected on the meaning of the words "prudence" and "humility." Every day, through a glance, the intonation of a voice, a misused word, a silence or a gesture, I realized I could have acted differently and I could have done better. I knew that my situation was an opportunity that life was offering me to take an interest in things I normally didn't think about. Incapable of acting in "the" world, I displaced my energy to act in "my" world. I was discovering another way of living, a life based less in action and more in introspection. I wanted to build a stronger, more solid self. The tools I had developed up to now were no longer of use to me. I needed another form of intelligence, another sort of courage, and greater endurance. But I did not know how to go about building those: It had taken over a year of captivity for me to just begin to question my own self.

God was surely right, and the Holy Ghost surely knew it, because he was so stubborn in not wanting to intercede in favour of my release. I still had a great deal to learn.

21

SECOND PROOF OF LIFE

The last time I saw Joaquín Gómez, it was to record the second proof of life. He came with other guerrillas, including Ferney, who I was very happy to see again.

I suspected that Ferney must have described to his superior some of the treatment I had been subjected to, and I thanked him for that, because there had indeed been a call to order. Andres granted permission for me to have powdered milk from time to time, and Edinson, the guard who captured us after the hornet attack, secretly brought me eggs that I "cooked" in boiling water, brought to me on the pretext of treating a rash. The greatest treat of all, however, was that Andres had once again allowed me to spend time in the *rancha*. I liked to be in the kitchen. I learned the techniques they had developed for creating a bread substitute, *cancharinas*, using a mixture of flour fried in boiling oil. Between two of his recent visits, Joaquín had kindly sent me a black bag full of good things. The militiaman who drove the motorboat received precise instructions not to open the black bag and to hand it to me in person. This was a wink from Joaquín, because on that first day when we went on our peripatetic walk, I'd complained about the way we were being discriminated against at mealtimes. When you have nothing, the most basic possessions take on an unbelievable importance.

When Joaquín arrived, we immediately set to work to prepare the video recording. He had given me his word that my family would get the entire text of my message, without changes. I would talk between fifteen and twenty minutes, from the little house with a sheet hung up as a background to hide any indication of where we were. Clara would also be allowed to send a proof of life. I planned to give my opinion on a delicate topic that had generated a debate on how to obtain our freedom. My family was firmly opposed to a military rescue operation. A few months earlier, a dozen prisoners, including the governor of the Antioquia region, Guillermo Gaviria, and his peace adviser Gilberto Echeverri, had been assassinated in the region of Urrao during an attempted rescue mission.* That had been a terrible shock to me. I did not know Guillermo personally, but I had found his commitment to peace in the Antioquia region courageous, and I was filled with admiration for his perseverance.

One afternoon at around four o'clock, as I was fiddling with a radio that Joaquín had brought me as a gift on one of his previous visits, I tuned in by chance to the news from Radio Canada, on shortwave. It was a little metal radio, not very powerful, that the guards made fun of because it had reception only very early in the morning or once night had fallen. It needed an antenna system to boost reception, and it was the guards themselves who helped me rig one up, using the aluminium wire from the scrub pads used to clean the casseroles. I had to hang it from the highest branches of the trees, sending one end up to the treetop with the help of a sling and wrapping the other end around the end of the radio antenna. The system worked fairly well, and I managed to listen to the news, particularly in the evening. It was a window onto the world. I would listen, and with the help of my imagination I could see everything. I had not yet found the frequency for Radio France Internationale, to which I would grow extremely attached later on, to the point of memorizing the names and voices of the journalists as if they were long-lost friends, or for the BBC, to which I would later listen religiously every day, a pleasure equal to the one I would have felt in civilian life of going to the cinema. For the time being, I was overjoyed just to have found Radio Canada and to hear French spoken.

---

* Known as the Massacre of Urrao, it took place on May 5, 2003.

But my pleasure turned to fright when I heard them say my name while explaining that Colombian hostages had been massacred by the FARC. I didn't know what they were talking about, but I sat there petrified, the radio up against my ear, trying to understand, afraid that at any moment I might lose the weak reception. Above all I did not want to miss the rest of the news bulletin. Several minutes later the entire story was repeated, and I discovered to my horror that Gaviria and Echeverri had just been assassinated. There was no other information, no further details. Then the subject changed, leaving me trembling. I went to sit on my bed, as I imagined with terror everything that must have happened for them to have been executed. And then I remembered the FARC's threat. After a year had gone by, they would begin to kill us, one after the other. And it was indeed just over a year since we had been taken hostage. That was it: the FARC had begun to carry out its plan. I ran from my house as if struck by lightning. I was breaking one of my own self-imposed rules about never going to speak with Clara without warning her ahead of time of my visit. But now I was charging down the path, followed closely by the guard who'd given me permission. Clara was sweeping her house.

"Listen, it's really serious. The FARC has just assassinated Gilberto and Guillermo."

"Oh, really?"

"It was on the radio. They just—"

"Right. Thanks for the information."

"I . . . I—"

"What do you want? There's nothing we can do. There it is, so what? What do you want me to say?"

I didn't insist and went back, devastated. I shut myself in my bedroom. I prayed, without knowing what to ask God. I imagined their families, their wives, their children, and my suffering was visceral, physical, I was bent over in pain, only too aware that such a fate might await my own family.

After nightfall my radio had powerful reception of the Colombian radio stations. Every ten minutes the voice of Yolanda Pinto, Guillermo's wife, was rebroadcast. She explained in detail the procedure required for recovering the corpses and the difficulties she faced, because access to the site of the massacre was under military control and forbidden to the families. The guard who was on duty called out to me. He wanted to know what was going on, too. I told him they had begun to execute the hostages and that I knew our turn would be next.

Andres came shortly afterwards.

"Ingrid, I just found out about the death of Guillermo and Gilberto. I want to assure you – the FARC is not going to assassinate you. It was an accident. The FARC was responding to a military attack."

I didn't believe him. After all these months, I knew that for the FARC, lying was merely a tactic of war.

And yet as the hours went by, the news seemed to be proving him right. The army had attempted a rescue operation. Only two of the hostages had survived the massacre. The broadcasts described how, when the commander had understood that they were surrounded by military helicopters, the prisoners had been brought together to be shot. Gilberto had gone down on his knees to beg for mercy. He'd been shot in cold blood by the commander himself. The survivors said that Gilberto had thought they were friends and reminded the commander of the fact, imploring him not to shoot.

I imagined the scene of the assassination down to the smallest details, convinced that it could happen to us, too, at any time.

That is why when Joaquín came for the proof of life, I insisted on expressing my support for a rescue operation by the Colombian army, knowing that many were against it after the bloodshed of Urrao. I understood that I could speak only for myself. But I wanted to stress the fact that freedom was a right and any effort to recover that freedom was a duty.

I also wanted the country to begin a deep reflection on what defending that right implied. The decision to undertake a military rescue had to be made at the highest level, and the president of the republic himself must bear total responsibility for the failure or success of the operation. I feared that in the labyrinth of political interests, our lives might no longer be worth anything; there might be greater interest in organizing some bloody fiasco and blaming the FARC for our deaths than in mounting any genuine rescue attempt.

Once the proof of life had been recorded, we waited for its broadcast on Colombian radio and television. The months in between were long. I had followed closely the story of a French aeroplane sent to the heart of the Brazilian Amazon, in the hope that the pressure to obtain the proof of survival might have some connection with it. A few days before the press released the information, a physician for the FARC had come to see us. He had studied medicine in Bogotá for a few years without obtaining his diploma and had been recruited as an instructor for nurses, as well as to head a bush hospital that I suspected must be close to our camp. To me his visit foretold liberation. It was in the best interests of the FARC to free its hostages in a condition that would enable the group to regain prestige in the eyes of the world. Perhaps the proof of life that the FARC had insisted upon so vehemently might be one of the conditions required by France to enter into negotiations, which, obviously, had to be kept secret. When the plane flew off again without us, I imagined that leaks in the media had probably caused the mission to fail. But there had been a moment of hope. France had taken a real risk to try to get me out of there. Dominique was searching for a way to snatch us from the FARC's claws. There would be further contact, other envoys would come, and new negotiations would take place.

When, a few weeks later, the militiaman who normally came with the supplies arrived with the order to take us away, for me this could only mean that the negotiations had succeeded. We were to depart the following dawn, so we had to pack up our things. I took only what was needed for the few days to reach the meeting place with the European envoys. I gave all the rest to the girls, including the dictionary and a full-colour map of the world that I had just finished making.

Andres organized a little get-together to say good-bye. The guerrillas shook my hand and congratulated me on the success of the negotiations and my imminent freedom. I didn't sleep all night, in a state of bliss. The nightmare was over. I was going home.

I was sitting on my belongings, ready to leave. The moon was still casting its silver reflection on to the lazy water of the river. At around five o'clock in the morning, they brought us a cup of hot chocolate and a *cancharina*. My companion was ready, too, sitting on the steps of her hut, with two large bags. She had no intention of leaving anything behind. I was filled with a strange happiness. It wasn't the euphoria I'd thought I would feel, just a quiet happiness. I was thinking about what this year of captivity had meant for me. I saw myself as some strange creature, an entity totally distinct from my present self. This person who had lived in the jungle all these months would stay behind. I would become myself again. A wave of doubt crossed my mind. Become myself again? What did that mean? Had I learned what I was meant to learn? I quickly let go of these silly notions. What did they matter now!

22

THE FORTUNE TELLER

August 22, 2003. An immaculate sky drew sharply above our heads, like a long blue snake between the trees on either side of the river. We were moving slowly. The river wound through the jungle at its own pace; we had to avoid dead logs in the hairpin turns. I was impatient. Despite my expectation of imminent release, my stomach was painfully tied up in knots. The smell of the engine, the bittersweet aroma of this chlorophyll world, the absence of any certainty forced me blindly back to the precise moment when I had felt the trap closing over me.

It had happened one week after we were kidnapped. They had moved us from camp to camp to a place on the top of a hill, where for the first time I had discovered the green ocean of the Amazon filling the horizon as far as the eye could see. El Mocho Cesar was standing next to me. He already knew that they intended to lose me in this impenetrable vastness.

They had set up a makeshift camp on the nearly vertical slope of a hill. We bathed in a transparent stream that hummed as it flowed over a bed of translucent pebbles. I saw my first monkeys. They gathered above us, entertaining themselves by tossing sticks at us from high on their perches to frighten us.

The forest was very thick, and it was impossible to see the sky. Clara stretched out like a cat, filled her lungs with all the air they could contain, and said, "I love this place!" It shocked me. I was so obsessed by the idea of escaping that I didn't even allow myself to appreciate the beauty around us, for fear it might decrease my sense of urgency. I was suffocating, and I would have felt just the same if I'd found myself imprisoned on an ice floe. Freedom was my only oxygen.

I was just waiting for nightfall to put our plan into action. I was counting on the full moon to make our escape easier.

A red truck appeared from behind a bend. Like ants, in less than two minutes the guerrillas loaded the truck. They had already dismantled the camp, and we hadn't realized.

We took the winding path down the hill. Two little houses with smoking chimneys stood sadly in the middle of a cemetery of trees. A child was running after a ball that was split open. A pregnant woman watched him from the doorstep, her hands on her hips, clearly in pain from her back. She disappeared quickly inside the house when she saw us. Then nothing more. Immense trees, one after the other, identical, for hours. At one point the vegetation changed. The trees, gave way to shrubbery. The truck left the dirt road and set off down a path that was scarcely visible among the ferns. Suddenly, straight ahead, as if put there by mistake, was a sturdy ironwork bridge, wide enough to allow the red truck to cross over easily. The driver stepped on the brakes and squealed to a halt. No one moved. On the far side of the bridge, emerging from the dark forest, were two individuals in camouflage uniform with big backpacks on their shoulders, walking resolutely toward us. I assumed they would climb onto the truck and we would cross the bridge. I hadn't noticed the river flowing beneath. Nor the large boat that was waiting for us, its engine already throbbing, ready to leave.

It was then that the memory came back to me. In November 2001, during my presidential campaign, in a pretty little colonial village in the region of Santander, I'd been approached by a woman who had urgently insisted on talking to me. The captain of the monoplane had agreed to delay our departure by half an hour so that I could meet with her. She was a beguiling young woman, serious, simply dressed, and she came up holding by the hand her little girl, who was no more than five. After she had asked the child to sit farther away, she explained nervously that she had visions and that her visions always came true.

"I don't want to upset you, and you will think I'm crazy, but I'll have no peace until I can tell you what I know."

"What do you know?"

She stopped looking me in the eyes, and her gaze was lost somewhere. I felt that she could no longer see me.

"There's scaffolding, something falling. Don't go under it. Stay away. There's a boat, a small craft on the water. It isn't the sea. Don't get on. Above all – listen to me, this is the most important – don't get on that boat."

I tried to understand her. This woman was not pretending. But what she was saying seemed totally incoherent. Still, I played along. "Why mustn't I get on the boat?"

"Because you won't come back."

"I might die?"

"No, you won't die . . . but it will take you many years to come back."

"How long?"

"Three years. No, it will be more. More than three years. A long time, a complete cycle."

"And then, when I come back . . .?"

"Afterwards?"

"Yes, afterwards. What will happen afterwards?"

The captain came to get me. The airport closed before sunset, at six o'clock sharp. We had to take off immediately.

I boarded the plane and forgot what the woman had told me.

Until the instant I saw the *canoa** beneath the bridge. Sitting at the front of the red truck, I was transfixed as I gazed at the launch waiting for us by the riverbank. *I mustn't. I mustn't.* I looked around me: It was impossible to escape; they were all armed. My hands were damp, and an irrational fear had taken hold of me. I didn't want to go there. One of the men grabbed me by the arm, thinking I was hesitant to go down the steep slope because I was afraid of slipping. The young men were skipping down breezily, proud of their training. They pushed me, dragged me. I put one foot in the small boat, then the other. I had no

---

* A *canoa* is a small boat.

choice. I was caught in the trap. For a long time, she had said. A complete cycle.

We sailed from twilight to dawn. It was the end of the dry season, so the river was at its lowest level; we had to keep the boat right in the middle of the stream to prevent it from running aground. From time to time, one of the guerrillas jumped into the water, fully dressed, submerged up to his waist, to push the boat and set it free. I was afraid. How could I get back? With every hour my feeling of claustrophobia grew.

In the beginning our convoy went past several small houses that watched us blindly. The enormous trees all around filtered the last rays of twilight, as if to show that just behind, the forest had been cut down to leave room for land that was ready to be cleared. But very quickly the density of the forest stifled any light, and we entered a tunnel of shadowy vegetation. There were no more signs of human life, not a trace of civilization. The sounds of the forest had become sinister and reached us in lugubrious echoes, despite the throbbing of the engine. I found myself sitting with my arms curled around my stomach as if to keep my guts in place. Dead trees, their branches bleached by the sun, lay like corpses in the water. As if they were still waiting for help from providence, their arms stiff, held out toward a speechless sky.

The captain had lit a powerful beam to see ahead. On the riverbanks little red lights shone as we went by — they were the eyes of crocodiles, hunting in the warm waters of the river. *Someday I will have to swim in this river to go home*, I thought.

With the night, the world we were entering was transformed into a phantasmagorical space. I was shivering. How would I ever get out of here?

After that the fear never left me. Every time I got into one of their *canoas*, I was inexorably thrust back into the sensations of that first descent into hell, on that black Caguán River that had swallowed me up.

Now, however, I could let myself go, to contemplate the marvels of luxuriant nature, celebrating life this beautiful morning of August 2003. But instead I had butterflies of fear in my stomach. Freedom. Was it was too good to be true?

23

AN UNEXPECTED ENCOUNTER

August 2003. The motorboat left behind the labyrinth of narrow, winding water to emerge onto the great river Yari. We headed against the current toward the opposite bank and dropped anchor among trees that were disappearing beneath the rising waters. They told us to disembark. I thought we must be alone, in the middle of nowhere. To my great surprise, hidden between the trees a group of guerrillas were striking their tents and packing up their personal belongings. Our captain unfolded a large plastic sheet in the shadow of a tall ceiba, for us to settle down on. We were used to waiting without asking questions. A young girl came up to us and asked if we wanted some eggs. Eggs! They reinforced the idea that they were giving us special treatment to prepare us for our imminent release. I had not noticed that a bit farther along they had made a *rancha* with a bonfire and there were stewpots hanging over the flame.

On our right, a man was sitting like us against a tree, observing me from a distance; he got up and started pacing back and forth. Eventually he gathered momentum and came over.

He was an elderly man, with a beard more salt than pepper covering his cheeks, and his eyes were swollen with black shadows and moist as if he were about to shed tears. His emotion upset me. Who was this guerrilla? Had I already seen him somewhere?

"Soy Luis Eladio, Luis Eladio Pérez. Fuimos senadores al mismo tiempo—"

Before he finished his sentence, I understood. The man I had taken for an old guerrilla was none other than my former colleague, Luis Eladio Pérez, captured by the guerrillas six months before I was. I'd been in Congress the day his abduction was announced. The senators used it as a pretext to interrupt the session in a sign of protest, and we all went home, glad to have the afternoon off. Everyone spoke highly of Luis Eladio, but I could not remember who he was. There were a hundred of us. I should have recognized his face in the photographs. But no, nothing. It was as if I'd never seen him before. I asked around to refresh my memory. "Yes, of course you remember him, he sits just behind us, just there." . . . "You've seen him a thousand times – he always says hello when you come in."

I was very angry with myself. I was drawing a total blank! And what was worse, I had spoken to him!

When I understood that it was Luis Eladio, I flung my arms around him and embraced him, holding back my tears. Dear Lord, it pained me so much to see him in such bad shape. He looked a hundred years old. I took his head between my hands. Those eyes, that gaze – where had I buried what I was searching for in vain? It was frustrating: I still could not recognize him, nor superimpose an image from the past on his face. And yet I had just found a brother. There was no distance between this stranger and myself. I took his hand and caressed his hair as if we'd known each other all our lives. We were weeping together, not knowing if it was from the joy of being together or from pity at seeing on each other's face the ravages of our time as hostages.

With similar emotion Luis Eladio hurried to embrace Clara.

"¿Tú eres Clarita?"

She held out a hand and, not moving, replied, "Call me Clara, please."

Luis Eladio sat down with us on the black plastic sheet, slightly disconcerted. His eyes questioned me. I answered with a smile. He began to speak to me for hours and hours, without stopping, hours that turned into days,

---

* "It's me, Luis Eladio, Luis Eladio Pérez. We were senators at the same time."
† "Are you Clarita?"

then weeks, an unending monologue. He wanted to tell me everything: The horror of two years in mandatory solitary confinement. (The commander did not like him and had forbidden the troops to speak to him or answer him.) The man's cruelty – with his machete he had killed a little dog that Luis Eladio had adopted. The fear that haunted him, that he would end his life here in the jungle, far from his daughter, Carope, whom he adored and whose birthday was that very day, August 22, the day we met on the banks of the Yari. His illness – he was diabetic and dependent on insulin injections, which since his abduction he had not been receiving – and the fear that at any moment he might fall into a hypoglycaemic coma that would kill him in no time at all or, worse, leave him a vegetable for the rest of his days. His anxiety about his family, for with his disappearance they had lost all their financial support. His dismay at not being there to guide his young son, Sergio, in his studies and career choice. His sorrow that he could not be by his elderly mother's bedside, for he feared more than anything that she would die in his absence. His regret that he had not spent more time at home with his wife, whom he loved deeply, but he had been too absorbed in his work and his political life. The feeling of weakness that haunted him, for having fallen into a trap and been captured by the FARC. He told me everything in one long go, with all the urgency of the solitude that he had so loathed.

We motored downstream under a pitiless noonday sun, until nightfall. During all the hours we travelled, I had not said a word. We sat side by side, and I listened, aware of his vital need to unburden himself to me. We grasped each other's hands, instinctively, for he wanted to convey the intensity of his emotion, and I wanted to give him the courage to continue. I wept when he wept, I fumed with indignation when he described the cruelty he had been subjected to, and I laughed with him to tears, because Luis Eladio could make a joke out of even the most tragic events. We instantaneously became inseparable. That first evening we shared together, we went on talking until the guards told us to shut up. The next morning we were delighted we could embrace again, and we went off hand in hand to sit in the motorboat. It mattered little where we were going. Quickly he became "Lucho" for me, then "my Lucho," and finally "my Luchini." I had adopted him for good, because his presence soothed me and gave me a powerful reason for living; better still, it gave a goal in my unchosen destiny.

After several days of travelling on the river, we came to a beach, where a well-maintained gravel road began. A truck that was closed at the back with a canvas sheet was waiting for us. To get us to climb on board, they did not need to insist. We were happy to be together so we could go on talking.

"Look," he said, "I know you're going to say no, because you must think I'm the kind of politician you don't like, but if someday we get out of here, I would really like to be able to work with you."

This touched me more than anything. I felt dirty, smelly. Dressed in my filthy rags, I was ashamed to be seen like this; I felt I'd aged and grown ugly. Yet Lucho still thought of me as the woman I'd been before. I tried to smile in order to give myself the time to respond.

To help me out of my confusion, he added, "But I warn you, we will have to change the name of your party – Green Oxygen, that's asking too much of me! After this I don't want to see any more green in my life!"

Everyone burst out laughing. The guerrillas, who had heard, applauded. Clara, too, was laughing wholeheartedly. I was bent over double. It felt so good to laugh. I looked at him. And for the first time, behind his white beard, behind his little shining eyes, I recognized him. I saw him sitting behind me in the semicircle of the Senate, greeting me with a mischievous air after throwing bits of paper at the neck of a colleague who sat opposite him and who turned around, exasperated. He had always made me laugh, even if invariably I strove to remain serious out of respect for our office. Behind his prisoner's mask, I had just placed him.

24

GIOVANNI'S CAMP

End of August, 2003. The truck stopped hours later, in the middle of the road that went through the rainforest. On our left, among the trees, we could just make out another FARC camp. They ordered us to get down. Clara and I carried potato sacks filled with our personal belongings. Lucho sported a FARC backpack made of waterproof green canvas, a rectangular shape, with straps on all sides from which he could hang everything, including his black plastic bowl, his tent rolled up like a sausage, and all the rest. He was fitted out like a guerrilla.

A surly-looking man was waiting by the side of the road, his legs spread, tapping impatiently against the top of his muscular thigh with a knife blade. He had shining very black hair, beady eyes, a little moustache, and three-day stubble. He was perspiring all over, probably having just finished some intense physical task.

He spoke to us in a gruff voice. "Hey, you! Come over here! I'm your new commander. You are now under the responsibility of the Eastern Bloc. Go in there and wait."

A barrier of trees partially concealed the camp. It was a beehive of activity. There must have been a lot of people, because wherever I looked, I could see *caletas* and men and women busy setting up their tents, no doubt hurrying so they would be ready before nightfall.

Lucho and I instinctively joined hands. "Our commander looks like a nasty piece of work."

"A regular murdering highwayman," whispered Lucho in reply.

"Yes. Our very own Norman Bates with his special knife," I added. "Don't worry. Around here it's the ones who look nice that you have to beware of! Not the others."

The commander came back for us, and we followed him cautiously. Ten yards farther, three *caletas* in a row had just been built. The wood, carefully stripped of its bark, was still oozing. Some of the men were busy finishing a big table with a bench on each side.

"Here, you're going to settle in here. The *chontos* are just behind you. It's too late now to take a bath, but tomorrow morning I'll send the receptionist to escort you to the bathhouse. I'll have some food brought to you. If you need anything, just call me. My name is Giovanni. Good night."

He disappeared, leaving two guards on either side of the imaginary rectangle within which we could move.

"Guard? To go to the *chontos*?" I asked.

"That way, follow the path, behind the screen of palm leaves. Be careful, there are tigers."

"Yes, tigers, and tyrannosauruses, too!"

The guard looked as if he were stifling a laugh, and Lucho glanced at me, delighted. Why did they always want to frighten us?

We settled in for the night, hoping that this was the meeting point for the emissaries sent to secure our release. I looked at what Lucho was unwrapping, and he looked over my way, too. He had a plaid woollen blanket that I had my eye on; I had a little mattress covered with waterproof canvas that you could fold in three: Lucho seemed to covet it. We smiled at each other. "Would you like to borrow my mattress?" I whispered.

"What about you? How are you going to sleep?"

"Oh, I'll be all right. They put some palm leaves over the *caleta*. It will be enough."

"You want me to lend you a blanket?"

"No, I have my jacket. It keeps me warm," I answered unconvincingly.

"But I have two blankets. Besides, I would rather you took it. I'd have fewer things to carry."

We were both so pleased with our trade! I asked for permission to go and sit with Lucho at the table, and the guard agreed. It was already dark, and this was a special moment to share secrets.

"What do you think?" Lucho asked in a hushed voice.

"I think they're going to release us."

"I don't think so. I was told they're taking us to another camp with all the other prisoners."

The guards let us talk and didn't try to interfere. The air felt good, with a warm breeze coming through the trees. I found real pleasure in listening to this man. Everything he said interested me, everything seemed structured and thoughtful. I knew that his presence was doing me a world of good. It was a sort of therapy, to be able to share with someone else everything that was boiling in my head. I hadn't realized the extent to which I'd missed having someone to confide in.

At daybreak we were cheered unexpectedly by the arrival of a pretty blonde guerilla who introduced herself as our receptionist. Lucho had woken up in very good spirits, and he began to bombard her with compliments. The girl teased him in return. We were all laughing. Lucho had no way of knowing that this charming girl was the commander's girlfriend. When Giovanni came to see us at the end of the day, he was a changed man. He held out his hand to greet us and invited us to join him at the table. His *socia* must have put in a good word for us, I thought. Giovanni proved to be an excellent conversationalist and stayed until late in the night, telling us his life story.

"We were in the thick of the battle. The paramilitaries were thirty yards across from us, and they were firing in all directions. There were a lot of casualties on both sides. At one point, when I was crawling along the ground to get near the enemy lines, one of my men called out to me over the radio. He was shit-scared. There I was, bullets whistling right by my ears. I tried to talk to him as best I could, as if I were talking to my own son, to get him to keep going and give him courage.

"Can you picture the scene? As I am speaking into the radio, I see the enemy. He doesn't see me – he's right there in front of me, talking on the radio. I approach very quietly, like a snake – he doesn't see me coming – and what do you know! I realize *he* is the one speaking to me over the radio. It was awful. I thought I was talking to one of my guys, and he thought he was speaking to his chief. But the jerk was speaking to me! And now I've got him right there in front of me, and I have to kill him. I was going crazy! I couldn't kill him – he was just a kid, you understand? He wasn't an enemy any more.

"So I pushed him, took his gun, and ordered him to get the hell out of there. He had a close call, the idiot. If he's alive, I'm sure he still remembers."

Giovanni was pretty young himself, not yet thirty. He was a very sharp guy, with a great sense of humour and an innate talent for command. All his troops adored him. I observed his behaviour with interest. He was very different from Andres. He trusted his men, but he also demanded a lot from them, and he controlled them. It was easier for him to delegate than it was for Andres, and his men felt more worthy. With this group I no longer felt I was being spied on. There was surveillance, of course, but the guards' attitude was different. Among themselves, too, the atmosphere was completely different. I saw no trace of the mistrust between the FARC that I'd seen before, with the others. They knew that their comrades were not spying on them. Everyone seemed to breathe more easily under this commander.

Giovanni got into the habit of coming every afternoon to play a game that Lucho devised, which consisted of moving pieces along a board – using beans, lentils, and peas – while eliminating the other players' pieces along the way. I never managed to win. The real duel began when only Lucho and Giovanni were left face-to-face. It was a sight not to be missed. They would goad each other mercilessly, with every political and social prejudice they could think of. It was hilarious. The troops came to watch the match the way you'd go to a show.

Very quickly we got used to Giovanni's familiar, pleasant company. We asked him outright if he believed we were going to be released. He thought we were. It would take a few more weeks, because they had to put together the "final details," and that still exclusively depended on the Secretariado. But we should get ready for our release, he said. That soon became the dominant topic of our conversations.

In very little time, we learned the names of all the guerrillas in the group. There were thirty or so. Giovanni had done his best to integrate us, going so far as to invite us to the "salon" for their evening activities. That had greatly surprised me, because in the camp we'd just left, Andres had been very strict, making sure that we could never hear what he said, even from a distance. This was an hour to relax, when the younger guerrillas enjoyed playing team games. They had to sing or invent revolutionary slogans, unravel riddles, and so on. It all took place in a very good-natured atmosphere. One evening as I was leaving the salon, one of the guerrillas came up to me.

"They're going to let you go in a few days," he told me. "What are you going to say about us?"

I looked at him with surprise. Then, trying to smile, I replied, "I'll say what I saw."

His question left me with a bitter taste. I was not sure my answer was the best one.

We were eating our morning meal when I heard the sound of engines. I gestured to Lucho. Before we could even react, the place was filled with excitement. Jorge Briceño, alias "Mono Jojoy," perhaps the best known of the FARC leaders after Marulanda, made his entrance. I almost choked on my drink. He came forward slowly, with his eagle's gaze, and took Lucho in his arms, embarrassing him with a huge hug. Mono Jojoy was a formidable man, probably the most bloodthirsty of all the FARC leaders. He had earned his reputation, rightfully, as a hard and intransigent man. He was the great warrior, the military man, the steely combatant, and he aroused the admiration of all the young people that the FARC had recruited, mainly from the poor regions of Colombia.

Mono Jojoy must have been in his fifties. He was a man of medium height, stocky, with a big head and practically no neck. He was blond, his face was bloated and red, and he had a prominent belly that made him walk like a bull.

I knew he had seen me, but he did not come over immediately. He took his time to speak with Lucho, although he must have been aware that Clara and I were waiting for him, standing outside our *caletas,* practically saluting. What had I become? Prison psychology distorted our simplest behaviour.

The last time I'd seen him, he was next to Marulanda. It was the day I went with Piedad Córdoba to Los Pozos, in the demilitarized zone. He hadn't wanted to say hello to me, and I had hardly noticed him. I wouldn't have noticed him at all had it not been for the unpleasant remark that he'd made to his comrades: "Oh, you're with the *políticos*? You're wasting your time! The best thing we can do with them is take them as hostages. At least that would keep them out of harm's way. And I'll bet that if we kidnap some *políticos*, this government will have to release our comrades from jail!"

I had turned to Marulanda and confronted him with a laugh. "Well! Really? You'd contemplate kidnapping me just like that, in the middle of the road?"

The old man had made a gesture with his hand, as if to wave away the bad idea Mono Jojoy had just given him.

But now, barely four years later, I was forced to concede that Mono Jojoy had carried out his threat. He finally walked over to me and hugged me tightly, as if he wanted to crush me.

"I saw your proof of life. I like it. It's going to be released soon."

"At least it's clear I'm not suffering from Stockholm syndrome," I retorted.

He gave me a nasty look that chilled me. In the second that followed, I understood that I had just sealed my own fate. What was it that he resented? Probably the fact that I didn't want his approval. I should have kept quiet. That man hated me; I was his prey, and he would never let me go.

"How are you treated?" He looked at Giovanni, who came over.

"Very well. Giovanni is very good to us."

There, too, I felt I had given the wrong answer.

"Make your list of all the things you need and give it to Pedro, I'll make sure everything is sent to you quickly. I'm going to leave you in the company of my nurses. They'll do a report on your health. Tell them if there is anything wrong."

He went away, leaving me immersed in an inexplicable anxiety. Everyone agreed that Commander Jorge was courteous and generous. I could see that much myself, but I knew instinctively that his visit was a very bad omen. I sat next to Pedro, while Lucho went for his medical checkup, and I dictated my list of needs to him, according to Mono Jojoy's precise instructions. The poor man was sweating hard, unable to spell the names of the products I needed. Lucho, who was listening, was writhing with laughter under the nurse's stethoscope. He could scarcely believe I dared to add beauty and care items to my list. "Ask for the moon while you're at it!" he teased. I added a Bible and a dictionary.

The next morning one of the nurses came back. She was massaging Lucho's back; he had been suffering terribly. Now he was in seventh heaven and let her have her way with him.

I lifted my head when I heard a squeal of brakes on the road. It all happened very quickly. Someone barked orders.

Giovanni came running over, looking pale. "You have to pack everything. You're leaving."

"Where are we going? And you?"

"No, I'm staying. I've just been relieved of my mission."

"Giovanni . . .?"

"No, don't be afraid. Everything will be fine."

A guy came in at a run and whispered something in Giovanni's ear.

Giovanni struck his thighs with his fists. Then he took hold of himself and said, "I have to blindfold you. I'm sorry. I'm really sorry. Oh, shit!"

The world collapsed. Shouts, guards running all around. Shoving me, pulling me. They bound my eyes with a thick blindfold, I couldn't see a thing. Except the image of Mono Jojoy's venomous gaze that stayed etched in my memory, pursuing me, unfolding before my closed eyes like a curse.

25

IN THE HANDS OF THE SHADOW

September 1, 2003. I was blindfolded and tied up. I lost all confidence, and an instinctive fear paralysed me; I didn't know where to put my feet. Two men took my arms on either side. I made an effort to stand up straight and walk normally, but every two steps I stumbled and found myself being held up by my watchers, making headway despite myself, dispossessed of my balance and my will.

I heard Lucho's voice just ahead of me. In the hope of reassuring me, he was talking loudly so that I would know he was not far away. I could also hear Giovanni's voice somewhere off to my right. He was talking with someone, and was not pleased. I thought I heard him saying that he had to stay with us. Then there were more shouts, and orders coming from all sides. There was a muffled sound. I ducked my head into my shoulders, as if I expected to receive a blow or to bang into something.

We were out on the road. I could tell from the gravel under my feet and the immediate heat of the sun on my head. An old engine was throbbing nearby, belching fumes of acid that stung my throat and nose. I wanted to scratch, but the guards thought I was trying to take off the blindfold. They reacted violently, and my protests only managed to irritate them further.

"Hurry up! Load the cargo!"

The man who'd just spoken had a thundering voice that pained me. He must have been standing right behind me.

A moment later I was being hoisted into the air and thrown onto what I supposed was the back of a truck. I landed on some old tyres and tried to get comfortable. Lucho joined me within a few seconds, as did Clara and half a dozen guerrillas who pushed us back into the truck. I groped around for Lucho's hand.

"Are you all right?" he breathed.

"Be quiet!" shouted someone sitting opposite me.

"Yes, I'm okay," I whispered, squeezing his fingers, clinging to him.

Someone covered the back of the truck with a tarp, a door was closed fast with much creaking and clicking, the vehicle grunted before lurching forward as if it were going to fall apart for good, and then it headed off at a crawl in a grotesque din. The air was very hot, and the exhaust from the engine filled our space. The stinking fumes got stronger, asphyxiating us. We were overcome by headaches, nausea, and anxiety. After an hour and a half, the truck stopped with a squeal of brakes. The guerrillas jumped down and, I believed, left us alone under the tarp. We must have been in a little village somewhere, because I could hear music coming from what I imagined to be a *tienda*, a sort of makeshift café where you could find a bit all sorts of things, drinks in particular.

"What do you think?"

"I have no idea," replied Lucho, shattered.

Trying to cling to one last hope, I said, "And what if this was the meeting place with the French envoys?"

"I don't know. What I can tell you is that I don't like it. I don't like it one bit."

The men climbed back into the truck. I recognized Giovanni's voice. He was saying good-bye; he would be staying in the village. He had come part of the way with us. The truck started up again and went through the village. The voices of women and children and young people playing soccer grew fainter and finally disappeared. All that was left now were the explosions of the engine and the horrible fumes that attacked our throats straight from the nearby exhaust pipe. We went on like this for over an hour. The uncertainty of not knowing what was going to become of us gnawed at me. Eyes blindfolded, hands tied, I tried to drive away the signs that our captivity was about to go on indefinitely. What if our release had just been aborted? How could this be? They had all assured us that we were on our way back to freedom! What had happened? Had Mono Jojoy intervened to derail the negotiations? Taking political figures hostage to obtain the release of the guerrillas was a strategy that he had conceived, defended, and imposed upon his organization. When we left behind the Southern Bloc under the aegis of Joaquín Gómez to move to the Eastern Bloc, we had fallen into the web that Mono Jojoy had woven around us from the day of our abduction. He wanted to have us under his thumb, and now it was done.

The truck stopped abruptly on a slope, nose downward. They removed our blindfolds. We were once again by the edge of a powerful river. Two motor canoes moored to the riverbank were pitching impatiently on the rough water.

My heart leaped. If we were about to board a boat again, it must be the sign of the curse that was pursuing me. A little man with a barrel-like stomach was already sitting in one of the boats. He had short arms and a butcher's hands, a toothbrush moustache and a copper complexion. There were heavy bags full of supplies piled at the fore of each canoe. He gestured to us to hurry and shouted authoritatively, "The women here with me! The man in the other boat!"

All three of us looked at one another, the blood draining from our faces. The thought that we were about to be separated made me sick. We were human wrecks, and we clung to one another to keep from sinking. Because we had no idea what was going on, we felt that no matter what lay in store for us, if we could share it, it would become less painful.

"Why are you separating us?" I implored the man.

He looked at me with his round eyes, and as if he suddenly understood our torment, he said, "No, no! No one is going to separate you! The gentleman is going on the other boat so that we can divide up the weight. But they'll be next to us during the whole trip, don't you worry."

Then he added with a smile, "My name is Sombra. Martín Sombra. I am your new commander. I'm very honoured to meet you. I saw you on television."

Sombra: the shadow. He reached out his hand without getting up from his seat and shook ours energetically. Then, turning to his troops, he shouted instructions. There were fifteen men or so, all very well built, all very young. These were the troops of the Eastern Bloc. They were the FARC's elite troops, the pride of their revolutionary youth. Martín Sombra treated his squad roughly, and the young men hurried to show their obedience.

In less than two minutes, we were heading downriver, deeper and deeper into the Amazon jungle.

Martín Sombra didn't stop asking me questions during the journey. I paid careful attention to all my answers, trying to avoid repeating the same mistakes I'd made in the past. But I also wanted to establish the sort of contact that would ease communication with the man who would be our commander for the coming weeks, perhaps months, or – who knew? – even years.

He behaved cordially with me. But I had also seen him at work with his troops and knew that he could be nasty. As Lucho pointed out, we should be wary of the ones who seemed nice.

Under a baking sun, the boats stopped at a bend in the river, in the shade of a weeping willow. The men stood at the edge of the boat and entertained themselves by seeing who could piss the farthest. I asked if I could get off to do the same, only more discreetly. The jungle was denser than ever. The idea of running off and getting lost did cross my mind. But of course that would have been sheer madness.

I tried to reassure myself by thinking that the time would come for my escape, but I would have to prepare it, down to the smallest detail, if I were to succeed. In my belongings I was dragging around a rusty machete that El Mico had mislaid near the landing stage after going fishing, a few days before we left Andres's camp. Thinking that I was about to be released, I'd wanted to keep it as a sort of trophy. I had wrapped it up in a towel, and so far no one had discovered it. But this new group did not look as if they'd be easy to deal with. I would have to take more precautions. Just thinking about it made my heart beat wildly.

I came back to the boat, still anxious. Sombra was handing out soft drinks and cans that opened with a metal ring, containing *tamales*, a sort of full meal consisting of chicken, rice, and vegetables, typical of the Colombian region of Tolima. Everybody dug in, famished. I couldn't even open my can. I could not bear the thought of food. I gave my ration to Clara, who opened it, delighted. Lucho was looking at me. He would have liked me to give it to him, but he was too far away.

We continued on our journey, one boat behind the other, down a river that changed with each bend, becoming impossibly wide in some places and very narrow at others. The air was heavy, and I did not feel well.

Among the bushes blocking the riverbanks, I saw an enormous royal blue barrel bobbing on the water, caught in the mangroves. It was one of those used to transport chemical products for the cocaine laboratories. So there must be people somewhere around here, I surmised. Farther along we came upon another, identical one that also seemed to be lost in the water, and so it went – every twenty minutes we would see a barrel drifting. I scoured the banks in the hope of seeing some houses. Nothing. Not a soul. Only royal blue barrels in this green world. *Drugs are Colombia's curse.*

We must have gone nearly a hundred miles, zigzagging along with an endless stream of water. Sombra stared straight ahead, looking at each bend with a trained eye.

"We've just gone over the border," he said knowingly to the captain.

The captain answered with a grunt, and I got the impression that Sombra had tossed out this piece of information to mislead me.

We went around another bend, and the boat's engine stopped.

Ahead of us was a FARC camp. It was built at the water's edge. Small boats and pirogues were bobbing gently, moored to a massive mangrove. As far as you could see, the camp was submerged in a vast pond of mud. The troops' incessant comings and goings had turned the ground into a mess. *They should create a path with boards,* I thought. The boats glided prow-first to the shore. Girls in camouflage uniforms, their black rubber boots filthy up to their knees, emerged from their tents one by one when they heard the sound of engines. They stood in single file, at attention, lined up.

Sombra quickly got to his feet, stepped over the prow of the boat, and with his short legs jumped to the ground, splattering mud on the women who had come to salute him.

"Say hello to the *doctora*!" he ordered.

They replied in unison, "Hello, *Doctora*." Fifteen pairs of eyes were trained on me. In my heart I prayed, *Dear Lord, please don't let us stay here too long!* as I looked around at the sinister place, mud covering everything. On the ground were two huge, badly washed stewpots, and some pigs trotted over to them, their snouts protruding aggressively with every intention of rummaging around in there.

In contrast with the sheer filth of the place itself, the girls all displayed impeccable hairstyles – thick, cleverly woven braids that hung like gleaming black bunches of grapes on their shoulders. They were also wearing brightly coloured belts with geometric patterns that immediately caught my eye. The belts were made with a technique I did not know. In the depths of this hole, the FARC girls had created fashion trends. They gathered in small groups to whisper and look at us, giggling at our expense.

Sombra shouted again, and their gossiping evaporated, as each girl went off to take care of her own business. We were made to sit down on rusty gas bottles that were rolling around in the mud and were brought some food in enormous bowls. It was fish soup. I had an entire fish floating in my bowl, its dead eyes staring at me through a film of yellow fat, its huge hairy fins hanging over the side of the bowl.

Sombra ordered us to prepare our *caletas* for the night. Two girls were moved elsewhere temporarily so we could use their mats. As for Lucho, they set him up in the middle of the mud. Two gas bottles for a base and two wooden planks placed across them served as a bed, with a canopy stretched overhead in case of rain. The mud was simmering from the heat in the ground. Gases from fermentation broke through pockets of mud and rose to the surface. The unhealthy buzzing of millions of mosquitoes filled the space, and their vibrating drilled into my temples like the painful warning of a fit of madness. I had arrived in hell.

26

SOMBRA'S SERENADE

The next morning before dawn, the camp was bustling with activity. Thirty or more well-armed men set off before daybreak in the two motor-boats that had brought us here. All the women stayed at the camp, and Sombra ruled over them as if over a harem. From my mat I could observe the way he sprawled across an old, torn mattress while the guerrillas served him like a sultan.

I meant to go and say good morning to him, but the girl who was on guard duty stopped me. I could not leave my *caleta* without Sombra's per-mission. I asked her if I could speak to him, and my message was relayed to him. He made a gesture with his hand that was easy to interpret – he was not to be disturbed. His answer followed the same path back to me: "Sombra is busy."

I smiled. From where I sat, I could see him perfectly. He was indeed very busy with a tall brunette with Chinese eyes whom he held on his lap. He knew I was looking at him.

I could see no open space in the camp to house us, unless they built the *caletas* on piles, just where the pigs lived, in the swamp to the left of the camp. This seemed unlikely. And yet that is what they did. Three girls, assigned to the job, hurried onto the slope with shovels and furiously dug into the earth to create a wide enough ledge to accommodate our *caleta*, like a balcony overlooking the pig pond. They packed us off to our new shelter before the morning of our first day was out. Whiffs of putrefaction came to us in waves.

My rapport with Clara was tense once again. Clara was suspected of having taken the straps from the backpack of one of the *guerrilleras*. We could be subjected to a search. My companion knew that I was hiding El Mico's machete, and that if they went through our things, I would have a hard time explaining where it had come from. When I mentioned this to her, she had a fit.

Sombra came to see us. He made a show of checking our set-up and inspecting our belongings. I was relieved that I had taken my precautions. Then, in an authoritarian tone, he declared, "You have to get along among prisoners. I won't tolerate any dissension!"

Clear enough. Someone must have told him about the tension between my companion and me, and he had come to get involved, pleased to play the role of peacemaker. "Sombra, thank you for your interest, and I'm sure you've already been well informed about our situation. But I feel I have to tell you that any differences between my companion and me are our business. I ask that you not interfere."

Sombra had stretched out on Lucho's *caleta*. He was in uniform, his shirt unbuttoned halfway down, unable to restrain his huge stomach. He was looking at me with his eyes partially closed, not letting a single expression show through, weighing each of my words. The girls who were on guard duty were following the scene closely. The tall brunette with the Chinese eyes had come to listen and was leaning against a young tree a few yards away. The silence began to weigh.

He burst out laughing and came to take me by the shoulders. "No need to get angry like that! All I want to do is help you. Nobody's going to get involved in anything! I tell you what, just to make you feel better, I'm going to give you a serenade. It will relax you. I'll send someone to get you!"

He set off in a good mood, with his retinue of young women around him. I was speechless. A serenade? What was he thinking? He was making fun of me, that much was clear.

A few days later, when Lucho and I had already concluded that Sombra was talking nonsense, we were surprised to see a squad of girls arrive, inviting us to follow them to the commander's *caleta*.

Sombra was waiting for us, stretched out on his tattered mattress, his huge, round stomach squeezed into a khaki shirt, its buttons ready to burst. He had shaved.

Next to him stood Milton, a guerrilla of a certain age whom I had noticed the day we arrived. He was a skinny guy, with prominent bones. His pale white skin was permanently affected by rosacea. He was sitting uncomfortably on one corner of the mattress, as if he were afraid of taking up too much room, and between his legs he held a fine, well-varnished guitar.

Sombra gave the order to bring some empty gas bottles for us to sit on. Once we were settled, as if on pews in a church, he turned to Milton. "Okay, go ahead."

Milton took up his guitar nervously with his dirty hands and black thumb nails that grew like claws. His hands were suspended in the air, his eyes rolling in every direction, waiting for Sombra's signal, which didn't come.

"Well, go ahead, begin!" barked Sombra, annoyed. "Play anything! I'll follow you!"

Milton was petrified. I didn't think he could get the slightest sound out of his instrument.

"Ah! What an idiot! Come on, play the Christmas tango! Yes, that's it. Slower. Start over."

Milton was trying his hardest, scratching at the chords of the guitar, his eyes riveted on Sombra's face. He played surprisingly well, using all of his swollen, scaly fingers with amazing dexterity. We began to encourage Milton and congratulate him spontaneously, which didn't seem to please Sombra too much.

Exasperated, he began singing in a deep taverner's voice. It was an infinitely sad song about an orphan who would have no Christmas presents. Sombra used the pauses between the verses to shout at poor Milton. The scene was truly comical. Lucho made a superhuman effort not to burst out laughing.

"Stop! Enough! You've played enough!"

Milton stopped abruptly, petrified once again, his hands in the air. Sombra then turned to us with a satisfied expression. All three of us hurried to meet his expectations, applauding as loudly as possible.

"Right, that's enough."

We stopped applauding.

"Milton! Let's sing the one the girls like. Go on, hurry up, for God's sake!"

And off Sombra went again in his powerful bass voice, singing false notes, ready to hit poor Milton on a whim or out of irritation. It made a hilarious show: one of them unrelentingly playing the guitar while the other sang at the top of his lungs as they both sank slowly into the mud. They looked like Laurel and Hardy.

Behind the ogre who frightened everybody was a man I could not possibly take too seriously, yet who moved me. I could not be afraid of him. I knew perfectly well that he could be abusive and remorseless. But his nastiness was his shield, not his deeper nature. In this world of war and violence, he could not afford to be taken for a fool.

27

THE BARBED WIRE

The activity in the camp worried me. Every morning at dawn, eighteen or twenty or so big fellows went off by boat upstream and came back just before twilight. Another group disappeared into the forest behind our *caletas*, above the slope. I heard them working with chain saws and hammers. On my way to the *chontos*, I could see permanent dwellings that were beginning to take shape through the trees, rising from the ground fifty yards or so behind the camp. I didn't want to ask any questions; I was too afraid of the answers.

Sombra came to see us shortly after the serenade, followed by his tall brunette, La Boyaca, and a jolly, fat girl named Martha. They were dragging huge oilcloth bags behind them, which they threw into our *caletas*: "This is from Mono Jojoy! Take out your checklist. If anything is missing, tell me."

Everything we had asked for was there. Lucho could not believe his eyes. The day when we'd drawn up our lists, when he saw that I was including items that had hitherto been forbidden, such as flashlights, forks, and knives, or plastic buckets, he'd ventured to ask for shaving cream and aftershave lotion. He was laughing like a kid when he discovered that his boldness had paid off. As for me, I was in raptures on discovering a little Bible, bound in leather and closed with a zipper. As a bonus Mono Jojoy had sent us sugary treats, which we shared among ourselves with reluctance, as well as T-shirts in gaudy colours that none of us fought over.

I was surprised at the amount of supplies that were being delivered to the camp. I commented on this one day to Sombra, who wised me up. "The *chulos* can spend all they like on aeroplanes and radar to look for you. But as long as they have corrupt officers, we will always be stronger! Look, the zone where we are now is under military control. Everything that comes in has to be accounted for. We have to indicate who it's destined for, the number of people per family, their names, ages, everything. But all it takes is for one of them to want to supplement his income and their entire plan falls apart."

And then he added, maliciously, "And it's not just the lower-level officers who do it! It's not just the little guys . . ."

His comment puzzled me. If the army was trying to find us, it was true that the existence of corruption could mean additional months or even years of captivity.

That was the crux of Mono Jojoy's message, in supplying us the way he did: We had to be prepared to hold out for a long time. The FARC deemed that there was no way to negotiate with Uribe. Since his election a year earlier, he had waged an aggressive campaign against the guerrillas. Every day he inflamed people's minds with incendiary speeches against them, and his approval rating soared. Colombians felt they had been tricked by the FARC. The peace negotiations that the Pastrana government had begun were seen as proof that the Colombian state was weak and that the FARC had taken advantage of this to strengthen their position. Colombians were disgusted by the arrogance of the Secretariado, and they wanted to be finished once and for all with an insurrection they repudiated, because it attacked the rich and the poor indiscriminately and spread terror throughout the country. Uribe had a good grasp of the nation's mood, and he would not budge. There would be no negotiating for our release.

In the evening I went to speak with Lucho in his *caleta*. He put the radio on loud enough to cover our voices, and we settled in to play chess on a folding magnetic chessboard that Sombra had lent us.

"What do you think they're going to do with us?"

"They're building some huge thing back there!"

"Maybe it's going to be their barracks."

"Whatever it is, it's too big for the three of us."

We were listening to *The Bolero Hour*, a programme that broadcast music from the 1950s. I liked this programme. I knew by heart all the words to the songs they broadcast, because Mom had sung all of them all day long from the moment I was born. It was also the hour of depression, bleak breakdowns, and the sorrowful stock-taking of time lost forever. Lucho and I took turns in unveiling the fathomless depths of our sadness.

"I am afraid of dying here," he repeated.

"You're not going to die here, Lucho."

"You know, I'm very sick."

"Not at all. You're in terrific shape."

"Stop making fun of me, I'm not joking. I'm diabetic. It's serious. I can go into a coma at any moment."

"Okay. Explain, what do you mean exactly?"

"Yes, it's like fainting, but it's much more serious. You can burn your brain and become a vegetable."

"Stop! You're frightening me!"

"I want you to know, because I might need you. If ever you see me go pale or pass out, you must give me sugar immediately. If I have a seizure, you have to hold my tongue—"

"Nobody can hold your tongue, dear Lucho!" I replied, laughing.

"No, I'm being serious, listen to me. You have to be careful that I don't choke on my own tongue."

I listened intently.

"When I regain consciousness, you have to keep me from sleeping. You have to talk to me all day and all night, until you are absolutely sure that I have my memory back. In general, after a hypoglycaemic crisis, you want to sleep, but you must not, because you might never wake up again."

I listened carefully. He was dependent on insulin. For two years he had not had a shot of insulin. He wondered what miracle was keeping him alive. I knew. I could see it in his eyes. He was clinging to life with a fierce determination. He wasn't alive because he feared death. He was alive because he loved life.

He was in the middle of explaining to me that the candies we had received could save his life, when the guard called out to us. "Hey! Stop listening to music, you're missing the news!"

"So what?" we replied in unison.

"So what! They're broadcasting your proofs of life."

We jumped up out of our chairs as if we had been given an electric shock. Lucho was hurriedly fiddling with the dial to tune in Radio Caracol. The voice of Darío Arizmendi, the station's star journalist, came through loud and clear. He was giving a recap of our messages that had just been broadcast on television. I managed to hear only certain snippets of my speech, and I couldn't check whether my recording had been edited. But I could hear my mother's voice, and Melanie's statement. Their exultation surprised me. In a way it hurt me, and I was almost angry with them for being happy about so little. There was something monstrous about the relief granted to them by my kidnappers, relief that was nothing more than a ruse to prolong our separation. I was filled with pain at the idea that we had fallen into their trap: This proof of life was not a condition for our liberation. There were no negotiations with France. It was a cruel way to inform us that our captivity was to be prolonged. They had managed to exert pressure without any intention of freeing us. We were trophies in the hands of the guerrillas.

As if to echo my thoughts, Fat Martha, who was on duty, came over to me.

"Ingrid . . . they're building a prison."

"Who is building a prison?"

"The *muchachos*."

"What for?"

"They're going to lock you all up."

I had refused to face the truth. I felt dizzy, as if I were standing on the edge of a precipice, moving ever closer to the edge. "Who do you mean by 'all'?"

"All the prisoners who are in the camp half an hour from here and the three of you. There are political prisoners, three men and two women, and the rest are soldiers and policemen. They're the ones who are part of the 'humanitarian exchange.' They're going to put you all together there."

"When?"

"Very soon. Probably next week. The barbed wire goes up tomorrow."

I went pale.

"*Mamita,** it's going to be very hard for you," said Martha with compassion. "You'll have to be very strong and prepare yourself."

I sat down on my *caleta*, drained. Like Alice in Wonderland, I was falling, falling into a bottomless well. There was nothing to hold me back. This was my black hole. I was being sucked down, dragged down into the bowels of the earth. I was alive only so that I could witness myself dying. Was this my fate? I hated God for having abandoned me. A prison? Barbed wire? With each breath I suffered, I could not go on. But I had to go on — there were the others, all the others, my children, Mom. Furious with myself and with God, I clenched my fists against my knees, and I heard myself say to him, "Don't ever let me stray from you, Lord! Ever!"

My head was empty, and I stood up like a robot to share the terrible news with my companions.

Every time we went to the *chontos*, we would look to see how the construction was coming along. Just as Fat Martha had said, they put up a chain-link fence, topped with barbs all around, a fence that was twelve feet high. In one corner of the construction site, overlooking everything, they had built a watchtower, with stairs to climb up it. Through the trees you could make out three more identical turrets. It was a concentration compound in the middle of the jungle. I had nightmares and would awake with a start, covered in sweat. I must have been shouting out, because Lucho woke me up one night with his hand on my mouth. He was afraid there might be reprisals. I began to lose sleep, seeking refuge in insomnia so that I wouldn't be caught unawares. Lucho could not sleep either. We

---

* A colloquial term of affection among Colombians.

would sit on our *caletas* and talk, in the hope of banishing the ghosts of the night.

He would tell me about his childhood, when his mother cooked *tamales** for Christmas, a dish typical of the Tolima region where she was born. The recipe included hard-boiled eggs, and as a child Lucho would steal a few. The next morning there his mother would be in her bathrobe, counting her eggs and wondering why there were always some missing! He laughed so hard he cried as he remembered it all.

As for me, I went back to the Seychelles and to the happy memories of my daughter's birth. I returned to what mattered most to me: Being a mother.

The building of the prison shook me deeply. I repeated to myself that I was not a prisoner, that I was being held illegally. I had done nothing wrong, I was not paying for some crime. Those who had dispossessed me of my freedom had no rights over me. I needed this constant reminder to help me not to give in, not to forget that it was my duty to rebel. They called it a "prison," as if, through some magic trick, I had become a criminal and they were the authority. No, I would not submit.

Despite my efforts our daily life became gloomy. I noticed my companions' morose mood; we were all depressed. Lucho had got into the habit of taking his morning meal with Clara on a wooden platform that must once have served to store supplies and which seemed like a floating island in the pig pond now that the swamp water surrounded it. Lucho went there every morning, taking some of the cookies that he had received. He shared them with no concern for keeping any for later. Then one day he no longer went to the platform and instead ate his meal sitting on his *caleta*.

"What happened, Lucho?"

"Nothing."

"Go on, tell me. I can see that something is bothering you."

"Nothing."

---

* Chopped pork and chicken, cooked with rice and corn, mixed with boiled eggs and carrots and reheated in a banana-leaf wrap.

"All right, if you don't want to tell me, it can't be that important."

As I was coming back from the river after my bath, I saw that Lucho was arguing with Clara over by the plastic buckets the guerrillas had given to us. He had volunteered to fill the buckets in the river to have fresh water for brushing our teeth, washing our hands, and cleaning our bowls after meals. It was a difficult chore, because you had to carry the two full buckets up a muddy, slippery slope. It was late afternoon, and night was about to fall. Lucho had already completed his task for the day and taken his bath, and he was clean and ready for the night. But Clara had used the water in the buckets to soak her dirty laundry. There was no more water to wash the bowls or to brush our teeth on waking. Lucho was exasperated.

These minor incidents were poisoning our life, probably because our world had become so small.

I looked at Lucho in his anger and understood him only too well. I, too, had lost my temper dozens of times. I, too, had had bad reactions and bad attitudes. Sometimes I shocked myself with how little I knew about the inner workings of my own personality. For example, food did not interest me. And yet one morning I was angry because the largest piece in the rations they had brought us was not for me. It was ridiculous. That had never happened to me before. But in captivity I discovered that my ego suffered the moment I was deprived of something I wanted. It was over food that prisoners, urged on by hunger, waged silent battles. I observed a transformation in myself that I did not like. I could see how ugly the same behaviour was in other people. Deprived of everything – our lives, our pleasures, our loved ones – we had the misguided reflex to cling to what little was left: a tiny amount of space, a piece of cookie, an extra minute in the sun.

28

THE SATELLITE ANTENNA

October 2003. It looked as if the prison was finished. We were counting the days left to us on our slope, like borrowed time on death row. Sombra came to see me one morning. He was planning to put up a satellite dish. There was a television in the camp. Some of the instructions were in English, and he needed my help.

I told him that I didn't know anything about satellite dishes. He insisted nevertheless that I go with him to check the equipment. Two enormous wooden barracks had been built. There was a third building, smaller than the two previous barracks, with benches and dozens of plastic chairs piled up along the side. They were well supplied, there was no doubt about that. Boxes full of electronic equipment were stacked in the middle of the room, with the instruction booklets neatly placed on top. I went closer. And then I saw the prison, all of it, behind the heap of chairs. It was a sinister sight, with spikes of barbed wire everywhere and mud all around.

I acted as if I were reading the instruction manuals, fiddling with a few knobs, and then I declared, defeated, "I don't understand a thing, I'm sorry." I was unable to focus on anything else besides the living hell they had built for us. I returned to tell my companions about it, my heart sinking.

Sombra, however, would not accept defeat. The next morning just before noon, one of the boats that went up and down the river came back with a prisoner from the camp upstream.

He was a thin little man, his hair cut very short, his eyes sunk deep, his face deathly pale. All three of us were standing on our slope, curious to see the person whom Sombra had brought to install his antenna. He went right by us, probably unaware that there were other prisoners in Sombra's camp. Did he sense our gazes fixed upon him? He turned around and stopped short. For a few seconds, we looked at one another. We were going through the same mental process. Our expressions reflected surprise and horror, followed by pity. Each of us was staring at a human wreck.

Lucho was the first to react. "Alan? Alan Jara? *¿Eres tú Alan?*"

"Of course! Of course! Excuse me, I wouldn't have recognized you. You are all so different in photographs!"

Everybody greeted one another. "How are you?" I asked after some silence.

"Fine, fine."

"And the others?"

"They are fine, too."

Poked by the guard, Alan gave a sad smile, waved good-bye, and started walking toward the barracks.

The three of us, devastated, exchanged looks. Alan was a walking corpse. He was wearing a T-shirt that was little more than a rag, and a filthy pair of shorts. His legs were extremely thin, floating in rubber boots that were too big for him. It was as if a blindfold had been taken from our eyes. We were used to seeing each other like this, but we were in no better shape than Alan. Except that we had just received supplies. Without hesitating we went to get what was left of our supply of treats, to send them to the prisoners in the other camp.

There was some of the cake left that I had just made to celebrate the birthdays of Lorenzo and Lucho's son.

"We should send it to them," Lucho said. "It's the birthday of Gloria Polanco and Jorge Géchem."*

"Wait, how do you know it's their birthday?"

"In the messages on the radio, their families congratulated them for

---

* Jorge and Gloria had been taken hostage shortly before I was captured.

their birthday, it's the fifteenth or seventeenth of October, I can't remember. But it's in a few days."

"What messages on the radio?"

"My God, how is it possible? It can't be! Don't you know that every day there is a broadcast on RCN radio, *La Carrilera*, presented by Nelson Moreno, which transmits messages from all our families to each of us!"

"What?"

"Yes! Your family doesn't call in to that programme. But your mother sends you messages every Saturday on Caracol's *Las Voces del Secuestro*! The journalist, Herbin Hoyos, came up with the idea to set up radio contact for the hostages. Your mother calls in, and she speaks to you. I hear her every weekend!"

"I don't believe it! And only *now* you tell me?!"

"Look, I'm sorry, I thought you knew. I was sure you were listening to the programme, like me."

"Luchini, this is marvellous! I can listen to Mom the day after tomorrow!" I threw my arms around him. He had just given me the best present imaginable, and he wanted me to forgive him!

We prepared a package of candy and cookies along with the piece of cake we had put aside for Gloria and Jorge. I asked the guard to pass on our request to Sombra. His reply came quickly: We had thirty minutes to talk to Alan and give him our package.

I didn't need to be asked twice. I followed the guerrilla into the room with the stacks of chairs. Alan was waiting for me. We hugged as if we had known each other forever.

"Have you seen the prison?" I asked him.

"Yes . . . I think I'm going to be in your group."

"What do you mean?"

Alan had found out by bribing his guards with cigarettes that there were four civilian prisoners, two men and two women. Alan would rather be with the soldiers. "Still, if I'm with you, we'll get organized. I want to learn French."

"You can count on it."

"Listen, Ingrid, we don't know what's going to happen – you never know with them. But whatever happens, be strong. And be careful. The guerrillas have their informers everywhere."

"What do you mean?"

"I mean you have to be careful, even among prisoners. Some of them are prepared to snitch on their comrades for a lighter or a packet of powdered milk. Don't trust anyone. That's my best advice."

"Okay. Thank you."

"And thank you for the treats. Everyone will be happy."

They gave us exactly thirty minutes. Not a minute more. Alan's words had made a strong impression on me. I felt that I should indeed steel myself for a difficult time ahead. I could see the enclosure, the barbed wire, the watchtowers. But what I couldn't yet see was the world inside the prison – the lack of privacy, the crowding, the violence, the informing.

29

INSIDE THE PRISON

October 18, 2003. In the morning some guerrillas came up to our tent. Among them was a tall skinny one with a thin moustache and a venomous expression. He was wearing a ranger's hat, the kind the paramilitaries used. He wedged his mud-encrusted boot onto my *caleta* and barked, "Pack up your things! Everything has to disappear in five minutes." He didn't intimidate me – in fact, I thought he was ridiculous with his tropical cowboy outfit – but I was trembling all the same. I was nervous, as if there were two of me. My mind was cold and lucid, whereas my body was emotional. It annoyed me. I had to be quick – fold, roll, put away, tie up. I knew where to begin and where to finish, but my hands wouldn't follow. I could no longer find the gestures that usually only took a second. The guy with the moustache looked on, irritated, as I botched every effort. I knew he was thinking that I was a clumsy idiot, and this just made me clumsier. I was obsessed with the idea of doing everything perfectly, as if to prove to myself that my awkwardness was only temporary. So I started over again – folding, rolling, putting away, tying up again, obsessively. The guy with the moustache thought I was doing it on purpose to delay the execution of his orders. It was more than enough to make him dislike me.

Lucho was looking on, anxious because he sensed problems. No sooner had I finished tying up my poor old supply bag than the guy with the moustache snatched it from me and ordered me to follow him. We set off in single file in painful silence, surrounded by armed, sinister-looking men. I was memorizing every step, every bump in the earth, anything specific in the vegetation that might serve as a signpost for my future escape. I had my eyes riveted on the ground. Perhaps that's why I got the impression that the prison came down upon my head. When I saw it, I was on the verge of bumping into the fence and the barbed wire. My surprise was all the greater when I saw that there were already people inside. I had foolishly assumed that because we were so close to the prison, we would be the first ones to be sent there. Sombra had arranged it so that the others would be inside before we were, either so that we'd be less afraid of going in or to announce the fact that other masters of the house had got there before us. The guy with the moustache had us make a detour, which showed us that the prison was divided in two, with one very small building and another bigger one, back to back and separated by a narrow corridor just wide enough for the guards to do their rounds. The entrance to the little building was through a dirt courtyard. All the vegetation had been removed except for a few young trees, which cast their shadow on the huts to keep the zinc roofs out of sight of the military planes scouring the zone. The entire space was enclosed by a thick steel fence. A heavy metal gate was kept closed, doubled up with an imposing chain and a massive padlock.

The guy with the moustache took his keys out of his trousers, fiddled with the padlock to make it clear that it was not an easy manoeuvre, then opened the gate; it creaked as if it had been built in the Middle Ages. The four people who stood inside took a few steps back. He tossed in my bundle hesitantly, as if there were wild animals inside. The four hostages were staring at us, inspecting us thoroughly.

They looked physically ravaged, their features drawn, their expressions gaunt, and their hair white; they had deep wrinkles and yellow teeth. But more than by their physical appearance, I was moved by their attitude, barely noticeable: the way they all positioned themselves, the way they looked at us, their heads bent. You could be led to believe that everything was normal. And yet something was no longer the same. Like when a new scent is carried in the breeze and fills the air. The instant you notice it, it's already disappearing. You might wonder if you ever really smelled it, and yet it has infused your memory.

They were behind bars. For a few seconds more, I would still be outside. It was almost indecent to be looking at them; their humiliation was laid bare, irrevocably exposed. They were human beings who had been dispossessed of themselves while they waited for others to decide their fates. I thought of mangy dogs rejected and maltreated, who can no longer stave off blows, hoping only to be forgotten by their tormentors. It was the look in their eyes. There were two of them whom I used to know — we had sat together on the same benches in the Senate. I saw them now before me, unshaven, their clothes ragged, their hands dirty, standing straight, trying to save face and keep their dignity despite their fear.

I felt sorry, sorry to see them like this and sorry they would know they were seen. And they felt sorry for me, aware that I was to share with them, any minute now, the horror that they could read on my face.

The gate was open. The guy with the moustache pushed me through. Jorge Eduardo Géchem was the first to walk up to me and take me in his arms. He was trembling, his eyes filled with tears.

"My dear *madame*,* I don't know if I'm glad to see you again or very sad."

Gloria Polanco also gave me a strong embrace. We had never met before, but we greeted each other like old friends.

Consuelo came up, and Orlando. We were all crying, surely relieved to be together, to know we were alive, but our shared misfortune hung like a dark cloud over us. Orlando took our bundles and led us into the building. It was a wooden barracks, with a wire mesh covering the entire ceiling and walls on the inside. There were four bunk beds so close to one another that you had to stand sideways to get to your own. On one side the wooden planks of the wall had been cut three-quarters of the way up, which made a sort of big window facing the outside of the enclosure, completely covered over by the same wire mesh. The place was in

---

* Jorge used "*madame*" in French as a term of endearment in deference to my French origins.

perpetual half-light, and the bottom bunks were downright dark. A smell of mould rose unpleasantly the moment you came in, and over everything there was a film of reddish sawdust; it floated in the air, proof of how recently the barracks had been built.

"Ingrid, you're in charge of assigning the bunks. Choose your own first!"

The idea surprised me and put me on my guard. It was awkward to be asked to play boss. Remembering Alan's words, I thought that the best thing would be to stand back.

"No, that's not my role. I'll take the bed that's left once you all have chosen yours."

The tension rose. Some were nervous, others were stiff, and this made us realize very quickly that beneath their good manners our comrades had been engaged in a veritable war. The three of us ended up strategically placed so that we would act as a screen between our four companions: Clara at the end of the dormitory between Orlando and Consuelo, Lucho and myself between them and the other two. This arrangement seemed to satisfy everyone, and we settled in.

I explained to Sombra that we needed some brooms to sweep our lodgings and that cutting a big window on the façade of the barracks would afford those who were on the bottom bunks more light. Sombra listened to me, inspecting our accommodation, and went away assuring me that he would send one of his guys with the brooms and the chain saw.

My comrades gathered around me. Sombra's attitude was unusual for them.

"He's always said no to all our requests! You are really lucky he listens to you. Let's see if he keeps his word."

Heartened by the thought that we were about to have a new window, we began to make plans: With the planks that would be removed, we could make shelves. We'd request extra planks to build a big table where we could all eat together, along with a smaller table by the entrance door to put the pots bearing our meals.

This created a feeling of kinship. As the atmosphere became more relaxed, we'd meet in the courtyard, beneath the few trees still standing, to swap stories. Orlando was the first one captured, and he had immediately been sent to join the fifty or more officers and NCOs held by the FARC for years. Consuelo was captured next. Locked up with the soldiers and policemen, she had bleak memories of her months as the only woman in the FARC camp. Gloria had been abducted with her two sons and separated from them without warning, to be placed in a group of "interchangeables." Jorge had been kidnapped in a plane, three days before my capture. Gloria and Jorge were put together by the guerrillas a few weeks before being locked up with the rest of the group.

The escape attempts and betrayals had hurt some and estranged others. Suspicion had arisen among them, and wariness was rife. Their rapport with the guerrillas was shaky. They'd been in Sombra's hands for over a year now. They were afraid of him and despised him, but they didn't dare even admit it for fear we might tell on them. Sombra's troops maintained a reign of terror over the prisoners. They told us that one of the NCOs, after a fight with another prisoner, had been shot.

My companions wanted to speak, to confide in us, but the terrible things they had experienced kept them silent. I could easily understand. As you share memories, an evolution occurs. Some facts are too painful to be told; in revealing them you relive them. And then you hope that as time goes by, the pain will disappear and you'll share with others what you've experienced and unburden yourself of the weight of your silence. But often, even if you no longer suffer when you revisit the memory, you keep quiet out of a feeling of self-respect – a reluctance to expose your humiliation. Over time, you sense you must not distress others with the memory of your own misfortune. If you share certain things, they will stay alive in other people's minds. So the most gracious and appropriate thing to do would be to let them die inside you.

30

THE ARRIVAL OF THE AMERICANS

Late October 2003. The broom arrived as Sombra had promised. But not the chain saw. The guards on duty in the watchtowers were inaccessible. If we had a request, we were obliged to wait for the receptionist to come. For the first time in my experience, it was no longer a girl; only the men had permission to come to the prison. And as if to make things simpler, it was the big guy with the moustache and the ranger's hat, Rogelio, in the role. He opened the heavy metal gate first thing in the morning and put the pot with our meal down on the ground, without saying a word. Our comrades ran up to speak to him before he vanished, but he pushed them back inside, quickly closing the door and raging, "Later, later!"

During the day he passed by the fence several times, ignoring my companions' calls and solicitations. Rogelio laughed as he went away, pleased with how he had thumbed his nose at them. My situation had changed. Until now I'd had fairly easy access to the camp commander. The commander had been the one in charge of solving my problems. Now it was this young guerrilla. He was responsible for our contact with the outside world. He was the only one to whom we could make any requests. When my comrades tried to be pleasant to him, he responded with disdain.

Since we'd moved into the prison, our captors had taken several more turns of the screw. We were beggars now. I couldn't bear to hang on to the chain-link fence, mewing to attract his attention. I hated the idea of licking the boots of this character who was all fake smiles or hypocritical friend-liness. But the man loved to be flattered. Very quickly he established hierarchical relationships with us. There were those he liked and to whom he responded more quickly and listened to more patiently, at times even with interest. And then there were the others, those of us with whom he felt duty-bound to be discourteous. I found myself crudely rebuffed in front of everyone every time I needed something, whereas he would hasten to satisfy a request from someone who was in his good books. In the very first hours that followed our confinement, I watched with conster-nation how this network of complex relations was established. Those who had the presence of mind to unabashedly play the game of courtesy imme-diately acquired a higher status than the rest of us. And in an almost natural way, they gained the upper hand over us, as well, because it was through them that it remained possible to obtain certain favours, favours that at a given time might suddenly become vital.

A grave, intense division now arose among us. In the beginning it merely seemed superficial; those who had chosen to be obsequious, and in turn felt judged by the rest of us for doing so, would still help the others with their needs. Everyone had something to gain, and none of us could be sure that we wouldn't behave the same way at one point or another out of sheer need.

For Lucho and me, our need to protect ourselves from ourselves and to maintain the unity of the group compelled us to call on our comrades to write a letter of protest to the members of the Secretariado. It was highly unlikely that our letter would ever end up in the hands of Marulanda. But we hoped in this way to establish a direct channel to the leaders, even if it were only to Sombra. The receptionist had to go, or at least be neutralized. I wanted, moreover, to make a written declaration, a testimony of our refusal to accept the treatment to which we were subjected.

They had no right to lock us up in a concentration camp, even in the eyes of their revolutionary doctrine. I did not want the members of the FARC to go about quietly finding ways to justify themselves and feel good about it. Plus, I dreaded that we might end up growing used to it.

I talked about this with Lucho for a long time. He also thought that one of us would be liberated soon and that we should write a secret letter to

Uribe asking him to authorize a military operation for our release. He believed that I would be the one who would get out, thanks to France's intervention.

So we all got together for a conference inside the barracks. There was a downpour; our voices would be muffled by the sound of the rain on the metal roof. Those who were in more frequent contact with the receptionist were afraid that our letter might bring on reprisals. But sensing that they might be accused of cowardice or collaboration with the FARC, they argued about the form of the letter. The secret message to Uribe was less problematic. In principle everyone was ready to sign it, probably because they all assumed it would never reach its destination. Gloria was the only one who abstained. She had been kidnapped with her two oldest sons, then brutally separated from them without warning. She did not want to authorize a military rescue operation that might endanger the lives of her children, still held hostage by the FARC. Everyone understood her position.

We spent a whole afternoon writing the letter to the Secretariado. Lucho went back and forth between us, like a good conventioneer, to add this or remove that, so that everyone would be satisfied. The rain had stopped and I saw one of our fellow prisoners speaking through the fence with the receptionist. I thought I could detect a servile attitude, but I rejected my impression to avoid disturbing the harmony of our group. Later I saw that same person talking for a long time with Clara. In the evening when we were all getting ready to sign the letter to the commanders, Clara refused because she didn't want any problems with Sombra. I didn't insist. Those who were getting cold feet about continuing our protest used this escape hatch to declare that we all had to be united and that if we weren't, they would also abstain. So the letter to the Secretariado was abandoned.

The letter to Uribe was signed by half of our newly created company, secretly, so that the others who had refused to sign wouldn't know about it. The ones who had gone through with it were running the risk that it might fall into the FARC hands and that they would be punished. The group's division seemed sealed. They entrusted me with hiding the letter, something I did for many years, keeping it even long after we had parted and scattered into different camps. No one ever found it, despite numerous searches. I had folded it, wrapped it in plastic, and sewn it inside the reinforcement at the elbow of my jacket. I reread it several times, long after we had all written and signed it, and it always gave me a twinge of sorrow. In those days we were still able to hope.

On a morning when we remained disheartened by our lack of success and by the split that had divided us, the prison awoke in an uproar. We could hear the sound of engines. Several fast boats had just arrived. The guards were in their parade uniforms. Rogelio wore a vest covered with ammunition and a parachutist's beret that hung over one ear and had the FARC tab embroidered on the front. He was so proud of himself! It wasn't hard to get the information out of him: Mono Jojoy was here on an inspection tour.

We rapidly agreed on what we would say when he came to greet us, thinking this would be the opportunity to express the indignation we'd meant to convey in our aborted letter. We set up our hammocks in the yard – because space was at a premium, we had made minute calculations and agreed the day before on where to hang everyone's hammock – and we waited for Mono Jojoy.

Space was perhaps the only advantage that the military hostages had over us and we envied them for it. The day we arrived in the prison, I saw them for the first time. I was in the middle of exchanging my first words with Gloria when I turned around at the sound of a metallic clanking. There were men's voices angrily calling behind me. For a moment I thought it was guerrillas chasing after pigs that had gone astray, because that had happened before.

Forty or more men in rags emerged from the bushes, with long hair, stubble on their faces, and a huge chain around their necks binding them together. Flanked by armed guards, they were walking in single file, carrying heavy backpacks, laden down with enormous old pots, mouldy mattresses that were half split open and rolled up against their necks, chickens attached by their feet swinging upside down from their belts, pieces of cardboard and empty oil drums wedged behind the straps of their bundles, and radios all dented and patched together, hanging from their necks like an additional yoke. They looked as if they had come out of a labour camp. I couldn't believe my eyes.

Guerrillas were circling them, shouting stupid orders to keep them walking. Holding to the bars of my prison's metal gate, breathless, my eyes popping out, I watched as this terrifying procession went by. I could make no sound. I recognized Alan. He turned around, and when he saw me, he smiled uneasily and said, "*Hola, Ingrid . . .*"

The other soldiers all turned around, one after the other. "It's Ingrid, it's the *doctora*."

They stopped walking. Some greeted me from a distance with a friendly wave, others raised their fists in a sign of resistance, some barraged me with questions I couldn't answer. The boldest among them came up to the gate to offer their hands through the bars. I touched them, wishing that my hand's contact could convey the emotion I felt and bring them some comfort. These bedraggled men of the jungle had been persecuted, tortured, and yet they had the guts to smile, to forget themselves, to act with dignity and courage. The guards shouted insults and threats to stop them from talking to us. The men were quickly locked back up in the building behind ours. We couldn't see them, but we could hear them. As a result we had conversations with them, speaking in hushed voices, placing our lips against the cracks between the planks on either side of the narrow passage where the guards performed their rounds. Communication between the two buildings was forbidden.

That is how we learned that Sombra had kindly granted them the space to practise some sports, a privilege we didn't have. In the vastness of the jungle, where everything was lacking except for space, the guerrillas had chosen to confine us in a narrow, insalubrious place whose conditions led to nothing but crowding and conflict. The few hours of cohabitation we'd shared had already unveiled the tensions created by our needs as individuals to defend our own space. As it did in primitive societies, space had become once again the essential, basic property, and its fundamental value lay in assuaging our injured pride: Whoever had the most felt superior.

Settled in our hammocks as if we were in an observation post, we could follow Mono Jojoy's inspection tour. He kept a safe distance from the fences and circled our enclosure so that our voices couldn't reach him, and he avoided meeting our eyes. If he'd been inspecting his cattle, he wouldn't have acted otherwise. Then he vanished.

Half an hour later a group we didn't know emerged from the northern wing of the prison. Three men – two mature tall blonds and a third, younger man, all wearing shorts and carrying lightweight backpacks, surrounded by half a dozen heavily armed guerrillas – walked alongside our fence, close by, on the wooden walkway that the guerrillas had just set up that went all the way around the outside of the prison. They were looking straight ahead, and they went on walking until they reached the soldiers' barracks.

"Hey, gringos! How are you? Do you speak English?"

The soldiers were thrilled to practise their few words of English. We looked at one another, disconcerted. Of course. They must be the three Americans who had been captured a year earlier and who were also part of the group of "interchangeables."

One of our companions who had the closest rapport with Rogelio announced knowingly, "Yes, those are the Americans. They're going to put them in here with us."

"Here?"

"I don't know, with the soldiers or with us. I think it's going to be with us."

"What do you mean? There's no room!"

He frowned at me. Then, as if he'd found the thing that would hurt, he let out slowly, "They're prisoners like us. And we welcomed you when you came. You have to do the same with the others."

I was embarrassed. Yes, of course, we had to welcome them as best we could.

31

THE BIG ROW

The metal gate opened, and the three Americans entered, their jaws clenched, their gazes apprehensive. We shook hands, introduced ourselves, greeted one another, and made room for them to sit down. The companion who had just lectured me took them under his wing and showed them the facilities. There were no bunks for them. Everybody began to speculate about what the guerrillas would do. We had the answer within the hour.

Brian, who was one of the strongest guerrillas in the group, showed up with the famous chain saw on his shoulder. Two other men followed him, carrying wooden planks and rough-hewn beams. They asked us to remove all our belongings and go out. In a few minutes, one of the bunks was cut from its base and pushed over to one side up against the wire mesh beneath the opening that served as a window. In the space that remained, they managed to fit a new bunk, squeezed in between the two others, with just enough room to reach it from one side. We all watched without saying a word. The room was once again covered in a reddish sawdust that stuck to one's nostrils.

Brian turned to me, bathed in sweat. "Right, where is it you wanted a window?"

I was flabbergasted. I thought that Sombra had forgotten our request.

"I think we should have a window here," I answered. With my finger I drew a huge imaginary rectangle on the wooden wall that looked out over our inner courtyard. Keith, the one of the three who had entered the prison first, was murmuring something behind me. He didn't seem pleased with the idea and was complaining to himself. One of our companions tried to calm him down, but communication was difficult, because he spoke so little Spanish. He managed to convey that he wanted the wall to remain intact. He was afraid of being cold at night.

"Come on, make up your minds!" Brian remonstrated.

"A window, a window!" exclaimed the others, worried that Brian might just turn around and depart.

The incident left a tension in the air. Keith came over to me to smooth things out. He spoke in English.

"Do you know that when you were kidnapped, our mission was to look for you? We flew over the region for days. Who would have thought that we'd eventually find you . . . only here!"

This was news. I was unaware that the American embassy had contributed to the search. We began to talk eagerly. I told him how Joaquín Gómez had bragged about the FARC's having shot down their plane.

"That's completely wrong. They didn't bring us down. We had engine failure. That's all."

Then, as if he were confiding something, he leaned close to my ear. "In fact, they're really lucky, because we are the only prisoners who truly count here, the three of us and you. We're the jewels in their crown."

I kept silent for a moment. His comment disturbed me. Then I answered, weighing my words, "We are all prisoners here. We're all the same."

That made him angry. He felt I had criticized him, and he didn't like it. And yet the last thing I wanted was to have him think I was lecturing him. I smiled and added, "You'll have to tell me your story in detail. I really would like to know what you've been through up to now."

Lucho was behind me. I hadn't seen him come up. He took me by the arm, and the conversation ended there. We were beginning to build some shelves. Orlando had managed to get some nails and borrow a hammer.

We had to hurry, since we had the use of it only until the end of the afternoon. We set to work.

That night the barracks rattled with everyone's snoring. It was like the sound of a factory. The day had been intense, and everyone had gone to bed exhausted. I stared at the ceiling and, in particular, the wire fencing over it, a few inches above my nose. They had built everything so quickly that to get to the upper bunks we had to crawl and roll over to lie down, since there was so little space between the beds and the ceiling. It was impossible to sit up, and to get down from the bunk you had to let yourself go gradually, into the void, hanging from the fencing like a monkey until you landed below. I didn't complain. At least it was sheltered, with a wooden floor that would keep us dry. The new window was a success. A warm breeze came into the barracks and cleaned the air, heavy with the breathing of the ten unfortunate souls crowded inside. A mouse ran along the beam supporting the wire mesh just above my eyes. How long would we have to live packed in here, on top of one another, before we were set free?

In the morning Lucho and I woke up to an unpleasant surprise: All the shelves we had struggled to build the day before were already filled with other people's belongings. There was no more room! Orlando was laughing to himself as he looked at us. "Go on, don't make such a face. It's no big deal. We'll ask for some more boards, and we'll put some other shelves over there, behind the door. It will be better for you – you'll have them opposite your bunks."

Gloria came over. She thought it was an excellent idea. "And we could make another shelf on this side of the fencing!"

I wasn't too happy, quite simply because I thought it was unlikely that the guerrillas would give us any more boards. To my astonishment, at Orlando's request the boards arrived that very same day.

"You'll have a lovely shelf! I'll make a desk for you, fit for a queen!"

Orlando went on making fun of me, but I was relieved, and my spirits improved. With Lucho they set about building a piece of furniture that could be both a table and a shelf. They also planned on putting together a little bookshelf for the corner where Gloria was. I wanted to help. But I sensed I was getting in their way.

I went back out to the courtyard to set up my hammock while they finished the job.

The place that had been allotted to me had now been taken by Keith, unaware that before their arrival we had agreed how to divide up the space. There was only one tree left where I could hang my hammock, but in that case the other end would have to be fixed to the chain-link of the enclosure. This entailed two problems. First of all, they might not allow me to hang it from the outside fence. Secondly, the rope on my hammock might not be long enough. Luckily, Sombra was doing his rounds of the barracks, and I was able to ask him directly. He agreed, and on top of it he provided the extra rope I needed. My companions looked at me askance. They knew that if I'd had to go through Rogelio, I wouldn't have got anything. These were little things, but our lives were made up of nothing but these little things. When Rogelio brought us the evening stewpot and he saw that I had hung my hammock to the fence, a dark shadow passed over his eyes. I knew I had definitely fallen out of his good favour.

A few days later, Tom, the oldest of our new companions, who had initially set up near Keith, migrated and came to hang his hammock over by me. He'd obviously had a falling-out with his compatriot. When he saw Lucho coming over to join us, he raised his voice, grumbling. We would have to share the same tree for our hammocks. I tried to explain to him that we all had to make an effort to settle together because space was limited. Exasperated, he snapped back at me. Lucho took my defence, also raising his voice. Tom was easily irritable, in the midst of a cold war with his companion. I understood that he wanted to create some distance. It was also in Keith's interest to see Tom go elsewhere. He went to the fence while Tom and Lucho were arguing, and whispered to Rogelio. The metal gate suddenly opened, and the man swept in.

"Ingrid, are you shit-stirring? Here everyone is the same. No one prisoner is more important than the others."

"But—" I fell silent, instantly realizing that this was not simply some misunderstanding over the hammocks.

"I don't want to know. You're not the queen here. You have to obey, that's all there is to it."

I didn't know what to say.

"I'll chain you up so you'll learn your lesson. You'll see!"

What I *could* see was that my companions, the ones who had inflamed Rogelio, were holding their sides laughing.

Rogelio was delighted, too. His comrades in the watchtowers were following his performance. He spat on the ground, put his ranger's hat back on his head, and walked out, strutting like a peacock.

Lucho took me by the shoulders and shook me tenderly. "Come on, we've been through worse. Where's your smile?"

It was true. I had to smile, even if it was hard. Then he added, "They're just making you pay. I heard what you said when the guy told you that they were the jewels in the crown . . . I don't think you've made a friend."

In these early days of cohabitation, we shared everything, even tasks, which we distributed as equitably as possible. We decided to sweep the barracks, the wooden walkway, and the toilets. We made brushes for cleaning the bowls using shreds of T-shirts. Every day we'd clean the facilities in teams of two.

When it was our turn, Lucho and I got up at dawn. In the beginning we had argued, because Lucho categorically refused to let me clean the latrines. He insisted on washing the toilet shed all by himself. This was a job that required a lot of elbow grease, and I didn't want him to exacerbate his diabetes by overexerting himself. There was nothing I could do. He always pretended to get angry with me and would block my way. So I fell back on the barracks and cleaned them vigorously, because I knew that as soon as he was finished with his chore, he would come and take the broom from my hands to finish my job. This whole business amused no one except Lucho and me. It was a sort of game between us to prove our affection. But it seemed as if our companions didn't appreciate our way of doing things. Criticism became a popular sport. What I wanted most was to build on this fledgling harmony, but that was becoming increasingly difficult. Each of us had a story of pain, spite, or vexation. None of it was really serious. It was just that little things were blown out of all proportion, because each of us was suffering in one way or another.

Any odd look or misplaced comment was taken as a grave offence and became a source of resentment, to be chewed over obsessively.

Add to that the way each individual's behaviour toward the guerrillas was perceived. There were those who had "sold themselves" and those who "remained dignified." This perception was a product of speculation, because all it took was for someone to speak to the receptionist to be accused of dishonest collaboration with the enemy. In the end, sooner or later, every one of us had to ask for something we needed. If you "obtained" what you had asked for, the others were filled with pathological envy at not having been granted a similar favour. We all eyed each other with suspicion, caught in our absurd divisiveness in spite of ourselves. The atmosphere had grown heavy.

One morning after breakfast, one of our new companions came to see me, looking as if he was in a foul mood.

I had just that minute begun a lively conversation with Lucho, Gloria and Jorge. They wanted me to give them French lessons, and we were getting organized. The intrusion annoyed my friends, but I followed my companion, knowing we would have plenty of time to continue discussing our project later.

He said that he'd "heard" that when they arrived, I'd remarked that I did not want them to be with us. Was this true?

"Who told you that?"

"It doesn't matter."

"Yes, it does, because that is a malicious and distorted claim."

"Did you say it, yes or no?"

"When you arrived, I asked how we would all fit in. I never said that I didn't want you to join us. So the answer is no, I never said that."

"Well, it's important, because it hurt our feelings."

"Don't listen to everything people tell to you. Rely on what you can see for yourself. You know that since you arrived, we have all done our best to make you feel welcome. As for me, it's a pleasure to talk with you. I enjoy our conversations, and I would like for us to be friends."

He got up, calmer, held out his hand in a cordial gesture, then apologized to my companions for having taken me away for a few minutes.

"That's the way it works: divide and conquer," said Jorge, the most cautious among us. Then, tapping me on the back of my hand, he added, "Come on, *madame*. We'll start our French lessons, and that will force us all to think about something else."

32

ROLL CALL

November 2003. I began my day with an hour of gymnastics in the space between Jorge's and Lucho's bunk beds, making the most of their being at the far end of the barracks, where I wouldn't bother anyone. Then I would go and wash in the shed, at the exact hour I had been granted in the strict schedule we had drawn up for the use of the "bathroom". The entrance was covered with a black plastic sheet and it was the only place where we could get undressed without being seen. We would all get together before lunch – Lucho, Jorge, Gloria, and I – and sit cross-legged on one of the lower bunks, good-humouredly working on our French lessons, playing cards, and inventing projects to work on together for the day when we would be free.

When the lunch pot arrived, it was chaos. In the beginning, people tried to be courteous. We would go up with our bowls in our hands and help each other. The men let the ladies go first, observing rules of etiquette. But, over time, our conduct gradually changed.

One day someone decided that we should line up. Then someone else ran to get to the front as soon as the clicking of the padlock could be heard. Another day one of the biggest men insulted Gloria, accusing her of elbowing her way so she could help herself to more. What should have been a time to relax became a pitched battle, each of us pointing fingers at the others for wanting to have the best part of this revolting pittance.

The guerrillas had dozens of pigs. We could often smell the roasting meat in the camp, and there was never any for us. When we mentioned this to Rogelio, he brought us back a stewpot with the skull of a pig on a bed of rice. The pig had so many teeth it looked as if it were smiling. *A laughing pig*, I thought. A swarm of green flies came as its personal escort swirling around. It was disgusting and that was what we were fighting over. We were hungry and suffering, and we all began to behave the way the guerrillas treated us.

I didn't want to be a part of this. I found it really distressing to be shoved by some and watched over by others, as if they were about to bite every time someone went near the pot. I could see their reactions, their sidelong glances. So we eventually agreed that it would be wiser for me not to go near the pot. I stayed in the barracks, and Lucho took my bowl and brought back my rice and beans. From a distance I observed our behaviour and wondered why we reacted this way. Rules of civility no longer applied. A different order had been established, one that appeared meticulously egalitarian, but in fact allowed the more aggressive and stronger among us to prevail over those who were smaller and weaker. The women were easy targets. Any protest on our part – once we were irritated and hurt – became an easy object of ridicule. And if one of us was unlucky enough to weep uncontrollably, the reaction was pitiless: "She's trying to trick us!"

I had never been a victim of overt sexism before. I had arrived in the political arena at the right time – discrimination against women was frowned upon, and women's participation in politics was promoted as a breath of fresh air in a world rotting with corruption. Confronted with this alpha-male behaviour made me think I could now understand why the Inquisition had managed to burn so many women at the stake.

One morning at dawn, when no one was up yet, the receptionist stood directly outside the window, together with another guerrilla, who stood just behind him as if to support him in a mission that, judging by how stiffly they stood, must be one of some importance.

Rogelio shouted in a voice that caused the entire barracks to jump out of their beds, "*¡Los prisioneros! ¡Se numeran, rápido!*"*

---

* "Prisoners! Head count, hurry up!"

I didn't understand what that meant. Count? What did he want from us exactly? I leaned over to speak with Gloria, who slept below, hoping she would have the answer. She had spent more time with Sombra's troops, and I imagined she must know what Rogelio was asking. It must be some routine I was unfamiliar with. "We each have to say our own number in turn. It's to count us. Jorge, who is right against the fence, will begin by saying 'One,' and then it will be my turn, and I'll say 'Two,' and Lucho will say 'Three,' and so on," explained Gloria, whispering hastily for fear of being told off by the guards.

We had to count! I found this monstrous. We were losing our identity – they refused to call us by our names. We were nothing more than cargo, cattle.

The receptionist and his acolyte were getting impatient when they saw how confused we were. No one wanted to start. Someone at the back of the barracks shouted, "Shit! Start! You want them to be pissed off at us all day long or what!"

There was silence. Then, in a loud voice, as if he were in a military barracks standing to attention, someone shouted, "One!" The person next to him cried, "Two!" The others followed: "Three!" "Four!" Then, when finally it was my turn, my heart beating, my throat dry, I said in a voice that did not sound as loud as I would have liked, "Ingrid Betancourt."

And in the panicked silence that followed, I added, "When you want to know if I'm still here, you can call me by my name and I'll reply."

"Go on, I don't have time to waste!" shouted the receptionist, to intimidate the others.

I heard a murmur in the back; some of my companions were grumbling about me. They found my attitude unbearable, thinking I was just being arrogant.

But it was not arrogance. I refused to be treated like an object, to be denigrated not only in the eyes of others but also in my own. For me, words had a supernatural power, and I feared for our health, our mental balance, our spirits. When I heard the guerrillas refer to us as "cargo," as "packages," I shuddered. These weren't just expressions. The point was to dehumanize us. It was simpler for them to shoot at a shipment of goods, at an object, than at a human being. I saw it as the beginning of a process of degradation, which I wanted to oppose. If the word "dignity" had any meaning, then we must not allow them to treat us like numbers.

Sombra came to see me during the morning. He had been told about the incident.

He said that roll call was a "routine procedure," to make sure nobody had escaped during the night. But he said he understood my reaction and had given instructions for them to call us by our names.

I was relieved. Waging the same battle every morning did not appeal to me. But some of my companions didn't like it. They refused to acknowledge that there was a point in not submitting.

33

HUMAN MISERY

I found I had a great need to isolate myself, which led me to withdraw into almost absolute silence. I understood that my silence might sometimes exasperate my companions, but I also noticed that there were moments in our discussions when there was no point in being rational. Anything anyone said was misconstrued and distorted.

At the beginning of my captivity, I had been talkative. But because I'd been rebuffed as much as I'd rebuffed others, my need for silence grew stronger. It was almost impossible to obtain it.

One of my companions, who always turned up when he was least welcome, became a real burden.

In a loud voice so others could hear, Keith told me stories of his very wealthy friends and his hunting vacations with them, in places to which we mere mortals would never have access. He couldn't help talking about other people's wealth. It was an obsession. He'd proposed to his fiancée because she was well connected. His favourite subject was his salary.

I was embarrassed for him. I normally retreated to my worktable halfway through his spiel. I could not understand how, in the midst of a drama like ours, anyone could continue living in his bubble, judging people's worth by what they possessed. If there were ever a time to dispel this crass illusion, surely it was here, now, in the jungle. We had nothing left.

Sometimes, however, I lost perspective on my own behaviour. One day while the guards had a tape player going full blast, with a nasal voice wailing shrill revolutionary refrains, I complained. The FARC was trying to develop a musical culture to accompany the revolution, as the Cubans had done with much success. Unfortunately, the FARC didn't have the same talent in attracting good artists. To my surprise, my companions responded in exasperation that they didn't want to listen to me complaining. I was put out. I had to listen to their ramblings for hours, but I was not allowed any complaints of my own.

Under normal conditions their reaction would probably have made me laugh. But in the jungle the slightest irritation could be very painful and I would overreact. These annoyances had accumulated in layers, day after day, month after month.

Lucho understood me, and he knew that I was sensitive because I was the target of all sorts of comments. On the radio my name was mentioned often, and that only fuelled the acrimony of some of my companions. If I remained aloof, it was because I looked down on them. If I joined in, it was because I was trying to dominate. Their irritation with me went so far that they would lower the volume of the radio at the mention of my name.

One evening when there was talk of some efforts on the part of the Quai d'Orsay* to obtain our release, somebody groused about it. "We're fed up with your goddam France!" he said. He went up to the *panela*† that Sombra had given us as a community radio, dangling from a nail in the middle of the barracks, and switched it off. Everyone laughed, except me.

Gloria came over and kissed me, saying, "They're jealous. You should just laugh." But I didn't think it was funny at all. I was too wounded to see that we were all going through a serious identity crisis. We had lost our bearings, and no longer knew who we were, or what our place was in the world. I should have realized how devastating it was for my companions not to be mentioned on the radio, for it made them feel they did not exist.

---

* The French Ministry of Foreign Affairs.
† This is another word for the radio "brick".

I had always fought against the FARC strategy of dividing us. In Sombra's prison my reflexes remained the same. One morning a few days after the Americans arrived, there was a delivery of foam mattresses– we could hardly believe such luxury! They were all different colours, and each of us could choose the one we wanted. Except Clara. The guard assigned her a dirty grey mattress that he stuffed through the gap in the metal gate. Lucho and I followed the scene. I went up to the gate and tried to reason with the guerrilla on Clara's behalf. He was about to go back on his decision when Rogelio showed up. He thought I was asking a favour for myself, so out came his usual line whenever I was around: "You're not the queen here. You do as you're told." And the matter was settled, with no further discussion.

Clara picked up the grey mattress without even looking at me and tried to exchange it with one of our comrades. Lucho took me by the arm and said, "You shouldn't have got involved. You have enough problems with the guerrillas as it is. And no one will thank you for it!"

And indeed Orlando, who had reluctantly agreed to exchange his mattress with Clara, turned on me, saying, "If you wanted to help, why didn't you just give her *your* mattress?"

Lucho smiled at me, knowingly. "You see, I told you so!"

Learning to keep quiet took time, and I was weary. Resigning myself to injustice was painful. Yet there was wisdom in not trying to resolve other people's problems, as I discovered one morning.

Sombra was beside himself with rage. The soldiers next door were sending messages to one of our companions, in violation of the rules. Consuelo received paper scrunched into balls from the barracks behind ours. We all joined in to pick up the letters, because they might fall anywhere, even on our heads when we were outside lying in our hammocks. So we were all willing accomplices, careful to pick up the bits of paper without alerting the guards standing in the watchtowers.

Sombra called out to Consuelo.

Seeing that she was in a tight spot, I asked Sombra to relax the rules he'd established, because we all wanted to speak to our soldier comrades in the other barracks.

Even Silence Has an End

I was completely thrown by the way he reacted. "They all told me you were the one stirring up the shit in here!" He said that if he caught me passing messages with my friends next door again, he'd lock me up in a hole, and then we'd see if I wanted to go on playing the smart alec.

No one came to my defence. This episode gave rise to a passionate debate during the French lessons. "Don't try any more! You'll only make the situation worse," said Jorge, who shared Lucho's opinion. "It's every man for himself here," added Gloria. "Every time you try to get involved, you make more enemies."

They were right, but I hated what we were being forced to become. I felt as if we were about to lose the best part of us and were being deluged in pettiness and baseness. This only increased my need for silence. Beneath the dreary skies of our everyday life, the guerrillas had sown the grains of a deep ill will. The guards spread the rumour that the three newcomers were infected with venereal disease. The guerrillas then told the Americans that we were saying malicious things about them, as if the rumour came from us. The guards pretended we were accusing them of being mercenaries and secret agents of the CIA, claiming that microscopic transmitters had been found in the soles of their shoes and localization chips camouflaged in their teeth. Finally they spread another story in which our three companions were negotiating their release with Sombra in exchange for the delivery of a certain number of cocaine shipments to the United States using American government planes. It took no more than this to breed a general mistrust.

One evening all hell broke loose. A misplaced word, and suddenly accusations were flying everywhere. Some were accused of being spies, others of being traitors. Lucho asked that the women in the camp be respected. Keith, in response, accused Lucho of plotting to attack him with the knives sent by Mono Jojoy! During the night there were discussions with the receptionist over by the fence.

They came to search us the next morning. Those who were behind this inspection murmured in satisfaction. It wasn't the knives that worried me – we'd obtained those "legally." It was the machete we had hidden in the mud under the floor of the barracks.

"You'll have to move the machete today, no later," Lucho said once the search was over. "If our companions find out where it is, they'll denounce us immediately."

34

LUCHO'S ILLNESS

Early December 2003. My second Christmas in captivity was drawing near. I had not lost hope in a miracle. The courtyard in our prison, which in the beginning had been nothing but a huge puddle of mud, was drying. Along with the sadness and frustration of being far from home, December brought an immaculate blue sky and a warm breeze redolent of vacation, which merely increased our melancholy. It was a time for regret.

Gloria had managed to get hold of a pack of cards, and we got into the habit of settling down after our morning wash to play bridge in a corner of the barracks. We had all understood from our first sessions that it was imperative to let Gloria and me win to maintain the good humour of the group. So there was an unwritten, unspoken rule stipulating that they would play to our advantage without us finding out. We were divided into two teams, the women and the men. Gloria and I did all we could to win our games, and Lucho and Jorge did what they could to lose theirs. This incongruous situation brought out the best in each of us, and any number of times I thought I would die laughing at the sight of the ingenious moves that our adversaries came up with to make us win. Lucho was becoming a past master of comedy and derision, going so far as to pretend he had fainted on the carpet, in order to mix up the cards and thus be able to ask for a new deal that would be in our favour. In the logic of this upside-down game of ours, where losing and trying to get the others to win had become the aim, we managed to make fun of our ravaged egos, to put aside our controlling reflexes, and in the long run to accept our fate with more tolerance. Jorge excelled at accumulating subtle errors, and we wouldn't notice the effect until a few turns later. Once we did, both Gloria and I would dance and give out wild Indian victory whoops.

Since my kidnapping, laughter had been absent from my life, and oh, how I had missed it! At the end of our games, my face would ache from laughing. This was most effective treatment against dejection.

I gazed at myself for hours in a compact mirror that had survived all the times we'd been searched. It was so small that I could see only a bit of myself at a time. I had noticed a first wrinkle of bitterness at the corner of my mouth – a discovery that frightened me, along with finding that my teeth were turning yellow, even though I couldn't remember their original colour. I did not like this surreptitious metamorphosis at all. I did not want to emerge from the jungle a shrivelled old woman, ravaged by acrimony and hate. I had to change – not to adapt, which would have seemed like a betrayal to me – but to rise above this morass of petty, base behaviour in which we had begun to wallow. I needed wings, I needed to fly far away above this fiendish jungle that sought to transform us into cockroaches. I didn't know how to go about it. I knew of no instruction manual for reaching a higher level of humanity and a greater wisdom. But I felt intuitively that laughter was the *beginning* of wisdom, as it was indispensable for survival.

So we settled into our hammocks, no longer fighting over our places, and we indulgently listened to one another. We were patient when one of our comrades repeated a story for the twentieth time. Sharing slices of our lives with the others let us see our memories as if we were staring at a movie screen.

That afternoon, on the radio, Christmas carols mingled with the traditional tropical music that was always played at parties in December. These familiar seasonal tunes conjured up for each of us specific memories. I was in Cartagena, aged fifteen. The moon shone lazily on the ocean bay, and the crests of the waves shimmered as they lapped against the shore. My sister and I were invited to a New Year's party. But we had fled when a handsome young man blessed with a godly tan and green cat's eyes had made indecent proposals to us. We left as fast as possible, running across the city through the festivities as if chased by the devil incarnate, and we nestled in Papa's arms until the strike of midnight, laughing and out of breath.

"You shouldn't have left," declared Lucho. "*Nadie le quita a uno ni lo comido, ni lo bailado!*"* Then he started to dance, followed by the rest of us, as we did not want him to have fun on his own, until the guards told us to lower the volume and we returned to our hammocks.

After a while, Lucho got up to go to the toilet; he came back covered in sweat. He was tired and wanted to go back into the barracks to lie down, he said. I couldn't see his face because it was dark, but something in his voice alarmed me.

"Do you feel all right, Lucho?"

"Yes, I'm fine," he groaned.

Then, changing his mind, he added, "Stand in front of me. I'm going to hold you by the shoulders, and you'll guide me into the barracks. I'm having trouble walking."

The moment we crossed the threshold, Lucho collapsed onto a plastic chair in the entrance. He was green, his eyes were glassy, and his face was gaunt, soaked in sweat. He could no longer articulate very clearly, and he had trouble holding his head straight. Just as he had warned, this was the onset of a diabetic crisis.

Lucho kept a supply of candy, and I hurried to go through his *equipo*† to find it. Lucho, meanwhile, was slumping, dangerously slipping from his chair, at risk of falling any moment, headfirst, on the floor.

"Help me!" I cried, without knowing whether it was better to hold him, to lay him on the floor, or to give him the candies I'd just found.

Orlando came over at once. He was tall and muscular. He took Lucho in his arms and sat him on the floor while I tried to get him to suck on one

---

* "Neither the food you have eaten nor your dancing can be taken away from you."
† Backpack.

of the candies I had in my hands. But Lucho was no longer there. He had fainted, and you could see the whites of his eyes. I chewed on the candy myself and put it into his mouth ground up. "Lucho, Lucho, can you hear me?"

His head was rolling in every direction, but he was grunting, making sounds to indicate that somewhere in his head he could still hear my voice.

Gloria and Jorge dragged a mattress across the floor so that we could put Lucho on it. Tom came in, too, with a piece of cardboard that he had found God knows where, and he started to fan Lucho's face vigorously to ease his breathing.

"I need sugar, quick! The candy isn't working!" I shouted, feeling Lucho's weak pulse.

"Call the nurse! We're losing him!" cried Orlando, who had just checked his heartbeat.

Someone brought a small plastic packet that held ten grammes or so of sugar. It was a treasure – it could save his life! I put a bit of sugar on his tongue, then mixed the rest of the sachet with a tiny bit of water and made him drink it in little swallows, half of which dribbled down the sides of his lips. He did not react.

The nurse, Guillermo, yelled to us from behind the fence. "What's all the fuss about?"

"Lucho is having a diabetic crisis. He's in a coma. You have to come and help us!"

"I can't come in!"

"What do you mean, you can't come in?"

"I need permission."

"Go get it! Can't you see he might be dying? Shit!" Orlando was practically shouting.

The man went off in no particular hurry, calling in a blasé voice from a distance, "Stop making all that noise. You'll get the *chulos* on our ass!"

Holding Lucho's head on my lap, I was terrified and filled with rage. How could that "nurse" go off without trying to help us, without lifting a finger?

My companions had gathered around Lucho, trying to help in one way or another. Some had taken off his boots; others were massaging the soles of his feet energetically; a third group was taking turns fanning him.

There was only one candy left of the twenty Lucho had in reserve. I'd made him swallow the rest. And yet he had told me that two or three ought to be more than enough to bring him back.

I shook him hard.

"Lucho, please, wake up! You don't have the right to leave! You can't leave me here all alone, Lucho!"

A terrible silence had fallen all around us. Lucho was lying like a corpse in my arms, and my companions had slowed down their efforts to reanimate him.

Orlando was shaking his head with dismay. "What swine! They didn't do a thing to save him."

Jorge came up and put his hand on Lucho's chest. He nodded and said, "Courage, *madame chérie*. As long as his heart is still beating, there's hope!"

I looked at the one remaining piece of candy. Never mind, it was our last chance. I crushed it with my teeth and inserted the little pieces into his mouth.

I could tell that Lucho had swallowed.

"Lucho, Lucho, can you hear me? If you can hear me, move your hands, please."

His eyes were closed, his mouth open. I could no longer hear his breathing. And yet after a few seconds he moved a finger.

Gloria gave out a shout. "He answered! He moved! Lucho, Lucho, speak to us! Say something!"

Lucho was making a superhuman effort to react. I forced him to drink a little bit of sweetened water. He closed his mouth and swallowed with difficulty.

"Lucho, can you hear me?"

In a hoarse voice that signalled he was back from the shores of death, he replied, "Yes."

I was going to give him some more water. He stopped me with a movement of his hand. "Wait."

Preparing me to deal with the possibility of a diabetic coma, Lucho had warned that the greatest danger was the damage to the brain that could follow.

"Don't let me go into a coma, because I won't come back," he'd instructed me then. "And if I pass out, it's vital you wake me up and keep me awake for the twelve hours that follow. Those are the most important hours for my recovery. You have to get me to talk by asking me all sorts of questions so you can make sure I haven't completely lost my memory."

I began right away, following the instructions he'd given me. "How do you feel?"

He nodded.

"How do you feel? Answer me."

"Fine."

He was finding it hard to respond.

"What's your daughter's name?"

He didn't say anything.

"What is your daughter's name?"

Still no answer.

"What is your daughter's name, Lucho? Make an effort!"

"Carope."

"Where are we?"

No answer.

"Where are we?"

"At home."

"Do you know who I am?"

"Yes."

"What's my name?"

No response.

"Are you hungry?"

"No."

"Open your eyes, Lucho. Can you see us?"

He opened his eyes and smiled. Our companions leaned over to take his hand, to welcome him back, to ask him how he felt. He replied slowly, but his gaze was still elsewhere, as if he didn't recognize us. Lucho was coming back from another world, and he looked a hundred years older.

All night long my companions took turns carrying on one-sided artificial conversations with Lucho to keep him actively conscious. Orlando got him to explain everything there was to know about exporting shrimp and kept him talking until midnight.

I took over from then until dawn. During those hours, I discovered that Lucho had regained his memory of relatively recent events. He knew we were being held captive. But he had no recollection of the events of his childhood or of the immediate present. The day before his coma had been completely erased. As for the dish his mother used to prepare religiously, the *tamale*, it no longer existed. When I asked him about it, clearly sensing that something was wrong, he looked at me with the eyes of a child who is afraid of being scolded and made up answers to keep me happy.

This hurt more than anything, because my Lucho, the one I had known, who told me stories to make me laugh, my friend and my confidant — that Lucho was gone, and I missed him terribly.

For months we had been dreaming about a political project that we planned to start work on as soon as we were released. After his diabetic crisis, he no longer had a clue what I was talking about. But what was possibly the most atrocious thing of all was that Lucho immediately forgot anything you'd just told him. Worse yet, he forgot what he'd just done. When he'd already had his lunch ration, he would start to complain because he thought he hadn't eaten all day and all of a sudden he was hungry.

Christmas was coming. We were all waiting for messages from our families, because more than ever it was a torment to be apart. Yet Lucho continued to be absent in spirit.

The only thing he never forgot was that he had children. Oddly enough, he talked about three children, although I had only been aware of the existence of two of them. He wanted to know if they had come to see him. I explained that nobody could come to see us but that we received their radio messages. He grew impatient to tune in to the show and listen to the latest messages, but he often became very dozy, and the next morning he had completely forgotten everything.

The longest broadcast with messages was on Saturdays at midnight. My heart felt as if it had shrivelled. There hadn't been a single message for Lucho. Unable to admit it to him, I found myself making up a story.

"What did they say?"

"That they love you and that they're thinking about you."

"Okay, but tell me what they talked about."

"They talked about you, how much they miss you—"

"Hold on, what about Sergio? Did he talk about his studies?"

"He said he's been working hard."

"Ah! That's good, that's very good . . . And Carope, where is she?"

"She didn't say where she was, but she said this would be the last Christmas without you, and—"

"And what? Tell me exactly!"

"And that she dreamed of being with you for your birthday and that . . . uh—"

"And what?"

"And that . . . she'll call you on your birthday."

My God! It made him so happy that I wasn't even ashamed of having lied to him.

In any event, I said to myself, to ease my conscience, *he's going to forget everything I just told him in two seconds.*

But Lucho didn't forget this. My little lie helped him to hold on to the present and, what's more, to get out of his labyrinth. He lived for the call. On his birthday he was back among us again, and he delighted everybody with his sense of repartee and good spirits. Keith, who had prompted the search for the knives, seemed to want to be forgiven. He gave Lucho a hug and explained in detail everything *he* had done to revive him with a fan. Lucho looked at him and smiled. He had lost a lot of weight; he looked fragile but he had regained his sense of humour. "Now I remember seeing you!" he said. "That's why I was so scared about coming back!"

One effect that prison had on us was, too often, to make us lose our perspective on things. The various quarrels among us were safety valves that pacified tensions stronger than any of us had ever known. Perhaps this explains why, after we'd been living crammed in Sombra's prison for over a month, it felt oddly like a family reunion to see Keith and Lucho getting together and chatting.

I sometimes thought this way about Clara. One day I said to her, "We are like sisters, because whatever happens, we have to go through this part of life together." We did not choose one another – it was fate – and we had to learn to put up with each other. It was a hard reality to accept. In the beginning I felt like I needed her. But in the long run, captivity frayed even this feeling of attachment. Our need became a burden. Yet the more I carried that weight, the lighter it seemed to grow. I found it easier to reach out to her, because I no longer expected anything from her.

This was also what I could observe between Lucho and Keith, and in a general fashion among us all. Accepting the other made us feel less vulnerable, thus more open. We were learning how to temper ourselves.

I went to get the presents I'd made for Lucho. Gloria and Jorge did the same – an extra pack of cigarettes (a huge sacrifice for Gloria, who had become a heavy smoker) and a pair of "almost new" socks from Jorge. The three of us began to sing around Lucho with our presents in our arms. One by one, all the others came over, each with some small thing to give.

Seeing that others were interested in him – and feeling that he was important to the rest of the group – fuelled Lucho's desire to live. He regained his memory completely, and with it a growing impatience to hear the messages his family had promised him. I was incapable of confessing to my white lie.

The following Saturday he stayed up all night, his ear glued to his radio But once again, as the previous Saturday, there was no message for Lucho. He went to get his cup of coffee early in the morning, as soon as he heard the sound of the pots, and came back with his head bowed. He sat down next to me, looked at me for a long time, and said, "I knew."

"What did you know, Lucho?"

"I knew they weren't going to call in."

"Why do you say that?"

"Because generally that's the way it is."

"I don't understand."

"Yes, look, when you want something very badly, it doesn't happen. If you don't think about it, then boom! It lands in your lap."

"Do you think so?"

"Yes, and in any case they had told me they were travelling over Christmas . . . They didn't call, did they?"

I didn't know what to say. He smiled at me affectionately and added, "Come on, I'm not mad. They were with me in my heart, all the time, like in a dream. That was the best birthday present of all!"

35

A SAD CHRISTMAS

December 2003. A few months before I was captured, I visited the Good
Shepherd women's prison in Bogotá. I had been impressed by those women
who wore makeup and wanted to lead a normal life in their isolated world.
Prison was a microcosm, a little planet of its own. I noticed sheets hanging
behind bars and laundry drying on every floor of the building. When I visited the men's prison, there was none of that. I felt sorry for the women, and
I was touched by the anxious way they had of asking for little favours, as if
they were asking for the moon: a lipstick, a pen, a book. I must have promised them things and then gone on to forget. I lived in another world then,
and I thought I was doing more for them by speeding up the legal pro-
ceedings on their behalf. How mistaken I was. It was the lipstick and the pen
that could have changed their lives. Now I understood.

After Lucho's birthday I promised myself I'd watch out for the others'
birthdays, too. But I came up against a wall of indifference. During the
month of December, there were three of us on the birthday waiting list.
When I suggested that we should celebrate one another's birthdays, my
companions went into a sulk. Some of them refused because they didn't
like the person whose birthday it was, while others adopted an attitude of
"What's the point?" Still others looked up suspiciously, as if to ask, "Is she
trying to give us orders?" Lucho laughed at my lack of success. "I warned
you!" he said. I decided to act on my own.

The week following Lucho's party, when I woke up, I heard on the radios – they were all switched on at the same time, to the same programme – the voice of Orlando's wife wishing him a happy birthday. It was impossible to pretend we hadn't heard it. Orlando was standing in line to get his cup of coffee while the others pretended to ignore the only event that might have changed our routine. It was written like a flashing neon sign all over Orlando's forehead: He was waiting for someone to congratulate him. I hesitated, to be honest. I wasn't very close to Orlando.

"Orlando? I'd like to wish you a happy birthday."

His eyes lit up. He was a sturdy man, and his hug was like a bear's. He looked at me differently for the first time. The others reacted and extended their birthday wishes as well.

The days leading up to Christmas were different. The radio was switched on all day long so we could hear the seasonal classics. Listening to this music was a truly masochistic experience for us.

We knew all the tunes and all the words by heart. I could see Consuelo playing cards with Marc, one of the American hostages, at the big table and furtively drying her tears on a corner of her T-shirt. The radio was playing "La Piragua." Now it was my turn to be sentimental. I could visualize my parents dancing next to the big Christmas tree at my aunt Nancy's house. Their feet glided on the white marble floor, perfectly synchronized. I was eleven years old and wanted to do the same. We could not escape the memories that came pouring in with every song. And besides, no one *wanted* to escape them. This sadness was our only satisfaction. It reminded us that in the past we'd had the right to happiness.

Gloria and Jorge had set up their hammocks in a corner that no one else ever fought over. Lucho and I tried to get closer to them, by hanging one hammock for two from the corner of the fence. It wasn't very comfortable, but we'd been able to chat for hours. One evening suddenly there was a loud thud. Jorge and Gloria had fallen out of the hammock and were sitting on the ground where they had landed, with all the dignity they could muster to avoid looking ridiculous. Everyone burst out laughing. Then we all rolled up our hammocks, creating some space to dance a few steps, to the sound of that music that beckoned us irresistibly. Was it the warm breeze blowing through the trees, a gorgeous moon overhead, the tropical music? I could no longer see the barbed wire or the guards, only my friends, our joy, our laughter. I was happy.

Then came a sound of boots, someone running over, shouting, threats, the flashlight beam upon us. "Where do you think you are? Switch off that fucking radio! Everybody inside the barracks – no more noise, no light, understand?"

The next morning at dawn, the receptionist came to inform us that Sombra wanted to speak with each of us, one on one.

Orlando came up to me. "Watch out, there's a plot against you!"

"Really?"

"Yes, they're going to say that you're monopolizing the radio and that you're keeping them from sleeping."

"It's not true. They can make up all the stories they like. I don't care."

I talked about it with Lucho, and we decided to warn Gloria and Jorge. "Let them say what they want, and we'll concentrate on asking for what we need," he advised. "It's not every day that old Sombra agrees to receive us!" As always, Jorge's words were full of common sense.

Tom was called in first. He came back with a big smile and declared that Sombra had been very amiable and had given him a notebook. The others followed. All of them came back delighted at their meeting with Sombra.

I found Sombra sitting in a sort of rocking chair in the corner of what he called his office. On a board that he used as a table, there were a dirty white computer and printer. I sat down where he showed me to sit, across from him. He pulled out a pack of cigarettes and offered me one. I was going to refuse, because I didn't smoke, but then I accepted. I could keep it for my companions. I took it and put it into my jacket pocket.

"Thank you, I'll smoke it later."

Sombra burst out laughing and handed me a brand-new pack of cigarettes from under the table.

"Here, have this. I didn't know you'd started smoking."

I didn't answer. La Boyaca was next to him. She observed me in silence. It felt as if she were looking right through me.

"Go and get her a drink. What do you want, a Coke?"

"Yes, thank you, a Coca-Cola."

Next to his office, Sombra had built a room that was completely fenced in and locked with a padlock. This was apparently where he stored all his treasures. I could see alcohol, cigarettes, candies and snacks, toilet paper and soap. On the floor next to him was a big wicker basket containing several dozen eggs. I averted my eyes. La Boyaca came back with my drink and placed it in front of me, then left again immediately.

"She wanted to say hello to you," said Sombra, watching her leave. "She likes you."

"That's nice. Thank you for telling me."

"It's the others who don't like you."

"Who are 'the others'?"

"Well, your fellow prisoners."

"And why don't they like me?"

"Maybe they thought they were going to have a party . . ." He said it in a mischievous way. I glared at him. "I was joking. I think they're annoyed because all the talk on the radio is about you."

I had so many things on my mind. "I don't know. There could be a number of explanations, but I think above all that Rogelio has poisoned them against me."

"What's he got to do with any of this, poor Rogelio?"

"Rogelio has been very rude. He came into the prison and insulted me."

"Why?"

"I was defending Lucho."

"I thought it was Lucho who always took your defence."

"Yes, that's true. Lucho is constantly taking my defence. And I'm very worried about him. When he had his diabetic fit, you behaved like monsters."

"What do you want me to do about it? We're in the jungle!"

"You have to get him some insulin."

He explained he had no way of refrigerating it.

"Well, then give him different food – fish, canned tuna, sausages, onions, any kind of vegetables. I know you have some. Even eggs!"

"I can't give preferential treatment to any of the prisoners."

"But you do, all the time. You have to help, Sombra. If he dies, you will be responsible."

"You really like him, don't you?"

"I adore him, Sombra. Life is horrendous in this prison. The only sweet moments I have in a day are because of things Lucho says, because of his company. If anything happened to him, I would never be able to forgive you."

He stayed silent for a while, then added, as if he had just made a decision, "Okay, I'll see what I can do."

I smiled and held out my hand. "Thank you, Sombra."

I got up to leave, and then on impulse I asked him, "By the way, why didn't you give me permission to make a cake for Lucho? It was his birthday a few days ago."

"You didn't ask me."

"Yes I did. I sent you a message, through Rogelio."

He looked at me, surprised. Then, suddenly very sure of himself, he added, "Ah, yes, I'm the one who forgot."

I imitated his gesture, pursing my lips, squinting my eyes, and said as I walked away, "That's right, I know you forget everything!"

He laughed and shouted, "Rogelio! Take the *doctora* back to the barracks!"

Rogelio came out from behind the house, gave me a murderous look, and signalled me to hurry up. Two days before Christmas, Sombra sent Lucho five cans of tuna fish, five cans of sausages, and a bag of onions. And it wasn't Rogelio who brought them. He had been replaced by Arnoldo, a smiling young man who made it clear from the start that he wanted to keep his distance from everyone.

Lucho picked up his cans and went, his arms full, into the barracks. He put everything down on the desk and came over to hug me, blushing with delight. "I don't know what you said to him, but it worked!"

I was as pleased as he was. He let me go to stand back and have a better look at me, and he added mischievously, "In any case, I know you did it more for yourself than for me, because now I'm going to have to give you some!"

We burst out laughing, and the echo resonated around the barracks. But I quickly restrained myself, feeling self-conscious to seem so happy in front of the others.

I felt embarrassed above all in front of Clara. It was her birthday. I had listened to the messages, and there weren't any for her. For two years her family had never sent her a single word. Mom always sent her greetings in her messages to me and sometimes mentioned that she'd seen or spoken to Clara's mother. One day I asked Clara why her mother never called in, and she explained that she lived out in the country and it was difficult for her.

I turned to Lucho. "It's Clara's birthday, today."

"I know. Do you think she would be pleased if we gave her a can of sausages?"

"I'm sure she would be!"

"You go ahead."

Lucho tried to avoid Clara as much as he could. Some of her attitudes were shocking to him, and he could not be swayed from his decision not to have anything to do with her. But he was a generous man, with a good heart. Clara was touched by his gesture.

Christmas Day finally arrived. It was very hot and dry. We passed the time taking siestas, because it was a good way to make the hours go faster. Our Christmas messages had come early, because the radio programme *Las Voces del Secuestro* was broadcast only from Saturday midnight until Sunday at dawn. And Christmas that year fell in the middle of the week. The programme, transmitted in advance, had been disappointing, because President Uribe had promised to send a message to the hostages, and in fact he hadn't done a thing. We did, however, have the heads of the army and the police, who addressed the officers and NCOs, hostages like us captured by the FARC, to ask them to stand firm. It was depressing. As for our families, they had waited for hours to go on air, with Herbin Hoyos, the journalist who had organized this live broadcast from the Plaza de Bolívar in Bogotá. It was a freezing night. We could hear the wind in the microphones, and the distorted voices of those who tried to say a few words in the cold. There had been the call of the faithful, in particular the family of Chikao Muramatsu, a Japanese captain of industry who had been kidnapped a few years earlier and who received messages from his wife religiously, speaking to him in Japanese, against a background of Zen music, which only served to enhance the pain conveyed by words I did not understand, obviously, but could grasp only too well. Then there was the mother of the boy David Mejia Giraldo, who had been kidnapped when he was thirteen years old and must now be about fifteen; his mother Beatriz was asking him to pray, and not to believe what the guerrillas said to him, and not to emulate his abductors. Recently young Daniela Vanegas's family had joined the faithful. The mother wept, the father wept, the sister wept. And I wept just as much. I listened to all the messages, one after the other, all night long. I waited for Ramiro Carranza's fiancée to call in. She had the name of a flower, and her messages were all poems of love. She never missed the occasion, and that Christmas she was there as usual, with all of us. The sons and daughters of elderly Gerardo and Carmenza Angulo were there too, oblivious to the passing of time, refusing the idea that the old couple might no longer be alive. Finally there were the families of the deputies from the Valley of Cauca. I was particularly moved by the messages from Erika Serna, the wife of Carlos Barragán. Carlos had been kidnapped on his birthday, which also coincided with the day his little boy was born: Andres had been growing up over the radio. We'd listened to his first gurgles and his first words. Erika was madly in love with her husband, and she had passed this love on to her little baby, who had learned to speak to his unknown father as if he'd just left him moments before. There was also little Daniela, the daughter of Juan Carlos Narváez. She must have been three years old when her father disappeared from her life. But she clung to his memory with a desperate tenaciousness. I was amazed by this little four-and-a-half-year-old girl who, on the radio, told herself the story of their last conversation, as if her father were the only one who could hear her.

And then there were our messages, the ones for us, for Sombra's prisoners. Occasionally I fell asleep during the endless hours of the programme. Did I doze for a minute or an hour? I had no idea. But I was filled with anxiety and guilt at the thought of missing Mom's message. She was the only one who called me without fail. My children surprised me sometimes. When I heard their voices, I trembled from the shock.

Years later, for example, the Christmas just before my release, I heard Melanie, Lorenzo and Sebastian, all three of them on my birthday, which happens to be on Christmas Day. I had felt particularly fortunate to still be alive, because the prisoners whose messages I used to hear had died in captivity: the hostages of the Valley of Cauca, the Japanese captain of industry, young Daniela Vanegas, Ramiro Carranza, the Angulos. At that time my children were in France with their father Fabrice. They had all sung for me, and each one had said a little loving word: Fabrice and Mela first, then Sebastian, and Lorenzo last. Nothing could be a better gift than their voices. They knew that I could hear them. But that was many years later.

On that Christmas of 2003, they did not know whether I was listening nor how to go about it. I had heard Mom's message; she was stoically awaiting her turn in the ghastly cold at Plaza de Bolívar. I had heard my sister, Astrid, and her children. There was my best friend, María del Rosario, who had also gone there with her young son Marcos, who did not complain about the cold and the very late hour, and my friend and faithful Oxígeno party activist, Marelby. There was no message from my husband. Had I fallen asleep for a moment without realizing?

I checked with Lucho, who had stayed awake. My other companions would not have told me. It wasn't just because it was me. I saw that even among friends they acted this way, pretending they hadn't heard anything and refusing to inform the person concerned. We were becoming like cockroaches, and we crawled under the weight of our frustration. I decided to work against this temptation by committing to memory the messages destined for others, making sure the next morning that they had all received them. But sometimes I could see that my attempts to help exasperated the very people they benefited, maybe because they did not want to owe anything to anyone. I didn't care. I wanted to break the vicious circles of our human stupidity.

And so one morning I decided to go up to Keith after I had heard a message in Spanish addressed to him. The Americans very rarely received any news from home. They listened to broadcasts on the shortwave from the United States, in particular the Voice of America, which sometimes recorded messages from their families and transmitted them over its Latin American service. This message was something different. I knew it was very important. The woman's voice announced that Keith had become the father of two little boys, Nicholas and Keith. My companion had also heard the message, but many of the words in Spanish were still unfamiliar to him. He seemed very happy and very worried at the same time. Finally he sat down, straddling one of the plastic chairs we had recently received, and confessed, "I feel trapped!"

Yes, I could understand. I was also trapped in my own obsession: My husband had not called, even for my birthday. In fact, he no longer called at all.

After the receptionist had left with our breakfast pans, I sought refuge on my bunk. I was going to celebrate one more year in a void. I lay down, trying to chase away any idea of celebration.

At midnight, that Christmas Eve, I awoke with a start. There was a flashlight right in my eyes — I was blinded. I couldn't see a thing. I heard laughter, someone counted to three, and I saw them all standing there next to my bunk, lined up like a choir. Then they started to sing. It was one of my favourite songs, by Trío Martino, "Noches de Bocagrande," with all the different voices, silences, and tremolos. "Nights of Bocagrande, / Beneath a silvery moon, / As the sea embroiders stars / On the thread of the shore, . . . / I'll swear my undying love, / As we swing in our hammocks."

How could I fail to adore them all, standing there in their shorts and T-shirts, with their hair rumpled and their eyes still full of sleep, nudging one another to call to order anyone singing off key. It was so ridiculous that it was magnificent. They were my new family.

Then there came a pounding on the wall from the soldiers' dormitory. "Shut up! Shit! Let us get some sleep around here!"

A moment later a guard showed up on the other side of the fence. "What the hell is going on? Are you crazy or what?"

No, we were simply being ourselves.

36

THE BICKERING

Clara had managed to turn everyone against her. Her behaviour upset those around us far more than it upset me, probably because the presence of others acted as a buffer between us. There was a huge fuss one morning because she had used the toilet and left it in an unspeakable mess. Orlando had summoned everyone to a meeting, to decide on "what action to take."

I had shrugged my shoulders. For me there was no "action to take" except that of cleaning it up. I'd lived with her long enough to know that trying to reason with her would be about as effective as banging one's head against the wall. And indeed, when they went to complain, Clara's response was to ignore them royally. One evening Clara snatched the communal radio from its nail and carried it over to her corner. Now and again one of us who was interested in a particular programme would go off with it for a few minutes. But in this case, she left the radio untuned, and all you could hear was the crackling of static. In the beginning nobody seemed to notice, and the noise was absorbed by our conversations. But once everyone was lying quietly in bed, this nuisance became unbearable. People gave signs of general unease, then more obvious impatience. Someone asked her to switch off the radio. A few minutes later, that person persisted and got no answer. Then we heard a loud noise, followed by the rough voice of Keith shouting, "The next time I catch you playing this game, I'll break that radio over your head."

He grabbed the radio out of her hands and turned it off. Then he put it back on the hook, and the chirring of the cicadas replaced the crackling sound.

It never happened again. I was reminded of my French teacher in my second year in high school, who told us that with some children from time to time the most appropriate response was a good smacking, because they were trying to get a reaction from authority that would help them regain control. I thought about it. In our enforced cohabitation, all my own parameters regarding people's behaviour were in a state of crisis. Instinctively I was against it. Nonetheless, I had to admit that the threat had worked in this case.

Lucho had concluded that hell was other people and he was considering asking Sombra if he could be locked up somewhere else on his own, away from the group. He told me that he had suffered a great deal from solitude, spending two years like a madman, talking to a dog, to trees, to ghosts. But that was nothing, he said, compared with the torture of this enforced communal life.

Each of us reacted unexpectedly toward the others. There was, for instance, the laundry affair. We did our washing by taking turns soaking our things overnight in plastic buckets that Mono Jojoy had sent us. A rumour went around that one of our companions was pissing in them, just to be nasty because he was jealous that he did not have a bucket of his own.

Another time we found the bathroom bench covered in excrement. The indignation was unanimous.

Each side that formed designated its culprit, chose a whipping boy. It provided an opportunity to vent. "I think it's So-and-So, who gets up at three o'clock in the morning to eat rotten food," or "So-and-So's mattress is full of cockroaches," or "So-and-So is getting dirtier and dirtier."

It was in this tense, defiant atmosphere that we started off the year. Clara came to speak to me one morning. I was stretched out on the ground between two bunk beds doing my abdominal exercises. I'd made a sort of curtain with the blanket Lucho had given me. She moved it aside and stood before me. Then she lifted up her T-shirt and showed me her belly. "What do you think?"

It was so obvious that it took me a moment to react. I swallowed my surprise before I replied that it was what she had wanted.

"Yes, and I'm very happy! How many weeks do you think I am?"

"I don't think it's just weeks, I think it's months. I think you must be near the fifth month."

"Right, I'll have to go talk to Sombra."

"Yes, you have to ask them to take you to a hospital. Ask to see that young doctor we saw in Andres's camp. He must be around here somewhere. Otherwise you'll at least need the help of a midwife."

"You're the first to know. Can I give you a hug?"

"Of course you can. I'm happy for you. It's the worst time and the worst place, but a child is always a blessing from above."

Clara sat down next to me and took my hand and said, "I'm going to call her Raquel."

"Fine. But think about some boys' names, too, just in case."

She remained thoughtful, staring into space. "I'll be a father and mother at the same time."

"The child has a father. You have to tell him."

"No! Never!"

She got up to go, took a step, and then turned around again. "Ingrid?"

"Yes."

"I'm afraid."

"Don't be afraid. Everything will be fine."

"Am I beautiful?"

"Yes, Clara, you're beautiful. A pregnant woman is always beautiful."

Clara went to make her announcement to the others. Their reception was cold. One of them came to see me. "How can you possibly tell her that this child is a blessing from heaven? You don't realize! Try to imagine what it will be like with the added screaming of a newborn child in this hell we're in!"

When our companions asked who the father was, Clara refused to discuss it, and this vagueness left them ill at ease. The men in the prison found her attitude threatening, because they suspected her of wanting to hide the guerrilla's identity in order to make them believe that the father could be one of them. Keith said they had a right to know who it was.

"It would be terrible if our families got wind of that and thought one of us could be the father."

"Don't worry," I replied. "No one is going to believe that you're the father. I'm sure that Clara will explain it's the child of one of the guards. But she doesn't have to give a name if she doesn't want to. She'll just have to confirm that the father isn't one of you."

My words did not calm him down. His personal history left him extremely touchy. He'd just had twins that he hadn't planned for, and he felt that if there were a scandal, the eyes of the entire world would be turned on him. He confronted Clara. He demanded that she reveal to him the name of the father, as a proof of her honest intentions.

"I don't give a shit about your family problems. I have my own to deal with," she said, to put a definite end to the discussion.

A few days later, in a confrontation with her over something unimportant, Keith exploded. "You're nothing but a slut! The whore of the jungle!"

Livid, Clara backed away. He ran after her, screaming insults at her. Lucho and Jorge restrained me, asking me to listen to them for once and not get involved. It was very distressing to watch. Clara tripped and reached out to plastic chairs to keep herself from falling in the mud. The next day everything was back to normal. Clara spoke with Keith as if nothing had happened. We had all learned the hard way: There was no point in bearing grudges. We were condemned to live together.

At that point Sombra took action. A guard came and ordered Clara to get her things together. Her belly had suddenly become enormous, and by the time she left the prison, she no longer tried to hide it.

For the rest of us, life went on as before, with a bit more room inside the prison. The news we heard on the radio became a topic of great debate. But there was very little information about us or about our families. Any measures taken that might eventually affect us were examined with a fine-tooth comb: a rise in the military budget, President Uribe's visit to the European Parliament, an increase in US aid for the war on drugs, the initiation of the Patriot Plan.* Each of us interpreted the news in light of our mood more than as the result of any rational analysis of the information.

I remained optimistic. Even when the news was bad, I looked for a glimmer of hope. I wanted to believe that those who were struggling on our behalf would find a way to get us out of there. My disposition irritated Lucho.

"Every day spent in this hole," he said, "increases exponentially our chances of staying here. The longer we are held captive, the more complicated our situation becomes. Everything is bad for us: If committees in Europe are active on our behalf, the FARC benefits from the exposure and sees no point in releasing us. But if the committees do nothing, we'll be forgotten and we'll spend ten more years locked up in the jungle."

During these debates I always found unexpected allies. Our American companions, just like me, looked for every possible reason to remain confident. They surprised me one day by explaining why, in their opinion, it was in Fidel Castro's interest to try to bring about our liberation, a hypothesis I endorsed. Other debates often turned sour. We were divided about the strategies to obtain our freedom. France had made our liberation a top priority in its agenda with Colombia, while the United States wanted to keep a low profile when it came to the American hostages, to avoid transforming them into trophies that the FARC would refuse to release. Uribe was waging a war against the FARC that excluded any negotiations for our freedom and counted on a military rescue. The discussions among us were fraught.

We would split up before the arguments disintegrated, in the hope that the next day another morsel of information might allow us to consolidate our beliefs and pick up where we'd left off the day before, with renewed ammunition. "He's as stubborn as a mule," we would say about the other person, to avoid being accused of the same fault.

We were all defending an attitude toward life, each in our own way, deploying a survival tactic. There were those who wanted to prepare for the worst and those, like me, who wanted to believe in the best.

---

* El Plan Patriota, a plan implemented by President Uribe to capture the leaders of FARC.

Eventually a feeling of harmony seemed to set in. Perhaps we'd learned to keep quiet, to let go of things, to wait. A desire to do things together returned. We dusted off some of the projects we'd set aside when confrontations had reached their peak. Marc and Consuelo spent all their time playing cards; Lucho and Orlando talked politics; I read for the twentieth time the copy of John Grisham's *Street Lawyer* that Tom had lent me as required reading for the English tuition he was giving me.

With Orlando we decided one morning to make some plastic mugs by cutting up the Quaker oatmeal containers we could get from the guards. Last Christmas in Andres's camp, Yiseth had made me one, and she'd shown me how. It was easy, but we had to borrow a machete to cut into the container and turn it inside out in order to make the handles for the cup.

Orlando obtained what we needed: the container and the machete. That was already quite a performance. We sat down at the big table outside in the courtyard. I was already sitting down, the container in my hand, the machete in the other, when we were startled by someone shouting behind us.

It was Tom, who was lying in his hammock and was suddenly overwhelmed by anger. I went on with my project, not realizing that in fact I was the object of his fury. I realized only when I saw Lucho arguing with him. Tom had lost his temper when he saw that the guard had lent me a machete, because he considered it a proof of favouritism. It was impossible to reason with him. In fact, he was delighted at the ruckus he'd stirred up. Sure enough, the prison gate opened. Two sturdy guards came in and took me by the arms. "Get your things together. You're leaving!" It happened so suddenly that all I had time to do was look at Lucho, in the hope of an explanation.

"They asked for you to be separated from the group," he said. "I didn't want to tell you about it. I didn't think they'd manage to do it."

I had no idea what was happening, particularly as all my companions got up one by one to hug me before I left.

37

THE CHICKEN RUN

March 2004. For a moment, when I heard the steel gates close behind me, I had a flash of hope: "And what if . . .?" I had my bundle over my shoulder and followed the guard along a muddy path that went around the camp. I could already picture myself in a boat, going upstream. But before we reached the river, the guard turned to the left, crossed a little bridge over a ditch, and made me go into the chicken run.

Behind the enclosure, in one corner there was a hut with a plastic roof. A woman came out. We were equally startled to see each other. It was Clara. "You'll be among friends," said the guard with a sneer. We looked at each other, not knowing what to say. We were not happy to see each other again, but perhaps deep down we were. There she was in her tiny hut, with just a bed and a little table. There was hardly any room. I didn't know what they wanted to do with me, and above all I did not want to disturb her in what was her space. She asked me to put my things down in a corner. Our spontaneous displays of politeness put us at ease and she seemed to become once more the Clara I'd known from before the jungle. I was very surprised to find her still here in the camp. I thought they'd taken her far away, where she would have access to hospital care. She had only one month left until her due date.

"I'm going to give birth here, on this bed," she said, inspecting the place for the hundredth time. "There's a girl who comes every day to massage my stomach. I think the baby is facing the wrong way."

Obviously, she was at risk. But what was the point of talking about it? The best thing would be to create a trusting environment, not to add anxiety to the long list of disturbing factors.

"I got the clothes you made for the baby. I love them. I'll keep them always – thank you!"

As she spoke, she brought out the bag with the things I'd sewn. There was a tiny sleeping bag, a little shirt with a round collar, mittens, matching booties, and – the thing I was proudest of – a kangaroo pouch so she could carry the baby with her hands free.

The sheet of pale blue gingham cloth I used had belonged to one of my companions. Lucho had helped me get it by bringing the wherewithal to barter. This cloth was an incredible godsend in the middle of the jungle. I had cut it out as best I could so as not to waste any, and from Orlando I had obtained the needle and thread I needed to get started. Finally I showed it to Gloria before sending it. She had given me some precious advice on how to get little buttons and zippers, and I'd finished it all with a decorative border scalloped in white thread. I had sent it to my companion through Arnoldo. I'd imagined that she was far away in a hospital in the middle of nowhere and that my package would take hours, by boat, to reach her.

We spent the rest of the day chatting, unaware of the passage of time. For me it was an opportunity to speak to her about her pregnancy and prepare her for what would follow. I told her it was important for her to talk to her baby before it was born. I tried to introduce her to the ideas of Françoise Dolto, because for me they had been fundamental. From memory I attempted to describe the clinical cases that had marked me the most when I read Dolto's books, the best illustration, in my opinion, of the importance of the bond of speech between mother and child. I also encouraged her to listen to music, to stimulate her baby's awareness of the outside world. And above all to be joyful.

The next day I saw her sit down to read out loud in the shadow of the big ceiba tree, caressing her protruding stomach, and felt I had accomplished something. That night, as on the previous one, I set up my hammock between one of the corner beams of the hut and a tree outside. Half of my body was outside, but it hadn't been raining for days, so there was a good chance I might spend a decent night. Clara came over to me, and somewhat formally she said, "I've been giving it a lot of thought: I would like you to be the child's godmother. If anything should happen to me, I would like you to look after it."

Her words caught me unawares. There was such a history between us. It was not a commitment to take lightly.

"Let me think about it. It's a decision that needs time to ripen, as it's an important one."

I thought about it all night long. If I accepted, I would be bound to her and to her child for life. But if I refused, it meant I was running away, and letting her down. Could I take on this role? Did I have enough love to give the child about to be born? Could I really adopt it, if the situation arose?

Early in the morning, I realized something: I was the only person who knew who the child's father was. Did that constitute a moral obligation?

"Well, have you decided?" she asked.

Silence fell upon us. I took a deep breath.

"Yes, I have. I accept."

She hugged me.

She was allowed fish soup for breakfast. She laughed as she told me that every day her receptionist went fishing for her on the order of the commander. The chicken run was, in fact, the solution that Sombra had devised to improve my companion's situation while avoiding accusations of favouritism. She still had no access to medical care, though, which was indispensable. I held on to the thought that they would call in the military nurse who was a part of the other group of prisoners.

I heard the sound of footsteps behind me. It was Sombra, furtively moving along behind the bushes, a hunting rifle over his shoulder. I waved to him.

"Shh!" he replied, looking around anxiously. "Don't tell anyone you saw me."

He moved away without giving me a chance to talk to him. A few minutes later, Shirley, a pretty girl who filled in as a nurse, appeared, equally stealthily. She came up to me and asked, "Have you seen Sombra?" When she realized I knew just what was going on, she added with a laugh, "I'm supposed to meet him, but if La Boyaca sees us together, she'll kill us!" She went away, delighted she'd found someone to confide in.

I stayed there, watching her leave, like some wild animal among the vegetation, and I wondered how they could live so carefree and at the same time work the strings to the drama of our lives.

I was lost in thought when I heard someone calling. I was startled and turned around: It was Lucho. He came over, his face lit up with a big smile. He was carrying a completely full backpack, while the guard trooped along behind him looking sullen.

"We had a fight over your departure, so I've been extradited, too!"

He sat down with Clara and me and gave us a detailed narration of the latest events inside the barracks.

"I don't want to go back to that prison," said Clara.

"Neither do I," said both Lucho and I in unison.

We burst out laughing, and then, more thoughtfully, Lucho concluded, "Here we are again, like in the beginning, just the three of us. Maybe it's better like this."

While we were chatting, a team of guerrillas came and energetically erected a hut identical to Clara's. In less than two hours, we all had a bed and a roof for the night. At the end of the afternoon, pretty Shirley came over; Sombra had sent her to inspect the premises. She'd just been appointed receptionist for the chicken run and as such was the only guerrilla authorized to come into the enclosure. She pouted as she looked at our hut.

"It's too dreary like this. Let me take care of it," she said, turning on her heel.

Ten minutes later she reappeared with a round table and two little wooden chairs. She made another trip and brought back some shelves. I was so happy that I gave her a hug. She had transformed our huts into veritable dolls' houses.

We sat down on our chairs, our elbows on the table, like old friends. It took Shirley ten minutes to tell me her life story and hours to relate her love affair with Sombra.

"How can you be with that ugly old potbellied guy?" I asked her. "Don't tell me that you, too, are a *ranguera*?"*

Shirley burst out laughing. "La Boyaca is a *ranguera*. She's got the big slice of the cake. I'm not entitled to anything. But I like the old guy. From time to time, he seems so lost it's touching. I like being with him."

"Wait, are you in love with him?"

"I think I am."

"And so . . . what about your *socio*?† Are you still together?"

"Yes, of course. He doesn't know anything!"

"He's a cute guy. Why are you cheating on him?"

"I'm cheating on him because he's too jealous."

"I think you're going too far."

"Well, you want to know the whole story? I saved old Sombra's life. It was during a bombardment. I found him with his head in the mud, collapsed on the ground. He was completely drunk. People were running past him, and no one was helping him. I put him over my shoulders and carried him. A minute later a bomb fell right where he'd been. Since then we've been good buddies. He likes me a lot, do you understand? He shows me a lot of tenderness, and he makes me laugh too."

We spent a good part of the night together. She had finished all her primary school, something she was very proud of, and she'd nearly made it to the secondary-school final exams. But then she fell in love with a guy who persuaded her to join the FARC. Shirley was an exception: As a rule, the guerrillas were poorly educated. Few of them knew how to read or write. When I asked her to explain the basis of her revolutionary commitment, she cleverly changed the subject. She became wary and kept her distance. Why had a girl like Shirley ended up in the FARC? She seemed to have a need for adventure, to live life to the fullest, that I hadn't found among her peers. The others had entered the ranks of subversion because they were hungry.

The next morning Shirley showed up early with a television in her

---

* Pejorative term the guerrillas use to designate a girl who sleeps with a commander for the perks associated with her "rank."
† Partner, a term used to designate a boyfriend.

arms. She put it on the table, plugged in a DVD player, and let us watch *Like Water for Chocolate*, based on Laura Esquivel's novel.

"I know this is the anniversary of your father's death," she said. "This will help take your mind off it."

It made me think of Mom, who had begged me several months before my abduction to go with her to the film. I had refused. I didn't have time. Now time was about *all* I had. I had no mom there with me, and I would never have my papa again. As I watched the film, I made myself two promises: If ever I got out of there, I would learn to cook for the people I loved. And I would have time, all my time, to devote to them.

Lucho was delighted to be in the chicken run. The absence of tension had restored his spirits. He took hold of a shovel to make *chontos* so large that they would last a month. At the end of it, he had huge blisters on his hands.

"I can't bear the thought of going back to that prison," he said.

"Hush. Don't even say it!"

As if echoing my fears, Shirley came to see me.

"Your fellow prisoners have been complaining because one of the guards told them that you have better living conditions than they do. They want you back."

I was speechless.

That night I had only just closed my eyes when I felt someone jump on me. Shirley, distraught, was shaking me vigorously.

"There are helicopters overhead. We have to leave right away. Take your things, and let's get out of here!"

I did as I was told. I pulled on my boots and grabbed my bundle. Shirley immediately took it from me.

"Follow close behind me," she said. "I'll carry your things. We'll go faster."

We headed into the darkness, with the helicopters just above our heads at the tops of the trees. How could I have slept and not heard them? They went back and forth along the river, making a hell of a racket. We arrived at the *economato*, a big shed with a zinc roof, surrounded by a thick fence, where bags of supplies were piled up to the ceiling.

Lucho and Clara were already there, anguish mingled with annoyance on their faces.

We were told to follow a line of guerrillas heading into the jungle.

"Do you think we're going to walk all night?"

"With them anything is possible!" said Lucho.

Shirley was walking ahead of us in silence. For a split second, the idea of suggesting she escape with us crossed my mind. But it was impossible – we had a pregnant woman with us. How could I even have thought of such a thing?

We would have to grin and bear it. After we'd walked for an hour, we stopped. They made us wait, sitting on our bundles, until dawn. At day-break the helicopters departed, and we were taken back to our chicken run.

After breakfast a team of guards appeared. In the space of fifteen minutes, they had dismantled our hut. We looked at each other with heavy hearts. We knew what this meant.

Clara took me by the arm. "I have a favour to ask you," she said.

"Yes, what can I do for you?"

"Don't tell anyone I'm here. Don't tell them we saw each other. I'd prefer they think that I've been taken to hospital. Do you understand?"

"Don't worry. I won't say anything. Neither will Lucho."

I embraced her before we parted, my heart aching.

38

BACK IN THE PRISON

March 24, 2004. Everything happened very quickly. On leaving the chicken run, I noticed Shirley as I went by: she wanted to reassure me, to tell me that everything would be fine.

When the steel gates of the prison creaked open, I felt that I was at the gates of hell again. I summoned all my courage and walked in. The morbid satisfaction on the face of one of my companions struck me like a blow.

"You didn't stay away long," he hissed viciously.

"I'm sure you missed us," answered Lucho curtly. "Maybe it was you who insisted we come back quickly?"

The man sniggered. "Well, we too have some influence."

His laugh turned sour when he saw that the guards were clearing a space next to the toilets. A plastic roof was set up. Shirley had sent along the little round table, the two chairs, and the shelf. In the courtyard of the prison, they were building a hut like the one in the chicken run.

Brian and Arnoldo were in charge of the operation. I looked on in silence. When they had finished their work, they picked up their tools and left.

Brian turned to me and spoke loudly, so that everyone could hear. "The commander doesn't want any more problems. You will sleep in here, and no one will bother you. If anyone behaves disrespectfully, you must call the receptionist."

I began to organize my little belongings so that I wouldn't have to face their angry gazes. I heard someone spit, "That's fine! Let her live in the smell of shit!"

I was mad at myself. Why did this still keep on hurting? I should have been immune to it by now. I felt an arm go around my shoulders. It was Gloria.

"Hey, come on. Don't start crying. Why give them the pleasure? Here, go on, I'll help you. You know, I'm very sad for your sake that they made you come back. But I'm so happy for my own – I missed you! And then, without Lucho, there was no more laughter in this prison!"

Jorge came over, as courteous as ever. He kissed my hand and used a few words of French that he had learned to welcome me. Then he added, "Now I don't know where to hang my hammock. I hope you'll invite us *chez toi, madame chérie.*"

Marc came over, shyly. He and I had only rarely spoken, and always in English. I'd often observed him, because he always stood apart from the group, and he was the only one among us all who had never got into a dispute with anybody. I'd also noticed that his two companions respected him and listened to him. The other two were always arguing, going from a spiteful silence where they ignored each other ferociously to verbal explosions that were short but harsh. Marc was the go-between, smoothing the edges. I could tell he wanted to keep at a distance, particularly from me. I had no difficulty imagining what he might have heard, and I hoped that over time he might change his attitude.

So I was surprised to see him standing there, unmoving, while we were cheerfully chatting away – Lucho, Jorge, Gloria, and me. Everyone's gestures were very calculated in the prison; none of them wanted to look as if they might be begging for anything or expecting anything, because that would have placed them in an inferior position. Yet there he was, waiting for the right moment to step in and join our conversation. We all turned around. He gave a faint, sad smile and said in his hesitant Spanish, where all the verbs were still in the infinitive, that he was happy to see us again, Lucho and me.

I was deeply touched, but caught in an inexplicable rush of emotion, I was unable to mutter anything more than a perfunctory thanks. In a way his gesture reminded me too cruelly of the others' animosity, and I was feeling sorry for myself. I was too vulnerable, and I felt ridiculous. In hell you don't have the right to show that you're in pain.

"Hey, I must be dreaming – you've started speaking Spanish! I leave for just three weeks, and before you know it . . . !" Lucho had just decided to count him in.

Everyone laughed, because Marc answered right back without missing a beat, in his fractured Spanish. He would translate American expressions literally, and to our delight they were miraculously just as caustic in Spanish. Then he politely took his leave and went back to the barracks.

The next morning something unexpected happened. The prisoners in the soldiers' barracks sent us a box of books. I found out that when they had been held in the demilitarized zone, during the negotiations with the Pastrana government, the hostages' families had managed to send them entire libraries. When the peace process failed and they were forced to flee from the army, they all took one or two books in their backpacks and exchanged the books among themselves. The march was very trying, and some of them, exhausted by the weight, had had to remove anything heavy or less important from their backpacks. So the books were first to go. The ones that now came to us were those that had survived. They were real treasures. There was a bit of everything – novels, classics, psychology books, Holocaust memoirs, philosophical essays, spiritual books, esoteric manuals, stories for children. They gave us two weeks to read them, and after that we would have to send them back.

It changed our lives. We were all off on our own, devouring as many books as possible. I began with *Crime and Punishment*, which no one else seemed to want, while Lucho was reading *The Mother* by Maxim Gorky.

I later discovered that someone had Maurice Druon's *Iron King*, and Gloria and I put ourselves on the waiting list to have a chance to read it before the deadline. To ensure that the books would rotate more quickly, we suggested making a shelf behind the door to the barracks so that they could be placed there when their readers weren't using them.

That enabled us to leaf through most of them and set our own priorities. There were some books that would be impossible to read, because everyone was waiting for them. I remember in particular *The Dark Bride* by Laura Restrepo, and *El Alcaraván* by Castro Caycedo. But the one I really wanted to read, and couldn't even get near, was *The Feast of the Goat* by Mario Vargas Llosa.

One morning Arnoldo came and took them all. It was a few days before the deadline. One of our companions, on a whim, had wanted to send them all back beforehand, without telling the others. I was particularly frustrated and felt betrayed by this fellow inmate.

I talked about it with Orlando, who had got into the habit of coming to chat with Lucho and me in the evening after lights-out. Orlando was very good at wheedling information from the guards. He was, in fact, the best informed among us. He noticed what the rest of us missed.

I had begun to feel affection for him because I'd realized that beneath his oafish manner he had a big heart, something he showed only at certain moments, as if he were embarrassed to. But it was above all his sense of humour that we enjoyed. When he sat down at the little round table to listen to the radio with us, Lucho and I knew that we were in for some serious banter, and we waited, enchanted, for him to shoot his first arrows.

He never indulged us, but he gave such a bald description of our situation, of our attitudes and failings, that we could only laugh and concede that he was right.

Some of our fellow inmates were sceptical about our friendship with Orlando. They didn't trust him and were ready to accuse him of every flaw on earth. Some came to warn me and put me on my guard against Orlando.

But I didn't want to listen to those kinds of remarks any more. We each had our own views. I wanted to give everyone the benefit of the doubt and reach my own conclusions.

Our return to the prison had obliged me to take stock. I looked at myself in the mirror of other people and saw there all the defects of humanity – hatred, jealousy, greed, envy, selfishness. But it was in myself that I observed them. I'd been shocked to realize this, and I did not like who I had become.

When I listened to remarks and criticism attacking others, I kept quiet. I, too, had run up to the stewpot in the hope of having a better piece. I, too, had waited on purpose for the others to help themselves in order to land right on the biggest *cancharina*. I, too, had envied a nicer pair of socks or a bigger bowl. And I, too, had stockpiled supplies of food to assuage my greed.

One day Gloria's supplies of canned food exploded. The cans were too old, and the temperature had risen too high. Everyone made fun of her. Most of the others were delighted that she had lost what they had already eaten while she patiently put her ration to one side. We were all alike, entangled in our ugly little pettiness.

I decided to monitor myself, to avoid doing the same. It was an ordeal. Sometimes my reason would pull one way, my guts the other. I was hungry. I ended up doing just the opposite of what my good resolutions dictated. My only solace was that I'd become aware of it.

I observed with consternation our behaviour toward our own families, in particular the scathing criticism and nasty comments that some of my companions made about their family members. In our prisoner psychology, there was a masochistic tendency to imagine that those who were struggling to have us released were doing it for opportunistic reasons. We could not believe that we were still worthy of their love.

I refused to accept that our life partners had turned our dramatic situation into a means of subsistence. The men suffered to think that their wives were spending their salaries. We women lived in fear that upon our return we might not find our home. My husband's prolonged silence prompted painful jibes. "He only calls you when there are journalists around," they would tell me.

Orlando's attitude changed as well. He became gentler, tried harder to make himself useful. He was very good at finding rapid solutions to little problems. When I told Orlando how frustrated I had been because they took the books away so quickly, he reassured me, "I have friends in the other camp. I'll ask them to send us some more books. I think they have the whole Harry Potter series."

The books arrived while I was in the washroom. They had all been handed out and the Harry Potter books were the first to go. Marc was reading *Harry Potter and the Chamber of Secrets*. I couldn't resist the temptation to go and look at the cover of the book. He smiled when he saw how excited I was. I was ashamed, and I tried not to linger too long with the book in my hands.

"Don't worry, I'm impatient to read it, too."

"I find it moving, because these were the first books Lorenzo, my son, ever read! I think it makes me feel closer to him," I said, to excuse myself. "And it's true I did devour volume one," I finally confessed.

"Well, for me it's my first book in Spanish! There are a lot of hard words, but already I can't put it down . . . Listen, if you want, we can read it at the same time: I'll read it in the morning, I'll hand it to you at noon, and you give it back to me in the evening."

"Really, would you do that?"

"Of course, but there's one condition."

I waited silently.

"You put it on my shelf at six o'clock sharp. I don't want to have to ask you for it every day."

"You're on."

39

RADIO ROUND-UP

April 2004. Our arrangement delighted me. I programmed my days so that I could devote every afternoon to reading, and I was particularly careful to leave the book at six o'clock sharp on his shelf. I had learned that we judged one another on these tiny details and, what's more, that it was on such a basis that friendships were built or conflicts ignited. The lack of privacy exposed us to other people's constant scrutiny. To be sure, we were watched over by the guards, but above all we were subject to our fellow captives' merciless surveillance.

If I'd been even one minute late, I knew that Marc would have sought me out with his gaze in the courtyard to find out why I was late. If the reason were trivial, he would have been offended and things would have got tense between us. We all worked this way. On the dot of noon, I would look up. I'd had time to do my gymnastics and wash up, and I waited impatiently for him to come out of the barracks with the book. This was a truly gratifying moment: For a few hours, I would plunge myself into the world of Hogwarts and I could escape, far from this enclosure and its barbed wire, its watchtowers, and its mud; I could return to the light-heartedness of my childhood. But my escape was making people jealous. I sensed that some of them would have liked to grab the book from my hands. I knew I could afford no false move.

One afternoon the guards arrived with the television that Shirley had brought to us in the chicken run. We were all very eager to see a film. But there was nothing at all relaxing about what they showed us – it was our three American companions' proof of life, recorded months before their arrival in our prison. The audience was moved on hearing their messages and the ones that their families had recorded in response, now part of a television programme that had been shown in the United States a few months earlier. To begin with, our companions were glued to the screen, as if it might have allowed them to climb into the picture and touch the people they loved. Gradually they sat farther back in their chairs, as if so much closeness were burning them. We stood behind them, painfully observing the families on television who, like our own, were racked with pain and anxiety. But above all I examined my companions, the way they reacted, as if they were being flayed alive on a public square.

There was something indecent about being there, watching the nakedness of their distress. But I was unable to tear myself away, fascinated by a spectacle of collective hara-kiri that reminded me of what I myself was going through.

I had at last put faces to the names of these strangers, who by now had become familiar, since I'd heard about them so often. I tracked their expressions on television, their gazes as they looked away from the camera, the trembling of their lips, their words – which were always revealing. I had been floored by the power of the image and the idea that we are all so predictable. I saw them for only two seconds, yet I felt as if I knew them intimately. They had all betrayed themselves; in front of the camera, none of us can mask the good and bad in our emotions. I was embarrassed, but there it was; we no longer had any right to privacy.

I observed my companions. The three of them behaved and reacted in ways that were utterly different from one another. One gave a running commentary on each image and would turn around to make sure the group had followed his explanations. He did say one thing that no one could fail to hear, while talking about his fiancée: "I know, she's not very pretty, but she's intelligent." Everyone stared at him. He blushed, and I could sense it wasn't because he was sorry about what he'd said. Sure enough, he went on to say, "I gave her a ring that cost ten thousand dollars."

Another was crouching off to one side, compulsively rubbing the stubble on his chin. His huge blue eyes filled with tears, and he said over and over in a low voice, "God, how could I have been such a jerk!" He aged a hundred years in a second. It was unbearable to witness his pain; his words were the same I heard in myself, because, like him, I bore a cross made of regrets. I thought to go and hug him. But I couldn't. For a long time now, we hadn't been speaking.

Marc was standing next to me. I didn't dare look over at him, because I thought it wouldn't be very tactful. I sensed he was motionless. And yet when the broadcast was over and I turned around to go out of the barracks, his expression stopped me in my tracks. He appeared in the grip of an inner anguish. He was staring into space, his head slumped forward, his breathing ragged, and he couldn't move, as if he'd had the sudden onset of a disease so powerful that it had swollen his joints and crushed his heart. I took no time to think, to debate with myself whether my gesture would be appropriate or not. I saw myself taking him in my arms, as if I might be able to break the curse under which he'd been placed. He burst into tears and tried to stem them by pinching the bridge of his nose and saying, over and over, hiding his face against me, "I'm okay, I'm okay."

He had to be okay. We had no choice.

A few hours later, he came to thank me. This was surprising, because I had taken him for a cold man, perhaps even insensitive. He had a great deal of self-control and often gave the impression of being elsewhere. Now that I saw him in a new light, I was intrigued and wanted to understand who he was.

From time to time, he came at dusk to talk with Lucho, Orlando, and me, and he made us laugh with his Spanish, which was getting better by the day but not necessarily with the most appropriate of words. He asked little favours of me, and I asked some of him. He had begun to embroider the names of his wife and children on his camouflage jacket. He was obsessed by his work and spent all day filling in with black thread the letters he had carefully outlined on the canvas. It looked as if he was not making much headway. I wanted to see what he was doing, and I was surprised at how perfect his work was.

One morning when I was trying to wear my body out by going up and down the stepladder, I heard his American companions congratulate him on his birthday. I thought that everyone else had heard, too, like me. But no one else greeted him. We had grown hard, probably in our efforts to isolate ourselves from everything so that living would be less painful. I decided to go up to him anyway. My initiative surprised and pleased him, and I thought we'd become friends.

Until the day Sombra ordered a raid on our radios. We were all caught unawares, except for Orlando, who had got wind of what was being said in the soldiers' barracks. He had stood with his ear up against the boards opposite their hut and heard that there was a general confiscation under way. He went around to all our fellow inmates and warned us one by one what to expect.

My blood drained away. Lucho was as pale as I was. If we gave them our radios, we would be cut off from our families for good.

"You give them yours, and I'll hide mine."

"Ingrid, you're out of your mind. They will realize."

"No. They've never seen mine. We always use yours, because that's the one they remember."

"But they know you have one."

"I'll tell them I threw it away a long time ago because it broke."

Arnoldo came charging into the enclosure with four of his acolytes. I just managed to throw my little radio, the one that Joaquín Gómez had given to me, under the floor of the washroom and to sit back down, looking as natural as possible. I was trembling. Lucho was green, beads of sweat forming on his brow. There was no going back.

"They'll catch us," he said again, anxiously.

Arnoldo stopped in the middle of the courtyard, while the four other guards sealed the premises.

There was nothing more important to a prisoner than his or her radio set. It was everything — the voice of family, the window on the world, the evening entertainment, a remedy for insomnia, something to fill our solitude. I watched as my companions put their radios in Arnoldo's hands. Lucho put his little black Sony down and grumbled, "It's out of batteries."

Moments like this alone were reason to adore him. He restored my strength.

Arnoldo counted the radios and declared, "There's one missing." Then, looking at me, he barked, "Yours."

"I don't have one."

"Yes you do."

"I don't have it any more."

"What do you mean?"

"It wasn't working."

He stared at me.

"I threw it out."

Arnoldo raised an eyebrow and looked closely at me. It felt as if he were counting every fold in my intestines. "Are you sure?"

Mom had always said that she was incapable of lying and that you could read it on her face. I had believed that it was a sort of providential flaw that obliged us, genetically, to be honest. At times it was so extreme that I blushed when telling the truth, just at the idea that anyone might think I was lying, and consequently it was not infrequent that I would think I had to practise lying to be able to tell the truth without turning red. In my civilian life, I could get away with it. But here I knew I was going to have to look him in the eye. I must not look away. The time had come when I had to learn to lie for a good cause. And that was what saved me. I was the only one who had hidden my radio. I did not have the right to lose my nerve.

"Yes, I'm sure," I said, holding his gaze.

He said no more about it. He picked up his pile of radios and batteries and went away satisfied.

I stood there petrified, unable to take a step, leaning on the table, within an inch of collapsing on the ground, soaked in a sickly outbreak of sweat.

"Lucho, could you tell I was lying?"

"No, nobody saw a thing. Please, talk normally, they're all looking at you from the watchtowers. Let's go sit at the little round table."

He held me by the waist and helped me take the few steps over to the little chairs, as if we were having a chat.

"Lucho?"

"What?"

"I feel like my heart is going to leap out of my body."

"Yes, and I'll run after it!" He burst out laughing and added, "Okay, now we're in a fine fix. You have to be prepared that one of these dog lovers might let the cat out of the bag. They'll make mincemeat of us if one of them betrays us."

It felt as if death were stroking my spine. At any moment the guards could come to search my hut. I changed the radio's hiding place a thousand times. Orlando, who was on the lookout, blocked me at the entrance to the barracks.

"You kept your radio, didn't you?"

"No, I didn't keep a thing."

I had answered instinctively. Alan Jara's words were resonating in my head: *Don't trust anyone.*

Lucho came to see me. "Jorge and Gloria have been wondering if we kept the radio."

"What did you tell them?"

"I didn't answer, I left."

"Orlando asked me the same thing. I said no."

"If we're going to listen to it, we'll have to wait a few days. Everyone is on the lookout, it's too risky."

Just then Gloria and Jorge came over.

"We have to talk to you. There's a terrible atmosphere in the barracks. The others have realized that you didn't hand in one of the radios, and they're going to denounce you."

The next morning Marc called out to Lucho. I could easily imagine the subject of their conversation, simply by the solemn manner they suddenly adopted. When Lucho returned, he was as nervous as I'd ever seen him.

"Listen, we have to get rid of the radio. They've found a monstrous way to blackmail us: Either we give them the radio or they turn us in. We have to meet in the barracks in ten minutes."

When we arrived at the barracks, the chairs had already been set out in a semicircle and I really felt as if I were in the dock. I knew I was going to have a hard time, but I was determined not to give in to their blackmail.

Orlando opened the discussion. I was surprised by his calm and kindly tone.

"Ingrid, we believe that you kept a radio. If that is so, we would like to have the possibility to listen to the news, too, especially the messages from our families."

This changed everything! It became clear that this would be the ideal solution. If there were no threats, no blackmail, if we could trust each other . . . I was thinking on my feet: It could also be a trap. Once I agreed to say that I had indeed hidden the radio, they could go and squeal on me. "Orlando, I wish I could answer you. But I can't talk openly. We all know that in our midst there are companions who are informers in the service of the guerrillas."

I looked at my companions' faces, one by one. Some of them looked down. Lucho, Gloria, and Jorge were nodding. I continued.

"Every time we have tried to do something as a group, one of us has gone to alert the guerrillas, like the day we wanted to write a letter to the commanders or the time we talked about going on a hunger strike. In our midst there are some *sapos*.* What guarantee do we have that anything said in this meeting won't be relayed to Sombra in the next half hour?"

My companions were staring at the ground, theirs jaws clenched. I went on.

"Let's just suppose one of us did keep a radio. What guarantee do we have that there won't be another search and that someone won't snitch?"

Consuelo was stirring on her chair. She said, "That may be true – there are surely some *sapos* here, but I would like to insist right away that it's not me."

I turned to look at her.

"You handed in your radio, you gave it to Arnoldo, you have nothing to worry about. But if ever one of us had a radio that you could use to get

---

* Literally, toads, but in the slang of young Colombians and schoolkids, a *sapo* is a snitch.

messages from your daughters and there was a search, would you be prepared to take responsibility, collectively, for the hidden radio?"

"No! Why should I have to take responsibility! I didn't hide it!"

"Let's suppose that during this hypothetical search the radio was confiscated for good. Would you be prepared to give yours, if they give it back
to you, in replacement for the one that was taken away?"

"Why me? No, it's out of the question! Why should I have to pay for
other people's stupidity?"

"Okay, I just wanted to illustrate how 'everybody' wants to make the
most of a hidden radio but nobody is prepared to take any risks. And that's
just the point: If you want a radio, you have to be willing to share the risk."

"We don't have to play your game," Keith exploded. "You're a politician,
and you think you can fool us with your fine speeches. We asked you one
question, we want one answer: Yes or no, have you got a radio hidden in
your *caleta*?"

His words stung me. I would have liked to find an outlet for the blood
that was boiling inside me. I asked Lucho to hand me a cigarette. It was the
first cigarette I'd ever smoked in captivity. Never mind, I wanted to remain
calm, and I thought that if I inhaled the smoke that was scraping my
throat, I might be able to keep my self-control. I snapped shut like a clam
and answered, "Deal with it yourselves. I'm not about to submit to your
pressure, your insults, and your cynicism."

"Ingrid, it's very simple: Either you give us the radio or I swear to you I
will go and denounce you this very minute." Keith was on his feet, threatening me, waving his finger in my face.

I got up, trembling, livid. "You don't know me. I have never given in to
blackmail. For me it's a question of principle. You didn't have the courage
to hide your radio, so don't come lecturing me. Go right ahead, tell the
guerrillas whatever you like. I have nothing more to say to you."

"Hey, we're out of here," Keith said, rallying his troops. "Let's go talk to
Arnoldo right away."

Marc got to his feet, looking at me with hostility. "Too bad, you asked for it."

I answered him in English. "What are you talking about! You didn't
understand a thing — you don't speak Spanish!"

"You're treating us like fools. That's enough for me."

If they were going to turn us in, I had to be ready. Lucho was as pale as I was; Jorge and Gloria were worried. "We warned you, they're monsters," said Gloria. "What are you going to do now?"

Before I was able to leave the barracks, Orlando got up and blocked my way, grabbing Keith by the arm.

"Stop it. Don't do anything stupid. If you report her, no one will get any news about anything!" Turning to me, he said, "Don't go out. Come with me. Let's go talk."

He led me to the other end of the barracks, and we sat down.

"Listen, I can understand why you're worried. And you're right. Someone here is going to tell the guerrillas everything. Except that this jerk, whoever he might be, needs you just now, because you're the only one who can give him access to his messages. That's it. No one can betray you, I guarantee. I'll offer you an agreement: In the morning I'll come and get the radio. I'll listen to the messages for everybody, and I'll inform the group. I'll bring the radio back at seven o'clock in the morning, after the programme with the messages and the news bulletins. If we have the slightest problem with the guerrillas, I'll take responsibility for everything together with you. Does that suit you?"

"Yes, that suits me."

"Thanks," he said, shaking my hand and giving me a big smile. "Now I have to go and convince those guys."

I told Lucho what we had agreed. He didn't seem pleased. "Sure – the least little hitch and all hell will break loose."

Gloria and Jorge didn't seem too pleased, either. "Why is it Orlando who gets to listen to our messages, and not us?"

I realized that it would be impossible to try to meet everybody's expectations. However, I thought that Orlando's suggestion at least had the advantage of easing the situation. I looked outside. Keith, Orlando, and the others were sitting around the big table. Keith was ranting.

"It's out of the question! Let's give her two hours to turn over the radio. If it's not in my hands at twelve o'clock sharp, I'll tell the receptionist!" To prepare for a possible search, I went to find a better hiding place for the radio under the floor of the washroom. I figured that if someone ratted on me, the guerrillas would concentrate their search on my belongings. Noon came, and no one got up. The day went by slowly, filled with tension, and fortunately there were neither reprisals nor suspicious movements among the guards. I breathed a sigh of relief, and Lucho did, too.

Orlando arrived at nightfall and went to sit at the little table between Lucho and me, as always.

"We have to find some headphones," he said. "Otherwise we might get caught."

"The reception on the radio is terrible," I said. "I think we're going to have to make an antenna, or we'll have been through all this for nothing. Right now even the headphones would serve no purpose."

"Well, are you going to bring out your radio or not?"

"Don't even think about it. It's not a good time."

"Yes it is. Lucho and I can carry on a normal conversation. Our voices will cover the radio. You stick it up next to your ear, put the volume on low, and we can test it to see what we need."

In the days that followed, we concentrated on improving the quality of the reception, doing what was necessary to arouse no suspicion. By now it was clear that my companions were not going to carry out their threat. The general belief was that their blackmail had been disgraceful. I was sorry that once again our quarrels had created permanent barriers between us.

In spite of everything, we set up a new routine. We would listen to the radio every evening and share all the information we had. Orlando devised a ground antenna by sticking an old battery in the mud, wrapped with wire as thick as the mesh of the fence and connected to a metal wire that was plugged into the jack for the radio headphones. The effect was astonishing: The volume and sharpness of the reception were now almost perfect. In the morning the connection had to be changed and the radio plugged into an aluminium wire that acted as an aerial antenna, a wire so thin that it became almost invisible, wound in the branches of one of the trees in the courtyard. At dawn, starting at four in the morning, the reception was excellent, but very quickly it would decline, and it became absolutely useless by eight in the morning.

There were only two times of day when it was easy to listen – at dusk and at dawn. Orlando waited impatiently for me first thing each morning, already on his feet in the barracks. We had finally worked out a procedure whereby I would listen to the messages until Mom had been on the air and then Orlando would take over.

For years Mom called in only on weekends, on Herbin Hoyos's programme that transmitted messages for hostages all night long, from Saturday evening to Sunday morning. She had just discovered *La Carrilera*, hosted by Nelson Moreno, a warm anchorman from the Valle del Cauca, which was broadcast every day of the week, from five to six in the morning. She'd become the most faithful participant, and she made it her duty to be on time, calling before dawn, to be the first to be aired.

This suited everybody, because when I handed over the radio to Orlando, the messages for our other companions had not yet been broadcast. Clara and our foreign companions received hardly any. So those of us who waited for our messages every day arranged to rotate the radio, taking turns listening to a part of the programme. In the long run, this made everyone feel more relaxed, since obviously we were all bound by the same secret.

Orlando came to see me one morning. He wanted to know if he could lend the radio to our fellow hostages. They wanted to listen to the news.

"Go ahead. Just make sure they don't give it to Arnoldo," I said wryly.

No sooner had I finished speaking than I was biting my lip. The wound had not healed; I still bore a grudge against them. Even less honourable was the sense that I would find it easier to forgive those who kept me locked up in prison – because in a way I expected nothing from them – than to forgive my own fellow captives, my comrades in misfortune, because I had always hoped for something better from them.

Once again we were divided in the camp, more intensely than ever. But I no longer felt isolated and, I no longer wanted to be. We went on with our French lessons, we played cards, and every evening we reinvented the world. I listened religiously to the news as soon as it was lights-out, and my companions took over from me for part of the evening. When a certain report or commentary drew our attention, we informed the others, and the topic of conversation immediately changed so that we could all debate the latest piece of news.

40

GLORIA'S CHILDREN

July 13, 2004. One evening I was listening somewhat distractedly to the radio, trying at the same time to follow the conversation between Lucho and Orlando, when my heart skipped a beat: They had just mentioned Jaime Felipe and Juan Sebastian, Gloria's children. I moved away and crouched down in the corner of my hut, cupping my hands over my ears. I wanted to be sure I heard properly. Gloria's children had been kidnapped at the same time as their mother. The guerrillas had stormed their building and forced everyone out in the street in pyjamas. Her youngest son, who hadn't woken up, had been spared during the raid, as had his father, who was away travelling. The guerrillas were demanding an outrageous ransom for their release. The father, thinking it was for the best, managed to get his wife elected, in absentia, as the local deputy for their department. At that time the general impression was that so-called political prisoners had a greater chance of getting out than the economic prisoners, above all more quickly, because the guerrillas had entered into peace talks with the Colombian government and a demilitarized zone had been allocated to the FARC. It turned out to have been the wrong move when the peace process failed. Gloria was separated from her children. The guerrillas had made her believe she would see them the next day, but she'd never seen them again. During all these months of cohabitation, I had held Gloria in my arms hundreds of times to comfort her, because the thought that her children were in the hands of the FARC drove her insane. We prayed together every day. She was the one who had explained to me how to use the rosary correctly, with the stations and devotions for each day.

She was a great woman with a big heart and a strong character, who didn't let others step on her feet and who knew how to put people in their place. I had seen her hold her own, even though some of our companions mistreated her. She refused to backpedal, even if I saw her weeping with rage afterwards, hiding up on her bunk.

Now the newscaster repeated the headlines. In fact, it was the top news on all the stations: Gloria's children had just been liberated. Their father was already with them. They'd been let go in San Vicente del Caguán, the place where I was headed when Clara and I were taken hostage.

My heart was racing. The journalist announced that the children would make their first statements to the press in just a few minutes. I ran into the barracks to find her. Lucho and Orlando were looking at me as if I'd gone mad. Trying to explain to them why I was so agitated, all I managed to say to them was "Gloria! Gloria!" while waving my hands frenetically, getting them into a panic as well.

"What about Gloria? Tell us! Speak, for Christ's sake!"

It was impossible to say anything more. I set off, stumbling, trying to adjust my sandals on the way, nearly falling over with each step. Gloria was sitting in the dark, and I didn't see her. I burst in, breathless, the radio hidden under my T-shirt.

She came up to me, alarmed. "What's going on?"

I put my arm around her neck and whispered into her ear, "The children, the children – they've released them."

She cried out, and I reached to stifle her cry with both hands, weeping like her, trying like her not to attract attention with our wild display of emotion. Dragging her over to the darkest corner in the barracks, I pressed the radio up to her ear. And there, huddled together in the dark, clinging to each other, we listened to her children, mindless of our fingernails painfully digging so hard into each other's skin that we bled. I was still crying, even though she had stopped, transformed by the joy of hearing their voices and the loving words they'd prepared especially for her. I stroked her hair and said, "It's over. It's all over."

We followed the children's voices on all the stations until there was nothing more. Gloria was transformed. She took me by the arm and leaned close to me to say, "I can't look too happy. I'm not supposed to know anything! Oh, my God, what if they come to tell me tomorrow? How am I going to hide my feelings!"

I kissed her before going back into my hut and warned her not to arouse the guards' curiosity.

"Wait, you've forgotten the radio."

"You're going to need to listen to it all night. They'll probably keep rebroadcasting the children's interviews, and tomorrow morning you'll have their messages on *La Carrilera*. Keep it." Strangely enough, while some of us were happy for her, others seemed dejected. In our world, one person's suffering could bring relief to another, by making him feel that his own fate was better. Likewise, another's joy could be just as unbearable.

The next day it was Guillermo the nurse who came to announce the news. Gloria did her best to look surprised. But more than anything she was relieved to be able to talk openly about the event and to express her joy unrestrainedly.

41

THE PETTY THINGS OF HELL

After the release of her children, Gloria became the target of petty little attacks. They made fun of her or imitated her in a rude way when her back was turned; they criticized her for smoking too much. Cigarettes came intermittently, and each of us was given a pack to do with as we liked. We nonsmokers gave our rations to the smokers. Or at least that's the way it was in the beginning. Gradually the attitude changed, and I noticed that there were nonsmokers who were keeping their cigarettes to barter for things from the guards or to obtain favours from fellow inmates. I found this repellent, and as soon as the packs were handed out, I gave mine to Gloria and Lucho. They were the ones who smoked the most.

One day one of our companions had the bright idea of asking the guerrillas *not* to give cigarettes to nonsmokers. He felt there was favouritism going on if some people had a double ration thanks to the others. Clearly, Gloria and Lucho were being targeted. The receptionist adopted their suggestion right away – the extra packs would be for him! When it was time for the next distribution, he asked that only the smokers come up. I demanded my pack, and he was about to refuse, so I had to smoke there in front of him to get it. He threatened me with reprisals if ever I tried to fool him. So with Gloria and Lucho, we agreed that from time to time I would smoke a cigarette very ostentatiously to avoid any controversy. The end result was ironic: After several weeks had gone by, I was smoking as much as they were. Instead of being a source of cigarettes, I had become a burdensome rival.

Likewise, some were jealous of the canned food that Lucho received for his diabetes. A bite of tuna fish was a luxury. Lucho had committed to sharing every can he opened with one of our companions in turn, so that we all could have some from time to time. He favoured Jorge, who was sick, and he never forgot me. Some were outraged by this; they would emerge from the barracks, fuming, when Lucho opened his nail clippers to attack his can of tuna.

Their attitude contrasted greatly with that of Marc's. During the final months of our stay in Sombra's prison, probably in anticipation of a planned departure – for the Plan Patriota was already under way – a series of chickens were slaughtered. The guerrillas brought the pot to us with the bird hacked in pieces, on top of the rice or floating in a suspicious-looking broth, head and feet included, curled up and sticking out of the pot. It was a repellent sight, especially as in general the neck had not been plucked properly and the bird's eye was wide open, taken by surprise when the sudden blow of death came. Still, this was like a banquet for us, and we all lined up to get our share. The strange thing was that Marc invariably ended up with the chicken head and neck. In the beginning no one paid it any attention. But because it happened so regularly, we began to place bets. Whether he stood at the front of the line or at the end, whether it was Arnoldo or someone else serving, Marc always got the head, with its quivering purple crest and staring eyes. He would look at his plate, incredulous, then sigh and say, "I always get it," and sit down. I admired his resignation and thought there was something noble about his detachment. I knew that all the others, myself included, tried to seek compensation wherever we could.

This realization helped to quell my animosity toward him. I had deeply resented the radio business and kept away from him afterwards. But I no longer wanted to nurture any feelings that might burden my existence.

When I heard in one of Mom's messages that Marc's mother was in Bogotá and that she would be trying to send him messages during the week, I put my resentment aside. For me information like this was sacred.

Every effort must be made so that he could hear his mother's voice. And I also thought that there were situations in life that made you come face-to-face with yourself, that were nods from fate: Without my radio, Marc wouldn't have known that she had come all the way to Colombia to fight for him.

When I gave him the news, he made no comment, but he took the radio after all the others had had their messages. And indeed the broadcaster mentioned Jo Rosano's presence. She hoped to speak with the authorities and in particular with the United States ambassador to Colombia. She felt that her son had been abandoned by her government, which was doing its best, she said, to consign him to oblivion. Marc was embarrassed by her declarations. He believed that the American authorities were working discreetly to obtain his release. However, the signs that were getting through to us were not favourable. The United States government had reaffirmed its refusal to deal with the terrorists; its response to the abduction of its citizens had been to increase military aid to Colombia. When they had first been abducted, I'd hoped that their presence would accelerate the release of all the hostages, as Joaquín Gómez had suggested. I'd reacted the same way my companions had when I myself had been kidnapped. But over time we had to face the facts: Their capture had made the hostage situation even more complicated. We all suspected that they would be the last ones to regain their freedom, and each of us liked to think that our fate was in no way connected to theirs. This idea had taken hold. From time to time, one of my American companions would say, "At least you've got France fighting for you. But nobody back home even knows what has happened to us."

Jo Rosano's visit to Colombia gave them courage. Everyone agreed that she was the only one moving things forward on the side of the Americans. My mother and Jo Rosano had met, immediately falling into each other's arms. Somehow or other they managed to make themselves understood, because Jo didn't speak Spanish and Mom's English was a distant memory from a stay in Washington with Papa at the very beginning of their marriage. But they were both of Italian origin, and that helped.

Marc came during the week, at dawn, and we sat down together to listen to the messages on *La Carrilera*, hoping to hear Jo, to no avail. What little information we had came from Mom – they'd had lunch together.

They'd met at Mom's to plan their joint action. Jo had come away frustrated from her meeting with the American ambassador. He'd been curt and ill-mannered, she said. Mom told me in her message that she wasn't surprised. "When I went to see him to ask for his support for the 'humanitarian agreement,'* he replied that it wasn't a priority for his government, that for them the hostages were as good as terminally ill patients and there was nothing they could do except wait!" Mom was audibly outraged. Marc was next to me. We had our ears by the radio and listened together to what Mom was saying. But he didn't understand everything, because she spoke quickly and Marc's Spanish was still very basic. I was relieved, since I didn't want him to understand everything I'd heard.

"Mom says that your mother came to have lunch with her, and they're going to take joint action. Your mother saw the American ambassador."

"And?"

"And nothing. She will surely call in on Saturday on *Las Voces del Secuestro*. It's very long. With a bit of luck, they'll be on early and we won't have to wait all night."

I dozed off between ten o'clock and midnight. I was terrified I wouldn't wake up in time. Without a watch, I had got into the habit of using the preceding programmes as a guide. I recognized the one that was just before our broadcast, an hour of tango music. So I knew then that I had to go on listening, and I pinched myself, hard, to keep myself awake.

That evening, like every Saturday, I roused from an uneasy sleep and switched on the radio. I hunted for the tango station in the dark. Marc had not come over yet, and I thought I was awake. But without realizing it, I fell back into a deep sleep.

Marc arrived later. He could hear the whispering of the radio and thought I was listening to the broadcast, stretched out on my bunk, and that I would hand him the radio if his mother called in. So he waited, sitting in the dark, for hours.

---

* The name given to negotiations with the FARC to obtain an exchange of prisoner.

I awoke with a start. They had just given the time on the radio. It was two o'clock in the morning. I had missed half the programme! I quickly got up and gave out a cry when I saw Marc in the dark, quietly waiting. I was confused.

"Why didn't you wake me up?"

"But I thought you were listening to the programme!"

"We must have missed all the calls."

I was so angry with myself. We sat back down, dejected, our heads close together and the little radio in the middle. The messages followed one another every two minutes. I listened attentively in the hope of finding a way to determine whether Mom had already called in. The programme was slow, and participants complained that some families would hog the broadcast as if it belonged to them. Herbin Hoyos, the director of the programme, apologized profusely and asked those who were waiting to prepare telegraphic messages to make the broadcast go faster. He named the people still to come: Mom and Jo were at the head of his list!

Marc was drowsy. He'd been waiting for so long that he could hardly keep his eyes open. I squeezed his arm. "Hang in there. They'll be on in a few minutes."

And sure enough, Mom's voice came on, with a lot of interference but still comprehensible. She was emotional. She informed me of an upcoming trip to Holland, where she would be receiving a prize in my name. Then the message was interrupted and someone else began to speak. We had to wait a long time until it was Jo's turn. Marc practically fell asleep on his chair. I roused him when his mother came on the air. Marc took hold of himself, but his entire body was stiff with emotion as he clutched the radio. I took his other hand and caressed it. It was one of Mom's gestures, and I did it instinctively to reassure him, to make him understand that I was there for him, to share this very intense moment. It was a gesture I'd also made with my children, and it helped me to concentrate on his mother's words, to record them in my mind. We were listening so intensely that it created a bond between us. Our quarrels no longer mattered. I knew exactly what he must be going through. I remembered the effect Mom's very first message had had on me – the sound of her voice, the timbre, her warmth, her mellow tone, all the physical pleasure I had in hearing the intonation of that voice I loved so much, the sensation of safety and well-being that had flowed over me. When she'd finished speaking to me, while I was still in the magical bubble that her voice had created around me, I realized I was incapable of recalling what she'd said.

I observed Marc's expression while his mother was speaking, the pain of absence transformed now into bliss, the need to absorb each word like an essential nourishment, the ultimate surrender to immerse one's entire being in an ephemeral happiness. When her voice vanished, Marc met my gaze with the eyes of a child. In that moment I understood that he'd been on the same journey. Then, as if he were suddenly waking up, he asked, "Wait a second – what did my mom say?"

I went over every moment of the message, one by one – the way she'd chosen to address him from a distance, the words of love she'd used to greet him, her entreaty to be strong and have courage in adversity, her own certainty that he had the strength to resist, and her absolute faith in God as she asked her son to accept God's will, for this was a trial, a way to grow spiritually. God would bring him home, she said. Marc wasn't listening to me; he was listening to his mother's voice inside his head, as if it were a recording he could hear through me. For a few moments, he made the same journey once again. When I finished, his face lit up, but his memory was absent.

"Sorry, I know I must seem stupid – can you tell me her message again?"

I would have repeated it to him a hundred times if he had asked. I was in the presence of a founding experience: A mother's words are magical and penetrate us intimately, even in spite of ourselves. Had I but understood this earlier! How much less demanding, how much more patient and reassuring I would have been with my own children. It was comforting to think that the words I'd said to them could have touched them in a way that was just as intense. During the week Marc asked me to repeat Jo's message, and each time I felt the same happiness. I noticed, after that, that his gaze had grown softer – not only the one he turned on the outside world, but also when he looked at me.

42

THE DICTIONARY

One morning Guillermo the nurse arrived with the big illustrated Larousse encyclopaedic dictionary that I'd been dreaming about. He called me over, put it in my hands, and said, "This is from Sombra."

He turned on his heel and went away.

I was dumbfounded. I'd asked for it incessantly. My best argument had always been that Mono Jojoy had promised it to me. But I didn't believe he would send it. I imagined that we were hidden in the far reaches of the jungle and that to get it here was unthinkable. So I could hardly contain my joy and excitement when at last I was holding it in my hands. The arrival of this dictionary transformed my life: It would alleviate boredom and allow me to make productive use of all the time I had on my hands and didn't know what to do with.

I'd kept my notebooks from Andres's camp, and I wanted to finish my research and track down lost information and learn. If I could learn, then I wasn't wasting my time. It was this that frightened me the most about my detention: The loss of my time was the cruellest of punishments. I could hear my papa's voice pursuing me: "Our life capital is measured in seconds. Once those seconds are gone, we never get them back!"

During my presidential campaign, he sat down one evening to help me do some planning and make an outline of the transformations I hoped to bring about. He got out his notebook, scribbled something, and declared,

"You will have only one hundred and twenty-six million one hundred and forty-four thousand seconds during your mandate. Think carefully — you won't have a single second more!"

I was haunted by his remark. Once I was deprived of my liberty, I was also deprived of the right to dispose of my time. It was an irreparable crime. It would be impossible for me to ever get back the millions of seconds that had been lost forever. The encyclopaedia was therefore my best antidote. It became my university in a box. I would wander around inside it following my whims and finding the answers to all sorts of questions that had been on a waiting list my whole life. This book was vital to me, because it enabled me to have a short-term goal and cleared me of the underlying guilt inherent in my condition, that of squandering the best years of my life.

But my contentment made some of my companions jealous. No sooner did I have the dictionary than one of my fellow inmates came to inform me that since it was the guerrillas who'd brought it, it didn't belong to me. I agreed with his comment in principle. When we were all waiting for the stewpot, I invited the rest of my comrades to use it.

"It will be available during the morning. I'll use it in the afternoon. Just help yourself, then put it back in its place."

Lucho warned me, "Be prepared that they'll do whatever it takes to get it away from you."

However, in the days that followed, there was less tension. Everyone took turns using the dictionary. Orlando offered to help me make a waterproof cover for it. Gloria provided the waterproof canvas from an old backpack she was getting ready to recycle. Just then Guillermo showed up again.

"Give me the dictionary. I need it."

His tone left me puzzled.

"Yes, of course, how long do you need it for?"

"A week."

"Listen, I'm working with it. Have it over the weekend if you like."

He looked me up and down, then eventually gave in. He brought the book back the following Monday and said, "Don't let it get ruined. I'll come and get it again next Friday."

The following week he tried a new strategy.

"The soldiers need the dictionary."

"Sure, no problem. Take it and ask them to send it back to me with the receptionist, please."

But this time he didn't bring it back.

There was a new commander in the camp. He was an older man, over forty, with greying hair and a hard gaze. His name was Alfredo. Everybody thought that Sombra was going to be dismissed, but in the end they settled into a power-sharing that seemed to function, despite obvious tension between them.

Commander Alfredo summoned the prisoners. I met with him, together with Sombra, for a whole afternoon, in what Sombra referred to as his "office." I immediately broached the subject of the dictionary.

"I want to know if I can use the dictionary as I please. Guillermo seems to think not. In fact, he has it now, and he hasn't given it back."

Sombra seemed embarrassed. Alfredo was staring at him harshly, like a raptor circling its prey.

"This dictionary is yours," declared Sombra, to make matters absolutely clear. I deduced he didn't want to give Alfredo any reason to report back to Mono Jojoy.

That was enough for me. The next morning Guillermo brought me the dictionary. He smiled as he handed it to me.

"*Él que ríe de últimas ríe mejor.*"*

His warning did not manage to spoil my satisfaction. I immersed myself once again in hours of spellbinding reading, seeking to find, to know, to understand, as if solving a puzzle.

---

* "He who laughs last laughs best."

43

MY FRIEND LUCHO

August 2004. Lucho and I became inseparable. The more I got to know him, the more I loved him. He was a sensitive soul, very wise, with a sense of humour that could withstand anything. His intelligence and wit were, for me, as vital as oxygen. Moreover, he was the most generous person on earth, which made him a rare pearl in Sombra's prison. I placed all my trust in him, and together we tried incessantly to think up ways to escape.

Orlando asked us about it one evening. He suggested we try to escape together. Lucho and I knew that this was impossible. We were convinced that Orlando would never dare, and we were not even sure that we ourselves would. Moreover, he was a big, heavyset man. We could not picture him making his way unnoticed through the chain-link fence and the barbed wire.

However, because we talked about it so much, we began to study the various options and to make plans. We concluded that it would take us months or even years to get out of this jungle, and that we would have to learn to live in it with no resources other than our ingenuity.

So we set to work making *equipos*, like the one Lucho had. Sombra had set up a leather workshop in the camp for making and repairing backpacks and the troops' equipment. When we presented our request, we were fortunate that the timing was right – not only was the material available but also, if we were to be evacuated, we would need something in which to carry our belongings.

Our plan was to make two each: One regular size, to be able to carry everything in case of an evacuation, and then a much smaller one, which Orlando called a "*mini-crusero*," for our escape. Orlando, who had done some leatherworking before, guided us through the basic techniques. Very quickly everyone in the prison joined in. Not only because we all sensed that sooner or later we would have to leave this camp (military planes were flying overhead on an almost-daily basis) but also because the opportunity to make a good backpack seemed to please everyone.

In the evening, Orlando would come and sit in my hut with a piece of wire that he'd taken from a corner of the fence and a big file that I'd lifted from a distracted receptionist. He wanted to make some fishhooks.

"This way we won't die of hunger!" he said proudly, brandishing a sort of crooked handmade hook.

"With that thing you'll only be catching whales," said Lucho, gently mocking.

I had managed to get a reserve of sugar from Sombra in case Lucho had a fit. We were also counting on this reserve for our escape. I worried about the shortage of sugar, because we really had only very little, and I was obliged to use it because Lucho often seemed on the verge of another diabetic coma.

I had learned to recognize the symptoms long before he felt he was in danger of a relapse. It began in the afternoon. His face suddenly became gaunt, and his skin would go grey. I would tell him it was time to take some sugar. As a rule he would reply mildly that he wanted to go lie down and that it would pass. But when he reacted badly, shouting at me that I was bothering him and no, he would not take any sugar, I knew that any minute now he would drop to the floor in a seizure. It was a real struggle. I had to use all sorts of tricks to get him to swallow his dose of sugar. Inevitably, at some point he would swing from aggression to apathy. By then he was completely at a loss, and I could get the sugar into his mouth. He would sit there dazed for minutes on end, then finally he became Lucho again and apologized for not having listened to me.

We were dependent upon each other, and this was both our strength and our vulnerability. Because of it we suffered twice as much – first of all from our own sorrow and then, just as intensely, from the other's afflictions.

It happened one morning. But I'm not so sure, it could have been at dawn, because sadness came upon us like an eclipse, and what I remember is a long day full of darkness.

We were sitting side by side, in silence, listening to the little radio together. It should have been a day like any other, but it wasn't. We were waiting for my mother's message; no messages for him, because his wife called him every Wednesday on Caracol, and this wasn't Wednesday. When he heard his sister's voice, his face lit up. He adored his sister, Estela. He was wriggling with happiness on his chair, as if to sit more comfortably, while his sister, in an infinitely tender, soft voice, said to him, "Lucho, be strong. Our little mother has passed away." I had a sudden violent memory of the asphyxia I'd felt on discovering my father's death in that old newspaper. Lucho was there beside me in the same overwhelming suspension of time, his breathing halted. His suffering reactivated my own, and I curled up on myself. I could not help him. He wanted to weep, as if to get his breath back, to get rid of his sadness and let it drain from his body, expel it. But he was weeping with dry eyes, and that was even more terrible. There was nothing to be done, nothing to say. This eclipse of emotions lasted for days, until the prison gate opened and Arnoldo shouted, "Take just what is absolutely necessary – hammock, mosquito net, toothbrush! We're out of here. You have two minutes."

They told us to line up one behind the other, and out we went. I took my dictionary. I wasn't nervous. I was slowly recovering from that long sadness, from that silence without thoughts. I wanted to go outside, I needed words.

"It will be good for us."

"Yes, it will be good for us."

"She was already dead."

"Yes, she was already gone. She had forgotten that I was no longer there." Then he added, "I was expecting it."

"You expect it, but you're never prepared."

We went slowly through the outside fence of the prison. Ahead of us the military prisoners walked, in chains, two by two. They had seen us, and now they waved, with big smiles across their hollow faces.

"Do you think we look like that?"

"I think we look worse."

We filed out of the camp, walking past the trenches for twenty minutes along the little path we'd taken with Shirley on the night of the raid.

We sat down among the trees, on our black plastic sheeting, far from the military prisoners, whom we couldn't see but whom we could still hear through the trees.

"Orlando, did you take the radio?"

"Yes, I've got it, don't worry."

Gloria went to set up her hammock, since it looked like we would be waiting a long time. She stretched out in it, then fell to the ground like a ripe fruit. This time it didn't make her laugh, although we did. We needed such moments to be lighthearted and silly. I went to give her a hug.

"Leave me alone, I'm in a bad mood."

"Oh, come on!"

"Leave me alone. I don't like it when you make fun of me. I'm sure it was Tom who untied the knots so I'd fall down."

"Not at all! Don't be silly! He didn't do anything to you, poor Tom."

They gave the order to set up tents. We would sleep three per tent. We were about to set ours up – Lucho, Orlando, and I.

"I warn you, I'm a terrible snorer," said Orlando.

Just then an increasingly loud roar made us raise our heads. We stopped everything.

"Helicopters."

"There are at least three of them."

"They're flying right over us – they're on top of us."

The forest began to shiver. We were all looking up. I could feel the sound of the engines in my breast.

"They're right nearby!"

The sky went dark. The metal birds seemed immense as they passed above us.

Orlando, Lucho, and I all thought the same thing at the same time. We had just put our *mini-cruseros* on our backs. I took Lucho's hand. With him I could face anything.

44

THE CHILD

The guards loaded their rifles and came closer. We were surrounded. I was praying for a miracle, some unexpected event. A bombardment that would create panic and allow us to slip away. A troop landing, even if it meant death. I knew that there was a standing order to kill me. Before any manoeuvre or change of location, a guerrilla was assigned to this mission. He had orders either to save me and pull me out of the way if there was crossfire, or to execute me if there was a chance I might end up in the hands of the *chulos*.

Some years later, during one of the long marches that became our martyrdom in the hands of the FARC, a young guerrilla woman bluntly explained the situation to me.

She was called "Fluff," and she deserved the nickname: She was petite and very cute. I liked her. She had a big heart. On this occasion I was having trouble walking and keeping up with the others. She'd been assigned as my guard, which was a relief to me. That day when we stopped somewhere to drink water, we heard a movement in the underbrush, and she loaded her revolver and aimed it at me. Her expression changed; I could hardly recognize her, she was so ugly and cold.

"What's going on?"

"You do what I say, or I'll shoot you."

I was speechless.

"Walk ahead of me. Start running straight ahead, and don't stop until I tell you to."

I began trotting ahead of her, weighed down by a backpack that was too heavy.

"Hurry up!" she shouted, annoyed.

She pushed me abruptly behind some rocks, and we stayed hidden like that for a few minutes. A *cajuche** ran straight ahead, a few yards from us, head down. Then came the entire herd, twenty animals or more, much bigger than the first one. Fluff took aim, fired, and hit one of the wild boars. The animal collapsed in front of us, steaming black blood running from the back of its skull.

"We were lucky it was only *cajuches*! But it could've been the army, and if it had been, I would have had to execute you. Those are the orders." She explained that the *chulos* would not be able to tell the difference between us, and they would shoot me. Therefore I had to learn to run fast, or else she would be the one shooting me. "So you've got no choice – or, better still, your best choice is me!"

I hovered behind Lucho. The helicopters shaved the treetops, went away, came back again, circled, and then went right over our heads again, without seeing us. They disappeared in the distance.

The day was nearly over, and there were a few minutes of light left. We had just enough time to put up our tent, spread out our plastic sheets, hang up our mosquito nets, and lie down for the night.

Orlando handed me the radio.

"Listen to the news tonight. Be careful, they're right nearby. Lucho and I will talk loudly to cover the sound."

The next morning at dawn, I handed him the radio after Mom's message and the one from Angela, Lucho's wife. I got up to go clean my teeth and stretch my legs while waiting for breakfast. Orlando was last to come out of the tent, long after us. All the blood had drained from his face. He looked like a walking corpse.

---

* A wild boar, greatly appreciated by the guerrillas for its meat.

Lucho took me by the arm. "My God, something's happened!"

Orlando looked at us without seeing us and walked like a robot down to the river to get some water. He came back with his eyes red and swollen, his face empty of any expression.

"Orlando? What's going on?"

After a long silence, he opened his mouth. "My mother has died," he said with a sigh, looking away.

"Shit! Shit!" shouted Lucho, stamping his foot on the ground. "I hate this jungle, I hate the FARC! How much longer is the Lord going to hound us like this?" he cried, looking up at the sky.

At the beginning of December, it was Jorge's mother who had passed away, then Lucho's, and now Orlando's. Death was pursuing us. Without their mothers my companions felt adrift, dispossessed of the women who safeguarded the memory of their lives. Now they were projected into a space where to be forgotten by others was to enter the worst of prisons. I shuddered at the idea that I might be the next victim of this curse.

As if fate wanted to make fun of us, life, like death, was also present in this makeshift camp. At least I thought so. During the night, in the silence of the trees, I'd heard the cries of a small baby. Clara had given birth, I concluded. On waking, I spoke of it to my companions, but they hadn't heard anything.

Lucho made fun of me. "That's no baby you heard – those are cats. The soldiers have a few. I saw them carrying them when they went ahead of us."

The helicopters didn't come back. We returned to Sombra's prison and to our belongings, which had been colonized by ants and termites while we were tramping around the forest, and as if to confirm Lucho's comment, some cats had shown up. There was a big tomcat with the coat of a jaguar and fiery yellow eyes that drew everyone's gaze, no doubt a cross between a cat and a jaguar. He was the king of the gang, surrounded by females all as extraordinary as he was, but more belligerent. He was immediately adopted by our group, and we all did what we could to contribute to his well-being. He was a magnificent animal, with a white chest and white paws that made him look as if he were wearing elegant gloves.

"I'm gonna take him home with me," said one of my companions. "Can you imagine if I sold the kittens? I'd make a fortune!"

But Tiger – that was his name – was a free creature. He had no master, and he treated us all with indifference, disappearing for days, and returning when we least expected him to. One of the females in his harem, just as fierce, had decided to come and stay with us. Right from the start, it was Lucho who conquered her affections. She jumped up on his lap and settled down, purring, mercilessly scratching anyone who tried to come near. Lucho was intimidated and thought it wiser not to get up off his chair until she condescended to leave. From then on, every day she did exactly the same thing. The cat had tamed Lucho, and not the other way around. She was an unloved, unnamed cat with a defect in one eye. She would show up in the evening, meowing, looking for him, and he opened his cans of tuna, not to feed himself or to share with us but to feed his kitty, whom we finally baptized Sabba. Sabba meowed like a crying baby, so for a while I thought that I'd been mistaken and the baby's cry I thought I heard must have been hers. But one evening while the cat was sleeping nearby, I again heard the cries. I no longer had any doubt. When Arnoldo showed up the next morning with the stewpot, I bombarded him with questions. Clara hadn't given birth yet, he said, and she was no longer in the camp.

I knew that he was lying, and my imagination ran away with me. In an awful dream that night, she was dead and her child lost.

In the morning I shared the dream with my comrades, insisting that she must be in danger. We all questioned the guards, each on our own, but they told us nothing. Then Sombra and Alfredo came one afternoon. They talked to us from behind the fence, as if we had the plague. The discussion turned sour, because Alfredo called our American companions mercenaries and CIA agents, and we didn't like it.

Before leaving, Alfredo declared, "By the way, your friend had her baby. It's a boy and his name is Emmanuel. She'll be back in a few days."

I was relieved, but my companions weren't. "It's going to be awful with a baby in the prison, screaming all night long!" said the very same person who had lectured me when the American captives arrived.

"I'll answer you with your own words: We have to welcome everybody here."

A few days later, Guillermo told us about Clara's labour. He had prepared for the operation by reading about the procedure on the computer. He said he'd saved the child's life, because it was almost dead when he'd intervened, and he had reanimated it. He then explained that Clara was already up and about.

Clara did indeed make an appearance one morning, with her little baby swaddled in her arms. We all greeted her with emotion, touched by this tiny being that had been born here in the jungle, in our prison, in our misfortune. He slept with his eyes wrinkled up, blind to the dreadful world in which he'd landed.

Clara put the baby down on my mattress and we sat together looking at him. She told me in detail what her life had been like since we'd last seen each other in the chicken run, then added, "I was very sick for days after the birth. The guerrillas took care of the baby. I never breast-fed him, and I only saw him once a day. I couldn't look after him. I've never given him a bath."

"Well, that's all right. We'll do it together, you'll see. It's a wonderful moment."

I took the baby in my hands to unwrap him, and I discovered that his left arm was bandaged.

"What happened?"

"When they took him out, they pulled a bit hard on his arm, and they broke it."

"My God, it must hurt him terribly!"

"He hardly cries at all. He must not feel it."

I was deeply moved. The weather was fine, the air was warm. We filled a basin that Lucho had found when we were at the pig pond. While I undressed the infant, I relived the moment Mom had taught me to give Melanie her bath. I copied Mom's gestures one by one, placing the baby on my forearm, holding his head in my hand, dipping his small body gently into the water, speaking to him, looking into his eyes, humming a happy little tune so that his first contact with water would become a sign of a pleasure, the way I'd seen her do. I scooped some water up with the palm of my other hand.

"You see, like this. Then you splash the water on his head, taking care not to let it get into his eyes, because that might frighten him. And you talk to him and caress his body, because it's a special moment, and each time it has to be a moment of harmony between the two of you."

Mom's words came back to me. Crouching above the basin with Clara's baby in my arms I understood all their significance. I was experiencing with Clara what I knew her mother would have liked to have the chance to share with her. Clara was fascinated, as I probably had been myself when I watched my mother's sure and experienced gestures. In fact, the point was not to transmit anything. My role was to liberate her from her fear and apprehension, so that she could discover in herself her own particular way of being together with her child.

45

THE STRIKE

I asked them to set up another hut next to mine, up against the fence, for Clara and her child. I wanted to be near her, especially at night, to help her take care of the baby without disturbing the others. I had tried to make my request at the right time, with the right words, in a tone that left no room for suspicion. But they refused, and Clara returned to her place inside the barracks with her child.

I was so sorry, particularly as, very quickly, Clara refused my help and limited my contact with the child. My companions rallied around her in turn, but she declined their help with equal stubbornness. It sank our hearts to witness her beginner's clumsiness as she rebuffed our advice. The infant cried all day, and the receptionist removed him, putting him in the care of one of the female guerrillas.

"You don't know how to do it!" Arnoldo shouted at Clara, exasperated.

I heard my companions telling her off, too.

"The bottle was scalding hot. You have to test it before you give it to him."

"You're going to make his nappy rash even worse if you go on wiping him with toilet paper! It's like sandpaper for him!"

"You have to give him his bath every day, but you mustn't move his arm. Otherwise it won't heal."

When they brought the baby back from his emergency caregiver, he looked much calmer. Too calm. I observed him from a distance. I spoke about it to Gloria and Consuelo. They, too, had noticed that something was wrong. The child wasn't following things with his gaze. He reacted to sound, but not to light.

It was very painful to look at him. There was no point discussing this with his mother. We thought the baby might be sick, but saying so out loud wouldn't help matters. If they had kept Clara in the camp to give birth, clearly they would do nothing to secure medical help for her child. They were prepared to let us die in prison, and that included newborn babies.

I would not forget the nurse impassively looking on while Lucho was having a seizure on the ground. Nor the way they had dealt with Jorge's heart attacks. Lucho had revived him, massaging his chest, something he'd learned from his sister, a doctor. We begged them to give us some aspirin to thin Jorge's blood and reduce the risk of a heart attack, to no avail. They eventually removed him from the prison, saying we had stressed him out, that we were responsible for his relapse because we fussed over him. He'd spent an entire week in the leather workshop, alone, lying on the ground.

We'd hoped that they gave him some medical care, but when he came back, he confessed that he'd had a series of other attacks and that the guard had done nothing to help him. Being alive, for every one of us, was becoming more and more miraculous.

Immersed in a world governed by cynicism, where our lives had become worthless, we had witnessed a reversal of values to which I could still not resign myself.

In the evening, stretched out in my hut, I followed with a heavy heart the petty trade that some of my companions had set up along the chain-link fence that surrounded us. Anything that might be the object of a transaction was brought there, with the aim of obtaining in exchange medication or food.

I had seen instances of fondling, when some of the guards, taking advantage of our distress and of our needs, pressed their demands ever further and increased our humiliation. Days would go by before I had the strength to say a word to the victim of such abuse.

It was disturbing to watch the way, for some, embezzlement was becoming a way of life. They justified it as a strategy to win the guerrillas' trust, with a view to improving their chances of survival. Whatever their true reasons were, they befriended our torturers. They strove to provide proof of their allegiance every time the opportunity arose.

Whenever a shipment of clothing arrived, which was rare – once a year, twice at the most with a bit of luck – one of our companions would generally receive the most coveted item in the lot. Then later he would come out and say he didn't want it, and instead of offering it to one of us, who could always have put it to good use, he gave it to a guerrilla he wanted to please. His gesture was duly appreciated, and in exchange he received favours of all sorts – like a greater quantity of better food in his bowl, or medication.

This attitude gained ground, and consequently some of us became mentally conditioned to see the guerrillas as figures of power and authority and to excuse them for all kinds of cruelty and abuse. Relations had been reversed, and, in contrast, fellow prisoners were viewed as rivals against whom aversion and hostility were nurtured.

We were beginning to behave like serfs trembling in the presence of a lord whom we would try to please to obtain favours, because we saw only the superiority of rank and not the human reality of the individual. We were becoming as obsequious as courtiers.

The suffering of Clara's baby acted as a healthy catalyst for rebellion among our little community. The baby would go from hysterical crying, caused by the pain of his broken arm, to apathy, under the effect of the strong sedatives that the guerrillas gave him unrestrainedly. Tom, who had previously refused to support our hunger strike to protest our treatment, agreed this time to join us in demanding that the child receive pediatric care. We all went on strike. Lucho made himself a dunce cap and a sign on which he wrote, DOWN WITH THE FARC! Following him in single file, chanting slogans of protest, we marched in circles around the courtyard. Orlando had the good idea of fermenting some *panela*, a piece of brown cane sugar that he'd been keeping in reserve for a long time, to make some homemade alcohol called *chicha*.

"We won't feel the hunger, and it will give us energy."

The effect was almost immediate: diarrhoea and intoxication all around! Our slogans degenerated. We went from demanding treatment for Clara's child to protesting against our lack of food: "Down with the FARC! We're hungry! We want corned beef!"

The spectacle was grotesque and we were so giddy that we ended up sprawled on the floor, unable to control fits of laughter whenever one of us had to run to the latrines for relief.

The guards looked on with consternation. We could hear our neighbours' commentary through the wall: The military prisoners wanted to join in and go on strike as well.

The prison gate opened. We expected reprisals. Arnoldo came in, surrounded by two other guards, dragging a hemp sack covered in dust.

Some captives immediately went up to excuse themselves, trying not to fall into disgrace. "Arnoldo, I'm really sorry. You have to understand."

The guerrilla stopped short, raising his hand. "Commander Sombra informs you that the prisoners have the right to protest and the FARC guarantees that right. He asks you to protest quietly, because your shouts might alert any *chulos* who happen to be in the area. Here are some cans of tuna to be distributed between you. Commander Sombra orders the child to be removed from the prison, as he isn't a prisoner. He will live freely among us, returning from time to time to see his mother. We're going to care for him and feed him well. You will be able to testify to this."

He dumped the hemp bag on the table and took the baby and all its things, then went away again, double-locking the gate, leaving us speechless.

The baby was growing and filling out before our eyes. Clara would take him, play with him for a few minutes, then hand him to the receptionist as soon as he began to cry. One evening it was Guillermo the nurse who brought him. We asked how they intended to care for his little arm. We demanded to know. He claimed that the baby had completely recovered, but we knew that was not true. Clara stopped the discussion. She thanked Guillermo for all he'd done for the baby and declared, "I wish you had been his father." There was a chill, and then everyone went back to his or her business.

I often thought about the child. In a way, by agreeing to be his god-mother, particularly in this jungle, I felt bound to him. When Arnoldo came, I would spend a few minutes interrogating him. I wanted to know how they were treating the baby's nappy rash and the heat rash he had all over his body, and more than anything I needed to know what sort of diet he was getting.

"We'll make a man of him," answered Arnoldo. "We give him strong black coffee in the morning, and he loves it."

That gave me the shivers. I knew it was a fairly common custom in Colombia. The poorest families could not afford powdered milk for infants, so they filled their babies' bottles with coffee.

I remembered a little girl I'd found in a cardboard box inside a rubbish bin in the north of Bogotá. I was on my way back from Congress, looking distractedly through the car window, and was startled to see a small hand emerge from a pile of rubbish. I jumped out of the car and found this little baby girl bundled up in a filthy blanket that stank of urine. She had fallen asleep with a feeding bottle in her mouth, full of black coffee.

Her older brother was playing nearby. He told me that the baby's name was Ingrid. Far less would have sufficed for me to see this as a sign from fate. I immediately called Mom to ask her if she had any room in her shelters for homeless children, for Ingrid and her brother who were sleeping on the street . . .

A bottle of black coffee for an infant. This was a result of extreme poverty to be sure, but also of ignorance. I explained to Arnoldo that coffee was too strong a substance and not suitable for a baby, that he must try above all to get some milk. He looked at me, offended, and said, "That's just bourgeois bullshit. We were all brought up like that, and we're doing fine."

Arnoldo had made it political. I knew that it was useless to insist. For little things and big ones, too, we were at the mercy of the guards' moods. Ferney had warned me: I had to wait for the right moment, use the right tone and the right words.

I'd failed miserably.

46

BIRTHDAYS

Unbelievably, September was nearly upon us. A painful cycle was beginning again. On the radio, tropical music was already announcing the Christmas season. I could not resign myself to the horror of being away from my children on their birthdays for the third year.

I wanted to celebrate my daughter's nineteenth birthday, and I dreaded that yet again I would do something wrong. I wanted to make a cake for Melanie, so I monitored Arnoldo's mood, looking for an opening to make my appeal.

But with each passing day, Arnoldo was becoming more tyrannical and disparaging, refusing to linger for a second to exchange a few words. And I did not want to make a big deal out of it. I knew that my plan had every chance of failing. Yet I also sensed, in an irrational way, that if I managed to celebrate my daughter's birthday once again, it would be a good omen. The idea took hold of me, and I waited for an opportunity.

And then there was a moment of respite from my frustration. Sombra decided we were to have our teeth examined. Shirley, who'd had some nurse's training, had been appointed the dentist. I seized the chance to ask for her help.

"I can't promise you anything. But I'll try to sell him on the idea for you to come and cook with us one afternoon. When is your daughter's birthday?"

But the days went by, and they didn't come to take me to the *rancha*.

I woke up on the morning of September 6, 2004, with a dream-kissed vision of my daughter before my eyes. I was glad I hadn't spoken to anyone about my idea — no one could mock my failure. *Learn to desire nothing*, I told myself over and over again, to banish disappointment.

But after lunch the creaking of the hinges alerted me.

Behind Arnoldo came La Boyaca, looking sullen. She was holding an enormous cake. Arnoldo shouted my name.

"It's for you. Commander Sombra has sent it."

The cake was nicely decorated and had written across it, HAPPY BIRTHDAY MELANIE, FROM FARC-EP. I jumped for joy, like a little kid, and spun around to share my emotion with my companions. Keith turned on his heel, furious. I recalled a conversation I'd had with him months earlier: Our daughters were born two days apart. The others brought their bowls, and I called to him, insisting he join us, too.

We still had some *chicha* left from our strike, so strong it was frightening. This was the perfect time to enjoy it.

Before slicing the cake, I raised my glass and said, "Today we are celebrating two important events: the birth of Lauren and the birth of Melanie. May God give them courage to be happy despite our absence."

When our little celebration was over, Keith gave me a hug. He looked at me, his eyes moist and his voice thick when he said, "I'll never forget what you just did."

On the radio news, the lead story was the deployment of troops in the Amazon as part of the Plan Patriota. The generals were going after Mono Jojoy, the report said; they were breathing down his neck, and he was sick and having trouble keeping up the pace. Mom was interviewed. She asked President Uribe to suspend operations and agree to negotiate with the guerrillas. She was afraid we would be massacred.

I also heard Fabrice, my ex-husband, interviewed on Radio France. I was happy to hear him. I was thankful he was an incredible father, and I knew that his fortitude helped keep our children going. However, this time he seemed very sad. He insisted on his right to fight for us at a time when doing so was perceived as a French intrusion into Colombian affairs. He wanted to send me a message. He wanted to give me hope, but as he spoke, he burst into tears. It broke my heart. I understood then how bad our situation was.

We began to prepare for departure, sorting through our things, choosing what to take. With the Plan Patriota, if the soldiers got any closer, we would be made to march into the jungle to shake them off.

I had never made any real marches. Orlando, on the other hand, was a veteran of marches that lasted for weeks. He said they had marched in pairs, chained together at the neck. When one fell down from the weight and fatigue, he would pull the other one down with him. The *equipos* they'd set off with were extremely heavy, and they had to throw out their treasures along the way to make them lighter. Their greatest fear was in crossing the tree trunks that served as bridges, because if you took a wrong step, both of you were in danger of being strangled or drowned.

With Lucho, we decided to prepare ourselves as best we could, above all to be in good physical condition to flee, in the event we were caught in the crossfire between soldiers and guerrillas. We had agreed on a set of signals to be able to rush off together at the slightest alert, in the hope of catching up with the army if the opportunity arose.

I spent mornings climbing up and down my footstool and carrying the *equipo* on my back, full of the things I planned to take with me. I hadn't favoured any one item over another, because I knew I needed everything. However, I made a list of the things that were emotionally important to me, that helped me carry on. Some of them I clung to as to my life.

The first of these was an envelope with a series of letters that Sombra had brought to me which had been delivered through the offices of the church. In my packet there was a long letter from Mom, which I read every day.

She had written it hurriedly, following a phone call from Monsignor Castro, who told her there was a possibility of contact with the FARC. Mom wrote, "I was angry with the Virgin Mary, because she wasn't listening to me. I had told her, if you don't give me any news of my daughter by Saturday, that's it, I won't pray any more."

Mom received a call to tell her that the proof of life had arrived Saturday before noon. She'd been startled on hearing in the video that I asked her to say the rosary with me, every Saturday on the dot of noon. She saw these coincidences as a sign, an answer, a protective and active presence. As for me, I made this Saturday prayer the high point of my week. Consuelo and Gloria never failed to remind me when it was time.

Reading Mom's letter had become part of this almost mystical routine I enacted to drive away the demons that had invaded my life. When I read it, I entered a world of goodness, rest, and peace. I heard her voice, echoing in my mind as I read the words she had formed in her lovely handwriting. I followed the pauses in her thoughts, the intonation of her voice, her sighs and smiles, and she appeared there before me. I saw her in the splendour of her generous nature, always beautiful, always content. With this little scrap of paper, Mom stopped time. I had her all to myself with each reading.

This letter was more precious to me than anything. I wrapped it up in some plastic I'd rescued during the most recent shipment of gifts, after a fierce, ridiculous struggle with one of my comrades who wanted it, too. I sealed it with sticky labels from deodorant bottles, to keep it dry if ever I fell into a river. I'd done the same with the photographs of my children that she had included in the letter, and the drawings from my four-year-old nephew, Stanislas. He had portrayed my rescue by the Colombian army, with a helicopter taking me away even though I was still asleep – and of course he was the pilot. There was also a poem from Anastasia, my sister Astrid's seven-year-old daughter, written with her inventive child's spelling, in which she asked her grandmother not to cry, to dry her tears, because her daughter would return to her one day, "in a moment of craziness, a moment of magic, a moment from God, in one day or three years, it doesn't matter. She will come back!"

Sitting cross-legged on my bed, I'd spread all my treasures out in front of me. Gazing at my children's photographs for a long time, I observed their faces, the expressions in their eyes, their haircuts, their features that sometimes looked so much like their father's and sometimes so much like mine. I analysed those instants that had remained frozen on a scrap of paper, and I found it so hard to look away. It was painful, wrenching. This luxury did not weigh a thing. I had folded it in such a way that it would fit into my jacket pocket. *If ever I have to leave at a run and abandon my backpack, I'll have saved my letters. And if they kill me, at least they'll know who I am.*

There were also the jeans that Melanie had given me. They were too heavy, but I was reluctant to leave them behind. When I wore them, I became myself again. And through them I was clinging still to my daughter's love. I couldn't let go. Worse yet, there was my jacket! It was fairly light to be sure, but so bulky. Finally there was the dictionary. It weighed a ton.

Lucho offered to carry my jacket so that I'd have room for it. Orlando agreed to take my jeans, Marc my Bible.

I was ready for the march. However, as the weeks went by, nothing happened. The rumours seemed to be just that – rumours. We settled back into our boredom, which now, with the dreadful prospect of a march, seemed like bliss.

It was my son's birthday. On that Friday, October 1, 2004, when the gates opened, I hurried over, sure that Arnoldo had come to take me to the *rancha*. But he was there for another reason.

He told us to prepare our bags as lightly as possible. We would be marching until Christmas. We would take supplies. There wouldn't be much food. "Sombra is also sending you bottles of vodka. Enjoy them – it's the last time you'll see any. Drink some before we leave, and it'll give you a boost to start the march. I warn you: It might be really tough. We have to walk quickly, and for long stretches. To console you, here's a piece of good news: You're having pork at lunch. You'll have a good meal before leaving."

Off in the distance, I could hear pigs squealing. Poor beasts, the guerrillas preferred to force-feed us than to leave anything behind for the military.

47

THE BIG DEPARTURE

October 1, 2004. I had thought I was ready, but when it was time to leave, I began to reconsider all my choices. I wasn't the only one. The barracks turned into a veritable bazaar. At the last minute, everybody added other things to his load. Then we all started thinking about taking our mattresses. Lucho convinced me to take mine under my arm, bound tightly with string, and I agreed, unaware of the burden I would have to carry.

I repacked my bag completely, and once the pack was closed, Lucho lifted it up to gauge the weight and said, "It's too heavy. You won't make it."

Too late. Arnoldo was already there with the stewpot, brimming with food.

"You have thirty minutes to eat, wash your bowls, and be ready to leave with your *equipos*."

We didn't eat — we stuffed ourselves. Obsessed by the thought of filling our stomachs, we couldn't taste anything we swallowed. We drank the vodka in the same way, just to add calories, not even taking the time to taste the liquid that went straight down and burned our throats.

I immediately felt as if someone were hitting me in the ribs. While I was rinsing out my bowl, shivers went up and down my spine. *I'm getting sick*, was all I had time to think.

Lucho had his hat on his head and his *equipo* on his back. The rest were already lined up. I heard Orlando say, "They're going to chain us, those bastards, you'll see!"

Lucho looked at me anxiously. "Are you all right? We have to leave right away! Come here, and I'll help you on with your backpack."

When the weight of my pack finally pulled on my shoulders, I thought Lucho had hung an elephant around my neck.

I leaned forward instinctively, but it was a position that would be hard to keep up while walking.

"I told you so. Your *equipo* is too heavy."

Of course he was right, but it was too late. The others were already leaving.

"Don't worry, I've been training. I'll manage."

Arnoldo gave the signal to depart. The armed guards slipped in between the prisoners, carrying backpacks that were twice as large as the ones I had seen on the guys from the southern front. I left last, glancing behind me. There were things scattered all over the prison, lifeless objects, leftovers. It looked like a Bogotá slum, with dirty clothing hanging from scraps of rope abandoned in the trees, sheets of cardboard, and empty cans everywhere in the mud.

This is what the soldiers will find when they get here. A tropical concentration camp. The guard who'd waited to escort me must have read my mind, because he exclaimed, "There's a team that's going to stay behind to pick everything up. We'll bury it all, just in case you left your names scratched on the boards."

I should have thought of it, of course. I should have left some clues to put the army on the right track. The guard realized that instead of getting me to talk, he had given something away. He bit his lips, and in a hoarse voice, adjusting his hat on his head, he barked, "Come on, get a move on! We're falling behind."

I jumped to obey, and made a superhuman effort to take ten steps forward. I couldn't understand what was happening. And yet I had trained, I was physically fit. My pride forced to me to march as if there were nothing wrong. I went by the group that had not yet left. *This must be the cleaning team.* One of the girls was leaning on a sort of railing that they had probably set up recently. She was playing with one of Sabba's little kittens, the fruit of her love affair with Tiger.

"What you going to do with the cats?" I asked the young girl as I went by.

"I'm going to take the kittens," she answered, lifting up her hat to show me where a second kitten was hiding.

"And the parents?"

"They'll manage on their own. They're hunters."

I looked sadly at the kittens; they wouldn't survive.

On my right was the pig pond and the place where we'd had our first *caletas*, on the hill. The river was ahead, swollen with the rains, the current rapid. They had also built a bridge; it wasn't there before. Sombra was leaning on it and watching my progress.

"Your load is too heavy. We're going to camp not far from here. You have to empty out your backpack. Don't even think of taking that mattress!"

I had put the mattress under my arm, without thinking. I felt ridiculous. I was sweating profusely, overwhelmed with a sticky fever.

I staggered across the bridge. The guard asked me to stop, took off my backpack, and fitted it on top of his own, behind his neck, as if he had just lifted up a feather. "Come on, follow me. We've got to hurry. It's going to be night soon."

After a quarter of an hour, at a slow jog, I saw my companions. They were all sitting in a row on their *equipos*. A few yards to the right, the soldiers had already set up their camp, with tents, hammocks, and mosquito nets filling the space.

My guard dropped my *equipo* on the ground and left before I could thank him. Lucho was waiting for me. "What happened to you?"

"I'm sick, Lucho. I think something's going on with my liver. I had the same symptoms after acute hepatitis a few years ago."

"It's not possible, not now, you can't do that to me!"

"I think it's the pork and the vodka. It was exactly the wrong thing to eat."

News of my condition spread. Guillermo was worried. This was really not the time to get sick. He gave me a box of silymarin, and I took the pills right away.

"Tomorrow I'm going to inspect your *equipo*," he said in a menacing tone of voice. "No one's going to carry it for you!"

I almost passed out. Before leaving I had removed the machete hidden under the prison floorboards and buried it in my *equipo*.

48

HEPATITIS

October 2004. Guillermo informed us that during the march he would be in charge of our group. He used his new power to make our lives impossible. He began by piling us up one on top of the other, stingily assigning our space in this huge jungle. Then he did his best to separate me from Lucho. Our reaction was immediate, and when we protested, he backed down. One of Lucho's arguments convinced him: "If she's sick, I'll look after her!" And it was indeed Lucho who set up my tent, my hammock, and my mosquito net. When they called to us to go and wash, I struggled to get up and get changed. Night was falling. The guard lit the way with a single flashlight beam for everyone. I was last in line and groped my way forward. We had to wash, the ten of us, in a tiny stream of water flowing in a deep and narrow gorge. The slope was steep, and you had to slide in there as best you could, clinging to branches so you wouldn't slip. By the time I got down to the stream of water, I was already covered in mud. My comrades were all standing upstream from the current. Water that had seemed clear to begin with was now brown with mud. I wasn't so much washing as getting dirty. In addition, this was the time of day when the mosquitoes were out in force.

Guillermo was barking at us to hurry up and finish when I hadn't even started. What should have been a moment of relaxation turned into an ordeal. The walk back was even worse. I reached my *caleta* dirtier than when I left, scratching uncontrollably and shaking with fever. The night was coal black, and we were all hastily unpacking clothes to change into and hanging up the ones we'd taken off, which were soaked in sweat and heavy with mud. We wrung out the T-shirts and shorts that we had worn to get washed, and in the chaos I slipped the machete beneath my towel, then went to see Lucho.

"Guillermo told me he was going to go through my pack tomorrow before we leave."

"Yes, I know. How do you feel?"

"Terrible. Listen, before leaving, I put the machete in my things."

"That's crazy, you have to get rid of it right away! You can't keep that in your *equipo*!"

"I can't throw it out either – there are guards everywhere. And it might come in useful someday."

"No, I won't carry it!"

"Please. They're not going to go through your things. You'll give it back to me later."

"No, no, no!"

"What am I supposed to do, then?"

"I don't know. Throw it out somewhere."

"Okay, I'll see what I can do."

"Ah, what the heck! Give it to me. I'll take care of it. Go get some sleep. You have to be in shape for tomorrow."

I opened my eyes to see Guillermo's face peering into my mosquito net. It was already daytime, and I jumped up. I knew we had to strike camp at dawn.

"Is it time to leave?" I asked anxiously.

"No, the departure has been postponed until tomorrow. I'm going to set you up with a drip. Sit down."

He was carrying a kit with needles, tubes, and compresses. He asked me to hold a pouch containing fluid above my head, while he jabbed me inside my elbow in the other arm, looking for a vein. I clenched my teeth, looking in disgust at Guillermo's hands, his long and black fingernails. He made numerous attempts before he found a vein that satisfied him, leaving my arm covered in bruises from the wrist up.

"Show me that backpack. We're going to make it a hell of a lot lighter!"

Guillermo laid out a black plastic sheet on the ground, emptied the contents of my pack onto it, and stopped short upon seeing the dictionary. His eyes shone with malice. He turned to me and said in an authoritarian tone, "The dictionary stays!"

"No, I'd rather leave everything else – not the dictionary."

I had answered straight back. My tone was so final I surprised even myself. He began, conscientiously, to go through the heap of objects spread on the ground. None of the books made it, except my Bible, Tom's García Márquez that he refused to part with, and my dictionary.

Orlando handed me Mela's jeans. "I'm really sorry. I have too much stuff. You've got room in your backpack now."

I was afraid that Marc might do the same. But he reorganized his *equipo* and kept my Bible in his things. Lucho, however, was very worried.

"If ever they search me, they'll kill me. It's too dangerous to go walking around with this thing."

But he went on carrying the machete in his backpack.

Mine was still too heavy. Or perhaps I was too weak. As I was about to put on my backpack to leave, my legs collapsed under the weight. I fell on my knees and didn't have the strength to stand up again.

Guillermo appeared, looking triumphant. He stood in the middle of the group and shouted, "Follow me, in silence, one by one, each of you with your guard behind you! You're in luck, there are no chains for you. The first one who does something stupid gets shot! Ingrid, you go last. Leave your pack – we'll carry it for you."

I was relieved that they were carrying my pack, but something told me it wasn't a good sign. I fell in following the person in front of me, praying mechanically on my rosary.

The hour of walking through the jungle was very trying. My feet got caught in all the roots and lianas. Every other step I stumbled, and it required an incredible effort just to make my way through the vegetation. I fell behind the rest of the group, and there was no one left in front of me, so I couldn't find my way and had to guess by looking for the line of shrubs cut here and there, on either side of an imaginary track.

My guard, irritated, decided to go ahead of me, violating the instructions. I had no intention of running away. I had enough trouble as it was, putting one foot ahead of the other to follow him. I tried to stay close to him to avoid having to catch up. All it took was for him to get two strides ahead of me, and the vegetation made him invisible. If I stuck too close, the branches he shoved aside would come snapping back in my face like a whip. "Learn to keep your distance!" he brayed. I really did feel incredibly stupid. I was constantly losing my balance, and I couldn't think straight. The little bit of self-confidence that remained to me crumbled. I was at their mercy.

After half an hour, I caught up with the rest of my companions, sitting in a circle in a little clearing. We could hear the sound of a chain saw not far away. But the foliage around us was very thick, so it was impossible to see anything.

The rest stop was brief, and I was drained. Gloria came over to see me. She put her arm around my shoulders and gave me a kiss. "You look dreadful," she said.

Then she leaned over to whisper, "The others are absolutely furious. They say you're faking it. They're upset because the guards are carrying your *equipo*. Watch out, they're going to make your life impossible."

I didn't answer.

No one was surprised when the order came to leave. Everyone got up and tamely fell back in line in the same order. We marched slowly until we came to a bend and the river suddenly appeared, roaring, pouring through a deep gorge at full speed. They had felled a huge tree that when it landed on the other shore, became a majestic bridge. I saw some guerrillas crossing, and I felt dizzy just looking at them. Lucho was right ahead of me, and he turned around and took my hand, squeezing it, whispering, "I'll never be able to do that."

I watched one of the female guerrillas crossing with an enormous *equipo* on her back, her arms extended on either side, seeking her balance like a tightrope walker.

"Yes, we'll manage. We'll do it together, very slowly, one step at a time. We'll make it."

Everyone crossed over. The guerrillas took the *equipos* from one bank to the other for those who were having difficulty crossing. Brian, one of the guerrillas, came back over to our side when it was our turn. He took me by the hand and told me not to look down. I crossed over blinded by a fog of nausea. I looked behind me and saw Lucho trembling all over, frozen at the middle of the trunk, carrying the backpack he'd refused to give to the guerrillas for fear they might decide to go through it. At one point he placed his foot awkwardly on an indentation on the trunk and tipped backward with the weight of his *equipo*, as if in slow-motion. My throat filled with bile, I murmured to myself, "He's going to break his neck."

Our eyes met at that very moment, and he thrust himself forward, precariously keeping his balance. Brian leaped onto the tree like a cat and ran to grab him by the arm to help him cross.

My muscles seemed to have seized up and become twisted in a cramp. I felt a lump surging below my rib cage. My liver, if that's what it was, had doubled in volume. The least little gesture triggered unbearable pain. I could hear Mom's voice. Was it one of the messages she'd read on the radio, coming back to me like a recording? Or had I invented these words myself in my rambling? *Don't do anything that will endanger you. We want you alive.*

For over ten minutes, I went on trying to walk. Most of the troops were just waiting for us to keep going. I caught up with them, bent double, one hand on my chest to hold the ball inside my ribs.

One of my companions glared at me. "Stop pretending. You're not sick, you're not even yellow!"

I heard Lucho behind me say, "She's not yellow, she's green. Leave her alone!"

Sombra was at the very head of the group. He'd been watching everything and came limping up to me now. I'd never noticed his limp before.

"What's the matter?" he barked, incredulous.

"Nothing."

"Come on, be brave. We have to go now."

I didn't know what to say.

"Look at me," he ordered.

I looked away from him.

Sombra shouted to one of the guerrillas standing toward the front. "The Indian! Come here."

The man came trotting up to us with his enormous backpack.

"Leave your *equipo* here."

He was a young guy, smaller than I was, thickset, with a chesty torso and brawny arms. He was built like a buffalo.

"You'll carry her on your back. I'll send someone to get your *equipo*."

The Indian gave a big smile, revealing his fine white teeth, and said, "It won't be very comfortable, but let's get going."

I set off on the back of this man who ran through the forest, jumping like a goat at full speed. I clung to his neck while his sweat seeped into my clothes, and I tried to hold on and not slide off. With each jerk I said to myself, *My liver is not going to burst. Tomorrow things will be better.*

49

GUILLERMO'S FRISK

My liver did not burst, but the next day things were not better. I had arrived at the campsite before the others, but I got my *equipo* only once it was dark. I had just knotted my hammock to one of the trees when the skies opened above us. A torrent of water formed in just a few minutes, and it came rushing down the hill, sweeping away everything in its path, Gloria's and Jorge's *caletas* included. My companions had to spend part of the night on their feet, with their belongings in their arms, beneath one of the nearby tents, while they waited for it to stop raining and for the flood to abate.

The next morning at dawn, I realized what Guillermo had done: He had searched my *equipo* at his leisure, which is why the previous day he hadn't given it to me till late in the evening. He'd taken my dictionary and Mela's jeans. I was crushed. He'd managed to get his hands on the very things he'd always had his eye on. When I went and demanded he return them, he didn't even take the time to explain himself. "Go and complain to Sombra," he replied arrogantly, after he told me he'd tossed everything out in the jungle. I knew it wasn't true. Seven of the ten belts I'd made for my family had been handed out among the troops. I'd seen Shirley wearing the one I'd made for Mom. Guillermo had fooled me, and I was angry with myself for not having taken precautions. But I also realized that in the state I was in, the battle was lost before it began. No one was prepared to drag a two-thousand-page dictionary around in the jungle, except for the two of us, who cared for it more than anything. This helped me to contain the hatred I nurtured against Guillermo. In a way, if he used the dictionary with as much passion as I did, then, fair enough. It was better for him to have it, because he could carry it and I couldn't.

It was harder to let go of Mela's jeans. That gave rise to a cruel feeling of guilt, as if my agreeing to let someone carry them for me were tantamount to betraying my daughter's love. Gradually, however, time did its work. This wound also closed. I decided that what was important was not managing to keep the jeans with me, but rather understanding how much my daughter's gesture (because I'd imagined her trying to decide what to give me that last Christmas we'd had together) had stayed with me during these years of misfortune and given me reason to smile.

The following morning the Indian did not come to get me. Sombra appointed Brian to carry me. He was considered the strongest guy of all the troops. I liked Brian; he'd always been pleasant with everyone. I figured that with him things could only get better.

He had me straddle his back, and off he went at a run, leaving the rest of my group behind. From the very first moment, I realized there was something wrong. After an hour had gone by, poor Brian was exhausted. He was as surprised as I was, and couldn't understand how the previous day the Indian had run for hours without getting tired, whereas Brian had only just started and already couldn't take it any more.

His pride had suffered a blow; his lack of stamina would prompt jibes from others. He disliked me from then on, complaining that I was failing to collaborate, and he did everything he could to humiliate me whenever we met another guerrilla on the path.

"Wait for me here," Brian said as he set off at a run to get his backpack, leaving me in the middle of the forest, knowing that I wouldn't move. My riding on his back had turned into a dreadful ordeal for both of us. He was making me pay for his effort by shaking me like a plum tree. I felt like I was dying. While I lay on the ground waiting for him to return, black bees, attracted by the smell, attacked my clothes and swarmed all around me. I was terrified; I must have lost consciousness. Unconscious or asleep, I heard the buzzing of thousands of insects around me, and I imagined it to be a truck moving as fast as it could to run me over. I woke up with a start and opened my eyes onto a cloud of insects. I got to my feet screaming, which only served to excite them further. They were everywhere – in my hair, in my underwear, clinging to my socks inside my boots, poking into my nostrils and my eyes. I went crazy trying to get away from them, wind-milling my arms in the void, stamping my feet, slapping at them as hard as I could, but I didn't manage to make them go away. I killed a lot of them and stunned others, and the ground was littered with them, but, amaz-ingly, they hadn't stung me. Exhausted, I eventually resigned myself to coexisting with them and collapsed onto the ground, defeated by my fever and the heat.

As the day went on, I got used to the company of the black bees. My smell must have been drawing them from miles around, and whenever Brian left me somewhere, they always found me again. They were trans-forming the horrible stench that impregnated me into a perfume. As they took the salt away, they left honey on my clothes. It was like I was stopping for a cleaning session. I also hoped that their massive presence would discourage other, less convivial bugs, and their company enabled me to doze off while I waited for Brian to come and get me.

50

UNEXPECTED SUPPORT

During one of the breaks in our journey, I collapsed like a tramp beneath a bridge. I stank to high heaven. I was filthy, with clothes I'd worn for several days, always damp with the sweat from the day before and covered in mud. I was thirsty, and the fever was dehydrating me as much as were the heat and my efforts to cling to my porter's back. It felt as if my brain was playing tricks on me. When I saw the column of chained men marching one behind the other, advancing toward me, I thought I was dreaming. I was lying on the ground, and I could feel the vibration of their steps in the earth. I imagined that a herd of wild beasts was coming at me and that I just had time to lift myself up on my elbows to see them emerge from the jungle behind me. They were moving closer, pushing aside the vegetation as they approached. I thought they hadn't seen me and that they would step on me. Then I was ashamed for them to see me like that, my hair all over the place and permeated with a smell that even *I* found revolting. I stopped thinking about myself when I saw them closer up, with their ashen features, like men carrying death, marching in time like convicts, burdened with years of calamity on their shoulders. I wanted to cry.

When they came upon me, practically tripping over me, their faces lit up.

"*Doctora* Ingrid! Is it you? Hang in there – we'll make it out of here!"

They held out their hands, stroked my hair, blew me kisses, and made the signs for victory and courage. These men – who were infinitely more unfortunate than I was, with long years of captivity behind them, longer than mine, chains around their necks, sick, famished, forgotten by the world – these hostaged Colombian soldiers and policemen were still capable of feeling compassion for someone else. That moment would stay with me forever. They had transformed my dusty green hell into a garden of smiles. We met the Indian on the path, and the Indian had smiled at me, as if he could read other people's thoughts. Humbly, almost shyly, he offered to carry me part of the way. Brian hesitated. He did not want to admit defeat. But the offer was all the more tempting because we'd come to a region where the geography had gone wild. They called it a *cansaperros*, a "dog-tiring" place; there was a series of steep hills to climb up and down, a change in level of thirty yards or more each time. It was as if a giant hand had crumpled the cloth of the earth, producing a series of tight, close pleats. In my geography books, the Amazonian jungle appeared to be a vast plateau. Nothing could be further from the truth. The terrain in this world was like this world itself – unpredictable. Whenever we came down a slope, in the small gorge between two hills there was a stream. We crossed it in one stride to begin climbing up the other slope. When they got to the top, the guerrillas would hurry down the slope to drink from the next stream. But climate change had found this region: Half the streams were dried up, and there was nowhere to drink.

Brian was suffering with me on his back. I did try to walk to relieve him now and again, but on one particular descent I fell and slid down on my butt. The troops that had gone ahead of us had turned the path into a toboggan run of mud. I landed hard in this stream, and for once it was filled with water, and I was covered with mud. Ahead of us was a steep climb that would require using our hands and feet to hold on. Brian took off his T-shirt, plunged it in the water while he washed his face, and removed it to wring out the water before he put it back on. He looked sideways at the Indian and said, "Take her. I'll take your *equipo*."

The Indian wiggled his shoulders and removed a huge backpack. "*Tengo todo el parque.*"*

"*No interesa, camarada, páselo.*"†

Brian would rather carry a pack full of ammunition than carry me. He put on the straps and adjusted them, then began his climb without looking back, carrying the *equipo* effortlessly. Five minutes later he got to the top, looked down at us, delighted to be himself again, and vanished into the wilderness.

"Our turn," said the Indian.

I jumped on his back, trying to be as light and motionless as possible. He clambered up the steep hill as quickly as Brian had done and headed off at full speed, scrambling downhill and up again, jumping from one drop in height to another so that I had the impression that I was bouncing in the air, while his feet hardly touched the ground.

Brian was waiting for us, leaning against a tree, smoking a cigarette and looking proud. We had nearly reached the campsite.

"None of the prisoners have arrived yet," he said, offering his companion a cigarette.

He didn't even think to look at me. The Indian took the cigarette, lit it, inhaled deeply, and handed it to me without saying a word.

I had no desire to smoke. But the Indian's gesture touched me. It was nothing, but it was everything. It took so little to make a difference.

Brian was in a good mood again. Then he turned to me, and said, "*Cucha, tírese allá, detrás de los que están cortando varas No se mueva hasta que le den la orden.*"‡

His words were like a slap in the face. My eyes were moist when they met the Indian's gaze. He smiled faintly, then quickly turned away; he was already busy readjusting the straps on his *equipo*. I felt idiotic reacting this way – it was surely my fatigue. I was used to being treated like that. It was standard practice. If I'd been alone with Brian, I would have swallowed his

---

* "I have all the ammunition."
† "It doesn't matter, comrade, give it to me."
‡ "Old woman! Get lost over there, behind the guys who are cutting wood. Don't move from there until we order you to."

scorn without any qualms. But with the Indian there, I became a human being again; his compassion allowed me to feel hurt. I became weaker as a result, more fragile.

We had overtaken the convoy of military prisoners. The clanking of their chains made me look around. The guerrillas were arrogantly barking orders at them. They settled in to wait, good-natured, fifty feet or so farther away, speaking animatedly in little groups, still chained to each other in pairs.

One of them saw me. They conferred among themselves Two came close and squatted down to speak to me behind a bush that acted as a screen.

"Are you okay?" whispered one.

"Yes, I'm okay."

"My name is Forero. This is Luis, Luis Beltrán."

Luis politely removed his hat in greeting.

"*Doctora*, we have a little present for you. We've made you a *ponche*. But you have to come closer. Don't worry! We've got the guard eating out of our hands."

The last time I'd heard about *ponche*, I must have been five years old. It was in the kitchen in my grandmother's house. She'd told us she was going to make some, and all my cousins had jumped for joy. I didn't know what it was. The kitchen gave onto an indoor patio. My oldest cousin was sitting on the ground with a bowl full of egg yolks that she was beating energetically. Mama Nina poured things into the mix with a knowing air while my cousin went on beating. The thought of it made my mouth water. But of course this *ponche* must be something else altogether. There were no eggs in this jungle!

They handed me a bowl full of freshly beaten egg yolks.

"Where did you get this?" I asked, ecstatic.

"They're hard to carry, but we managed. We don't have many left – we ate most of them during the march. We had four hens in the prison, and they were generous. They laid lots of eggs. We carried them all day long. But we had to put them in the pot already the first evening, or they would never have survived the *cansaperros*!"

I listened to them, flabbergasted. What? Hens in the prison?! Eggs?

For a second the idea that the eggs might make me sicker crossed my mind. I immediately rejected it. If my body didn't feel disgusted, then this couldn't hurt it, I decided. I swallowed it all, my eyes closed.

I was five years old again, sitting next to my cousin, and my grandmother was there. I opened my eyes with satisfaction. Forero was watching me with a big smile, nudging Luis Beltrán with his elbow.

The soldier called Luis pulled a pouch of powdered milk from his T-shirt. "Hide it quickly," he said. "If they see it, they'll confiscate it. Mix it with sugar. It's good for your hepatitis."

I took Forero's and Luis's hands and squeezed them in mine, and I kissed them. Then I made my way back, and squatted down, eager to tell Lucho everything that had happened.

Guillermo was leading the march, my companions following behind. When I saw him, the smile that was still on my face vanished.

"It's forbidden to talk to the soldiers. If I catch anyone fooling around, I'll put them in chains," he threatened.

I had to wait until that night's camp was built before I could have a word with Lucho. We were hastily preparing for our wash. The soldiers had already done all their chores, and they called Sombra, who came over right away.

One young man spoke up on behalf of all of them.

"That's Lieutenant Bermeo," explained Gloria. We were all watching the scene, our eyes riveted on Sombra. The soldiers had made a pile of the supplies they had taken out of their packs.

"We're not carrying another thing," declared Bermeo.

We heard snatches of conversation. But Sombra's attitude was unequivocal. He wanted to calm the rebellion.

"We should do the same thing," said Lucho. "We are poorly fed, they treat us like dogs, and on top of it they make us carry their food!"

"Hey, I want to eat," Keith interjected. "I'll carry whatever they ask me to carry."

He glared at the guard who was following our conversation with interest, then went to lean against the tree by his tent and crossed his arms.

"We should show some solidarity toward the soldiers," said Tom, and he began to remove the bags of rice he was carrying in his pack. The others followed suit. None of us spoke, so we could hear what was going on with the soldiers.

Bermeo went on talking, and he said, "You have no right carrying her like that. You're going to kill her. If it was one of your own bunch, you would carry him in a hammock."

I could not believe my ears. These men were standing up for me! My throat was tight, and I turned around, trying to find Lucho's gaze.

51

THE HAMMOCK

We didn't find out what happened with the soldiers' boycott. A snake had shown up in our area, and when Gloria cried out, everybody went looking for it. It had disappeared behind the *equipos* that were right on the ground and might resurface during the night, curled up inside one of them. I felt uncomfortable watching them search. With the exception of trapdoor spiders, for which I felt no pity, I always took the side of the creature we were persecuting. I hoped that the snake would escape and manage to save its skin, much as I myself would have liked to escape from them. My attitude toward snakes surprised even me. They didn't disgust me, and I was far from feeling the aversion that I'd witnessed in others, the need to annihilate them, to kill them. I just found them very beautiful. In Andres's camp I had come upon a red, white, and black collar snake on the ground against one of the poles of the hut. I was about to pick it up when Yiseth had shouted, "Don't touch it! It's a twenty-four hours."

"What's a twenty-four hours?"

"They kill you in twenty-four hours."

FARC members carried antivenins on them, but those didn't always work. They would make their own antidotes, drying the gallbladder of a rodent they called the *lapa*. They considered this homemade brew more effective than any laboratory serum. Maybe because I believed I felt safe knowing they had their antivenins, or maybe I thought some supernatural force was protecting me for whatever reason, but I could approach snakes without fear. Even the monster that the guards had killed in Andres's camp, which they had caught while they were watching one of the female guerrillas at bath time, had fascinated me. After they killed it, they laid the skin out in the sun to dry, stretched with stakes along the riverbank in the open air – to the delight of thousands of greenbottle flies that swarmed around, attracted by the terrible smell it gave off. The skin stayed there exposed to the elements for weeks. Finally it rotted, and they threw it into the dump. I thought about all the luxury handbags that had been lost in their wasteful operation. I was then haunted by this thought, as the very fact that it had crossed my mind seemed obscene.

The snake that Gloria had seen was a *cazadora*, a "huntress." It was long and fine, an attractive apple green colour. It came straight at me, terrified. Without giving it too much thought, I tried to pick it up so that I could get it out of there, out of sight of my companions. I knew it wasn't a poisonous snake. Surprised by my touch, it turned around to attack me, opening its mouth wide and making a fearfully dissuasive rattle. I didn't want to frighten it. I stopped moving so that it would become trusting again, which it immediately did, turning around to confront my companions, who had all gathered around, as if it sensed that it was safe with me. The guard was laughing as he watched the show. I left the snake on the lowest branch of a huge tree, and we watched it disappear, slithering from branch to branch to the treetops.

I went back to my *caleta* to prepare a mix of sugar and powdered milk with a bit of water, just enough for two spoonfuls, one for Lucho and one for me. The march had been very hard on him. He was all skin and bones. I was afraid it might trigger a diabetic coma.

Two new guerrillas arrived with a long pole the next morning. I understood that the young lieutenant's protest had worked. I was about to hand them my hammock so that they could set it up when Lucho stopped me.

"Take mine. It's sturdier than yours, and yours will only get filthy and dusty," Lucho said. "You won't be able to sleep in it."

"And you?"

"I can sleep on the ground. It will be good for me. I'm beginning to get a backache."

This was a lie.

The guards set up his hammock, right against the pole. They put it on the ground so that I could slip into it. In no time the pole was on their shoulders and they set off at a run, as if they had the devil at their heels.

My bearers' initial enthusiasm was put to a rude test crossing a succession of deep swamps with thigh-high water. Miraculously, I emerged still dry, which only served to irritate everybody, the bearers to start with, who were angered by my comfort and forgot that I was sick; they felt humiliated, lugging a princess around. My companions – soaked to the bone, with blisters on their feet because our days spent marching were getting longer and longer – were also angry. Jealousy had returned to poison our relations. I heard one of them talking with the guards, asserting that this was all a strategy on my part to slow up the entire group. He claimed that I had confessed as much to Orlando, who allegedly had then told him.

My companions' gossip worked like a meticulously distilled venom. Every day a new pair of men was assigned to carry me, and every day they would show up ever more inflamed against me. Finally along came Rogelio and a young guerrilla we all made fun of, because he seemed to think he was Zorro, with his flat-brimmed hat with a string chin tie and trousers that were too tight.

"We'll be dancing today!" they said, winking at each other.

I could sense they did not wish me well, and before we left, I made the sign of the cross, expecting the worst.

The forest had become even denser, and the vegetation had changed. Instead of ferns and shrubs in the shade of gigantic ceiba trees, we were now going through a dark, humid region thick with palms and banana trees. The trees were so close together that it was difficult to weave our way between them; the pole was too long, which made it impossible to get around the bends in the terrain. The bearers often had to back up and try a different angle. Every step was a negotiation between the man in front and the man behind, and they argued, each one wanting to impose his opinion on the other. They got angry, sweaty, and tired. The trunks of the banana trees were swarming with ants of all kinds, big and little, red, yellow, and black. The appearance of human beings on their territory drove them crazy. As we were obliged to brush against the banana trees to push our way through, the ants would hurry onto the leaves to attack us, cling to us, bite us or piss on us. Their urine was by no means the worst thing. They secreted a powerful acid that burned our skin and raised oozing blisters. Stuck in my hammock as if it were a capsule, I couldn't move. I had to lie there with my arms along my body, and I suffered stoically the offensives of these creatures as they invaded the most intimate parts of my body. I couldn't say a thing: The guys were suffering more than I was, with their naked torsos and their burden pressing into their shoulders.

After the banana trees came the brambles. We were going through a dense forest of bushy palm trees that protected themselves against the outside world by means of barbed spines wrapped all around their trunks. Once again the trunks were so close together that it was hard not to bump into the sharp spikes that covered them. Rogelio was beside himself. He took his revenge by swinging the hammock more than was necessary, so that with each sideways motion I was projected against the spines that dug deep, first through the layer of protective cloth and then into my flesh. I came out of that palm forest looking like a hedgehog, covered with spines.

But that wasn't all. Once again there were swamps to wade through, even deeper than the earlier ones, in which a particular vegetation covered in thorns was growing. My bearers waded through this lukewarm water, with the altered mood that any human being will feel after hours of being soaked against his will, feeling their way forward with their feet, not knowing what they would find at the bottom of this blackish water. Often they lost their balance and I would be half submerged in the swamp, thus becoming even heavier. Every time one of them stumbled, his reflex was to reach out for the nearest tree trunk. By the end of the day, their hands were gashed and bleeding.

We didn't go quickly that day, or in the days that followed, or in the weeks that came one after the other. In the end we all lost track of the hours we wandered through that endless jungle, crushed by the mere effort of moving on, no matter what. There was nothing left to eat, or hardly anything. Guillermo came each morning with a pot of rice, less and less of it every day. The ration had to last until evening, and once the camp was set up, the *rancheros* had to dream up a new soup of water boiled with whatever they'd found along the way. The march stopped at around five o'clock in the evening. We had only one thought in mind: to build our shelter for the night and dress our wounds. We had barely an hour to put up the tents, fix the hammocks, take a bath, hang the clothes we would put on again the next morning, still dripping – and come back to collapse under the mosquito net before nightfall.

At dawn, when it was still dark and cold, we would put back on the soaking wet uniform we would wear for the march. This was a real torture. I had decided that if I had to choose between muddy, wet clothes and clean, wet clothes, I'd rather continue to wash my outfit every day, even though the effort drained me.

There was no time for other people; it was every man for himself. Except for Lucho, who made a point of helping me with the tiniest things. My condition was getting worse. I begged Guillermo to give me some silymarin, but he said, "For you there's no medication."

52

SELLING HOPE

We were always woken before dawn. One morning our marching orders did not come. Speculation about our fate was rife. Some said that our group was going to be split up. Others claimed there would be some releases. We were moved into a clearing, where the trees were farther apart and a thick carpet of dead leaves was strewn across the ground. The sky was overcast. It was a sinister place. They ordered us to sit in a circle. The guards stood all around us, pointing their guns at us.

"They're going to kill us," said Lucho.

"Yes," I agreed, "they're going to slaughter us."

My heart was beating wildly. I was sweating profusely, like all my companions, despite the fact that we weren't moving, only sitting on our *equipos*, with our backs turned to the guards. I changed my position.

"Don't move!" shouted one of the guards.

"If you're going to kill us, I want to look death in the face!" I replied.

The guard shrugged and lit a cigarette. We went on waiting. We had no idea what was going on. It was almost noon. I imagined our bloody bodies on that bed of leaves. They say that before you die, your life flashes in front of your eyes. Nothing was flashing before mine. I had to go to the toilet. "Guard! The *chontos*." Now I spoke the way they did, I smelled as bad as they did, and I was as insensitive as they were.

They gave me permission to go off to one side. When I came back,

Sombra was there. He asked who among us could swim. I raised my hand. Lucho, too, but Orlando didn't. Was he pretending? Maybe Orlando knew something. Maybe it was better to say that we didn't know how to swim?

They had us line up, and we began marching again. Twenty minutes later we came to the banks of a huge river. They made us get undressed, down to our underwear and boots. A rope had been stretched between the two riverbanks. Ahead of me a young guerrilla woman was getting ready to go into the water with her *equipo* tightly wrapped in black plastic. I looked all around. There was a bend in the river just ahead, and after the bend it was three times as wide. Where we were now, the river must have been two hundred yards wide.

The guerrilla woman took the rope and entered the water, moving one hand after the other along the rope as she crossed. Soon it would be my turn. Going into the water was invigorating. It was just cool enough to refresh my body. Thirty feet out, the current was very strong. You had to be careful not to let it carry you away. I let my body float without putting up any resistance, and I made headway solely by moving my hands along the rope. The technique seemed to be working. Once I got to the other side, I had to wait for my clothes and my backpack, in a cloud of thirsty mosquitoes. They used a small boat to bring across fat Sombra and the baby. It came back and forth but it almost sank under the weight of all the *equipos*. I spent the rest of the afternoon drying my things, and I tried to rescue the few remaining dry items for the night. I thanked heaven that Sombra had decided to set up camp right there and spare us more hours of marching.

We all set about repacking our backpacks and throwing out anything we could to make them lighter. Marc came to see me. He wanted to give me back my Bible; he was loaded down. Clara, too, wanted to come into my *caleta*, but with the baby. She was allowed to have him for an hour. I laid out a plastic sheet on the ground and a towel to place him on. A fat female guerrilla with enormous breasts brought him over, nestled against her belly in the kangaroo pouch I'd made for Clara at his birth. The baby was smiling. He seemed quite alert as he followed our fingers with his eyes and listened attentively to the songs we sang him. He seemed to be in good condition, but his arm still hadn't healed. Clara played with him for a while. After a moment the infant began to cry, and the guerrilla with the big breasts came over at once and took him away without saying a thing. That was the last time I saw Clara's son in the jungle.

Night fell suddenly. I didn't even have time to pick up the hammock Lucho had lent me for my transport, which normally I rolled up on top of my pack for the night, to avoid a termite attack. I fell asleep listening to the sound of a fine drizzle around me. My things would be soaked tomorrow, I thought. Never mind, I was too tired to move.

Around midnight the camp was awakened by the sound of Clara's screams. A guard switched on his flashlight beam. Her *caleta* had been invaded by ants. The *arrieras* were devouring everything in their path – they were red and small, and had protruding jaws that enabled them to chew through almost anything. Clara's hammock was in shreds, as were the marching clothes she'd hung up on a rope. A sea of ants covered her mosquito net. The guard did the best he could to get rid of them, but many had already got inside. Clara wanted to take down her hammock to shake them off, but the ground, too, was swarming with insects, and she didn't have her boots. Then I realized, too late, that the sound of the drizzle was in fact the sound of the *arrieras* moving over the ground. They had invaded the camp and had already been through my *caleta*.

Daylight revealed that we had all been attacked. The hammock Lucho had lent me was like a sieve. The straps of my *equipo* no longer existed. There was nothing left of Orlando's jacket but the collar, and every tent had holes in it. We had to patch things quickly. I put my *equipo* back together as best I could and quickly repaired the hammock. It was time to leave.

A unit of guerrillas had come with supplies from a neighbouring FARC camp, so we saw some new faces. They'd provided the rowboat for Sombra and the baby. We were all hoping that the end of the march was in sight. Despite better food, we were walking slowly. The guerrillas were complaining. Everyone was finding it hard to go on. That day we stopped after two hours. Sombra was furious. He came up to me, fuming. "Tell those Americans not to take me for a fool. I understand every word they say. If they want to fuck around, I'll chain them up, all three of them!" I looked at him, alarmed. Half an hour later, I saw Orlando and Keith arrive, chained together at the neck. Jorge followed after them with Lucho. The others lagged behind. Guillermo went ahead of them the moment he saw me.

"Go sit farther away," he barked at me, to keep me from speaking to my companions. Keith was extremely nervous, holding both hands around the chain hanging from his neck. Orlando sat down next to me, crowding into the space Guillermo had allotted us.

He pretended to be playing with his feet, and said, "That idiot began kicking his backpack. Guillermo thought he didn't want to carry his things any more. He told Sombra that we were trying to hold up the march. Now I'm the one who takes the rap."

While he was talking to me, Keith had got up and was speaking to Sombra with his back to us. Sombra began to laugh, removed Keith's length of chain, and threw it over at Orlando.

"As for you, you can keep yours for a few days! That'll teach you to try to be clever with me."

Keith walked away, rubbing his neck, not daring to look at Orlando. Guillermo came back with a big stewpot filled with water. He shared it out with everybody, let us all drink, then screamed, "Line up, in marching order! Now! Get a move on!"

My companions jumped to their feet like robots, slung their backpacks on their shoulders, and headed down the path back into the jungle in single file. I had to wait for my bearers to come back; I would be on my own until then. Sombra hesitated. Then, deciding to leave me, he said, "Don't worry about the dictionary. Where you're going now, it will be easy to get you another one."

"Sombra, you have to remove Orlando's chains."

"It's none of your business. Think about what I just told you. The French are in the process of negotiating for you. You'll be free much sooner than anyone can imagine."

"I don't know about any of that. What I do know is that Orlando has a chain around his neck, and that you have to remove it."

"Come on, hang in there! It'll all be over soon," he said, scarcely hiding his irritation. He limped away and disappeared. My bearers arrived. There was a new one, because the man who'd been carrying me in the morning had dislocated his shoulder. He'd been replaced by the Indian, still smiling, still friendly. The moment we were alone for a second, he said, "They're going to release someone. We think it's going to be you."

I looked at him, incredulous. I hadn't believed a word of what Sombra had said before. "What? What are you saying?"

"Yes, some of them are going to the Sierra de la Macarena,* and others are going to leave with the First Front. But you're going to the leaders."

"What leaders? What on earth are you talking about?"

"If you want more information, give me your gold chain."

I burst out laughing. "My gold chain?"

"Yes, as a pledge."

"A pledge of what?"

"That you won't inform on me. If ever anyone finds out that I spoke to you, I'd be court-martialled and shot."

"I don't have a gold chain."

"Yes you do! It's in your *equipo*."

I was startled. "It's broken."

"Give it to me and I'll tell you everything."

His teammate arrived. I slid into my hammock again, lost in thought. The chain had belonged to my grandmother. I had broken it, lost it, found it again miraculously, and hidden it carefully between the pages of my Bible. They'd made a *very* thorough search.

When we reached the site, while we were setting up the tents for the night, I mentioned it to Lucho.

"They're searching through everything," I told him. "You can't go on carrying the machete."

"What should we do?" he answered, nervous.

"Wait, I have an idea."

The soldiers' camp was once again right next to ours. I sought out my

---

*An elevation in the middle of the Llanos, between the Andes and the jungle.

friends. They were chained two by two and had to coordinate their moves. They were happy to see me and served me some milk and sugar.

"I've come on a delicate mission. I need your help."

They crouched down to listen attentively.

"I've been keeping a machete on me, because I'm going to try to escape. There's going to be a search, probably tomorrow. I don't want to just toss it out somewhere. Can you hide it in your things for a few days, only long enough until they've done their search?"

The men looked at each other in silence.

"It's dangerous," said one.

"Very dangerous," said the other.

A guard was shouting. I had to go back. I looked at them anxiously. We had only a few seconds.

"What the hell, we can't leave you in a fix. You can count on us," said one of them.

"Take this towel. After your bath, wrap the machete up in it. You'll give it back to us when it's dark. You can say I lent you my towel and that you had to give it back," said the other.

My eyes were full of tears. I hardly knew them, and yet I trusted them, totally.

I went back to tell Lucho.

"I'll go and give it back to them. I want to thank them in person," he said, deeply touched. We knew all too well the risk they were taking for us.

At dawn the next morning, there was a search. Our friends were starting their march, and they waved to us before leaving. We could rest easy. When it was my turn, Guillermo opened my Bible. He took the chain and toyed with it for a moment. Then he put it back between the pages and carefully closed the zipper of the leather case protecting the Bible. *He won't dare!* I thought.

Once again the Indian was assigned the chore of carrying me. He clearly wanted to speak to me but was waiting for the right moment. As for me, I was more and more intrigued by his story. I was eager for good news. Even if it wasn't true, I wanted more than anything to be able to cling to a beautiful dream. I said to myself that in any case, if Guillermo had his eye on my grandmother's chain, sooner or later he would find a way to get it. So when the Indian approached me, I was ready to buy his lies.

The Indian sat with me, on the pretext that I mustn't stay alone, because we were getting close to an area patrolled by the military. His teammate was only too happy to go off and haul his *equipo*.

"I'm going to tell you everything. I'll leave the rest to your conscience," he declared by way of introduction. He explained I was going to be handed over to another commander, whose mission was to take me to Marulanda and that I was going to be released. "Mono Jojoy wants to have a big ceremony with all the ambassadors and a lot of journalists. He's going to deliver you into the hands of the European envoys. Your companion will be sent to the First Front of the Eastern Bloc. Her child will go and live with a family of militia, who will take care of him until he grows up." He declared that when Emmanuel was old enough, he would become a guerrilla. He would be sent to a hospital to have his arm operated on. Then the Indian added, "The Americans will leave for the Macarena. The others will be divided in groups and sent to the Amazon.

"There," he finished, "you know everything. I hope you'll keep your word."

"I haven't promised you a thing."

"I told you everything. Now you're alone with your conscience."

I knew that the Indian was lying. I knew that among the guerrillas, lying was considered the sign of a good warrior. It was part of their apprenticeship, an instrument of war that they were encouraged to master. They knew how to go about it. They had acquired the wisdom of the shadows that is used to do evil.

But the Indian had started me dreaming. By pronouncing the word "freedom," he'd opened a box that I'd kept double-locked. I could no longer stop the flood of raving visions that submerged me. I could see my children, my bedroom, my dog, my breakfast tray, my ironed clothes. I could smell Mom's perfume. I opened the fridge, I closed the door to the bathroom, I lit my bedside lamp, I wore high-heeled shoes. How could I shove all that back into oblivion? I wanted so badly to become myself again.

Even doubt was a source of hope. Without it, all I had was an eternity of captivity ahead of me. So yes. Doubt was a reprieve, a moment of rest. I was grateful to him for that.

I decided to give him the chain. I adored my grandmother. She was an angel who somehow had wandered onto the earth. I'd never heard her say a nasty thing about anyone. I suppose that is why we all went to her with our family quarrels. She would listen and laugh and say, "Don't pay that any attention, forget about it!" She had the gift of healing a wounded ego, because each of us always got the impression she was taking our side. But she made it easier to forgive, because she put things into perspective, and she knew how to make our resentment seem unimportant. She and I were very close – she knew all my secrets. She had always played an important role in my life, and her love had been constructive. It was not a demanding love, and that's probably one of the most beautiful lessons of life she taught us. There was no bargaining with her, she gave everything without expecting anything in return. She didn't manipulate or make you feel guilty. She forgave everything. My grandmother had a host of grandchildren, and each one of us was convinced of being the favourite. Mom had given me her chain as my inheritance. My grandmother had always worn it, right up to her death, and I wore it after that, until it broke.

Giving it now to a man who had shown compassion, I felt I was honouring my grandmother's goodness. I knew that she would be nodding to me from on high. I also reasoned that others had already noticed my chain, and there was a good chance it would disappear before the march was over. But I was no fool. The Indian had sold me hope in a box. For days I was floating in bliss, the expectation of happiness being more enjoyable than happiness itself.

After a particularly difficult day where the "dog-tiring" terrain was unusually steep and high, the Indian strolled over to our section. He had come for his chain. I took it out of its hiding place and placed it furtively in his big, callused hand. He hastily closed his fist around it and disappeared like a thief.

In the days that followed, he gave me a wide berth. One evening I encountered him all the same; he had come to help Gloria set up her *caleta*. I called out to him. He lowered his eyes, incapable of meeting my gaze.

I hadn't told Lucho any of the story. What hurt the most wasn't that my release was a pipe dream. It was that the Indian no longer smiled or sought to help me. He had become just like the others.

53

THE GROUP OF TEN

One afternoon Milton* ordered me to walk and sent the bearers back to the end of the line. I dragged myself along through the jungle like a zombie, with Milton by my side. He tried to be firm and raised his voice in the hope it would encourage me to walk faster. But it had nothing to do with my will. My body obstinately refused to cooperate. When night began to fall, I was still hours away from the campsite.

A group of girls caught up with us. They'd left the earlier campsite much later than we had, charged with cleaning up any trace of our passage. They had to bury any evidence and camouflage all the different clues we prisoners had left in the hope of being located by the Colombian army.

They arrived in a good mood. They had just done five hours at a jog with their *equipos* on their backs, whereas our group had taken nine hours to go the same distance. The girls saw me sitting on the ground, head between my knees, trying to gather my strength. Without waiting for an order, they decided to carry me. The girl who took the initiative crouched behind me, put her head between my legs, and in one go she lifted me up astride her shoulders.

---

* He was the guerrilla who had accompanied Sombra on the guitar during the serenade, third in command after Alfredo and Sombra.

"She hardly weighs a thing," she announced.

Off we ran, like an arrow. All the women took turns carrying me, in twenty-minute shifts. Two hours later we came to a stream that meandered silently through the trees. A mist seemed to rise from the surface of the water, which still shone in the last rays of light. We could already hear the sound of the machetes. The camp had to be nearby.

Sombra was sitting a bit farther along the path, surrounded by half a dozen young men who were admiring him. The girl who was carrying me jogged up to him and left me at his feet. She made no comment but looked at him for a long time. They all seemed shocked, and I didn't really know why. Sombra gave me the answer. "You look terrible," he said.

Guillermo was there in the group. He immediately understood he had to take charge of the situation. He tried to hold me by the arm, but I pulled away. Everyone was returning from bathing. Lucho came up to me, aghast. "You have to get some treatment. Without medication you'll die, and it will be their fault!" he said loudly, to be sure that Guillermo heard him.

Orlando also came up to us. He put his arm around me – he still had a chain around his neck. "Don't do those bastards the favour of dying here. Come with me, I'm going to help you."

I was already inside the mosquito net when Guillermo showed up carrying a pile of small boxes in his hands. He shone his flashlight beam right in my face.

"Cut it out!" I protested.

"I'm bringing you some silymarin. Take two after each meal."

"What meals?" I answered, sure he was making fun of me.

"Take them whenever you have something to eat. This should keep you going for a month."

As he went away, I heard myself saying, "My God, please let me be home in a month."

The following morning, there was an indescribable commotion over by the guerrillas' camp. It was six o'clock, and there was no sign of departure yet. I'd arrived too late the night before to notice that the military prisoners were encamped with us. My companions made the most of the opportunity to talk to them, and the guards let them.

When Lucho came back from his conversation with our new friends, he was in shock.

"They're going to split us up," Lucho reported to me. "I think the two of us are going to go with another group."

That was exactly what the Indian had told me. My heart leaped. "Where did you hear that?"

"The soldiers are well informed. Some of them have buddies in Sombra's ranks. Look!"

I turned around: walking toward us was a tall young guy with copper skin, a neatly trimmed moustache, and an impeccable uniform.

Before he reached us, Gloria went up to him and bombarded him with questions. The man smiled, delighted by the importance we were according him.

"Come here, all of you!" he shouted, friendly and authoritarian at the same time.

Lucho went up warily, and I stood behind him.

"Are you Betancourt? You look terrible. You've been very sick, or so I've been told."

I hesitated to answer, not really knowing what to say.

Gloria broke in, "This is our new commander. He's going to give new radios to everybody!"

The group gathered more closely around him, everybody wanting to know more, and above all trying to make a good impression.

The man began to speak again, knowing how important it was to weigh his words. "I won't be everyone's commander, just a part of this group. *Doctora* Ingrid and *Doctor* Pérez are going elsewhere."

I felt a spasm somewhere in the region of my liver. Out of pride I refused to allow myself to ask the hundreds of questions going through my mind. Fortunately, Gloria asked all of them for me in the space of thirty seconds. That much was clear: Lucho and I were going to be separated from the rest. Who knew for how long – perhaps forever.

Jorge came over to take me in his arms. He squeezed me so tightly that

I could hardly breathe. His eyes were filled with tears, and in a broken voice, trying to hide his face on my shoulder, he said, "*Madame chérie*, take good care of yourself. We're going to miss you."

Gloria came up behind him and scolded him. "Not here, in front of them!"

Jorge got hold of himself and went to embrace Lucho. I was doing my best to restrain my tears too. Gloria took my face between her hands and looked me right in the eyes. "Everything will be fine. I will pray for you, all the time. Don't worry."

Clara came up. "I wanted to stay with you," she said.

As if to downplay what she'd said, she began to laugh, then concluded, "They're bound to put us back together again in a month or two!"

Guillermo came back to get us.

We went through our section, then through part of the guerrillas' camp, and finally along the stream for a few minutes before coming to a place covered in sawdust, where they obviously had set up a temporary sawmill. I sat down on a tree trunk the moment Guillermo ordered us to wait. There was already a guerrilla in place to guard us.

I began thinking. What could it all mean?

I didn't have time to answer. Coming toward us was a group of eight soldiers chained together in pairs. They were ordered to wait. I got up to welcome them and hugged them one by one. They were smiling and kind, and they looked at us with curiosity.

"I suppose we're all going to be in the same group now!" said Lucho by way of introduction.

We started talking right away. They all had their own ideas, opinions, ways of seeing things. They listened carefully to one another, courteously, weighing their words, so as not to give the impression that they were contradicting one another.

"How long have you been prisoners?" I asked.

"I've been with the FARC longer than most of these kids," replied a pleasant young man. Then, turning to the guard, he said, "Hey, friend, how long ago did you enlist?"

"Three and a half years ago," answered the adolescent guard proudly.

"You see? Just as I said! I've been rotting here for nearly five years." His eyes became red and shining. He swallowed his tears, gave a laugh, and began to sing, *"¡La vida es una tómbola, tómbola, tómbola!"** It was a song they played constantly on the radio. Then he became serious again and added, "My name is Armando Castellanos, at your service, subintendent† of the National Police."

Our new group was made up of eight other men. Jhon Pinchao, also from the police, was chained to an army officer, Lieutenant Bermeo, the same one who had asked for me to be carried in a hammock. Castellanos was chained to Sublieutenant Malagón, Corporal Arteaga with Flórez, who was also an army corporal. Finally there was Corporal William Pérez, the army nurse, chained to Sergeant José Ricardo Marulanda, who was visibly the oldest of all these prisoners.

Their presence immediately made me feel at ease. My separation from my companions suddenly seemed like a relief; I determined to take the time to create direct relations with all of them and to avoid any situations that might create tension between us. They were open and interested in getting to know us. They had also been through difficult times and had learned from them. Their attitude toward Lucho and me was radically different from that of my former companions.

Lucho remained wary. "We don't know them. We have to wait."

"I would feel better if we could also change commander," I whispered to Lucho.

It was Sombra who came to get us. He stood before us, legs spread, his hands on his hips. I had not noticed the guard who must have overheard my comment, because he said, as if it were a secret, "You're out of luck. You're going to have Sombra for a long time still!" And he laughed.

The next morning we woke up to a torrential downpour. We had to wrap up all our things in the storm and begin the march soaking wet. We had to begin by climbing an incredibly steep slope. I was too slow and above all too weak.

---

* "Life is a lottery . . ."
† A rank of the Colombian police force.

After the first half hour, my guards decided that they would rather carry me than wait for me. So there I was once again, hanging for hours in a hammock that was soaked and filled with rainwater, which the guerrillas would drain by shaking me on the ground whenever the terrain allowed it. Most of the time, they would hoist me up, then drag me, one man tugging in front, the other pushing from behind. Several times they let go of the pole and I slid perilously, picking up speed, to crash against a tree that stopped my downward slide. I pulled the hammock over my eyes so I wouldn't see. I was beaten black and blue. I prayed, repeating prayers whose meaning I'd forgotten but which kept my mind full of words and stopped me from thinking and yielding to panic. He who could hear my heart knew that I was crying out for help.

Going down the other side, they would leap like mountain goats and land on tree roots that restored their balance, with my weight on their shoulders, my hammock swinging violently, banging against the trees. They didn't even try to avoid them any more.

The next day my companions left the camp before dawn. I stayed where I was, alone, waiting for instructions. The bearers had gone ahead to drop off their *equipos*, and they would come back to get me during the morning. Sombra had left a girl named Rosita to guard me. I had noticed her during the march. She was tall, with an elegant way of walking and a face of refined beauty. She had radiant black eyes and a perfect smile.

While we were waiting, under a fine, irritating drizzle, I set about rearranging the few things I had left. Rosita watched me in silence. I didn't feel like talking. She came up to me, crouched down, and began to help me.

"Ingrid, are you all right?"

"No, I'm not all right."

"Me neither."

I looked up. She seemed to be terribly upset about something.

She wanted me to ask her why. I wasn't sure I wanted to. I maintained the silence as I finished packing my *equipo*. She stood up and made a shelter on a tree trunk that was rotting on the ground. She put the backpacks under it and invited me to come sit with her beneath the shelter.

"Do you want to tell me what's wrong?" I asked her, resigned.

She looked at me, her eyes full of tears, smiled, and said, "Yes, I think if I don't speak to you, I'll die."

I took her hand and whispered, "Go ahead, I'm listening."

She spoke slowly, avoiding my gaze, lost in her memories. Her mother was a *paísa*, the term used to describe inhabitants, of Spanish descent, of the Antioquia region, and her father was from the Llanos, the Colombian grass plains. Her parents were hardworking but didn't manage to feed all their children. Like her elder siblings, Rosita had left the family home as soon as she was old enough to work. She had enlisted in the FARC so she wouldn't end up in a brothel.

As soon as she'd joined, a minor leader, Obdulio, wanted to make her his girlfriend. She resisted, because she wasn't in love with him. I knew Obdulio. He was a man in his thirties, with silver chains dangling from his neck and wrists, already bald, half his teeth missing. I had seen him only once, but I remembered him because I thought he must be a cruel man.

Obdulio had been sent to provide backup to Sombra's units. He belonged to another front and took his orders from another commander. In the group he'd put together to join forces with Sombra, he had included Rosita, in the hope of overcoming her resistance.

She eventually had to agree to sleep with him. In the FARC it was frowned upon to turn down a leader's advances. A girl had to show proof of camaraderie and of revolutionary spirit. Women in uniform were expected to assuage the sexual desires of their brothers-in-arms. In practice, there were two days a week when the guerrillas could request to share a *caleta* with someone else: Wednesdays and Sundays the young men handed the commander their requests to sleep with a *guerrillera*. A girl could refuse once, twice, but not three times, or she would be called to order for a lack of revolutionary solidarity. The only way to avoid censure was to declare, officially, that you were part of a couple and to obtain permission to live together under the same roof. But if a leader had his eye on one of the girls, it was unlikely that another guerrilla would try to intervene.

So Rosita had capitulated. She had become a *ranguera*, a girl who "associated" with a high-ranking officer, someone who had access to certain luxuries, FARC style – better food, perfume, little pieces of jewellery, small electronic devices, and nicer clothes. Rosita didn't care about any of that. She was unhappy with Obdulio. He was violent, jealous, and petty.

When she arrived in Sombra's unit, Rosita met a young man called Javier. He was good-looking and brave. They fell madly in love. Javier asked to share his *caleta* with Rosita. Sombra agreed to the young couple's request, and this only served to infuriate Obdulio. He was not Javier's leader, so he could only take it out on Rosita. He inundated her with chores. Jobs that were increasingly exhausting – the hardest and most disgusting ones – were systematically reserved for her. This just made Rosita fall all the more deeply in love with Javier. And when the young man finished his work, he would run to help her with her chores.

During this march, I had seen Javier rushing past like a crazy man to be the first to arrive at the camp. He'd thrown down his *equipo* and gone straight back to get Rosita's. He put it on his back, took Rosita by the hand, and they ran off laughing toward camp.

The following morning they had divided the groups of prisoners. Javier went off with his unit in one direction, and Obdulio got Rosita back. He wanted to force her to return to him.

"That's the way it is in the FARC! I belong to a different front. I'll never see Javier again," said Rosita in tears.

"Run away with him. Leave the FARC, both of you."

"We don't have the right to leave the FARC. If we do, they'll go and kill our families."

The bearers had come up, and we hadn't noticed. They were standing in front of us, scowling.

"Get out of here," one of them barked at Rosita.

"Come on, get in the hammock. We don't have all day!" said the other one to me, with venom in his voice.

I looked at Rosita. She was already on her feet, her Galil rifle on her shoulder.

"Get the hell over to the camp. And don't drag your feet if you don't want to end up with a bullet in your head." Then, turning to me, "And you, too, just watch it. I'm in a foul mood, and I would love to put a bullet between your eyes."

I cried throughout the rest of the day. Because of Rosita. She was my daughter's age. I wanted to comfort her, to give her tenderness and hope. Instead I'd left her in fear of reprisal.

I often think about her. One thing she said stayed with me, a dagger in my heart: "You know, for me the most horrible thing of all is knowing that he will forget me."

I lacked the presence of mind to tell her that it was impossible; she was simply unforgettable.

54

THE ENDLESS MARCH

October 28, 2004. We were the last to leave and the first to arrive at the campsite, ahead of Lucho and the rest of my new companions. I was told they had got lost, but as I listened to conversations, or at least what I could gather from their whispering, I learned that my companions had narrowly avoided disaster. They'd been a few hundred yards from an army squadron.

It was still raining, a stubborn little rain that never let up. It was cold. Just enough to chasten me but not enough to make me get up and walk around. Here time stretched to infinity; ahead of me there was nothing. I heard a commotion above my head. A group of fifty or more monkeys were making their way through the foliage. It was a well-populated colony, with the big males leading and the mothers with their babies clinging to them bringing up the rear. They had seen me from above and were looking down at me with curiosity. Some of the males became aggressive, shouting and dropping down just above me, hanging from their tails, making faces at me. I smiled. These rare moments when I came into contact with animals restored my desire to live. I knew that it was a privilege to be there among them, to be able to look at them as equals, their behaviour unaffected by the barbarity of men. The moment the guerrillas got out their guns, the enchantment would vanish. It would be the story of little Cristina all over again. The monkeys pissed on me, bombarded me with broken branches, in the innocence of their ignorance.

The guards had seen them too. Through the bushes I watched as they grew excited and gave the order to load their guns. I couldn't see anything any more; I could only hear their voices and the monkeys' cries. And then a first detonation, and a second, and yet another, the sharp sound of branches cracking and the thuds on the carpet of leaves. I counted three. Had they killed the mothers to capture the babies? Their perverse satisfaction in killing disgusted me. They always had good excuses to give themselves a clean conscience. We were hungry, we hadn't eaten a real meal for weeks. All that was true, but it wasn't a good enough reason. I found hunting difficult to tolerate. Had I always felt like this? I was no longer sure. I'd been profoundly upset by the business with the guacamaya that Andres had killed for pleasure, and by the death of Cristina's mother. She had fallen from her tree, and the bullet had gone through her stomach. She'd put her finger in her wound and looked at the blood coming out. "She was crying, I'm sure she was crying," William had said to me with a laugh. "She showed me the blood on her finger, as if she wanted me to do something about it, and then she put her fingers back in the wound and showed me again. She did that a few times, and then she died. Those animals are just like humans," he concluded. How could you kill a creature that has looked you in the eye, with whom you've established contact, for whom you exist, who has identified you? Of course, none of that mattered when you had already killed a human being. Could I kill? Oh, yes, I could! I had every reason to think I had the right. I was filled with hatred for those who humiliated me and took so much pleasure in my pain. With every word, every order, every affront, I stabbed them with my silence. Oh, yes – I, too, could kill! And I would feel pleasure in seeing them put their fingers in their wounds and look at their blood as they became aware of their imminent death, waiting for me to do something. And I wouldn't move. I would watch them die.

That afternoon, under that wretched rain, curled around my unhappiness, I understood that I could be like them.

My companions arrived, exhausted. They'd made a long detour that had obliged them to go through a mosquito-infested swamp, and they'd had to cross over a steep pass in order to reach us. They could hear crossfire not far away. There had been exchange of fire with the army. The guerrillas had managed to "save" them.

We began to look for a place to set up our tents.

"Don't trouble yourself with that, *Doctora*," said one of the soldiers, "between Flórez and me, we'll have those tents up for you in no time."

This was Miguel Arteaga, a young corporal with a pleasing smile. "We've perfected our own technique. Flórez cuts the stakes, and I drive them in," he explained.

And they were indeed very nimble at the job and made it look very easy. I couldn't help admire them both for their skills and for their heart. They always offered to help me set up my tent during the following four years we were together.

The trees opened in circles above our heads, revealing a heavenly vault full of constellations I was by now familiar with. We all sat on the ground on our plastic sheets to wait for them to bring us some food. Our conversation quickly focused on our shared anxiety. Some were whispering, not to be overheard by the guards – one of us had received information alleging that we would be handed over to another front.

The guard arrived, lugging two huge stewpots.

"Bring your bowls!" he shouted. "Today you're spoiled – you've got *mico* and rice!"

"Stop lying," said Arteaga. "You'll have to come up with something better. You really expect us to believe your story about monkey meat?"

I leaned over the stewpot. It was indeed monkey meat. They might have skinned it and cut it into pieces, but you could identify it – the arms, forearms, thighs. The meat had been cooked so thoroughly, probably on charcoal, that the muscles were charred.

I could not eat a bite. It felt like partaking in some sort of experiment in cannibalism.

I said I wouldn't eat any, and this gave rise to a general outcry.

"You're pissing us off with your Greenpeace behaviour!" said Lucho, mocking me. "Before you start showing so much concern about endangered species, you'd do better to show some concern about *us*. We're the ones on the verge of extinction."

"I don't think it's monkey meat," said someone else. "It's too scrawny. I think it must be one of us." And he began counting heads.

Meat was one of those rare things we dreamed about the most. Nobody wanted to know where it came from, still less to ask existential questions about whether it was appropriate to eat it or not.

For me the situation was different. I'd been shaken by my own murderous impulses. If I was capable of acting like them, then I was in danger of becoming like them. The worst would not be to die; the worst would be to become something I abhorred. I wanted my freedom, I clung to my life, but I was determined not to become a murderer. I would not kill, even to escape. Nor would I eat monkey meat. I don't know why the two seemed to go together in my mind, but it made sense.

It was our first day of rest since we'd left Sombra's prison on October 1, and the men spent the day sewing and repairing their *equipos*. I spent mine sleeping. Guillermo came. I was not glad to see him, although he brought me some more boxes of medicine. I'd made the inventory of my possessions. He had taken everything for himself. All he left me was my Bible.

I found it easier to let go of the objects that were precious to me than of my grudge against him. I had hoped that he would be staying with the other group and that I'd never have to see him again. He could sense the unpleasant effect his presence had on me, and his pride was wounded. Oddly enough, he did not react with his usual scorn and insolence. On the contrary, he suddenly became friendly and charming, and he sat at the foot of my hammock to tell me his life story. For many years he had worked for the mafia, in charge of finances for a drug trafficker operating somewhere in the Colombian Llanos region. He described the luxury he'd lived in, the women and money he once had at his disposal.

I listened, in silence. He went on to explain that he had lost an important sum of money and his boss had put a price on his head. He had joined the FARC to escape from that, becoming a nurse out of necessity, to meet the FARC's requirements for study. He had taken some training courses and the rest he'd learned on his own, reading and doing research on the Internet.

Nothing he told me made me feel sorry toward him. For me he was a barbarian. I knew he was capable of putting a gun to my head and pulling the trigger without hesitating. What irrepressible pleasure I took in bombarding him with a detailed list of all the things he'd pocketed! I saw him shrinking by the second, surprised that I was able to account for everything so quickly.

"Keep it all," I said, "because clearly you don't know how to make people obey you."

He was irritated when he left, and for the first time in many months I didn't care. In Sombra's prison the group pressure had been so strong that I'd slipped into a cautiousness that sometimes turned into obsequiousness. I didn't like to see it in other people, even less in myself. I had often been afraid of Guillermo, of his ability to detect my needs, my desires, and my weaknesses and to use his power to hurt me. When I had to confront him, my voice trembled, and I was angry with myself for my lack of self-control. Sometimes I would spend an entire day preparing how to ask him for a certain medication or for some absorbent cotton. My attitude would trigger in Guillermo reactions of impatience, abuse, and domination.

The wheel of life had turned: I was reminded of María, a secretary who had worked with me for years. She was greatly intimidated by me, and her voice broke when she wanted to speak to me. I felt myself becoming like María, disturbed by power, paralysed by the awareness I had of the need to please the other in order to obtain whatever, at a given moment, might seem vital. How many times had I been Guillermo? Had I also answered impatiently, annoyed by the other person's fear? Had I believed I was truly superior because someone else needed me?

I hardened my heart while listening to Guillermo, because I was condemning everything in him that I did not like in myself. I was beginning to understand that humility, wherever one might be on the wheel of fortune, was the key. I'd had to go to the bottom of that wheel to understand.

The next day Sombra came over. He seemed to want to talk, and he had time. He sat down on a tree trunk and signalled me to sit next to him.

"I was a little boy when your mother was a beauty queen. I remember her well. She was magnificent. That was another era, when queens were truly queens."

"Yes, Mom was very beautiful. She still is," I answered, more out of politeness than because I felt like talking.

"Your mother is from the Tolima region, like me."

"Oh?"

"Yes, that's why she has such a strong character. I listen to her every morning on the radio. She's right, what she says to you. The government isn't doing anything to obtain your release. In fact, for Uribe it would be better if you don't get out."

I didn't know what to say.

"Is she still looking after the orphans?"

"Yes, of course she is. It's her life."

"I was an orphan, too. My parents were massacred during the *violencia*. I was well on my way to becoming a crook. At the age of eight, I had already killed a man. Marulanda took me in, I followed him everywhere, up to now."

I was silent.

"I've always been Marulanda's right-hand man. For a long time, I was the one who was in charge of the FARC's treasure. It's hidden in a cave, in the Tolima region. There's only one way in, and I'm the only one who knows it. You can't see it from outside – it overlooks a ravine. You have to climb up the rocks. The FARC has accumulated mountains of gold; it's fabulous."

I wondered if he'd gone mad, or whether the story he was telling me was a yarn he'd made up for my benefit. He grew very animated, and there was an unusual gleam to his eyes.

"There's a castle nearby. It's a very well-known place – I'm sure your mother has been there. The land belonged to a very rich man. He was killed, so they say. It's all abandoned nowadays. Nobody goes there any more."

He believed his story. Maybe he'd made it up a long time ago and repeated it so often that he could no longer distinguish truth from make-believe. I was also under the impression that the story derived from his childhood memories. Maybe he'd heard it as a child and made it his own story now. I was fascinated to see him lost in this mystical world that belonged to him alone. I had learned at a very young age that in Colombia anything could happen. Reality was never circumscribed by what was possible. The barriers of the imagination were impermeable, and everything could live together in the most natural way.

Sombra's tale, with his mountains of gold, his secret passages, the curse he maintained would fall on anyone who tried to remove any of the treasure took me back to the imaginary world of Colombian folklore. I asked him outlandish questions, and he replied, delighted that I was interested, and for a moment we both forgot that he was my jailer and I was his victim.

I would have liked to despise Sombra. I knew he was capable of the worst things, that he could be cruel and cynical, and the prisoners loathed him.

But in certain situations I also glimpsed, as if through the cracks in his personality, a sensitivity that touched me. I had found out, for example, in the jumble of gossip that went around the prison, that La Boyaca was pregnant. When he came back from his little trip, with the letters from my mother, I congratulated him, thinking he must be happy to become a father. It was as if my words had stabbed him, and I quickly apologized, dismayed at the pain they seemed to cause him. "It's just that . . ." He hesitated. "The commanders decided it wasn't a good time for La Boyaca to be pregnant. The army is everywhere . . . She had to have an abortion."

"That's terrible," I replied. He nodded in silence.

Clara's child was born a few months later. I would often see Sombra playing with the baby, walking around the camp with him in his arms, happy to be pampering a little one.

I had accumulated countless grievances against him, but when he was there next to me, I found it hard to hold all that against him. I had to confess I had a liking for this vulgar, despotic brigand of a man. I sensed he must feel similarly conflicted about me. I must represent everything he'd always hated, everything he'd fought against his entire life, and the guards had supplied him with every possible and imaginary piece of gossip, so he must mistrust me as much as I mistrusted him. And yet every time we spoke together again, our compass showed us a different north.

While we were talking, one of the guards called out. Sombra looked up. Two men I'd never seen were waiting for him. He talked with them for a long while, then limped back over to me. "Your time with me is over. Let me introduce your new commanders. You must obey them from now on. You know the rules. I haven't had any trouble with you. I hope they won't have any either."

There must have been a note of joy in my voice when I held out my hand to Sombra to say, "I don't suppose we will ever meet again."

He spun on me like a snake who's been trampled on, and he hissed, "You are mistaken. I'll be your commander again within three years."

The poison immediately took effect. I had never entertained the possibility of staying in the hands of the FARC for five years. When Armando had revealed to me that he'd been in captivity for five years, I looked at him as if he were a Chernobyl survivor, with a mixed feeling of horror and commiseration, plus relief at the thought that no, that wouldn't happen to me. Sombra's words unleashed a flood of anxiety. All through the march, he'd been dangling the glimmering lure of release. When he had spoken about the French and the negotiations they'd begun with the FARC, it was only a strategy to make me hold out, a strategy to keep me moving. In one second I saw before me the film of that endless march – the swamps inundated with clouds of mosquitoes, the roller coasters of the *cansaperros*, the ravines, the rivers infested with piranhas, entire days under a baking sun, the rain, hunger, and sickness. Sombra had played a clever trick on me, and he had come out the winner.

Two men were appointed to take over and ensure my transportation. I stood before them and said, "I don't want to be carried in the hammock. From now on I'll walk."

Sombra's eyes nearly popped out of his head. He had thought of everything – except this. He looked at me angrily, particularly as I was making him lose face, but finally he decided to keep quiet. Sombra's troops were lined up along the path. I was proud to set off on my own two feet, to leave those people behind. And with them the prison, the humiliation, the hatred, and everything that had poisoned our existence for a year. I felt it like revenge: They were the ones who were staying. I lacked the strength to carry my backpack, and even just putting one foot in front of the other made me dizzy. But I felt as if I had wings, because I was the one leaving.

55

CHAINS

Early November 2004. From the first minutes of my contact with Jeiner, the young commander who had taken over from Sombra, I felt as if I'd stepped onto another planet. He walked by my side, taking my hand to help me cross a little stream and stopping the entire group so that I could catch my breath. Before the end of my second day in their company, Jeiner sent a contingent of young boys to bring back supplies. They were waiting for us on the path with fresh *cuajada* and *arepas*.* I chewed every bite religiously, savouring all the juice and texture. For so long we'd eaten nothing but little portions of rice. The delight was like a fireworks display. The effect lasted for hours; my taste buds were on fire and my guts had gone wild, rumbling indiscreetly like an unoiled gear suddenly beginning to work.

The weather was fine, and the jungle was at its most magnificent. We entered a new world. The light pierced through the foliage, scattering beams of colour as if we were walking through a rainbow. Crystalline waterfalls leaped over gleaming polished rocks and set the fish free; they took flight and landed, wriggling, at our feet. The water wound its way between the trees, leading to a bed of emerald green moss, where we sank up to our knees. We continued without hurrying, as if we were on a stroll.

---

* Soft curd cheese and corncakes.

We even camped for a few days around a turquoise-blue pool carpeted with fine sand. It was at the base of a waterfall that zigzagged through the trees to disappear mysteriously into the forest. I would have liked to stay there forever.

The team that Jeiner commanded was made up of children, the youngest hardly ten years of age, and they carried their rifles as if they were playing war games. The eldest girl was Katerina, a black girl scarcely out of adolescence, who had been appointed to prepare my meals according to very strict instructions from Jeiner, intended to speed my recovery. I was not allowed any salt, and everything had to be boiled in disgusting medicinal plants whose most obvious property was to ruin the taste of all the food. Katerina was scolded one evening because I hadn't eaten the noodles she prepared, and I felt bad for her. I later understood that the second-in-command, a young guy called "the Donkey," had it in for her because she'd refused his advances. Her girlfriends were particularly hard on her and asked to have her replaced immediately by somebody else. The world of children could be even harder and crueller than that of adults. I saw her crying in her corner, and I tried to smile and talk to her whenever I ran into her during the march.

We had come to a house, in the middle of the virgin forest, where enormous fruit trees intertwined their branches with the jungle foliage. On one side of the house, there was an enormous satellite dish, as if a huge blue mushroom had grown there under the effect of ionizing radiation.

It was there that I met Arturo, one of the commanders of the First Front of the Eastern Bloc, Jeiner's superior. He was a black giant of a man, with an intelligent gaze and a self-confident swagger. When he saw me, he rushed up to me and smothered me in his arms, saying, "We've been worried as hell about you! Are my guys treating you right?"

He handed out precise orders, then did half the work he'd delegated by himself. His army of children gathered around him, and he would hug them as if they were his own. *If these children were looking for a father, they have surely found one*, I thought, imagining what must have happened in these children's lives for them to end up as cannon fodder in the ranks of the FARC.

"You are mistaken," pointed out Lieutenant Bermeo. "These kids have a greater chance of surviving in war than the adults do. They are braver, more agile, and sometimes more ruthless. The FARC is all they know. There are no borders between play and reality. It's later on that it gets complicated, when they realize that they've lost their freedom and they want to run away. But by then it's too late."

My new companions had been observing the guerrillas for years, and nothing could fool them. When I mentioned how bad I felt about the business with Katerina, Bermeo warned me, "Don't let your feelings show. The better they get to know you, the more they'll manipulate you. They managed to put pressure on you, and you started walking. That's what they wanted, for you to feel guilty about being carried in a hammock, although it's their job. They take us hostage, and we're supposed to thank them on top of it!"

That was the same evening I met Arturo. He seemed delighted to speak to me. We sat down next to each other on a dead tree and spoke about who we were in civilian life. He described his childhood on the Pacific coast, on the *esteros** of the Río Timbiqui, in a jungle as thick as this one. I knew the region well. Arturo began to talk about his African origins. Centuries before, men like him had been brought as slaves to work in the mines and sugar plantations. "My ancestors ran away. They preferred the jungle to having a chain around their necks. I'm the same. I've chosen the jungle, not to be enslaved by poverty."

Without thinking, I blurted out, "You've never had a chain around your neck, but you still talk about the ones your ancestors carried. How can you stand to see soldiers subjected to the same treatment, knowing that you are responsible, that it's your fault?"

He was speechless, immobile, absorbing the blow. My companions were across from us, far enough away that they couldn't hear. They were dragging themselves along with the chains that hindered their movements, that obliged them to go through all kinds of manoeuvres to avoid choking each other whenever they stepped too far apart. Arturo seemed to be

---

* Estuaries.

looking at them as if for the first time, although we'd been together for days.

I hammered the nail a bit further. "I cannot understand how a revolutionary organization can end up behaving worse than the very people it is fighting."

Arturo stood up, rubbing his knees. There was something feline about his perfectly defined muscles. He held out his hand to conclude our discussion and went on his way.

After the evening meal, Jeiner arrived with a handful of keys that Sombra had given to him. He inserted them, one after the other, into each padlock, until all the chains were removed. The chains were so heavy that two men were needed to help him carry them. They were taken to Arturo.

56

THE HONEYMOON

Without the chains we all felt lighter. There was a good atmosphere in the camp. Arturo led the march, and the kids behaved like kids. They played, and fought among themselves, and ran after one another, and rolled in the moss hugging each other. We looked like a tribe of nomads.

I spoke a great deal with Lucho. During quiet hours, when there was a break in the march, we would discuss the reforms and the projects we dreamed of for Colombia.

I was obsessed with the idea of high-speed rail, a supersonic machine travelling through space like a meteor, winding its way through my country's Andes Mountains, balanced above the void on a gravity-defying elevated track. I wanted it to travel from the north coast of Colombia through the *páramos** and valleys to serve the inhabitants of inaccessible, forgotten villages that were dying of solitude, then wind its way westward, to open a route to the magnificent Cauca Valley and reach the luxuriant, and abandoned Pacific coast. I wanted it to be a means of transportation for everyone, rich and poor, to make the country accessible to everyone, because I was convinced that only through a spirit of unity and sharing would it be possible to achieve greatness. Lucho told me I was crazy. I answered that I was free to dream. "Just imagine for one moment

---

* High elevations in the Andes.

that you could, on an impulse, get a train and two hours later be dancing salsa on the beach in Juanchaco. Completely safe."

"In a country crawling with guerrillas, that's impossible!"

"Why should it be impossible? The conquest of the American West took place with stagecoach robbers everywhere, and that didn't stop them. It's so important that we could buy the luxury of having armed guards every five hundred yards. You wanted to create jobs for them, why not the railroad?"

"Colombia is up to its ears in debt. We can't even pay for the Bogotá Metro! And now you want a high-speed train!"

I argued that it would be a great investment opportunity, and it could be financed by selling stocks.

"It's a crazy idea — but it could work!" said Lucho.

"It would be a huge building site. It would provide jobs for professionals, engineers, and others, but also for all those young people who at the moment have no other way out than to offer their services to organized crime."

"And what about corruption?" Lucho would add.

"Citizens would have to get organized to keep an eye on the project on every level, at every stage. With the law behind them, to protect them, it can be done."

It was time to bathe. We went to a huge swamp formed by the overflow of the river. They had set up two parallel planks across the surface of the water between half-submerged tree branches over fifty yards or so. You had to walk across them, keeping your balance, to reach the place that had been assigned to us for washing and laundry. We were all spread out on either side of these planks, guerrillas and hostages alike, scrubbing.

This was the hour my comrades preferred, because the *guerrilleras* bathed in their bras and underwear, then paraded along the footbridge to go get dressed on solid ground. Jeiner's companion, Claudia, was the most admired of all. She was blonde, with green eyes, and her skin had a silvery shine to it that seemed luminescent; moreover she had a natural flirtatiousness that became more noticeable when she knew you were looking at her. The day the front leader arrived, nobody was in any hurry to go and meet him. Claudia was ordered to get out and dress elsewhere.

The war name of the commander of the First Front was Cesar* – again. He was standing there in his fancy khaki uniform, a beret over his forehead, Hugo Chávez style, and a big chemical-white smile that made us envious. When, acting the great lord, he asked us what we needed, we answered in unison that we wanted a dentist. He promised he would take care of it, particularly as fat Sergeant Marulanda had illustrated how years of captivity had taken their toll: Right before Cesar he opened his mouth wide and pointed to the enormous hole left by a dental bridge lost during a march. Cesar deemed that this evidence was enough.

Cesar also allowed us to make a list to order supplies. I could recite from memory the list I'd made a couple of years earlier for Mono Jojoy, and I added a radio, because we desperately needed one. Since we'd been brought together, we all had to share my worn-out little radio, which was now behaving in a very capricious way, the reception erratic and completely unreliable.

The soldiers' excitement at the thought they'd be able to order what they needed contrasted sharply with Lucho's despondency.

"They're not going to release us," he said, his heart sinking, confessing that in fact he had shared some of my hope.

"The soldiers told me that when the recruits were liberated,† the FARC had dressed them in new clothes from head to toe," I answered stubbornly.

"I need to get out, Ingrid. I can't stay here. I'm going to die."

"No, you're not going to die here."

"Listen. Promise me something."

"Yes."

"If we're not liberated by the end of the year, we'll escape."

I didn't say anything.

"Yes or no?"

"It's really hard . . ."

---

* I met three commanders called Cesar: El Mocho Cesar, who was present at my capture; Young Cesar, the first commander who was assigned to us; and this Cesar, member of the Oriental block under Mono Jojoy's command, chief of the First Front.
† FARC liberated a group in 2001.

"Yes or no, answer me."

After a moment of silence, I said, "Yes."

Cesar had set up a tent, and in this tent he had built a table out of young tree trunks. From his bag he pulled a metallic, ultralight laptop computer. It was the first VAIO I'd ever seen in my life. I looked at it awestruck, like a child watching Mary Poppins open her magical bag. The scene was utterly incongruous, and fascinating at the same time. Here we had a technological marvel before us, a cutting-edge device placed on a table worthy of the Neolithic era. As if echoing this perception, they brought us some logs to sit on. Cesar had been kind enough to bring us a film, and the screening was about to begin. He wanted us all to cluster around the little screen, which we did, casually enough, until we saw him fiddling somewhat nervously with the computer applications.

Bermeo read my thoughts more quickly than I could myself. He nudged me with his elbow and said, "Watch out, he's trying to film us!"

His warning spread like wildfire. In a split second, we all scattered and agreed to come and sit back down only once the film had started. Cesar laughed, like a good loser, but now we were all wary. Nothing he asked us from that point on would get a spontaneous answer. What I remember from that dialogue of the deaf was the incidental information I managed to grasp in passing. Cesar was the commander of the First Front. He was a rich man, and business was doing incredibly well. Cocaine production was filling his coffers to the brim. "We have to fund the revolution somehow," he said with a laugh. His girlfriend was in charge of the finances, and she was the one who approved expenses and who could authorize, among other things, the purchase of gadgets like this laptop computer Cesar was so proud of. I also concluded that because Cesar never missed an opportunity to refer to this young Adriana by name, he must be madly in love.

I was not the only one who had noticed. Pinchao whispered to me with a mischievous laugh, "I hope Adriana will be in a good mood when she gets our list!" Two days later (in record time), we received our order. Everything except my dictionary. That evening Arturo introduced us to another commander.

"Jeiner has been called away on another mission. Mauricio will be looking after you from now on."

Mauricio was a big guy with a hawk-like gaze and a carefully groomed moustache above thin lips, and he wore a light cotton poncho, like the one Manuel Marulanda wore as a scarf. Mauricio used his to hide a missing arm.

Unlike Jeiner, he had come in like a cat, doing the rounds of the *caletas* with a suspicious air. The soldiers had got out of their hammocks to speak with him, and they called us over.

"What do you think of him?" asked Lucho when Mauricio had left.

"I preferred Jeiner."

"Yes, good things never last with them."

In the morning we had a visit from a group of very mischievous young *guerrilleras*. In the same manner as Mauricio, they lurked around the *caletas*, laughing among themselves and eyeing the prisoners. Eventually they peered into my tent. One of them, a voluptuous girl with prominent breasts, long black hair braided to below her waistline, and almond eyes rimmed with thick lashes that seemed endless, said in a childish voice, "Are you Ingrid?"

I laughed and, wanting to make her feel at ease, called my comrades over to introduce them.

Zamaidy was Mauricio's girlfriend. She called him "Pata-Grande" (Long Leg), and she had clearly put his promotion to good use, for she in turn reigned over a court of young girls who followed her devotedly. She wore a revealing fluorescent tank top that enhanced her curves, the envy of all her girlfriends. Her girlfriends obviously wanted to strive for the same effect, but they weren't as successful, which served to increase Zamaidy's ascendancy over them. If Zamaidy walked somewhere, they followed; if she sat down, they did, too; and if Zamaidy spoke, they fell silent.

Zamaidy's appearance had paralysed our camp. The soldiers would shove each other aside for a chance to talk to her. She repeated her name to them only too willingly, explaining that it was not a very common name, and that you spelled it with a Z – another way for her to make it clear she knew how to read and write.

When the nurse who had just been appointed came in to introduce himself, only Lucho and I were there to talk to him. Camilo was a quick, intelligent young guy, with a friendly face that made everyone like him. We took to him immediately, particularly when he confessed that he didn't like to fight and that his vocation had always been to relieve the pain of others. At midnight, after we'd hiked for a while in the dark and total silence, the river appeared before us in all its majesty. A fine mist was floating on the surface, half concealing an enormous boat waiting by the riverbank. We were about to begin an endless journey into the bowels of the jungle. As usual they made us wait for hours before boarding. The moon had vanished, and the mist on the water had thickened. Camilo cast off, and the *bongo** throbbed throughout its steel hull, sounding like an old submarine, and we could only guess at the unfathomable depths of the waters we were sailing.

Each of us found a place to spend the night, while the *bongo* plunged deep into the bowels of an ever denser jungle with its cargo of armed children playing on the deck, and its tired prisoners curled around their regrets. Mauricio was at the prow, with an enormous projector clamped between his knees throwing a beam of light through the fog in the tunnel of water and vegetation before him. With his one arm, he gave instructions to the captain who was standing at the stern, and I could not help but think that we were in the hands of a new breed of pirates.

After an hour had gone by, Camilo took a metal bucket he'd found on the deck, wedged it between his legs, and turned it into a drum. The diabolical rhythm he produced roused everyone's spirits and sparked a fiesta. He mingled revolutionary songs with popular tunes; it was impossible not to join in. The girls improvised *cumbias*,† swaying their hips and whirling in place, possessed by a dizzying urge to live. They were driven wild by the onlookers' full-throated singing and vigorous hand clapping.

---

* Amazonian barge.
† Colombian folk dance, originally performed by slaves from the high Magdalena, in the city of Monpox. It is inspired by African songs using Carib, Indian and Spanish instruments.

Camilo banished the cold and boredom, and probably the fear, too. I looked at the starless sky and the endless river and this cargo of men and women without a future, and I sang all the louder, searching in this semblance of joy for an aftertaste of happiness.

At one of the *bongo*'s stops, during the night, we came alongside a phantasmagorical abandoned camp, where suddenly a nasal voice taunted us from the treetops.

"Hello there, silly goose, you eat alone, and die alone, *ja, ja*!"

Then the voice grew closer.

"You don't see me, but I see you *ja, ja*."

It was a starving parrot who had not forgotten what he had learned. He let us feed him but kept a careful distance. His freedom was precious to him. As I observed him, I thought that he was far cleverer than we were. When the time came for us to leave, the parrot disappeared. Nothing could get him to come down from his treetop.

Farther along the river, Pata-Grande made arrangements to build a permanent camp. The location was on the bank, among some scattered peasant houses we'd glimpsed from the *bongo*. Once again it was an abandoned camp. We arrived in the middle of the night, during a violent storm. The young men set up our tents in the blink of an eye, using the old frames which were still solid.

When it stopped raining, I noticed one little boy, with a thicket of blond hair and the looks of a cherub, ill at ease holding an AK-47 in his hands.

"What's your name?"

"Mono Liso," he mumbled.

"Mono Liso? Is that your nickname?"

"I'm on duty, I can't talk," he said to me.

Katerina was going by, and she made fun of him, telling me, "Don't pay any attention to Mono Liso. He's a real pest."

Any desire to establish relations with my captors had vanished. Jeiner's departure had dampened the good-natured atmosphere that had reigned for a few short days. From my experience, the troops modelled their attitude on their leader's. I was convinced that over time there would be an inevitable deterioration into abuse.

A few months before my abduction, I'd switched on the television and come upon a fascinating documentary. In the 1970s, Stanford University had undertaken a simulation of prison conditions to study the behaviour of ordinary people. The findings were astonishing. Well-balanced, normal young people disguised as guards, with the power to open and close doors, turned into monsters. Other young people, equally well balanced and normal, masquerading as prisoners, let themselves be mistreated. One guard dragged a prisoner over to a closet, where he could only stand, not sit, and left him there for hours, until he passed out. It was a game. However, faced with peer pressure, only one of them had been able to react "out of character" and demand that the experiment be stopped.

I knew that the FARC was playing with fire. That we were in an enclosed world, without cameras, without witnesses, at the mercy of our jailers. For weeks I had observed the behaviour of these armed children, forced to act as adults. I could already detect all the symptoms of a relationship that could easily degenerate and turn poisonous. I thought it was possible to fight against it, by preserving one's own character. But I also knew that peer pressure could turn those children into the guardians of hell.

I was lost in thought when I saw a very short man, with glasses rammed on his nose and close-cut hair. He walked like Napoleon, his arms crossed behind his back. His presence disturbed me. There was a dark aura around him.

He came up to me from behind and whispered, "Hello, I am Enrique, your new commander."

57

AT THE GATES OF HELL

Very quickly it became clear to all of us that the arrival of Enrique would change things a great deal. He had been sent to oversee Pata-Grande, who visibly resented the fact. The cold war between the two men became obvious. They avoided each other and communication between them was kept to a bare minimum. Mauricio spent a great deal of time with the military hostages, and my comrades liked him. We had received a little radio with multiple bands in our shipment, as well as a big *panela* radio from Cesar. Finally, a third *panela* radio with big speakers arrived, which Mauricio lent to us to play *vallenatos* at full volume all day long. He knew that the soldiers enjoyed it, and he made use of this to plant in their hearts the seeds of dislike he himself felt toward Enrique.

As for Enrique, he did everything he could to make people despise him. The first order he gave was to forbid the girls from talking to the hostages. If any of them came up to us, they would be punished. The second was to oblige the guards to inform their leaders of the slightest communication they had with us. Any request we might make had to be cleared by him. In the space of a few weeks, the children's faces resembled adults', dark and scowling. I no longer saw them rolling in the moss, hugging each other. There were no more hysterical peals of laughter. Zamaidy had lost her following of young girls; Lili, Enrique's *socia*, had gone off with them.

The day he arrived in the camp, Enrique had taken her to his bed. Lili

was a fine specimen, no doubt about that. Her faintly copper skin emphasized her smile and her perfect teeth. She had smooth, silky dark hair
that she swung gracefully as she walked. She was flirtatious and mischievous, and her eyes shone when she spoke to the soldiers, to make them
understand that she considered herself exempt, at least in part, from
Enrique's order; she called him "Gafas," Specs, with obvious familiarity.
She had immediately, and joyfully, taken on her role as *ranguera*.

The rivalry among the men had spread to the girls. Zamaidy stayed off
to one side, also avoiding contact with her rival. From one day to the
next, Lili became a little tyrant and took great pleasure in ordering everyone around. The treatment we received began to deteriorate. The guards,
who had spoken to us respectfully, now began to take certain liberties, to
which I reacted coldly. The soldiers saw nothing wrong with it; they didn't
mind a bit of heavy-handed camaraderie. But I feared that if a certain level
of courtesy was lost, we would spiral into the kind of rude behaviour so
prevalent in Sombra's prison. My fears proved well founded. Very quickly
the tone went from joking to barking. The young boys felt they were
gaining ascendancy over their peers if they ventured to give us orders on
the slightest pretext. They couldn't help but see that there was a power
struggle between Gafas and Pata-Grande. Because Pata-Grande was close to
the soldiers, Enrique felt entitled to dictate precise directives regarding the
guerrillas' behaviour toward us, in order to point a finger at Pata-Grande.
The kids were clever enough to grasp that Enrique would encourage any
form of severe treatment toward the prisoners.

As for Pata-Grande, he wanted to play the mediator. He believed that by
maintaining control over the prisoners he could convince Cesar that
Enrique's presence was pointless. So he insisted on having us invited to
what he called "cultural hours." The young people loved it, and our presence stimulated them. They sat us down on freshly cut tree trunks. There
were riddles, recitals, songs, and spoofs, and we were all invited to take
turns and join in. My heart wasn't in it.

I saw myself with my cousins, in the old house where my grandmother
lived, making up a show to honour our parents. We ran up the old
wooden stairs that led to the attic in a stampede, and I could hear my

grandmother downstairs shouting that we were going to bring the house down. In the attic there was a chest where Mom kept her ball gowns and the crowns she'd been given when she was a beauty queen, and we all took turns dressing up in them. We would recite and sing and dance, just like in this jungle, because children's games are the same everywhere. Invariably one of my cousins would shout "A mouse, a mouse!" and there would be a frantic retreat in the other direction to throw ourselves down the stairway into my grandmother's arms before she could scold us. This little Proust's madeleine came to remind me of what I had lost. I didn't feel like playing. The time that these people were stealing from me, keeping me away from my children, could not be dressed up in some cultural hour. My comrades said that my attitude was contemptuous and that I was preventing the others from having some fun. The only one who understood how wrenching this was for me was Lucho.

"We don't have to go," he said, patting my hand. And then, with a touch of humour, he added, "Yes, we can stay here and be bored. We could even have a contest to see who's the most bored between the two of us."

I didn't insist, but my reservations were reported to the guerrillas. Pata-Grande came to warn us, "Everyone takes part or no one does."

One day there was an exceptional arrival of fruit salad from a neighbouring village. There must have been a road leading to the camp, and I was relieved to know that civilization was not completely inaccessible. The fruit salad was distributed only to the guerrillas, but because I was convalescent, Gafas allowed me to have a cupful. I've never eaten anything so good in my life. The fruit was fresh and just ripe. There was mango, apricot, plum, watermelon, banana, and medlar. The flesh was firm, juicy, and tender, melting in my mouth, topped with an unctuous sugary cream that stuck to my palate. I was unable to speak after the first mouthful, and by the second I focused on running my tongue all around my mouth to capture every flavour. I was about to take my third bite when I stopped short, my mouth still open. "No, the rest is for Lucho."

One of my comrades saw me as I was handing Lucho my cup. He leaped from his hammock as if he were on a spring and called out to Mauricio. He wanted to complain about the preferential treatment I was getting. We were all prisoners, so why should I get more to eat than they did? The very next day, they gave another turn of the screw. We'd been in the habit, ever since Jeiner's time, of going to the *chontos* without having to ask permission from the guard. I was on my way there when the guard called out curtly, "Where you going?"

"Where do you think?"

"You have to ask me for permission, get it?"

I didn't answer, thinking that things would only get worse. And they did, but for other reasons. A squadron of helicopters passed right over the camp, turned around several miles away, and then flew directly overhead again, covering us with their shadow for a few seconds.

Mauricio gave the order to strike camp that very minute and to hide with our *equipos* in the *manigua*. We waited, crouching in the vegetation. From dusk until midnight, I was devoured by microscopic ticks that took possession of every pore in my skin. I couldn't even think straight, struggling against a torture of itching.

Ángel, a young guerrilla, was determined to chat with me. He was a nice-looking boy, not mean, I thought, though somewhat slow. He was listening to the radio, sitting on his heels, and seemed impatient. "Have you heard the news?" he said, opening his eyes wide to get my attention.

I went on desperately scratching, unable to grasp what could be attacking me like this.

"Those are *cuitibas*. Stop scratching, you're just feeding them all the quicker. You have to pull them out with a needle."

"*Cuitibas?* Microscopic ticks! How awful! They're everywhere . . ."

"They're tiny."

He switched on his flashlight and aimed the beam onto his arm.

"There, see that dot moving? That's a *cuitiba*."

He dug his fingernail into his skin until he bled and then declared, "It got away!"

Someone ahead of us shouted, "Switch off your lights! Shit! You want them to bomb us? Pass it on!" The voices echoed around us, every guerrilla repeating exactly the same thing, one after the other, all along the column, until it came to Ángel, who recited it reproachfully to his neighbour, as if it had nothing to do with him. He eventually switched off the flashlight and was laughing like a child caught doing something naughty.

He continued in a whisper, "So! Have you heard the news?"

"What news?"

"They're going to extradite Simón Trinidad."[*]

Simón Trinidad had been present at the meeting at Pozos Colorados[†] between all the presidential candidates and the FARC leaders. I remembered him well; he hadn't opened his mouth, just sat taking notes and passing bits of paper to Raúl Reyes, who was officiating as group leader. During the peace negotiations he had declared that international human rights were a bourgeois concept. His speech was all the more astonishing in that he himself came from a bourgeois family from the Caribbean coast, had studied at the Swiss school in Bogotá, and taken courses in economics at Harvard. I had stood up before the end of the conference to go and get some air. The session had been endless, and it was very hot. Simón Trinidad got up behind me and followed me out. He had been gallant, opening the door for me and holding it while I went through. I'd thanked him, and we exchanged a few words. I found there was something hard and brittle about the man. Then I forgot about him.

Until the day he was captured in a shopping centre in Quito, Ecuador, without his ID. The FARC's immediate reaction was to make threats. Trinidad's capture, according to them, meant the failure of the talks with Europe for my release. They claimed he had been in Quito to meet with representatives of the French government.

However, every time the arrival of European envoys was announced on the radio, the Colombian government dragged the bait of the "humanitarian agreement" back out of the closet, and the FARC lost interest in any contact with outsiders. My enthusiasm always ended in disappointment, because of their inability to initiate any negotiations.

According to Lucho, Trinidad's arrest was a central obstacle to our

---

[*] Simón Trinidad was the nom de guerre of high-ranking FARC leader Juvenal Palmera Pineda.
[†] Near San Vicente del Caguán.

release. I felt, on the other hand, that it was a new variable that could lead to negotiations. The FARC had very quickly announced that Simón Trinidad must be added to the list of prisoners they wanted to exchange for us. But the revelation of Trinidad's possible extradition confirmed our greatest fear. "If they send Trinidad to the United States, the Americans will never get out of here. And neither will you!" Lucho had already said, months earlier back in Sombra's prison, when we were analysing the various possibilities.

We were all sitting in a row in the dark. Two other guerrillas had slipped in between Lucho and me. Gafas had given the order that prisoners must be physically separated by guards. When Ángel told me the news of Trinidad's extradition, I turned instinctively to speak to Lucho. "Did you hear?"

"No, what you talking about?"

"They're going to extradite Simón Trinidad."

"Oh, no, what a shit!" he exclaimed spontaneously, visibly distraught.

The guerrilla who was between us interrupted. "Comrade Trinidad is one of our best commanders. Keep your insults to yourself. We don't like the use of vulgar words here."

"No, you're mistaken. Nobody is insulting Simón Trinidad," I said.

"He said he was a shit!" Ángel retorted.

58

DESCENT INTO HELL

The enormous *bongo* arrived at midnight. We were ordered to board in complete silence. The guerrillas tied their hammocks to the metal bars that supported the canvas roof of the *bongo* and went to sleep. Shortly after four o'clock in the morning, the *bongo* shook and the rattling and banging as we came in to dock woke everyone up. Enrique announced that we would be disembarking. A huge house overlooking the river seemed to be waiting for us. I prayed to God who was listening to let us spend the rest of the night there. I wanted to hear Mom's voice. She was the only one who could calm me down. My little radio wasn't working very well. It needed an antenna, and this was something I could only set up at a fixed campsite. The other radios had been stored away and were inaccessible. With our *equipos* on our backs, we were made to walk single file down a path alongside the house, then we left it behind to cross immense pastures, perfectly enclosed with impeccable white picket fences. It was already a quarter to five. Where were we? Where were we going?

The sky was ochre, precursor of dawn. The thought that Mom would be speaking to me in a few minutes was paralysing me. It was as if I no longer knew how to walk. I stumbled over flat, even ground that presented no obstacles other than the mud which clung to my boots and the long oblique shadows that changed the aspect of the terrain. Ángel was walking alongside me and he made fun of me, saying, "*Parece un pato.*"*

That was enough to make me slip and end up lying in the mud. He helped me back to my feet with a forced, exaggerated laugh, looking all around him as if he were afraid someone might have seen us.

I went to smooth off my clothes, now coated with mud, and then I wiped my hands on my trousers and pulled out my radio. It was three minutes to five.

Ángel looked at me, enraged. "No way! Keep moving, we're behind."

"Mom is going to speak to me in three minutes."

I fiddled impatiently with my radio, shaking it in every direction. He took his M-16, pointed it at me, and shouted, "Start walking, or I'll shoot!"

We walked all day long under a baking sun. I stayed walled up in relentless silence as we passed through elegantly maintained estates, one after the other, with cattle as far as the eye could see, all surrounded by virgin forest.

"*Todo esto es de las FARC,*"† Ángel boasted, before we entered the undergrowth.

Ángel stopped under a gigantic tree to pick up some strange-looking, grey-velvet fruit that were strewn over the ground. He handed one to me.

"This is the *juanchaco*, the chewing gum of the jungle!" he announced, as he peeled the fruit with his teeth and began sucking its flesh. It tasted sweet and sour and, as he had warned, the flesh was very chewy. It gave us both a timely boost to our energy.

We penetrated a wall of vegetation, made of creepers as thick as a man's body that intertwined to build an impenetrable weave. The scouts had been through hours ahead of us, hacking away with their machetes on either side to open the path. It took us hours to keep on their tracks and find our way out of the labyrinth, and that was only thanks to Ángel's concentration, for he could tell where we'd already been, although the dense tangle of plants offered no landmarks.

---

* "You look like a duck!"
† "All of this belongs to the FARC."

Stunned, we stumbled out onto a veritable freeway, wide enough for three huge trucks to roll side by side, and we followed it without stopping until twilight, crossing grandiose bridges made from the millennial trees they had gutted with a chain saw.

"*Ésto lo hicieron las FARC,*"* he pointed out.

Hours later I saw the others, sitting down far ahead of us. They were drinking Coke and eating bread. Lucho had removed his boots and socks, which were drying over his backpack, covered with greenbottle flies. His toes were purple, and the skin of his feet was peeling off in shreds. I made no comment. I trembled at the thought of amputation.

A white jeep showed up. We were driven along miles of mud and dust for hours. We went through a ghost village, with pretty, empty houses set in a circle around a little arena, with its wooden bleachers and sandy ring – for the *corridas*. The car's headlights had swept over a sign that read BIENVENIDOS A LA LIBERTAD.† *How ironic, we have arrived at "Freedom,"* I thought. I knew La Libertad was in the region of Guaviare.

The militia drove through La Libertad with the same contentment as El Mocho Cesar when he went into La Unión-Penilla. Lucho was sitting next to me. He gave me a sad smile as he whispered, "La Libertad . . . Fate is snubbing us."

And I answered, "No it's not, it's good omen!"

The car stopped at a pier beside an immense river. The guerrillas had already set up tents all around. It was cold, and there was the smell of a storm in the air. Gafas did not allow us to take out our hammocks. We waited until dawn under the fine drizzle, so tired we did not have the strength even to swat flies, watching as the guerrillas found shelter and slept. With the first light of day, a *bongo* came in to dock. We had to squeeze up in the bow, in a space too small for all of us, packed in together to make room, asphyxiated by the stink of diesel coming straight at us from the engine. The guerrillas spread out over the entire deck. At least here we could sleep.

---

* "The FARC did this."
† "Welcome to Freedom."

The journey lasted nearly two weeks, reaching farther and farther into the depths of the jungle. We sailed at night. At dawn the *motorista*,* who was not the captain, would find a place to moor, according to Gafas's precise indications. Then we had the right to set up our hammocks, take a bath, and wash our clothes. I had been listening to Mom religiously. She did not mention Simón Trinidad; she was getting ready to spend Christmas with my children.

One dark night the *bongo* stopped. We were made to get off. On the far shore, the lights of a large village were like a magical apparition. The river was scattered with stars. It was all inaccessible to us.

We went along the opposite riverbank, jumping over rocks; we discovered there were rapids, and that is why we'd had to leave the boat behind. Another *bongo* was already waiting a distance downriver. It immediately bore us away from the village, far from the lights and the people.

The next morning, farther down, still more *cachiveras*† blocked the river. They were impressive. They stretched over hundreds of yards, in a tumultuous expanse of raging water. We repeated the manoeuvre.

Children were playing on the opposite shore, by a little peasant house across from the rapids, and there was a rowboat upstream from the *cachiveras.* A dog was running around the children, barking. They hadn't seen us. We were hidden behind the trees.

I could hear the sound of a motor: a speedboat.

They appeared on our right, heading rapidly upstream. It was an outboard, driven by a young guy in a uniform, with two others leaning against the prow, one in civilian clothes, the other in a khaki outfit. They sped straight ahead, as if the idea of going over the *cachiveras* was perfectly natural. The boat leaped up over the first line of rocks, bounced over the second, and on hitting the third, it exploded. The passengers flew into the air, propelled like missiles, and disappeared into the turbulent, foaming currents.

Gafas was sitting opposite me. He did not bat an eyelid. I rushed forward at the same time as Lucho to the edge of the river. The children had

---

* Mechanic in charge of the boat's engine.
† Rapids.

already jumped into their rowboats and were rowing as fast as they could to reach the pieces of the wreck surfacing on the river. The dog was standing at the prow and barking, the children's shouts exciting it even more.

A head had surfaced. The dog jumped in the water and struggled desperately against the current. The head disappeared again in the swirling water. The children shouted ever louder and called to their dog. The animal, disoriented, turned on himself and was borne away by the current, until he managed, courageously, to swim back to the rowboat. Gafas did not move. Mauricio was already running to and fro along the bank, carrying a pole he had just cut, using his machete with amazing dexterity, not to be expected from a one-armed man, and he kept staring stubbornly at the river. The troops looked on in silence. Finally Gafas opened his mouth. "That will teach them to act like idiots." Then he added, "Rescue the engine."

I was grieving. Lucho was holding his head in his hands. My comrades gazed at the river, aghast. Around us life went on without any transition. A makeshift *rancha* was set up, and we all went to get our own bowl and spoon.

At night we climbed into a rowboat similar to the children's, with the rescued outboard on it. We drifted on the current for hours, until dawn. We saw no more houses, or lights, or dogs.

Next morning, when the sun was already high in the sky and we were still travelling, Gafas gave the order to stop, and then he suddenly hurried forward like a madman.

"My rifle!" he shouted to Lili.

It was a tapir.

"Aim for the ears," somebody said.

It was a magnificent animal, bigger than a bull, and it swam powerfully as it crossed the river. Its chocolate-coloured skin gleamed in the sunlight as it lifted its snout out of the water, revealing a bright pink mouth, which gave it a certain feminine allure. The animal swam toward the boat, unaware of the danger, and looked at us mildly through its curling eyelashes, almost smiling with ingenuous curiosity.

"Please don't kill it," I begged. "These are endangered animals. We're very lucky to see one."

"They're all over the place!" shouted Lili.

"It's your steak," Enrique said, shrugging his shoulders. Then, turning to my companions, "If you're not hungry . . ."

We were all hungry. However, no one said anything, and Enrique interpreted this as an answer.

"Fine," he said, putting away his gun. "We know how to protect nature."

He gave us a huge grin, but his gaze was murderous.

59

THE DEVIL

We arrived at a steep bank that dropped straight into the river. It was the dry season, and the water level was very low. We were at a meeting of two rivers. One small tributary came to join the main river at right angles. We could see only the gorge of the secondary river, deep and narrow, with a stream of water winding its way through. This was a regular feature. Wherever we went, the flow of water had decreased phenomenally. I asked the Indians among the troops whether this had always been the case. "It's climate change!" they declared.

Gafas announced that this would be our permanent camp. I shuddered at the thought. Living as a nomad was hateful, but at least I could nurture the illusion that we were headed toward freedom.

Our *cambuches** were constructed inland, a mile or so from the riverbank but very near the *caño*,[†] where a small dam was built, to provide for bathing and laundry. Lucho and I asked for palm leaves to use as mattresses in our *caletas*, and Tito, a little man with a lazy eye, took the time to teach us how to weave a carpet.

While he was working, we listened to the *panela* that was hanging

---

* *El cambuche* designates a dwelling place (tent and bed). The word *caleta* is used to designate a bed built on the ground. Sometimes *cambuche* and *caleta* can be used interchangeably.
[†] A small stream.

from a nail in Armando's *caleta*. We heard President Uribe making a proposal to the FARC, and this brought a halt to all our work setting up the camp. He said he was prepared to suspend Simón Trinidad's extradition to the United States if the FARC would release the sixty-three hostages they'd detained by December thirtieth. A feverish excitement overtook the camp, among jailers and hostages without distinction. It was a daring proposal, and the guerrillas liked the sound of it. They all thought Trinidad's extradition would be a painful blow to the organization.

Pata-Grande came to discuss it with the military prisoners, and he claimed that the FARC leaders were considering Uribe's proposal in a positive light. Months earlier the FARC had declared in a press release that "the time to negotiate had come," but the leaders were asking for a demilitarized zone in order to proceed with the negotiations. Uribe would not budge. He didn't want to make the same mistake that Pastrana's government had – giving the FARC a huge territory, which it had then turned into a sanctuary to carry out criminal operations.

However, the card Uribe was playing now might indeed break the deadlock. Up until this moment, I'd thought the guerrillas were attempting to negotiate our liberation and that it was Uribe's government that was causing such initiatives to fail. However, the offer not to have Trinidad extradited had me start to doubt. I wondered whether the FARC had simply never had any real intention of setting us free in the first place. In a way we had become the organization's calling cards. They needed to keep us, because we were more useful to them as trophies than as bargaining chips.

Tension in the camp began to rise. The rivalry between Mauricio and Gafas had reached its peak. When I asked for some sugar for Lucho, I created a huge fuss. Mauricio came to see me with a large package that he handed to me in front of everybody. "I have brought you my personal supply of sugar, because Gafas refuses to have some delivered to you. You will have to speak about it to Cesar!"

Our relations with the guards were also becoming tense. Gafas had made our regime even tougher. The guerrillas who hoped to find approval in the boss's eyes knew only too well that they'd be praised if they acted ruthlessly.

Watchtowers had been built at each corner of our compound. Young Mono Liso with the cherubic face was on duty one morning, his revolver in his fist, taking his job as sentinel very seriously. One of my companions went off to the *chontos* and forgot to inform him. In truth, it wasn't even necessary, because the *chontos* were perfectly visible from the guard post. "Where are you going?" screamed Mono Liso from his perch. My companion turned around, thought he was talking to someone else, and continued on his way. Mono Liso pulled out his revolver, aimed at my companion's legs, and fired three times.

The silence of the grave fell over the camp. Mono Liso was a good marksman. The bullets had grazed my companion's boots but hadn't wounded him.

"Next time I'll wedge one in your thigh to teach you to respect the rules."

My comrade was white as paper, and so were we. "We have to get out of here," whispered Lucho.

Some of the guerrillas offered to supply us with the things we needed, in exchange for sewing, or radio repair, or cigarettes. Every time we needed something – and that was every day – we were obliged to offer something in exchange. In the beginning the guards had been willing to help us, but now they realized they had absolute power over us, and they became increasingly bullying and irritable.

Lucho and I suffered more than the others. The order had been given to isolate and humiliate us. The slightest request we made was systematically denied.

"It's because we refuse to work for them," Lucho warned me.

At one point there was an outbreak of leishmaniasis, first among the guerrillas and then among us. I had never seen the effects of the disease up close. Although we often talked about it among prisoners, I also had not realized how serious it was. It was commonly called jungle leprosy, because it caused a degeneration of the skin to begin with, then spread to other organs, which decomposed as if they were rotting in place. It would begin with a little pimple, which, as a rule, no one would pay any attention to. But the disease went on doing its dirty work inside. I saw the damage it wrought on the leg and forearm of Armando. He had a big hole in his skin, softened as if acid had been poured on it. You could place your finger in the hole without his feeling any pain. When Lucho showed me a small spot that had just appeared on his temple, I merely shrugged; I could not imagine for a moment that it was the dreaded *pito*.*

Our ignorance in jungle diseases contrasted with our knowledge of FARC tricks. Pata-Grande came to inform us that there would be a Christmas celebration in our honour. Lucho and I sensed that they were setting a trap for us. We had seen Enrique in the *bongo* taking pictures. We talked about it with Bermeo and the others. Our companions, too, were on their guard. We were afraid that the guerilla would use this occasion to film us in secret and show the outside world how well they took care of us. But the idea of a party was too tempting to turn down.

The guerrillas had built a rectangular space, set off by tree trunks that served as benches, and the ground had been smoothed and covered with sand. They'd put a crate full of beer in one corner, and all the *guerrilleras* were sitting in a row waiting for us. It looked just like a dance floor. Sometimes you end up doing the opposite of what you planned to do. It happened to me that evening. The sound system was very loud. The music caused the trees all around us to quiver. The girls all got up at the same time and invited the military hostages to dance. It was impossible to refuse. When Ángel came all the way across the camp, walked onto the dance floor, and offered me his arm, I felt stupid. I sought Lucho's eyes. He was sitting with a beer in his hand, watching me. He shrugged and nodded. He obviously thought that if I refused, the guerrillas would take it badly. Everyone was staring. I could feel the pressure weighing heavily on me, and I hesitated for a few seconds. Finally I got up and agreed to dance. I had been around the dance floor twice at the most when I saw it: Enrique had a digital video camera, small and compact, aimed right at me. He was

---

* Another slang term for leishmaniasis.

hiding behind a tree. The little red light that came on to show that the camera was filming betrayed him. My heart leaped, and I stopped dancing then and there. I let go of Ángel and left him alone on the dance floor to go and sit down, turning my back on Enrique. I could have kicked myself for being so stupid. Ángel had already left with a laugh, delighted that he'd done such a good job.

In the jungle my upbringing was a handicap. I refrained from being blunt out of a fear of offending other people. I told myself repeatedly that I must forget all the codes of courtesy to survive in that jungle. Once my annoyance had dissipated, I took hold of myself. No, on the contrary, I decided. Each time I must try to be more polite. But Gafas's trap caused me to reevaluate all my good intentions. I could no longer go on reasoning as if I could apply the rituals and codes of the outside world to my present life. I was kidnapped. I could not expect these women and men to behave any differently. They lived in a world where evil was good. Killing, lying, and betrayal were all part of what was expected of them. I went up to Lucho, who was beside himself.

"We have to talk to Enrique. He had no right to film us without our consent."

The music stopped in the middle of the song. The girls disappeared, and the guards armed their rifles. They pushed us boorishly back to our camp. Our Christmas ended there.

Enrique came to see us the next day. Lucho had insisted on talking to him. The discussion turned sour. At first Enrique denied that it was all staged, but in the end he said that the guerrillas could do whatever they liked, which was tantamount to a confession. When Lucho said he was offended by his attitude, Enrique changed his stance and accused him of being a vulgar man and of having insulted Commander Trinidad. "You said he was a piece of shit."

They parted on very bad terms. We concluded that we could expect the worst from Enrique. Sure enough, the guards were ordered to treat us ruthlessly. One morning Lucho got up, worried. "We can't take this. We have to escape. If by December thirtieth the FARC has not accepted Uribe's proposal . . . we'll start to get ready to leave."

On December 30, the FARC remained silent. That afternoon, Simón Trinidad was put on board an aeroplane bound for the United States, extradited for drug trafficking. Long years of captivity lay ahead of us. We had to fill the day and not think about the future.

In our anxiety, the cases of leishmaniasis seemed to grow faster. The little pimple on Lucho's temple was not getting any bigger, but it hadn't disappeared. We remembered back to the night waiting for the bongo near La Libertad Guaviare – it was the perfect spot for the *pito* to bite. We decided to ask William his opinion, since he was an army nurse and the only one whose judgement might be reliable. His diagnosis removed any doubt.

"You have to begin treatment immediately, before the disease reaches your eye or your brain."

Enrique took revenge on Lucho, refusing to allow him the necessary treatment. We knew that the guerrillas had substantial supplies of Glucantime. They bought phials in Brazil or Venezuela; in Colombia the medication was embargoed, because of the war against the FARC. The army knew that the guerrillas were the main consumers of the drug, because they operated in zones where the disease was endemic.

Gira, who was in charge of healthcare, was a serious, cautious woman. Unlike Guillermo, she had not transformed the distribution of medicine into a black market. She came to examine Lucho and declared, "It's a lengthy treatment. You have to have at least thirty phials of Glucantime, at a rate of one injection a day. We'll start tomorrow."

The next day Gira did not show up, nor on the following days. She eventually claimed there was no more Glucantime, although we knew she was administering it daily to the other prisoners. I watched anxiously as the ulcer progressed, and I prayed. One evening when Tito (the guard who'd taught us to weave palm mattresses) was on duty, he came over and said, "It's the *cucho** who doesn't want to authorize your treatment. We have crates full of Glucantime, and we're waiting for some new ones. Tell Gira that you know there are phials in the pharmacy, and she'll be obliged to discuss your case in *el aula*."

---

* The commander, in this case Enrique, alias Gafas.

We followed Tito's advice and witnessed Gira's embarrassment when we pressured her.

"This is a crime against humanity," I declared, outraged.

"The notion of crimes against humanity is a bourgeois notion," retorted Gira.

60

NOW OR NEVER

January 2005. I had begun to prepare seriously for our escape. My exit plan was simple. We had to leave the camp on the pretext of going to the *chontos* and get to the river. Lucho was not happy with the idea of swimming for hours. So I thought I could make life jackets, using the *timbos*, the two old plastic oil containers that my companions had tossed out because they'd managed to get some brand-new ones in.

I also succeeded in getting a machete. Tiger, an Indian who had taken an immediate dislike to us because we hadn't wanted to give him Lucho's watch in exchange for some herbs that were supposed to cure leishmaniasis, had left it lying around when he was building Armando's *caleta*. Enrique threatened to apply severe sanctions if the machete was not found. I had hidden it in the *chontos*. They searched the camp from top to bottom, and I lived through torture, feeling as if all their suspicions were focused on me.

At the end of January, we were told, to our great surprise, that we would be going on an "outing": Enrique wanted to take us to swim in the *cachiveras* upstream. Now that the level of the river had risen, the *cachiveras* had become an ideal swimming hole. The soldiers were all very enthusiastic about the idea. As for me, I feared that this was another strategy to get us away from our *caletas* to do a thorough search. The order was peremptory: Everyone must go. The days leading up to it were torture for

Lucho and me. What would they do if they found us out? I believed that it would be the end of the world.

My companions set off as happy as children. Lucho and I were wary. However, it turned out to be a useful exercise. I observed the lay of the land, the vegetation, the distance we covered in a given time, and I included it all in my plan.

We were allowed to fish, and they set us up with the necessary gear – some hooks and a bit of nylon line – and I watched how Tiger found bait and cast his line. I applied myself to learning, and I managed it with a certain degree of success. "Beginner's luck," said Tiger sarcastically. The main thing was that we managed to pocket a few hooks and a few yards of line, on the pretext that our original line had broken.

Tiger had found some tortoise eggs while exploring the rocks. He had swallowed two of them whole right there in front of me, ignoring my exclamations of disgust. I had done the same. They smelled strongly of fish but had a different taste, which wouldn't have been all that bad if the texture of the yolk had not been unpleasantly sandy.

On the way back, I decided I would return the machete. The vegetation on either side of the river was not that dense, and we wouldn't have to fight against walls of creepers or go through bamboo forests like those I'd seen elsewhere. I couldn't go on living in this debilitating paranoia. To run away, and make our escape successful, we would need to keep our wits. The outing had put our situation in perspective: It was possible to survive.

It became all the more important not to run the risk of being caught because of Tiger's machete. I chose a moment when the men were behind the *chontos*. They'd been ordered to cut as many palm leaves as possible to make a *maloka*.* I left the machete where they were working. Ángel found it and took it to Enrique, holding it up defiantly. To my great relief, that was the end of the matter.

It felt like a sign from fate when Gafas came to see me and asked me to translate the instructions, in English, for a GPS unit that he'd just received.

---

* A native hut, with a roof made of palm leaves.

It was a little yellow-and-black device with satellite reception, an electronic compass, and a barometric altimeter.

"Yes, of course I understand what it says," I answered, "but I have to look after Lucho. He's very worried about his leishmaniasis. It's getting worse, and there's no Glucantime for him."

The next morning Gira arrived grinning from ear to ear. She had just received a new shipment of medication.

"That's strange," remarked Pinchao. "I didn't hear any engines."

We didn't say anything. Gira knew to disinfect the skin with alcohol where she would apply the injection of Glucantime, a procedure that other nurses seemed to consider superfluous. The shot was particularly painful, because the medication had the consistency of oil, and on injection it produced an extreme burning sensation.

The illness had spread considerably, and Gira was dismayed. Intensive treatment was called for. She decided to inject some of the phial directly beneath the skin of the boil. The effect was immediate. Lucho lost consciousness, and above all he lost his memory.

When Enrique asked for the translation of his instruction manual, I accepted in the hope that it would be a way to get adequate food for Lucho. I knew that the guerrillas went fishing every day. They had made *potrillos*, which are a sort of canoe hewn from the trunk of the balsa tree, whose bark is not unlike birch and known to float like cork. These canoes were ideal for moving down the river, and they could reach the deepest water, where the fishing was plentiful. There were tons of fish but Enrique would not allow them to give us any.

When Lucho came round, he had lost not only his childhood memories but also, what was worse this time, the memory of our plans. William said it had been a mistake to inject the medication on his temple. I, on the other hand, wanted to believe that if we treated his diabetes, he would recover his entire brain and, most importantly, we would find all of him again.

Enrique sent some fish, and I set to work on his Garmin GPS. I had the device in my hands for an entire morning, and I noted the information it contained. In particular there was a place that had been recorded under the name of *Maloka*, with the following coordinates: N 1 59 32 24 and W 70 12 53 39. *Maloka** could be the name Enrique had given to the camp. I was surprised that he'd left me in the presence of this information, but of course they must have thought I did not know how to decipher it, which was true, except that I remembered the basic lessons of cartography learned at school.

Armed with my new knowledge, I went to speak with Bermeo. We agreed that we had to find a way to get hold of a map with longitude and latitude on it. This secret information was essential for all of us. He recalled having seen one in a little notebook that Pinchao had, a tiny map of Colombia with a grid. Then I remembered that I myself possessed a set of world maps that were in the yearly planner I had on me when I was kidnapped.

I'd kept it to see the series of appointments I'd made for the days and weeks and months that followed my capture, appointments I'd missed. This same yearly planner became an essential tool against boredom. I had set about learning all the world capitals, their size and population. Sometimes with Lucho, to pass the time, we tried to make each other slip up on our geography. "What's the capital of Swaziland?" "Easy: Banana!" replied Lucho playfully, poking fun at our silly mnemonics.

So I had a map of Latin America, with a little Colombia on it, the equator, and a few latitudes and longitudes with sketchy coordinates. Pinchao's map was much smaller, but more clearly marked. In addition, along the edge there was a tiny printed scale, and we copied it onto a pack of cigarettes to have the best estimate possible. All we had to do was divide the distance between two parallel lines to figure out where the second latitude was located. A little higher than the equator and we had a good idea of the coordinate 1°59 N. The lines of longitude ran from right to left, from 65 west, which went through Venezuela and Brazil, to 70, which was right on Colombia, to 75, west of Bogotá. So 70°12 put us a few millimetres to the left of the 70th meridian. Visibly we were in the Guaviare.

I spent hours mesmerized by Pinchao's map. If our calculations were correct, we must be in a little horn of the department of Guaviare that

---

* House.

followed the course of the river Inírida, at the frontier of the Guainía department. This river belonged to the Orinoco Basin. If we were on one of its tributaries, the current would take us to Venezuela. I dreamed of it. With my makeshift ruler, I measured the distance between the imaginary point that we called Maloka and Puerto Inírida, the capital of Guainía, where we were bound to end up. It was a bit more than 180 miles in a straight line, but the river took a very winding course, which could easily triple the actual distance to travel. If we thought about it, Puerto Inírida was not the goal of our journey. All we needed was to find a human being along the way who did not belong to the FARC and who would agree to help guide us out of the labyrinth.

I felt like I was the master of the world. I knew where we were, and that changed everything. I was aware that we would have to prepare to last a very long time in this jungle. The distances were enormous. They had chosen their hiding place well. There was nothing definite for a hundred-mile radius, through the thickest of jungles. The closest town was Mitú, to the south, exactly sixty miles, but there was no navigable way to get there. The idea of marching through the forest without a compass seemed like a greater madness than what I sought to undertake. Was it possible to embark on such an expedition with a sick man? The answer was, I would never leave without him. We would have to learn to survive with what we found and take the risk. It was better than waiting to be killed by our captors.

One day Gira's boyfriend came to dig some *chontos*. He was a huge Indian with a deep gaze. I hoped to chat with him for a few minutes. But I wished I hadn't. He said, straight out, "The FARC doesn't like you. You are everything we are fighting against. You'll only get out of here twenty years from now. We have all the organization it takes to keep you as long as we like."

This reminded me of Orlando, talking about one of our fellow inmates: Look, he's behaving like a cockroach. They sweep him out, and he scurries back in again. As I tried to befriend that Indian, I saw myself as a cockroach. *There is no greater stimulant to finding the determination to escape*, I thought.

The fish did wonders for Lucho. Two weeks later his memory was back in place. While he'd been absent, I'd felt as if I were talking to a stranger.

When he became normal again and I could confide in him at length, telling him how I'd suffered to see him like that, he played at frightening me, pretending to have new memory lapses that panicked me. He would burst out laughing and hug me, sheepish but delighted to see how much I cared for him.

Everything was ready. We had even decided to leave and interrupt the Glucantime treatment. It was endless, and Lucho wasn't getting any better. We could still improve our supplies, but we planned to find things to eat in nature, in order to travel as light as possible. We began to wait for the right moment: A terrible storm at six-thirty in the evening. We expected it every evening. In this tropical forest where it rained every day, the year 2005 was one of unprecedented drought. We waited a long time.

61

THE ESCAPE

February 2005. To keep busy we decided to start up our French classes again. Only Jhon Pinchao, a young policeman who had been taken hostage almost as soon as he enlisted, decided to join in. He was convinced he'd been born with bad luck and, according to him, the chain of events that had brought him to Maloka was proof that his entire life was doomed to fail. He nourished a deep sentiment of injustice, which left him bitter, and he would get angry at the entire world. I liked him. He was intelligent and generous, and I enjoyed talking with him, even though most of the time I would leave him annoyed, declaring, "You see! It's impossible to talk with you."

He was born in Bogotá, in the poorest neighbourhood in the city. His father was a bricklayer, and his mother worked wherever she could. He had spent his childhood in utter poverty, shut up with his sisters in a rented room in a slum. His mother locked them inside during the day, since she could not look after them. At the age of five, his oldest sister prepared their lunch on a portable stove that his mother left right on the floor. He remembered often being cold and hungry.

He adored his father and revered his mother. Eventually his parents managed – the fruit of intense labour and unlimited courage, with their own hands and after work hours – to build a little house and give their children a decent education. Pinchao finished high school and then enlisted in the police, because he had no money to continue his studies.

From the very beginning of our French lessons, I noticed that Pincho, the nickname we all used, was a very fast learner. He had a great thirst for knowledge and asked all kinds of questions that I tried to answer as best I could. He was delighted when, after he'd squeezed me like a lemon all day long, I would admit defeat and confess I didn't know a particular answer.

He became bolder and asked me to introduce him to what he called "my universe." He wanted to know about the other countries I'd visited and lived in. I took him for a walk through my memories, through different seasons, something he knew nothing about. I explained that I liked autumn best for its baroque splendour, even though it was so short; that springtime in the Luxembourg Gardens was a fairy tale; and I described snow and the delights of winter sports, which he thought I'd made up just to please him.

After our French lessons, we would immerse ourselves in another subject. Pincho wanted to learn all about the rules of etiquette. When he first asked me, I immediately thought I was the wrong person for the task.

"To be honest, my poor Pincho, you're out of luck! If my sister were here, she would give you the best possible training. I really don't know much about etiquette. But I can show you at least what I learned from my mom."

He was very excited at the prospect. "I've always thought I would panic if I had to sit down one day with a pile of forks and lots of glasses lined up in front of me," he said. "But I was always ashamed to ask."

We made use of a shipment of planks one day to build a table, on the pretext that we needed it for our French lessons.

I asked Tito to use his machete to chop bits of wood to make pretend knives and forks, and we played tea party, together with Lucho, who took our classes in *savoir faire* very seriously and delighted in correcting my every other word.

"Forks on the left, knives on the right," I began.

"Yes, but on the right you can also put a soup spoon or snail tongs," said Lucho.

"Wait a minute, what are snail tongs?" Pincho wanted to know.

"Don't listen to him, he's trying to impress you."

"But how do I know which one to use?" insisted Pincho, dismayed.

"No need to guess. They are placed in the order you use them."

"And if you hesitate, just look at your neighbour," Lucho piped up again.

"That's good advice. Moreover, you must always wait for the host to set the example. You must never do anything before he does."

"If you do, you might have the same thing happen to you as happened to an African head of state – actually, I don't know if he was African, but he was invited to dinner with the Queen of England. They had put finger bowls on the table, and the man thought it was a cup to drink out of, so that's just what he did. To spare the man any embarrassment, the Queen drank from her finger bowl, too."

"What's a finger bowl?"

We spent entire afternoons talking about how to set the table, how to serve the wine, to help oneself, to eat, and we went off into a world of courtesy and refined pleasures.

I swore that the day I finally got home, I would pay attention to detail, I would always have flowers in my room and wear perfume, and I would no longer forbid myself to eat ice cream or cakes. I understood that in my life I had abandoned too many little pleasures, taking them for granted. I wrote it down somewhere, so that I would never forget, because I sensed that the unbearable lightness of living could condemn me to forget what I'd experienced in captivity. But like everything I wrote in the jungle, I burned it to avoid its falling into the wrong hands.

I was thinking about all this, sitting in my *caleta*, planning my French lessons for the next day, when I suddenly heard a long, creaking sound – it was painful, horrible, the way it echoed, as if it were increasing in volume to surprise us and oblige us to look up. I saw a rustling of leaves over by the *chontos*, and then I saw Tiger dash hell bent for leather through the camp, abandoning his guard post. The tallest tree in the forest had chosen that particular moment to die, and it had come crashing down like a felled giant. Our surprise was equal to that of the young trees it brought down with it, which smashed with a thundering sound as they landed on the ground, raising a huge cloud of dust in the blast generated by the fall. Parrots flew away, terrified. My hair was swept backward by the shock wave; my face was coated with a cloud of particles that covered all the tents and the surrounding foliage. The sky had opened, revealing frayed yellow clouds. Everyone ran to take shelter. It didn't even occur to me to do so.

I could have died, I said to myself, stunned, realizing that a branch of the giant tree had landed six feet from my foot. But it was a beautiful sight.

I was delighted that this providential opening would allow us to gaze at the sunset and the stars.

"Forget it!" warned Lucho. "You'll see, they'll make us change camp."

And indeed, a few days later Mauricio gave the signal: We had to pack. The place where we set up camp was set back from the river. As at the Maloka camp, there was a *caño* to the left of our site. It was much wider, and it split into a fork before reaching the river. The larger branch served the guerrilla camp.

Very quickly we all slipped back into our habits. We threw our aluminium-wire antennas into the trees to connect with the world. I didn't miss a single one of Mom's messages. After Trinidad was extradited, she undertook to get in touch with anybody who might have the ear of President Uribe. It was her intention to win over the president's wife. Mom made a point of saying all this in public, on the air, as if it were just the two of us talking.

"I don't know what to try next," she said. "I feel terribly alone. People are bored with your story. I feel as if all the doors are closing. My friends no longer want to see me. They say I depress them with my tears. And it's true, my darling, that I speak only about you, because it's the only thing that interests me, and all the rest seems superficial to me now. As if I could spend my time chitchatting when I know you are suffering!"

I wept in silence, repeating in a hushed voice, "Stay strong, my little mum. I have a surprise for you. In a few days, I will arrive somewhere, in a village by the side of the river. I will go and hide in the church, because the guerrillas will be looking for me everywhere, and I will be frightened. But from a distance, I'll see the church tower, and I'll find the priest. He will have a telephone and I'll dial your number. That is the only one I have not forgotten: '*Dos doce, veintitrés, cero tres.*'* I will hear it ringing – once, twice, three times. You're always busy doing something. Finally you'll pick up. I will hear the sound of your voice, and I will let it echo for a few moments in the void, just long enough to offer up my thanks. I will say, 'Mom?' and you will reply 'Astrica?' because our voices are similar, and it can only be her. And then I'll say, 'No, Mamita, it's me, Ingrid.'"

My God! How many times have I imagined that scene?

Mom was in the midst of preparing an appeal with the support of all the NGOs in the world, to ask President Uribe to appoint a negotiator for the humanitarian agreement. She was counting on the unconditional support of one of the country's leading lights. Former president Alfonso López, looking on from his ninety years of age, continued to have an influence on Colombia's destiny.

All through my years in politics, I had maintained a certain distance from President López. In a way, he incarnated for me the old political class.

A few days before my abduction, I received an invitation to go see him. I arrived early at his house, one Saturday morning, with the only one of my security escorts whom I trusted fully. I was startled as I rang at the door, because it opened instantly and it was President López himself who greeted me.

López was a very tall man, handsome despite his advanced age, with eyes an aquatic blue that changed according to his mood. He was elegantly dressed, with a cashmere turtleneck, a dark blue blazer, and impeccably ironed grey flannel trousers. He asked me to follow him into his library, where he settled into a large armchair, his back to the window. I have no memory of opening my mouth for the two hours our meeting lasted. I was won over. By the time I left him, I realized that he had rid me of all my preconceived ideas about him.

---

* "Two-one-two, two-three zero-three."

Through my radio I learned that López had been to Neiva, a city as hot as a devil's cauldron, to take part in a demonstration organized on our behalf. Along with his wife, who had subjected herself to the same ordeal, he'd brandished photographs of the hostages during the march. Mom was there, with all the families of the other hostages. Intolerance had reached its apex. Some people in Colombia thought their demands for our liberation were an inadmissible compliance with the guerrillas' blackmail and an act of treason toward the country. President López had lent his support to our plight at a time when so many were turning a blind eye. He died when I was still chained to a tree. I suffered. I had come to truly love him. But by the time he left us, he had won his last battle: Fighting for our freedom had become politically correct in Colombia.

It was his voice I heard first on the radio when we disembarked and it made me like the new place. Our new camp had been designed in a strange way. We were isolated from the barracks that the guerrillas were building for themselves, and we had only two guards at either end of our camp. I had sketched out a plan that seemed perfect. Moreover, Lucho's treatment was finished. He had received 163 injections of Glucantime over six months, five times more than the normal dose. The side effects had caused him to suffer, in particular, pain in his teeth and bones. But the sore on his temple had healed. All that was left was a slight indentation of the skin, which would be a lifelong testimony to the prolonged struggle he'd waged against leishmaniasis.

We were still waiting for the providential storm at six-thirty in the evening that would allow us to escape. Every evening we fell asleep disappointed that we'd not been able to leave but secretly relieved that we'd been able to sleep another night in a dry place.

One morning Mono Liso and a group of five other guerrillas came very early, with enormous squared beams that they had cut at the base to make posts. They drove them into the ground every five yards around our camp. Simultaneously we were all moved inside what would in all likelihood become an enclosure. I thought I would die. They wouldn't have time to finish it that day. The mesh and barbed wire would be put up the following day.

"It's our last chance, Lucho. If we want to leave, we have to do it tonight."

July 17, 2005. My sister's birthday was the following day. I got our *mini-cruseros* ready, and I put everything in a corner of my *caleta*, inside the mosquito net. Mono Liso went by at that very moment, and in spite of the black veil of the insect shield, our gazes met. He looked at me, feigned indifference, but in that very second I understood that he had read my thoughts. I went to stand in line for my last hot meal with my bowl in my hand, thinking that I was mad, that he couldn't have seen my intentions, and that everything would be fine. I confirmed that Lucho was also ready, and I asked him to wait for me to come and get him. I had faith.

Big black storm clouds were gathering in the sky above. There was already the smell of rain. And sure enough, big raindrops began to fall. I made the sign of the cross inside my *caleta* and asked the Virgin Mary to take care of me, because I was already trembling. I had the feeling she'd ignored me, for in the distance I saw Mono Liso headed my way. It wasn't time for the changing of the guard. My heart sank. The boy was coming along a wooden walkway on piles that the guerrillas had just finished, to connect their camp to ours. The walkway went all around the camp, just three yards from my tent. It was already raining quite hard. It was exactly six o'clock. Mono Liso stopped just in front of me and sat on the walkway, his legs dangling, his back to me, indifferent to the storm.

It was my fault. I'd been too nervous, and I'd set off the alarm. Tomorrow they would lock us up in a prison with barbed wire, and I would not get out of this jungle for twenty years. I was trembling, my hands were damp, I was overcome with nausea. I started to cry.

The hours went by, and Mono Liso went on sitting there right before me, on guard, without moving. The other guards were changed twice, but he didn't abandon his post. At around half past eleven, "El Abuelo," another, older guerrilla came to replace him. It went on raining. Mono Liso had gone away soaked through to the bone. The new guard went to sit beneath a temporary tent where they stored the cooking pots. He was diagonally across from me and could see all the angles around my *caleta*. He stared straight ahead, lost in his thoughts.

I turned to Mary, imagining that God was too far away to be reached. I prayed for a long time, with the force of despair. "Mother Mary, I beg you, you're a mother, too. I have to see my children. Today it's still possible, tomorrow it will be too late. I know that you are listening. I wish I could ask you to help me with something more spiritual — to become better, more patient, more humble. I'm asking all that of you, too. But now, I beg you, come and get me."

Mom had told me in her letter that one Saturday, nearly losing her mind with pain, she rebelled against Mary. She was informed that the same day the guerrillas had sent my second proof of survival.

I no longer believed in coincidences. Ever since I'd been abducted, in this space of life outside time, I'd been able to look back over my life like someone who has too much time on her hands. I'd concluded that you had to be patient and wait for the purpose of things to become visible. And then coincidence ceased to exist.

I spoke to her like a madwoman for hours, using the most elementary emotional blackmail, sulking, getting angry, throwing myself at her feet again. The Virgin Mary whom I prayed to was not some idealized image. Nor was she a supernatural being. She was a woman who had lived thousands of years before me but who, through exceptional grace, could help me. Frustrated and exhausted by my pleading, I collapsed into a dreamless sleep, convinced I was still keeping watch. I felt that someone was touching my shoulder; then, when I did not respond, whoever it was began to shake me. That's when I understood that I was sound asleep, because my return to the surface was heavy and painful, and with a disjointed leap I found myself springing back in time, to sit up, my eyes wide open, my heart pounding. "Thank you," I said out of politeness. Nothing divine, just a sensation of a presence.

I did not have time to ask myself any more questions. El Abuelo had stood and was staring in my direction. I held my breath, because I realized he was fed up and had decided to leave. I didn't move, banking on the probability that the darkness would not enable him to see that I was sitting up.

He stayed there motionless for a few seconds, like a wildcat. He headed off, went around the walkway, then came back in my direction. "Mary, I beg you, make him go away!" He again inspected the surrounding darkness, took a breath; reassured, he cut through the woods to go back to his camp.

A rush of gratitude overwhelmed me. Without waiting another second, I left my mosquito net and crawled along on all fours, constantly murmuring, "Thank you, thank you." The two other guards were standing behind the row of tents and hammocks where my companions were sleeping. They could have seen my feet if they'd squatted down to look, but they were just as I imagined, rolled up in their black plastic sheets, shivering with cold and boredom. It was 1.50 in the morning. We had only two and a half hours to get away from the camp. It was enough time for us to vanish into the jungle and lose them. But we had only ten minutes before the next change of guard.

I groped my way toward the soldiers' tents. I took the first pair of boots I found on my way and crept up closer to the guards to get another pair. I knew that there were orders to keep a close watch on Lucho and me. The first thing the new guards would do would be to make sure that our boots were there by our mattresses. They would see the soldiers' boots I had just put there and unsuspectingly go away.

I went up to Lucho's *caleta* to wake him.

"Lucho, Lucho, it's time."

"Huh . . . what . . . what's going on?"

He was sound asleep.

"Lucho, we're leaving, hurry up!"

"What? What are you thinking? We can't leave now!"

"There are no more guards! This is our only chance!"

"Damn! You want them to kill us or what!"

"Listen, you've been talking about this escape for six months."

He was silent.

"Everything is ready. I even have the soldiers' boots. They won't notice a thing."

Suddenly Lucho's destiny was staring him in the face, and so was I. He transformed his fear into anger.

"You want us to leave, okay! They're going to shoot us, but maybe that's better than dying here."

He made a sudden movement, and a pile of pans, bowls, cups, and spoons he had balanced against a post went flying in a terrible clatter.

"Don't move," I said, to restrain him in his suicidal recklessness.

We crouched behind the mattress, hidden by the mosquito net. A beam of light shone over our heads, then moved away. The guards were laughing. They must have thought we'd had a visit from a rat.

"Okay, I'm coming! I'm ready, I'm coming!" said Lucho, grabbing his two oilcans, his tiny backpack, his sun hat, and the gloves I'd made for him for the occasion. He walked off, taking large strides. I was about to follow, then realized I'd lost a glove. In my panic I groped my way back toward the soldiers' tents. *This is stupid! We have to leave now!* I thought. Lucho was already climbing over the walkway, charging straight ahead, trampling all the plants in his path. There was a horrible rustling of leaves as they clung to the polyester trousers he was wearing. I turned around. How could the guards fail to hear the deafening clamour we were making? And yet behind me there was total calm. I looked at my watch: In three minutes the other guards would arrive. They were surely already on the way. We had to jump over the walkway and run across the cleared terrain ahead of us to have time to hide in the undergrowth.

Lucho was already there. I was afraid he might head in the wrong direction. We had to take a sharp turn to our left to jump into the *caño* and swim to the other side. If he kept straight ahead, he'd end up on Gafas's lap. I made the sign of the cross and began to run, certain the guards must have already seen us. I arrived breathless behind the bushes, just in time to catch Lucho's hand and pull him to the ground. Crouching close together, we took a good look through the branches to see what was going on. The relief had just arrived. They were training their flashlight beams first on our boots and mosquito nets, then over our way, sweeping the empty space in every direction.

"They've seen us!"

"No, they haven't seen us."

"Let's go. We're not going to wait for them to come and get us."

I put my oilcans in their cover, hung them around my neck, and tied them to my belt. They hampered my progress. We had to climb over a tangle of branches and bushes piled up there after the spot had been cleared to build the camp. Lucho grabbed me with one hand, his oilcans in the other, and he ran straight toward the bank of the stream. The plastic cans seemed to explode whenever they hit the dead trees, and dry wood cracked painfully beneath our weight.

We had reached the riverbank. Before sliding down the slope, I looked behind me. Nobody. The flashlight beams were still sweeping along the tents. One more step and I literally rolled over on top of Lucho to land on the fine sandy beach where we used to come every day to wash. It had almost stopped raining. The noise we were making wouldn't be covered by the rain. Without another thought, we threw ourselves like stampeding cattle into the water. I tried to keep control over my movements, but I was quickly caught by the current.

"We have to cross, quickly, quickly!"

Lucho seemed to be drifting toward the other arm of the tributary, the one that led to Enrique's camp. I was swimming with one arm, holding Lucho with the other, by the straps on his backpack. We were no longer in control of our movements; we were paralysed with fright and were trying at best simply not to drown.

The current helped us. We were borne over to the left, to the other arm of the tributary, into a curve where the speed of the current increased. I couldn't see the guerrillas' tents any more, and for a moment I had a sensation that this was possible. We headed deeper, farther, into the warm waters of the Amazon Basin. The *caño* closed around itself, thick, dark, noiseless, like a tunnel.

"We have to get out of the *caño*. We have to get out of the water," I said repeatedly to Lucho.

We landed unceremoniously on a bed of thick leaves, which led to a passage between brambles and ferns.

This is perfect, I thought to myself. *No traces.*

I knew instinctively which way to go.

"It's this way," I said to Lucho, who was hesitating.

We plunged into increasingly thick, tall vegetation. Beyond a wall of young bushes with sharp brambles, we came upon a clearing of moss. I hurried onto it in the hope of decreasing the resistance of the undergrowth so that we could go more quickly, but I fell into an enormous ditch that the moss concealed like mesh above a trap. The ditch was deep, I was in moss up to my neck, and I couldn't see what was below me. I imagined that all sorts of prehistoric monsters must live there, waiting for prey to land in their mouths as I had just done. Panicking, I tried to get out, but my movements were clumsy and I made no headway. Lucho dropped down into the same ditch and tried to calm me.

"Don't worry, it's nothing. Keep walking, we'll get out of it."

A bit farther along, some tree branches helped us hoist ourselves out. I wanted to run. I could sense that the guards must be on our tail, and I expected to see them burst from the scrub to pounce on us.

The vegetation changed abruptly. We left behind the shrubs of bramble and thorns to penetrate into mangroves. I saw the mirror of water shining through the roots of the trees. A bit farther still, a beach of grey sand sloped to the rush of the river. There was a last row of trees caught in the flood of the river, and after that lay the vast silver surface, waiting for us.

"We're there!" I said to Lucho, not knowing whether it was relief or the vision of our upcoming ordeal that was terrifying me.

I was hypnotized. This water flowing rapidly before us: This was our freedom.

I looked behind me once again. No movement, no sound, just the deafening pounding of my heart.

We ventured cautiously into the warm water up to our chests. We pulled out our ropes, and I conscientiously went through the gestures I knew by heart, having practised them daily during the long months leading up to this moment. Every knot had its own purpose. We had to be firmly attached to each other.

We couldn't use sliding knots, but they had to be ready to release in case of emergency. I meticulously checked our life jackets. They had to be placed on our chests in such a way that they would not rise up against our necks, which would hamper our movement in the water. Our little back-packs had to be firmly against our spines so that they wouldn't pull us backward. One set of ropes had to be intertwined over our boots so that they would stay firmly against our calves and we wouldn't lose them to the current. Lucho had trouble keeping his balance in the water.

"Don't worry. Once we start swimming, you'll get your balance."

We were ready. We held hands to walk forward until we lost our foot-ing. We let ourselves float, gently paddling until the last line of trees.

The river opened up before us, grandiose, beneath the vault of sky. The moon was immense, luminous, like a silver sun. I was aware that a pow-erful current was about to suck us up. There was no going back.

"Careful, it's going to go fast," I warned Lucho.

In one second, once we had gone through the last barrier of plants, we found ourselves rapidly propelled into the middle of the river. The shore went by at great speed before our eyes. Behind us I could see the guerril-las' landing stage growing smaller and smaller, and I was overwhelmed with a feeling of plenitude, as vast as the horizon that we had just redis-covered.

The river went around a bend, the landing stage disappeared for good. There was nothing left behind us. We were alone. Nature had conspired in our favour, putting all her strength at the service of our flight. I felt pro-tected.

"We are free!" I cried at the top of my lungs.

"We are free!" shouted Lucho, laughing, his eyes in the stars.

62

FREEDOM

We had made it. Lucho was no longer struggling; he let himself be carried peacefully, trustingly, and so did I. The idea of drowning no longer seemed possible. We were in no danger. The current was very powerful, but there were no undercurrents. The river flowed quickly forward. There were a hundred yards or so to the bank on either side.

"How are we going to get to the shore?" asked Lucho.

"The current is strong. It's going to take some time. We'll begin by swimming slowly to the opposite shore. If they're looking for us, they'll start by inspecting their own side. They'll never believe we could have crossed this river."

We began to swim, a gentle, sustained, rhythmic breaststroke, careful not to get tired. We had to keep our bodies warm and work our way to the right in order to get beyond the pull of the current that was keeping us in the middle of the river. Lucho was slightly behind me, and the rope between us was still taut, which reassured me, because I could keep moving without looking at him yet know he was there.

I knew that the greatest danger in the water would be hypothermia. I had always suffered from it. I have memories of Mom pulling me out of the swimming pool when I was a child, wrapping me in a blanket, rubbing me vigorously as I shivered uncontrollably, angry that I had been interrupted in my childish games, surprised at my body's reaction, which I had not noticed until that very moment. "Your lips are blue," she would say, as if in apology.

I loved the water. Except when my teeth began to chatter. I would do everything to ignore it, but when that happened, I knew I had lost the struggle and that it was time to get out. When I went diving, even in tropical water, I made a point of wearing a thick wetsuit, because I liked to stay at the bottom for a long time.

So it was the onset of cramps I feared. I wasn't thinking about anacondas; I thought that in the water they stayed near the shore to wait for their prey. I thought that the *guíos** must have reserves of food that were more accessible than we were.

I was more worried about the piranhas. I had seen them at work, and I was unable to distinguish between myth and reality. Several times I'd gone to bathe in the *caño* when I had my period. Surrounded by men as I was, my sole preoccupation had been that no one notice my condition.

In captivity I had always suffered from the condescending attitude with which the guerrillas treated female needs. There was a far greater guarantee of shipments of cigarettes and their distribution than of the supply of sanitary towels. The guard in charge of bringing them to me always shouted, to the amusement of his companions, "You'd better not waste them! They have to last!" They never lasted long enough. Even less so if we were on a march, because my companions raided my supply to put them in their shoes when their blisters were torturing them. When I prepared our escape, the thought of having to swim in this condition had compelled me to devise a form of personal protection, but I wasn't certain it was working.

Now, in this dark brown current, I swirled the water around me, as much to make headway as to drive off any creatures attracted by our presence.

We swam, propelled by the momentum of our euphoria, for three hours. The luminescence of the moonlight-bathed landscape changed gradually as dawn approached. The sky was again cloaked in a black velvet. Darkness fell on us, and with it the chill that precedes daybreak.

---

* Anacondas.

My teeth had been chattering for a while, without my being aware. When I tried to speak to Lucho, I realized I could hardly say anything.

"Your lips are blue," he said anxiously.

We had to get out of the water.

We came closer to the bank, or rather the foliage along the river. The level of water had risen so high that the trees at the fringes were completely submerged, and only the treetops were still visible. The bank had withdrawn inland, but to get there, we had to plunge into the foliage along the edge.

I hesitated. The idea of being engulfed by this secretive nature terrified me. What might there be beneath this silent greenery, that was impervious to everything save the powerful current? Might an anaconda be lurking, waiting for us there, curled around the highest branch of that half-submerged tree? How long would we have to swim toward the interior before finding solid ground? I stopped trying to choose the best spot, because there wasn't one.

"Let's go in here, Lucho," I said, ducking my head beneath the first branches resting on the surface.

The undergrowth was dark, but we could just make out the shapes of things. Our eyes adjusted. I went slowly forward, closing the distance between Lucho and myself so I could take his arm.

"Are you all right?"

"Yes, I'm okay."

Sounds were muffled. The roar of the river had given way to the muted sound of quiet waters. A bird flew along the surface and just missed us. My gestures had lost, instinctively, some of their expansiveness, as if I feared bumping into something. And yet nothing I could see was any different from what I'd already seen thousands of times. We were swimming among the branches of the trees like the *bongo* thrusting its way, opening a course. The sound of water lapping told us we were near the riverbank.

"Over there!" whispered Lucho.

I followed with my gaze. To my left, a bed of leaves and, farther along, the roots of a majestic ceiba tree. My feet had just found the land. I came out of the water, heavy with emotion, shivering, so glad to be standing on solid ground. I was exhausted. I needed to find a place to collapse. Lucho climbed the gentle slope at the same time, and he pulled me over to the roots of the tree.

"We have to hide. They could show up at any moment."

He opened the black plastic sheet he kept in his belongings and helped me off with my backpack.

"Hand me your clothes one piece at a time. We have to wring them out."

I did as he said, only to be immediately attacked by *jejenes*, tiny little midges that are particularly voracious and move around in dense clouds. I had to do a war dance to keep them away.

It was nearly six o'clock in the morning. The forest was so dense where we were that daylight was taking its time to reach us. We decided to wait because we couldn't see what was around us. *My God, today is my sister's birthday!* I thought, happy to have remembered. The light reached the undergrowth at that very moment and spread like wildfire.

We were not in a good spot. The roots of the huge ceiba tree – the "tree of life" – were the only dry place in the surrounding swamp. A few yards away, a round ball of dry earth hanging from the branch of a young tree reminded me of the time we'd been pursued by a swarm of hornets. It was a beehive.

"We have to get away at once and go inland," declared Lucho. "Besides, when it rains, everything will be covered with stagnant water."

Someone on high must have heard him, because it began to rain that very second. We cautiously took our leave of the nest and headed deeper into the forest. It was raining harder. We stayed on our feet, carrying our things, with plastic sheets over us as umbrellas, too tired to think of anything better. When finally a pause in the rain gave us a truce, I spread the plastic sheet on the ground and collapsed on it.

I awoke with a start. Around us there were men shouting. Lucho was already crouched down, on the lookout.

"They're here," he murmured, his eyes popping out of his head.

We were in a clearing, easily visible, with very few trees around us. It was the only dry spot in the swampland. We had to find a place to huddle behind, if there was still time. I looked desperately for a hiding place. The best thing was to lie flat on the ground and cover ourselves with leaves. Lucho and I thought of the same thing at the same time. It seemed to me that we were making as much noise pulling the leaves over us as the men who were shouting.

The voices came nearer. We could hear their conversation distinctly. It was Ángel and Tiger, and a third man, Oswald. They were laughing. I had goose bumps. I remembered the time the guerrillas had recaptured Clara and me, after the attack of the African wasps. Edinson had let off a volley of bullets into the air, roaring with laughter. For that's what it was, a manhunt. Surely they had seen us.

Lucho lay motionless beside me, camouflaged beneath his carpet of dead leaves. I would have liked to laugh if I weren't so frightened. And to cry, too. I didn't want to give them the satisfaction of getting their hands on us again.

The guerrillas were still laughing. Where were they? Over by the river to our left. But the vegetation there was very dense. Then the noise of an engine, more voices, and the metallic echo of men boarding a boat, the clicking of rifles, the motor again, going away this time, and the silence of the trees. I closed my eyes to give thanks.

Night fell very quickly. I was surprised to feel at ease in my wet clothes, which trapped the heat of my body. My fingers hurt, but I had managed to keep my fingernails clean, and the cuticle that gave me problems so often was not irritated. I had woven my hair into a tight braid, and I had no intention of touching it for a long time. We had decided that we would always eat something before going back to the river, and for this first day we had one cookie each and a piece of *panela*.* They would start their hunt again at dawn, just when we left the river to hide among the trees. We had to leave at two o'clock in the morning, to have three hours on the river before daybreak. We wanted to be on shore with the first light of dawn, because we dreaded the thought of plunging blindly into the vegetation. We agreed on all of that, crouching among the roots of our old tree, as we waited for the rain to stop so we could curl up on our plastic sheets and get some sleep.

---

* A square of brown sugar.

The rain didn't stop. We dozed off all the same, curled up against each other, incapable of struggling against sleep any longer.

I was awakened by a resounding noise. Then nothing. Once again the sound of something twisting in the swamp, striking the water violently. All I could see was darkness. Lucho searched for the flashlight and switched it on for a second.

"It's a *cachirri!*"* I cried, horrified.

"No, it's a *guío*," said Lucho. "He's taking his prey down into the depths to drown it." He was probably right. I remember a *guío* killing the rooster in Andres's camp, I heard it from my wooden house splashing into the river taking its squirming prey down with it. It made the same sound.

We remained silent. In a few minutes, we would have to go back into that black water. It was already two o'clock in the morning.

We waited. A deadly calm reigned.

"Right, it's time to go," said Lucho, tying the ropes around his boots.

We went into the river apprehensively. I bumped against the trees as I moved forward. Once again the current took hold of us abruptly, grabbing us from beneath the dome of vegetation to project us out under the open sky in the middle of the river. It was even stronger than the day before, and we were swept ahead, whirling on ourselves uncontrollably.

"We're going to drown!" cried Lucho.

"No, we're not going to drown. It's normal, it's been raining all night. Let yourself go."

We were moving so fast I felt as if I were spiralling downward. The river was winding, and it seemed narrower to me. The riverbanks were higher, and sometimes the line of trees gave way to a sudden steep embankment, as if a bite had been taken out of the shore. The bare, bloody earth opened like a gaping wound in the middle of the curling darkness of foliage.

When I felt my first shivers and the thought of leaving the river became urgent, the flow was less powerful and we were able to swim to the opposite shore, to the side where the vegetation seemed less dense. We hadn't even reached the riverbank, and already it was broad daylight.

---

* Cayman.

Desperate, I struggled to go faster. We were easy prey for any posse out looking for us.

With relief we plunged into the greenery, sheltered in the gloom.

At the top of the incline, the terrain was very dry and dead leaves crackled under our feet.

I collapsed on a plastic sheet, my teeth chattering, and fell sound asleep.

I opened my eyes and wondered where I was. There were no guards. No tents, no hammocks. Carnival-coloured birds squabbled on a branch above my head. When I managed to make my way through a labyrinth of scattered memories to place myself back in reality, I was overwhelmed by the happiness of a time gone by. I didn't want to move any more.

Lucho wasn't there. I waited, tranquil, till he returned. He had gone to inspect the surroundings.

"Do you think there's any civilian transportation on this river?" he asked.

"I'm sure there is. Remember the boat we saw just after we left the Maloka camp?"

"Should we try to intercept one?"

"Don't even think about it! Odds are two to one that we'll come upon the guerrillas."

I knew the dangers of our escape. But the one I dreaded most was our own weakness. The surge of adrenalin at the time of our escape subsided once we felt we were out of danger, and we were letting our guard down. It was at times when we relaxed that the dark thoughts arose, and we could lose the prospect of the sacrifice we'd made. Hunger, cold, and fatigue started to become more insistent than freedom itself, because now that we'd regained our freedom, it seemed less important in the light of our urgent needs.

"Come on, let's eat something. Let's treat ourselves."

"How much longer will our supplies last?"

"We'll see. But we have our fishhooks. Don't worry. With every passing day, we're getting closer to our families!"

The sun had come out. Our clothes had dried, and that boosted our spirits. We spent the afternoon envisaging what we must do if the guerrillas came anywhere near.

We left earlier that day, in the hope of making better progress. We were nurturing the illusion that on our way we would find signs of human presence.

"If we could find a boat, we could sail all night without getting wet," said Lucho.

We found a spot to shelter that seemed promising, because the riverbank was visible through the foliage and stretched along a beach for thirty yards or more. We had arrived at dawn, and we chose it because one of the trees that reached far out into the water had branches that grew horizontally, which would enable us, we thought, to take turns keeping watch on the river.

The sun from the day before had put us back on our feet, and it looked like today would be hot again. We decided to try to do some fishing, to boost our morale. We would have to last for a long time – weeks, perhaps months.

While Lucho was looking for a good branch to make a fishing rod, I focused on finding some bait. I had noticed a tree trunk that was rotting, halfway in the water. I gave it a good kick, the way I'd seen the guerrillas do, and split it open. Inside, a colony of purple, sticky worms was writhing. A bit farther along, there were bird-of-paradise plants in abundance. With the smooth, fresh leaf from one of them, I fashioned a cone that I filled with the unfortunate creatures. I attached the nylon thread and a hook to Lucho's fishing rod and conscientiously hooked the bait, telling myself that what I was doing was very cruel, to be pinning this poor creature, still alive, to a hook before tossing it into the water. Lucho looked on, disgusted and fascinated at the same time, as if the ritual I was performing made me the keeper of occult powers.

I hadn't had time to take a step, and already I was pulling from the water a fine *caribe*, which is a more reassuring name for a piranha. I found a branch to use as a stake and planted it next to me, then impaled my catch on it, confident that after such good fortune luck would continue to smile on me. Beyond all my expectations, the fishing was miraculous. Lucho was laughing wholeheartedly. We had three stakes of fish in no time. All our anxiety vanished. We could eat our fill every day until we managed to find our way out.

We were unaware that we'd begun talking loudly. We heard the engine only after it had already gone by. A heavily laden boat, sitting low on the water, with ten people or more crowded in a row – women, one of them with a baby, men, young people, all of them civilians wearing colourful clothes. My heart leaped. I cried for help when the boat had already gone by, and I realized they could no longer see us, or even hear us. For a few seconds, they had been so close to us. We saw them motor by before our eyes, paralysed by fear and surprise; I remember every detail of this apparition. Our best opportunity to find our way out of the jungle had just eluded us.

Lucho looked at me, his face like that of a whipped dog. His eyes welled with tears.

"We should have been watching the river," he said bitterly.

"Yes, we're going to have to be more vigilant."

"They were civilians," he said.

"Yes, they were civilians."

I no longer felt like fishing. I took my nylon line and the hook to put them away.

"Let's make a fire and try to cook the fish," I said, looking for something to do to hide our disappointment.

The sky had changed. Clouds were piling up overhead. Sooner or later it would rain. We had to hurry.

Lucho gathered a few branches. We had a lighter.

""Do you know how to make a fire?" asked Lucho.

"No, but I don't think it is very difficult. We need to find a *bizcocho*,* that's the tree they use in the *rancha*."

We spent two hours trying to get it started. I remembered hearing the guards say it was best to peel the wood when it was damp. We had scissors, but despite all our efforts it was impossible to remove the bark even from a small branch. I felt ridiculous: With my lighter and all this wood around us, and yet we could not kindle the tiniest flame. We didn't talk about it, but we were in a race against time.

---

* Wood, used for cooking, that will burn even when wet.

Sooner or later Lucho's sickness would recur. I kept a close watch for any of the warning signs. So far I hadn't seen anything alarming, other than his expression of sadness when the boat went by, because sometimes before a diabetic crisis he would lapse into a similar state of affliction. In those cases his morose mood had no specific cause; it came on as a symptom of the deregulation of his metabolism, whereas the dejection I had just noticed had an obvious cause. I wondered if the disappointment that had overcome him could be enough to trigger his illness, and the thought of it tortured me more than hunger or fatigue.

"Right, listen, it's not a problem. If we can't light the fire, we'll eat our fish raw."

"No, never!" cried Lucho. "I'd rather starve to death."

His reaction made me laugh. He went off at a run as if he thought I'd be in hot pursuit, to force him to swallow the caribes raw, with their sharp little teeth and their staring, gleaming eyes.

I took the scissors, and on a leaf from the bird-of-paradise plant I cut little fillets of translucent caribe flesh and meticulously lined them up. I was careful to toss the scraps into the water, and they were instantaneously fought over in a splashing of voracious fish.

Lucho came back, wary, but he watched me, bemused.

"Mmm. It's absolutely delicious," I said without looking at him, my mouth full. "You're wrong not to try it. This is the best sushi I've ever had!"

On the leaf there were no more dead fish, just finely sliced strips of fresh meat. The sight of it reassured Lucho, and, driven by hunger, he ate first one, then a second, and finally a third.

"I'm going to throw up," he said in the end.

I was already reassured. I knew that next time we would eat it without a problem.

This was our first real meal since we'd run away from the camp. The psychological effect was instantaneous. We immediately started to get ready for the next leg of our journey, gathering all our little things, making the inventory of our treasures and our supplies. The day ended on a positive note. We had saved two cookies, and we felt good.

Lucho cut some palm leaves and wove them together at the foot of the tree, spread the plastic sheets, and put our bags and the oilcans down on them. We were about to stretch out when suddenly the storm was upon us without warning. We barely had time to take up our things and cover ourselves with the plastic sheets, only to watch with resignation as all our efforts to stay dry were foiled by a pitiless lateral wind. Defeated by the gusts, we sat on what was left of the rotten trunk, waiting for the rain to stop. It was three o'clock in the morning when the storm finally subsided. We were exhausted.

"We can't go into the river in this state. It would be dangerous. Let's try to get some sleep, and we'll leave tomorrow on foot."

A few hours of sleep restored us. Lucho set off ahead of me with a determined stride.

We came upon a path that went along the riverbank and that visibly had been cleared years before. The shrubs that had been cut on either side of the path were already dry. I thought there might well have been a guerrilla camp somewhere nearby, and this worried me, because I could not be sure that it had been abandoned for good. We were walking like robots, and with every step I said to myself we were taking too many risks. And yet we kept on going, because our desire to get somewhere prevented us from being reasonable.

On our way, I recognized a type of tree that Tiger had shown me once. The Indians would say that if you brushed past it, you should go back and swear three times to avoid the tree cursing you. Lucho and I didn't respect the ritual; we felt it did not apply to us.

At the end of the day, we stopped on a tiny beach of fine sand. I cast my lines and pulled in enough fish for a decent meal. Lucho ate the raw fish with some effort, but eventually admitted that it wasn't bad.

The moon came back out and gave enough light for us to react when an ant farm suddenly began to attack us.

That night another plague lay in wait: the *manta blanca*. It covered us like snow, spreading over our clothes and into our skin, inflicting painful bites that we could not avoid. *La manta blanca* was a compact cloud of microscopic pearl-coloured midges with diaphanous wings. It was hard to believe that these fragile things, so clumsy in flight, could inflict such painful bites. I tried to kill them with my hands, but they were insensitive to my efforts, because they were so tiny and light that it was impossible to crush them against my skin. We had to retreat and take the path to the river earlier than planned. We plunged with relief into its warm water, scratching our faces with our nails to try to free ourselves from the last relentless insects chasing us.

Once again the current sucked us out to the middle of the river, just in time. Behind Lucho I saw the round eyes of a caiman that had just surfaced. Had he decided we were too big to be prey for him? Had he decided not to leave the riverbank behind? I saw him swing his tail, then turn around. Lucho was uncomfortable, trying to adjust his floating plastic bottles to find better balance; the waves were constantly pushing him over. I didn't say anything. But I decided that next time I would leave the shore equipped with a stick.

For hours the current swept us this way and that. It was hard not to roll on top of each other, and the rope that tied us together often tangled on itself capriciously as if trying to strangle us. After a bend the river became wider, flooding the land to a frightening degree. It was as if tall trees had been planted in the middle of the river, and I was afraid that an awkward manoeuvre might send us crashing into one of them at the speed of the current.

I did my best to head toward either shore, but the river and Lucho's weight seemed to be pulling in the opposite direction. We were going faster and faster and had less and less control.

"Do you hear that?" asked Lucho, almost shouting.

"No, what?"

"There must be waterfalls here somewhere, I think I can hear the sound of rushing water!"

He was right. A new sound had joined the familiar roar of the river. If the acceleration I'd noticed was due to the existence of some *cachiveras* downstream, we had to get back to shore as quickly as possible. Lucho knew this, too. We swam energetically in the opposite direction.

A tree trunk came hurtling along in the current, dangerously near. Its branches, bleached by the sun, stuck out of the water like sharp iron stakes. It was rolling and pitching with rage, coming closer to us by the second. If our rope got caught in its branches, the rolling of the trunk would be enough to sweep us along and cause us to sink. We had to do whatever we could to avoid it. Somehow we managed to, only to go crashing into a tree right there in the middle of the river. Lucho ended up on one side and I on the other, held together by the rope that straddled the trunk.

"Don't worry," I said, "it's nothing. Let me take care of it. I'll come over to you."

I managed to make my way over to Lucho by pulling on the rope, which had somehow got twisted and knotted around one of the submerged branches of the tree. We couldn't let go of each other to try to free it, since the current was too strong. I had to duck underwater and follow the rope's path backward in order to untie all the knots.

By the time we were free again, it had been daylight for a long time. Luckily, no boats belonging to the guerrillas went by. We managed to get ashore and hide again. Only then did I realize that I had left my fishing hook back on the beach where the ants were.

63

THE CHOICE

This was a hard blow. We didn't have many hooks. I had one left, just like the one I'd lost, and another slightly larger one, and half a dozen very rudimentary hooks that Orlando had made back in Sombra's prison.

I told Lucho so only when I felt sufficiently serene to announce it to him without getting upset. I added that we still had others in reserve.

We were on a little beach, hidden by mangroves that led to an elevated terrain. We immediately climbed up, well aware that in a storm this beach would disappear completely when the waters rose.

The elevated terrain opened onto a clearing of felled trees piled in a jumble in the middle, as if to open a skylight in the thickness of the forest, allowing a baking sun to concentrate its rays. The access to this sunlight coming straight upon us like a laser beam was a godsend. I decided to wash our clothes, rubbing them with sand to remove the smell of mould and spread them out in the implacable noonday sun. The bliss of wearing dry, clean clothes helped me forget the misfortune of my lost fishhook. As if to discipline ourselves, we sacrificed a day of fishing and fell back on the sugared powder they'd given us in the camp shortly before our escape.

We had daydreamed all afternoon, stretched out on our plastic sheets looking at the clear sky. We had prayed together, with my rosary. For the first time, we spoke of the risk of a diabetic coma.

"If that happens," said Lucho, "you'll have to go on alone. You'll make it out of here, and if you're lucky, you can come and get me."

I thought carefully before I answered. In my mind I pictured the moment, with freedom in one hand and Lucho's life in the other. "Listen to me. We escaped together. We'll get out of here together or we won't get out at all."

Put like that, it became a pact. Our words echoed in the air, beneath a heavenly dome that wore the dust of diamonds sprinkled alongside the constellations of our thoughts. Freedom – such a precious jewel, one we were prepared to risk our lives for – would lose all its brilliance if it were to be worn in a life of regret. Without freedom our awareness of self deteriorated until we no longer knew who we were. But now, lying on my back admiring the grandiose display of the stars, I felt a lucidity that comes of freedom so dearly regained.

The self-image that captivity returned to me had brought back all my failures. All the insecurities unresolved during my teenage years, insecurities that later shaped my failings as an adult – they all came back like a hydra, inescapable.

I had fought against it in the beginning, more from idleness than discipline, obliged to live in a cycle of time that was forever starting again, where the irritation of discovering that I was still there with all my petty little weaknesses, unchanged, drove me to strive once again for a transformation that seemed inaccessible.

That evening, under a starry sky that recalled faraway years of happiness in the days when I'd counted shooting stars in the belief that they carried the promise of a future of grace to come, it dawned on me that I had just experienced one of those moments that allowed me to bring back the best part of myself.

We went back into the river beneath a shower of stars. The river had slowed, and this gentler movement of the waters led us to hope that the *cachiveras* were not so big after all, or might not even exist. On either shore entire swathes of earth had crumbled away, exposing the roots of the trees that had not collapsed but still clung to a scarlet wall only waiting for the next high water to give way, too.

We progressed without difficulty, carried along in the opaque, warm water. In the distance a couple of "water dogs"* were frolicking near the shore, with their siren tails interlaced as they played their love games. I turned to Lucho to point them out. He was letting himself be carried by the current, his mouth half open, his eyes glassy. We had to get out right away.

I pulled him toward me with the rope, nervously hunting in my pockets for the bottle where I kept the sugar for emergencies. He swallowed the handful I put on his tongue. And then a second one, that he carefully savoured.

We went ashore by the roots of a dead tree. We had to climb the wall of crimson clay to reach the riverbank. Lucho sat on a trunk, his feet in the water, while I opened a passage. Once we were both up there, I set about preparing to fish while Lucho rested.

I settled on my trunk, but the fish weren't biting there. So I walked farther out. Right then Lucho called to me, and I heard an engine coming up the river. I figured that I would have time to hide. But just as I was about to retrace my steps, the nylon line went taut. The hook was caught in the branches of the trunk below the water. We could not afford to lose another hook. Too bad. I dove in. I could hear the sound of the engine getting closer. I clung to my obsession of getting the hook, but it was solidly stuck in a tangle of branches. I tugged in despair and brought up the nylon line, a full quarter-length shorter. The hook was missing. I rose to the surface, very nearly out of breath, in time to see a man go past me, standing next to his engine, in a boat filled with crates of beer. He hadn't seen me.

Lucho was gone. I climbed up, anxious, and found him collapsed in the trancelike state that preceded his hypoglycaemia. I took all the supplies of sugar out of my bag and gave them to him, praying that he would not lose consciousness.

"Lucho, Lucho, can you hear me?"

"I'm here, don't worry, I'll be all right."

---

* River otters.

For the first time since our escape, I looked at him with the eyes of memory. He had lost a great deal of weight. His features seemed to have been etched with a penknife, and the twinkle in his eyes had vanished.

I took him in my arms. "Yes, you'll be all right."

I had made my decision.

"Lucho, we'll stay here. It's a good spot, because from here we can see the boats coming."

He looked at me with immense sadness. The sun was at its zenith. We put our rags out to dry, and we prayed the rosary together, watching the majestic river winding at our feet.

During our flight we often debated hailing passing boats, concluding that it was a risky option. The guerrillas dominated the region and controlled the rivers. There was a good chance that those who picked us up would be militia taking orders from the FARC.

We no longer had the option of continuing to go downstream. Lucho needed food. Our chances of making it depended, more than anything, on our ability to feed ourselves. I had only one hook left, and we had finished our reserves.

So we waited, sitting on the edge of the embankment, our feet dangling. I did not express my fears, because I could tell that Lucho was struggling against his own.

"I think we might have to retrace our steps to get the hook we forgot at the campsite with the ants."

Lucho made a sound of acknowledgement and incredulity. The sound of an engine drew our attention. I got up so I could see better. Coming from our left was a boat filled with peasants on their way upstream. Some were wearing straw hats, others white caps.

Lucho was looking at me in a panic.

"Let's go and hide. I don't know. I'm not sure they are peasants."

"They are peasants!" shouted Lucho.

"I'm not sure!"

"And I am. And in any event, I have no choice. I'll die here."

The world stopped. I saw myself beneath the dust of stars, like a wink from life taking me at my word. I had to choose.

In seconds the boat would be opposite us. It was crossing the river over by the far shore. We would have only one chance to make ourselves seen. After that the boat would move on and we would disappear from the occupants' line of sight.

Lucho was clinging to me. I took his hand.

We stood up together, shouting at the top of our lungs, waving our arms energetically.

On the far side of the river, the boat stopped, manoeuvred quickly, its prow pointing toward us, and then accelerated in our direction.

"They've seen us!" exclaimed Lucho, overjoyed.

"Yes, they've seen us," I repeated. As the boat drew closer, I discovered with horror the faces beneath the white caps: Ángel, Tiger, and Oswald.

64

THE END OF THE DREAM

They approached, like a snake moving toward its prey, cutting through the water in their boat, staring intently, enjoying the terror they caused. There was an unfamiliar dark purple tinge about their complexions, and they had bags under their red eyes, which only accentuated their mean look. "*My God,*" I said, frozen, making the sign of the cross. I stiffened. The sight of these men made me clench my teeth. I turned to Lucho. "Don't worry," I murmured. "Everything will be fine."

I knew I could be angry with myself, I could berate the heavens for not having saved us. But there was no room for any of that now. All my attention was focused on observing these men and their hatred. Before my eyes was the physical incarnation of evil. Mom used to say, "People wear the face of their soul." In that boat, beneath the mask of familiar features, were the glaring faces of pride and anger, as if possessed by the devil.

"Well, the white caps did the trick," whistled Oswald perfidiously, with his Galil assault rifle on his shoulder, so that I could see it.

"You took long enough!" I said, to save face.

"Shut up, take your things, and get on board!" said Erminson, an old guerrilla who was trying to rise in the hierarchy. Between his teeth he added, "Hurry up, if you don't want me to drag you by the hair." And he laughed. He gave me a sidelong look, to see if I was surprised. I didn't expect this from him. He used to treat me with a certain kindness. How could his heart now be so miserly?

Lucho got our things. I would have preferred to leave them there. With our *timbos* and our backpacks, they would know we had swum down the river, and I didn't want to give them any information.

When I stepped on board the boat, I remembered the warning from the fortune teller. I sat to the fore, with a mad desire to jump and thwart destiny. Lucho, next to me, was filled with despair, his head between his hands. I heard myself say, "Mother Mary, help me understand."

Going back, I did not recognize the river we had travelled down. Behind me the guerrillas were swapping jokes, and their laughter hurt. Lost in thought, trying to imagine what was in store for us, I had the impression that the return trip took no time.

"They're going to kill us," Lucho said breathlessly.

"Unfortunately, we won't be that lucky," I answered, before they told us to shut up.

It began to rain. We took cover under a plastic sheet. There, sheltered from their gaze, Lucho and I agreed. We must not say anything.

On the landing stage, with his arms crossed in front of him, Enrique was waiting, holding his AK-47 with both hands, motionless. He watched us climb out of the boat with his unmoving little eyes and pinched lips, then turned around and went away. The first blow of a rifle butt between my shoulder blades propelled me forward on the wooden walkway, but I refused to hurry. The prison rose up among the trees, its wall of barbed wire over ten feet high. There my companions lived their lives. *Like in a zoo*, I thought, observing one of them delousing another's scalp. A henhouse door opened up before me, and a second blow landed me inside the prison.

Pinchao ran up to hug me.

"I thought you'd be already in Bogotá by now! I've been counting the hours since you left. I was so glad you managed to slip away from us!" Then he added reproachfully, "Some of the people here are very happy you got caught."

I did not want to hear that. I had failed. It was hard enough as it was. The mirror we held up to one another was so immediate, so close, it was difficult to bear. I knew this, and I did not hold it against my companions. The frustration of being a hostage was all the more overwhelming when others managed to carry off the very exploit we all dreamed of. I felt an unspoken affection for these men who had been captives for so many years and who were relieved to see us return, as if our failing could somehow lighten their ordeal. They all wanted to tell us what had happened after the night of our escape, and their words helped us to accept our defeat.

The prison door swept open. A squadron of men in uniform appeared. They threw themselves on Lucho. They tied a huge chain around his neck, closed with a heavy padlock that hung on his chest.

"Marulanda," one of them called out.

The sergeant stood up, glancing about him warily. They fastened the other end of Lucho's chain around his neck. Lucho and he looked at each other, resigned.

The guerrillas began to walk toward me in a circle, slowly, to surround me.

I was walking backward, hoping to gain some time to reason with them. Very quickly I was stopped by the barbed-wire fence. The men rushed me, twisting my arms while blind hands pulled me backward by the hair and wound the metal chain around my neck. I struggled wildly. In vain, because I knew in advance that I had lost. But I was not there, in that place and time. I was in another time, elsewhere, with men who had hurt me and who were just like these, and I was struggling against them, struggling to no avail, struggling for everything. Time was no longer linear; it had become impermeable, a system of communicating valves. The past returned to be lived again like a projection of what might come.

The chain was heavy, and it burned me to carry it. It reminded me of how vulnerable I was. And once again, as before when I had escaped alone, I found in myself a strength of a different nature. That of submitting, in a confrontation that could only be a moral one, tied to the idea of honour. An invisible strength, rooted in a value that was futile and cumbersome but that changed everything – because it saved me.

We stared at one another: They were inflated by their power, I was holding on to dignity.

They attached me to William, the military nurse. I turned to him and apologized. "I'm the one who's sorry," he replied. "I don't like to see you like this." Bermeo, too, came up to me. He felt awkward. He was mortified by the scene he'd just witnessed. "Don't try to resist them any more. They dream of nothing better than to have the opportunity to humiliate you."

When I managed to regain some calm, I saw he was right.

Gira, the nurse, came through the prison door. She was doing her rounds among her patients to say that there was no more medication.

"Reprisals," said Pinchao behind me, almost imperceptibly. "They're going to begin to tighten the screw."

She walked right by me, staring at me, her gaze full of reproach.

"Yes, look at me carefully," I said to her. "Don't ever forget what you see. As a woman you should be ashamed to be part of this."

She went pale. I could see she was trembling with rage. But she continued her rounds, without saying a word, and went out.

Of course I should have kept my mouth shut. Humility begins with holding one's tongue. I had a great deal to learn. If God didn't want me to be free, I had to accept that I wasn't ready for freedom. This notion became a lifebuoy.

It was cruelly distressing to see my Lucho. We were forbidden to be near each other, or even to speak. I would see him sitting there, chained to fat Marulanda, alternately looking at his feet, then at me, and it took an excruciating effort to hold back my tears.

President Uribe had made a proposal that the guerrillas had rejected. The idea was to release fifty guerrillas detained in Colombian prisons, in exchange for the liberation of a few hostages. The FARC attached a condition to any negotiation: the prior evacuation of troops from the municipalities of Florida and Pradera, at the foot of the Andes, where the chain let the Río Cauca through. The government gave the impression that it would accept, then retracted the offer, accusing the FARC of manipulating public opinion with offers that really only sought tactical military advantage to find an escape for its guerrillas who had been cordoned off by the Colombian army.

I was tired of listening to the commentary about the government's offer on the opinion programmes. The country was divided in two. Anyone who supported the creation of a secure zone in order to open a dialogue with the government was immediately suspected of collaborating with the guerrillas. It was no longer a question of trying to put an end to our tragedy. For the government and the guerrillas alike, it was a question of saving face. And our lives had simply become bottle corks bobbing in raging oceans of hatred.

I yearned to hear my mom's messages again. I wanted for her to tell me about her daily life, what she was eating, what she was wearing, who she was spending time with. I did not want to hear the usual lamentations and the hollow litanies that our loved ones repeated tirelessly.

I sat uncomfortably on the remaining floorboards. The order had been given to gather up everything. The guerrillas were afraid that, with the efforts they'd made in looking for us, the military might have got wind of our presence.

The guerrillas had confiscated a large part of my belongings. I had managed to save Mom's letters, the photograph of my children, and the newspaper clipping where I had read about Papa's death. I cried without tears.

"Think about something else," William said, not looking at me.

"I can't."

"Why are you scratching?"

I didn't answer.

William stood up to look more closely at me. "You're covered in *cuitibas*.* After the bath you'll have to get some treatment."

There was no bath, not that evening nor any that followed. Enrique put us on a *bongo* that was only a third the size of the ones we'd known before. He squeezed ten of us into a tiny space that was six feet by six, next to the engine, with a drum of gasoline in the middle. It was impossible to sit without having someone's head or legs in the way. He had arranged the chains so that we were attached to one another and to the metal bars of the boat at the same time. If the boat sank, we sank with it. He covered our hole with a thick tarpaulin, and beneath it our breath mingled with the fumes of the engine. The air was suffocating. He obliged us to stay like that

---

* Ticks.

day and night, using the river for a toilet, clinging to the tarpaulin, in front of everybody. We were like worms crawling over one another in a match-box. Gafas was experienced; he didn't need to raise the tone of his voice or bring out a whip. He was a torturer who wore gloves.

The stifling, condensed, contaminated air that burned our throats till we coughed, the heat rising under the tarpaulin, the murderous sun, our bodies stewing in sweat – all of this, of course, was the collective price paid for our escape.

Yet not one of my companions ever blamed us.

65

PUNISHMENT

Late July 2005. I couldn't sleep. How was I supposed to sleep with a chain around my neck that pulled painfully every time William moved? My companions' legs were tangled around me, and I was obliged to shrink into myself to avoid any inappropriate contact – a foot against my ribs, another one behind my neck. I was crushed in a vice of bodies, where no one had enough room.

I lifted a corner of the tarpaulin cautiously. It was already daylight. I put my nose out to fill my lungs with fresh air. The guard's foot stomped my fingers to punish me for my boldness. Then he sealed the tarpaulin. I was mortally thirsty, and I badly needed to urinate. I asked for permission to relieve myself. Enrique shouted from the prow, "Tell the *cucha* she can piss in a pot!"

"There's no room," said the guard.

"She can make room," replied Gafas.

"She says she can't do it in front of the men."

"Tell her she doesn't have anything that the men haven't already seen."

I blushed in the darkness. I felt a hand reaching for mine. It was Lucho. His gesture brought down the dam inside me. For the first time since we'd been recaptured, I burst into tears. *What more must I endure, Lord, to earn the right to go home!* Enrique removed the tarpaulin for a few seconds. My companions' faces were distorted, dry, corpselike. We looked all around us, straining our necks anxiously, not knowing what to think, blinking, our eyes blinded by the harsh midday sun. For a brief moment, we had a vision of the expanse of our misery. We were in a place where four vast rivers met. Water crisscrossing through an endless forest, with us, an infinitesimal spot pitching dangerously in the turbulent eddies where the currents collided.

The *bongo* stopped heavily one morning, on a whim of Enrique's. The guards disembarked. We didn't. Lucho swapped places to sit by me.

"Things will get better, you'll see," I told him.

"That's what you think. It can only get worse."

Finally, after three days, they had us get out in the middle of nowhere. "If it rains," said Armando, "we'll all get wet." It rained. My companions managed to stay dry under their tents. Enrique chained me to a tree, away from the group. I was under the storm for hours. The guards refused to let me use the plastic sheet my companions sent to me.

Drenched and shivering, I was once again chained to William. He asked for permission to go to the *chontos*. The guerrillas had just dug some. They removed his chain. When he came back, I asked to go in turn. Pipiolo, a potbellied little man with chubby fingers, from Jeiner and Pata-Grande's group, stared at me while he was slowly replacing the padlock around William's neck. He remained stubbornly silent. And then he went away.

William looked at me, embarrassed. Then he hailed the guard. "Guard! She needs to go to the toilet, didn't you hear?"

"So what? It's none of your business! Are you asking for trouble or what?"

He wanted to suck up to Enrique. This meant the end of Pata-Grande's reign. Pipiolo broke off a twig to use as a toothpick and glared at me.

"Pipiolo, I need to go the *chontos*," I repeated monotonously.

"You want to take a shit? Do it here, in front of me. Squat here at my feet. The *chontos* are not for you!" he shouted.

Oswald and Ángel went by, carrying logs on their shoulders. They burst out laughing and slapped Pipiolo on the back to congratulate him. Pipiolo pretended to catch himself on his Galil 5.56 mm assault rifle, delighted to have an audience.

I would wait for the changing of the guard.

William began to talk with me. As if nothing had happened. He wanted me to pretend to ignore Pipiolo, and I was grateful to him for that. Pipiolo came up to me. He planted himself before me.

"You shut up, get it? Now it's my turn to have fun. As long as I'm here, you keep your mouth shut."

Enrique let Pipiolo stay on guard all day long. There was no relief until evening.

The troops were working flat out, building something we could just discern between the trees. In one day the prison was set up – fences, barbed wire, eight *caletas* close together in a row, and two others in the corner on either side. Right up next to one of them, hidden from sight by a screen of palm leaves, they had built a latrine. On the other side, there was a tree. In the middle a reservoir of water. All around the *caletas*, there was a muddy pond.

I was assigned to the *caleta* between the latrine and the tree, to which I was chained. I had enough slack to be able to go from my hammock to the latrine, but if I tried to reach the pool of water, I choked. Lucho was on the far side of the reservoir, also chained. They removed our boots, making us walk barefoot. I was not allowed to communicate with anyone.

Being next to the latrine was a refined form of punishment. I lived in the permanent stench of our sick bodies. The nausea never left me, as I was the unhappy witness to all my companions' physical afflictions.

I retreated to my bubble, under my mosquito net. I sought refuge from the attacks of *jején, pajarilla, mosca-marrana** and contact with men. I spent twenty-four hours curled up in my cocoon, huddled in my hammock, clinging to a silence with no end.

Eventually I switched on the radio. One day I came upon a preacher who was broadcasting from the West Coast of the United States. He was preaching the Bible as if it were a philosophy class. I encountered his programme several times, and I was disdainful. I thought that he was one of those cranks who had made God their milk cow. But then I stopped to

---

* Different sorts of gnats.

listen. He was analysing a passage in the Bible, dissecting the texts, basing his erudite arguments on the Greek and Latin versions of the text. Every word took on a deeper, more precise meaning, and it was as if he were cutting a diamond there before me. It was one of the first paragraphs in chapter twelve of the second letter from St. Paul to the Corinthians.* It should be read like a poem, without any preconceived ideas. I thought it was universal and could be used by anyone seeking for a meaning in suffering.

I began to hibernate. There was no longer any day or any night, any sun or any rain. Noise, smells, insects, hunger and thirst, everything disappeared. I read, listened, meditated, sifted each episode of my life through my new thoughts. My relationship with God changed. I no longer had to go through others to have access to him, nor did I need rituals. Reading his book, I saw a gaze, a voice, a finger that showed the way and transformed things. The human condition that was revealed in the Bible became a mirror that sent my own reflection back to me.

I liked that God. He spoke, he chose his words, he had a sense of humour. Like the Little Prince charming the rose, he was cautious.

One evening when I was listening to the nighttime rebroadcast of one of the preacher's lectures, someone called me. It was ink black outside, and it was impossible to see anything. I raised my head and listened, and the voice came closer.

"What's going on?" I cried, afraid that it might be the alert to strike camp.

"Shh! Stay calm." I recognized Mono Liso's childish voice.

"What do you want?" I asked warily.

He had put his hand through the wire fence and was trying to touch me, saying obscene things that sounded ridiculous in his little-boy's voice.

"Guaaard!" I screamed.

"What!" answered an irritated voice from the other end of the prison.

"Call the *relevante!*"*

---

* "And he said to me, My grace is sufficient for you: for my strength is made perfect in weakness . . . for when I am weak, then am I strong."

"I'm the *relevante*! What do you want?"

"I have a problem — Mono Liso."

"We'll see about it tomorrow," he said curtly.

"He has to learn respect!" shouted someone from inside the enclosure. "We heard everything. He's a foul-mouthed brat!"

"Shut up!" the guard shouted back.

The *relevante* circled with his flashlight beam, and it caught Mono Liso, who leaped back from the fence and pretended to be cleaning his AK-47.

The next morning after breakfast, Enrique sent Mono Liso with the keys to the lock hanging from my neck. He sauntered over, proud as a peacock.

"Come here!" he shouted, with the smugness of authority acquired too soon.

He opened the padlock and tightened the chain around my throat. I could hardly breathe. Pleased with his work, he went back out, rolling his shoulders. Once he was outside, he gave some useless instructions to the men on duty. He wanted everyone to know that he had just been promoted to *relevante*.

I went back to my hammock and opened my Bible. I no longer left my hammock.

After several days had gone by, Enrique decided to visit the prison. He got the military prisoners together and acted all chummy with them. He pretended to write down everyone's requests. In the end, when he saw that everything had gone smoothly and no one had any reason to protest, he asked if anyone had any special requests.

Pinchao raised a finger. "I do have one for you, Commander."

"Tell me, my boy, I'm listening," Gafas said in a syrupy voice.

"I would like to ask you" — Pinchao paused to clear his throat — "I would like to ask you to remove my companions' chains. They've been chained up for nearly six months and—"

Gafas interrupted him. "They'll be chained up until they leave here," he said, a touch too spitefully.

---

* A superior in charge of the changing of the guard.

Then, thinking better of it, he got up and smiled and said, "I don't suppose there's anything else? Right. Good night, *muchachos!*"

The next morning at around six, planes flew right over the top of the camp. And a few minutes later, there was a series of explosions, about twelve miles away.

"They're bombing!"

"They're bombing!"

My companions didn't know what else to say.

The first thing I put into my *equipo* was my Bible. I anxiously sorted through my belongings. All I wanted to keep were the things that reminded me of my children. They had just turned twenty and seventeen. I had missed all their adolescent years. Did they still remember my face? My hands were trembling. I had to throw out all the rest – recycled pots, patched scraps of clothing, my men's underwear. Permanent contact with mud, insects, and athlete's foot had made my feet a frightful mess. My legs had atrophied, and I had lost most of my muscle mass.

When the guard came to announce our imminent departure, I was ready to march.

66

THE RETREAT

November 2005. While we were walking in single file, silently, bent, I prayed, with my rosary in my hands. No one had told us anything, but I imagined that we must be in the same part of the country as our former companions, Orlando, Gloria, Jorge, Consuelo, Clara and her little Emmanuel. I prayed that the bombing had not caught any of them in the line of fire.

We went through changing forests, and every step entailed risk. Those at the front of the line had their faces deformed by brambles and bee stings. "They're Chinese," said the others, making fun of them. I marched with a hat pulled down over my head, a mosquito net covering my face, and gloves that I had made from old camouflage uniforms. *I am an astronaut*, I told myself, feeling like an alien landed on a hostile planet. I was absent, lost in my prayers, concentrating on the effort, and I did not see the mountain coming. I looked up, and the wall of vegetation disappeared into the clouds. The climb was very hard, I could not keep the pace. My companions were far ahead of me, excited by the physical effort – who would go fastest, carry the most, complain the least.

"I'll never make it," I said quietly.

Ángel was getting impatient. "Hurry up!" he shouted, pushing me.

"Hand me your *equipo*," said someone behind us with false resignation.

It was Efrén, a tall, muscular black man who never spoke. He had just caught up with us at a slow jog. He was meant to come last. We were the last ones in the group, and he didn't want to get left behind because of me.

He took my *equipo* and wedged it behind his neck above his own backpack.

"Go ahead," he said with a smile.

I looked one last time toward the top and began to climb, clinging to everything I could get my hands on. Three hours later, after crossing waterfalls, rock faces, and an astonishing esplanade of stones piled in pyramids like the ruins of an ancient Inca temple, I reached the top.

Sitting in a row on the slope, my companions were eating rice. Lucho sat against a tree, his cheeks hollow with fatigue, unable to lift his food to his mouth. I moved toward him.

Ángel called out in a nasty voice, "Come back here! You will sit where I tell you to."

Enrique gave the order to start marching again. We didn't even have time to rest for a moment. Efrén, exhausted, protested against Enrique's decision. He took off my *equipo* to give it back to me. He was called up front, then came back, tail between his legs. Enrique had not appreciated his complaint; he would have to go on carrying my *equipo* as a punishment. Ángel, too, protested. He was fed up with being last because of me and losing his chance to eat. He was relieved from his mission and replaced by Katerina, the black girl who'd looked after me when we left Sombra. I did my best to hide that I was overjoyed.

"Let's not let them get ahead," she said, mingling authority with complicity.

We crossed a high, desert-like plateau, where the clay ground baked beneath the sun. The open horizon revealed the expanse of the jungle. A green line carved through the blue sky around the 360 degrees of our field of vision. To the left a huge river stretched lazily, in traceries of India ink. *That must be the Río Negro*, I thought.

At the far side of the plateau, we entered a cloister of scraggly dry trees with neither leaves nor shade, growing in a tangle. They tore at my hat with their clawed branches, held me back by the straps of my pack, blocked my way whenever I could squeeze my *equipo* between them, and finally sliced through my boot with a branch as sharp as a blade that was sticking up from the ground. "I'll have water in my socks," I muttered, cursing. We had a dizzying descent, down a slope built in terraces, which we could hurry down, jumping, at the risk of missing our landing and rolling the rest of the way in freefall. The last part of the descent gave onto an expanse of rainwater captured in the moss and bushes, and I had to jump from one tree root to the other to avoid water getting into my damaged boots. The next morning the terrain was flat and dry. Out of nowhere came a huge dirt road. "We've found our way out," said Katerina. We'd made good time, not letting the others get ahead.

"Let's stop here," she said. "I'm tired."

I put my pack on the ground.

"What do you like to eat?" she asked, lighting a cigarette.

"I like pasta," I answered.

Katerina pouted. "Normally I'm pretty good at pasta. But here, with nothing, it's hard. Do you like pizza?"

"I love pizza."

"When I was little, my mother sent me to live with my aunt in Venezuela. She worked for a very rich lady who liked me a lot. She would take me to eat pizza with her children."

"Were they the same age?"

"No, there were older. The boy said that when he grew up, he would marry me. I would have liked to marry him."

"Why didn't you stay there?"

"My mother wanted me with her. She lives in Calamar with her new husband. But I didn't want to come back. And when I did, there were problems. We didn't have any money, and I couldn't leave again."

"Did you like it in Calamar?"

"No, I wanted to go back to my aunt, in that nice house. They had a swimming pool. We ate hamburgers. Here they don't know what that is."

"Were you studying in Calamar?"

"I was in school at the beginning. I was good in school. I liked drawing a lot, and I had nice handwriting. Later on I needed money, so I had to work."

"Work where?"

She hesitated for a moment, then said, "In a bar."

I didn't say anything. Most of the girls had worked in a bar, and I knew what that meant.

"That's why I enlisted. Here at least, if you have a boyfriend, you don't have to wash his laundry for him. We women and men are the equal."

I listened to her, thinking that it wasn't quite true.

What was true, on the other hand, was that the girls had to work like men. I can still see Katerina in her tank top and camouflage trousers, an axe in her hand, swinging her arms back with a spectacular twist of her waist to land a precise blow at the base of a fine tree she chopped down without any difficulty. It was a vision that had left my companions breathless, this black Venus displaying a physical prowess that emphasized every muscle on her body. How could a girl like her could stay in a place like this?

"I would have liked to be a beauty queen," she confessed. "Or a model," she added dreamily.

Her words stabbed my heart. She was carrying her AK-47 the way others carry a book and a pencil.

The march went on, every day more trying. "We won't be there in time for New Year's," said Gira's boyfriend. I didn't want to believe him. I thought he was just saying that to make us go faster. I had no intention of walking faster. This blind effort, with no idea where we were headed, was sapping my energy.

One particularly rough day, with *cansaperros* one after the other, like pearls strung together by an invisible hand, a storm broke. The only order we had was to keep going. Ángel took pleasure in forbidding me from covering myself. I kept going, dripping with rainwater.

I caught up with Lucho, who was leaning against a tree in the middle of a climb, his gaze adrift. "I can't take it any more, I can't take it any more," he said, looking up at the sky as it raged against us.

I went up to him to give him a hug, to take his hand.

"Keep moving!" shouted Ángel. "Don't try to trick us with your stories. We know the game you two play to slow up the march."

I didn't listen to him. I was fed up with his insults, his fits, his threats. I stopped, tossed my backpack on the ground, and took out the sugar I always carried on me.

"Here you are, my Lucho, take this. Let's carry on together, gently."

Ángel cocked his M-16 rifle and poked the barrel into my ribs.

"Never mind," said a voice that I recognized. "We're already there. The troops are resting fifty yards from here."

Efrén picked up Lucho's pack and said, "Come on, sir, just a little more effort."

He took out the black plastic sheet on the side of his equipment and handed it to him. Lucho wrapped himself in it and held my arm, and he was still saying, "I can't take it any more, Ingrid, I can't take it any more." He couldn't tell that I was crying along with him, because it was pouring so hard that my face was streaming with rain.

My God, this is enough! I screamed in the silence of my heart.

When I got to the top of one hill, I was ready to pass out. I had forgotten to fill the little plastic bottle I used for water. Ángel was drinking from his, water dripping down his neck.

"I'm thirsty," I said, my mouth all furry.

"There's no water for you, you old hag," he brayed.

He was looking at me with the cold eye of a reptile. He raised his canteen to his mouth and drank for a long time, never taking his eyes from me. Then he turned it over, and two drops fell out. He screwed the top back on. Enrique was doing his rounds. He walked the length of the column, frowning. He went right by me. I kept silent.

"Prepare the water!" he shouted when the last of us had arrived.

A sound of pots banging cheered the silence of the mountain. Two guys struggling to carry a cauldron filled with water stopped a few feet from us. They tossed in two packs of sugar and some sachets of the strawberry-flavoured powder. They stirred it all up with a branch they broke off a tree.

"Who wants water? Come on up!" shouted one of them like a street vendor.

Everybody rushed up.

"Not you!" screamed Ángel, in a foul mood.

I squatted down, my head between my knees. "I'm not as thirsty as before. Pretty soon I won't be thirsty at all."

The water left in the cauldron was poured out on the ground. We went on marching. Efrén came running up to me.

"Lucho sent this for you!" He tossed me a bottle filled with red water, which landed at my feet.

67

THE EGGS

On December 17, 2005, the march stopped at ten o'clock in the morning. We had just jumped two small streams, with a bed of little pink and white pebbles. The rumour immediately spread that we'd be camping at the top of a hill a few yards high.

"We made it before Christmas," I said, relieved.

In a few hours, the camp was built. I was chained to my tree at the far end and Lucho to his at the other. I was allowed to build some parallel bars for exercise. They wanted me to be in better shape for marching, I thought. They opened the padlock that attached me to the tree, and I had to keep the whole chain wrapped around my neck when I climbed on the bars. I did my spins while the guards looked on, amused. *I'll fall, and the chain will stay caught on the bar, and I'll die, strangled*, I thought wryly.

I had one hour for my exercises and my bath. "You have to get some muscles in your arms," said the young guy who had replaced Gira as nurse. I found it very difficult to do push-ups, and I tried to raise the weight of my entire body, hanging from one of the bars, to no avail. *I'll do it every day, and I'll make it*, I promised myself.

My companions watched and felt sorry for me. Arteaga was the first one to break the silence imposed on me. He spoke without looking at me, continuing to work on sewing caps, advising me on which exercises to do and how many, right in front of the guards. There were no comments, no reprimands. One by one, my companions began speaking to me again, more and more openly, except for Lucho.

One afternoon on my way back from the bath, I could see that Lucho wasn't feeling well. He needed sugar. I hurried to find it in my things, my hands trembling because I knew it was urgent. I gave Lucho the sugar and stayed with him for a while to be sure that he felt better. From behind, Ángel pulled my chain violently.

"Who do you think you are?" he screamed. "Either you are stupid, a mental retard, or you're taking us for fools! Don't you get it? You're not allowed to talk to anyone. Has your old donkey's brain stopped working? I'll get it to work, all right, with a bullet between your eyes, you'll see!"

I listened to him without batting an eyelid. He dragged me like a dog to my tree and chained me up, relishing every second. I knew I'd done the right thing, maintaining my self-control. But the rage I felt against Ángel distracted me from my good resolutions. I was almost angry with myself. During the night I replayed all the possible versions of the same scene, above all the imagined slap I delivered to his face, and I delighted in picturing Ángel's defeat when I put him in his place. Nonetheless, I knew the best thing had been to keep quiet, despite the white-hot burn of his insults.

Ángel made a point of not allowing me to forgive him for degrading me. He persecuted me with his spite and shared it with the guerrillas like Pipiolo or Tiger, who got off on the self-aggrandizing pleasure of attacking me. The slightest pretext for abuse was a delight. They knew that I waited impatiently for my morning drink. They insisted on serving me last, and when I held out my bowl, they hardly filled it at all or threw out the rest in front of me.

They knew I liked bath time. I was the last one to go to bathe, but they would hurry me from the water faster than anyone else. I was not allowed to sit in the stream to wash; I had to do it standing up, because they said I got the water dirty. My companions had set up a plastic curtain so that I could have some privacy when bathing. Everyone could use it except me.

One morning when I was washing, I noticed some movement over by the forest. Soaping myself, my eyes on the trees, I saw Mono Liso, his pants around his ankles, masturbating.

When the guard came to lock my chain around the tree, I demanded he call Enrique. Enrique didn't come. But "the Dwarf," his new second-in-command, answered my request.

The Dwarf was a strange man, first of all because he was well over six feet tall and then because he looked like an intellectual lost in the bush. I had never been able to decide whether I liked him or not. I believed he was weak and a hypocrite, but perhaps he was simply disciplined and cautious.

"I wanted to let you know that if the FARC is not capable of educating that brat, I'll do it myself."

"The next time it happens, let us know."

"There won't be a next time. If it happens again, I'm going to give him a thrashing he'll blush about all his life."

The next morning no one came to unchain me, so I couldn't do my exercises at the bars outside my *caleta*. I was reduced to doing push-ups below my hammock.

Many months had passed by when I saw the hen. She had just jumped onto Lucho's *caleta* and had settled onto the mosquito net he left rolled up at the end of his bed during the day. It must have been a more pleasant nest. She stayed for hours, motionless, unbeknownst to anybody, with one eye closed, sitting straight up as if she were sleeping. She was speckled grey, with a lovely blood-red crest, well aware of the strong impression she made. *What a looker*, I thought as I observed her. She got up, clucking, then cackled energetically, ruffling her feathers, before going off without further ado.

Every day at the same time, Lucho's hen came to visit. She regularly laid an egg for him on the sly. At twilight we observed the guards.

"She was in the camp this afternoon."

"She must have laid an egg here somewhere, among the trees."

The egg was already in our bellies. It had come to me in a roundabout way, so that I could cook it. I had perfected a technique for heating my bowl by burning the plastic handles of the disposable razors delivered to the camp. I kept all of them. With a single razor handle, I could cook an egg, which Lucho then shared out to our comrades in spoonfuls, taking turns.

When it rained, I could cook continuously — the rain hid the smoke, the smells, and the sound. And we would eat all the eggs we'd saved one by one.

We had just discovered a new one in the folds of Lucho's mosquito net. The hen had made a great fuss, to Pinchao and me, to tell us about her egg. We were really happy, because it was Mother's Day, and it would allow us to celebrate.

We could not have imagined that the date would be marked in a very different way. They hadn't made a sound; by the time we heard them, they were already on top of us.

68

MONSTER

May 2006. The Dwarf arrived, out of breath.

"Take your *equipos* just as they are. Don't take anything more. We're leaving right away."

The helicopters were whirring above our heads, their rotors slowly stirring the air with a deafening sound of cataclysm. William, the nurse, ran off right away. He was always ready. The rest of us always wanted to slip something precious in our packs at the last minute.

I didn't try to go any faster. Papa always said, "Get dressed slowly if you are in a hurry." And death? I didn't give a damn. A bullet – quick, clean, why not? I didn't believe it would happen to me. I knew that was not my destiny. A guard was barking ferociously behind me. I looked up. Everyone had left.

The guard pushed me, took my *equipo*, which was still open, and left at a run. Above my head a helicopter was hovering. A man was seated in the door, his feet dangling, looking at the ground. He was wearing big goggles, and his gun barrel was aimed at the same spot he was looking at. How could he not see me, right there below him? Maybe it was my camouflage trousers. He might take me for a guerrilla and shoot me. I had to signal that I was a prisoner. I'd show him my chains. Maybe it would be too late, and they'd leave me lying there in a puddle of blood, and the military patrols would discover my body.

"*Vieja hijue' madre, quiere que la maten?*"*

It was Ángel. He was hysterical, bent over behind a tree with my *equipo* in his arms. The blast from the helicopter was making him squint, his head to one side as if he were in pain.

A hail of bullets raked the forest. I jumped. I ran straight ahead, grabbing Lucho's mosquito net, with the egg still inside, and I landed next to a tree, to crouch beside Ángel.

There was no let-up in the firing, just next to us but not at us. The helicopter went on circling above us. Ángel didn't want to move. In a row of trees in front of ours, other guerrillas were waiting, like us.

"Let's go!" I said. I wanted to move.

"No, they're shooting at anything that moves. I'll tell you when to run."

I still had the egg in my hand. I wondered what I could do with it now. I slipped it into my jacket pocket and tried to roll up the mosquito net so it could fit into my *equipo*.

"Now's not the right time," said Ángel, growling.

"You bite your fingernails, I put my things away – you have your way, I have mine!" I answered, annoyed.

He looked at me, surprised, and then he smiled. I hadn't seen that side of him for a long time. He took my *equipo* and tossed it neatly over his head to wedge it on his own pack against his neck. Then he took me by the hand and looked me straight in the eye.

"On the count of three, we run, and you don't stop until I do, got it?"

"Got it."

Other helicopters were coming toward us. The one directly above climbed higher and went into a bank. I could see the soles of the soldier's boots getting smaller. Ángel ran, the devil on his heels, and I followed.

Three-quarters of an hour later, we were making our way through the bush once again. We caught up with the rest of the group. I showed the egg to Lucho. "You're silly," he said, delighted. The egg was all that mattered. Having the army come to rescue us seemed like an impossible dream.

*

---

* "You old bitch, do you want them to kill you?"

The forest was dressed up in pink and purple. This happened twice a year with the flowering of orchids. They grew around the tree trunks and they awoke all at the same time, in a flurry of colour that only lasted a few days. I picked them as we walked, to put in my hair, tucked behind my ears and wove them through my braids. My companions would hand me some, pleased to rekindle gestures of gallantry they had forgotten.

We walked for days, and then we would find the *bongo* farther away. Enrique always crowded us together in the stern, next to the fuel cans, but we were too tired from the march to mind.

Behind a little cluster of trees, the grey-blue water of the river seemed immobile, like a mirror. Gradually the light changed. The trees stood out, as if drawn with Japanese brushstrokes against artificial paradise of the pinkish red background. The cry of a pterodactyl broke the air. I looked up. Two guacamayas soared across the heavens in a trail of rainbow colours and gold dust. "I'll draw them for my Mela and my Loli."

The sky darkened. There was nothing left but stars when the *bongo* arrived.

We came to a disused FARC camp. We set up off to one side, on a slight slope overlooking a deep, narrow stream that capriciously formed a right angle just in front of us, creating a pool of blue water above a bed of fine sand.

Enrique magnanimously authorized each of us to bathe when it suited us. My *caleta* was built first, in the row going up the slope. I had an incomparable view over the pool. I was as happy as I could be. The water flowed icy and crystal clear. Early in the morning, it was covered in vapour, like thermal waters. I decided to go for my swim just after the morning meal, because no one seemed to want to argue over that time slot, and I wanted to stay in for a long time. The current was strong, and a tree trunk lodged in the curve was an ideal support for swimming on the spot.

The next day Tiger was on duty, and his vicious gaze did not leave me during the entire time I did my exercises. *He's going to make my life hell*, I thought. The day after that, Oswald replaced him at the same time.

"Get out," he brayed.

"Enrique said we could stay in as long as we like."

"Get out."

When the Dwarf came on his rounds, I asked him for permission to swim in the pool.

"I will bring it up with the commander," he replied, the model FARC guerrilla.

With the FARC not a single leaf on a tree could be cut without permission from the leader. This centralized power meant that things moved very slowly. But it proved very useful for putting a spanner in other people's works when it suited. If a guard wanted to turn down a prisoner's request, he would reply that he'd ask his superior. The Dwarf's answer was the equivalent of a refusal. So I was surprised when he came back the next day and declared, "You can stay in the water and swim, but watch out for the stingrays."

Tiger and Oswald moved their rifles to the other shoulder. If they were on duty when it was my bath time, they would try to outdo each other repeating, "Watch out for the stingrays!" just to annoy me.

I hung some sheets that my companions had given me around my hammock so that I could change without having anyone look at me.

Monster arrived one afternoon, introducing himself to the prisoners in a friendly way. I was surprised by his name, and at first I thought it was a joke, but then I remembered that they did not speak English and that "Monster" must not have the same resonance for them as for me. He asked me a few questions, acting in a very friendly way, but when he went away again, I said to myself, *Otro Enrique.**

That very evening Oswald was on duty. He came and planted his uptight person before me and roared, "Get this shit out of here!" pointing to the hanging sheets.

This was a hard blow. I really needed some privacy.

Exasperated, Oswald pulled down my sheets himself. I asked to speak to

---

* Another Enrique.

Monster, hoping that he had not yet been contaminated. It was worse than that. He knew that he'd get a standing ovation if he treated me harshly.

From that day on, Monster began to despise me with an easy conscience. No matter what I asked, he invariably said no. *It's character-building,* I kept telling myself.

Before Monster arrived, I had begged them to build us a screen of leaves in front of the *chontos.* They had dug them right next to the *caletas,* and I could see my companions when they squatted down. Huddling behind a big tree whose roots hid me, I made a hole with the heel of my boot and relieved myself, praying that the guards wouldn't compel me to use the hole in front of everybody. One evening on my way back, my foot caught in a root. As I fell, I rammed a sharp branch into my knee. I understood what had happened before I even felt it. I got up cautiously and saw that the tip of the branch was soaked in blood from a gaping hole in my knee that was opening and closing spasmodically. *I've done something nasty there,* was my instant diagnosis.

As I expected, I was denied any medication. So I decided not to move from my *caleta* until the wound closed, and I just prayed to the heavens that there would be no raids until my knee had scarred over. I thought it would be a matter of two days; it took two weeks of complete immobilization.

Lucho was worried and asked around for some alcohol. One of our companions had a permanent stock, and he had the last squeeze of a tube of some anti-inflammatory cream – miraculously, they both ended up in my hands. He also got permission from Monster to bring me a jug of water from the stream every day so I could wash, giving us the chance to exchange a few words, a privilege that brought me all the happiness I could hope for.

I quickly told Lucho about the business that had so upset me. One evening before I hurt my knee, Tito shook me in my hammock. He wanted to speak to me in secret. I feared a repetition of Mono Liso's advances, so I rejected him. Before returning to his guard post, he whispered, "I can get you out of here, but we have to be quick!"

I paid no attention. I knew how the guerrillas liked to set traps, and I imagined that Enrique had sent him to sound out my intentions. But I didn't see Tito again.

Efrén came to see me. He brought a brand-new notebook and some coloured pencils. He wanted me to draw the solar system.

"I want to learn," he said.

I rummaged in my memory to situate Venus and Neptune, filling the paper with a universe that I created at my whim, with balls of fire and giant comets. He loved it and asked for more, and he came back every day for his notebook and his new drawings. He had a thirst for knowledge, and I needed to keep busy. I invented all kinds of subterfuges in order to bait him with subjects I knew well, and he would take the bait, delighted to come back for more the next day. So it was that I discovered, in casual conversation, that Tito had run away with his girl and another guy. They had been caught and shot. Tito's face, with his lazy eye, came to haunt me in my nightmares. I regretted that I hadn't believed him. The chain I wore around my neck twenty-four hours a day now seemed heavier than ever. My one consolation was that Lucho no longer had to wear his during the day.

I got out of my bath and dried off quickly: The morning pot had arrived. We didn't eat much, and this was the only meal that sated my hunger. I rushed over, forgetting my good manners, wondering how I could manage to get the biggest *arepa*. Marulanda was in front of me. I was jubilant – he would get the little one, and mine would be the big one, the next on the pile. Tiger was serving, he saw me coming, he looked at the *arepas* and understood why I was pleased. He took the pile and turned it over. Marulanda got the big one and I the little one.

I was ashamed of myself for succumbing to such petty desire. So many years fighting against my basic instincts, to no avail. I vowed not to look at the size of the portions any more and take whatever I was served.

However, the next morning when they unlocked my padlock, despite my resolution to behave like a fine lady, the demon in me got out when it smelled the *arepa* and I realized to my dismay that my eyes were boring into the pile of *cancharinas* and that I was ready to bite the hand of anyone who tried to take my turn.

So I decided I would wait until the very last moment to go for my food. Unfortunately, the moment the pot arrived, another "me" took over. *This isn't normal*, I reflected. *My ego is interfering*. Much to my dismay, there was no way around it. Day after day I failed the test.

69

LUCHO'S HEART

It was on one of those mornings, as I was standing in line to get my first meal, that I saw our three American companions coming along the path that led to the guerrillas' camp. I was surprised, it made me so happy.

Marc, Tom, and Keith were all smiles. I hurried to greet them, with a warmth that proved contagious to my fellow prisoners. Tom hugged me affectionately and began speaking English, knowing how happy I would be to resume our English lessons.

Monster scowled at me as he went by and heard me talking to Tom. The next morning he announced with obvious glee, "The prisoners are allowed to talk among themselves. Except to Ingrid." Everyone forgot the rule when a poor stingray drifted into the pool. I saw it while I was taking my bath. It had tiger stripes, like the ones I'd sometimes seen in Chinese aquariums. Armando gave the alert, and the guard came to hack off its tail with a blow from his machete. Then it was put on display, not for the exceptional patterns of its skin, but because the guerrillas ate its genital organs for their aphrodisiac properties. The prisoners gathered to examine the poor specimen, clearly a source of great interest, due to its resemblance to human male organs.

That day, Enrique agreed to let the hostages enjoy watching DVDs.

Some of our companions who were on good terms with the guerrillas insinuated that it might be therapeutic for the depression coming in waves among the prisoners. It's true that at night we were often awakened by one of our companions screaming. My *caleta* was next to Pinchao's, and his nightmares were more and more frequent. I tried to rouse him from his dream by calling his name, putting on my best sheriff's voice.

"The devil was attacking me," he would confess, still in the grip of a vivid vision.

I did not want to admit that we were all as disturbed as he was. It was happening to me more often. The first time, Pinchao woke me. I said, horrified, "Someone was strangling me."

"That's the way it is," he whispered to reassure me. "You don't get used to it. It only gets worse."

Enrique hadn't wanted to appear weak by entertaining his "detainees." Maybe he changed his mind to impress the Americans. Maybe he was concerned about our mental health. Whatever. The guerrillas liked films with Jackie Chan and Jean-Claude Van Damme. But the ones they knew by heart starred their Mexican idol, Vicente Fernández. I watched the men as they watched the movies and was intrigued to discover they always identified with the good guys and had tears in their eyes during the soppy love scenes.

One afternoon we left the stingray camp, unhurriedly and halfheartedly, and went once again deep into the *manigua*. On occasion I had been at the front of the line during the marches, because Enrique knew that I walked slowly, so he made me leave earlier. Very quickly some of my companions would catch up, ready to trample over me to get ahead. I would often wonder why grown men would bother vying to be in the lead of a line of prisoners.

Late October 2006–December 2006. The new camp boasted two places to bathe. One was the river itself, which was rare, because they generally tried to hide us from places where there was traffic, and another was on a little waterfall with turbulent water, farther inland.

When we went down to the river, I would swim upstream and manage to go a few yards. Some of my companions followed my example, and bath time became a sort of sports competition. The guards didn't go after anyone but me. So I swam in circles or on the spot, convinced that my body was benefiting from it just as much.

When, for reasons that were not revealed, they ordered us to take our bath in the waterfall, we had to go past a clearing that they had made into their volleyball court, which they had created with sand from the river, then along the outside of their camp. As we went by, in their *caletas* I could see papayas, oranges, and lemons, which I looked at longingly.

I had asked Enrique for permission to celebrate my children's birthdays. For the second year in a row, he refused. I tried to imagine how different my children's faces must be. Melanie had just turned twenty-one, and Lorenzo was eighteen. Mom said his voice had changed. I had never heard it.

The flatness of life, the boredom, time that was forever starting over again just the same – it all acted like a sedative. I watched the girls practising a dance for the New Year on the volleyball court. Katerina was the most talented. She danced the *cumbia* like a goddess. These good-natured activities filled me with melancholy and impatience to recover my freedom.

We were all obsessed by our need to run away. Armando grew very excited as he explained in detail the escape he had planned, always for sometime soon. He even claimed he'd already gone through with it once.

"But I had to come back. You see, I was wandering around like that at night, and I saw the commander headed straight for me. I thought he was going to kill me. But he didn't. It was too dark. He didn't recognize me. 'Where are you going, son?' he asked. 'I have to take a leak, comrade!'"

"That's a shameless lie! You never even set foot outside your mosquito net."

"You don't believe me? You'll see, I'll surprise you all!"

I, too, could think of little else but the idea of escape. They had eased my regime considerably. I was allowed to speak with Lucho for an hour a day during lunch break and with the others without restriction, although English was strictly forbidden.

When my hour with Lucho was over, Pinchao took his place. It had become usual to make appointments between prisoners. We took pride in making it clear when we didn't want to be disturbed. Living together twenty-four hours a day with hardly anything to do led us to raise imaginary walls. Pinchao came over for our daily chat.

"When I grow up," I liked to say playfully, "I'll build a city in the Magdalena where the *desplazados** will have fine houses with the best schools for their children, and I'll make Ciudad Bolívar into a Montmartre, with lots of tourists, good restaurants, and a place of pilgrimage for the Virgin of Freedom."

"Do you really want to be president of Colombia?" asked Pinchao.

"Yes," I answered, just to annoy him.

One day he asked, "Aren't you afraid?"

"Why are you asking?"

"Yesterday, just to try it, I wanted to go outside my *caleta* without asking the guards' permission. It was so dark I couldn't even see my hand."

"And?"

"I was too frightened. I'm a coward. I'm useless. I'll never be able to escape the way you did."

I heard myself say very softly, "Every time I left the camp, I thought I would die of fear. Fear is normal. For some people it acts as a brake; for others it's an engine. The important thing is not to let it control you. When you make the decision to escape, it's a cold, rational decision. Preparation is essential, because in the midst of action, when fear takes hold of you, you mustn't think about it – you have to act. So you do it in stages. I have to take three steps forward, one, two, three. Now I get down and I go under that big branch. Then I turn to the right. Now I start running. The movements you make must take all your concentration. You feel your fear, but you accept it and you put it aside."

A few days before Christmas, we moved to a makeshift camp that was less than half an hour from where we were. Hastily built, it had no *caletas*, no hammocks; everybody slept on plastic sheets on the ground. Everything

---

* People displaced by the war between paramilitaries and guerrillas.

was somewhat improvised, and the guards were not as attentive, so I was able to sit next to Lucho.

"I think that Pinchao wants to escape," I confided to him.

"He won't get far. He doesn't know how to swim."

"If there were three of us, we'd have a better chance."

Lucho looked at me, a new glow in his gaze. Then, as if he refused to show any enthusiasm, he said, frowning, "Have to think about it!"

I hadn't realized until now that during our entire conversation he'd been ill at ease, shifting position, worried, as if he were having trouble getting comfortable with his own body.

"Ah, I've got a cramp," he said breathlessly.

He stretched out his arm, and I thought he'd hurt himself.

"No, not there. It's in the middle of my chest. It really hurts, as if someone were pressing on it, right here in the middle."

He went from white to grey. I had already seen this. Papa to begin with and then, in a different way but just as acute, Jorge.

"Lie down and don't move. I'll get William."

"No, wait, it's nothing. Don't make a fuss."

I let go of him and reassured him. "I'll be right back."

William was always wary. He'd often gone running to look at a patient, only to find a gifted actor scheming to get more food.

"If I help you, out of friendship, the day we really need medication, they'll refuse," he'd explained, back in the days when we were chained up together.

"You know I wouldn't come and get you if I didn't think it was serious," I said.

William's diagnosis was instantaneous. "He's having a heart attack. We need some aspirin right away."

Oswald gave me a chilly reception.

"We need some aspirin, quickly. Lucho has just had a heart attack."

"There's no one around. They're all working on the site."

"And the nurse?"

"There's no one, and as far as I'm concerned, the old guy can die."

I leaped back, horrified. Tom had witnessed the scene. When I came over to him, Lucho opened his closed fist to show me his treasure: Tom had just given him a spare aspirin he'd been keeping since Sombra's prison.

Even when the nurse eventually came, there was no aspirin for Lucho. As if to apologize, old Erminson told me in confidence, "They had to clear some land to plant the coca. Enrique's going to sell it, because we have no more money, and the Plan Patriota cut us off from our suppliers. That's why there's nothing left and we're all busy."

The men had been complaining about the hard work they had to put in. Harsh blue smoke had wafted over us as they burned the land, making it hard to breathe, and we'd noticed that they changed the guard only twice a day. They were all very busy.

Two days before Christmas, we went back to the old camp by the river, and we set up our antennas to listen to the programme devoted to our families. Saturday, December 23, 2006, was a strange night. Wrapped up in my hammock and my solitude, I heard my mother's faithful voice and the magical ones of my children. Mela spoke to me in a wise and maternal voice that broke my heart.

"I hear your voice in my heart, and I repeat all your words. I remember everything you told me, Mom. I need you to come back."

And I cried just as hard when I heard Lorenzo's voice. It was his voice, my little boy's voice. But it had changed, and in it there echoed a second voice. My father's voice, his grave, warm tone, like velvet. As I listened, I saw my child and I saw Papa. And not just Papa, but also his hands, his big hands with square fingers, dry and smooth. It gave me such happiness that it made me sob. And I also heard Sebastian. He had recorded his message in Spanish, although his mother tongue is French, and this brought him closer to me. I felt blessed in hell. I could not listen any more. My heart couldn't take this much emotion. "Have I told Sebastian how much I love him? Dear Lord, he doesn't know. He doesn't know that purple has been my favourite colour because of that purple pareo he gave me and that I refused to wear." I laughed at my memories and my guilt. "I will get out of here alive to be a better mother," I said, resolved. At dawn, with swollen eyes and my hammock soaked, I got up so they could free me to use the *chontos*.

As early as it was, the guards were already drunk. This was the only time I ever saw them drunk. Armando swore he would carry out his plan that same day, and I wanted to believe him. The night was moonlit, and the guards were even drunker by this time. It was a perfect night, but Armando didn't escape.

The next morning Pinchao came up to me. "Armando didn't leave. He'll never be able to."

"And you, could you?" I asked.

"I don't know how to swim."

"I'll teach you."

"My God! It's my dream to learn, because I want to teach my son to swim. I don't want him to feel ashamed, like I do."

"We'll start tomorrow."

Pinchao returned the favour. He appointed himself my trainer, and he put together a strict routine of exercises that he performed by my side. Hardest for me were pull-ups. I couldn't get the weight of my body up even one inch. In the beginning Pinchao held my legs. But some weeks later my body kept going until my eyes were above the bar. I was thrilled. I was able to do six pull-ups in a row.

We were working out, far from the ears of the guards, when I asked him straight out.

"You can count on me," he said immediately. "With you and Lucho, I would go to the end of the earth."

We started work right away. We had to gather supplies.

"It's easy. We'll exchange our cigarettes for dark chocolate and *farinha*," I suggested.

I had only recently discovered *farinha*. They'd given it to us during the march. It was cassava flour, dry and coarse. If you mixed it with water, it tripled in volume and cut your appetite. It came from Brazil, which made me think we must be somewhere far in the southeast of the Amazon region.

Pinchao easily got hold of a supply of nylon line and hooks; he often helped the fishermen in the camp, and they liked him. I set about making some new *mini-cruseros* and getting some flotation devices, and I collected all of our cigarettes, much more easily now because Lucho had stopped smoking after his heart attack. I used them for barter with Massimo, an old black man from the Pacific coast; he had a good heart, and he liked Lucho, because his family had always voted for him.

When we heard rumours that the army was in the region, we knew we could be moving camp. We quickly got together to figure out how to distribute our extra food supplies, eight pounds of chocolate and *farinha*. Carrying them would be a torture.

Lucho could not commit to taking on more weight than his present load. My load capacity was around zero.

"Never mind, we'll have to throw out the rest. We'll get new supplies in the next camp," I declared, too boldly.

"No, it's out of the question. If need be, I'll carry everything," said Pinchao.

Enrique ordered us on a new march. For days we struggled through a labyrinth of creepers so entangled that the opening the scout made with the machete closed on itself immediately and it was impossible to find the way. We had to form a human chain to keep the passage open, and this required constant concentration from all of us, without respite. Then we had to clamber down a cliff 150 feet high and repeat the effort, up and down, again and again, because the cliff extended all along the river and in some places it was the only way to advance.

Pinchao was scrambling like an ant, furious to be so loaded down, and I prayed that he wouldn't drop the bars of chocolate on my head. He showed up with his feet bleeding and the straps of his *equipo* cutting into his shoulders.

"I'm fed up!" he shouted, throwing his backpack angrily to one side. Then the guard announced that a *bongo* would be coming for us at nightfall. Only then did Pinchao agree to keep our precious supplies.

We landed in a sinister place. Swamps with slimy brown water extended from a murky river. Trees leaned into the water as if they were being stifled by fetid green moss. The sun hardly shone through the tropical canopy.

70

PINCHAO'S ESCAPE

"I have a bad feeling about this place. It is cursed," I murmured to Lucho.

We all fell sick. At twilight I was lying cramped in my hammock when I felt as if I were being caught up by a centrifugal force that was sucking me out from within, making me tremble from my neck to my toes, like someone in a rocket ready to blast off. I had contracted malaria. We had all come down with it. I knew that it was a filthy disease. I had already seen my companions shaking with convulsions, their skin shrivelling on their bones.

But what the body was preparing once the convulsions ceased was even worse. Acute fever pulled on your ligaments like the strings on a bow and left you motionless, your entire body shrill, as if a dentist's drill were boring into an exposed nerve. In a trance, after having to wait in excruciating pain for the guard to give the alert and for someone else to find the keys and another guard to come and open my padlock, I had to get up, in agony, and dart to the *chontos*, overwhelmed by a flood of diarrhoea.

Afterwards I was surprised to be still alive. The guerrilla in charge of medical supplies came in the morning, wanting to question whether it was indeed malaria. He agreed to put me on medication only after three crises identical to the first one, and when I thought I was already dead.

He arrived like a wizard with his boxes of various drugs. For two days I took two huge tablets that smelled like bleach, then little black pills –

three on the third day, two on the fourth, three again, and finally just one to finish the treatment.

This treatment regime seemed crazy, but I wasn't about to disobey orders. The only thing that really mattered to me was the ibuprofen. He gave it sparingly, counting every pill and it was the only antidote to the painful bar above my eyes that pressed against my sinuses, skewed my vision, and muddled my thinking.

Convalescence was slow. My first gesture when I came back to life was to wash my hammock, my clothes, and my blanket. I put up a laundry line in the one place where the sun seemed to be making its way through. I went there after my bath with my burden, too heavy for me, wanting to get the task behind me quickly. Ángel was lurking at his guard post, spying on my every move. The moment I started hanging the laundry on the rope, he pounced on me.

"Get that out of here. You have no right to put up your laundry here."

I was speechless.

"Take it down immediately, I said. You're not allowed out of the perimeter of the camp."

"What perimeter? I don't see any perimeter. Everybody puts lines up next to their *caletas* – why can't I?"

"Because I said so."

I looked at the rope and wondered how I would manage with all that laundry in my arms. A sour voice called out, "Making trouble again? Chain her up!"

It was Monster, arriving on cue.

Massimo, on guard on the other side of the camp, saw everything. After his shift he came over. In his sleeve he had hidden a bar of chocolate he owed me – I had given him a pack of cigarettes in exchange for a bar of chocolate, and he hadn't yet paid his debt.

"I don't like to see them treating you like that. It really upsets me."

I didn't know what to say.

"I feel like a prisoner here, too. There are days I feel like I'd like to leave."

"Leave with me," I said, thinking of Tito.

"No, it's really tough. I'll get killed."

"You'll get killed here, too. Think about it. There's a big reward on our heads. More money than you've ever seen in your life. And I'll help you to get out of the country. You'll come and live with me in France. France is a beautiful country."

"It's dangerous, very dangerous." He looked around nervously.

"Think about it, Massimo, and give me your answer quickly."

In the evening when I was already chained up in my hammock, Massimo came over to me.

"It's me, don't say anything" he whispered. "We'll leave together. Shake my hand."

"There are two others with me."

"Three is too many!"

"Take it or leave it."

"I'll go with two, not three."

"There are three of us."

"Let me see, we need a boat and a GPS."

"I'm counting on you, Massimo."

"Trust me, trust me," he whispered, shaking my hand.

With a guide we were sure to make it. I couldn't wait for dawn to share the news.

"We have to be very careful. He could betray us. We have to ask for some guarantee," warned Lucho.

Pinchao remained silent for a long while. "Already three would be difficult. But four, that's impossible," he said finally.

"We'll see. For the time being, the main thing is for you to learn to swim."

He devoted himself to the task. During our bathing time I supported him beneath his stomach to simulate the sensation of floating and showed him how to hold his breath underwater. Then Armando took him under his wing. One morning Pinchao called to me, overjoyed. "Look!"

That day Pinchao became a swimmer and Monster ordered my chains removed for the entire day. I regained courage: Once again escape became a possibility.

*

Luck continued to smile on us. Pinchao had offered to make a drawing in one of the guards' notebooks. As he was leafing through it, he found precise instructions for making a compass copied out in a childish handwriting. It was simple. You had to magnetize a needle and place it on a surface of water. The needle would swing to line up in a north-south axis. And the rest you could figure out from the position of the sun.

"We have to try."

We settled inside my tent, on the pretext that we wanted to sew a jacket, a project that I'd had in mind for some time, to run away in something lighter and better adapted to the jungle. Everybody was always sewing something; no one would suspect anything.

We filled an empty deodorant bottle with water and magnetized our needle by rubbing it against the speakers of Pinchao's *panela*. The needle floated on the level surface of the liquid, turned, and pointed northward. Pinchao hugged me.

"It's our key out of here," he said.

The next morning he came back and sat down, once again to play at being a tailor. My plan was to remove the seams from two identical pairs of trousers, one belonging to Lucho and another that I'd been given. I wanted to recycle the fabric and the thread to make my jacket. Pinchao showed me a way to pull out lengths of thread long enough to be used again, a process that required infinite patience. While we were busy at our task, he said, "I've broken my chain. It's perfect. You can't tell. I'm ready to leave right away. We have everything we need."

Lucho and I had to figure out a way to get free of our chains during the night. The trick would be to ensure that the links of the chains were not too tight around our neck – we needed to attach them with nylon thread to eliminate the gap between them. Once we broke the thread, the chain would grow longer and we would be able to put our heads through. With luck, the guard closing the lock at night wouldn't notice.

"I'll try it," promised Lucho.

That night when I got up to pee, the guard who was on duty right next to my *caleta* insulted me. "I'll make you stop wanting to get up during the night! I'll put a bullet in your pussy!"

I'd often had to swallow their vulgar taunts. It was stupid. I should really have felt contempt for them, but instead I felt outrage.

"Who was the guard next to me last night?" I asked the guerrilla who showed up in the morning to unfasten our padlocks.

"It was me."

Jairo was a smiling young kid, always courteous.

"You were shouting those obscenities at me last night?"

He puffed up his lungs, swayed his hip to one side as if to defy me, and proudly said, "Yes, it was me."

Without thinking I grabbed him by the neck and pushed him, spitting in his face. "You stupid jerk, you think you're so strong with your big rifle? I'll teach you how to behave like a man. I warn you, do it again and I'll kill you."

He was trembling. My anger vanished as quickly as it had come. Suddenly I found it hard not to laugh. I shoved him again. "Now get out of here."

He was careful to leave the chain around my neck, out of revenge. Never mind. I was pleased. I had warned them any number of times. They never dared to address the men in such a coarse way, because they knew that the reaction could easily be a fist in a jaw. But with me they liked to play rough; a woman's reaction could always be ridiculed. My outburst was reckless. I could have ended up with a black eye. I'd been lucky – Jairo was a short kid with a slow wit.

As soon as he was out of sight, I began thinking about the reprisals that might ensue. I waited, indifferent. Nothing they did could affect me. Their ruthlessness had made me grow insensitive.

I was having my breakfast, leaning against my tree, when Pinchao arrived. He reached his hand toward me, ceremoniously, and said, "*Chinita, estoy muy orgulloso de ti.*"* He knew what had happened, and I was eager to hear what he'd have to say.

"Those chains you are wearing, wear them proudly, because they're the most glorious of medals. Not one of us would have dared to do what you did. I feel vindicated!"

---

* "Girl, I'm very proud of you."

I took him by the hand, touched by his words. He added in a whisper, "There's been a delivery of boots. Make a hole in yours so that they'll give you some new ones. With the old ones, we can make little boots for our departure. We'll say we need them for gym. I'll tell Lucho."

Before long, Monster came by to check the condition of our boots and ask us our sizes.

"You won't be getting any," he said when he saw me.

When Massimo came into our enclosure to take up his shift, I asked permission to go to the *chontos*. He came with keys to open the padlock. "Well, Massimo?"

"We're leaving tonight."

"Okay. Find me some boots."

"I'll bring them. If anyone asks you, you say they're your old ones."

They mustn't see us having long conversations. Within the FARC everybody told on everyone else. Their surveillance system was based on snitching.

Massimo was very frightened. Efrén had reported us, saying that he saw us speaking and found our behaviour odd. Massimo was called before Enrique. He claimed we'd been discussing the Pacific coast, a region I knew well, and Enrique swallowed his story. But Massimo was being watched, and he was less and less eager to leave.

He came that night to my *caleta*, making a horrible crackling sound walking over the dry branches. He had boots for me. *This is my guarantee*, I thought as I listened to him.

"The situation is tough. All the boats are locked up for the night. The GPS that Enrique sometimes lends us isn't working."

"The guy's not serious," said Pinchao, the next morning. "We have to leave now, before he sounds the alert."

"I can't leave now," said Lucho. "My heart feels weak. I don't think I could make it, running through the forest with those guys on our heels. If Massimo comes with us, that's different. He knows how to survive, we'll be okay."

When Pinchao came to see me on April 28, 2007, with his spool of neatly rolled thread and the fabric of the trousers ready to be cut, I was overcome by an inexplicable sadness.

"Thank you so much, my dear Pinchao. You've done a hell of a job."

"No, I have to thank you. You gave me something to do. You helped me to cure my boredom."

He looked me right in the eye, the way he did whenever he was going to confess something to me.

"If I leave tonight, then, I take the path toward the *bañadero*⋆ and then I take the boat they left moored in the little pond and head down the river, right?" he said.

"If you leave tonight, you'd better not take the boat in the little pond, because they've put a guard on duty, deliberately. You should leave from your *caleta* and cross the guards' perimeter."

"They'll see me."

"Not if you go across when they change shifts. The *relevante* will go past with the relief, one post after the other, assigning each guard to his place. But the first one, the one he'll take himself and which is just opposite your *caleta,* that post will be empty for two minutes while he finishes his round."

"And then?"

"And then you'll go straight ahead into the *manigua*. Not too far — otherwise you'll end up in their camp. Say maybe a dozen yards or so, just far enough to hide your footsteps. If it's raining, make a sharp turn to the left to get away from our enclosure and then left again to go around us and reach the river, farther than their boats and the little pond."

He waited for me to go on.

"And then you put your empty bottles on and you let the current carry you as far as you can before you get cramps. Remember to swim, to move. It will help you."

"And if I get cramps?"

"You've got your flotation device, you let them pass. And you get over to the shore and get out."

"And I get out and walk straight ahead."

"Yes, and be careful where you put your feet. Try to get out where

---

⋆ Washing area.

there's a bed of leaves, or in the mangrove. You have to make absolutely sure not to leave any traces."

"Okay."

"Wring out your clothes, set up your compass, and walk due north."

He listened.

"Stop every forty-five minutes and take a good look around. And use the time to call upstairs, so that he'll give you a hand."

"I don't believe in God."

"It doesn't matter, he won't be offended. You can call him anyway. If he doesn't reply, call Mary – she's always available."

He smiled.

"Pinchillo,* I don't like this place, it gives me goose bumps. I feel almost as if it is cursed . . ."

He didn't answer. He was already taut like the string of a bow, ready to fly away.

In the three years or more that we'd been together, there had never been any demonstrations of affection between us. It just wasn't done. Probably because I was the only woman among so many men, excessively thick walls had risen between us.

And yet in that moment, in the presence of this young kid I'd come to know and grown fond of, when I understood we were saying farewell and I knew that he wouldn't get a second chance – because he was a member of the armed forces and would be shot if he were retaken – I felt a crushing pain. I knew he was waiting for me to give him a final thumbs-up before he set off to accomplish his exploit. I reached out my arms to hug him, aware that our gesture would attract attention. I saw my companions watching us, and I pulled back, restraining myself to only wishing him well. "May God be with you every step of the way." Pinchao hurried off, more moved, more tense, more tormented than I had ever seen him.

Suddenly there was a commotion. The guards were shouting, and the tension in our enclosure had once again reached new heights. *He won't leave,*

---

* I have many nicknames for Pinchao.

I said to myself just as Monster's flashlight blinded me. I was already huddled in my nighttime cocoon.

The storm broke shortly before eight o'clock in the evening. *If he's going to
leave, now would be the ideal time*, I thought. *But if he's too afraid, he won't leave.* I
lapsed into a deep sleep, relieved I would not have to face the wrath of the
gods in such weather.

It was already late in the morning when they came to remove our
chains. When I emerged from my tent with my toothbrush and my water
bottle, my companions were all looking at the *relevante*, who went away
cursing.

"What's going on?" I asked Marc, whose tent had been set up opposite
mine.

"Pinchao's not there any more," he whispered, not looking at me.

"Oh! My God, that's fantastic!"

"Yes, but now we're the ones who are going to pay."

"If it is so that one of us can get free, I don't care."

71

THE DEATH OF PINCHAO

April 29, 2007. Soon there was talk of nothing else. Everyone speculated on how Pinchao must have escaped, and no one was willing to bet that he would succeed. *The weather is good. He's making headway,* I thought, reassured.

Rumours went around that the guerrillas had found him. One of the guards leaked the information to a prisoner he trusted. *As long as I don't see him, I won't believe it,* I said to myself. But the order was given to pack our things, because we were leaving. I was released from my tree, and I wrapped my yards of chain around my neck and put away all my gear without hurrying. *Please let him escape from them.*

They made us wait by our beds with our tents folded up all morning long. Then they gave the order to get ready to have our bath, and we had to unpack everything again. We stood in single file between the guards, who drove us like cattle and, as on every day, we went along the little path down toward the swamps.

We passed five bare-chested men on their way through our enclosure with shovels over their shoulders. Massimo was one of them. He was walking energetically, careful not to lift his eyes from the ground so they would not meet mine.

Once we were in the water, with our soap in our hands, Lucho whispered, "Did you see?"

"The men with the shovels?"

"Yes, they're going to dig a grave."

"A grave?"

"Yes, for Pinchao's body."

"Stop it with your bullshit!"

"They executed him, so the guards told some of our men. They say it was our fault."

"What do you mean, *our* fault?"

"Yes, they say we dragged Pinchao into it."

"Lucho!"

"And they also say that if he is dead, it's our fault!"

"What did you tell them?"

"Nothing . . . But what if he is dead and it *is* our fault?"

"Listen, Lucho dear, stop right there. Pinchao left because he wanted to. He made his decision as a grown man, the way you and I did. Don't worry about it. You're not to blame, and I'm very proud of what he did!"

"And if they killed him?"

"They can't possibly have found him."

"But they did find him. Can't you see? We're leaving, for Christ's sake!"

Our return from the bath was like a funeral march. We met the same guards, on their way back again, soaked in sweat, their shovels dirty. "They dug holes to bury the rubbish," I said, increasingly unsure.

Once we were dressed again, we had to go closer to the shore, onto a sporting ground they had made for themselves. The guards didn't react when I sat down next to Lucho to talk. The hours went by, an endless wait.

There was some movement among the troops at the back of what was left of our enclosure. I could hear voices, distorted by the echo of the vegetation. I could see shadows moving behind the rows of trees.

"They've brought Pinchao back," said Armando. "They're going to rough him up for a while. Then we'll all leave. The *bongo* is already waiting."

I turned around. Sure enough, where we had taken our bath a few hours earlier, there was a big *bongo*, like an iron monster. The thought that Pinchao had been taken made me sick. "Why don't they bring him here?" asked Armando, tired of waiting.

I looked at patches of sky through the dome of foliage above us. *The blue sky has changed to purple*, I thought, increasingly worried as I felt the coolness of twilight draw over us. Lucho was silent, answering only in grunts when someone spoke to him.

Suddenly the agitation at the back of the camp started up again. Shadows, voices. There was the sharp report of a gun being fired, piercing through the muffled latticework of vegetation. A murder of blackbirds flew up above the trees, soaring straight to the sky above our heads. *Those birds are a bad omen*, I thought. Another shot, a third, another, and yet another.

"I counted seven," I whispered to Lucho.

"They just executed him," replied Lucho, drained, his lips dry and trembling.

I took his hand and squeezed it tight. "No, Lucho, no! It's not true!"

Everybody thought the same thing. Enrique didn't come. Nor did Monster. Another guerrilla whom we'd seen a few times showed up; we didn't know his name. I called him "El Tuerto" because he was one-eyed. He came over to us, and in a loud voice to intimidate us, his hands on his hips and his legs spread, he laughed, "Well this ought to discourage you from wanting to run away, right?" He felt the weight of our gazes upon him, holding our breath, hanging on to his every word. "I've come to inform you that that son of a bitch is dead. He was trying to swim across the swamps. A *guío* got him. We saw him when the snake was already twisted around him, and he was squealing for help like some little woman. I ordered them to let him get off that shit on his own, and the creature dragged him down to the bottom. That's what you get when you want to play the hero. Take it as a warning."

His story didn't make sense. *They killed him, they're the ones who killed him!* I thought, horrified.

"I want to see Pinchao's body. I don't believe you," I said, breaking our silence.

"But didn't you hear what the commander just said? An anaconda got him! How do you want them to go and get his body?" shouted Armando, beside himself.

I was angry with him for interrupting. I wanted to know what the commander had to say. *His body is in the grave they just dug, with seven bullets in his skull,* I thought, aghast.

"Put your *equipos* on your backs and follow me in silence," he ordered, ending the discussion. "Ingrid, you'll board last."

Above the river the sky seemed to be smeared with blood. I looked at my companions as they climbed on board the *bongo.* Some of them were cracking jokes. In the space reserved for the guerrillas, the young girls were doing their hair, busy making pretty braids for one another. "El Tuerto" was flirting with them like a sultan in his harem. *How can they go on living, so carefree?* I didn't want to look at the spectacular sunset, or the pretty girls, or the *bongo* sailing through the tranquil velvet waters of the river. Soon a dome full of stars covered our world and my silence. I sat hidden behind Lucho and wept hot tears as if from a hole in my heart. I put my hands on my cheeks to catch them before anyone could see I was crying. *My Pinchao, I hope you can't hear me and that you're not up there yet.* For days we sailed on the *bongo.* I didn't want to think. Immersed in my pain, and in Lucho's, I tried not to listen to what they were saying.

"It serves him right," said one of our companions.

"With his rabbit teeth and smile, who did he think he was? Did he think that he was better than us?"

My companions were speaking loudly so that the guerrillas would understand that they weren't involved in any way.

I hated them for that.

"He died because he had it coming to him. He shouldn't have listened to such bad advice," said someone else, sitting next to Lucho.

Lucho was tormented and I wasn't much help to him with my weeping.

The *bongo* went farther into the jungle, crushing its way through nature like an icebreaker with its reinforced hull; it opened a passage into the bowels of hell, heading up channels that had been virgin until then. We were protected under the tarpaulin, while the world crumbled around us and the steel monster moved stubbornly and slowly forward. *He must be rotting on the ground. They probably threw him there like a piece of meat.* I could not stop tormenting myself.

When Mother's Day came that year, we ourselves were rotting in the bowels of the *bongo*. Glued to my radio, at four o'clock in the morning I listened to a message from Pinchao's mother, as well as the clear, wise voices of his sisters. *Who's going to tell them? How will they find out?* I felt terrible, knowing he was dead and listening to their message for him.

We finally stopped at the mouth of a channel, on a small beach of fine sand. We disembarked and stretched our bodies from the forced immobility of recent weeks in front of a little house all of wood, surrounded by a garden of fruit trees. We were sent to the back of the house, where a roof of corrugated metal supported by twenty or so beams covered an expanse of earth. We all hurried to take possession of a beam to hang up our hammocks. A big pot of chocolate in boiling water was brought in. Everyone hurried to stand in line, lost in thought. I stood up, shaken and aching, and looked around me at our new reality.

"Companions!" I shouted, in a voice that I wished were louder. "Pinchao is dead. I would like to ask you to observe a minute of silence in his honour."

Lucho nodded. The guard narrowed his eyes. I concentrated on my watch. Our companion who was thick with the guerrillas brushed past me and went up to the guard, talking in a loud voice. The others hurried to do the same when they saw Enrique coming. Everyone found their own way of breaking the silence; with some it was more premeditated than with others. Only Lucho and Marc went to sit to one side and refused to open their mouths. The minute seemed to last forever. When I looked at my watch and saw it was over, I thought, *My poor Pinchillo, I'm glad you're not here to see this.*

We went on walking toward nowhere, fleeing from an invisible enemy that was breathing down our necks. Marches alternated with journeys on the *bongo,* and I did not know which was worse, because in both cases the guards made it their duty to harangue me with their spite.

"She's the one who helped him to escape," they muttered behind my back, to justify their vile behaviour. In the evening, sitting all around us, they would speak loudly to be sure we heard. "I can still see Pinchao with the holes in his head and blood everywhere. I'm sure his ghost is coming after us," one of them said. "Where he is now, he can't hurt us any more," scoffed another.

One evening when we had just set up camp on a terrain infested with *majiñas** and we were suffering from the burns they had inflicted, I was stretched out in my hammock and could not even reach out for the radio to listen to the news, when I suddenly heard Lucho roaring, "Ingrid, listen to Caracol!"

I jumped.

"What? What is it?" I stammered, trying to emerge from my torpor.

"He made it! Pinchao is free! Pinchao is alive!"

"Shut up, you bunch of idiots!" shouted a guard. "I'll shoot the first person who opens their mouth."

Too late. I myself was shouting, I couldn't keep it in.

"Bravo, Pinchao, you're our hero! Hurray!"

We all switched on our radios at the same time. The voice of the reporter announced the news, and it echoed around the camp. "After seventeen days of walking, police subintendent Jhon Frank Pinchao has found his freedom and his family once again. Here are his first words."

Then I heard Pinchao's voice, full of light on our starless night:

"I would like to send a message to Ingrid. I know she's listening to me at this moment. I want her to know I owe her the greatest gift of all. Thanks to her, I have found my faith again. My little Ingrid, your Virgin Mary was there for me when I called to her. She put a police patrol on my path."

---

* Microscopic red ants that defend themselves by pissing acid.

72

MY FRIEND MARC

May 2007. Now that their lies had been exposed, the commanders merely became more aggressive. Their rage against Pinchao's exploit increased their hatred toward me. It was enhanced by all the little things that made me different in their eyes. They nicknamed me "the Heron." I was too thin and too pale. They made fun of me, irritated me in every little way that could cross their mind. They wouldn't let me sit where I wanted and obliged me to sit where it was wet or dirty. They found me precious and ridiculous, because I wanted to keep my face and nails clean.

I had always had an image of myself as self-assured and well-balanced. After years of captivity, that image had become blurred, and I no longer knew whether it corresponded to me in any way. For the better part of my life, I had learned to live between two worlds. I had grown up in France, discovering myself through contrast. I had eagerly sought to understand Colombia in order to explain it to my friends at school. As a teenager, I'd thought of myself as a tree with branches in Colombia and my roots in France. Before long I knew it would be my fate to try to keep my balance between my two worlds.

When I was in France, I dreamed of *pandeyucas*,* *ajiaco*,† and *arequipe*.‡ I

---

* Cheese bread made with yucca flour.
† A special dish from the central Andean region, potato soup with chicken and sweetcorn.
‡ A dessert of sweet, smooth caramel paste.

missed my family, my vacations spent with cousins, full of music. When I came back to Colombia, I missed everything about France – the order, the perfumes, the beauty, the rhythm of the seasons, the reassuring sound at the street cafés.

When I fell into the FARC's hands and lost my freedom, I also lost my identity. My jailers did not think of me as Colombian. I didn't know their music, I didn't eat what they ate, I didn't speak like they did. So I was French. That idea alone sufficed to justify their bitterness. It allowed them to channel all the resentment they'd accumulated in their lives.

"You must have been able to wear a lot of designer clothes," said Ángel with a fake smile.

Or to make conjectures about my future. "You'll go and live in another country, won't you? You're not from here!" said Lili, Enrique's companion bitterly, referring to the improbable day when I would regain my freedom.

My companions in misfortune shared this resentment to some degree. We had followed the 2006 World Cup soccer tournament with a passion. We would all turn on our radios and tune in, so we listened to the games in stereo, the sound coming from every *caleta*. The final between France and Italy divided the camp in two. Initially the guerrillas sided with Italy, because France, to them, meant me. My companions had done the same. The ones who had a bone to pick with me for having the support of France expressed their aversion in a very aggressive way with every goal. Those who felt close to me celebrated, screaming and dancing every time France scored a goal, right up to the final. We were still in the stingray camp then. I was chained to my tree and almost choked when Zidane was expelled during the final game. And I understood that the more they resented me for being French, the more French I became.

France had opened its arms to me with the generosity of a mother. For Colombia, however, I had become a burden. Rumours justified the need to forget me.

"It's her fault. She went looking for it," a voice said on the radio.

"She's in love with one of the FARC leaders."

"She's got a kid with the guerrillas."

"She doesn't want to come back – she's living with them."

All this nasty gossip was circulating in the hope that France would stop showing concern over us. It hurt me deeply, because I felt it created doubts, and those who were struggling so self-effacingly for our release might begin to doubt. I felt as French as I did Colombian. But without the recognition of my love for Colombia, I no longer knew who I was, or why I had fought, or why I was in captivity.

We docked at three o'clock in the morning in the middle of nowhere, ramming our way into the mangrove to get to land. It was the height of the rainy season. We waited for the order to disembark so we could set up our tents before the storm that raged every day at dawn.

Monster came over once the troops had already disembarked to inform us that we would be sleeping inside the *bongo*. The tarpaulin had already been removed in order to cover the *rancha*; I'd overheard them making the decision.

"What are we going to cover ourselves with?" I asked, perfectly aware we couldn't put up our tents on the *bongo*.

"It won't rain tonight," hissed Monster, turning on his heel.

Lucho and I started getting our things ready, thinking we might be able to set up our hammocks next to each other. But Monster, as if he had read our thoughts, turned around and came back over, pointing his finger at us. He barked, "You two! You know you don't have the right to speak to each other. Lucho, go set up your hammock at the stern. Ingrid, follow me. You're going to set yours up here in the prow between Marc and Tom."

And he went away again with a caustic laugh, revealing once again his hatred of me.

Ever since I'd been forbidden to speak to my American companions, I sensed that they had been doing whatever they could to avoid me, to stay out of trouble. It was as if I had the plague.

Monster knew only too well which way the wind was blowing. He'd put me where I would be the least welcome. The hammocks had been hung up in a row from starboard to port, using the hooks that were for the tarpaulin. Marc and I were the last ones to set ours up. There were only three hooks left. Our two hammocks would have to share one of the hooks. I was already dreading this first negotiation. I knew that it was very hard to agree on anything among prisoners, and I must have looked confused. I didn't want to set mine up and leave my companion with a fait accompli.

Marc anticipated the problem.

"We can hang both our hammocks from this one," he suggested kindly.

I was surprised. Courtesy had become a rare thing.

I hung up my hammock, stretching it as taut as I could so the weight of my body wouldn't make me touch the wet deck of the *bongo* once I was inside. *If it rains, this will be one huge puddle*, I predicted. *Anyway, it's bound to rain*, I concluded, taking out my biggest plastic sheet to hang it over me as a makeshift roof. It was big enough to drape over either side but too short to cover me from head to foot. *I'll get soaked*, I thought, resigned. So I settled into my hammock, with my plastic sheet above my head and my feet exposed, falling into a deep sleep heavy with fatigue.

It was a terrible tropical storm, as if the sky had broken. I waited apprehensively for the water to soak into my socks and up my legs until all of me ended up drenched in my hammock. And yet, after a few minutes had gone by, I didn't feel a thing. I wiggled my toes in case my feet had gone to sleep, but all I could feel was the dry warmth of my body in my plastic wrapping. The plastic must have slipped farther down. The water would get in through my neck, I figured, groping about cautiously with my hand to see where the edge of the plastic sheet was. But everything was where it should be. *I must have shrunk*, I decided, and went back to sleep, relieved.

By daybreak the storm was still raging. I ventured to lift the corner of my black roof to take stock of the situation and saw Tom still asleep, swimming in a veritable pool. He had no plastic sheet, and his hammock had filled up to the brim with water. The storm gave way to a light rain; there was movement on the *bongo*. They all wanted to get out of these makeshift shelters to stretch their legs. That was when I discovered what had happened: Marc had thought to share his plastic sheet with me. He had covered my feet.

I stood there under my plastic with my hastily folded hammock. My throat was tight. Such compassion was so unusual between hostages.

Surely he hadn't done it on purpose. Perhaps he hadn't realized that he had covered my feet, I thought in disbelief. When Marc finally came out of his hammock, I approached him.

"Yes, you would've been soaked otherwise," he answered, almost apologetically. He smiled gently, in a way I had never seen before. It made me feel good.

When the morning meal arrived and we had to stand in line to get our hot drink, I slipped between the prisoners to share a few words with Lucho and reassure him. He, too, had managed to sleep and looked rested. To know that Pinchao had made it lifted a huge weight from him. Our companions were gathering around him to speak to him, trying to put behind them the unpleasant comments that had hurt him so deeply. Lucho held no grudges.

I went back to my spot in the bow and set about tidying my backpack. It was a nuisance, but it had to be done, because the storm had soaked everything. I took out my rolls of clothing one by one, dried the plastic bags that contained them, and rolled them up again, finally resealing the bags with a rubber band at either end to make a waterproof package. This was the way the FARC did it, to stave off some of the disadvantages of life with 80 per cent humidity. Marc decided to do the same.

Once I'd finished that chore, I conscientiously cleaned the board where I'd put my things and placed my toothbrush and bowl there for the next meal. Finally I took a rag to clean my boots and make them shine.

Marc watched me with a smile. Then, as if he were sharing a secret, he whispered, "You behave just like a woman."

His comment surprised me. But in a curious way, it flattered me. It was not a compliment, among the FARC, to be seen to behave like a woman. In fact, I'd been dressing like a man for five years, and yet everything in me reminded me I was a woman: It was my essence, my nature, my identity. I turned my back on him, and on the pretext of brushing my teeth I took my brush and my bowl and moved away, to hide my confusion. When I came back, he hurried over, concerned, and said, "If I said anything that—"

"No, on the contrary, it was really nice of you!"

The guards were watching but let us talk, as if they'd been ordered not to interfere.

Officially, I hadn't been allowed to speak to my companions for over two years. I did surreptitiously from time to time, driven by loneliness. Pinchao and I had managed to foil their surveillance, because our *caletas* had often been set up next to each other and we could pretend to be busy with our things while speaking in very low voices. I had felt doubly isolated since Pinchao left, given the reaction from the rest of the group regarding his escape and the restrictions imposed on my time with Lucho.

When Marc and I began to have real discussions, driven by restlessness and boredom, waiting aimlessly in the prow of that *bongo*, I realized how cruel the guerrillas' punishment was and how heavily my enforced silence weighed upon me.

Oddly enough, we picked up old discussions left unfinished in Sombra's prison, as if there had been no interlude between the two. *Time spent in captivity is circular*, I thought.

And yet clearly, for Marc and me, time really had counted. We resumed the same arguments that opposed us years before, regarding subjects as controversial as abortion or the legalization of drugs, and we managed to find links, points in common, where in the past we had merely been irritated and intolerant. We would end our hours of discussion exhausted and surprised. And when we parted, we were surprised to find we were no longer filled with bitterness and spite the way we used to be.

When we understood that the *bongo* was not about to move any time soon, we set about trying to come up with a shared activity. Marc called it "our project." We had to try to obtain permission to cover the *bongo* to protect ourselves from the evening storms. I watched as he formulated his request, in his Spanish that was getting better by the day, and to my surprise his idea was approved.

Enrique sent Oswald to oversee the project. He cut poles and prongs that were placed at regular intervals in order to hold the huge plastic sheets from the *rancha* and the *economato* that weren't being used at the moment, to cover the entire *bongo*. My contribution had been minimal, but we celebrated the completion of the project as if it had been our shared work.

When the *bongo* headed off down the river again and we reached our destination, I felt a profound sadness. The new camp was deliberately set up on a very narrow terrain. Two rows of tents faced each other, squeezed together, separated by a path from a small cove by the river that would be used for washing, to the other end where they dug the *chontos*.

Enrique himself assigned our space, and to me he allotted twenty square feet of land to set up my tent, over a spot where a huge colony of *congas** had the entrance to their nest. They were perfectly visible, walking along one behind the other on their long, black, stilt-like legs. The smallest ones were at least an inch long, and I knew the pain their venomous sting could inflict. I had been stung by one before, and my arm had quadrupled in size and hurt for forty-eight hours. I begged to be allowed to set up my tent elsewhere, but Gafas would not budge.

The poles supporting my hammock were buried on either side of the entrance to the *conga* ants' nest, and my hammock was hanging right above it. I went to get Massimo to help me, but since Pinchao's escape he had changed completely: He had been very frightened, and now it was impossible to envisage any attempt to escape. He wanted to stay clear of any problems, and so he avoided me. Nevertheless, when he saw the unending ballet of insects underneath my hammock, he agreed to intercede on my behalf so that they would send me a pot of boiling water to kill them. He also cut me a sharp stick while he was on duty so that I could impale them one by one.

"Be careful, they can be deadly if several of them attack."

There was no respite. I spent all my time killing any *conga* that came near me, in what seemed to me a losing battle. I looked enviously at my companions. They had all finished setting up camp, and were relaxing, resuming their usual routines: Arteaga and William were sewing, Armando was weaving, Marulanda was bored in his hammock, Lucho was listening to the radio, and Marc was busy at his latest project, repairing the straps to his backpack.

---

* Giant, poisonous ants.

I wish I could talk to him, I thought, surrounded by a cemetery of *conga* ants; the fetid odour would not go away. Like Gulliver in the presence of the Lilliputians, I could not afford a moment's inattention while I waited for the boiling water Enrique had promised.

Marc walked by my *caleta* on his way to the *chontos* and looked at me, astonished.

"I've got millions of *congas* in my *caleta*," I explained.

He laughed, thinking I was exaggerating. On the way back, as he saw I was still absorbed by my *conga* combat, he stopped. "What are you doing?"

I came out of my tent and was about to explain, when I saw his eyes widening in horror.

"Whatever you do, don't move," he said, speaking very clearly, his frightened gaze focused on something on my shoulder.

He came toward me very slowly, his finger raised. Filled with dread, I followed his gaze and turned my head just enough to see an enormous *conga,* with a gleaming coat of armour and hairy legs and threatening pincers extended, only a few millimetres from my cheek. I was about to run off, but I stopped myself in time, when I realized it would be wiser to wait for Marc to flick the monster away. He went about it calmly, despite the fact that I was nervously stamping my feet and moaning. There was a hollow click as he made contact with the insect, and then it soared like a missile to crash against a giant tree trunk.

I watched it all out of the corner of my eye, at the risk of giving myself a stiff neck, and then I jumped for joy. Marc was laughing so hard he was on the verge of tears, bent over double.

"You should have seen your face! I wish I could have taken your picture! You were just like a little girl."

Then he gave me a hug, and said proudly, "It's a good thing I was here!"

When at last Enrique sent the kettle of boiling water, the water washed out more floating corpses than survivors. As for Marc, our victory over the *congas* sealed our friendship.

73

THE BAN

I climbed out of my hammock one blind-black night to answer a call of nature, delighted that I could step outside and no longer fear an attack from those infernal creatures. Suddenly I heard a whistling sound of something brushing past my hair. I stood paralysed in the darkness, aware that something had fallen through my tent with a thud, just inches from my nose. The guard refused to come and shine his flashlight beam, and I preferred to go back to the safety of my mosquito net rather than wander anywhere near whatever it was that had shaken my dwelling.

At dawn I got up quickly, to see that my tent was in shreds. A pod the size of a man's head had fallen from a neighbouring palm tree, wrapped in a thick leaf that tapered into a point as sharp as a spear. It had come loose from the trunk and had fallen more than sixty feet and had landed deep in the ground, right next to me, ripping my roof in two. *If I'd gone one step farther . . .* I thought, not that this was any consolation for my ruined tent. It would take hours to repair, I realized with resignation.

I had to borrow a needle and some thread, and when I was ready to start, it began to rain. Marc came up to me, wanting to give me a hand. I accepted, astonished. This wasn't done, among prisoners. Requests for help were met with moodiness and disdain. Each of us wanted to show that we were self-sufficient. But I always needed help, and Lucho – who would always give me a hand – was forbidden to approach me. If I didn't ask for help, it was to avoid conflicts. I already owed people for their needles and thread. That was enough.

Marc's help turned out to be very timely. His advice helped me to finish faster. We spent nearly two hours together, busy at our task, laughing over the slightest little thing. When he went away again, I watched with regret. Lucho was always reminding me that I mustn't get attached to anything. The next morning Marc came back. He asked me for some waterproof canvas to patch his own tent and to help him glue patches over the holes that the *arrieras* had made in the canvas.

Asprilla, a big muscular black guy, had just become second-in-command. Together with Monster, he was responsible for the hostages' camp, a task they shared in turn. He'd been kind enough to unchain me during the day, and now he brought a big pot of glue so that Marc could repair his tent. He came back in the afternoon and found us there, like children, our fingers all sticky. I could see the way he looked at us. *I'm too happy, and he can see it*, I thought, worried.

Marc went on laughing, putting glue on the square pieces of canvas that we had carefully cut out. *This is ridiculous*, I thought, trying to banish my apprehension. *I'm getting paranoid.*

The morning after that, I saw Marc sitting on the ground with his radio in pieces, spread out before him. I was hesitant to go up to him, then decided there was no harm in it, and I would see if I could help him. The connection of his antenna to the electronic circuits had been damaged. I'd watched my companions repairing their radios in similar situations, so I volunteered to fix his.

Very quickly I managed to repair the connection before Marc's admiring gaze. I was glowing with satisfaction. This was probably the first time I'd ever managed to repair anything all by myself. The following day Marc came to get me to help him cut his plastic sheets. He wanted to roll them up in his boots, for the next march.

We sat silently, absorbed in our efforts to cut them neatly at right angles. It was hot, and the slightest movement made us sweat. Marc thrust his hand toward my ear and caught something in the air. His gesture surprised him as much as it did me. He apologized, confused, and explained shyly that he wanted to remove a mosquito that had been pestering me for a while already. His shyness was charming, and the thought of it confused me, too. I got up quickly to go back to my tent. I would have to find a pretext to come back and spend more time with him. This growing friendship surprised me. For years our paths had crossed, and it had never really occurred to us to spend time together. I'd always had the impression that we'd been doing whatever we could to avoid each other. And now I had to admit that I woke up in the morning with a smile, and I waited with childlike impatience for a chance to speak to him. *Maybe I'm becoming intrusive*, I thought. So I held back and for a few days kept myself from going up to him.

He came the following week and offered to help me set up my radio antenna. I had tried to do it myself, to no avail, because Oswald and Ángel, who were considered the battery-throwing champions, had refused to lend me a hand.

My battery throwing reached no higher than fifteen feet at the most, which made everyone laugh. Marc spun the battery like a sling. Flying to the sky on the third spin, my antenna landed higher than anyone else's.

"Just dumb luck," he confessed.

My radio was rejuvenated. I could hear Mom perfectly. It was as if she were right next to me. She was planning a trip to rally support.

"I don't like leaving Colombia. I'm afraid you'll be released and I won't be here to welcome you," she said.

I loved her for this.

In the morning, taking advantage of the fact that I was in the breakfast line, I laughed about it with Lucho.

"Did you hear your mother? She doesn't want to go, as usual."

"And, as usual, she will go," I answered, delighted.

It was one of our favourite jokes. Mom always hesitated until the last minute. Then I would get her message from the other side of the planet, because she always managed to be there for our appointment on the radio, wherever she happened to be. Her trips were good for both of us. I figured if she met other people, it would help her to be patient, the way that hearing her voice, invigorated by her activity, helped me. I really appreciated Marc's help.

One morning Marc came to borrow my Bible. When I handed it to him, he asked me, "Why didn't you come back and talk to me?"

His question took me by surprise. I tried to keep my thoughts clear as I answered.

"First of all, because I don't want to impose upon you. Secondly, because I'm afraid I might begin to enjoy it too much and that the guerrillas will find a way to pressure me."

He gave me a sweet smile. "Don't think about all that. If you have a moment, I'd like to have a talk this afternoon."

He went away, and I realized in amusement that I had an appointment! Boredom was a poison with which the FARC injected us to weaken our resolve, something I dreaded more than anything. I smiled. I'd gone from a life filled with too many appointments, engagements, time slots to suddenly having none. Now, in this jungle miles from anywhere, the idea of an appointment pleased me.

I began to speak to Marc using *tú* quite naturally, another, more familiar way to say "you" in Spanish.

"I don't know how to use *tú*," he said.

He seemed to be fascinated by the nuances of this usage, totally nonexistent in English. But he had grasped the meaning— and the familiarity it conveyed. "*Quiero tutearte*,"* he said.

"*Ya lo estás haciendo*,"† I replied with a laugh.

We opened the Bible. He wanted me to read one of my favourite passages to him. Finally I decided on a passage where Jesus insistently asks Peter whether he loves him. I knew the Greek version of the text. Again, it was all about nuance. Jesus used the term "*agape*" when addressing Peter, to refer to the quality of superior love, a love that demanded nothing in return, that sufficed unto itself through the action of loving. Peter replied using the word "*philia*," to mean a love that expected something back,

---

* "I want to use *tú* to talk to you."
† "You are already doing so."

that sought reciprocity. The third time that Jesus asked the question, Peter seemed to have understood the subtlety and replied using "*agape*," which bound him to unconditional love.

Peter was the man who had betrayed Jesus on three occasions. The Jesus who was asking these questions was the resuscitated Jesus. Peter had been a weak man and a coward, but through the strength of that unconditional love he had been transformed into his opposite, a strong, courageous man who would be crucified for defending Jesus's legacy.

I had been living in captivity for five years, and despite the extreme conditions I'd endured, changing my character proved immensely difficult.

We were deep in discussion, sitting side by side on Marc's old black plastic sheet. I had no idea what language we were using – probably both. Absorbed in our discussion, at one point I paused, intrigued by the silence in the camp. To my great embarrassment, I realized that our companions were following our conversation with interest.

"Everybody's listening," I said in English, lowering my voice.

"We are too happy. It's attracting their attention," he replied without looking at me. It made me worried. In an effort to recover peace, I continued: "See what we've become in this camp, how hard it is for us to unite against these guerrillas when they intimidate us and threaten us . . . The apostles were afraid and only John came to the foot of the cross. But after the Resurrection, they no longer behaved in the same way. They went to the four corners of the earth and were massacred for bearing witness to what they had seen. They were decapitated, crucified, skinned alive, stoned to death. Each one was able to surpass his fear of dying. Each one chose who he wanted to be."

We gradually opened our hearts to speak of things we did not dare admit to ourselves. Marc had had no news from anyone except his mother in years. In her messages there was not much information about his family or the life of the people he loved. "It's as if I were looking at my world through a keyhole," he said, trying to express his frustration. "I don't even know if my wife is still waiting for me."

I understood him only too well. My husband's voice had disappeared from the airwaves, long ago. When he did occasionally show up again, my companions were sarcastic. Nobody commented when a journalist from *La Luciérnaga*,* one of the programmes we listened to in the evening, made a comment about him, adding, "I'm referring to Ingrid's husband, or rather her ex-husband, since we've been seeing him with someone else for some time now." I had wanted to move on, but the words tore at me.

One morning when I was waiting, stretched out in my hammock to be freed from my chains, I felt someone shaking my feet. I jumped. It was Marc, on his way to the *chontos*. "Hi, Princess!" he whispered, leaning toward my mosquito net.

It will be a happy day, I thought.

We settled down as on previous days, side by side on Marc's plastic sheet. Pipiolo was on duty, and he looked at me the way an eagle stares at its prey. I shuddered, knowing he was up to something nasty. We had just started talking when Monster's voice boomed like a cannon: "Ingrid!"

I immediately jumped to my feet and went out into the central path, trying to see him through the tents that blocked my view. Finally he appeared, his hands on his hips, his legs spread wide, and his eyes full of venom.

"Ingrid!" he shouted again, even though I was standing in front of him.

"Yes?"

"I told you, you are not allowed to speak to the Americans. If I catch you communicating with them, I'll chain you to the tree!"

There was no room for tears, for words, for gazes. I closed in on myself, my contact with the outside world having shrunk to nothing. I could hear, as if from a world far in the distance, Marc's voice. But I could no longer see him.

---

* *The Firefly.*

74

THE LETTERS

It will be like always — he won't care, he will want to avoid having any problems, I thought, going back to sit on the root of the tall tree that ran across my *caleta*. I had to get busy doing something — sew, wash, tidy up, fill the space with movement to act as if I were alive. *I didn't think it would hurt this much*, I told myself, after catching a glimpse of Pipiolo's carnivorous leer. My gaze met Lucho's. He smiled at me and motioned to me to calm down. He was there for me. I smiled back. Of course it was not the first time they'd gone after me like this. I was used to being chained up or let go according to their mood swings. I'd been waiting for them to do this. From the moment I started my conversations with Marc. In a way I felt a certain relief. *It can't be any worse*, I heard myself murmur.

"Can we speak in Spanish, the way we do with the other prisoners?" I heard Marc ask Monster, standing haughtily by his tent.

"No, those are orders. You can't speak to her."

On our way to bathe, Marc came up behind me and whispered, in English, "I really enjoyed talking to you. We have to go on communicating."

"Yes . . ." I mumbled, my eyes wet.

"How?" he asked.

I was thinking on my feet, quickly, quickly. Afterwards we wouldn't have the chance to talk.

"Write me a letter," I whispered.

"Come on, move!" shouted one of the guards behind us.

In the river, while I was washing my hair with a piece of blue laundry soap, Marc managed to find a place to stand where the guards couldn't see him. He was gesturing to have me understand that he would write to me that very same day. I had to bite my tongue not to betray my joy. Lucho looked at me, astonished. I spoke to him, handing him my soap to fool the guards, "I feel better," I whispered.

All I could think about was his letter. I was sure he was going to pick up our conversation exactly where Monster had interrupted it. Above all I wondered how he'd manage to get it to me. I could see from my *caleta* into his. As soon as he was dressed again, he began to write.

Night fell too quickly. *The letter will be a short one*, I told myself, in anticipation. But the night seemed very long. I had relived the scene a thousand times: Monster with his hands on his hips, threatening. I was afraid again.

The letter came to me when I was least expecting it. I was on my way back from the *chontos* at dawn, just after the guard had unchained me. Marc was third in line. The path was narrow. He took my hand as I was brushing past him, and put into it a paper folded in four. I kept on walking, my hand trailing behind me. I thought everyone must have seen and that I would faint on the spot.

When I got to my *caleta* and looked back out, I was surprised to see that everything was normal. The guards hadn't noticed anything.

Impatiently, I waited until breakfast to read the letter. It was short. Just a page and a half, a handwriting of carefully formed letters, that of a conscientious child. It was written in English, with all the standard procedure and polite formulas. It made me laugh; it was as if I were reading a letter from a stranger. He told me how sorry he was that we were forbidden to speak and went on to ask me courteous questions about my life. I read the letter several times, always with the same emotion, not because it had been forbidden but because it enabled me to hear the voice I had recorded in my head whenever I wanted to.

I'm going to write him a fine letter, I thought. *A letter he'll want to reread several times.*

I looked at my supply of paper – it wouldn't last long. I wrote my letter in one sitting. I didn't wear kid gloves and tossed out the conventional "Dear Marc" right from the start. I wrote as if I were face to face with him.

"Hi, Princess," he replied in his next letter, once again himself.

Before long, we devised a secret language with hand signals he described to me in his letters and demonstrated when he saw that I'd finished reading his message. I sent him a few of my own devising, and soon we had a second, very efficient means of communication to alert each other when a guard was observing us or when we went to place a new message in the "letter box."

We had agreed to leave our notes at the base of a tree stump not far from the *chontos*. It was a good spot, because we could go there alone without arousing any suspicion. I had sewn some little black canvas bags to slip our messages into, to protect them from the rain and so that the white paper would not attract the guards' attention.

The guards must have noticed something, because one morning when I had just picked up my letter for the day, they followed me and went over the area with a fine-tooth comb. So we decided to alternate the letter box with other, more accessible ways of sending our missives, although they were just as risky. Sometimes Marc would stand next to me during the morning rush for breakfast and slip the bag into my hand, and sometimes I would motion to him to go to the wash area where I had just filled my water bottle, and he could fetch my letter.

I was very worried. I'd noticed a resurgence of entangled feelings. Our pleasure in being together had made some people jealous. Some demanded that I be separated from the group. Massimo warned me: One of our comrades had explicitly requested as much. It gave me nightmares. I refrained from mentioning it to Marc, because I didn't want to jinx us. But I was suffering more and more, fearful that what had become a lifeline to me might break.

Writing was the only important thing of the day. I kept the letters he'd sent me and I reread them while waiting for the next. A strange intimacy was flowering between us. It was often easier to pour my heart out in writing. Another person's gaze might prevent me from revealing my feelings, and sometimes what I intended to share remained caught in a silence I simply could not overcome. In writing, however, I discovered a distance that was liberating. I could always, so I thought, refrain from sending what I'd written, and that possibility made me bold. But once the secrets of my mind came to light, they seemed simple to me, so there could be no harm in sharing them. Marc played the game with far greater mastery than I did, and I enjoyed his openness. There was something very elegant about his ideas, and I was never disappointed by the person he revealed. It seemed as if the most recent letter was always the best, until I read the one that followed. The more I craved his friendship, the more I began to worry. *They're going to separate us*, I thought as I conjured Enrique's perverse glee if he discovered Marc's importance to me.

Enrique organized a search in a very underhand way. They made us believe we were preparing for a new march. Marc's letters had become my greatest treasure, and I instinctively tucked them into the pocket of my jacket before closing my *equipo* to put it on my back. They made us walk a hundred yards or so to the place they used as a sawmill. There they asked us to empty out our packs. Marc was right next to me, livid. Had he managed to hide my letters?

He gave me a meaningful look, then turned around and said he had to relieve himself and went behind a big tree. He came back, his eyes riveted on his shoes, except for a brief moment when he gratified me with a confident smile, as fleeting as the wink that I alone could see.

I let a few minutes go by, and then I did exactly the same. Once I was behind a tree, I hid the letters inside my underwear, then came back to tidy away my *equipo* after the search. I noticed that the old talcum powder bottle, where I had painstakingly rolled my most precious documents to preserve them from the humidity, had disappeared. Inside, there were my mother's letter, my children's photographs, my nephew's drawings, and the ideas and projects that Lucho and I had worked on for three years.

"You'll have to ask Enrique for it," said Pipiolo, enjoying every word.

This was a bitter blow. Mom's letter had been my lifesaver every time I felt a black mood come upon me. I rarely looked at my children's photographs because they gave me a physical torment I could not endure. But just knowing they were within reach lent me a feeling of security. As for the programme of reforms I had written up with Lucho, I really wanted that, too. It represented hundreds of hours of work and discussion. Still, I could not dispute the fact that I felt immensely relieved they hadn't found Marc's letters. Nor would they find my diary. I had taken the precaution of burning it.

Just when we thought the search was over, four more guards showed up. They'd been sent to perform a "personal" search. They asked the men to get undressed, while Zamaidy told me to follow her.

Zamaidy stood before me, apologizing in advance for what she was about to do. In my pockets she found small pieces of cloth cut up in squares.

"What's this?" she asked, intrigued.

"I haven't had any sanitary towels for a long time now. I asked for some, but apparently Enrique gave the order to stop supplying me."

She grunted. "I'll get you some."

Consequently she stopped her search and sent me back to the rest of the group. I let out a long breath; I hated to think what I would have had to invent to explain anything else she might have found.

Marc was waiting anxiously for my return. I smiled to him, and he understood that I'd made it through the search. Lucho, violating every rule, asked me if everything was all right. I told him about Enrique's confiscation of my bottle of talcum powder.

"You have to get it back!" he scolded.

That seemed like an impossible mission. After the fright that Enrique's search had given us, Marc and I were twice as careful and our correspondence grew even more intense. We told each other everything about our lives, our relationships, our children. And our guilts, as if by describing them we might make our wrongs right. Condemned to distance, we had become inseparable.

One morning Marc came up to me when I was in the first line to go to the *chontos* and said he had to speak to me no matter what. An irrational fear took hold of me. *He's going to tell me that we mustn't write any more!* I thought. I was filled with dread until we were the last two left in the line.

The things he told me made my blood run cold. The last of his thoughts was about our current ban. He wanted us to ask Enrique to lift the restriction imposed by Monster. At the same time, I saw Pipiolo glaring at me; my head was spinning. He saw Marc speaking to me, he saw the effect his words had on me. We had disobeyed orders. He would be only too happy to make us pay.

Later I wrote a long answer to Marc. I told him how worried I was that Enrique might try to separate us, and I relayed what Massimo had said: Some of our companions were plotting against us.

To add to my grief, as I was getting ready to brush my teeth one morning one of the men tried to grope me. He was a man who was prey to his obsessions, and I'd already had problems with him. Enrique had put him next to me just to humiliate me even more. Lucho happened to be going by, dragging the night's jug of urine in one hand to go toss it into the *chontos.* He instantly realized what was happening. The guards had already informed Enrique of these attacks, but he'd merely replied, "All the prisoners are equal. She can just stick up for herself." Lucho knew this. He threw down his jug of urine and jumped on the man. In reply the other man punched him in the stomach, and Lucho went wild, knocking him to the ground and pummelling him. The guards were laughing till they burst, lapping up the spectacle. I was horrified. This could give them a pretext to take me away.

But nobody came. Neither Enrique nor Monster nor Asprilla. I felt reassured, thinking that Enrique would lay down the law and the matter would be closed. Marc's letter that day was more tender than usual. He didn't want me to suffer for what had happened.

When I heard Mom's message on the radio at dawn, I trembled. I'd been completely turned upside down by the man's assault. No matter how I told myself he was deranged, and that his behaviour was the result of ten years in captivity, knowing that he was nearby made me ill at ease.

I hated the way he spied on me, even holding a mirror up to his eyes to stare at me while he had his back turned.

Mom's voice was gentle and serene, as on her good days. She was calling me from London, pleased with the steps taken to garner support for our release. "Don't lose heart, whatever happens, don't lose heart. Look up at the sky and rise above all the nastiness around you. Very soon you will get out and move toward a new life." So I looked at the sky. The weather was fine; this sunny morning could only bring good things.

But fate decided otherwise. The radio informed us that eleven of the twelve members of the Valle del Cauca Regional Assembly who were also being held by the FARC had been massacred. I'd just heard the message that the sister of one of the victims had sent, fighting for him in London. But he was already dead and she did not know. I was sickened.

Still chained to my tree, I put my head out of my *caleta*, stifled by the horror of it. I listened to the messages for them every day, in particular at dawn on that June 18, 2007. Their families had probably just heard the news the way we had. They had left children behind; one of them, Carlos Andres Barragán, was born the day before his father was abducted. I had heard little Carlos Andres grow up through the sound of his voice, as if he were a member of my own family. I sought out Marc's eyes in his *caleta* and met his gaze, as distraught as my own.

When I thought the situation of the day couldn't get worse, I was told by Asprilla to pack my things because I would be leaving. I was annihilated. Marc asked for permission to come and help me. Being in the physical presence of each other, our demonstrations of affection felt awkward under the close scrutiny of the guards and of our fellow hostages.

"Send me your Bible. I'll send it back to you with my letters," he said, taking down my tent. The guards were busy clearing a space for me near the wash area. That's where they were going to put me.

"At least we'll still be able to see each other. Promise me you'll go on writing every day."

"Yes, I'll write to you every day," I assured him, bent double with the pain. I had just been wounded to my core, and I was only just beginning to realize it. Before the guards came to get me, he handed me the little black bag. When had he had time to write? I saw that his eyes, too, were moist.

Then I heard Oswald's nasal voice: "Go on, move it!"

I couldn't.

75

THE SEPARATION

Where they took me, I could still see them from a distance. I clung to this thought, thanking the heavens for not burdening me with an even heavier load. Silence fell upon me like lead; everything rang hollow. A crushing, twisting pain in my guts forced me to remember to breathe: Inhale, and then, with excruciating effort, exhale. *This jungle is damned.*

I arranged my things on an old board they had condescended to give me. I didn't owe them anything, and I didn't want to ask for anything. I shut myself away. No one would see that I was suffering. Some girls were sent along to help me set things up. I didn't say anything. I sat down on a rotten tree trunk, and I contemplated the extent of my misfortune.

My hammock became my refuge. I wanted to stay there all day long with the radio stuck to my ear, grinding my loneliness. That Saturday night, when *Las Voces del Secuestro* broadcast Renaud's song "In the Jungle", I hoped it was a sign. Renaud was one of the most loved French composers alive. Hearing him mentioning my name, singing that he was waiting for me, gave me an urgent thirst for blue open skies. I went to swim in the pond without anybody daring to harass me. I could see Lucho and Marc through the trees.

Asprilla came to check on me, all smiles. "It's only for a few weeks. You'll come back to the camp afterwards," he explained, although I had not asked him.

Marc wandered through all the tents, inspecting the premises, and eventually found a spot where I could see him without him being seen. Using signs, he conveyed that he'd be going to the *chontos* and from there he would throw me a piece of paper.

I followed his instructions. With a bit of luck, his missile might reach me. The paper landed outside my designated area, but I rushed into the bushes to pick it up. It was a letter on a tiny space filled with a jumble of overlapping words, a space too small for all he had to say.

Settled in my hammock beneath my mosquito net, I read the letter. It was so sad and funny at the same time. I could see him standing, keeping a lookout, waiting for me to finish reading it to see the effect of his words on my face.

Very soon we made a routine of sending each other messages this way, until Oswald's girlfriend, who was on duty, found us out and instantly reported us to Asprilla. We would have to find another system. Marc asked Asprilla if we could share the Bible, and he agreed. That became our new letter box. He came to get my Bible in the morning and brought it back in the evening. We wrote in pencil in the margins of the Gospels and indicated where to write the answer. If it occurred to Asprilla to leaf through the pages, he wouldn't find anything, just words in the margins, sometimes in Spanish, sometimes in French or English, the fruit of five years of reflection, carefully annotated.

This daily contact allowed Marc to gain Asprilla's trust, and the guerrilla informed him that Enrique was going to divide the group in two and that we would be in the same group as Lucho. This news filled me with hope.

I asked to speak to Lucho and to Marc. Asprilla advised me to wait patiently; he didn't want Enrique to refuse and decide to prolong my isolation. A shipment of chains arrived. The new ones were much thicker and heavier than Pinchao's. I was the first one to try them out — one huge padlock around my neck and then another one just as enormous to attach my chain to the tree. I witnessed my American companions' anguish when they understood that for the first time they would also be chained up. The sight of that enormous chain shining around Marc's neck made me sick.

On that day his letter was distraught. He explained to me how you could snap the lock on a padlock by rusting it with salt, how you could release the inner latch with some tweezers or nail clippers. He explained that we had to be near each other to be able to run if the military suddenly attacked. There we were, naked before our fear of death, but we didn't want to face it without each other.

At dawn we prepared to leave the camp, and I was hurriedly packing my things, impatient to be together again with Marc and Lucho. It was a splendid day, unusual for the rainy season. I was ready before everybody. But there was no hurry. Sitting on my rotten tree trunk, chained by the neck, I watched the hours go slowly by, while the sounds from the guerrillas' camp indicated that it was being totally dismantled in a slow and organized way. The hollow sound of metal banging against the riverbank announced the arrival of the *bongo*. It wasn't a march, I concluded, relieved.

Late in the afternoon, Lili, Enrique's girlfriend, showed up. Her friendly attitude misled me. As I waited to be reunited with my group, I let down my guard.

Lili began talking about this and that, making pleasant comments about Lucho. Then she spoke about some of the other prisoners and asked me about Marc. Something in her tone of voice rang an alarm bell, but I was unable to identify the danger. I paused before I replied that Marc and I had indeed become good friends. As if she'd got what she'd come for, she left without even saying good-bye. I closed my eyes with the horrid impression that I had fallen into a trap.

Then I saw old Erminson. He came up to me acting as cold as an executioner and tried the keys on a heavy key ring he held pompously until he found the right one to open my padlock. He took it off the ring and brandished it victoriously, shouting to Asprilla and Enrique that everything was ready.

The guards ordered us to put on our backpacks. Then they separated my companions into two groups. Marc and Lucho's group was told to go to the fore of the boat without me. *No, it can't be! Lord, don't let this happen!* I prayed with all my strength. Lucho stopped to hug me, even though this infuriated the guards. Marc went by last; he took my hand and squeezed it tight. I saw him go off, his *equipo* filled to the brim with useless things, and I told myself that our lives were worthless.

When the second group headed off, I was ordered to follow. Massimo was next to the *bongo,* and he took me by the arm to help me on board. I looked everywhere for Lucho and Marc. They were sitting at the bottom of the hull, and their heads were hardly any higher than the level of the guardrail where I was walking. Enrique had built a dividing wall by piling up our *equipos,* and I had to sit down on the other side with the second group. I longed to hear Monster, "El Tuerto", or Asprilla telling me that I had to sit with my friends. But all I heard was Enrique's voice, cold and cruel, addressing us as if we were dogs. "Move it! At the back, on the other side, hurry up!"

Zamaidy was on guard, holding a Galil rifle pointed at us as she watched me go down into the hole where the rest of my companions were already arguing over the best spots. She maintained a stony silence in the middle of all the shouts and noise the troops were making as they boarded. Night fell instantly, and the *bongo* moved off like an ogre emerging from its sleep. The engine filled the air with nauseating bluish fumes, and its throbbing drowned out all else. We were once again on the smooth track of a great river. A huge full moon rose in the sky like the eye of a cyclops.

I no longer had any doubt. My fate was hounding me, relentlessly, like an avalanche sweeping before it everything I cared about. I didn't have much time left; we were going to be separated for good. Marc moved to the wall of backpacks that divided us. I crept up there, too, and put my hand over the wall, hoping to find his. Zamaidy looked at me. "You have a few hours," she said, placing her body as a screen. This was the first and last time Marc and I held each other's hands. Our companions were already sleeping, and our words were muffled by the sound of the engine.

"Tell me about your dream house," I urged him.

"It's an old house, the kind you find in New England. There are two big fireplaces on either side and a wooden staircase that creaks when you go up it. There are trees all around, and gardens. There are two cows in the garden. One is called Ciclo and the other is Tímica."

I smiled. He was playing with the syllables of the first word I'd taught him in Spanish. *Ciclotímica.**

"But this house won't be my home until I share it with the person I love."

"I've never yet seen such a beautiful, sad night," I confessed.

"They may separate us, but they can't prevent us from thinking about each other," he said, caressing my hand. "Someday we'll be free, and we'll have another night like this one, beneath the same fantastic moon, and it will be a beautiful night. And it won't be sad any more."

The *bongo* slowed heavily to its mooring. The air suddenly became heavy. The first group were ordered to disembark. Lucho came up to me. "Don't worry," he said. "I'll look after him, and he'll look after me," he added, looking at Marc. "But you promise me that you'll hang in there!"

We held each other. I was torn apart.

Marc took my face between his hands. "I will see you soon," he said, planting a kiss on my cheek.

---

* Word used to describe a person who is prone to mood swings.

76

STROKING DEATH

August 31, 2007. I stood there gasping for breath, frozen in a void, absent from the commotion around me. The guerrillas were loading and unloading *equipos* and bags of supplies. I waited for the *bongo* to move off again. I needed some distance. But the commotion had given way to a calm that was even more despairing, and I eventually understood that our group would spend the night in the hull. It was bound to rain. I looked around me at the inscrutable faces of my companions. They were each setting out items to mark their territory. The man who had assaulted me was restless in his corner. *Enrique did this on purpose*, I thought. Diagonally across from me, as far away as possible, there was one small free spot. William was looking at me. He smiled faintly and motioned to me. I crouched down in the empty space, drawing my body in as much as I could.

I have to sleep. I have to sleep, I repeated relentlessly, hour after hour, until dawn. *I can't go through another night like this one.*

"*Doctora*," someone murmured close to me.

Doctora? Who was calling me that? For years no one had called me that, ever since Enrique had ordered them not to. I was Ingrid, *la vieja*, *la cucha*, the Heron. But not *Doctora*.

"*Doctora*, psst!"

I turned around. It was Massimo.

"*Doctora*, go tell him. He's there, go get him! He can have you change groups."

Indeed, Enrique was standing at the prow, in the same spot where they had disappeared. *How can I go on living?* I thought, as I moved along the railing in spite of myself. Enrique had already seen me. His entire body stiffened, like a spider who can sense its prey struggling in its web. *Dear Lord, I'll go down on my knees before that monster*, I thought, horrified. He knew. He pretended to chat with a *guerrillera*; he was being hard, sharp, humiliating the girl. He deliberately made me wait and refused to look over for a long time. For so long that on the boat, everything stopped, as if the world were holding its breath not to miss a word of what was about to be said.

"Enrique?"

He refused to turn around.

"Enrique?"

After a long, exacerbated silence, he grumbled: "What do you want?"

"I have a request to make."

"I can't do anything for you."

"Yes you can. I'm asking you to change me to the other group."

"That's impossible."

"For you everything is possible. You're the leader here. You're the one who decides."

"I don't want to."

"Why do you hate me so much?"

"I can't do it."

"Yes you can. You're a god here. You can do whatever you want."

Enrique puffed himself up, and his gaze glided down over the world of humans. From on high, pleased with his genius, he declaimed, "It is the Secretariado who decides. I received a precise list; your name is in Commander Chiqui's group." He pointed to a small, round man with pink, porcine skin and a bushy little beard.

"I humbly beg you to show some compassion toward us."

He took a deep breath of contempt, certain that the world belonged to him.

"I beg you, Enrique," I said again. "They're my family, the one that happened to be here in this jungle, in this captivity, in this hell. Don't forget that the wheel turns. Treat us as you would like to be treated if ever you were taken prisoner."

"I shall never be taken prisoner," he retorted. "I would kill myself before I let myself be taken. And I would never lower myself to ask for anything from my enemy."

"Well, I do. My dignity does not depend on this. I'm not ashamed to beg you, even if it costs me a great deal. Because, you see, the strength of love is always greater."

Enrique gave me a vicious look, squinting, searching in me for his own dark abyss. He was aware that everybody was listening, and as if he were tossing his gloves onto a piece of furniture, he said disdainfully, "I will pass on your request to the high command. That's all I can do for you."

He turned his back on me, caressed the head of the *guerrillera* who was on duty, and jump-landed on the ground with a sharp sound, like the blade of a guillotine falling on a neck.

The *bongo* shuddered and floated away from land again, and the deafening sound of the engine throbbed and shook the empty shell of my inert body. The canal grew increasingly narrow. Oswald and Pipiolo, armed with a chain saw, were attacking the immense trees that had grown horizontally across the watercourse, blocking the way. *Everything is upside down now*, I thought.

Two hours later El Chiqui, standing poised on the prow, motioned for the boat to moor.

An Indian girl called Consolación, with a long black braid, in green uniform, had just brushed my shoulder with her hand. I shivered on opening my eyes. I followed, stooped under my heavy load. Ahead of me was a steep incline, which I set about climbing like a mule, my eyes staring at the ground. I stumbled against one of my companions who had stopped, and I realized that we were unloading right there.

I collapsed against a young tree off to one side and sank into limbo. Someone was shaking me. The meal had just come. The idea of food disgusted me. It felt impossible to move. They began constructing the camp.

Where my tent was, there were no trees within reach of my chain. They had set up a huge post by my tent. *Now it's the post that's chained to me.* Pipiolo came with the key ring. He was overjoyed. He spoke to me, sticking his face right up against mine, spluttering. I recoiled from his rancid breath. Pipiolo took his revenge by tightening the chain around my neck, several links. I could feel it painfully when I swallowed.

He wants me to beg him, I thought. He went away. *Don't ask for anything, don't desire anything.*

The days were nothing but a succession of meals. I forced myself to get up and pass my bowl. Above all to avoid any comments. I felt a chronic nausea welling up in waves – whenever I smelled the pot, whenever I heard the sound of the changing of the guards or felt the padlock being closed too tightly after I'd been shuttled to the *chontos*.

Someone had given me a brand-new school notebook with a pirated picture of Snow White. I was still writing to Marc, but it was no longer fun, because he was not there to answer. I reread his letters, a small bundle that never left my pocket, to hear his voice. Those moments were the only ones I could look forward to, and I pushed them back as far as I could, to a time just before twilight.

I'm hibernating, was my explanation to myself for my insurmountable lack of appetite.

My trousers were beginning to float on me. Before, I used to alter the trousers so they would fit. Now I used the belts that I'd woven for the children. *They'll rot otherwise,* I said to myself.

I was startled one morning by the horrified look on the face of one of my companions standing in line with his bowl. I turned around, ready to see a monster behind me. He was staring at me. All I had was a little piece of a broken mirror that I hardly used. I could only see myself in bits – an eye, my nose, a quarter of my cheek and my neck. I was green, with purple shadows around my eyes like spectacles; my skin was dry.

I had made a hole at the foot of my post with a little stick to bury the strands of hair that I picked up every day. My comb never failed to come away with a dusty clump that I hid so that the wind wouldn't blow it over to the neighbours. They'd complain. They'd say I was dirty. I wasn't.

Through sheer will I put on the damp, stinking shorts I euphemistically called my "bath outfit," which were decomposing because they could never actually dry out, covered with a transparent sticky film of mildew. We had to run down a steep slope and climb back up it to get to the wash area, carry our jugs of water, and the clothes we invariably had to wash.

I've turned into a cat, I mused, stunned, thinking of my grandmother's sweet expression. When she was a child, no one had warned her about the transformations of puberty. Terrified to see how her body was changing, she concluded she was under a spell and changing into a feline.

My mutation was less spectacular. I began to despise contact with the water. I would slip into it tensely at the last minute and come out shaking, blue, my scalp as painful as if some invisible hand were pulling my hair. My boots filled with water, my legs and arms were taut; I would struggle back to my *caleta*, hoping that with the next step I would fall and never get up.

El Chiqui's camp was built the first week of August, 2007. I had remained secluded in my hammock for months, oblivious to time and space. *Melanie is going to be twenty-two.* These words contained all the horror in the world. I went to the *chontos* and vomited blood.

I was drinking hardly anything, and I ate nothing. When I went to the toilet, which was constantly, a greenish, slimy liquid left my body, excruciating, and I threw up blood, more out of weariness than from some violent urge; my skin was covered with burning pustules that I scratched until they bled to stop the itching. I got up every morning to brush my teeth. That was all I did all day long. I went back to my hammock and held my radio up against my ear, but I listened without hearing as I wandered through the labyrinth of illogical thoughts made up of memories, images, patchwork ideas with which I filled my eternal boredom. Nothing awoke me from my introspection except my Mom's voice and the music of the Colombian artist Juanes singing "Sueños" – "Dreams." I shared my dreams so badly.

Pipiolo came to me one evening and stared at me, his voice honeyed. He opened the padlock and gave me some slack around my neck, loosening the chain by a few links. He wanted me to thank him. "You'll feel better like this. You'll get your appetite back."

Poor idiot. I hadn't noticed the chain for a long time.

I was finding it harder and harder to make the simplest gestures of life. One day I gave up bathing and remained prostrate in my bed. *I'm going to die, like Captain Guevara.** *Everyone dies for the new year, it would be a perfect cycle,* I thought, without emotion.

Massimo came to see me from time to time. "Nothing," he said, because he knew I was still waiting for an answer from the leaders. Each time I felt the same pang. "I'm going to write a letter to Marulanda," I decided, as a last resort. The prospect of undertaking something in order to be with my friends again propelled me for a few days into a state of near-delirious energy. "If you write a letter for the Secretariado, Gafas has to make sure it gets there, or he'll be punished," asserted Massimo. "Give it to Asprilla, or to El Chiqui, so that there are witnesses. They will have to give it to Enrique first, but it will end up in Manuel Marulanda's hands."

Asprilla, who was in charge of the other group, came to say hello and did not hide his surprise when he saw me. "Your friends are doing very well," he confirmed. "They're eating well and doing exercise every day."

I almost begrudged them their good form. Still, I handed him the letter I kept inside my pocket. He opened the sheet, folded in four, glanced at it, and folded it up again. I got the impression that he didn't know how to decipher it.

"I can read it to you," I offered, to allay any suspicion.

He shrugged and said, "If you're asking to change groups, don't count on it. Enrique won't budge."

I didn't hear anything else. I felt as if my life had stopped there. I fell victim to a new outbreak of pustules, I went on vomiting, and I felt I was losing contact with reality. I didn't want to leave my *cambuche* any more.

They forced me to go bathe. On my way back, I discovered that all my belongings had been searched. They had taken my notebook, with the messages I went on writing in English for someone called Marc who was no more than a name, an echo, an idea, perhaps even some sort of madness — did he really exist? I was afraid they would break into my secret world, and I sank ever deeper into wretchedness.

---

* Captain Julián Guevara fell ill in December 2006 and the FARC refused to treat him. He died shortly after. He was in a camp not far from ours that was also under the command of Enrique.

I put the radio on every morning, a mechanical gesture, which by dawn had drained me of all my energy. My radio was constantly playing tricks on me; it would stop working just as Mom was beginning her message. I'd been getting ready since four in the morning for her five o'clock message, and when, miraculously, the radio worked, I stayed motionless, holding my breath, hypnotized by the tender, caressing tones of her voice. When Mom's voice disappeared, I could not remember what she'd said. One afternoon William came to see me. He had asked for permission, and they'd unchained him for a few minutes. This was a special concession that the guerrillas granted only to William because he acted as a doctor for the camp.

"How are you?" he asked blandly.

I was going to give a standard polite reply when a wave of tears overwhelmed me. Between spasms I tried to assure him that everything was fine. This went on for over a quarter of an hour. When at last I managed to control myself, William asked outright whether I had heard Mom's message. All I could do was shake my head, so he left, unable to help.

The next morning at dawn, two guerrillas packed all my things to move elsewhere. Chiqui had ordered them to build an isolated *caleta*, far away from the other prisoners. As a form of special treatment, I would have only women watching over me. Consolación, the Indian girl with the black braid, was on duty. "We're going to take care of you," she said, as if this were good news.

They dropped off a box filled with intravenous-drip supplies. Fluff had just been appointed as a nurse, and she came up to me, trembling, with the order to get started by practising on my arm. Once, twice, three times, inside my elbow, her needle went through my vein without finding the correct position. "Let's try the other arm." Once, twice, three times. On the fourth try, she decided to search for a vein in my wrist. Monster came by to take a look at my ordeal and went away delighted. "That'll teach you," he said mockingly, turning on his heel.

"Call Willie," I pleaded eventually. Asking me to be patient, Consolación went off at a run. She must have been incredibly convincing, because half an hour later she came back with William and Monster following close behind.

William looked at my arms, frowning in a way that made everyone ill at ease. "I refuse to try to prick her again. She's getting phlebitis. We have to wait until tomorrow." Then, turning to me, he said gently, "Chin up, I'll look after you."

I lost consciousness. When I opened my eyes again, it was already dark. The Indian wasn't there any more. In her place was Katerina, an AK-47 over her shoulder, watching me with curiosity.

"You're in luck!" she said admiringly. "William said he wouldn't take care of anyone else unless you are treated properly."

Consolación was back at dawn. She was working, cutting and stripping wood. I didn't even think to ask what she was doing. "I'm going to build you a table and a bench. You'll be able to sit here and write." I hated her. They hadn't returned my notebook, and here she was taunting me with a privilege I no longer desired. The Indian must have seen the dark shadow over my face, for she said, "Stop worrying, you're going to get better. They're going to make you a good fish soup." Her gentleness was a burden. I just wanted to be left alone. The table was built by the time the pot arrived. A big piranha was floating in it. The girl put the pot down respectfully in front of me, as if enacting a sacred ritual. From the neighbouring camp, I could hear the guard barking at the prisoners that it was time to eat. I sighed, absorbed in my contemplation of the beast in the pot. "I never managed to persuade Lucho to eat the eyes," I mused.

I had once been to a dinner among diplomats when the father of my children was posted in Quito. The wife of the officer hosting the dinner had prepared a superb fish, which lay splendidly in the middle of the table. The hostess had been born in Vientiane, Laos. I have never forgotten her, with her black hair pulled back into a shining chignon and her multicoloured silk sarong. She explained gracefully that in Laos the most prized dish was fish eyes. As she spoke, with a refined gesture she removed the creature's slimy eye and lifted it to her mouth. "I should try," I urged myself one hungry day in captivity. "It's like caviar!" I had to admit Lucho always looked at me and laughed, absolutely disgusted. Tom was the only one who followed my cue, and he had become as crazy about fish eyes as I was.

Willie's voice roused me from my torpor; he was already holding my arm, looking for a vein.

"Did you hear the message from your mother and daughter this morning?"

"Yes, I think I heard them."

"What did they say?" he asked, as if asking me to recite my lesson.

"I think they were talking about a trip?"

"Not at all. They were telling you that your dog Pom died. Melanie was very sad."

Now it came back to me. *La Carrilera* had started with a beautiful song from Yuri Buenaventura composed for the hostages. I had the impression he was singing my story, and I was deeply shaken. I heard Mom next. She told me that Pom had been sniffing everywhere, trying to find my smell. She nuzzled my clothes and went from room to room inspecting every little corner. *My little Pom, she's gone ahead to prepare my arrival.*

I thought I was ready to go, too. There was a certain order to it all, and I liked that. Then I disconnected myself from the world, the needle in my arm filling my vein with a deadly chill.

I came back suffering terrible convulsions. I wanted to disconnect the drip; I felt instinctively that it was killing me. The panicked guard forbade me and began shouting for help. Monster came running. He tried to make me stay down flat in my hammock, and when he felt that my body was rushing away at a gallop, he ran, disappearing in a panic the way he had come.

William arrived and immediately disconnected the drip. The convulsions stopped. He wrapped me in a blanket, and I fell asleep again, dreaming that I was an old glove.

The drip eventually stabilized my condition. William came to see me very often. He massaged my back and talked to me about my children. "They're waiting for you, they need you." He would feed me fish broth, spoon by spoon: "One for your mother, one for your daughter, one for

Lorenzo, one for Pom." Then he stopped there, knowing I would refuse any more, and came back later to try again. When I thanked him, he got angry. "You have nothing to thank me for. Those monsters agreed to let me come because they need a proof of life."

77

THIRD PROOF OF LIFE

October 2007. This news upset me greatly. In a spiral of depression, I clung to the words I had loved, to keep from falling. I reread Marc's letters. And I recited poems I had always kept in my memory: *"Je suis le ténébreux — le veuf, — l'inconsolé . . ."** I savoured the words as if they were the finest nourishment. *"Porque después de todo he comprendido / que lo que el árbol tiene de florido / vive de lo que tiene sepultado."*† I saw Papa, standing with his finger raised, aware of the mesmerizing effect he had on me; in reciting these verses, he was arming me for life. It was his words that I heard in my words. *"'There is no silence that does not end,'"‡* he said and I repeated after him, killing my fears with Pablo Neruda's claim over death.

This immersion in the past boosted my spirits. It wasn't the IV that had allowed me to recover. It was the words! Back in my secret garden, the world I could observe through the peephole of my indifference seemed less insane.

Enrique came by one morning at the end of October when I was already seated on my bench. At the sight of him, the nausea grabbed me by the throat, like a cat.

"I have some good news!" he shouted from a distance.

---

* From the poem "The Disinherited" by the French poet Gérard de Nerval.
† From a sonnet by the Argentinian poet Francisco Luis Bernárdez.
‡ From the poem "Para Todos" by Pablo Neruda.

I played blind and deaf. He came toward me, acting mischievously, hiding behind trees playing peek-a-boo. Consolación watched him, amused, giggling at her boss's clowning. *Dear Lord, forgive me, but I hate him,* I professed silently, looking at the toes of my impeccably clean boots.

He went on acting the buffoon, seeming more ridiculous by the second. He must have realized that he was getting nowhere with me. Finally he planted himself before me.

"I have some good news," he said again, not backing down. "You're going to be able to send a message to your family," he continued, scrutinizing my reaction.

"I have no message to send," I replied firmly.

I've had plenty of time to think about it. I only wanted to write a letter to my mother, a letter just for her, a sort of testament. I would not be part of the circus that the FARC wanted us to perform in.

Naturally, I had got wind of President Hugo Chávez's efforts to obtain our release. He was trying to sell the FARC on the idea that releasing the hostages could be a jackpot for them in political terms. He was the only one who could talk with the FARC, probably because Marulanda saw him as an ally, a fellow revolutionary. He had also won the trust of the Colombian president, Uribe.

Uribe initially gave Chávez free rein to deal with the FARC; I thought Uribe was convinced, as I was, that the FARC would never yield. They wanted to make us their window display, never selling their goods. Uribe probably hoped to unveil their true intentions, show the world that the FARC had no peace plans and therefore no interest in letting us go.

But Chávez was moving fast. He had already met with the FARC delegates, received a letter from Marulanda, and even announced that the Secretariado was going to entrust him with our proofs of life. He would hand them personally to President Nicolas Sarkozy during his trip to France, scheduled for the end of November. I couldn't believe there would be a positive outcome for us; it was just a game to show the FARC off.

I would have no part of their manipulative pretence. My family was suffering enough as it was. My children had grown up in anxiety, and they had reached adulthood chained, as I was, to uncertainty. I had made my peace with God. I felt there was a sort of lull in my suffering, because I'd accepted what had happened to me. I hated Enrique. But in a way I knew that I could let go and not hate him if I wanted. When he had looked at me and said, "You know I can get this proof of life no matter what," he'd already lost. I almost felt sorry for him. Of course he would get it, but it didn't interest me any more. There lay my victory. He no longer had a hold on me. Because I had already accepted that I could die. For my entire life I had believed I was eternal. My eternity had stopped here, in this rotten hole, and the presence of imminent death filled me with a peace of mind that I savoured. I no longer needed anything; there was nothing I desired. My soul was stripped bare. I was no longer afraid of Enrique.

Having lost all my freedom and, with it, everything that mattered to me – my children, my mom, my life and my dreams – with my neck chained to a tree – not able to move around, to talk, to eat and to drink, to carry out my most basic bodily needs – subjected to constant humiliation, I still had the most important freedom of all. No one could take it away from me. That was the freedom to choose what kind of person I wanted to be.

With this realization came the understanding that I was no longer a victim. I was free to choose to hate or not to hate. I was a survivor.

When Enrique went away, he was satisfied. So was I. I would write a letter to my mother and nothing more. I had emptied the space around me. I had only a day to do it. I put down the sheets of paper sweet Consolación had hastened to bring to me, on her little table. I wanted my words to bring Mom to me, where I was. I wanted her to smell me and breathe me. I wanted to tell her that I had been listening to her, because she didn't know. And I wanted my children to speak to me. To prepare them at last, as I had prepared myself, to face death without regrets. To restore their freedom and give them wings for life.

I did not have much time to put myself back into a conversation that had been interrupted six years earlier. I had to go straight to the essential. But I knew they would find meaning in every word, in all our codes of love; they could smell my skin in the way I formed my letters and hear my voice in the rhythm of my sentences.

It was a monologue that lasted eight hours, without interruption. The guards didn't dare disturb me, and my bowl sat empty next to me the entire day. My hands carried me over thousands of words at a dazzling speed, following thoughts that had flown thousands of miles away.

When Enrique reappeared to take my letter, I hadn't finished. He left again, grumbling with irritation, but I'd obtained an extra hour to say good-bye. It was wrenching. I had just spent a day with my loved ones, and I didn't want to let them go.

Enrique came back just as I was signing, and he snatched up the letter with a covetous impatience. I felt naked in those sheets of paper he was slipping so inelegantly into his pocket. *I should have made an envelope*, I thought.

"I see you're in great shape," he said.

He was so stupid, I was no longer listening to him. I was tired. I wanted to go back under my mosquito net to my cocoon.

"Wait, we haven't finished. I have to film you."

"I don't want you to film me," I said, surprised and weary. "We agreed that I would write a letter and that was all."

"The commanders agreed to the letter, but they also want images."

He pulled out his digital camera and aimed it at me. The red button lit up and went out again.

"Go on, say something. Say a little hello to your mom."

The red light came on for good. He had lied to me. The letter would never reach my mother. I sat stiffly on Consolación's bench. *Lord, you know that this proof of life exists against my will. May your will be done*, I prayed in silence, and I swallowed my tears and my pride. I did not want my children to see me like this.

Before leaving, Enrique deposited my notebook on the table – the one they had taken away in the last frisk. I didn't have the strength even to rejoice.

I was surprised when, three weeks later, the radio announced that Chávez did not give the proof of life to Sarkozy. Was Mono Jojoy playing his own game, trying to abort a mediation process I now wanted to believe in, against my better judgement? Sarkozy had made the Colombian hostage situation an issue of global importance, working relentlessly since his election to advance the talks with the FARC.

If Marulanda had announced proofs of life, and if they had been collected in time, why didn't Chávez get them? Was there a latent struggle within the FARC between a militaristic wing and a more political faction?

I discussed it with Willie endlessly. I knew that this was Willie's tactic to get me to take an interest in the world again. He had shown himself to be unfailingly constant, checking on my recovery hourly. He persuaded the guerrillas to provide me with some energizing supplement pills, and he sat down next to me to make sure I took them when our meals arrived.

But with Willie we spoke primarily about my children and Mom. He came every day to ask me if I had listened to their messages, and I thanked him for repeating their words to me, because it gave me the opportunity to talk about them.

"And you, why don't you receive any messages?" I asked him once.

"It's hard for my mother. She works all the time."

He closed up like a clam, avoiding any topic that concerned him. One day, however, he sat next to me with the intention of talking to me about *his* lost world, too.

I wanted to know more about his father. But Willie refused to say anything about him. As if to excuse himself, he eventually said, "I think I still hold it against him, but it's less and less true. I would like so much to take him in my arms and tell him how much I love him."

The next morning on the radio programme, his mother sent him a message. I was startled when they announced her presence, knowing how much joy it would give him to hear her, and I listened intently.

Her voice was that of a very sad woman, carrying a burden that was far too heavy on her shoulders.

"My son," she said, "your father has died. Pray for him."

Willie came as on every day. We sat side by side in silence for a long time. There was nothing to say. I didn't even dare to look at him so that he wouldn't be ashamed of his tears. Finally I uttered, very quietly, "Talk to me about him."

We left the camp. I couldn't carry my backpack, so they spread my things out among the guerrillas. Half of them I would never see again. It hardly mattered. I had my Bible and my letters on me.

Suddenly the radio announced that the army had seized some videos from young militia hiding in a neighbourhood south of Bogotá. They were the proofs of life that Chávez had never received. Chávez's mediation had just been suspended as the result of a virulent confrontation with Uribe. Mom was crying on the radio. She had learned I'd sent her a letter, because excerpts had been published in the press, but the authorities refused to give it to her. The images Enrique had recorded were also seized.

Lucho and Marc had reacted just as I had, refusing to speak in front of Enrique's camera, I discovered. Marc had also written a letter to Marulanda that had been found with the proof of life. He had asked to be reunited with me. Without knowing, we had fought in the same way. This gave me great peace of mind. We were connected by our gesture of protest, united against all the forces that had tried to destroy our friendship.

Something had happened with the discovery of these proofs of life that revealed our mental and physical conditions. For the first time in so many years, there was a change of heart. Testimonies of compassion and solidarity were being heard everywhere.

President Sarkozy sent a harsh televised message to Manuel Marulanda. "A woman in danger of dying must be saved (. . .) You bear a heavy responsibility, I urge you to rise to it," he had declared. *It's the end of the nightmare*, I thought. I fell asleep, as if lulled by an incantation. Words – the words of others – had healed me. The next morning, for the first time in six months, I wanted to eat.

It was December 8, the feast of the Virgin, and an urgent need to listen to music from the outside world grabbed hold of me. I had a thirst for life again. By chance I heard a countdown of Led Zeppelin's best songs, and I wept in gratitude. "Stairway to Heaven" was my hymn to life. Hearing it reminded me that I was born for happiness. I had collected all their records, and they were my treasure back in the days when music came only on vinyl.

I knew that among die-hard fans it was frowned upon to like "Stairway to Heaven." It had become too popular. Connoisseurs were not supposed to share the taste of the masses. But I never disowned my first loves. From the age of fourteen, I'd been convinced that the song was written for me. On hearing the song again in that impenetrable jungle, I wept at the promise of freedom made to me long ago, which I had never understood before:

> And a new day will dawn
> for those who stand long
> And the forests will echo with laughter.

78

LUCHO'S RELEASE

El Chiqui had warned us we'd be marching at New Year's; this was only a temporary camp, despite the commotion there was that morning. It was not the signal of a new departure, since the guerrillas' tents had not been dismantled.

At around eleven o'clock, the girls showed up carrying paper plates with chicken and rice, nicely decorated with mayonnaise and tomato sauce. I had not seen anything like this in my nearly six years of captivity. Then, in the middle of the table that had been built the day before, they set down an enormous fish cooked in banana leaves. I was disconcerted.

The guerrillas were calling to me, coming up to me with bags full of wrapped presents. Behind me my companions were shouting joyfully at the sight of this unexpected Christmas. I felt a sudden rush of anxiety. Instinctively I looked all around. The girls were getting ready to hug me, and it would be anything but gratuitous. That is when I saw Enrique, hidden behind the bushes. Once again the red light betrayed him. He was filming in secret with his little digital camera. I rushed to take refuge under my mosquito net, leaving unopened the package the girls had placed in a corner of my *caleta*.

I switched on my radio, furious, to distract myself from the shameful charade that Enrique had cooked up. I was sure that this new footage he was making had no other aim than to improve the FARC's image, for it had been seriously tarnished by the discovery of our proofs of life. The images of the human rags and bones into which they'd transformed us had given the FARC bad press.

I was brooding over this when the radio programme was interrupted by a news alert. "The FARC has announced the pending liberation of three hostages." Consuelo, Clara, and her son, Emmanuel, were going to be released! I leaped from my hammock and ran over to my companions, who greeted the news with hugs and smiles. Armando came up, swaggering. "We're next!" A wave of well-being washed over me. "It's the beginning of the end," I repeated over and over, imagining Clara's and Consuelo's happiness. We prisoners shared a theory: If one of us got out, the others would follow. Pinchao had paved the way. His success had echoed within us like a signal. It must be our turn soon.

We moved to another camp the next day, down the river, our tents bunched together, which meant the real beginning of a march. Guerrillas I hadn't seen for a long time walked through our camp, carrying heavy wood on their shoulders. "Look," said William, "those are the guards from the other group. They must be right nearby."

Christmas came, and with it the hope that we would all meet again. It was a hot day. As we were making our way back from the bath session, clinging to tree roots as we climbed a very steep riverbank, a torrential storm shook the forest and drenched us before we reached our *caletas*. Everything was torn by the raging wind and soaked through by a lashing, horizontal rain. *It's the dry season*, I thought. *It shouldn't be raining*. It almost made me forget my birthday.

I had spent my time imagining what my children must be doing. I'd heard them call in, after midnight, together with their father, to wish me a happy birthday. It gave me great peace of mind to know they were all together. I knew they had read my letter, and I felt that something essential had been accomplished. They had heard my inner voice. There was a lightness and hope in their words. Wounds had begun to heal.

Sebastian, Melanie and Lorenzo were growing their wings, strong in their knowledge of my love. Mom and Astrid were as solid as a rock, building my resilience with the tenacity of their faith. And I liked to think that if Fabrice had been here with me, he would have lifted up my back-pack and given me his hand and not let go.

The day after Christmas 2007, we began marching again. Though I was carrying hardly anything in my backpack my muscles seemed to have melted, and I trembled with every step.

From the beginning, Willie had been very attentive. He helped me to fold up my tent, to close my *equipo*. He buttoned my jacket up to my neck and pulled my hat down over my ears, put on my gloves, and handed me a bottle of water.

"Mind you drink as much as you can," he ordered, like a doctor; he left with a group after me but arrived first at the site of the new camp.

When I got there, everything was ready for me. He had collected the belongings that others had carried for me, and he'd put up my tent and set up my hammock. I arrived at nightfall, very tired.

I slept fitfully, anxious at the thought of the next day's march, and I got my things ready before the guards called so that when Mom was on the air, nothing would distract me from her words. My sister was there again. I loved Astrid's messages. Her judgement was always sharp, like my father's. *It's been years since she had a Christmas, or a New Year's, or a birthday party*, I thought with a heavy heart. Along with Mom she had asked President Uribe to let Chávez mediate with the FARC once again. Armando had also heard their message, as well as his mother's, who called in every day.

"They're optimistic. You'll see, we'll be next!" he said.

I hugged him, wistfully. I didn't think we'd be so lucky.

We stopped the march on December thirty-first. New Year's was the only feast the guerrillas allowed themselves to celebrate. We came to a marvellous place, with a waterfall of crystal-clear water winding merrily through huge trees. We were a day's walk from the other group. My companions found items belonging to Lucho, Marc, and Bermeo in the spots we were going to use after them to put up our tents and hammocks. William was pleased; Monster had given him a good location for his *caleta*, next to the water.

I was hesitant, as I knew he didn't like the rituals that connected us to the outside world. "William, I would like to ask you a favour."

He looked up, amused. "I don't have time," he answered jokingly. We had nothing to do.

"Well, it's Mom's birthday. I'd like to celebrate it in one way or another. I thought of singing 'Happy Birthday,' but I believe the sound waves have a better chance of reaching her if there are several of us. To be honest, I don't want to sing alone."

"You want me to act like a clown just to make you happy?" he said, unconvinced. "Go on, you begin!"

We sang, in low voices, and it made us laugh, like two children up to mischief. Then he pulled out a little packet of cookies he'd saved from Enrique's fake Christmas party, and we pretended to be sharing a cake.

"It's the last day of the year," I told him. "Let's make a list of all the nice things that have happened to us this year, to thank the heavens." I smiled. In the jungle I no longer prayed prospectively, for what I hoped to come, but rather for what I had already received.

"No, no," said Willie. "I haven't been talking to God for a long time. I'm mad at him, just as he is surely mad at me. You see, I am a Christian. I was raised very strictly and with high moral standards. I can't start talking to him if I haven't set things right."

"Look at it as a question of being polite. If someone does something for you, you say thank you."

Willie clammed up. I had just overstepped the bounds. I tried to back-track.

"Okay, let's just make a list. Look, there was Pinchao's freedom, and now there's Consuelo, Clara, and Emmanuel."

"And we also have the release of the politicians from the Cauca Valley," he replied bitterly.

I knew that he was talking about their tragedy so as not to have to talk about his own. Then, as if he were coming from far away, he said, "This is a very nice place. We're lucky to be waiting for New Year's here. Let's call the place Caño Bonito."

It was a real ordeal to start the march again. We climbed a sheer mountainside, sleeping several nights in succession on a steep slope, clinging to the earth like lice. We washed in a waterfall tumbling from the heights, splashing on enormous stones polished by the current. The water was icy, and the sky was grey. It made me dizzy to look down. If I slipped, I'd kill myself.

Then we crossed a plateau that I immediately recognized– the granite rocks, the ground like slate, the small forest of dry bushes, the pyramids. Our companions had just been through there, walking across the same ground in the same place, and I looked down, hoping they'd left some sign for me.

Armando, who was ahead of us, came upon a small, pink, fluffy animal rolled around a tree branch. It was an odd-looking animal, with two long fingers each ending in a single, long, curved claw. When the guard explained this was a *Gran Bestia*, I thought he was making fun of us. I had heard about the *Gran Bestia* on several occasions and was under the impression it was a monster, anything but the cute, inoffensive creature before us. Legend had it that the *Gran Bestia* had extraordinary powers, including one with which I was obsessed: It could escape from anywhere without leaving a trace. Once we made camp for the night, the *Gran Bestia* was firmly attached to a post and shut in a box. I sat down and stared at it until it was time for us to bathe. I had only looked away for a second when one of my comrades alerted us. The *Gran Bestia* had disappeared. The troop's disappointment contrasted with my delight. I felt there was some justice.

When we reached the bottom of the mountain, by a wide river, our caravan stopped abruptly. One of the guerrillas had stumbled over a strange instrument planted in the ground, in the middle of our track.

The metal shaft was the visible part of a sophisticated device buried three feet beneath the ground. In all likelihood there was a battery connected to a solar panel set up somewhere among the trees, with a camera and an antenna. It was all contained in a metal box that the guerrillas initially took for a bomb.

Enrique had it dug up very cautiously, then laid out everything conscientiously on an enormous plastic sheet. All the components had captions engraved in English, and he called for a translator to be brought over to decipher them.

Maybe it would be Marc! On my way to the river to get some water, I might be able to see him. But it was Keith who volunteered. He spent hours with Enrique, going over all the materiel. Information reached us almost simultaneously. It was an American system used by the Colombian army. The camera was supposed to send images via satellite link. The system was equipped with a sensor that turned on the camera when it detected vibrations on the ground. If an animal or a person passed by, the camera would start filming. Someone in the United States, or in Colombia, had seen us go by, in real time.

I was overjoyed. Not at the thought that the Colombian army might have located us, which for me remained mere speculation, but to know that my friends were only a few hundred yards from there and that we might be reunited.

My other comrades, the captive Colombian soldiers, were furious. I could hear them talking among themselves, whispering with their backs to the guards, visibly exasperated.

"What's wrong?" I asked Armando.

"This is treason. This information shouldn't get into the hands of the enemy," he said, frowning like a policeman ready to give a ticket.

We reached the river late in the afternoon. On the opposite shore, two hundred yards from us, we saw our companions from the other group taking their baths. I made huge signs with my arms. They didn't respond. Maybe they hadn't seen me. The riverbank on their side was bare, but not on ours. Or maybe their guard was a hard case.

We came to a disused FARC camp a week later early in the afternoon under an apocalyptic storm, like shipwrecked sailors. Lucho and Marc's group had already set up camp a few yards away. Enrique magnanimously opened some crates of beer that were sitting there, abandoned in the camp. While we waited for the order to set up our tents, I switched on my radio. The reception was terrible, but I clung to it in the hope of more details about Clara's release scheduled to happen that same day. My comrades were doing the same. The broadcast lasted a long time, and when we had finished installing our tents, we could still hear an untiring Chávez greeting our companions.

"There will be more releases," he announced.

It's not my turn yet. I sighed, listening to a press conference where Sarkozy applauded the major efforts being made by thousands of people rallying to demand our freedom. He appealed for perseverance.

Where were we headed? Probably nowhere. I felt as if we'd been going around in circles for weeks. We were marching, lost souls, in this impenetrable jungle, constantly on the verge of starvation.

At the end of the month, we came to a camp that was already set up. I didn't recognize it right away, but when I saw the volleyball court, I realized we had come back to the camp where we'd spent Christmas a year earlier, where Katerina had been dancing the *cumbia.*

Everything had rotted. My *caleta* had been invaded by ants and termites. I found a bottle I'd left behind and a hairpin I'd lost. We set up our tents in a row on the volleyball court.

Armando called to me, shouting, "Look, your friends are here!"

Sure enough, behind a row of bushes not fifty yards away, Marc and Lucho's group had set up camp. Lucho was on his feet and waving to us. I couldn't see Marc.

When the order came to prepare for the bath, I was ready immediately. To go to the river, we would have to go right by their camp. I was stirred at the prospect of greeting them. And Marc and Lucho were waiting for us by the side of the path, their arms crossed, their lips set. I wore my bath outfit, more patched than ever. My joy gave way to confusion. I could tell by their eyes that they were dismayed to see me in such a state: I had got used to myself like this, all the more so because I had no mirror. I felt suddenly self-conscious. They seemed in better shape, more muscular, and curiously enough, that hurt me.

I did not hurry back from the bath. They were gone. With their bowls. I saw their guard busy handing out the evening meal. It was Saturday, I went back to my *caleta* and prepared myself mentally to listen to the messages after midnight. I checked that the alarm on the watch Cesar had given me when we first met had been set properly and prepared myself for the night.

I had already heard my family's messages when at midnight the radio interrupted its usual programming with a bulletin:

"The FARC has announced that they will release three more hostages."

I leaped up, clinging to my radio; I could hardly get my breath.

Lucho's name was among them.

I stifled a cry that caught in my throat. I fell to my knees under my mosquito net, my chain around my neck, thanking the heavens between sobs. My head was spinning from the emotion. "Dear God, did I hear properly?" The silence around me worried me: What if I'd misheard? All my companions must have been listening to the same programme. And yet there was no movement, not a sound, not a voice, no emotion. I waited for the news to be repeated, stamping my feet with impatience. Lucho, Gloria, and Orlando were being set free.

I rushed out of my tent at the first glow of dawn. Still chained around my neck, I strained to see the spot where I'd noticed Lucho the night before. He was there, he was waiting.

"Lucho, you are free!" I screamed when I saw him.

I was jumping, wildly enough to snap my neck, just to see him better.

"Lucho, you are free!" I cried with all my lungs, tears streaming down my face, indifferent to the guards' admonishments and the grumbling of my comrades, irritated by a happiness they could not share.

Lucho waved no with his finger, his hand in front of his mouth. Weeping.

"Yes, yes!" I answered, stubbornly, nodding fiercely.

What? Could it be he hadn't heard? I went on, more stubborn than ever. "Didn't you listen to the radio last night?" I shrieked, miming my words to illustrate my question.

He nodded, laughing and crying at the same time.

The guards were beside themselves. Pipiolo insulted me, and Oswald ran off to the commanders' shack. Asprilla came hastily and said something to Lucho with a tap on the shoulder, then ran over to me.

"Calm down, Ingrid. Don't worry, they'll give him time to say good-bye to you."

I understood that they would separate Lucho from his group in the coming hours. *They'll keep me from talking to him.*

The order was given to move our tents to our old spots in the camp. From there it was impossible to see Lucho. However, in their obsession with forbidding any communication between us, the guerrillas overlooked the fact that the other group's *chontos* were only a few feet from our spot. It was awkward for them, but no one complained. Marc was the first one to realize. We spoke with signs; he promised to get Lucho.

Lucho was very tense when he came. We spoke without closing the thirty feet or so that separated us, as if there were a wall between us. On a sudden impulse, I turned to the guard, the same one I had once grabbed by the neck to punish for being so vulgar.

"Okay, go ahead," he said. "You have five minutes."

I ran over to Lucho, and we held each other tight.

"I won't leave without you."

"Yes, you have to leave. You have to tell the world what we are going through."

"I won't be able to."

"Yes you will. You have to."

I removed from my waist the belt that I was wearing and said, "I want you to give this to Melanie."

We held each other's hands in silence; it was the greatest blessing we could receive. There were so many things to say to him! When I felt that the time was running out, I knew I must secure one last promise from him.

"Ask me whatever you want."

"Promise me . . . that you'll be happy, Lucho. I don't want you to spoil the happiness of your release by feeling sorry for me. Swear that you will live life to the fullest."

"I swear that every second of my new life I will not stop working for your return, that's what I'll swear."

The guard's voice brought us back down to earth. We flung our arms around each other one last time as tears streamed down my face, and I couldn't have said whether they were mine or his. I saw him walk away, his back bent, his steps heavy. In his camp the tents were already being dismantled.

We no longer saw the members of Marc's group, although I imagine we couldn't have been very far from each other. On February 27, three weeks after we said good-bye, Luis Eladio, along with Gloria, Jorge Eduardo, and Orlando, landed at the Maiquetía airport in Venezuela. Their release was a diplomatic triumph for President Chávez.

In chains, curled up inside our mosquito nets, we listened to the broadcast, trying to visualize the images we couldn't see. It must have been six o'clock in the evening; the twilight sky must be cooling the dusty Caracas air. I imagined the plane must be quite a big one. You could hear the song of the cicadas above the turbines of the plane— or was it around my *caleta* that the cicadas were singing?

Lucho's voice was full of light. He'd got stronger during the weeks leading up to his release; his words were clear, his ideas sharp. What must he be feeling at that moment? He was back in the world, and now the reality I was still living had moved into the past for him, as if by magic, with a snap of someone's fingers. He will hit a switch to turn off the lights tonight, and he'll have clean sheets on a real bed, and hot water just by turning the tap. Will he be immediately swallowed up into that new world? Or will he pause before he switches on the light and think about us, and think again about us as he lies down, and remember us when he chooses his dinner? *Yes, at dinner he'll be back here for a few seconds*, I thought. Armando shouted from his *cambuche*, "We'll be next!"

I felt pain in my heart. No, not me. I wouldn't be on the list of the FARC's releases. I was sure of that.

79

THE DISAGREEMENT

March–April 2008. The march went on, aimlessly. We spent several days sleeping on a granite bed by the side of a lazy river, pestered by flies dismembering the stinking remains of fish caught among the rocks when the waters subsided. Then we crossed over to the other side of the river.

"They're going to get us some supplies," explained El Chiqui, pointing his chin toward Monster and two other boys leaving with empty *equipos*. So we waited patiently. They allowed us to fish with hooks that they would collect again when night fell. This improved our rations. I ate the bones and fins of the fish to ensure an intake of calcium.

One evening El Chiqui came to inform us that we had to pack everything up, because we would leave as soon as the *bongo* arrived. We made a short crossing and spent the rest of the night on a muddy river-bank. In the morning we were ordered to hide in the woods, not to speak or use radios or put up tents. At noon we saw our companions from the other group go by in single file behind Enrique. They were held on leashes like dogs by guards who walked behind, rifles pointed at them.

I could not get used to the sight of a chain around a man's neck. Our companions went by us, practically stumbling over us, but they didn't want to speak or even look at us. Marc went by – I had got up to look at him, in the hope that he would turn his head. He didn't.

Then we followed them. We, too, walked in silence, kept on a leash. Monster had just been killed by an army patrol; one of the young guerrillas had managed to flee and give the alarm. We were surrounded by the army.

Our flight was exhausting. To get the army off our trail, Enrique ordered us to march in *cortina*,* which meant we no longer followed each other but moved forward elbow to elbow in a single row in the same direction, like a front line.

So we had to clear our own passage through the vegetation, being careful not to break any branches or damage the ferns. It was hand-to-hand combat with nature. Each of us was on a leash held by a guard. My guard got angry with me because I tended to go where my neighbour had already cleared the way, and so I fell behind and broke the front line.

I was slowing everybody down; perhaps I was hoping, even unconsciously, that the army would catch up with us. As we clambered through the barriers of thorns, climbing over the white corpses of dozens of charred trees blocking our passage and fought our way through the creepers and roots of hostile vegetation, I pictured the sudden arrival of commandos, their faces smeared with colourful green paint.

Every day I prayed for the commandos, even if the risk of dying was considerable. It was not just the idea that the bullets would spare me no matter what. It was stronger than that. It was above all a need for justice. The right to be defended. A vital aspiration, to reconquer my own dignity. But I couldn't do much.

This advance, this struggle against the elements with a chain around my neck, was all the more painful and humiliating because it forced me to invest will and ingenuity in "fleeing" from what I desired most: my freedom. And I hated myself for every step I took.

---

* In a "curtain."

More than once we left behind the edge of the forest to wander across the land of huge *fincas* that had been recently burned by the antidrug squads. A few head of cattle watched terrified as we went by, filling our pockets with guavas and mandarin oranges from the lush trees spared by the fire. Then we disappeared again into the thick cover of jungle. One afternoon in April, as we were going toward a wide river with tranquil waters and I was hoping for nothing more from life than a bath and a moment of rest, El Chiqui came up to me and pulled me out of the line we had formed to wait.

"We've received a message from the Secretariado. We've been ordered to change your group."

I shrugged, only half believing what he said.

"Get your things ready. We'll proceed immediately with the exchange."

A few minutes later, I was sitting on the ground, filled with anxiety, trying as best I could to stuff my backpack with my belongings.

"Don't worry," said William, standing behind me, "I'll help you."

We followed El Chiqui across a small stream with a bed of pink pebbles and went up the steep slope of the bank. Camouflaged among the trees a hundred yards from us, the other camp, already set up for the night, was a beehive of activity. Enrique was standing with his arms crossed, looking daggers at me. "Over there!" he muttered, motioning with his chin.

I looked over to where he had indicated, and I saw my companions gathered together. I trembled with impatience at the thought of seeing Marc again.

His tent was the first one in the campsite. He had already spotted me and was standing right outside his *caleta*. He didn't move. He had a huge chain around his neck. I walked up. The joy I felt on seeing him again was not what I had anticipated. It was a melancholy joy, a happiness made weary by too many trials. *He's in good shape*, I thought as I observed him more closely, as if to justify my resentment.

We hugged, with restraint; we clasped hands for a moment, then let go, intimidated by rediscovering a closeness we'd never really achieved.

"I've been thinking about you a lot."

"Me, too."

"I was afraid."

"Me, too."

"We'll be able to speak now."

"Yes, I think so," I answered, not altogether sure. The guard behind me was getting impatient.

"I'd like to have my letters back."

"Yes, if you want . . . and will you give me back mine?"

"No."

"Why?"

"Because I want to keep them, too."

I was surprised. I had the letters in my pocket. I could simply hand them to him. But I didn't. "We'll see tomorrow," I said, thinking that we would have to work at rebuilding the bridges between us.

My companions went on with their occupations without a fuss. They kept to themselves, mindful not to disturb their neighbour or ruffle anyone's susceptibilities.

Over the coming days, Marc and I cautiously resumed our conversations. I felt the same great joy that I'd known before, sharing these moments with him once again, but I restrained myself, forcing myself to dose out my freedom to speak with him carefully.

"Did you hear that Monster was killed?" I asked one day.

"Yes, that's what I heard."

"And?"

"Nothing. And you?"

"It did affect me. I saw him leave the camp with his empty *equipo*. He was on his way to die. No one knows the place or the time. All the ones who were so hard on us came to a bad end. Did you know that Sombra was captured?"

"Yes, I heard it on the radio. Rogelio died, too, in La Macarena."

"Rogelio? The receptionist at Sombra's prison?"

"Yes. He was killed in an ambush. He had got really nasty with us. And Shirley, the pretty girl who acted as a nurse and dentist at Sombra's camp, what happened to her?"

"I saw her not long ago. She's in a group of soldiers with Romero and

Rodríguez. They're part of the convoy that's ahead of us. She's with Arnoldo now, the one who took over from Rogelio at Sombra's prison."

This was our world now. These men and women who held us prisoner were our community, our social references.

Marc and I started doing gymnastics together. We were constantly changing camp, but it was no longer a continuous march. We spent two weeks by a stream, three weeks by a river, one week behind a coca field. Wherever we went, we would find a way to set up parallel bars and something to make weights with. Our training routine had a precise goal, that of preparing our escape.

"We have to flee toward the river. Then we have to go wherever the helicopters are," said Marc obstinately.

"The helicopters are constantly moving around. We can't predict where they'll be. We have to do what Pinchao did. We have to head north."

"That's totally crazy, to head north! We'll never have enough supplies to get as far as Bogotá!"

"It's even crazier to think we could reach the helicopter base. It's never permanent. One day they're here, the next day they're somewhere else."

"All right," Marc eventually agreed, "we'll go to the river where the helicopters are, and then we'll head north."

But our plans to escape were running into more and more difficulties.

The business of the letters became a serious source of tension. I tried to avoid the topic, but he kept coming back to it. I gradually put more distance between us, limiting our moments together to our workouts. I felt sorry, but I couldn't see my way out of this absurd confrontation over the letters.

One evening after a discussion that was more heated than usual, one of the guards came to see me.

"What's your problem with Marc?" he asked.

I replied evasively.

Later William lectured me. "They're the ones in charge here," he warned me. "They can search you at any time."

I knew he was right. At any moment our letters could end up in the guerrillas' hands. I decided to burn those I had in my possession, certain that Marc wouldn't give me back mine. During one of the short marches that were now routine, I managed to burn a few without being seen.

Or at least that's what I thought, because one of the *guerrilleras* had watched me at it and notified Enrique. I was summoned. William took me to one side and said, "Tell us the truth. They already know about the letters."

Enrique was short with me. "I don't want any problems between prisoners. Give your comrade what belongs to him, and I'll make him give you what is yours," he said.

Despite the humiliation the situation caused me, Enrique's attitude gave me some peace of mind. He didn't seem to be interested in the letters per se. He was delighted to be able to play the referee between Marc and me. It was his personal revenge for having me back.

Marc, too, was summoned. We were in a different camp, right in the middle of a budding coca plantation, with fruit trees in the centre and, along the periphery and at each corner, tall, solitary papaya trees. There were also two adjacent wooden houses and an open-air clay oven. They had put us off to the side of the plantation, in the woods. Enrique had pitched his tent right behind the wooden houses, in the garden, before the edge of the forest.

Marc stayed talking with Enrique for a long time. When he returned, I went up to him. He seemed in low spirits, and he made me wait until he'd finished putting his things away before he would give me his attention. This whole business was really stupid. It would have taken just one word for the walls rising between us to crumble. His dark look stopped me from speaking, though. I handed him the roll of letters, and he took it without glancing at it. I thought about telling him that they weren't all there, and I waited stiffly, unsure about how to say it. Misunderstanding my reason for waiting there, he said, "I'm sorry, but I'm keeping yours, too."

I could not understand why he wanted to keep my letters. What did he want with them? I had become increasingly suspicious.

The next morning after breakfast, Enrique sent El Abuelo as courier. We had to take our *equipos* and go into one of the little wooden houses.

"We're going to show you some films," he announced.

El Abuelo convinced no one, because the order to take our backpacks with us could only mean something else.

The group was divided in two. El Abuelo asked Marc to open his bag and took out all his belongings. He carefully inspected every single object and was particularly interested in Marc's notebook, the one he used as a diary. He called me over.

"Does this belong to you?" he asked, showing me the notebook.

I stood where I was in the little house, refusing to cross the space between us. Another guard came up.

"Get a move on. Can't you see the comrade is calling you?" he said, exasperated. The little houses were built on posts three feet from the ground. I jumped down and walked over.

"It's not mine," I answered.

For a moment Marc seemed troubled, and then, as if to regain his composure, he said, "Can I put my things away now?"

El Abuelo scowled at him. His two other companions were shouting and waving their arms in exasperation, outraged that they'd been made to wait there with their *equipos* too. El Abuelo was irritated by Marc's comment and their impatience. He was about to leave, his mission over, but then he changed his mind.

"You! Open your *equipo*!" he said, raging against Keith. There was a deadly silence.

I heard the other guard shout, sharp as ever, "That will teach him to act like Rambo!"

The other guerrillas who were standing near the oven, busy cooking, burst out laughing. Massimo was there with them. He came over to me as he watched the scene.

"Ouch!" he said, shaking his hand as if it hurt. "What a viper's tongue that guy has!"

This wave of reactions left me a bitter taste. *What a waste*, I thought, sadly, watching Marc pack up his belongings. I didn't care for the letters any more. His friendship was the only thing worth fighting to keep.

80

THE SACRED HEART

June 2008. I was overcome with melancholy. That I couldn't speak to Marc – not because the guerrillas had separated us, but because of our own stubbornness – left me feeling disgusted with everything.

Before we got to the campsite with the two little houses, when we were still on the march, Asprilla had brought me a big Larousse dictionary, the one I'd asked for from Mono Jojoy years earlier. I had known for a long time that it was in the camp. Consolación and Katerina had first told me, back in the days when they were my guards, during my isolation and convalescence in Chiqui's group, that the Larousse had arrived.

Monster had been carrying it around. He had later let me leaf through it for a few days, in exchange for which he wanted me to explain the history of the Second World War. The girls were delighted to be able to use it, too, and together we had looked through the dictionary while they braided my hair. Once Monster died, I figured no one wanted to carry it.

I waited for Marc to give some sign that he'd like to use it, but he refused to show any interest. Keith often asked for it, and we agreed that I would leave it for him beside my *equipo* while I was working out so that he could use it at his convenience. But his curiosity quickly faded, and in the end only William remained absorbed by it.

One afternoon when I was waiting for William to finish using it and I was killing time fiddling with the dial on the shortwave radio, a man talking about the promises of the Sacred Heart caught my attention. Perhaps because as a child I often went to the Basilica of the Sacré-Coeur in Paris, or maybe because the word "promises" had struck a chord, the fact remains that I stopped turning the knob to listen to what the man had to say.

He was explaining that June was the month of Jesus's Sacred Heart, and he made the list of graces that would be granted to those who invoked it. I quickly went to fetch a pencil and a cigarette pack, and I wrote down the promises I'd managed to remember.

There were two in particular that seemed to express my deepest hopes: "I will give blessings on all their plans" and "I will touch even the hardest hearts." My plan was none other than our freedom. It had become an immediate reflex. Likewise, the transformation of hardened hearts was a promise tailor-made for me. During my discussions with Pinchao, we often used the same expression. There were too many hardened hearts around us – the hard hearts of our jailers, of those in the outside world who maintained we must be sacrificed for reasons of state, and of those who were simply indifferent and turned their backs on us.

Without thinking, I appealed to Jesus. "I don't dare to ask for my immediate release, but if your promises are true, I want to ask you for one thing: During this month of June, which is yours, help me to understand how much longer we will have to live as captives. You see, if I knew how long it is going to be, I could hold on. Because I would know that there is an end in sight. If you tell me, I promise you I will pray every Friday for the rest of my life. That will be the proof of my devotion to you, and that you did not let me down."

But the month of June yielded little hope. Of course I listened to the appeals of the Green parties, of members of the European Parliament, of the support groups demanding the release of all those who were still in the jungle. There had been huge marches at the beginning of the year, not only in France and the rest of Europe but also, for the first time, in Colombia. The support groups campaigning in favour of the hostages had grown in number, and there were now thousands of activists everywhere. All the presidents of Latin America had expressed their support for talks with the FARC, and in Argentina, during Cristina Kirchner's inauguration as president, she had opened the doors so that our families could appeal for help from her peers.

But during June, our situation seemed more deadlocked than ever. Operation Phoenix, led by the Colombian army on March 2, 2008, into Ecuador to kill Raúl Reyes, the FARC's second-in-command, created a serious diplomatic crisis between Colombia, Ecuador, and Venezuela. Talks for the release of new hostages were suspended.

On March 24 the announcement of the death of Manuel Marulanda, the FARC's leader, chased away our last hopes. As Reyes, who would have been Marulanda's immediate successor, had been killed two weeks earlier, the organization seemed to have been beheaded. The exchange of prisoners would be postponed indefinitely.

There won't be anything for you, I thought, to avoid nurturing any illusions. However, on June 28, I had a surprising visit. Enrique crept quietly up to my *caleta*, trying to find his way in, visibly intending to sit down and speak to me. I assumed that new misfortune was about to befall me. I didn't like seeing Enrique. I froze, my muscles tense.

"A commission of Europeans will be coming to see you. They want to talk to you all and check on the health of the hostages. You have to be ready. We will have to move. There's a possibility that one or several of you may be released."

I had learned not to show my emotion. Nevertheless, my heart leaped from my chest like a fish from a bowl. I did not want Enrique to think he could fool me. He would have taken too much pleasure in my disappointment. I pretended not to be interested.

"I've ordered new clothes and smaller backpacks to be delivered to you. Take just the bare essentials — no tent, no mosquito net, just your hammock, a change of clothes, and that's all. Leave your *equipos* here with all the rest."

He went around the *caletas*, talking to everyone in the same weary, conscientious tone, no doubt following his orders. Members of the FARC were not encouraged to act on their own initiative. Once Enrique had left our camp, everyone had a personal interpretation of what he'd said. There was a flurry of debate. I had only one thing in mind: I'd just been given the answer I was waiting for. Right before the end of June, the Colombian government had authorized European delegates to travel into the Amazon to meet with Alfonso Cano, the new FARC leader. These delegates were Noël Saez and Jean-Pierre Gontard, two men who had devoted years to our cause. If they restored contact with the FARC, then there was a chance that negotiations might be forthcoming.

The next morning Lili came into the camp with her arms full. There were plaid shirts and new trousers for the men and for me some jeans and a turquoise T-shirt with a low scoop neck. Marc refused to wear the new clothes and handed them back to Lili. Tom put on his new plaid shirt right away. You could tell they wanted to put us on stage. I'd wear my old clothes, I decided, emulating Marc's gesture.

81

THE TRICK

When our *cambuches* were dismantled and they had picked up everything, we were made to go up to one of the little wooden houses. We were very surprised to find the hostages from the other two groups already chatting in one of the houses. Armando and Arteaga were having animated discussions with Corporal Jairo Durán, and police lieutenant Javier Rodríguez, Corporal Buitrago, who was known as Buitraguito, and the ever courteous Sergeant Romero. We were all happy to see them. We'd become friends during the marches, because we sometimes had long waits for the *bongo* together. We'd go from one person to the next, wanting to find out all the news in a minute, exchanging our reactions and our feelings about what was coming. Nobody knew a thing. No one dared ask if they believed there'd be releases, because none of us dared to admit we hoped there might be.

I went up to Armando. I liked his company and his irrepressible optimism. He hugged me, delighted. "You'll be next!" I laughed with him – he didn't believe it any more than I did. "Look, Arteaga's got a girlfriend," he said, changing the subject. I turned around to have a look. It was sweet. Miguel had a little tame *cosumbo* on his shoulder, and he was kissing it on the nose.

"Who gave him the *cosumbo*?"

"It's not a *cosumbo*, it's a coati!" said Armando, the specialist.

"Hey, what's a coati?"

"It's like a *cosumbo*."

We were laughing, for no reason. The idea of a change in routine made us lighthearted.

"So where are we going?"

"Nowhere. We're staying in Cambodia," he said sarcastically.

That was his favourite expression, to imply that anything could happen and that we were in the worst possible mess, as if we were in the hands of Pol Pot. It always made me laugh. On the surface it might have seemed incongruous. And yet it was so true – the same jungle, the same extremism and fanaticism wrapped up in the same communist rhetoric, and the same cold-blooded cruelty.

"He eats more than leishmaniasis!" Armando said, pointing behind his back.

I laughed even though I didn't know who he was talking about. Off to one side in a corner, huddled over his bowl, Enrique was gorging himself on the morning's leftover rice.

Our old *equipos* were piled up in a room in the little house, behind a door locked with a big padlock, and the key ended up in Enrique's pocket. *We'll never see them again*, I thought, glad that at the last minute I had taken out the belts I'd woven for Mela, Lorenzo, and Sebastian years earlier. Enrique was cleaning his new AR-15 Bushmaster, an upgrade on his previous AK-47, and seemed oblivious to time. Lili came to inform him. The *bongo* was waiting.

The passage was surprisingly short. They had covered our heads with a huge tarpaulin, but I managed to see the opposite shore, with a scattering of neat little buildings painted in bright colours.

Where are we? I wondered, surprised to see so many civilians.

We moored below an imposing estate. A fine garden, planted with palm trees fanned out in the middle of an impeccable lawn, led up to a house on piles that was divided into three perfectly harmonized sections. The central part looked like it must be a sort of common room. A huge table with a multitude of plastic chairs seemed lost in a big room that was anything but crowded, despite the presence of an equally huge billiards table in the far corner.

We were immediately led into the left wing of the building. As a rule we were put inside henhouses or laboratories, not in real houses. We were told to set our backpacks on the ground, at the back of the house, and to take out our bathing things. In no time at all, we were in the river.

"You're a real soldier now," said Rodríguez jokingly.

Someone brought out a half-full bottle of shampoo.

"Wow!" said everyone in unison.

Shampoo was a treasure that normally was not shared. But today everyone was feeling good-humoured, and the bottle was passed around. The scent of the shampoo made me long for another life, and I sank into the water to play mermaid as I rinsed out my hair.

"Betancourt, out!" barked Oswald.

I picked up my piece of soap and got out before the others. I smiled, thinking that someday this would all come to an end, and I walked up to my *equipo* to change quickly, before the mosquitoes started attacking.

One of the guards opened the side door of the left wing of the building.

"Take your backpacks inside and get your chains ready," he said smugly.

I saw my companions crowding together to be the first ones in. I looked at the sky one last time. The night was clear. Not a cloud. Above me the first star had just twinkled.

My companions hurried around a pile of torn mattresses. By the looks of it, there wouldn't be enough to go around. William had grabbed two of them, and he showed me the spot he'd saved for me.

The guard rattled his key ring. Everyone found a spot, and the guard came by to lock our padlocks and fasten the chains to the posts supporting the beds. Once he had left, I took out my little radio and, as on every evening, tuned in to the Colombian programmes. It felt good – to be under a roof, in a bed, upon a mattress.

I woke up at three o'clock in the morning and took out my rosary. It was a Wednesday.

That day I prayed with even greater joy, because I was convinced that my pact with Jesus had been sealed. *He has kept his word*, I thought, even if I had absolutely no idea what to expect.

Mom's voice came to me at dawn. "I have to take the plane this afternoon," she said, "but I don't want to leave you." I smiled, thinking of Lucho. *Tomorrow she'll call me from Rome*, I thought, amused. Melanie, too, came on the air. She was calling from London and I thought there'd be nobody to meet me on my arrival, if I should be released now.

Fabrice came on immediately afterwards. From my letter to Mom, he had learned that I could hear the radio messages, so he called in from everywhere, and he always ended up having to put the phone down, because his voice became too emotional. This time he managed to tell me that they were with Marc's mother and that Jo was fighting like a lioness for him. Fabrice had been speaking to me in French, and no one but me could tell Marc.

The guard was already coming along to open the padlocks. To my great surprise, he removed my companions' chains and put them away. *Don't go getting ideas. He's going to leave yours on*, I thought when I saw that it was Oswald at work. However, this time, he removed mine too.

I looked up at the sound of dishes. A guerrilla came in with a china bowl in each hand, filled with soup. He handed it to my companions, going back and forth every two minutes. Soon they were all silently bent over their plates, focused on fishing the small pieces of potato out of the bowl.

A sudden stir announced a new arrival. Commander Cesar had just come in and was speaking with each of my companions, courteously, one by one, until he came to me.

Everyone had cleared out, probably as much out of courtesy as out of a desire to make the most of a sunny morning without chains and a good breakfast. I was left alone with the leader of our front.

"We are the army of the people," said Cesar, like an orator.

They're just like the old Colombian political class, I thought. He made his statement in due form, explaining why they were keeping the "detainees" – a euphemism for "hostages" – and why it was a good thing they were using drug money to finance their activities, because it meant they would not have to take economic hostages.

I looked at him impassively, knowing that there had to be a purpose behind everything he was saying. What was he afraid of? Did he want me to serve as witness? Did he want to pass on a message? Leave himself a way out? Whom were we going to meet? Foreigners? FARC leaders? I sighed. Years ago

I would have resisted, would have tried to pull his arguments to threads. Now I felt like an old dog. I no longer barked. Sitting down, I observed.

An hour later Cesar was still going on and on. My soup was cold. I had put the bowl down on the flea-infested mattress where I'd slept. When it seemed he had finished, I asked him what we might expect from the rest of the day.

"Some helicopters will be coming to get you. We'll be going to talk with Alfonso Cano, probably. After that I don't know," he confessed. "Maybe you'll be transferred to another camp."

Marc was by his bunk bed, putting his bowl into his backpack. We were alone in the room. I hesitated, then went up to him. "Marc, I wanted you to know that on the radio this morning I heard that your mother is in London. She's with my family at a forum on peace, or human rights, I think. Fabrice told me she's fighting like a lioness for you."

Marc had gone on closing his bag while I was speaking. Finally he looked up, his gaze so gentle that I was ashamed of my official tone. He thanked me, and I went away so as not to prolong a tête-à-tête that might turn awkward.

Outside, there was the clatter of approaching helicopters. All my companions were already there, looking up at the clouds, searching the sky. I began sweating at once, my stomach in a painful knot; my body was reacting as if it were a military raid. "How stupid. . . I know it's not and yet I react all the same," I mumbled. My mouth felt furry, and I was still trembling when old Erminson screamed at us to return to the barracks with our backpacks. He made us walk single file into the billiards room. We were being searched. Yet again.

There was one guard for each prisoner, so the search went very quickly. They confiscated anything that could cut, even nail clippers. Mine were in my pocket and survived the search. Still in single file, we were taken down to the *bongo*.

I had an assigned guard following close behind, a girl I'd never seen before. She was very nervous, and she would scream at me, sticking the end of her rifle into my ribs.

"Take it easy, gently," I said, to calm her down.

We crossed the river in the *bongo* and moored on the opposite bank, by a field of coca behind a little shack. In the middle of the coca field, a grassy expanse surrounded by a fence seemed to be the spot the guerrillas had chosen for their helicopter pad. There were two choppers circling high above, disappearing into the clouds and reappearing immediately afterwards. One of them began its descent. It was all white, with a red band beneath the rotors. The sound of the rotor became deafening and seemed to take on the same rhythm as the pounding in my heart. The closer it came, the more the vibrations spread through my body. It landed, and the door opened immediately.

Enrique had ordered most of his troops to stand in a circle all around the enclosure. The guards were looking ill-tempered, and their nervousness was as tangible as the hot air shimmering just above the ground. We prisoners were gathered in a group; we had instinctively clustered against the barbed wire to be as close as possible to the helicopter, so we couldn't be overheard by the guards. I stayed slightly to the rear. I was wary.

Several people jumped out of the chopper. There was one very tall man, with a white cap on his head, who walked bent to one side, as if he were afraid the wind from the rotors might knock him over. Another thin man with a blond beard ran behind him, along with a little woman in a white lab coat, holding forms in one hand and a pen in the other. A sturdy guy with very dark eyes and a piercing gaze walked along the side. He looked Arabic. Behind and to the left was a dark little man with a movie camera in his fist; he wore a white vest and a Che Guevara T-shirt and was filming everything. Next to him was a young reporter wearing a red bandanna and brandishing a microphone, visibly trying to speak to the commanders.

"Are they Europeans?" My companions nudged me, eager for an answer.

I was trying to get a good look at them, but my sight was affected by the glare. And it was hotter than a furnace.

"No, they're not Europeans."

The tall man with the white cap stopped just on the other side of the barbed wire and bombarded us with stupid questions, while his acolyte took notes.

"Are you in good health?"

"Do you have any infectious diseases?"

"Do you get vertigo in aeroplanes?"

"Do you suffer from claustrophobia?"

He wasn't interested in anyone in particular, and he went from one person to the next without waiting for any answers.

I got closer to look at the laminated ID badge hanging from his neck: INTERNATIONAL HUMANITARIAN MISSION, it read, written against a pale blue background bearing the logo of a dove with its wings spread, like the one on a bar of Dove soap. *This is a trick*, I thought, in dismay. The men were obviously foreigners; they might be Venezuelan or Cuban. Their accent, in any event, was Caribbean.

This was no international commission. There wouldn't be any releases. We were going to be transferred God knows where. We'd still be prisoners ten years from now, I concluded.

The man with the white cap had given an order to unload some crates of soft drinks from the helicopter; acting the grand gentleman, he gave them to Cesar.

"These are for your troops, *compañero*," was what I managed to lip-read, and then they gave each other the prescribed greetings. The guards were posted every two yards in a circle around us. There must have been sixty or more. Obviously Cesar had brought in new troops. They were proud, standing to attention, eagerly observing everything going on. Enrique wasn't talkative; he was withdrawn in comparison with Cesar, who was lapping it up, full of himself.

The man with the white cap addressed us in what was meant to be an authoritative voice, declaring, "*Muchachos!* Let's be quick now. We can't stay on the ground any longer. We have a commitment to the FARC, and we're going to make sure it's respected. Everybody has to get into the helicopter, hands tied. Line up. The guards have the handcuffs we brought. I ask you to please cooperate, so we can guarantee the success of our mission."

Unexpectedly, and for the first time ever, there was a rebellion among the hostages. No one wanted to get into the helicopters. All the prisoners

protested. We would not accept from these strangers what we'd been tol-
erating for years from the guerrillas.

The guards readied their rifles, in case we needed reminding. Some of
my companions lay down on the ground, kicking whoever approached.
They were viciously handcuffed by the guards and forced at gunpoint to
climb into the aircraft. Others wanted to testify to the camera and were
pushed away again, hands tied, and forced into the helicopter in turn.
The guard who was binding our hands was a young guy with a violent
temper. He bound my wrists so tightly that he nearly lost his balance. I
didn't say a thing. I was crushed by the thought of what might be next.

The nurse offered to help carry my backpack. I refused outright.
Those images they were filming, endlessly, were meant to convey to the
world the picture of a humane guerrilla movement. I wanted no part in
their game. I didn't say a word, and I climbed into the helicopter like a
beast going to the abattoir. Inside, on every seat there was a white parka.
We're going to the páramo, I thought, biting my lips. *To Alfonso Cano*, I
concluded.

I was sitting between Armando and William, very near the door,
because we were the last ones to board. I had my backpack between my
legs, and I was trying in secret to pull off my handcuffs to get my blood
flowing again. That was fairly easy, since it was a system not unlike the
straps for suitcases used in airports.

"Put them back on. It's not allowed," warned Armando, shocked.

"I don't care," I answered testily.

Enrique took his seat, and the door closed. The helicopter took off. I
looked through the porthole behind me: The guerrillas were standing at
attention, watching us leave. Soon they became tiny, until they were a line
of black dots in the greenery. We could overpower them and take control
of the helicopter, I thought, looking toward the cockpit.

The nurse came up to me again and offered me something to drink. I
didn't want anything from her, for she was taking part in an operation to
prolong our captivity. I rejected her coldly, irritated by her friendly look.

Then I saw it. A quick movement, and Enrique fell out of his seat. The big
Arab was on top of him. My companions were kicking him. I didn't know

what was going on. I couldn't even dare to believe what was happening. My thoughts seized up. My brain was blocked. Nothing seemed coherent.

The tall man in the white cap stood up, the Arab was holding his position, on top of Enrique. All I could see was the victory of these giants over the man I had hated so much. Everybody turned around to look at them. The colossus threw his white cap in the air as he yelled with all his might, "*¡Somos el ejército de Colombia! ¡Están libres!*"*

The sound of the engine filled my head with vibrations, and I couldn't comprehend what was going on. The words took some time to penetrate the carapace of incredulity that had hardened over so many years around my brain. The words soaked in like the first rains after a long winter, gradually filling me through layers of pain and despair that had grown rock hard inside me, and with those words came back a surge of power, rising like lava, deep from my entrails, burning its way out, about to explode.

A long, long, and very painful cry came breaking through, like a burst of flames reaching to the skies, forcing me open, like a mother in childbirth. When I finished emptying my lungs, my eyes opened to another world. I had just been catapulted into life. A rich, intense serenity flooded over me, I felt like a lake with deep waters, its surface reflecting an image of snowy peaks all around.

I kissed my rosary in an inexpressible élan of gratitude. We were hugging, whimpering with tears. William was clinging to me and I to him, suddenly afraid and breathless in front of this void of freedom opening up before us. As if we were about to take flight, our feet on the edge of a cliff.

I turned my head away. My eyes met Marc's for the first time on the other side of life, in the world of the living, and at that precise moment I saw the kindred spirit I had discovered in the jungle, when we were in chains and had written to each other. Marc smiled. *What we become is what we are*, I thought.

At my feet, curled up like a foetus, his hands and feet bound, lay Enrique. No, I didn't like our violence, nor the kicks we had given him. That wasn't us. I took William's hand. Next to me he was weeping.

"It's over," I said, caressing his head. "We're going home."

---

* "We are the Colombian army! You are free!"

82

THE END OF SILENCE

William put his arm around my shoulders. Only then did I realize that I, too, was weeping.

But in fact it wasn't me crying – it was my body that had gone to pieces trying to become whole again, through tears, submerged by a multitude of disparate and disconnected feelings colliding. I walked barefoot for a few more moments on the planks of precious wood they had cut with the chain saw in the camp of horror and which was now rotting in the past with the thousands of trees sacrificed during those six and a half years of waste. I thought about my body that had not regained its female functions since my near death and which now seemed to have stopped hibernating at the most inopportune moment. It was the first time in my life that the thought of it made me happy.

My companions were jumping around Cesar's and Enrique's recumbent bodies in a war dance of our victory with shouts and cheers. I watched as Armando was singing in Enrique's ear, "¡La vida es una tómbola, tómbola, tómbola!"

The helicopter's going to crash, I thought, startled by a rush of adrenalin, suddenly fearful that our euphoria would disturb the aircraft. I sat back down, tense. What if the curse still followed us? I imagined the accident, I couldn't help it. "How soon do we land?" I screamed, hoping for someone to hear.

In the cockpit the mechanic turned around with a huge smile, showing me five fingers.

My God, I thought, *five minutes! That's an eternity!*

The tall man with the white cap stood before me and lifted me from my seat in a bear hug that took my breath away. He introduced himself. "Major in the Colombian army," he said, telling me his name. He had the build of a Thracian gladiator, I thought immediately.

He put his mouth up to my ear, his hands cupped. "I left my family over a month ago to take command of this mission. I couldn't tell anyone anything – we were sworn to the utmost secrecy. My wife kissed me before I left and said, 'What you're doing is incredibly important. I know you're going to get Ingrid. My prayers go with you. You'll succeed, and you'll be back. And remember that whatever happens, I know I have shared my life with a hero.' . . . I wanted you to understand, Ingrid, that we've all been behind you, every day, bearing your pain like our own cross, all Colombians."

I was hanging on his words, clinging to him, as if in his arms I could be safe from all misfortune.

I gave thanks to God, not for releasing me but for *this* release. For the selfless love of these men and women – whom I had never met before and whose sacrifice had given a transcendent meaning to all that I had lived through.

An immense serenity came over me. Everything was as it should be. Out of the porthole behind my seat, the little village of San José del Guaviare, in a garden of greenery, grew larger and larger beneath my feet. *There is the oasis, the promised land,* I thought. Was it possible?

The door opened. My companions leaped out of the helicopter, jumping over the bodies of the two subdued men. Enrique looked unconscious, stretched out on the floor in his underwear. I felt a pang. There was nothing to cover him. He would be cold. The woman who had played the nurse during the operation took me by the arm. "It's over," she said gently. I stood up and squeezed her tight. She pushed me toward the door, and I jumped with my backpack onto the tarmac.

At the end of the runway, the presidential aerorplane was waiting to fly us to Bogotá. A man in uniform opened his arms to me. It was General Mario Montoya, the man who was responsible for Operation Jaque. His exuberant joy was contagious. My companions were dancing, waving their handkerchiefs around him.

In the aeroplane he filled me in on the details of the operation and the preparations made to ensure its success. In the depths of the jungle, the military helicopters had been painted white, at a secret camp where for one month the team had rehearsed the operation down to the smallest detail. They had intercepted communications between Cesar and Enrique, and their leader, Mono Jojoy. Jojoy thought he was speaking to his subordinates, but it was the Colombian army. Cesar and Enrique in turn thought they were getting their orders from Jojoy, not suspecting that it was Montoya's men. The initial order was to identify the group of hostages under Enrique's command and then to put us all together in the same group. When they saw that their orders had been carried out, they took their bold enterprise one step further, ordering Cesar to put us in the helicopter belonging to the fake international commission. They had copied the procedure that had been set up for unilateral releases at the beginning of the year. The operation seemed to follow the same logic as the previous ones, and it worked. The death of the FARC leadership, Manuel Marulanda and Raúl Reyes, made the premise of an interview with the new leader, Alfonso Cano, believable, which explained why Cesar and Enrique were so eager to travel in the helicopter. Like a giant jigsaw puzzle, all the pieces came together just as they should, in the right place at the right time.

I listened to the general. He was describing my children in detail and giving me news of Mom and my sister.

"Does my family already know?" I asked.

"At exactly one o'clock this afternoon, we announced the news to the entire world."

Then, without thinking, I asked for permission to go to the toilet. He said nothing, just looked at me. "You don't need to ask permission any more," he whispered. He courteously stood up and offered to take me there.

I changed and braided my hair in a real mirror, behind a real locked door, and I laughed at the idea that I'd never again have to ask permission.

We were about to land. I found Marc toward the front of the plane, lost in his silence. I motioned to him, and we went to sit in a corner with some empty seats. "Marc, I just wanted to say . . . I want you to know that those letters that I didn't give back to you, I burned them—"

"It's not important," he said gently, interrupting me. Our hands clasped, and he closed his eyes to murmur, "We are free."

When he opened his eyes again, I found myself saying, "Promise me that when you are back in your life, you won't forget me." He looked at me as if he'd just found his bearings in the sky and assured me with a nod. "I'll always know where to find you."

The plane landed, and General Montoya greeted the minister of defence, who was still standing at the entrance to the aircraft. I had not seen Juan Manuel Santos in many years. He kissed me affectionately and said, "Colombia is celebrating, and so is France. President Sarkozy is sending a plane. Your children will be here tomorrow." Then, without giving me the time to react, he took me by the hand and led me out of the plane. I went down the steps in a dream. On the tarmac a hundred or more soldiers cheered our arrival. All those men and women in uniform kissed me, and I was giving myself to them as if I needed their gestures, their voices, their smells to believe that this was real.

The minister handed me a mobile phone. "It's your mother."

If you believe what you say, words become reality, I told myself, for I had imagined this moment so many times. I had wanted it so badly and waited for it for so long.

"Hello, Mom?"

"Astrid, is that you?"

"No, Mom, it's me, it's Ingrid."

Mom's happiness was just as I had imagined. Her voice filled with light, and her words seemed to flow on from the ones I'd heard at dawn on the radio that very day. We had never left each other. I had lived through these six and a half years of captivity hanging on to life from the thread of her voice.

We left Tolemaida, a military base a few minutes from the capital, where we had made a stop. During the flight to Bogotá, I closed my eyes in an exercise of meditation and saw again everything I'd experienced since my capture, as if in a film screened at high speed. I saw my entire family, just as I'd pictured them during all those years we'd been apart. I had an inexpressible fear, as if I might not recognize them any more, or they might brush past me without seeing me. Papa was almost more alive for me than they were, or at best they were as far away from me as he was. I knew I had to resolve to bury him for good, and this was still very painful. I would need my sister's help to mourn him. How could I possibly accept him as being dead when I was coming back to life? That was an immense task awaiting me. I would have to find out myself, in my home among my loved ones, knowing all the while that I was now so different, almost a stranger to them.

My greatest worry was reestablishing the connection with my children; founding our relationship on a new basis to create trust, complicity; starting from scratch while delving into our past to restore the codes of our love. My son was still a child when I was captured. What memories might he have kept of his mother from his childhood? Would there be room for me in his life as a young man? And Melanie – who was Melanie? Who was this determined, thoughtful young woman who insisted I not give up? Would she be disappointed by the woman I had become? Could she, could I, recover the intimacy that had bound us so deeply before my disappearance? Papa was right: The most important thing in life is family.

This new world, about which I knew nothing, had meaning for me only in my family and through my family. During the years of agony, they had been my sun, my moon, and my stars. I had escaped from that green hell every day, carried away by the burning memory of my children's kisses, and so that the memory of our past happiness would not be confiscated, I had buried it in the stars, near the constellation of Cygnus that I had given to my daughter when she was born. Deprived of everything, I had devoted my energy to the coming happiness, of hearing the voice of my son change into that of a man and, like Penelope, I had woven and unwoven my work, waiting for that day to come.

Only a few more hours and I would see them all – Mom, my children, my sister. Would they be sad to see me so worn down by captivity? I took a deep breath, with my eyes closed; I knew that we were transformed. I saw it when I looked at Willie, Armando, Arteaga. They were all different, as if radiating from within. I must be, too. I kept my eyes closed for a long time. When I opened them again, I knew precisely what I would do and say when I came off the aeroplane. I felt neither impatience nor fear nor exaltation. Everything I had thought during those interminable cycles of marches and camps, season after season, was ready, was ripe in my heart.

At last the door opened.

On the tarmac Mom was waiting, intimidated by so much blessedness, and on her face, as if she would have liked to hide them from me, were the traces of her years of suffering. I liked her new fragility. It was familiar to me. I descended the steps slowly, to have time to admire her, to love her better. We embraced with the energy of victory. A victory that we alone could understand, because it was a victory over despair, over oblivion, over resignation, a victory solely over ourselves.

My companions, too, had disembarked. Armando took me by the hand and led me along. We looked forward with our arms around each other's shoulders, as happy as children, on clouds. I felt with a shiver that everything was new, everything was dense and weightless at the same time, and in the explosion of light everything had disappeared, been swept away, emptied, cleansed. I had been born once again. There was nothing left in me but love.

I fell to my knees, looking ahead to the world in front of me, and I thanked the heavens for everything that was still to come.

ACKNOWLEDGEMENT

To Susanna Lea, who inexaustibly sustained my writing and my soul.

www.virago.co.uk

virago

To find out more about Ingrid Betancourt and
other Virago authors, visit:
www.virago.co.uk

Visit the Virago website for:

- Exclusive features and interviews with authors,
  including Margaret Atwood, Maya Angelou,
  Sarah Waters and Nina Bawden

- News of author events and forthcoming titles

- Competitions

- Exclusive signed copies

- Discounts on new publications

- Book-group guides

- Free extracts from a wide range of titles

PLUS: subscribe to our free monthly newsletter